W9-AFG-633

The Story of a Life

About the Author

Born in 1892 into a railroad worker's family in Moscow, Konstantin Paustovsky studied at the Universities of Moscow and Kiev. When World War I broke out he left school to become an ambulance driver. He later worked at a steel mill, as a tram conductor, as a free-lance newspaperman, and as a fisherman in a small village by the Black Sea. A professional writer since 1925, a friend of Pasternak and survivor of Stalin, Paustovsky wrote numerous books and articles. He died in the U.S.S.R. on July 14, 1968.

The Story

OF

A LIFE

Konstantin Paustovsky

TRANSLATED FROM THE RUSSIAN BY
Joseph Barnes

PANTHEON BOOKS

NEW YORK

Translation Copyright © 1964 by Random House, Inc.

All rights reserved under International and Pan-American Copyright Conventions. Published in the United States by Pantheon Books, a division of Random House, Inc., New York, and simultaneously in Canada by Random House of Canada Limited, Toronto.

LIBRARY OF CONGRESS CATALOGING IN PUBLICATION DATA

Paustovsky, Konstantin, 1893-1968.
The story of a life.

Translation of Povest'o zhizni.
1. Paustovsky, Konstantin, 1893-1968—Biography.
2. Authors, Russian—20th century—Biography. I. Title.
PG3476.P29Z4713   891.73′42 [B]   81-22466
ISBN 0-394-71014-2   AACR2

MANUFACTURED IN THE UNITED STATES OF AMERICA
FIRST PANTHEON PAPERBACK EDITION
1982

Contents

THE FARAWAY YEARS

The Death of My Father	3
My Grandfather Maxim Grigorievich	10
Carp	16
Pleurisy	20
The Trip to Chenstokhov	23
The Pink Oleanders	29
The Elderwood Balls	37
Svyatoslavskaya Street	44
The Winter Carnival	50
The Naval Cadet	57
What Paradise Looks Like	61
The Bryansk Forests	66
Swarmers	72
Water from the Limpopo River	80
The First Commandment	88
The Linden Blossoms	96
I Was, of Course, a Little Boy	105
The Little Red Lantern	114
The Deserted Crimea	120

Disaster	131
Artillerymen	137
The Great Tragedian Kean	143
Alone on the Big Road	149
Wild Alley	152
The Autumn Battle	156
Living Languages	160
"Messrs. Gymnasium Pupils"	166
The Hook-nosed King	172
From Empty to Emptier	175
The Inn on the Braginka	181
Sleep in My Grandmother's Garden	196
"Golden Latin"	203
Teachers of the Humanities	207
The Shooting in the Theater	212
Razgulyai	218
A Story About Nothing	231
Certificate of Maturity	236
A Summer Night	243
A Small Dose of Poison	250

RESTLESS YOUTH

"Here Lives Nobody"	257
The Unprecedented Autumn	261

contents [vii]

The Copper Line 268

To One Side of the War 276

The Old Man with the Hundred-Ruble Bill 282

Lefortovo Nights 287

Medical Orderly 291

Russia in the Snowdrifts 296

The Bugler and the Torn-up Paper 302

Rain in the Carpathian Foothills 306

By the Muddy San River 315

Spring by the Wieprz River 320

The Great Swindler 325

The Ocean-going Steamship Portugal 333

On the Road of Defeat 348

Two Thousand Volumes 361

The Village of Kobrin 366

Treachery 371

In the Marshy Woods 374

Under the Lucky Star 380

The Bulldog 392

The Putrid Winter 398

A Sad Fuss 405

The Suburb Chechelevka 412

Just One Day . . . 420

The Great Britain Hotel 429

Notebooks and Memory 439

The Art of Whitewashing Huts 451

The Raw February 460

❀   ❀   ❀

THE START
OF AN EXTRAORDINARY ERA

The Whirlpool	481
The Blue Torches	494
The Journalists' Café	506
The Room with the Fountain	524
The Zone of Silence	533
Revolt	539
Notes for a History of Moscow Private Houses	544
Some Explanations	550
The Heated Boxcar	553
The Neutral Zone	561
"Our Vagabond Hetman"	564
The Violet Ray	585
A Bolshevik Wedding	596
The Crimson Riding Breeches	602
Puff Pastry	614
The Cry in the Night	622
The Wedding Present	627
The Silversides, the Water Pipe, *and Small Dangers*	643
The Last Shrapnel	656

The Faraway Years

The Death of My Father

I WAS IN MY LAST YEAR OF SCHOOL IN KIEV WHEN THE TELEGRAM came saying that my father was dying on a farm at Gorodishche, near Belaya Tserkov.

The next day I went to Belaya Tserkov, stopping at the house of an old friend of my father, Feokistov, who ran the post office. He was a nearsighted old man with thick glasses and a long beard. He wore a postal official's jacket with the brass insignia of his job sewed on its worn cloth.

It was near the end of March. Rain came down in a steady drizzle. The naked poplars loomed up through the mist.

Feokistov told me the ice had broken up the night before on the fast-flowing Ros River. The farm where my father was dying was on an island in the middle of this river, some twenty versts [about fourteen miles] from Belaya Tserkov. A stone causeway led across the river to the farm. The water was now pouring over this causeway in high flood, and naturally no one would want to take me to the island, not even the most desperate driver in town.

Feokistov pondered for a long time: who was the most reckless driver in Belaya Tserkov? In the half-darkened drawing room his daughter, Zina, a schoolgirl, was diligently practicing the piano. The music made the leaves of a potted fig tree tremble. I stared at a pale, squeezed piece of lemon on a plate, and kept silent.

"Well, why not? Let's call Bregman, the old rascal," Feokistov decided finally. "He's not scared of anything."

Before long the driver, Bregman—"the most downright old rascal" in Belaya Tserkov—walked into Feokistov's office, a room filled with volumes of *Niva** in gold-lettered bindings. He was a thickset little Jew with a sparse beard and blue eyes like a cat's. His weathered cheeks were as red as apples. He twisted a little whip in his hands, and listened skeptically to Feokistov.

"Oy, what misfortune!" he said at last in a falsetto voice. "Oy, what bad luck! Pan Feokistov, my carriage is flimsy and my horses are weak. They're only gypsy horses! They'll never pull us through. We'll all drown, the horses and the carriage and the young man and the old driver. And nobody will even write about it in the paper. That's what I can't stand, Pan Feokistov. But of course we can go. Why not? You know yourself that an old driver's life is only worth three silver rubles, or five, I won't object—or let's say ten."

"Thank you, Bregman," Feokistov said. "I knew you'd agree. You're the bravest man in Belaya Tserkov. For this I'll subscribe to *Niva* for you to the end of the year."

"Well, if I'm as brave as all that," Bregman whined, "then make it *Russian Invalid* instead. There I can read about the soldiers' sons, and the men who win medals. In an hour the horses will be at the door, Pan."

And Bregman walked out.

There had been a curious sentence in the telegram I had received in Kiev: "Bring a priest from Belaya Tserkov, either Orthodox or Roman Catholic—it makes no difference which, provided he will come."

I knew my father, so this phrase disturbed me. My father was an atheist. His jokes about priests and clergymen had involved him in endless fights with my grandmother, a Pole and a religious fanatic like almost all Polish women.

I guessed the demand for a priest had been made by my father's sister, Feodosia Maximovna or—as everyone called her—Aunt Dosia. She had broken with all church ceremonies except the remission of sins. Her Bible had been replaced by Shevchenko's *Kobzar*,† hidden deep in her ironbound trunk and just as yellowed and wax-spotted as a Bible. Aunt Dosia would take it out sometimes at night and read "Katerina" by candlelight, wiping her eyes steadily with a dark-colored handkerchief.

She cried over Katerina's fate, which was so like her own. In the damp woods behind her cottage was the green grave of a son

---

* *Niva*, an illustrated weekly, was published in St. Petersburg from 1870 until 1917 by the firm of A. F. Marks; it appealed chiefly to middle-class readers.

† Taras G. Shevchenko (1814-1861) was probably the greatest of all Ukrainian poets. *Kobzar*, published in 1840, was his first collection of poems.

who had died a long time ago when Aunt Dosia was still quite young. This fellow was—as people then used to say—her "illegal" son. The man she loved had betrayed Aunt Dosia. He had abandoned her, but she remained true to him unto death, expecting him always to return; for some reason she was sure he would be sick, penniless, injured by life, and, after cursing him out as he deserved, she knew she would grow used to him in the end and treat him kindly.

None of the Orthodox priests would agree to go to Gorodishche, all of them pleading illness or previous engagements. Only one young Catholic priest agreed to go. He warned me that we would first have to drive to the church for the holy sacrament needed to administer the last rites to a dying man, and that it was strictly forbidden to carry on conversation with anyone carrying the holy sacrament.

The priest wore a long-skirted black overcoat with a velvet collar and a strange round hat which was also black. It was gloomy in the church, and cold. Some red paper roses hung at the base of the crucifix. Without candles, without the sound of church bells, without the rolling of organ music, the church was like the wings of a theater in daytime.

At first we traveled in silence. Bregman smacked and hurried his skinny brown horses, scolding them with the little sounds all drivers use. The rain drummed on the low-lying gardens. The priest held the chalice containing the holy sacrament wrapped up in a piece of black cloth. My gray schoolboy's overcoat became soaked, and turned dark in color.

Out of the haze made by the rain, the famous Alexandrian Gardens of Countess Branitskaya rose, it seemed, right to the sky. These were big gardens, comparable in size, Feokistov had told me, to Versailles. The snow was melting in them, wrapping the trees in trails of cold steam. Bregman turned around and said there were wild deer in the gardens.

"Mickiewicz* was very fond of these gardens," I said to the priest, forgetting that he was supposed to be silent all the way. I had wanted to say something pleasant to him in gratitude for his agreeing to this hard and dangerous trip. The priest smiled in answer.

Rain water stood on the fields around us. Reflected in it, you could see the jackdaws flying over, cawing. I turned up the collar of my coat and thought about my father and how little I knew

* Adam Mickiewicz (1798–1855), Polish poet and patriot, was the leader of the Romantic school in Polish literature; after a term in a Tsarist prison, he lived in Russia for five years.

him. He was a statistician who had worked almost all his life on various railroads—the Moscow-Brest, the Peterburg*-Warsaw, the Kharkov-Sevastopol, and the Southern-Western lines. We moved often from town to town, from Moscow to Pskov, then to Vilna, then to Kiev. Everywhere my father got along badly with his superiors. He was very sure of himself, an eager, good man.

A year before, my father had left Kiev and taken a job as statistician at a factory near Bryansk, in Orlovsky province. Having worked there only a little while, and without any apparent reason, he suddenly quit the job and went back to his father's old farm at Gorodishche. His brother Ilko, a village teacher, and Aunt Dosia were living there.

My father's inexplicable conduct upset all his relatives, but most of all my mother. She was living at this time with my older brother in Moscow. A month after my father's arrival in Gorodishche, he became ill and now he was dying.

The road led downhill through a ravine. At its end you could already hear the persistent roaring of the water. Bregman pulled in his horses.

"The causeway!" he said in a quavering voice. "Now's the time to pray to God."

The causeway suddenly appeared around a bend in the road. The priest half rose in his seat and grabbed Bregman by his faded red belt. The water was flowing very quickly, confined between the river's granite sides. At this point, the Ros River breaks in a fury through the Avratinsky Hills. The water was overflowing the stone causeway in a wide, clear wave, falling down like thunder, and filling the air with a cold mist.

Across the river, at the other end of the causeway, an enormous poplar seemed to leap into the sky, and I could see a small white house in the distance. I recognized the farm on the island where I had lived in early childhood—its trees and wattled hedges, the beam which raised water from the well, and the rocks along the shore. Sometimes my father and I had fished for minnows from those rocks.

Bregman stopped the horses near the causeway, dismounted, adjusted the harness with his whip handle, looked untrustingly at his carriage, and shook his head. Then for the first time the priest broke his vow of silence.

"Jesus Maria," he said in a low voice. "How will we get across it?"

"Eh, eh!" Bregman answered. "How should I know? Just sit quiet. The horses are already shaking all over."

* St. Petersburg.

The brown horses tossed their noses in the air, snorting, and walked into the rushing water. It pushed and twisted the carriage toward the unprotected edge of the causeway. The carriage slipped slantwise toward one side, grinding the iron hoops around its wheels against the stones. The horses trembled and leaned down until they were almost lying in the water so it would not rush them off their feet. Bregman swung his whip over his head.

In the middle of the causeway where the water was flowing fastest, making a kind of jingling sound, the horses stopped. The foaming rapids swirled around their spindly legs. Bregman cried out in a wailing voice and began to beat the horses unmercifully. They fell back a little and moved the carriage to the very edge of the causeway.

Then I saw Uncle Ilko. He was galloping up from the farm to the causeway on a gray horse. He yelled out something, and swung a coil of thin rope around his head. He came out onto the causeway and threw the rope. Bregman tied it somewhere underneath the horses and then the three of them—the gray and the two brown horses—finally dragged the carriage onto the island.

The priest crossed himself with a big Catholic crucifix, Bregman winked at Uncle Ilko and said that people would remember such a driver for a long time, and I asked about my father.

"He's still alive," Uncle Ilko answered, and he kissed me, scratching my face with his beard. "He's waiting. But where's your mother, Maria Grigorievna?"

"I sent her a telegram to Moscow. She'll probably get here tomorrow."

Uncle Ilko looked at the river. "It's still rising," he said. "It's bad, my dear Kostik. Well, perhaps it will get better. Let's go."

Aunt Dosia met us on the steps, all in black, with dry, cried-out eyes.

The badly ventilated rooms smelled of mint. I didn't recognize my father right away in the yellow old man, covered with gray bristles, who was waiting for me. My father was only fifty. I always remembered him as slightly stooping but well-proportioned, elegant, with dark hair, an unusual sad smile, and gray, attentive eyes.

Now he sat in an armchair, breathing hard, and he looked steadily at me, and a tear started down his dry cheek. It disappeared in his beard and Aunt Dosia wiped it away with a clean handkerchief.

My father couldn't speak. He was dying of cancer of the throat.

I sat beside him all night. Everyone else slept. The rain stopped. The stars shone coldly outside the windows. The river's noise grew steadily louder. The water was rising fast. Bregman and the priest could not get back and were marooned with us on the island.

In the middle of the night my father stirred and opened his eyes. I leaned over him. He tried to put his arm around my neck but he could not do it, and he said in a whistling sort of whisper:

"I am afraid . . . your lack of firmness . . . will destroy you."

"No," I answered quietly. "That won't happen."

"You'll see your mother," my father whispered. "I have treated her badly . . . May she forgive . . ."

He was silent, and he pressed my hand weakly.

I did not understand his words then, and only much later, after many years, did their bitter meaning become clear to me. It was also much later that I understood that my father had not really been a statistician at all, but a poet.

He died at dawn, but I did not realize it right away. It seemed to me that he was sleeping quietly.

An old man named Nikifor lived with us on the island. He was summoned to read the psalms over my father. He would interrupt his reading often to go out in the corridor and smoke *makhorka,* a cheap tobacco. There he would whisper to me uninteresting stories which had somehow stirred his imagination: about a bottle of wine he had drunk the summer before in Belaya Tserkov, about how he had once seen General Skobelyev near Plevna so close—"as close as that hedge"—about an extraordinary American threshing machine powered by a lightning rod. Nikifor was, as they said on the island, "not a serious man"—a babbler and a liar.

He read the psalms all day and all the following night, picking the wax off the sides of the candles with his black fingernails, falling asleep on his feet, starting to snore, then waking up and continuing to mutter his inaudible prayers.

On the other side of the river that night, someone started to wave a lantern and shout. I went out to the riverbank with Uncle Ilko. The river was racing. It tore across the causeway in a cold cascade. It was late and dark, and there was not a single star over our heads. Moisture rising from the thawing earth beat at our faces with a wild freshness. And all the time someone was shouting slowly on the other bank and waving a lantern, but because of the river's noise not a word could be understood.

"It must be Mama," I said to Uncle Ilko. But he made no answer.

"Let's go," he said quietly. "It's cold on the bank. You'll catch cold."

I did not want to go back to the house. Uncle Ilko was quiet a little longer, and then went away, but I stood there and watched the faraway lantern. The wind blew stronger and stronger, it shook the poplars, and from somewhere it brought the sweetish smell of straw.

We buried my father in the morning. Nikifor and Uncle Ilko dug a grave in a grove of trees on the edge of the ravine. From there you could see the woods far beyond the Ros, and the white March sky.

We carried the coffin out of the house on wide, embroidered hand straps. The priest went first. He looked straight in front of him with his quiet, gray eyes, saying Latin prayers in a low voice.

When we had carried the coffin out onto the steps, I saw an old carriage on the far side of the river, with unharnessed horses tethered to it, and a small woman in black—Mama. She was standing motionless on the bank. She could see how we were carrying my father. She sank to her knees and let her head fall to the ground.

A tall, lanky driver went up to her, leaned over her, and said something, but she went on lying there motionless. Then she jumped up and ran along the bank to the causeway. The driver grabbed her. She sank down helplessly on the ground and covered her face with her hands.

We carried my father along the road to the woods. At the turn, I looked back. My mother was sitting just as before, her face hidden in her hands.

Everyone was silent. Only Bregman kept rapping his whip against his boot.

At the grave the priest raised his gray eyes to the cold sky and said in Latin, slowly and clearly:

"Requiem aeternam dona eis, Domine, et lux perpetua luceat ei."

The priest stopped, and listened. The river roared. Some titmice were chirping in the branches of the old elm trees over our heads. The priest sighed and began to talk about eternal longing for happiness and about this vale of tears. These words fitted my father's life amazingly. They made my heart ache. Since then I have often felt the same anguish in my heart at any thought of man's thirst for happiness or of the inadequacy of human relations.

The river went on roaring, the birds whistled a little, and the coffin, now smeared with dirt and clay, slowly settled down into the grave.

At this time I was seventeen years old.

MY GRANDFATHER MAXIM GRIGORIEVICH

I stayed on at Gorodishche for several days after my father's funeral. It was only on the third day that the river fell and my mother could get across the stone causeway.

Her face had a pinched, dark look. She was no longer crying, but she sat for hours by my father's grave. There were no fresh flowers and the grave was covered with paper peonies. They had been made by girls in a neighboring village. They loved to braid these peonies in their hair, with silk ribbons of different colors.

Aunt Dosia tried to comfort and divert me. She got a chest full of old things out of a closet in the storeroom. Its cover opened with a loud noise. In the chest I found a yellowed hetman's charter deed,* written in Latin, a copper seal with a coat of arms, and a St. George's Medal for the Turkish War, several smoked-out pipes, and some very delicate black lace.

The charter deed and the seal had been handed down in our family from our remote ancestor, the hetman Sagaidachny. My father used to laugh about his hetman ancestors, and he loved to explain that our forefathers had plowed the land and harvested their grain as simple, patient farmers even though they considered themselves scions of the Zaporozhskaya (Dnieper) Cossacks.

When the Zaporozhskaya Cossacks were broken up under Catherine II, some of them were settled on the bank of the Ros River around Belaya Tserkov. The Cossacks settled unwillingly on the land. Their turbulent past was still boiling in their blood. Even I, who was born at the end of the nineteenth century, heard tales from old men of bloody battles against the Poles, campaigns against the Turks, great slaughters, and the Cossack hetmans.

Filled with these stories, I used to play battles with my brothers at Zaporozhskaya. We played in the ravine behind the farm where the dew was heavy on the wattled fences and on the thistles. Their red flowers and prickly leaves gave off a sickly smell in the heat. The clouds stood still in the sky over the ravine, lazy and mag-

* Originally a Polish military title, the word "hetman" has been retained by Cossack leaders and cavalry commanders.

nificent, the true clouds of the Ukraine. And so strong are the impressions we form in childhood that ever since then battles against the Poles and the Turks have been linked in my imagination with this wild field of full-blown thistles and their dusty prickles. The flowers of the thistles were like drops of Cossack blood.

The Zaporozhskaya turbulence diminished over the years. By the time of my childhood it survived only in long-drawn-out, abusive lawsuits against Countess Branitskaya, and in Cossack songs. These were sung to us, his grandchildren, by my grandfather Maxim Grigorievich.

He was a little man, all gray, with colorless but kindly eyes. All summer long he used to live in a hut near his beehives, in flight from the angry disposition of my Turkish grandmother.

In the distant past, Grandfather had been a Ukrainian oxcart driver. He went with his oxen as far as Perekop and Armyansk for salt and for dried fish. It was from him that I first heard that somewhere beyond the sky-blue and golden steppes of the Empress Catherine's country and the Khersonshchina lay the heavenly land of the Crimea.

Before he became an oxcart driver, Grandfather had served in the Tsar's army, had gone off to fight the Turkish War, had been captured, and had brought back a beautiful Turk as his wife, from the town of Kazanlik in Thrace. Her name was Fatima. When she married my grandfather, she took a new Christian name—Honorata.

We were as scared of our Turkish grandmother as my grandfather was, and we tried never to catch her eye.

Sitting next to his hut among the yellow pumpkin blossoms, Grandfather would sing for us the old Cossack songs and the oxdrivers' songs, in a wheezing tenor voice, or he would tell us all kinds of stories.

I loved the ox-drivers' songs for their sadness. One could sing songs like these for hours on end over the squeaking of cart wheels, lying on the cart and looking at the sky. The Cossack songs, too, always produced an incomprehensible sadness in me. They seemed sometimes to be the weeping of conscripts dragging their Turkish chains, sometimes solemn marching songs set to the melody of horses' hoofbeats.

What didn't my grandfather sing! Most often of all he sang our favorite song:

> *The Cossacks whistled*
> *Marching in the night.*
> *Marusenka cried*
> *Her clear eyes out.*

The story of his that we liked best was the tale of the lyre player Ostap. I don't know if you have ever seen a Ukrainian lyre. One can be found now, probably, only in a museum. But in those days you could find blind lyre players not only at fairs in little towns but often on the streets of Kiev itself.

A blind man would walk along holding on to the shoulder of a small barefoot boy in a ragged shirt, who would be leading him. Bread, onions, and salt, wrapped up in a clean rag, were stowed away in a canvas bag on his back, and the lyre hung in front. The lyre looked something like a violin, but a handle had been added to it, and a wooden rod with a little wheel. The lyre player turned the handle, the wheel revolved, rubbing against the strings, and they vibrated in different chords, just as if a hive of tame bees were buzzing around the player, accompanying him.

The lyre players almost never sang. They spoke their songs in a kind of recitative chant. Then they would stop, listen for a long time to their lyres humming and dying away, and then, staring straight in front of them through sightless eyes, they would ask for alms.

They did not beg like ordinary beggars. I remember one lyre player in the town of Cherkasy. "Throw me half a kopeck," he said, "for me, a blind man, and another for my boy, because without a boy a blind man can get lost and never find his way to heaven when he dies."

I do not remember a single fair without a lyre player. He would sit there, leaning against a dusty poplar tree. Compassionate old women would crowd around him, sighing, and throw greenish copper coins into his wooden bowl.

The memory of lyre players is always linked for me with Ukrainian fairs, early markets when the dew is still shining in the grass, cold shadows lying across the dusty roads, and a bluish smoke streaming across the land already lit up by the sun. With misted jugs of ice-cold milk, wet marigolds in pails of water, buckwheat honey, hot cheesecakes with raisins, sieves full of grapes, the smell of sea roach, the lazy ringing of church bells, the eager wrangling of chattering old women, the lace parasols of young provincial ladies of fashion, and the sudden rumble of a copper pot carried on the shoulders of a wild-eyed Rumanian. All the old men felt themselves obliged to rap the pot with their whip handles to see if the Rumanian copper were any good.

I knew the story of the lyre player Ostap almost by heart.

"It happened in the village of Zamoshe, near the town of Vasilkov," my grandfather would begin. "Ostap was the blacksmith in that village. His forge stood near the exit of the village, under dark willows which hung right over the river itself. There was nothing Ostap couldn't do well: he shoed horses, made nails, forged axles for the oxcarts.

"On one summer evening, Ostap was blowing on the coals in his smithy when a thunderstorm broke, stripping the moldering willow trees of their leaves and scattering them in the puddles. Ostap blew on his coals and suddenly he heard the stamping of fiery horses being reined up outside his smithy. And someone's voice—a woman's, a young voice—called for the blacksmith.

"Ostap went out, and stood stock-still. At the very door of his smithy a black horse was prancing, and on it was a woman of fabulous beauty in a long velvet dress, carrying a whip and wearing a veil. Her eyes were laughing behind the veil. And her lips were laughing. And the velvet of her dress was soft and blue, and the drops of water falling on her after the rain, from the black willow trees, were shimmering. Next to her, on another horse, was a young officer. A regiment of Uhlans was quartered about this time in Vasilkov.

" 'Blacksmith, my pigeon,' the lady said, 'shoe my horse for me, he's lost a shoe. The road is terribly slippery after the rain.'

"The woman dismounted from her saddle and sat on a log. Ostap began to shoe the horse. He worked away, but he watched the woman, and she suddenly grew troubled, too, lifted her veil, and looked at Ostap.

" 'I've never met you before,' Ostap said to her. 'You're not from around here, are you?'

" 'I come from Peterburg,' the woman answered. 'You handle that forge very well.'

" 'What are horseshoes?' Ostap said to her quietly. 'Worthless things! For you I could forge out of this steel such a thing as no empress in the whole world has.'

" 'What kind of a thing?' the woman asked.

" 'Whatever you like. Well, for example, I could forge you the most delicate rose, with leaves and thorns.'

" 'Good,' the woman answered, just as quietly. 'Thank you, blacksmith. I'll come for it in a week.'

"Ostap helped her into the saddle. She gave him her gloved hand for support, but Ostap could not restrain himself, and he held onto her hand ardently. She couldn't withdraw it before the officer hit Ostap with a violent backhand blow of his whip across the face, and shouted: 'Don't forget your place, peasant!'

"The horses reared and pranced. Ostap grabbed his hammer to

strike the officer. But he couldn't. He could see nothing in front of him. Blood was flowing down his face. The blow had hurt one of his eyes.

"But Ostap pulled himself together, worked for six days, and forged his rose. Several persons looked at it and said that such craftsmanship did not exist, probably, even in the land of Italy.

"In the evening of the seventh day someone rode up quietly to the smithy, got off a horse, and tied it to the hitching post. Ostap was afraid to go out and show his face. He covered his eyes with his hands, and waited.

"He heard gentle steps and light breathing and then someone's warm arms went around him and one, solitary tear fell on his shoulder.

" 'I know, I know everything,' the lady said. 'My heart has been sick for all these days. Forgive me, Ostap. Your great misfortune happened because of me. I have driven him away, my fiancé, and now I am going back to Peterburg!'

" 'Why?' Ostap asked in a low voice.

" 'My darling, my heart,' the woman said, 'people wouldn't let us be happy together.'

" 'It's as you wish,' Ostap answered. 'I'm a simple man, a blacksmith. For me, just to think about you—that's happiness.'

"The lady took the rose, kissed Ostap, and rode slowly away. Ostap went out on the threshold, looking after her, listening. Twice the lady stopped her horse. Twice she wanted to turn back. But she did not return. The stars whirled in the sky and fell down into the steppe; it was as if heaven were weeping over their love. That's how it was, my boy!"

At this point, Grandfather always paused. I sat there, afraid to stir. Then I would ask, in a whisper:

"So they never saw each other again?"

"No," Grandfather answered, "that's true, they never saw each other again. Ostap started to go blind. He decided then to walk to Peterburg so he could see her again before he became completely blind. He got to the Tsar's capital, and learned that she had died— I guess she couldn't survive the separation. Ostap found her grave in the cemetery; it was made of white marble. He looked at it, and his heart stopped beating—his steel rose was fixed to the stone. The lady had ordered the rose to be put on her grave. Forever. So Ostap began to play the lyre, and there it is. He must have died somewhere along the road, I guess, or at some market fair under a cart. Amen!"

The shaggy dog Ryabchik, with shreds of turnip on his muzzle, would yawn loudly while Grandfather told this tale. I would kick him in the side in indignation, and Ryabchik, not a bit insulted, would rub up against me to be petted, sticking out his warm tongue. There were only the debris of teeth in Ryabchik's jaws. The autumn before, when we left Gorodishche, he had bitten onto the carriage wheel—he wanted to stop it—and broken his teeth.

Ah, Grandfather Maxim Grigorievich! It's to him I owe my susceptibility to impressions, and my romanticism. They transformed my childhood into a series of collisions with reality. I suffered from this, but I still knew that my grandfather was right, and that a life made up of sobriety and good sense might be fine, but it would be burdensome to me, and fruitless. "To every man," as Grandfather used to say, "his own recipe."

Perhaps this was why Grandfather could not get along with his old woman. Or, rather, why he hid from her. Her Turkish blood gave her not one single attractive trait except her beautiful but threatening exterior.

The old lady was despotic, and captious. She used to smoke a pound of the strongest black tobacco every day. She smoked it in short, hot pipes. She did the housekeeping. Her black eyes caught the slightest disorder in the house.

On holidays she wore a satin dress edged with black lace. She would walk out of the house, sit down on the small mound of earth along the outer walls of a peasant's house, smoke her pipe, and watch the swift Ros River flowing by. Sometimes she would laugh out loud at her own thoughts, but no one ever dared to ask her what she was laughing at.

The only thing that won us even a little to the old lady was a hard, rose-colored bar of something like soap. She kept it hidden in her cupboard. Occasionally she would take it out and proudly give it to us to sniff. The bar gave off the most subtle fragrance of roses.

My father told me that the valley around Kazanlik—my grandmother's birthplace—was called the Valley of Roses, that attar of roses was made there, and that the wonderful bar was some kind of substance made from this oil.

Valley of Roses! The words themselves moved me. I could not understand how a person could grow up in such a poetic place with such a harsh spirit as my grandmother.

CARP

While I stayed on now in Gorodishche after my father's death, I recalled my childhood and the times we used to come here from Kiev, happy and carefree, for the summer. My mother and father were still young then, and my grandfather and his Turkish wife had not yet died. I was still the littlest kind of little boy and I made up a fabulous world out of the simple things around us.

The Kiev train pulled into Belaya Tserkov in the evening. My father hired a flashy driver in the station square. We got to Gorodishche in the night. Through sleep I heard the tiresome jangling of the cart springs, then the noise of water around the mill, then the barking of dogs. The horses snorted. The night shone with uncountable stars. Out of the wet dark came the smell of weeds.

Aunt Dosia would carry me asleep into the warm farmhouse, its floor covered with different-colored mats. The house smelled of boiled milk. I opened my eyes for a minute, to see around my face the elegant embroidery on Aunt Dosia's snow-white sleeves.

In the morning the hot sun woke me up, striking against the white walls. Red and yellow hollyhocks waved back and forth outside the window. Together with them, a nasturtium blossom looked in the window; a hairy bee sat inside it. Lying quite still, I watched how angrily the bee turned and twisted to get out of the narrow flower. Rays of light ran endlessly across the ceiling, reflections from the river. The river itself ran noisily beside the house.

Then I heard my funny Uncle Ilko say to someone:

"Well, the sun is barely up, of course, but the parade has started! Dosia, put the cakes and the cherry brandy on the table!"

I jumped up, ran barefoot to the window, and saw the parade. A file of old men in straw hats was approaching the farm over the causeway from the other side of the river, tapping the ground with their crooked sticks. Their medals jingled and glittered on their brown robes. These were the estimable and respected elders of the neighboring village of Pilipchi, come to greet us and to congratulate us on our safe arrival. In front walked the pockmarked village elder Trofim, with his copper badge around his neck.

Fuss and bustle swept through the house. Aunt Dosia spread a cloth on the table. Wind blew through the room. Mama hurriedly put cakes on dishes and sliced some sausage. My father opened bottles of homemade cherry brandy, and Uncle Ilko set cut-glass tumblers on the table.

Then Aunt Dosia and Mama ran off to change their dresses, and my father and Uncle Ilko went out on the porch to meet the old men who were approaching as solemnly and inevitably as fate itself.

At last the old men came up, quietly kissed my father and my uncle, sat down on the mound of earth around the little house, and all sighed together. Then the village elder Trofim, after a small preparatory cough, uttered his traditional sentence:

"I have the honor to welcome you most respectfully, Georgi Maximovich, on your arrival among us, in this dark and quiet place!"

"Thank you," said my father.

"Yes-s," the old men all said together, sighing again with relief. "It's so, of course."

"Yes-s," Trofim repeated, and he looked through the window at the table where the bottles were shining in the morning light.

"That's just how it should be, of course," said an old soldier with a crooked nose.

"Yes-s, that's clear!" A small and very curious old man named Nedolya moved into the conversation. He was the father of twelve daughters. He forgot their names in his old age, and he could count only five on his fingers: Hannah, Parasya, Gorpina, Olessya, Frossya . . . then the old man would grow confused and start the count all over again.

"So it is!" the old men said, and for a little while they were quiet.

By now my grandfather, Maxim Grigorievich, had come out of the cottage. The old men stood up and bowed deeply to him. Grandfather bowed in answer, and the old men, sighing noisily, sat down again on the ground, grunted, were silent, looked at the earth. At last Uncle Ilko guessed, from some mysterious clue, that everything was ready inside the cottage, and he said:

"Well, thank you for the conversation, good people. If you please, let us now eat what God has sent us."

Mama, in a smart summer dress, greeted the old men inside the cottage. They kissed her hand, and in reply she kissed their brown hands—such was the custom. Aunt Dosia, pretty and red-cheeked, with prematurely gray hair, in a blue dress and a scarf with crimson roses, bowed to the old men from the waist.

After the first glass of the sticky cherry brandy, Nedolya, tortured by curiosity, began his questioning. All the things we had brought from Kiev astonished him. Pointing at them, he asked: "What's that? What's it for?"

My father explained to him that that was a brass flatiron, and this was an ice-cream freezer, and there, on the cupboard, that was a folding mirror. Nedolya nodded his head each time in sheer delight.

"There's a tool for everything!"

"That's so, of course," the old men all agreed, and they took another drink.

Summer came into its own at Gorodishche—hot summer with its terrifying thunderstorms, the noise of the trees, the cold currents of river water, the catching of fish, the blackberry thickets, the sweet sensation of carefree, constantly changing, days.

The island on which we lived was, of course, the most mysterious place in the world. Behind the house were two large, deep ponds. It was always gloomy there, with old willows and dark water. Beyond the ponds and up the hill rose a grove of impenetrable nut trees. And beyond this grove began the fields, standing waist high in flowers and so fragrant that on hot days they made your head ache.

Beyond the fields, where the beehives were, a thin streamer of smoke curled up from the little cabin where Grandfather lived. And beyond this cabin were the unexplored lands—red granite cliffs covered with creeping little bushes and wild strawberries.

In the hollows of these cliffs stood little lakes of rain water. Small wagtails, shaking their colored tails, drank the warm water. Clumsy, impudent bumblebees spun around dizzily and buzzed when they fell in the water, calling vainly for help.

The cliffs presented a sheer wall to the Ros River. We were forbidden to walk here. But we snaked our way sometimes to the edge of the cliffs and looked down. The river flowed in a tight limpid torrent. Under the surface of the water, thin quivering fish swam slowly up against the current.

On the other side of the river Countess Branitskaya's forest reserve sloped upward. The sun could not break through the massive green of these woods. Only once in a long while did a beam of light break through the foliage and open to our eyes the fantastic power of this vegetation. Small birds flew like specks of dust in this beam of light. They chased each other with little peeps and dove into the leaves as if into green water.

But the ponds were my favorite places. Every morning my father would go there to fish. He took me with him.

We went out of the house very early, walking carefully on the heavy wet grass. The willow branches shone in quiet gold stripes among the dark foliage. The carp swam in still water. Water lilies grew in the ponds, and water buckwheat hung over the black abyss.

A mysterious world of water and plants opened before me. The charm of this world was so great that I could sit on the shore of a pond from sunrise to sunset.

My father would fix his lines quietly, then start to smoke. The tobacco smoke drifted across the water and disappeared in the bushes along the shore.

I filled a pail with water from the pond, threw grass into it, and waited. The red floats stood motionless in the water. Then one of them would begin to bob, starting ripples of light, or would plunge suddenly down, or be yanked quickly to one side. My father pulled the line tight, the walnut rod bent in an arc, and a gurgling, splashing sound started in the mist over the pond. The water churned. Water beetles scattered hurriedly to all sides, and at last in the mysterious depths there appeared a golden flash. It was impossible to distinguish what it was until my father had pulled the carp out onto the trampled grass. It lay on its side, gasping, flapping its fins. The surprising smell of an underwater kingdom rose from its scales.

I put the carp in the pail. It twisted there in the grass, then suddenly flapped its tail and covered me with drops of water. I tasted the drops with my lips, and I wanted very much to drink from the pail, but my father would not permit this.

It seemed to me the water in the pail with the carp and the grass should be just as fragrant and tasty as the rain which falls in thunderstorms. And all the boys on the island drank this thirstily, and knew that it would make a man live to be a hundred and twenty. This, at any rate, was what Nikifor assured us.

PLEURISY

Thunderstorms were frequent in Gorodishche. They began usually on Ivan Kupala Day* and lasted all through July, piling up enormous clouds of many colors over the island, with lightning and thunder enough to make our house shake and to frighten Aunt Dosia into a dead faint.

My memory of my first love affair is connected with these thunderstorms. I was nine years old.

On Ivan Kupala Day the young girls from Pilipchi used to come to our island, all dressed up, to float wreaths on the river. They made the wreaths out of wild flowers and in the center of each wreath they put a crosspiece made of twigs and fastened a wax candle end to it. The girls would light the candles at twilight and float the wreaths on the river.

The girls were telling their fortunes: the one whose candle burned the longest would be the happiest. But luckiest of all was the girl whose wreath floated into a whirlpool and slowly turned in circles within a pool in the river under the steep bank opposite where we stood. It always seemed quieter there, the candles burned with a special brightness in the whirlpool, and even from the bank where we stood we could hear the sputtering of their candlewicks.

All the grownups and we, the children, dearly loved these wreaths on Ivan Kupala Day. Only Nikifor would grunt scornfully and say: "It's stupid! There's no sense to those wreaths!"

One of the girls was Hannah, my second cousin. She was sixteen. She used to braid orange and black ribbons into her reddish hair. She wore a necklace of dull coral beads, and her eyes were green and shining. Whenever she smiled, she would drop her eyes and then lift them slowly, as if it was hard work for her to raise them. Her high coloring never left her cheeks.

* June 24: Ivan Kupala Day is a Russian religious holiday celebrating the birth of John the Baptist but also linked with many local rites and superstitions marking the summer solstice; fire and flame, to ward off evil spirits and protect the harvest, play an important part in its celebration.

I sometimes heard Mama and Aunt Dosia pitying Hannah for something. I wanted to know what they were saying, but they always stopped talking as soon as I came near.

On Ivan Kupala Day I was allowed to go with Hannah to join the girls by the river. On the way, she asked me:

"What are you going to be, Kostik, when you grow up?"

"A sailor," I answered.

"Ah, no, you mustn't," Hannah said. "Sailors are drowned in the deep. Then some girl will have to cry her beautiful eyes out because of you."

I paid no attention to Hannah's words. I hung onto her warm, dark-colored hand and told her about my first trip to sea.

Earlier in the spring my father had had to go to Novorossisk on a three-day business trip and took me with him. We saw the sea first from a distance; it looked like a dark blue wall. For a long time I couldn't understand what it was. Then I saw a green bay and a lighthouse, I heard the noise of waves on a breakwater, and the sea flowed into me as a magnificent, not very clear, dream flows into one's memory.

Two black warships with yellow funnels stood in the roadstead —*The Twelve Apostles* and *The Three Saints*. My father and I visited them. I was astonished by the tanned officers in white tunics with gold daggers, and by the oily warmth of the engine rooms. But most of all I was astonished by my father. I had never seen him like this. He laughed and joked and talked eagerly with the officers. We even went into the cabin of one of the naval engineers. My father drank cognac with him and smoked rose-colored Turkish cigarettes with Arabic letters printed on them in gold.

Hannah listened, lowering her eyes. I felt sorry for her, for some reason, and I told her that when I became a sailor I would certainly take her on my ship.

"But what will you take me as?" Hannah asked. "As cook? Or as laundress?"

"No!" I answered, on fire with boyish enthusiasm. "You will be my wife."

Hannah stopped and looked me sternly in the eyes.

"Take an oath!" she whispered. "Swear it on your mother's heart!"

"I swear it!" I answered without hesitation.

Hannah smiled, the pupils of her eyes turned as green as sea water, and she kissed me ardently on the eyes. I could feel the warmth of her lips. We were silent the rest of the way to the river.

Hannah's candle went out first of all. A smoky cloud was mov-

ing up over Countess Branitskaya's woods. But we were so fascinated by the wreaths that we didn't notice it until the wind hit us,
the bushes bent whistling to the ground, and the first lightning
flashed, followed by a deafening clap of thunder.

Squealing girls threw themselves under the trees. Hannah took
the scarf off her shoulders, covered me with it, grabbed my hand,
and we both ran. She was dragging me, the cloudburst was catching up with us, and I knew we'd never get home in time.

The downpour hit us close to Grandfather's hut. We were
soaked to the skin when we got there. Grandfather was not in the
hut.

We sat close to each other in the little cabin. Hannah dried my
hands. She smelled of wet cloth. She kept on asking me, in a
frightened voice:

"Are you cold? Oh, if you get sick, what will I do?"

I shuddered. I was actually very cold. Fear, terror, and love
followed each other in Hannah's eyes.

Then she held on to her throat and coughed. I could see a vein
throbbing in her soft, clean throat. I put my arms around her and
laid my head on her wet shoulder. I wished I had a mother who
was as young and as good.

"What's the matter with you?" Hannah asked me in confusion,
still coughing and stroking my head. "What's the matter with you?
Don't be frightened. The thunder won't hurt us. I'm here with you.
Don't be frightened."

Then she pushed me gently away, covered her mouth with the
sleeve of her blouse, which was embroidered with red oak leaves;
next to them there showed a spot of blood on the fabric, just like
the embroidered oak leaves.

"I don't need your oath," Hannah whispered, looking guiltily
and sullenly at me, and she smiled a bitter kind of smile. "I was
only joking."

The thunder was now rumbling far beyond the edge of the
enormous earth. The downpour had stopped. The only noise was
the patter of raindrops on the leaves.

That night I ran a fever. The young doctor Napelbaum came
out the next day from Belaya Tserkov on his bicycle, examined
me, and found that I had pleurisy.

Napelbaum went from us to Pilipchi to see Hannah, came back,
and told my mother in the next room, in a low voice:

"Maria Grigorievna, Hannah has galloping consumption. She
won't live till spring."

I cried, called Mama, hugged her, and noticed that the same

tender vein throbbed in Mama's throat as in Hannah's. Then I cried still harder and couldn't stop for a long time, but Mama stroked my head and said:

"What's the matter with you? I'm here with you. Don't be frightened."

I got well, but Hannah died that winter, in February.

The next summer I went with Mama to her grave and put a bunch of oxeye daisies, tied with black ribbon, on the little green mound. Hannah used to braid them in her hair. And somehow I felt awkward, because Mama was standing next to me holding a red parasol against the sun, and because I had not come to Hannah alone.

THE TRIP TO CHENSTOKHOV

In Cherkasy, on the Dnieper, lived my other grandmother—Vikentiya Ivanovna, a tall old Polish woman. She had a lot of daughters, who were my aunts. One of them, Yefrosinya Grigorievna, was the director of the girls' *gymnasium** in Cherkasy. My grandmother lived with this aunt in a big wooden house.

Vikentiya Ivanovna always wore mourning, with a black head-dress. She first wore mourning after the defeat of the Polish uprising in 1863 and had never abandoned it afterwards. We were all convinced that Grandmother's fiancé must have been killed during the uprising, and that he must have been a proud Polish revolutionary, not at all like her cross old husband, my grandfather, who had formerly been a notary public in Cherkasy.

I remember this grandfather only dimly. He lived in a little attic which he seldom left. Grandmother had banished him there away from everyone else because of his intolerable addiction to smoking.

* A *gymnasium*, in pre-1917 Russia, was an eight-year secondary school. Between the ages of ten and eighteen, students studied subjects roughly comparable to those taught in high school and college years in the United States.

Sometimes we would visit him in his room, which was bitter and cloudy with smoke. Tobacco lay in piles on the table, spilled out of its packages. Grandfather sat in an armchair, rolling cigarette after cigarette in his sinewy fingers. He never used to talk with us. He would rub the hair on the back of our heads with his heavy hand, and give us the lilac-colored paper from his tobacco packages.

We used to go often from Kiev to visit Vikentiya Ivanovna. She had one regular habit: every spring she would go on a pilgrimage to the Roman Catholic holy places in Warsaw, Vilna, or Chenstokhov. But sometimes she would take it into her head to visit Orthodox saints instead, and then she would go to the Troitsko-Sergievskaya Monastery, or to Pochayev.

All her daughters and sons-in-law laughed at this, and said that if it went any further Vikentiya Ivanovna would begin to visit Jewish synagogues and would end her days as a pilgrim to Mohammed's grave in Mecca.

Once when my father was going to a conference on statistics in Vienna, a violent quarrel between him and my grandmother was produced by her decision to take me with her on one of her pilgrimages. The decision pleased me, and I couldn't understand my father's indignation. I was eight years old.

I can remember the limpid spring in Vilna and the Ostra Brama Chapel where Grandmother walked up to receive the sacrament. The whole city was shimmering in the green and gold brilliance of the first leaves of spring. At noon, on Castle Hill, they fired a cannon of Napoleonic vintage. My grandmother was a very well-read woman and she explained everything to me in great detail.

Her religious feelings never conflicted at all with her progressive ideas. She was deeply moved by Herzen and also by Henryk Sienkiewicz.* Portraits of Pushkin and Mickiewicz always hung in her bedroom next to icons of the Chenstokhov Madonna. During the 1905 revolution she hid revolutionary students in her home, and she hid Jews, too, at the time of pogroms.

From Vilna we went to Warsaw. I can remember only the monument to Copernicus, and a café where Grandmother treated me to "upside-down coffee": there was more milk in it than coffee. She also gave me cakes—meringues which melted in my mouth with

---

* Alexander I. Herzen (1812–1870), Russian writer and revolutionary leader, left his country for good in 1847 and many of his writings were banned by Tsarist censors. Henryk Sienkiewicz (1846–1916), the best-known Polish novelist, author of Quo Vadis, won the Nobel prize for literature in 1905.

a buttery, cold sweetness. We were served by fidgety waitresses in crimped aprons.

From Warsaw Grandmother and I went to Chenstokhov to visit the famous Catholic monastery, Yasna Gora, where the miracle-working icon of the Black Madonna is preserved.

This was the first time I ever encountered religious fanaticism. It astonished me and frightened me. From this time a terror of fanaticism and an aversion to it entered my consciousness. For a long time I could not free myself from this terror.

The train got in to Chenstokhov early in the morning. It was about a mile and a half from the station to the monastery, which stood on a high green hill. The pilgrims poured out of the train— Polish peasants with their wives and a few city folk in dusty derby hats. A fat old priest and some young boys in surplices were waiting at the station for the pilgrims.

The procession formed up on the dusty road next to the station. The priest blessed it and mumbled a prayer through his nose. The crowd fell to its knees and crawled toward the monastery, singing psalms.

The pilgrims crawled on their knees all the way to the monastery. A gray-haired woman with a white, ecstatic face went first. She was holding a black wooden crucifix in her arms.

The priest walked slowly and indifferently in front of the crowd. It was hot and dusty. Sweat poured down his face. People panted hoarsely, and looked back angrily at the laggards.

I grabbed Grandmother's hand.

"What is this for?" I asked in a whisper.

"Don't be frightened," she answered in Polish. "They are all sinners. They want to ask forgiveness from Pan God."

"Let's get away from here," I said to my grandmother. But she pretended she hadn't heard my words.

The Chenstokhov Monastery turned out to be a medieval castle. Rusty Swedish cannonballs were imbedded in its walls. Green water stood putrid in the moat. Dense trees rustled on the ramparts.

The access bridges were lowered by steel chains. We drove across one of them, in a hired carriage, into the wilderness of court-yards, passages, back streets, and arcades which made up the monastery.

A lay brother with a rope around his waist led us to the hospice. They gave us a cold, vaulted room. The inevitable crucifix hung on one wall. On one brass foot of Christ, pierced by its nail, some-one had hung a wreath of paper flowers.

The monk asked Grandmother if she were not suffering from

some disease. Grandmother was always anxious about her health, and she complained at once about a pain in her heart. From the pocket of his brown cassock, the monk took a handful of small hearts, arms, heads, and even toy babies, all made of silver, and scattered them across the table.

"There are hearts," he said, "for five rubles, for ten, and for twenty. They have already been blessed. All you have to do is to hang one with your prayer on the icon of the Mother of God."

Grandmother bought a plump little heart for ten rubles.

She told me we would be going to the Catholic Church that night for a High Mass. She poured me some tea, we ate some stale rolls we had brought from Warsaw, and she lay down to rest. She fell asleep. I looked out the narrow window. A monk walked by in a handsome faded cassock. Then two Polish peasants sat down in the shade next to the wall, took some gray bread and garlic out of their bundles, and started to eat. They had blue eyes and strong teeth.

I grew bored, and I went out cautiously into the street. Grandmother had ordered me not to speak Russian in the monastery. This scared me because I knew only a few words of Polish.

I got lost, and found myself in a narrow passageway between high walls. It was paved with cracked flagstones. Plantains were growing in the cracks. Iron lanterns were fastened to the walls, but it must have been a long time since they had been lighted—in one of them I saw a bird's nest.

A small door in the wall was half open. I looked through it. An apple orchard, dappled by sunshine, stretched down the slope of the hill. I walked in, warily. The trees were dropping their blossoms; yellowed petals were falling on the ground. A thin but pleasant sound of music floated down from the church bells.

A young Polish peasant woman was sitting under an old apple tree, suckling her child. The baby frowned and cried. A white-faced peasant lad was standing next to the woman. A blue satin ribbon was sewed onto his new felt hat, with a peacock's feather pinned to the ribbon. The fellow kept looking at his feet out of small, round eyes, and didn't stir.

A short bald monk with gardener's shears in his hand sat down on a stump facing the woman. He looked at me carefully, and said:

"Praise be to Our Lord, Jesus Christ!"

"Forever and ever," I answered, just as Grandmother had taught me. But my heart stopped beating in sheer terror.

The monk turned around and began again to listen to the woman. A lock of white hair fell across her face. She brushed it away gently with her hand and said, complainingly:

"When my son was in his fifth month, Mikhas shot a stork. He brought it back to our cottage. I cried, and I told him: 'What have you done, you fool? You know that God takes a child away from people for every stork they kill. Why did you shoot it, Mikhas?' "

The fellow in the felt hat went right on looking impassively at the ground.

"And since that day," the peasant woman went on, "our son has been turning blue, and the disease has started to choke him in the throat. Will the Mother of God help him?"

The monk looked evasively to one side, and made no answer.

"Ah!" the woman said, and she began to scratch her throat with one hand. "Ah!" she cried and she pressed the baby to her breast.

I remembered the little toy babies made of silver which the servant had shown Grandmother in the hospice of the monastery. I felt sorry for this woman. I wanted to tell her that she ought to buy one of those babies for twenty rubles and hang it on the Chenstokhov icon. But I didn't know enough Polish to give such complicated advice. Besides, I was afraid of the gardener-monk. I walked out of the orchard.

When I came back, Grandmother was still sleeping. I lay down, without undressing, on a hard cot, and I fell asleep at once.

Grandmother woke me in the middle of the night. I washed in cold water in a big glazed bowl. I was trembling with excitement. Outside the windows I could see hand lanterns, and I could hear the stamping of many feet, and church bells.

"Tonight," Grandmother said, "the Cardinal will celebrate Mass, the Papal Nuncio."

It was hard to find our way to the church through the dark.

"Hold on to me!" Grandmother said in the darkness.

We groped our way into the church. I could see nothing. There was not a single candle, not a glimmer of light in the stifling blackness, penned in by the high church walls and filled with the breathing of hundreds of people. The pitch black darkness had the sweetish smell of flowers. I could feel a worn iron floor under my feet. I took a step, and bumped into something.

"Stand quietly," my grandmother whispered to me. "People are lying in a cross on the floor. You'll tread on them."

She began to recite a prayer while I waited, holding on to her elbow. I was frightened stiff. The people lying in a cross on the floor were breathing quietly. A sad kind of rustling drifted around us.

Suddenly the sobbing noise of an organ broke through the heavy blackness. At the same moment, hundreds of candles were lighted. I shrank into myself, blinded and scared.

The great golden curtain which covered the icon of the Chen-

stokhov Madonna began slowly to rise. Six old priests in lace vest-
ments were kneeling in front of the icon, their backs to the crowd.
Their hands were held up to heaven. Only the thin Cardinal, in a
purple cassock with a broad, violet-colored girdle around his slender
waist, stood at full height—also with his back to the praying people
—as if he were listening to the dying chords of the organ and the
sobbing of the crowd.

I had never before seen such a theatrical and incredible spectacle.

After the midnight Mass, Grandmother and I walked down a
long vaulted corridor. It was growing light. The praying people
knelt along the walls. My Grandmother also knelt, and forced me
to kneel with her. I was afraid to ask her what all these people with
their mad eyes were waiting for.

The Cardinal appeared at the end of the corridor. He was walking easily and swiftly. His purple cassock billowed out and brushed
against the faces of the praying people. They caught at its edge and
kissed it with passion and humility.

"Kiss his robe," my grandmother told me in a quick whisper.

But I wasn't listening. I was pale with resentment, and I looked
straight in the Cardinal's face. There must have been tears in my
eyes. For he stopped, put his dry little hand for a moment on my
head, and said in Polish:

"The tears of a child—are the best prayer to God."

I looked at him. His sharp face was covered with brown leather.
A sort of dim glow lit up his face. His black, squinting eyes looked
expectantly at me.

I stayed stubbornly silent.

The Cardinal turned sharply around and went on down the corridor, just as swiftly as before, raising a little breeze.

My grandmother grabbed me by the arm so tightly that I almost
cried out with the pain, and led me out of the corridor.

"Just like your father!" she said when we had come out into
the courtyard. "Just like your father! The Chenstokhov Mother of
God! Ah, what is going to happen to your life!"

THE PINK OLEANDERS

Oleanders grew in green tubs in the gallery of my grandmother's house in Cherkasy. They had pink flowers. I loved their grayish leaves and their pale blossoms. They were linked in my imagination somehow with the sea—far away, warm, washing the shores of countries flowering with oleanders.

Grandmother was good at growing flowers. Fuchsias always bloomed in the winter in her bedroom. In the summer so many flowers grew in her garden, up to the fences choked with burdock, that they seemed to make a solid bouquet. The fragrance of the flowers reached even up to my grandfather's attic and drove the smell of tobacco out of it. He would slam the window shut in anger. He used to say that the fragrance reactivated his old asthma.

Flowers fascinated me then; I thought of them as living people. Mignonette was a poor young girl in a gray patched dress. Only her amazing fragrance betrayed her fabulous origin. Yellow tea roses seemed to me young beauties who had lost their fine coloring by overindulgence in drinking tea.

The flower bed with pansies seemed to me a fancy-dress ball. These weren't flowers, but happy, cunning gypsies in black velvet masks, and many-colored dancers, some blue, some lilac, some yellow.

I didn't like the daisies. They reminded me of the boring dresses worn by the daughters of my grandmother's neighbor, the teacher Tsimmer. These girls had no eyebrows and were tow-haired. Every time you met them they curtsied, showing their muslin little-girls' petticoats.

Portulaca was, of course, the most interesting flower of all, creeping along the ground and blazing with clean, strong colors. Instead of leaves, portulaca had soft, juicy needles. I had only to squeeze them and the green juice would spurt out into my face.

Grandmother's garden and all her flowers acted with extraordinary force on my imagination. My passion for travel must have started in this garden. When I was a child I invented for myself a faraway country where I would go some day, a plain with hills on it and filled to the horizon with grass and flowers. Towns and cities drowned in them. When express trains crossed this plain, pollen coated the sides of the cars in a thick layer.

I told all this to my brothers, my sister, and Mama, but nobody wanted to understand me. In my oldest brother's answer I heard for the first time the scornful epithet: "dreamer."

My Aunt Nadya was perhaps the only one who understood me. She was the youngest of my grandmother's daughters. She was twenty-three at that time. She had studied singing at the Moscow Conservatory. She had an excellent contralto voice.

Aunt Nadya came to Grandmother's in Cherkasy for Easter and the summer. At once the quiet spacious house became noisy and full of life. She used to play with us, skimming over the polished floors and laughing. She was a well-proportioned, slender girl with blond, tousled hair and a slightly open, fresh-looking mouth.

Flecks of gold shone in her gray eyes. These eyes laughed at everything, at any joke, at a happy word, even at the disgusted face of Anton, the cat, who didn't like our cheerfulness.

"Nadya doesn't care a fig for anything!" Mama used to say with a slight reproach in her voice.

Aunt Nadya's happy-go-lucky good spirits were proverbial in our family. She was always losing her gloves, her powder, her money, but it never bothered her. On the day of her arrival we always raised the top of the piano, and it stayed open until Aunt Nadya had gone back to her cheerful, hospitable Moscow.

Piles of music accumulated in the armchairs. The candles smoked. The piano murmured all day long, and sometimes I went to sleep to the sound of a tender voice singing a barcarolle.

> *Float, my gondola,*
> *Lit by the moon.*
> *The barcarolle sounds*
> *Over the sleepy waves.*

And in the morning an ingratiating voice would wake me up, singing almost in a whisper into my ear, with Aunt Nadya's hair tickling my cheeks. "Get up at once," she would sing. "Aren't you ashamed to be asleep, giving yourself up to dreams? The robins have been singing for a long time, and the roses have opened just for you."

I would open my eyes, she would kiss me and immediately disappear, and a minute later I would hear her circling the drawing room in a fast waltz with her brother, a cadet, Uncle Kolya. Some-

times he too came from Peterburg to celebrate Easter with my
grandmother.

And I would jump up, feeling sure of an impetuous, happy, unexpected day.

When Aunt Nadya sang, even my grandfather would partly
open the door from his attic onto the stairway, and later he would
ask my grandmother: "How was it that only Nadya got this gypsy
blood?"

Grandmother asserted that Aunt Nadya's blood was not gypsy,
but Polish. Quoting literary examples and the history of Poland, she
showed that such irresistibly happy, extravagant, and lighthearted
women are often to be found among the Poles.

"That's exactly right!" my grandfather said caustically and he
closed his door tightly behind him. "Exactly right!" he repeated
loudly behind the closed door as he sat down to roll a cigarette.

Once, I remember, Easter came late in the spring. The gardens
in Cherkasy were already in bloom. We came from Kiev on a river
steamer. Then Aunt Nadya came from Moscow.

I loved Easter, but I dreaded the pre-Easter days because I was
required to grind almond flour for hours, or to beat whites of eggs
with a spoon. I grew tired from this, and even cried a little, quietly.

Besides, great confusion reigned in Grandmother's house just
before Easter. Women with their skirts tucked up washed the fig
plants, the rhododendrons, the windows, and the floor, beat the
carpets and the upholstered furniture, polished the brass handles
on all the doors and windows. They drove us without respite from
room to room.

After the cleaning came the religious rites—my grandmother
always made the dough for the *kulich* or Easter cake. In our family we always called it "the satiny baba." They covered the tub of
yellow, bubbly dough with quilted towels, and, until the dough had
risen, we couldn't run through the rooms, slam the doors, or talk
loudly. When a horsecab drove down the street, Grandmother would
take alarm: the slightest vibration might make the dough fall and
then good-by to the tall spongy *kulich* smelling of saffron and covered with sugar icing.

Besides the *kulich* Grandmother baked a great many different
mazurkas—dry little cookies with raisins or almonds. When the
pans with these hot cakes were taken out of the oven, the house
was filled with such an odor that even my grandfather began to
grow nervous in his attic. He would open his door and look down
into the drawing room where the long marble table was already
covered with heavy tablecloths.

Finally, on Holy Saturday, the house was filled with a refreshing cleanliness and quiet. In the morning we were each given a glass of watery tea and some dry biscuits, and then we ate nothing all day until the fast-breaking after matins. This slight hunger pleased us. The day seemed very long. Grandmother's command not to chatter so much put us all in a mood of celebration.

In the middle of the night we set off for matins. They dressed me up in long sailor's trousers and a sailor's blouse with brass buttons and they parted my hair with a brush, and it hurt. I looked at myself in the mirror, saw a strangely excited and flushed little boy, and was very pleased.

Aunt Yefrosinya Grigorievna came out of her rooms. She alone took no part in the holiday preparations. She was always sick, spoke very rarely, and just smiled pleasantly in answer to our happy chatter. She came out in a vague blue dress, with a gold watch chain around her neck and a red sash pinned to her shoulder. Mama explained to me that this sash was the reward for graduation with honors from the institute where Aunt Yefrosinya Grigorievna had studied.

Mama put on her holiday gray dress, and my father a black suit with a white waistcoat.

Then Grandmother appeared—festive and beautiful, dressed all in black silk with artificial heliotrope flowers as a corsage. Her smooth gray hair could be seen under her lace headdress. Her dress rustled and she moved with great lightness—my grandmother always grew younger on this night. She lit the lamps, then drew on her black lace gloves, and my father held out her cloak.

"You're not going to the service, of course?" Grandmother asked him in a pleasant but cool voice.

"No, Vikentiya Ivanovna," my father answered with a smile. "I'll lie down for a while. They'll wake me up when you get back from church."

"Ah," Grandmother said, shrugging her shoulders to make her cloak fit better. "I have only one hope now, that your jokes have bored God at last and that He will stretch out His hand to you."

"I, too, am counting heavily on that," my father answered courteously.

Grandmother went up to the attic for a moment to say good-by to my grandfather. When she had returned, Aunt Nadya came into the hall. She was always late. She didn't really come in—she flew in, like some slender, skimming bird, in a white dress of light silk with a long train. She was breathing heavily, and a yellow rose moved up and down on her breast. It seemed to me as if all the light and all the happiness in the world were held in her dark eyes.

Grandmother stopped on the stairs and put her handkerchief to her eyes. She couldn't hold back tears at the sight of her youngest daughter's beauty. Each time my grandmother, obviously, was wondering what would happen to Aunt Nadya, how things would go for her in this rough life, and these thoughts made the old lady cry in spite of herself.

When we returned from the church this time, my father was not asleep. He had partly opened the drawing-room window onto the garden. It was very warm.

We sat down at the table to break our fast. The night stood by our side. The stars flickered in our eyes. The cheeping of birds could be heard in the garden. No one talked much, and we listened to the now-swelling, now-disappearing, sound of church bells in the dark.

Aunt Nadya sat there pale and tired. I noticed that my father had handed her a blue telegram in the vestibule when he had helped her off with her cloak. Aunt Nadya had blushed, and crumpled the telegram in her hand.

After eating I was sent to bed at once. I woke up late, when the cups were already clattering in the dining room and the grownups were drinking coffee.

After dinner Aunt Nadya said she had received a telegram from her friend Liza Yavorskaya in the neighboring town of Smela. Liza was inviting Aunt Nadya to visit her for a day at her country place near Smela.

"I want to go tomorrow," Aunt Nadya said, looking at Grandmother, and she added: "And I'll take Kostik with me."

I turned red with happiness.

"God be with you," Grandmother said. "Go along, but be careful you don't catch cold."

"They are sending horses for us," Aunt Nadya said.

From Cherkasy to Smela took an hour in the train. Liza Yavorskaya, a big, good-natured girl, met us at the station. We drove in a carriage with two horses through a clean, beautiful little town. The Tyasmin River flowed from quiet pool to quiet pool under its high green banks. Its slight current became silvery only in the middle of the pools. It was hot. Dragonflies darted over the river.

When we drove into a deserted park beyond the town, Liza Yavorskaya said that Pushkin had loved to walk there. I couldn't believe that Pushkin had actually been there, that I was now in a place where he had been. At that time Pushkin was a legendary being for me. His brilliant life, it seemed to me, must have been lived far away from these Godforsaken Ukrainian places.

"There's Kamenka, which used to be the Rayevskys' estate," Liza Yavorskaya said. "He lived with them for a long time, and wrote some wonderful poems here."

"Which ones?" asked Aunt Nadya. Liza recited a verse.

I couldn't understand some of the words, but the singing strength of the lines, the soaring park around us, the century-old linden trees, and the sky filled with clouds—all these put me in a fairy-tale mood. The whole day has stayed in my memory as the great event of a quiet, lonely spring.

Liza Yavorskaya stopped the carriage next to a broad path. We got out and approached the house along a side path cut through thick sweetbriar.

Suddenly a sunburned bearded man without a hat appeared around a bend in the road. A double-barreled hunting gun was hanging from his shoulder. He held two dead ducks in his hand. His jacket was unbuttoned and I could see his strong brown neck.

Aunt Nadya stopped, and I noticed how pale she grew.

The sunburned man broke off a big branch of sweetbriar in bud and gave it to Aunt Nadya. She took the prickly branch carefully and held out her hand; the man kissed it.

"Your hair smells of gunpowder," Aunt Nadya said. "And your hands are all scratched. You should take out those thorns."

"They're nothing," he said, and he smiled.

He had very even teeth, and now, close up to him, I could see that he was by no means an old man.

We went up to the house. The bearded man talked very strangely about everything all at once—how he had come from Moscow two days before, how wonderful it was here, how he was going to take his pictures to an exhibition in Venice the day after tomorrow, how a gypsy—the artist Vrubel's model—had cast a spell over him, and how he was in general a hopeless man and how only Aunt Nadya's voice could save him.

Aunt Nadya smiled. I looked at him. I liked him a great deal. I guessed he was an artist. He really did smell of gunpowder. His hands were covered with sticky pine resin. From the black ducks' bills clear blood dropped occasionally onto the road.

There were cobwebs, pine needles, and even a big twig in the artist's thick hair. Aunt Nadya took him by the elbow, stopped him, and took out the twig.

"Incorrigible!" she said. "Just a little boy," she added, and she smiled a little sadly.

"Just imagine!" he blurted out in an imploring voice, "how wonderful that was! I was going through little pine trees, I got torn to tatters, but what a fragrance! Spider webs, and red pine needles, and dry, white pinks—what a delight!"

"That is what I love you for," Aunt Nadya said in a low voice.

The artist suddenly took his gun from his shoulder and fired both barrels into the air. A wisp of blue smoke floated upward. The dogs barked and rushed around us. Somewhere a frightened chicken cackled.

"Salute to life!" the artist said. "It's devilishly wonderful to be alive!"

We went up to the house surrounded by excited barking dogs.

It was a white house, with columns and with striped blinds in the windows. Liza Yavorskaya's mother came out to greet us. She was a little elderly woman in a faded pink dress, with a lorgnette and with her hair in gray curls. She screwed up her eyes, clenching her fists, and spent a long time in ecstasy over Aunt Nadya's beauty.

A breeze blew through the cool rooms, rattling the blinds and blowing the newspapers *Russian Word* and *The Thought of Kiev** on the table. Sniffing dogs wandered everywhere. When they heard a suspicious sound from the park they would all break loose and, piling on top of each other and barking loudly, dash out of the house.

The sun was running away from the breeze through the rooms, picking out all kinds of things—vases, the brass castors on the piano, Aunt Nadya's straw hat tossed on the table, and the blue barrels of the gun. The bearded man had put it on the window sill.

We drank thick coffee in the dining room. The artist told me how he had caught fish in Paris from the river bank opposite the cathedral of Notre Dame. Aunt Nadya kept looking at him and smiling affectionately. And Liza's mother went on repeating:

"Ah, Sasha! When will you grow up? It's high time you started!"

After coffee the artist took Aunt Nadya and me by the hands and led us into his room. It was filled with brushes, squeezed-out tubes of paint, and general disorder. He hurriedly collected dirty shirts, shoes, pieces of canvas, and shoved them all under the couch. Then he filled his pipe from a blue tin box, lit it, and told Aunt Nadya and me to sit down on the window sill.

We sat down. The sun burned our backs. The artist walked over

* *Russian Word* was a daily newspaper published in Moscow from 1894 until 1917; it had a very large circulation. *The Thought of Kiev* was the most important provincial newspaper in pre-1917 Russia; after 1905 it was edited by Mensheviks and it was closed in 1918 by Petliura.

to a picture hanging on the wall and covered with a cloth, which he took off.

"Now look," he muttered in an embarrassed way. "Nothing came out right for me at all."

It was a picture of Aunt Nadya. At that time I knew nothing about painting. I had heard my father quarrel with Uncle Kolya about Vereshchagin and Vrubel.* But I didn't know a single good picture. Those which hung in my grandmother's house showed only enormous landscapes with boring trees or deer standing by mountain streams or brown ducks hanging head downwards.

When the artist unveiled this picture, I couldn't help laughing from sheer delight. The picture was itself a part of Aunt Nadya's shining springtime beauty, of the sun pouring in a golden waterfall into the park outside, of the breeze slipping through the room, and of the green reflection of the leaves behind us.

Aunt Nadya looked at her portrait for a long time. Then she ruffled the artist's hair lightly and walked quickly out of the room without having said a word.

"Well, God be praised!" the artist said with a sigh. "This means I can take the canvas to the exhibition in Venice."

Later in the day we went boating on the Tyasmin. The shadow of the woods lay like a green, jagged wall on the water. In the depths we could see the round leaves of water lilies which had not yet reached the surface of the water.

Before we left, in the evening, Aunt Nadya sang in the long, narrow ballroom. The artist accompanied her, and complained because his fingers, still smeared with resin, stuck to the keys.

> First meetings, last meetings,
> The beloved sound of a dear one's voice . . .

And then we drove back to Smela with the two horses. The artist and Liza went with us. The horses pounded their hoofs on the hard road. A dampness came up from the river, the frogs were croaking. Soon stars shone in the sky.

At the station Liza took me into the buffet to buy ice cream while Aunt Nadya and the artist stayed on a little bench in the station garden. There wasn't any ice cream to be had, of course, and when we returned, Aunt Nadya and the artist were still sitting there, thoughtful, on the bench.

* V. V. Vereshchagin (1842–1904) was a popular Russian painter who was known for his realistic battle scenes. M. A. Vrubel (1856–1910) was a Symbolist painter and muralist; one of his most famous pictures, in the Tretyakovsky Gallery in Moscow, is "The Demon," from Lermontov's poem.

Aunt Nadya soon returned to Moscow and I never saw her again. At Shrovetide the next year she drove to Petrovsky Park in a troika, and sang there in frosty weather. She caught pneumonia and died before Easter. My grandmother and my mother went to the funeral, and even my father.

I grieved deeply then. And until now I've been unable to forget Aunt Nadya. For me she has always been the epitome of all the delights of childhood, of tenderness, and of happiness.

THE ELDERWOOD BALLS

Soft, white balls rolled around in the box. I would drop one into a bowl filled with water. The ball would begin to swell, then it would open and transform itself into a black elephant with red eyes, or an orange dragon, or a rose with green leaves.

These fabulous Chinese balls made of elderwood were brought to me from Peking by my uncle and godfather, Iosif Grigorievich, or —more simply—Uncle Yusia.

"An adventurer, pure and simple!" my father would say of him, but not in censure and even with a certain envy.

He envied Uncle Yusia because he had traveled all over Africa, Asia, and Europe, not as a well-behaved tourist but as a conqueror —noisily, crashingly, with narrow escapes, and with an insatiable thirst for every improbable kind of affair in any corner of the world, in Shanghai or Addis Ababa, in Harbin or Meshed.

All these affairs ended in disaster.

"I should go to the Klondike," Uncle Yusia said. "I'd show them something, those Americans!"

Just what he intended to show the gold prospectors of the Klondike remained unclear. But it was quite plain that he would have shown them something so stupendous that his fame would have rumbled over all of the Yukon and Alaska.

Perhaps he had been born to be a famous explorer or discoverer, like Nikolai Przhevalsky or Livingstone. But life in Russia in those days—my father always used to call them "the premature days"— tortured Uncle Yusia. The noble passion for travel was corrupted by him into a disorderly and fruitless wandering. But I am still indebted to Uncle Yusia for the fact that after his stories the world seemed to me an incredibly interesting and inviting place, and that I have kept this feeling all my life.

My grandmother Vikentiya Ivanovna considered Uncle Yusia "a punishment from God," the black sheep in our family. When she was angry at me for some prank or for not paying attention, she would say:

"Be careful, or you'll turn out to be a second Uncle Yusia!"

My poor grandmother! She never suspected that this uncle's life seemed to me magnificent. It was my dearest dream to become "a second Uncle Yusia."

Uncle Yusia always showed up unexpectedly at our house in Kiev or at my grandmother's in Cherkasy, and disappeared just as unexpectedly, only to reappear with his deafening ring at our door a year or two later, filling the apartment again with his raucous voice, his coughing, his swearing, and his contagious laughter. And every time the cabdriver would follow Uncle Yusia with heavy trunks full of wonderful things.

Uncle Yusia was a tall, bearded man with a broken nose, with fingers of steel—he could bend a silver ruble in his hands—and with suspiciously quiet eyes in the depths of which there was always a kind of cunning.

As my father used to say, he "feared neither God nor the devil nor death" but he went all to pieces when he had to deal with women's tears or with the caprices of children.

The first time I ever saw him was after the Boer War. Uncle Yusia had joined the Boers as a volunteer. This action—disinterested and courageous—lifted him appreciably in the eyes of his relatives.

We children were fascinated by that war. We were sorry for the Boers, fighting for their independence, and we hated the English. We knew every detail of every battle taking place at the other end of the earth—the siege of Ladysmith, the defeat of Bloemfontein, and the assault on Diamond Hill. The most popular people for us were the Boer generals—De Wet, Joubert, and Botha. We despised the arrogant Lord Kitchener and we made fun of the British soldiers in their red uniforms. We were engrossed in a book called *Peter Marits, a Young Boer from the Transvaal.*

We were not alone. The whole civilized world followed the trag-

edy taking place on the steppes between the Vaal and the Orange
River with a sinking of the heart, aghast at the unequal fight between a small people and a great world power. Even the organ-
grinders in Kiev, who until then had been playing songs like "Separation," began to play a new song: "Transvaal, my country, you
are burning up in flames." For this they got our five-kopeck pieces
which we had been given for ice cream.

For little boys like myself, the Boer War was the wrack and
ruin of the exotic dreams of our childhood. Africa turned out to be
not at all what we had imagined it from the novels in the series
called "Around the World," or from the house on Vankovskaya
Street in Kiev that belonged to the engineer Gorodetsky.

On the walls of this gray house, which was built like a castle,
were sculptured representations of rhinoceroses, giraffes, lions,
crocodiles, antelope, and other animals native to Africa. Elephant
trunks made of concrete hung out over the pavement, replacing
the gutters. Water flowed out of the rhinoceroses' jaws. Gray stone
boa constrictors raised their heads out of dark recesses in the
building.

The owner of this house, the engineer Gorodetsky, was a passionate hunter. He went to hunt in Africa. It was in memory of
these expeditions that he decorated his house with the stone figures
of wild beasts. Grownups said that Gorodetsky was eccentric, but
we little boys loved his curious house. He helped to shape our
dreams of Africa.

But now we understood, even though we were still little boys,
that a great struggle for human rights had broken out on the enormous Dark Continent where, until then, we had thought only of
the trumpeting of wise elephants, of tropical jungles, and of
behemoths puffing quietly in the greasy ooze of great uncharted
rivers. Until then Africa had existed for us only as a land for explorers, men like Stanley and Livingstone.

Like many other little boys, I was sorry to break with this picture of an Africa where we had wandered in our dreams. It meant
no more lion hunts, no more dawns on the sands of the Sahara, no
more rafts on the Niger River, no more whistling of shots, furious
chattering of monkeys, and dark gloom of untrodden forests. There
danger had waited for us at every step. In our imaginations we had
often died, of fever or of wounds, behind the log walls of a fort,
hearing the whine of bullets, breathing the smell of wet, poisonous
grasses, looking with inflamed eyes into the black velvet sky where
the Southern Cross held reign.

How many times I died, regretting my young, short life, and

my failure to traverse mysterious Africa from Algiers to the Cape of Good Hope and from the Congo to Zanzibar!

We couldn't, of course, completely erase this picture of Africa from our memories. It turned out to have life in it. I find it hard to describe the intense but quiet delight I felt when our prosaic apartment in Kiev was visited by this bearded man, burned by the African sun, in his wide-brimmed Boer hat, his open-necked shirt, a cartridge holder on his belt—Uncle Yusia.

I followed on his very heels. I looked into his eyes. I could not believe that these eyes had really seen the Orange River, the Zulu Kraal, the English cavalry, and the storms of the Pacific Ocean.

This was about the time when the President of the Transvaal, the old and massive Kruger, came to Russia to ask for help for the Boers. Uncle Yusia came with him. He stayed for only one day in Kiev, and then went off to Peterburg with Kruger.

Uncle Yusia was convinced the Russians would help the Boers. But from Peterburg he wrote my father: "Overriding governmental considerations have forced the Russian government to a mean, ugly act—we will not help the Boers. This means everything is finished, and I am going back to the Far East."

My grandfather—my mother's father—had not been a rich man. He didn't have enough to pay for the education of all his children—five girls and three boys—except by sending all the boys to the Cadet Corps in Kiev. Education was free in the Cadet Corps.

Uncle Yusia had been a student there with his brothers. Four years went by satisfactorily but in the fifth year Uncle Yusia was transferred from Kiev to a branch at Volsk which was used as punishment for criminals. Cadets were sent to Volsk only for "serious crimes." Uncle Yusia had committed a serious crime.

The kitchen in the Kiev Cadet Corps was in the cellar. Just before a holiday, they had baked a quantity of rich buns and these had been left on the kitchen table. Uncle Yusia got a pole, fixed a nail to its end, fished out through an open window several dozens of the cakes, and organized a magnificent feast for the whole class.

Uncle Yusia spent two years in Volsk. In the third year they expelled him from the Cadet Corps and demoted him to a private's rank for striking an officer: the officer had stopped him in the street and bawled him out rudely for some small fault in his uniform.

So Uncle Yusia put on a private's greatcoat. They gave him a rifle and sent him on foot from Volsk to the town of Kutno, near Warsaw, to an artillery regiment. He walked the country from east to west in winter, checking in with the commanders on the way, asking for bread in the villages, sleeping wherever he found himself at night. He left Volsk a hotheaded youngster, and he arrived at Kutno an embittered soldier. He advanced there to the lowest officer's rank, and they made him an ensign.

Uncle Yusia continued his military career with the same lack of success. From the artillery he was transferred to the infantry. His regiment was summoned to Moscow to handle security at the time of the coronation of Nicholas II. His company was assigned the riverbank next to the Kremlin.

Early in the morning of the day of the coronation, my uncle saw his soldiers rush to the bank of the river, where a violent melee was taking place. He held on to his cap and ran after them. There in the mud on the bank he found an extraordinary creature with a copper head bound around with wires. The soldiers had knocked this creature down and piled on top of it while it awkwardly tried to kick them away with its heavy lead boots. One of the soldiers grabbed a rubber pipe near the creature's copper head and almost at once the monster relaxed, and stopped all resistance. My uncle realized that it was a diver and yelled at the soldiers, but, by the time he had opened the copper helmet, the diver was dead.

No one had warned my uncle that divers from Kronstadt had been assigned to check the bottom of the Moscow River that morning, searching for terrorist bombs.

After this incident, Uncle Yusia was discharged from the army. He went off to Central Asia where he worked for some time as head of a camel caravan going from Uralsk to Khiva and Bokhara. At that time Central Asia was not yet linked to Russia by a railroad, so all goods had to be reloaded onto camels at Uralsk and moved by caravan.

During his caravan trips Uncle Yusia became friendly with the Grum-Grzhimailo brothers, the explorers, and he hunted tigers with them. He sent my grandmother a tiger skin as a present; there was such a fierce expression on the face of this dead tiger that Grandmother immediately hid it away in the cellar, having first rolled it full of moth balls.

Uncle Yusia used to love to tell how he had once killed a jackal with a sneeze. He lay down in his camp on the desert, put his box of food under his head, and prepared to sleep. The jackals approached, their tails between their legs. When the boldest of them began carefully to pull the box out from under my uncle's head with his teeth, he produced an ear-shattering sneeze, and the cowardly jackal, without even a yelp, died on the spot of heart failure.

We believed this, because we knew very well how Uncle Yusia

used to sneeze in the mornings when he was getting ready for the new day. He could make the glass rattle in the windows, and the cat, out of its mind, would fly through the rooms looking for safety.

Uncle Yusia's stories were more interesting to us than the tales of Baron von Münchausen. We had to imagine von Münchausen, but Uncle Yusia was right there, alive, enfolded in clouds of tobacco smoke, shaking the sofa with his laughter.

An obscure period followed in Uncle Yusia's life. He wandered around Europe, gambled at roulette at Monte Carlo, people said, went off to Abyssinia and came back with an enormous gold medal given him for some reason by the Negus Menelik. The medal looked like one of the big plates used by courtyard janitors to mark the street number of a house.

Uncle Yusia never found his right place in life until he went to the fogbound Far East, to Manchuria and Ussurisky Province. It was as if this territory existed expressly for people like my uncle. There one could live in a big way, loudly, without knuckling under to any "fool's law," and with all the strength of a man's own character and enterprise.

This was the Russian Alaska—unpeopled, rich, and dangerous. No better place on earth could have been imagined for Uncle Yusia. The Amur, the taiga, gold, the Pacific Ocean, China, Korea, and farther still—Kamchatka, Japan, and Polynesia. A vast unknown world thundered like the surf on the shores of the Far East and inflamed men's imaginations.

Uncle Yusia took with him a young ascetic girl as wife—since nobody but an ascetic, in Mama's opinion, could ever be the wife of such a terrible man as Uncle Yusia—and went off to the Far East.

During the Boxer rebellion he took part in the defense of Harbin, in fights against the *hungusi* bandits, and in the building of the Chinese Eastern Railway. He interrupted this activity only to go to the Transvaal. After the Boer War, he went back to the Far East, this time to Port Arthur. He worked there as an agent for the navy. Uncle Yusia wrote us that he had come to love ships and that he regretted not having become a sailor in his youth.

About this time, his wife died. Uncle Yusia found himself with two daughters on his hands. He brought them up carefully and skillfully with the help of an old Chinese male servant who was named Sam Piu-chai. Uncle Yusia loved this devoted Chinese as much as his daughters. In general he loved the Chinese people; he used to say that they were a magnificent, goodhearted, wise people whose only fault was their fear of the rain.

During the Japanese War, Uncle Yusia was taken back into the army as a senior officer. He sent his daughters to Harbin with Sam Piu-chai. After the war he came back to Kiev to visit his relatives. This was the last time I saw him. He was already gray and more relaxed, but the violent, cheerful little sparks could still be seen, although rarely, in his eyes.

He told us all about Peking, the gardens of the Chinese emperors, Shanghai, and the Yellow River. After these stories China seemed to me a country of eternal warm, clear evening. Maybe this was because Uncle Yusia no longer made things up, no longer rolled his eyes or roared with laughter, but talked in a tired voice, continually tapping the ash off his cigarette.

This was in 1905. Uncle Yusia did not understand much about politics. He thought of himself as an old soldier, and he really was one—honorable and loyal to his oath. When my father would begin one of his sharp and dangerous speeches, Uncle Yusia would grow silent, walk out into the garden, sit on a bench, and smoke in solitude. He considered my father "the leftest of the leftists."

In 1905 there was a revolt in an engineers' battalion in Kiev. An artillery battery joined the uprising. The engineers moved into action through the city, beating off attacks by the Cossacks sent against them, and took up positions at the Demievsky Gate.

From there the rebel battery opened fire on the Governor General's palace and on the Cossacks' barracks. But the battery fired too little and badly, and not a single shell fell either on the palace or on the barracks.

Uncle Yusia was very nervous that day, smoking all the time, wandering around the garden, and quarreling in a low voice.

"Snotty-nosed children!" he muttered. "They're chicken killers, not artillerymen! Shame on them!"

During the day he suddenly left the house. Toward evening, the battery of the rebels opened up again, at last laying down a fast and accurate fire on the attacking Cossacks, on their barracks, on the fort, and on the Governor General's palace.

The uprising took over military control of the city for a short time. But under the cover of the artillery fire the engineers, who had already lost their own revolt, scattered to the woods and the swamps to the west of Kiev.

Uncle Yusia did not come back in the evening, nor that night, nor the next day. He never came back. It was six months later that we got a letter from his daughter in Harbin. She told us that Uncle Yusia had settled down in Japan and that he asked us to forgive him for his sudden disappearance.

It was much later that we learned that Uncle Yusia's heart, the heart of an old artilleryman, had not been able to stand the wretched firing of the rebels. He had left the house, joined the up-rising, taken over command of the battery, and, as he expressed it, "carved his initials" on the government troops.

Naturally, he had had to flee. He went to Japan where he died soon after in Kobe of cardiac asthma and the strange disease of homesickness, grief for his fatherland. Before his death this enormous, violent man would cry at the slightest reminder of Russia. In his last, half-joking letter, he asked us to send him in an envelop the most valuable gift he could think of—the dried leaf of a Kiev chestnut tree.

SVYATOSLAVSKAYA STREET

Our trips to Cherkasy and to Gorodishche were the holidays in my childhood, but the rest of the year was lived in Kiev, on Svyatoslav-skaya Street, where we lived through the long winters in a gloomy, uncomfortable apartment.

Svyatoslavskaya Street was filled with ugly apartment houses and pavements made of yellow brick. It led across a vast wasteland cut by ravines. There were lots of these empty spaces in the city. Each was called a *yar*.

All day long wagons filled with dirt drove by our house on Svyatoslavskaya Street. Their drivers filled in the ravines in the wasteland and leveled them off for the construction of new houses. The dirt spilled out of the wagons, the road was always muddy, and I didn't like Svyatoslavskaya Street at all.

It was strictly forbidden for us to go into the wasteland. It was a frightening place, the haven of thieves and beggars. But we boys assembled our forces sometimes and went anyway. We always took with us, for emergencies, a police whistle. It seemed to us as de-pendable a weapon as a revolver.

At first we looked cautiously down into a ravine. We could see the shimmer of broken glass, and of rusted basins. Dogs burrowed in the rubbish. They paid no attention to us at all.

Then we grew bold enough to go down into a ravine, where a dirty yellow smoke collected. This smoke came from caves and shanties. The shanties were made out of anything: broken plywood, old tinplate, broken boxes, the seats of chairs, mattresses from which the springs were sticking out. Dirty sacks hung in place of doors.

Bareheaded women in rags sat beside the fireplaces. They called us "young masters" or asked for a drink of vodka. Only one of them, a shaggy, gray old woman with a lioness's face, smiled at us with her single tooth.

She was an Italian beggar who was well known in Kiev. She used to walk from courtyard to courtyard and play the accordion. For an extra payment she would play the "Marseillaise." When she did this, one of the little boys would be sent to give warning in case a neighborhood policeman should appear. The beggar would not only play the "Marseillaise" on her accordion; she would also sing it in a piercing, raucous voice. She made the song sound like an angry challenge, like a curse of all the inhabitants of the Svyatoslavskaya *yar*.

Among those who lived in these shanties we recognized old acquaintances. There was Yashka Padushi, a beggar with white, vodka-like eyes. He used to sit constantly on the church porch of the Vladimir Cathedral and whine out one and the same sentence: "Goodhearted gentlemen, just look at my crippled-dippled condition."

At home Yashka Padushi was not at all the snuffling, quiet wretch he was on the church porch. He would drink a quarter-liter of vodka in one swallow, hit himself on the chest with all his strength, and howl tearfully: "Come unto me, all who are suffering or overburdened, and I will give you peace!"

There was a bald old man who peddled toothpaste on Fundukleyevskaya Street near the François Café, and a hurdy-gurdy man with a parrot.

Around the shanties smoke rose from clay stoves through which holes had been poked for the samovar chimneys.

I liked best of all the organ-grinder's shanty. He wasn't there in the daytime; he was walking from courtyard to courtyard in the city. A barefoot girl with a dirty face and with pretty, sullen eyes sat on the ground near the shanty, peeling potatoes. One leg was wrapped up in rags.

This was the organ-grinder's daughter, a gymnast, "a person without bones." She had formerly gone into the courtyards with her father, spread out a little rug, and demonstrated on it—thin, in blue tights—various acrobatic tricks. Now she had hurt her leg and could no longer work.

Sometimes I would find her reading, always the same book in a torn paper cover. By the picture on it I guessed that it was Dumas's *Three Musketeers.*

The girl would yell at us, unhappily: "What are you walking here for? Haven't you ever seen how people live?"

But after a while she became used to us and stopped yelling at us. Her father, the gray, short organ-grinder, finding us once in the wasteland, said:

"Let them look. Let them see how our world suffers. Maybe it will do them good when they get to be students."

At first we used to go there only in battalions. Then I grew accustomed to the inhabitants of the *yar* and started to go alone.

I hid this for a long time from Mama, but the organ-grinder's daughter gave me away. I had loaned her *Uncle Tom's Cabin* to read but then I got sick and didn't return for the book for a long time. She grew anxious and brought the book back herself to the apartment. Mama opened the door for her, and all was discovered. I could see this from Mama's tightly pressed lips and her icy silence.

There was a conversation between Mama and my father about my behavior that evening in the dining room. I listened to it from behind the door. Mama was very much upset, and she grew angry, but my father said that it was nothing terrible, that it would be hard to spoil me, and that he would prefer to have me make friends with these unfortunate people than with the sons of Kiev's merchants and officials. Mama countered that at my age it was necessary to protect me from painful, worldly impressions.

"Understand," my father said, "that these people show a kind of stanchness in human relations that we won't find in our circle. So what's this about painful, worldly impressions?"

Mama was silent, and then she answered:

"Yes, perhaps you're right . . . ."

When I got well, Mama brought me *The Prince and the Pauper* by Mark Twain, and said:

"There . . . take it yourself . . . to the organ-grinder's daughter. I don't know what her name is."

"Lisa," I said shyly.

"Well, there it is. Take this book to Lisa as a present."

From this time on, nobody at home was upset about my visits to the Svyatoslavskaya *yar*. I no longer had to sneak sugar stealthily from the buffet for my new friends, or Chinese nuts for the near-sighted parrot, Mitka. I asked Mama openly for everything. She never refused me. I was grateful to Mama for this, and my heart felt as light as only a boy's heart can when he has a clear conscience.

One day in early autumn the organ-grinder came into our courtyard without his parrot. He turned the handle of the organ without his heart in his work. It scratched out a polka: "Come on, come on, my darling angel, come on and dance with me." The organ-grinder stared at all the balconies and open windows, waiting for the moment when coins, wrapped in paper, would be thrown to him.

I ran out to the organ-grinder. He told me, without stopping his grinding:

"Mitka has some kind of disease. Sits there like a hedgehog. He won't even crack your nuts. Just watch, he'll be dead soon."

The organ-grinder took off his black dusty hat and wiped his face with it.

"What a hopeless existence!" he said. "An organ-grinder alone, without Mitka, can't even earn his vodka, let alone his bread. Who will pick out 'happiness' now?"

For five kopecks, the parrot would pick out, as desired, a green, a blue, or a red ticket with a prediction printed on it. For some reason, these tickets were always called "happiness." They were rolled inside little cylinders and placed like cigarettes in a box like a cartridge case. Before picking out the little ticket, Mitka would stamp for a long time on his perch and screech unhappily.

The predictions were written in an obscure language: "You were born under the sign of Mercury and your stone is the emerald, which signifies a dislike for worldly affairs and final mastery over them only in the years which are gray with age. Be on guard against blondes, and do not go out in the streets on the day John the Baptist was beheaded."

Sometimes there were shorter and more sinister phrases in the little tickets: "Tomorrow, in the evening," or "If you want to stay alive, never look behind you."

A day later, Mitka died and I buried him in the *yar* in a cardboard shoebox. The organ-grinder got drunk and disappeared.

I told Mama about the parrot's death. My lips trembled, but I did not lose control of myself.

"Get dressed," Mama said sternly. "We're going to Burmistrov."

Burmistrov was an old man with a beard which had turned green with age. He ran a dark, stuffy little shop on the Bessarabka. There this hard-of-hearing old man, who looked just like a gnome, sold the most wonderful things—fishing rods, many-colored floats, aquariums, goldfish, birds, ant eggs, and even decalcomanias.

Mama bought an old green parrot with a tin ring on his leg. We borrowed a cage from Burmistrov. I carried the parrot in it. On the way he grew angry and bit my finger to the bone. We went into a pharmacy where they bandaged my finger, but I was so excited that I hardly felt the pain.

I wanted to take the parrot to the organ-grinder as quickly as we could, but Mama said:

"I'll go with you. I should see this myself."

She went into her room to change her clothes. I felt ashamed that Mama would dress up before going to see beggars, but I didn't dare say anything to her.

She came out in a few minutes. She had put on a very old, patched dress. She wore a shawl on her head. For once she didn't pull on her elegant kid gloves. She had on shoes with worn-down heels. I looked at her in gratitude, and we started off.

Mama went courageously down into the ravine, walked by the ragged women, and not once did she raise her skirt so as not to dirty it on a pile of rubbish or ashes.

When she saw us with the parrot, Lisa sighed deeply, her gray face flushed with color, and she suddenly made Mama a curtsy. The organ-grinder was not at home; he was still drinking away his sorrow with his friends.

Lisa took the parrot and, blushing more and more, repeated the same words:

"But why do you do it? Why do you do it?"

"Can you teach him to pick out the 'happiness'?" Mama asked.

"Of course, in a couple of days," Lisa answered happily. "But why do you do it? God! My masters! Why? For he cost such a lot of money!"

When my father heard about this, at home, he laughed, and said:

"Female philanthropy! What a sentimental education!"

"Ah, my God!" Mama said sorrowfully. "I don't know why you have to contradict yourself so often. You do have a surprising character! In my place you'd have done the same thing."

"No," my father answered, "I would have done more."

"More?" Mama asked, and in her voice there was a kind of threat. "Well, all right! We'll see."

I didn't guess that my father had said this on purpose, to tease Mama.

The next day Mama sent Lisa a black dress of my sister's and her own brown boots. But my father would not lag behind. He waited until the organ-grinder came to our courtyard with his new parrot.

He had his red scarf tied around his neck. His nose shone triumphantly with vodka. In Mama's honor he played everything his organ could grind out: the march "Grief for the Fatherland," the waltz "The Waves of the Danube," the polka "Separation," and the song "Ekh, My Pack Is Overflowing." The parrot picked out the "happiness" tickets. Copper coins wrapped up in paper came showering down from the windows. The organ-grinder caught them skillfully in his hat.

Then he slung the organ on his back, and bending down as he always did he walked, not out onto the street, but up the stairs to ring at our door. He took off his hat and held it in his hand so that it touched the floor, and he thanked Mama and he kissed her hand. My father came out and invited him into his office. The organ-grinder put his organ next to the wall in the vestibule and, walking carefully, followed my father.

My father gave him a drink of cognac and said that he realized how hard his life must be and how unrewarding. He offered him a job as a guard on the Southern-Western Railroad. He would have his own little home, and a garden.

"Don't judge me too severely, Georgi Maximovich," the organ-grinder said very quietly, and he blushed, "but I'd be bored as a policeman. It's clear I must sweat out my time with my organ."

He walked out. Mama couldn't hide her satisfaction, but she kept quiet.

Several days later the police suddenly evicted all the inhabitants of the Svyatoslavskaya *yar*. The organ-grinder disappeared with Lisa—obviously, they had moved to some other city. But before this I had managed to be in the *yar* once more. The organ-grinder had invited me to spend an evening with them.

A plate with baked tomatoes and black bread stood on a turned-over box, with a bottle of cherry brandy and some dirty candy—thick sugar sticks striped in red and white. Lisa had on a new dress, and her hair was tightly braided. She took great pains to make sure that I ate "the same as at Mama's." The parrot slept, closing his leather eyelids over his eyes. Once in a while the organ gave out a singing sound all by itself. The organ-grinder explained that this was because some air had been trapped in one of its pipes.

It was already September. Twilight was coming on. Whoever
has not seen autumn in Kiev has no conception of the tender beauty
of these hours. The first star began to shine in the sky. The
magnificent autumn gardens wait for the stars in silence, because
they know that the stars must fall to earth and that the gardens
will catch them, as in a hammock, in the thickness of their leaves
and ease them down to earth so gently that no one in the town will
even wake up or know about it.

Lisa accompanied me home, gave me a sticky pink candy as a
farewell present, and then quickly ran down the stairs. For a long
time I couldn't make up my mind to ring the bell, afraid that I
would be scolded for coming home so late.

THE WINTER CARNIVAL

My father gave me a pair of Halifax skates for Christmas.

Boys of today would laugh if they could see those skates. But
then there were no better skates in the world than those from the
city of Halifax.

Where was this city? I asked everyone. Where was this old city
covered with snow called Halifax? All the children there went
around on skates like these. Where was this wintry country,
populated by retired sailors and bright schoolboys? Nobody could
answer me.

My oldest brother, Borya, said that Halifax was not a city at all
but the family name of the inventor of the skates. My father said
that it seemed that Halifax—yes, it was a little town on the island
of Newfoundland on the northern shores of America and it was
famous not only for its skates but also for its Newfoundland dogs.

The skates lay on the table. I looked at them and thought about
Halifax. As soon as I got the skates I made up the town, and I could
already see it so clearly that I could have drawn a map of its streets
and public squares. I would sit at the table for a long time over my

Malinin and Burenin arithmetic book—I was preparing that winter for my *gymnasium* entrance examinations—and think about Halifax.

This habit of mine frightened Mama. She was afraid of my "fantasies" and she used to say that beggary and death under the fence were waiting for boys like me. The gloomy prediction "You'll die under the fence," was very common at that time. For some reason death under the fence was considered especially disgraceful.

I heard the prediction often. But much more often Mama would say that my "brains were dislocated and not at all like other people's" and that she feared I would be nothing but a failure.

My father became very angry when he heard this, and he would say to Mama:

"Let him be a failure, or a beggar, or a tramp, or anything you like, so long as he doesn't grow up to be one of these damned Kiev philistines!"

In the end I too began to be a little afraid of my imagination, and ashamed of it. I seemed to be engrossed in nonsense while everyone around me was doing serious things: my brothers and sister went to school and crammed for their lessons, my father worked in the management of the Southern-Western Railroad, and Mama sewed and ran the house. I alone was living in a world divorced from general interests, wasting my time fruitlessly.

"You'd do better to go out skating than to sit there stupidly just dreaming about something," Mama said. "What a boy you are!"

I went out to the skating rink. The winter days were short, and dusk often found me still at the rink. A military band would come. Many-colored lights were lit. Schoolgirls in fur coats would skate in a circle, swaying, holding their hands in little muffs. The schoolboys skated either backwards or "pistol-style"—crouching on one leg and holding the other out straight. This was considered most stylish of all. I envied them.

I would come home flushed and tired. But I never stopped being anxious at heart, because even after skating I would feel the same dangerous desire to sit and dream and make up stories.

At the skating rink I often met my sister Galya's friend, Marusya Vesnitskaya, who was in one of the higher classes at the Fundukleyevskaya Female Academy. Marusya had Halifax skates, too, but hers were made of black burnished steel. My oldest brother Borya, who was a pupil at a technical school specializing in mathematics, was courting Marusya. He used to waltz with her on skates.

The skaters would clear a wide circle on the ice. They would cuff the street boys, darting under their feet on homemade skates, to keep them quiet, and then the slow, slippery dance would start. Even the bandmaster, a red-haired Czech named Kovarzhik, would turn to face the ice, just to see this dance. A saccharine smile would spread across his red face.

Marusya Vesnitskaya's long braids would swing in time with the waltz. They got in her way, and without stopping the dance she would hold them to her breast. She would look up arrogantly, with half-closed eyelids, at the delighted spectators.

I would watch Borya with malicious joy. He did not skate as well as Marusya. Sometimes he slipped a little on his much-vaunted Yacht Club skates.

Little did I imagine then that the life of Marusya Vesnitskaya was going to turn out more strangely than the fantasies I made up. At that time one of the sons of the King of Siam was a student in England, either at Cambridge or at Oxford. This prince could not stand ocean travel, so he went home from England by the long land route—across Europe, Russia and India.

During one of these trips the prince got pneumonia on the way near Kiev. The trip was interrupted. The prince was taken to Kiev, put up in the Tsar's palace, and attended by the city's best doctors. The prince recovered, but before continuing his journey to Siam, it was necessary for him to rest and convalesce. So the prince lived in Kiev for two months. He was bored. Everyone tried to distract him —they took him to balls at the Merchants' Assembly, to the circus, and to the theater.

At one of these balls the yellow-faced prince saw Marusya Vesnitskaya. She was dancing a waltz, just as on the skating rink, her braids hanging down over her breast and her deep blue eyes looking up arrogantly under their half-opened lids. The prince was fascinated. A small man, with slanting eyes and hair that shone like wax, he danced with Marusya until drops of sweat stood out on his round face.

The prince fell in love with Marusya. He went back to Siam, but he soon returned incognito to Kiev and asked Marusya to be his bride. She agreed.

This was a blow to every schoolgirl in Kiev. With one voice they declared that not for anything would they, in her place, have married an Asiatic, even if he was the son of a king.

Marusya went off to Siam. Soon the king died of some kind of tropical disease. Then the first two heirs to the throne died of the same disease. Marusya's husband was the king's third son. He had had very little hope of ever becoming king. But after the death of his brothers, he was the only heir, and succeeded to the throne.

And the cheerful schoolgirl from Kiev, Marusya Vesnitskaya, became Queen of Siam.

The courtiers hated this foreigner as their queen. Her very existence violated all the traditions of the Siamese court. On Marusya's demand, electric lights were installed in Bangkok, and this filled the courtiers' cup of hatred to overflowing. They decided to poison this queen who was upsetting all the old customs of the people. So they began little by little to put tiny pieces of glass from broken electric light bulbs in her food. In six months, Marusya died of intestinal hemorrhage.

The king built a monument over her grave. An enormous elephant of black marble, with a golden crown on its head and its trunk hanging down sadly, stands up to its knees in heavy grass. Underneath this grass lies Marusya Vesnitskaya—the young Queen of Siam.

Whenever I have visited that skating rink since then I have thought of Marusya, and of the bandmaster playing the waltz, "Summer Is Gone Forever," and of how Marusya used to wipe the snow off her forehead and her eyebrows with her mittens, and of her skates made of black steel—skates from the city of Halifax. Simplehearted retired sailors live in that town. Just try to tell those old men the story of Marusya Vesnitskaya. At first their mouths would fall open in astonishment, then they would turn red with anger against the courtiers, and they would shake their heads for a long time over the cruelty of human fate.

In the winter I was taken to the theater. The first play I ever saw was *The Storming of Ismaila*. I didn't like it at all, because I noticed a man in glasses and worn velvet trousers standing in the wings. He stood next to General Suvorov, then he pushed him hard in the back, and Suvorov flew skipping out onto the stage and crowed like a rooster.

But then my second play, Rostand's *The Faraway Princess*, utterly stunned me. It had everything needed to capture my imagination: the deck of a ship, enormous sails, troubadours, knights, a princess.

I fell in love with the Solovtzovsky Theater, its blue velvet upholstery and its little boxes. It was impossible to get me out of the theater until the lights were turned out. The darkness in the hall, the smell of perfume and old orange skins, everything about it was so entrancing to me that I dreamed of hiding under a seat and spending all night in the empty theater. When I was a child I couldn't distinguish between a play at the theater and reality itself, so I was really tortured and even ill after each performance.

My passion for reading grew ˙ after being introduced to the theater. I had only to see *Madame Sans-Gêne* to begin to devour all the books I could find about Napoleon. Epochs and people I saw in the theater came alive in the most wonderful way and were filled for me with extraordinary interest and charm.

It wasn't only the plays I fell in love with. I liked the corridors with their mirrors in tarnished gold frames, the dark cloakrooms smelling of the fur of overcoats, the mother-of-pearl opera glasses, and the clatter of horses' hoofs outside the theater exits.

In the intermissions I would run to the window at the end of a corridor and look outside. Everything was pitch black except for the snow whitening the trees. Then I would turn around quickly and see the lights of the richly decorated hall, the chandeliers, the light on women's hair, bracelets and earrings, and the velvet curtain stirring a little in a breeze. I would repeat this several times— looking first out of the window and then back into the theater— and it gave me enormous pleasure.

I didn't like opera. This was obviously because the first opera to which I was taken was Rubinstein's *The Demon.** A fat actor with a coarse face sang the Demon's part lazily and with a sort of waddle. He was hardly made-up at all. It seemed funny to me that they should dress this solid, potbellied man in a long black muslin shirt, sewed all over with spangles, and pin wings to his back. This actor rolled his r's, and when he sang "Accursed world, contemptible world," I could not hold back my laughter. Mama was indignant and stopped taking me to the opera.

Every winter Aunt Dosia came to visit us from Gorodishche. Mama loved to take her to the theater. Each time Aunt Dosia would spend a sleepless night. Several hours before the play began she would put on a swishing dress of brown satin embroidered with yellow flowers and leaves. She would throw a brown shawl over her shoulders, clutch a small handkerchief in her hand, and then, ten years younger and a little frightened, drive off to the theater in a cab with Mama. Like all Ukrainian women, Aunt Dosia used to wear a black scarf with little roses on her head. Everyone in the theater stared at her, but she became so engrossed in the play that she paid no attention to anything else.

We took her chiefly to Ukrainian plays—*Natalka Poltavka, Zaporozhets za Dunayem,* and *Shelmenko the Groom.* Once in the

---

* Anton G. Rubinstein (1829–1894) was a famous Russian pianist; he wrote *The Demon* in 1875, one of fifteen operas he composed in a career which also included the founding of the St. Petersburg Conservatory.

middle of a play Aunt Dosia jumped up and yelled at the villain on the stage, in Ukrainian:

"What are you up to, you scoundrel, you and your shameless eyes!"

The audience roared with laughter. The curtain came down. Aunt Dosia cried all the next day out of shame, and begged my father's pardon, and we didn't know how to reassure her.

The first time we ever went to the motion pictures was with Aunt Dosia. At that time they were called "illusions" or "Lumière's cinema." The first showing was organized in the opera house. My father was enthusiastic about the new device and hailed it as one of the most magnificent novelties of the twentieth century.

A wet gray cloth was hung on the stage. Then all the chandeliers were turned off. An ominous greenish light flickered on the cloth and black spots darted across it. A smoky beam of light streamed above our heads. It sizzled terrifically, as if they were roasting a wild boar behind our backs. Aunt Dosia asked Mama:

"Why does this illusion make such a noise? It won't burn us up, will it, like a chicken coop?"

After a long twinkling on the cloth the title appeared: "Eruption on the Island of Martinique. Travel Film." The screen trembled and on it, as through a heavy shower of dust, a volcano erupted. From its depths the lava poured out. The audience muttered, shaken by the spectacle.

Afterwards we were shown a comic picture about life in a French barracks. The drummer beat his drum, the soldiers woke up, jumped out of bed, pulled on their trousers. One soldier found a big rat in his trousers. It ran around the barracks and the terrified soldiers opened their eyes wide and climbed onto the beds, the doors and the windows. With this the picture ended.

"Clowning!" Mama said. "The only difference is that at the Contract Fair the clowns are much more interesting."

My father commented that people with no vision had laughed at Stephenson's steam engine, and Aunt Dosia, trying to make peace between my father and Mama, said:

"God be with it, this illusion! It's not something we women can understand."

The clowns were really interesting at the Contract Fair, which was the most important sugar market of old Russia.* We used to love this fair, and waited impatiently all winter for it to open. It

* One of the oldest fairs in Russia, the Contract Fair was moved to Kiev from Dubno in 1797; it has its name because the contracts made here each spring used to regulate sugar production throughout the country.

began every March in the ancient House of Contracts in Podol and in plank booths set up around the central building. Usually the day it opened coincided with the spring floods. The sharp smell of fair goods could be detected a long way off. This was a smell of new barrels, leather, cakes, and calico.

What I liked best at the fair were the merry-go-rounds, the toys, and the panopticon. Oily blocks of white and chocolate halvah crunched under the salesmen's knives. Transparent rose and lemon Turkish Delight gummed up our mouths. On enormous earthenware plates were piled pyramids of sugared pears, plums, and cherries—products of the famous Kiev candymaker Balabukhi.

On sacking spread out in the dirt stood rows of toy soldiers, crudely whittled out of wood and colored with sticky paints—Cossacks in tall sheepskin hats and wide trousers with raspberry-colored stripes, drummers with protruding eyes, trumpeters with elegant tassels on their trumpets. Earthenware penny whistles were heaped up in mounds. Cheerful old men wandered around in the crowd hawking other toys. One of them was entrancing—a shaggy little black devil who dived into the water inside a small glass cylinder.

A multitude of sounds deafened us—the cries of the peddlers, the screeching of wagon wheels, the Lenten chimes from the Bratsky Convent, the squeaking of rubber devils, the blowing of penny whistles, and the cries of the children on the merry-go-round. For an additional payment they would whirl the merry-go-round so fast that it turned into a many-colored blur of papier-mâché horses' muzzles and teeth, neckties, boots, billowing skirts, garters of different colors, laces and scarves. Sometimes the glass beads from a broken necklace would fly like bullets into the spectators' faces.

I was rather afraid of the panopticon, especially of its wax figures. The murdered President Carnot of France lay smiling on the floor, dressed in a frock coat with a star on it. Thick unnatural-looking blood, a little like red vaseline, flowed down his dress shirt. It looked as if Carnot were happy to have died so theatrically.

Queen Cleopatra clutched a black snake to her firm, greenish breast. A mermaid with lilac eyes lay in a zinc bathtub. A dull electric light was reflected in the mermaid's dirty scales. The water in the bath was muddy. A boa constrictor slept on an eiderdown in an open box covered with wire netting. Occasionally it would stretch its muscles, and the crowd would shy away.

A stuffed gorilla, surrounded by foliage made of painted shavings, was carrying an unconscious young girl with flowing golden hair into a wooded thicket. For three kopecks anyone could shoot at the gorilla with a rifle and save the girl. If you could hit a circle on the gorilla's chest, he would drop the ragged girl to the ground. Dust rose from the girl in clouds. Then they would close off the gorilla for a minute with a chintz curtain, after which he would again appear, carrying the girl just as fiercely into the same faded grove.

We also loved the Contract Fair because it heralded the coming of Easter, a trip to our grandmother's in Cherkasy, and then the always beautiful and extraordinary springtime in Kiev.

THE NAVAL CADET

Spring in Kiev always began with the flooding of the Dnieper. You had only to go out of town onto Vladimir Hill to see a great blue sea spread out before your eyes. But that was not the only flood which began then in Kiev; there was also a vast overflowing of sunshine, of freshness, of warm and fragrant breezes.

The pyramid-shaped poplar trees came into leaf along Bibikovsky Boulevard. They filled all the streets around with a smell of incense. The chestnuts broke out their first leaves, transparent, crumpled, covered with reddish down.

By the time the yellow and red candles had blossomed on the chestnut trees, spring was in its prime. Waves of freshness blew out of the old parks into the streets, with the damp breathing of young grass and the noise of fresh, unfolding leaves.

Caterpillars crawled on the sidewalks even as far as the Kreshchatik. The wind swirled fallen petals into little piles. Ladybugs and butterflies flew through the windows into the trolley cars. At night the nightingales sang in the gardens. The poplar pollen, like foam on the Black Sea, moved in waves along the pavements. Along the sides of the roads the yellow dandelions bloomed.

Striped awnings were pulled down against the sun over the wide-open windows of candy stores and coffee houses. Lilac stood in vases on restaurant tables. Young girls searched bunches of lilac for flowers with five petals. Their faces under their summer straw hats took on a yellow, lusterless color.

The season of Kiev's parks was starting. For whole days in the spring I wandered through the parks. There I played, there I did my lessons, there I read. I went home only to eat and sleep.

I knew every corner of the enormous Botanical Garden with its ravines, its ponds, and the heavy shade of its alleys of century-old linden trees.

But best of all I liked Marinsky Park in Lipki, which surrounded the palace. It hung out over the Dnieper. Walls of pink and white lilac, three times a man's height, bent and rustled with their weight of blossom. There were fountains in the middle of the lawns.

A wide belt of parks—the Marinsky and the Dvortsovi, the Tsar's and the Merchants'—stretched out along the red clay bank of the Dnieper. From the Merchants' Park there opened out the famous view of the Podol; the entire population of Kiev was proud of this view. A symphony orchestra used to play all summer in the Merchants' Park. There was nothing to interfere with the music except the drawn-out whistling of the steamboats, carried up from the Dnieper.

The last park on the Dnieper bank was on Vladimir Hill. The monument to Prince Vladimir stood there, holding a bronze cross in his arms. Electric lights, wired to the cross, were lighted at night, and the blazing cross hung high in the sky over the slopes of Kiev.

The city was so beautiful in the springtime that I could never understand Mama's passion for obligatory Sunday visits to the suburbs—Boyarka, Pushcha Voditsa, or Darnitsa. I was bored in the monotonous suburban quarters of Pushcha Voditsa, I looked with indifference at the stunted paths in the woods of the poet Nadson, and I didn't like Darnitsa, with earth heaped up around its pine trees and the sand mixed with cigarette butts.

Once in the spring I was sitting in Marinsky Park, reading Stevenson's *Treasure Island.* My sister Galya was sitting next to me, also reading. Her summer hat with green ribbons on it was lying on the bench. A breeze fluttered the ribbons.

Galya was nearsighted, very trusting, and with a good nature it was almost impossible to upset. It had rained in the morning, but now a clear sky shone over us. Only a few late raindrops pattered off the lilac bushes.

A small girl with ribbons in her hair stopped next to us and began to skip rope. This disturbed my reading. I shook the lilac. A little rain splattered down on the girl, and on Galya. The girl stuck out her tongue at me and fled, while Galya brushed the drops of water from her book and went on reading. It was just at this moment that I saw the man who was to fill my dreams for a long time to come.

A tall marine cadet was walking along the path. He had a quiet, sunburned face. A straight black sword hung from his highly polished belt. Black ribbons with bronze anchors on them fluttered in the slight breeze. He was dressed all in black. Only his bright gold stripes lightened his somber uniform.

In landlocked Kiev, where we almost never saw sailors, this was a stranger from the faraway and legendary world of sailing ships, from the frigate *Pallada,* from the world of all the oceans, all the seas, all the port towns, all the winds and all the fascinations that are linked with the picturesque occupation of sailor of the seas. His ancient-looking sword with its black hilt might have come right out of the pages of Robert Louis Stevenson into the Marinsky Park.

The cadet walked by, his footsteps crunching in the sand. I stood up and walked after him. Galya was so nearsighted that she did not notice my disappearance.

All my dreams about the sea had found reality in this man. I often used to imagine the sea to myself, in fog and in the golden still of the evening, on long voyages, when all the world changes like a rapid kaleidoscope through the windows of the portholes. My God, if anyone had thought to give me a grain of hardened rust from an old anchor, I would have hoarded it like treasure.

The cadet looked around. On the black ribbon of his sailor's hat I could read the mysterious word "*Azimuth.*" Later I learned that this was the name of a training ship of the Baltic Fleet.

I followed him down Elizavetinskaya Street, then along Institutskaya and Nikolayevskaya Streets. The sailor saluted army officers whom he passed, elegantly but a little carelessly. I felt ashamed, in his presence, of these clumsy earthbound warriors of Kiev.

He looked around several times, and at the corner of Meringovskaya Street he stopped and beckoned to me.

"Little boy," he said with a smile, "why are you following me?"

I blushed and couldn't answer anything.

"It's clear, he's dreaming about being a sailor," the cadet guessed, for some reason talking as if to a third person.

"I'm nearsighted," I answered in a falling voice.

The cadet put his lean hand on my shoulder: "Let's go along to the Kreshchatik."

We walked on side by side. I was afraid to raise my eyes and I could see only his boots, shining with an incredible polish.

On the Kreshchatik the cadet walked into the Semadeni Café, and ordered two portions of pistachio ice cream and two glasses of water. They served us on a little three-legged table with a marble top. The table was very cold and all covered with figures: the brokers from the Bourse used the Semadeni and they figured their profits and losses on the tabletops.

We ate our ice cream in silence. The cadet took a photograph of a magnificent corvette, with full rigging for sails and a big funnel, out of his notebook and handed it to me:

"Take it to remember me by. That's my ship. I sailed on it to Liverpool."

He shook my hand firmly and walked away. I sat there a little longer, until my sweaty neighbors began to stare at me. Then I walked awkwardly out and ran back to the Marinsky Park. The bench was empty. Galya had left. I guessed that the cadet had felt pity for me and for the first time I learned that pity leaves a bitter aftertaste in the heart.

For many years after this meeting I was tortured by the desire to become a sailor. I was spoiling for the sea. I had seen a little of it for the first time at Novorossisk where I had gone for several days with my father. But that was not enough.

I would sit for hours over the atlas, looking at the shores of the oceans, looking up unknown ports, islands, mouths of rivers. I thought up a complicated game. I made up a long list of steamships with nice-sounding names: *Polar Star, Walter Scott, Khingan, Sirius.* The list grew every day. I became the owner of the biggest fleet in the world.

Of course, I would sit in my own steamship office, surrounded by cigar smoke, attractive posters, and sailing schedules. The wide windows looked out, naturally, on the harbor. The yellow masts of the ships loomed up past the windows, and pleasant elm trees made a noise outside the office. Steam from the ships' boilers drifted through the windows to mix with the smell of old brine and new bast matting.

I dreamed up a series of amazing voyages for my ships. I followed them closely and knew accurately where the *Admiral Istomin* was today, and where *The Flying Dutchman*: the *Istomin* was loading bananas in Singapore, while *The Flying Dutchman* was unloading flour in the Faroes Islands.

I had to have a good deal of knowledge to run such a far-flung steamship operation. I ransacked timetables and dusty almanacs and everything which might have even the remotest connection with the sea.

It was then that I heard the word "meningitis" for the first time from my mother.

"God knows where his games will take him," Mama said one day. "If only it doesn't all end in meningitis!"

I had heard that meningitis was a little boys' disease which came from learning to read too young. But I only laughed at Mama's fears.

It all ended with my parents deciding to spend an entire summer at the sea. I can guess now that Mama was hoping to cure me of my passion for the sea by this trip. She thought I would be disillusioned—as always happens—by direct experience with something I had so passionately dreamed about. And she was right, but only partly right.

WHAT PARADISE LOOKS LIKE

One day Mama declared with some ceremony that in a few days we would be going to the Black Sea for the whole summer, to a little town called Gelendzhik, near Novorossisk.

No better place than Gelendzhik could have been picked, probably, to discourage my yearning for the sea and the south. Gelendzhik was then a dusty, hot little town without any vegetation. Everything green had been destroyed for many kilometers around by the harsh Novorossisk winds—the northeasters. A few little bushes of Jerusalem thorn and some stunted acacia with dry, yellow little flowers were the only things that grew in the gardens. A baking heat rolled down from the tops of the mountains. A cement factory smoked away at the end of the bay.

But the bay itself was very nice. Big jellyfish swam in its warm, transparent water like red and blue flowers. Dappled flounder and goggle-eyed bullheads lay on its sandy bottom. The surf threw up on to the shore red seaweed, and rotten pieces of the floats of fishing nets, and pieces of dark-green bottle glass worn smooth by the waves.

After Gelendzhik, the sea did not lose its charm for me. It became simpler, and all the more beautiful, than in my fancy dreams.

I became friends in Gelendzhik with an old boatman named Anastas. He was a Greek, his family came from Volo. He had a new sailing sloop, white with a red keel and a deck scrubbed to a fine finish. Anastas took the cottagers around in his sloop. He was well known for his skill and his cool head, and Mama sometimes let me go out alone with him.

Anastas took me out beyond the harbor once, into the open sea. I will never forget the fear and the delight I felt when the sail, filling out with wind, bent the boat over until water came right up to the gunwale. Enormous thundering waves came at us, green and translucent, pouring salt mist over my face.

I grabbed onto the shrouds. I wanted to be back on shore, but Anastas, gripping his pipe in his teeth, hummed something and then asked:

"How much did your Mama pay for those slippers? Ah, they are fine slippers!"

He pointed at the soft Caucasian slippers I was wearing. My legs were shaking. I made no answer. Anastas yawned, and said:

"Never mind! A little shower bath, and a warm one. You'll have a good appetite for dinner. You won't have to be asked—you'll eat like your Papa and Mama."

He turned the sloop around casually but skillfully. It scooped up the water and we darted across the harbor, plunging and leaping from wave crest to wave crest. The water came out from under the stern with an enormous thunder. My heart sank.

Suddenly Anastas began to sing. I stopped trembling and listened in amazement to his song:

> *From Batum to Sukhum*
> *Ai-vai-vai!*
> *From Sukhum to Batum*
> *Ai-vai-vai!*
> *A little boy ran, he carried a box.*
> *Ai-vai-vai!*
> *The little boy fell, the box broke.*
> *Ai-vai-vai!*

With this song he let down the sail and our momentum carried us quickly to the wharf where a pale Mama was waiting. Anastas picked me up in his arms, placed me on the dock, and said:

"Now you have him back salted, madame. He's already used to the sea."

One day my father hired a wagon and we drove out of Gelendzhik to the Mikhailovsky Pass. The road, made of broken stone, wound at first around the sides of bare, dusty mountains. We crossed bridges over ravines in which there was not a drop of water. Exactly the same clouds, made of dry, gray cotton waste, hung all day long over the mountains as if tied to their summits.

I wanted a drink. Our red-headed Cossack driver turned around and said that I should wait until we got to the pass—there the water would be cold and tasty. But I didn't believe the driver. The dryness of the mountains and the absence of water frightened me. I looked back in sorrow at the dark fresh strip of sea. We couldn't drink it, but at least we could have bathed in its cool water.

The road ran higher and higher. Suddenly a freshness struck us in the face.

"Here's the pass itself!" the driver said. He stopped the horses, got down, and fixed a steel brake to the wheels. From the top of the mountain we could see an enormous, close-grown forest. It ran along the mountains in waves to the horizon. Red granite cliffs stuck out in places from the green, and in the distance I could see the peak, covered with ice and snow.

"The northeast wind doesn't blow here," the driver said. "Here is paradise."

The wagon started to descend. At once dense shadows covered us. In the impenetrable thicket of trees we could hear the gurgling of water, the cheeping of birds, and the rustling of leaves moved by a midday breeze.

The lower we went, the thicker the woods became and the more darkly shaded the road. A limpid little brook now ran along its side. It washed over different-colored stones, swirled its water around little violet-colored flowers, and forced them to bend over and shake, but it could not tear them from the stony soil and wash them down with it to the gorge below.

Mama scooped up a cup of water from the brook and gave me a drink. It was so cold that the cup was immediately covered with frost.

"It smells of ozone," my father said.

I sighed deeply. I didn't know what I could smell around me, but it seemed to me I had been handed a bunch of twigs drenched in fragrant rain.

Vines clung to our heads. Now here, now there, some kind of

little flower would peep out from behind a stone on the edge of the road and look curiously at our wagon and at the gray horses holding up their heads and marching ceremoniously, as if on parade, in order not to break into a gallop and upset the wagon.

"There's a lizard!" Mama said.

"Where?"

"Look, there. Do you see the nut tree? And to the left of it, a red stone in the grass? Look higher. Do you see a yellow corolla? That's azalea. A little to the right of the azalea, on the fallen beech tree, near its roots. There, don't you see a shaggy little red root in the dry ground there and some tiny blue flowers? Right next to that."

I saw the lizard. But while I was finding it, I had made a miraculous journey via the nut tree, the red stone, the azalea flower, and the fallen beech tree.

"So this is what it's like, the Caucasus!" I thought.

"Here is paradise!" the driver repeated, turning off the main road onto a narrow grassy lane cut through the woods. "Now we'll rest the horses and have a swim."

We drove through such a thicket and the branches beat us so heavily in our faces that we had to stop the horses, get out of the wagon, and go on foot. The wagon slowly followed us.

We came out onto a meadow in a green gorge. Masses of dandelions stood like white islands in the succulent grass. Under thick beech trees we saw an empty barn. It stood on the bank of a noisy mountain stream. The water was pouring over the stones in a transparent cascade, boiling and mixing a multitude of air bubbles in with the water.

While the driver unharnessed the horses and went off with my father to look for brushwood for a fire, we washed in the little river. Our faces burned as with fever after we had washed them. We wanted to go up the river right away, but Mama spread a tablecloth on the grass, got out the provisions, and said that she wouldn't let us go anywhere until we had eaten.

I gave in, ate ham sandwiches and cold rice with raisins. But it turned out that I was hurrying for no purpose—the stubborn copper teapot refused to boil on the fire. It must have been because the water from the stream was like ice.

Finally it boiled, so suddenly and furiously that it boiled over onto the fire. We drank the strong tea and started to hurry our father to go into the woods with us. The driver told us we must be careful because there were many wild boars in the woods. He explained that if we found little holes dug into the ground these would be the places where the boars slept at night. Mama was upset

—she couldn't go with us because she was short of breath—but the driver calmed her, pointing out that a boar must be deliberately aroused before it will attack a man.

We walked along the little river. We broke our way through a thicket, stopping every minute to call each other to look at the granite basins worn smooth by the water, at trout which flashed like blue sparks in the river, enormous green beetles with long whiskers, foamy waterfalls, horsetail plants higher than we were, wood anemones, and clearings full of peonies.

Borya found a little dusty hole, shaped like a child's bathtub. We walked around it carefully. Obviously, this was a place where a wild boar had spent the night.

My father went in front. He began to call us. We caught up with him through buckthorn, going around enormous mossy boulders. Father was standing next to a strange construction, overgrown with blackberries. Four enormous, smoothly polished stones were capped, as by a roof, with a fifth stone. It made a kind of stone house. There was a hole in one of the side stones, but so small that even I couldn't squeeze through it. There were several similar stone constructions in the vicinity.

"These are dolmens, or cromlechs," my father said. "Ancient burial grounds of the Scythians. But perhaps they're not burial grounds at all. The scholars don't know yet who built these dolmens, or why, or how."

I was convinced that the dolmens were the houses of long-extinct dwarf people, but I didn't tell this to my father, because Borya was with us, and he would have laughed at me.

We got back to Gelendzhik deeply burned by the sun and drunk with fatigue and the forest air. I fell asleep and through my sleep I could feel the breath of heat on me, and I could hear the faraway murmur of the sea.

So I made myself the owner, in my imagination, of another magnificent land—the Caucasus. Thus began my enthusiasm for Lermontov, for mountaineers, and for Shamil.* Mama grew worried again.

Now, at a ripe old age, I remember my childhood enthusiasms gratefully. They taught me a great deal. But I wasn't at all like

* M. Y. Lermontov (1814–1841), Romantic writer and poet, served twice on military missions in the Caucasus and was much influenced by the region. It was the setting for his poem "The Demon," probably the most universally popular poem in late nineteenth-century Russia. Shamil (1798–1871) was the leader of a stubborn Caucasian revolt against Tsarist Russia, a religious fanatic but a romantic warrior who captured the imagination of many Russians.

those excited and noisy little boys who can't swallow their spit for their emotion, and who give nobody any peace. On the contrary, I was very shy, and I didn't pester anyone with my enthusiasms.

THE BRYANSK FORESTS

In the autumn of 1902 I was supposed to enroll in the preparatory class of the First Kiev *Gymnasium*. My middle brother, Vadim, was studying there. After his tales I began to be afraid of the *gymnasium*. Sometimes I even wept, and I implored Mama to let me stay at home.

"Do you really want to be an extern?" Mama asked me, frightened.

Externs were the boys who studied at home and went to the *gymnasium* only to take examinations every year. From what my brothers had told me, I could imagine very well the nightmare fate of these externs. They were failed on purpose in their examinations; everyone made fun of them, and demanded more knowledge from them than from the ordinary *gymnasium* students. There was nowhere an extern could turn for help.

I pictured these poor boys to myself, worn out from cramming, in tears, their ears sticking out red with embarrassment. It was a sorry picture. I gave in, and said:

"Well, all right, I won't be an extern."

"Well, well! Aren't you the good boy!" Borya yelled from his room. "Sniveler!"

"Don't you dare hurt his feelings!" Mama intervened.

She considered Borya heartless and she was always wondering out loud where he could have got his calloused character. Obviously, from our Turkish grandmother. All the rest of our family were remarkable for our unusual responsiveness, our affectionate nature with people, and our impracticality.

My father knew about my fears, my tears, and my emotions

and he found, as he always did, an unexpected cure for these miseries. After a slight skirmish with Mama he decided to send me by myself to visit my uncle, Mama's brother Nikolai Grigorievich.

This was the same cheerful cadet, Uncle Kolya, who used to come from Peterburg to visit my grandmother at Cherkasy and who loved to dance waltzes with Aunt Nadya. By now he had become a military engineer, had married, and was serving in the town of Bryansk in Orlovsky province at an old factory where they made artillery gun carriages. The factory was called an arsenal.

Uncle Kolya had taken a cottage for the summer on the ancient and neglected Ryovna estate in the Bryansk forests, and he invited us all to go there. My parents agreed. But they couldn't leave until my sister and my brothers had finished their examinations. So they sent me ahead by myself.

"Let him get used to it," my father said. "It's good for little boys who are so shy."

My father wrote a letter to Uncle Kolya. I didn't know what he wrote in it. Mama, furtively wiping away her tears, packed a small trunk for me in which nothing was forgotten, with a note in it listing all kinds of instructions. They bought me a second-class ticket to the station at Sinezerki. My uncle's country house was about ten versts [six or seven miles] from there.

Everyone went with me to the station, even Borya. My father said something to the gray-haired conductor and gave him some money.

"We'll take him there as gently as a snowflake," the conductor said to Mama. "Don't let yourself worry, ma'am."

Mama asked my neighbors in the compartment to look after me and not to let me get out at the stations. My fellow passengers agreed willingly. I was very embarrassed, and pulled guardedly at Mama's sleeve.

After the second bell, everyone kissed me, even Borya, although he also gave me, unnoticed by the others, what was then called a "pear"—a painful tap with his thumb on the top of my skull.

They all went out of the train onto the platform. But Mama still couldn't leave. She held my hand and kept on saying:

"Be good. Do you hear? Be a bright boy. And be very careful."

She looked at me with searching eyes. The third bell rang. She hugged me and then walked quickly, her dress rustling, to the door. She got off just before the train started. My father caught her, and shook his head.

I stood by a closed window and watched how quickly Mama

walked ahead of everyone else down the platform, and only then did I see how pretty she was, how tiny, and how tender. My tears poured down on the dusty window frame.

I looked out of the window for a long time, although I could no longer see either Mama or the platform, but only the freight tracks, some switching engines, and the new Gothic Roman Catholic church, which seemed to be revolving, on Vasilievskaya Street. I was afraid to look around for fear my neighbors in the compartment would see that I had been crying. Then I remembered that a telegram had been sent to Uncle Kolya about my arrival. A feeling of pride that an actual telegram had been sent about me quieted me a little, and I turned around.

The compartment was upholstered in red velvet. It was warm and cozy. Little motes of dust began to fly in the sunshine from one corner to the other, all at once and as if by command, and then to fly back again just as quickly. The train was pulling out of the tangled outskirts of Kiev and was rounding a big curve.

I had been placed in a compartment reserved for ladies. Mama had insisted on this. I looked at my companions carefully. One of them, a dark, dried-up Frenchwoman, nodded quickly at me, smiling and showing her horse's teeth, and offered me a box of crystallized fruit. I didn't know what to do, but I thanked her and took the candy, getting my hands all sticky.

"Put it in your mouth, quickly!" a second passenger said—a sixteen-year-old *gymnasium* student in a brown schoolgirl's dress, with slanting, cheerful eyes. "Chew it, don't think about it!"

The Frenchwoman, obviously a governess, said something crossly in French. The schoolgirl made a face, and then the Frenchwoman began to speak quickly, angrily, and for a long time in French. The schoolgirl did not hear her out, but got up and went out into the corridor.

"Ah, youth!" said my third fellow passenger, a fat little old lady with a mouth like a ring-shaped roll. Behind her back, hanging in a string bag, were some ring-shaped rolls, covered with poppy seeds. "Ah, what has happened to young people!"

"O-o!" The Frenchwoman nodded her head. "It's just disobedience. Just *fif!* Just whims!"

I did not know what the word *fif* meant but I guessed it was something bad, because the old lady raised her eyes to the ceiling and sighed so deeply that even the Frenchwoman looked at her with interest.

I wanted to look out of the window so I went out to the corridor. The high school girl was standing next to an open window.

"Ah, Vitya!" she said to me. "Stand next to me here, we'll look out together."

"I'm not Vitya," I said, blushing.

"It doesn't make any difference. Stand here."

I knelt on the radiator and leaned out the window. The train was crossing the Dnieper on a bridge. I could see the Kiev Lavra,* in the distance, and the Dnieper washing the sandy islands around the foundations of the bridge.

"She's the devil's own old hag!" the girl said. "Madame Demifemme! But don't be scared of her. She's really a goodhearted old lady."

My first train trip left me very tired, because I spent the whole time, except at night, next to the open window. But I was happy. For the first time I was feeling that traveler's serenity in which you don't have to think about anything at all but just look out of the window at the fields of rye, the woods, the little stations where barefoot old women are selling milk, at the little streams, the railroad watchmen, the stationmasters in their dusty red caps, the geese, the village children running after the train and yelling: "Uncle, throw me a kopeck!"

It was a long, roundabout road to Bryansk in those days, via Lvov and Navliya. The train didn't get to Sinezerki until the third day.

It didn't hurry, and stood for a long time at stations, puffing at the water towers. The passengers would jump down, run to get hot water for tea or to the buffet, to buy strawberries or roast chicken from the old women. Then everything would grow calm. Long past the time to leave, a sleepy quiet would reign over the station, the sun would shine, clouds would drift over us dragging blue shadows along the ground, the passengers would doze, and the train would just stand and stand. Only the locomotive would sigh loudly, and boiling oily water would drop out of it onto the sand.

At last the fat conductor would come out of the station in his canvas coat, stroke his mustache, put a whistle in his mouth, and blow a shrill blast. The locomotive would not answer, but just go on puffing. Then the conductor would walk lazily up to the locomotive and blow his whistle again. There would be no answer. Only at the third or fourth whistle would it at last emit a short unsatisfactory snort of its own and slowly start to move.

I would lean out of the window because I knew that just beyond the signal tower there would be slopes covered with clover and

* The Lavra was the oldest and most important of the pre-1917 Russian monasteries. It stands on the Pechersky Hill above the city of Kiev.

bluebells, and then would come a pine forest. When the train entered it, the sound of the wheels would become much louder and the echoes would bounce back, just as if cheerful blacksmiths had begun to wield their hammers all through the forest.

I was seeing central Russia for the first time. I liked it better than the Ukraine. It was emptier, more spacious, and wilder. I loved its woods, its overgrown roads, and the talk of its peasants.

The old lady in our compartment slept all the time. The Frenchwoman calmed down and made lace, and the schoolgirl sang, leaning out of the window, and skillfully snatched leaves from the trees flying past the train. Every two hours she would get the provisions basket, eat for a long time, and force me to eat, too. We ate hard-boiled eggs, roast chicken, and little cakes filled with rice, and we drank tea.

Then we would hang out of the window again, a little lightheaded from the fragrance of the blossoming buckwheat. The shadow of the train ran along the fields and the train was filled with such an orange light from the setting sun that in our compartment you couldn't tell one thing from another in the flaming haze.

The train pulled into Sinezerki at twilight. The conductor put my suitcase on the platform. I expected my Uncle Kolya, or his wife, Aunt Marusya, to meet me. But there was nobody on the platform. My fellow passengers began to be troubled.

The train stopped only a minute. It went away, and I was left there with my suitcase. I was certain that Uncle Kolya had been delayed but that he would come soon.

A bearded peasant, in a coat and black visored cap and with a whip stuck in the top of his boot, stumped up to me. He smelled of horse sweat and hay.

"Aren't you Kostik?" he asked me. "I've been waiting for you. Your uncle the captain ordered me to meet you and to keep you safe. Give me your little bag. Let's go."

This was the final test prepared for me by my father. He had written Uncle Kolya not to meet me at Sinezerki.

The driver—he was called Nikita—muttered something about my uncle, the captain, seated me in a wagon filled with soft hay covered with a blanket, untied the horse's bag of oats, sat down on the coachman's box, and off we went.

At first we drove for a long time through the evening fields. Then the road wound upward through woods. Sometimes the wagon rattled over a wooden bridge, and black swamp water glittered underneath. A raw freshness engulfed us, smelling of marsh sedge. Over the woods and some little groves of trees hung a crimson moon. A bittern hooted, and Nikita said:

"Our district is wooded, there are very few people. We have lots of water. It's the nicest place in all Orlovsky province."

We drove into a pine forest and began to descend along a narrow road to a river. The pine trees hid the moon and it grew very dark. We could hear voices along the road. I began to feel a little scared.

"Is that you, Nikita?" my uncle's familiar voice called out of the darkness.

"Whoa!" Nikita yelled, violently reining in the horses. "Sure, it's us. Whoa, may the goblins take you!"

Someone picked me up and lifted me out of the wagon. In the failing sunset light I could see my Uncle Kolya's laughing eyes and his white teeth. He kissed me and handed me to Aunt Marusya. She fondled me like a baby, laughing deep in her chest. She smelled of vanilla—probably she had just been kneading some sweet dough.

We sat in the wagon, and Nikita walked by its side. We crossed an old black bridge over a clean, deep river, then a second bridge. Under it a fish slapped the water loudly. At last the wagon drove past a stone gatepost into such a dark, tall park that it seemed to me the tops of the trees were lost in the stars.

In the very depths of this park, under a canopy of linden trees you couldn't see through, the wagon stopped next to a little wooden house with lighted windows. Two dogs, a white one and a black one called Mordan and Chetvertak, began to bark at me and to jump up at me, trying to lick my face.

I lived all that summer at Ryovna, a former estate of Prince Potemkin, among the dense Bryansk forests, the rivers, the gentle Orlovsky peasants, in an ancient park so vast that nobody knew where it ended and the forests started. This was the last summer of my real childhood. The *gymnasium* started right after it. Our family disintegrated. I was left alone very early, and I earned my own living in my last years at the *gymnasium* and considered myself entirely grown up.

From this summer on, forever, I have felt tied by all my heart to central Russia. I know no country which has such immense lyrical power and such moving beauty—with all its melancholy, its calm, and its spaciousness—as the central belt of Russia. It is hard to measure the size of this love. Everyone knows it for himself. You love every blade of grass sparkling with dew or hot from

the sun, every cup of water from a forest well, every sapling leaning over a pond, its leaves trembling without any breeze, every bird
cry, and every cloud drifting across the pale, high sky.

And if I want sometimes to live to a hundred and twenty, as old
Nikifor predicted, it's only because one life is very little in which
to experience all the charm and all the healing strength of nature
in our Russian land.

My childhood ended. It's too bad that we begin to understand
the delights of childhood only when we are already grown up.
Everything was different when we were children. We looked at the
world with lighter and cleaner eyes, and everything looked much
clearer to us.

The sun was brighter, and the fields had a stronger smell, the
thunder was louder, there was more rain, and the grass grew
higher. And the human heart was bigger, and grief more bitter,
and the earth was a thousand times more puzzling, our native
earth, this most magnificent earth given to us for our lifetime. We
should cultivate it, take care of it, and defend it with all the
strength there is in us.

SWARMERS

I was not jealous, like other little boys, of the military cadets in
Kiev who wore white shoulder straps with yellow monograms and
stood at attention in front of generals. I wasn't jealous of the
gymnasists, even though their overcoats, made of gray officer's
cloth with silver buttons, were considered very handsome. From
my childhood I was indifferent to every kind of uniform except a
sailor's.

When I first put on long trousers and a *gymnasist's* jacket, in
the autumn of 1902, I was awkward and uncomfortable, and for a
while I didn't feel like myself. I became a strange little boy with a
heavy cap on his head. I didn't like those hard blue caps with their

stiff coats of arms, because all my comrades—pupils in the entering class—always wore them so that their ears stuck out. When they took off their caps, their ears would become normal again. But as soon as they put them on again, their ears would stick out. It was as if they had been designed so that the inspector Bodyansky, taking a beginner by the ear, could say to him in his frightening voice:

"You're late again, miserable creature! Stand in the corner and think about your bitter destiny!"

So as soon as Mama bought me a cap, I imitated my older brothers and took out its little steel hoop and tore out its satin lining. This was the tradition: the more shapeless the cap, the more valiant the schoolboy. "Only grinds and lickspittles go around in new caps," my brothers told me.

You were supposed to sit on your cap, carry it in your pocket, and use it to knock down ripe chestnuts. Then it would take on that battered look which was the pride of every real *gymnasist*.

They bought me a satchel made of deerskin with a silk lining, a pencil case and some squared paper, some thin textbooks for the beginning class, and Mama took me to the *gymnasium*.

Grandmother Vikentiya Ivanovna was visiting us in Kiev at that time. She made the sign of the cross over me and hung a little crucifix on a cold chain around my neck. She straightened the collar of my black jacket with trembling hands, tucked the crucifix under my shirt, turned around, and pressed her handkerchief to her eyes.

"Well, go on!" she said in a low voice and she pushed me slightly. "Be a bright boy. Study!"

I went out with Mama. I kept looking back at our house as if I were being led away from it forever.

We were living then on shaded, quiet Nikolsko-Botanicheskaya Street. Enormous chestnut trees stood as if lost in thought around our house. Their dry, five-pointed leaves were beginning to fall. It was a sunny day, with a blue sky, warm, but with cold shadows—a normal autumn day in Kiev. Grandmother stood at the window and waved to me until we had turned on to Tarasovskaya Street. Mama walked along in silence.

When we got to Nikolayevsky Square and I could see the yellow building of the *gymnasium* through its greenery, I started to cry. I probably understood that my childhood was finished, that I would have to work now, and that my work would be bitter and long and nothing like the quiet days I had spent at home.

I stopped, pressed my face against Mama, and cried so hard

that the pencil box in the satchel on my back bounced and clattered as if to ask what had happened to its small owner. Mama took off my cap and wiped away my tears with a scented handkerchief.

"Stop," she told me. "Do you think this is easy for me? But this is what we must do."

This was what we must do! No other words had ever entered my consciousness with such force as these, said by Mama: "This is what we must do."

The older I grew, the more often I heard grownups say that one should live "the way we must, and not just as we want to or as it pleases us." I couldn't adjust to this for a long time, and I used to ask grownups: Doesn't a man really have the right to live the way he wants to? Must he always live just the way others want him to? But the answer they gave me was that I was judging something I didn't understand. And Mama said to my father one day: "It's all your anarchist way of bringing him up!" My father drew me close to him and, pressing my head against his white waistcoat, said jokingly:

"We're not understood, you and I, Kostik, in this house."

When I had calmed down and stopped crying, Mama and I went into the *gymnasium* building. A wide iron staircase, shined by heels until it looked like lead, led upward where we could hear an ominous throbbing, like the humming of an enormous beehive.

"Don't be frightened," Mama said to me. "They're changing classes."

We climbed up the staircase. At first Mama did not hold my hand. Two older boys suddenly started down. They made way for us. One of them said, addressing my back:

"They're bringing in another unhappy swarmer!"

This was how I became a member of the beginners' class, a restless and helpless society of little boys or, as the upperclassmen called us scornfully, "swarmers." They called us this because, small and nimble, we swarmed and tangled between the legs of older people when pupils were moving from one classroom to another.

Mama and I went through a white assembly hall hung with portraits of the emperors. I remember especially Alexander I. He was holding a green cocked hat against his thigh. Red sideburns adorned the sides of his catlike face. I didn't like him, even though cavalrymen in plumes were galloping over a hill behind him.

We went through this room into the office of the inspector, Bodyansky, a stout man in a large uniform coat like a lady's cape.

Bodyansky laid a pudgy hand on my head, thought for a long time, and then said:

"Do your lessons, or I'll eat you up!"

Mama was forced to smile. Bodyansky called the proctor, Kasimir, and ordered him to take me to the beginners' class. Mama nodded to me, and Kasimir took me by the shoulder and led me down a long corridor. He held on to my shoulder tightly, as if he were afraid that I'd break away and run back to Mama.

Classes were going on in the classrooms. It was empty and quiet in the corridor. The quiet seemed especially surprising after the incredible tumult between periods. It had left dust floating in the sunbeams which came in from the park outside. This was the famous park of the First Kiev *Gymnasium*—a century-old park filling an entire city block.

I looked out the window and wanted to cry again. Chestnut trees stood there with the sun shining through them. Rustling pale-lilac poplar leaves were dancing in the breeze.

As a little boy I already loved parks and trees. I didn't break off branches and I didn't rob birds' nests. Perhaps this was because Grandmother Vikentiya Ivanovna had told me that "the world is wonderful and good, and a man should live in it and work in it just as in a big garden."

Kasimir noticed that I was getting ready to cry. He dug out of a pocket of his clean, old coat a sticky candy called a *zubrovka* and said, with a Polish accent:

"Eat this candy when the classes change again."

I thanked him in a whisper and took the candy.

I talked only in a whisper and was afraid to raise my head during my first days in school. Everything flabbergasted me: the bearded teachers in their long coats, the old vaults, the echoes in the endless corridors, and finally the director, Bessmertny—an elderly, handsome man with a little golden beard and a new dress uniform. He was a gentle, enlightened man, but for some reason we were supposed to be afraid of him. Maybe it was because he sat in a very high office with a portrait of the surgeon Pirogov, a stucco ceiling, and a red carpet. The director seldom left his office. According to the rules, we stopped and bowed to him, although we could greet the teachers without stopping.

Kasimir led me down a resounding corridor. Wandering along it and looking into the classrooms through the glass panels in their doors were the supervisors "Melon," "Shponka," "Snuff," and the only supervisor whom the schoolboys liked, Platon Fedorovich. This corridor, on which was the beginners' classroom, was under

Platon Fedorovich, and this saved me from much unpleasantness in the first few days.

It was up to the supervisors to follow closely the behavior of the boys and to report to the inspector everything they did. Penalties were meted out—being held back for one hour or two "without dinner" (in other words, the anguish of sitting in an empty class-room after lessons were finished), a bad mark for conduct, or, finally, a summons to the parents to come to the director's office. This last penalty we were afraid of most of all.

In the older classes there were other punishments: temporary suspension from the school, expulsion with the right to apply else-where, and the most fearful of all—expulsion with a "wolf's ticket," without the right to matriculate again in any secondary school.

I saw only one upperclassman expelled with a wolf's ticket. This was when I was already in the first class. They said he had slapped the face of the German teacher, Yagorsky, a rude man with a greenish face. Yagorsky had called him a blockhead in front of the entire class. The schoolboy demanded that Yagorsky apologize. Yagorsky refused. So the schoolboy hit him. It was for this that he was expelled with a wolf's ticket.

The day after the expulsion, the boy came back to school. None of the supervisors could make up his mind to stop him. He opened the classroom door, took a Browning revolver out of his pocket, and pointed it at Yagorsky.

Yagorsky jumped out of his chair and, covering himself with a newspaper, ran down between the desks, trying to hide behind the pupils' backs. "Coward!" the expelled boy said to him, then he turned around, walked out on the stair landing, and shot himself in the heart.

The door of our classroom opened onto the same landing. We heard a sharp crack, and the sound of breaking glass. Something fell and clattered down the stairs. The classroom teacher rushed to the door. We ran right after him. The freckled pupil lay on the stairway. He raised his hand, clutched at the baluster, then his arm grew limp, and he was still. His eyes looked at us with a surprising smile.

The supervisors were rushing around him. Then the director, Bessmertny, walked quickly up. He fell to his knees beside the schoolboy, tore open his jacket, and then we could see the blood on his shirt. First-aid orderlies were already climbing up the stairs, in brown uniforms and with French caps on their heads. They quickly put the body on a stretcher.

"Lead the children away from here, at once!" the director said to our classroom teacher. But he, probably, didn't hear, so we all stayed there.

Yagorsky came out of his classroom and walked, all hunched over, toward the teachers' room.

"Get out of here!" the director suddenly said, to his retreating back.

Yagorsky turned around.

"Get out of my school!" the director said quietly. And Yagorsky suddenly ran, cowering, down the corridor.

The next day Mama didn't want to let me go back to school, but then she changed her mind and I went. We were all released from school after the second class. They told us that any of us who wanted could go to the dead boy's funeral.

And we all went—little, frightened, in our long-skirted overcoats, carrying our heavy satchels on our shoulders.

It was a cold, foggy day. The entire school walked behind the coffin. There were a lot of flowers on it. The director held the arm of a gray-haired, badly dressed woman—the dead boy's mother.

At that time I didn't understand such worldly incidents very well, but still I understood that life was giving us a first lesson in comradeship. We walked up to the grave in turn, and each of us threw in a handful of dirt, as if we were taking an oath that we would always be kind and just to one another.

But this took place much later, and now Kasimir was just leading me into the beginners' class.

The classroom teacher Nazarenko, a loud man with a wavy blue beard like an Assyrian emperor's, was sitting behind a table. The upperclassmen called Nazarenko "Scientific Informer." They claimed that he worked in the Secret Political Police Department.

All year long, until we were promoted into the first class, Nazarenko tortured us, his young pupils, in a stentorian voice, giving us bad marks, jeers, and stories about how he had had his ingrown toenails operated on. I feared him and I hated him. I hated him most of all for his stories about this operation.

I sat at a little desk which had been heavily carved with a penknife. I could hardly breathe. The sour smell of ink was everywhere. Nazarenko was dictating: "One day the swan, the crayfish, and the pike . . ." A sparrow sat on a twig outside the open window, holding a dry maple leaf in its beak. I wanted to change places with the sparrow. The sparrow looked into the classroom, chirped in sympathy, and dropped the maple leaf.

"New boy," Nazarenko thundered at me, "get your notebook,

write, and don't look around unless you want to go without dinner!"

I got my notebook and started to write. Tears streamed down on the blotter. Then my neighbor, a dark little boy with cheerful eyes, named Shmukler, whispered to me:

"Swallow your spit, then you'll get over it."

I swallowed my spit, but I didn't get over anything. For a long time I couldn't breathe except in little gasps.

This was the beginning of my first year in the *gymnasium*. Dust, running about between classes, constant terror that someone would call me to the blackboard, inky fingers, my heavy satchel and—as hangovers from a lost life—the melodic sounds of the Kiev trolley cars outside the windows, the distant tune of an organ-grinder, and the whistles of the locomotives floating up to us from the railroad station. There the big trains started up and, puffing steam, chugged through forests and harvested fields while we, hunched over our desks, breathed hard from the chalk dust floating in dry clouds off the blackboards.

Directly opposite the beginners' room was the physics laboratory. A narrow door led into it. We often looked in while we were changing classes. It had benches raised to the ceiling in an amphitheater.

Upperclassmen went there for their classes. We were always swarming between their legs, of course, and they probably grew bored with this. One day a tall, pale upperclassman gave a long whistle. His fellows began to grab us swarmers, and to drag us into the physics laboratory. They scattered on the benches, holding us prisoners between their legs.

At first this delighted us. We looked with great curiosity at the mysterious things on the shelves, black disks and flasks and copper spheres. Then the first bell rang in the corridor. We began to squirm. The upperclassmen wouldn't let us go. They held us tightly, and they gave the "pear" to the most rebellious of us.

The second bell rang ominously. We began to struggle with all our strength, to plead and to cry. But the upperclassmen were unyielding. The pale student was standing at the door.

"Watch out," his comrades yelled to him. "Be sure you have it timed just right!"

We didn't understand a thing. We were half dead with fright. The third bell was about to ring. Nazarenko would come back to an empty beginners' classroom. His anger would be formidable. Rivers of our tears would not be able to put out that anger.

Then the third bell rang. We howled with all our voices. The pale student raised his hand. This meant that the physics teacher had appeared at the end of the corridor. He was walking slowly, listening with apprehension to the yells coming from the physics room.

This teacher was a very fat man. He had to go through the narrow door sideways. The upperclassmen's trick was based on this. When the teacher was already in the door, the pale student dropped his hand. They all released us and we, out of our minds, seeing nothing, understanding nothing, and filling the laboratory with our lamentations, rushed back toward our classroom. We literally flew over the frightened physics teacher. For a moment a whirlpool of shaved children's heads swirled around the door. Then we popped the teacher like a cork out into the corridor, swarmed around and between his legs, and regained our room. Fortunately, Nazarenko had been held up in the teachers' room, and he noticed nothing.

The upperclassmen managed to play this treacherous trick on us only once. Afterwards we were more careful. Whenever they appeared in the corridor, we would hide in our own room, closing the door and barricading it with desks.

It was the tall, pale student who had thought up this entertainment which cost us so many tears. His name was Bagrov. Some years later he fired a revolver in the Kiev Opera House at Stolypin, the Tsar's prime minister, killed him, and was hung for it.

At his trial, Bagrov seemed calm and lazy. When the sentence was read to him, he said:

"It's all the same to me whether I eat two thousand more cutlets in my life, or don't eat them."

Grownups talked a great deal about Bagrov then, and tried to guess if he was really a revolutionary or an agent of the Secret Political Police Department who had organized the killing of Stolypin for the Tsar's benefit. (Nicholas hated Stolypin because he couldn't dominate him.) My father declared that any man who could pronounce such cynical words just before his death could not possibly be a revolutionary.

WATER FROM THE LIMPOPO RIVER

Bottles of yellowish water, sealed with sealing wax, stood on the table in our classroom. There was a label on every bottle. On the labels was written in an old-fashioned, rounded handwriting: "Water from the Nile," "Water from the Limpopo River," "Water from the Mediterranean Sea."

There were a lot of bottles. They held water from the Volga, the Rhine, the Thames, Lake Michigan, the Dead Sea, and the Amazon. But no matter how much we looked at the water, all the bottles seemed to have the same yellow, boring kind of water in them.

We asked the geography teacher Cherpunov to let us taste the water from the Dead Sea. We wanted to find out if it really was salty. But Cherpunov wouldn't let us sample it.

A short man, with narrow eyes and a long gray beard reaching almost to his knees, Cherpunov made us think of a sorcerer. He always brought all kinds of exhibits to his classes. He loved most of all to bring these bottles of water. He told us how he had got the water from the Nile himself, near Cairo.

"Just look"—he shook the bottle—"how much sediment there is in it. The sediment of the Nile is worth more than diamonds. Egyptian culture grows in it. Markovsky, explain to the class what culture is."

Markovsky stood up and said that culture was the growing of cereal grains, raisins, and rice.

"Stupid, but related to the truth!" Cherpunov commented, and he began to show us other bottles.

He was very proud of the water from the Limpopo River. One of his former students had sent it to Cherpunov as a present.

Cherpunov thought up visual techniques to help us remember all kinds of geographical facts. For example, he drew a big letter A on the blackboard. In the right corner of this letter he drew another smaller A. In this he drew a third, and in the third he drew a fourth. Then he said:

"Remember: this—is Asia, in Asia—is Arabia, in Arabia—is the city of Aden, and in Aden—there sits an Anglo-Saxon."

We remembered this at once and for all our lives.

Older boys told us that Cherpunov had organized a small geographical museum in his apartment, but the old man invited no one to see it. He was said to have a stuffed hummingbird there, and a collection of butterflies, a telescope, and even a nugget of gold.

When I heard about this museum, I began to build my own. It was, of course, not a very rich collection, but it blossomed in my imagination into a kingdom of amazing things. Different stories were connected with every item, whether it was a Rumanian soldier's button or a dried-out praying mantis.

I ran into Cherpunov once in the Botanical Gardens. He was sitting on a bench which was wet with rain, and poking the ground with his cane. I took off my cap and bowed.

"Come here!" Cherpunov called me and he held out a fat hand to me. "Sit down. Tell me. They say you've collected a small museum. What have you got?"

I listed shyly my simple treasures. Cherpunov laughed.

"Most commendable!" he said. "Come and see me on Sunday morning. You'll see my museum. I wouldn't be surprised, since you are attracted by this so young, if you turned out to be a geographer or a traveler."

"With Mama?" I asked.

"What about Mama?"

"Should I come to see you with Mama?"

"No, why should you? Come alone. Mamas don't understand geography."

On Sunday I put on my new *gymnasium* suit and went to call on Cherpunov. He lived in Pechersk, in a low outbuilding on a courtyard. The building was so heavily overgrown with lilacs that it was dark in the rooms. It was late autumn but the lilacs had not yet turned yellow. Mist dripped off the leaves. River boats were whistling below on the Dnieper. They were going away to spend the winter in backwaters somewhere, and they were saying good-by to Kiev.

I climbed up on the porch and saw a little copper cup set in the wall with a round handle for the bell. I pulled the handle. A little bell rang inside the building. Cherpunov himself let me in. He had on a warm gray jacket, and felt slippers.

The marvels began in the vestibule. A small *gymnasium* student, red with confusion, trying to unbutton his coat with chilled fingers, was reflected in an oval mirror. I didn't understand at once that this boy was myself. For a long time I couldn't manage the buttons. I finally undid them, and looked at the frame of the mirror. It wasn't a frame, but a wreath of insipidly colored glass leaves, flowers, and bunches of grapes.

"Venetian glass," Cherpunov said, helping me take off my coat and then hanging it on the hall stand. "Look more closely. You may even touch it."

I approached the round object carefully. The glass was frosted, as if dusted with powder. In a beam of light which came in from the next room it shone with a reddish fire.

"It looks just like Turkish Delight," I commented.

"Stupid, but related to the truth," Cherpunov muttered.

I blushed until my eyes burned. Cherpunov clapped me on the shoulder.

"Don't be offended. That's a way I have of speaking. Well, let's go in. You'll have some tea with us."

I started to refuse, but Cherpunov had me by the elbow and he led me into the dining room. We entered a room like a garden. To get to my place at the table, I had to move carefully a philodendron leaf and a branch with odorous red cones which hung down from the ceiling. A fan-shaped palm hung over the white tablecloth. Vases with rose-colored, yellow, and white flowers stood on the window sills.

I sat down at the table, but jumped up at once. A short young woman with shining gray eyes had walked swiftly into the dining room, rustling her dress.

"Here, Masha," Cherpunov nodded at me, "is that young *gymnasium* student I was telling you about. The son of Georgi Maximovich. He's embarrassed, naturally."

The woman held out her hand. A bracelet tinkled.

"Are you really going to explain everything to him, Pyotr Pyotrovich?" she asked, looking at me and smiling.

"Yes, after tea."

"Then I'll walk into town while you do. To the candy store. To Kirkheim's. I need to buy something."

"As you wish."

The woman poured me tea with lemon, and offered me a bowl of Viennese rolls.

"You must build up strength before the lesson."

After tea, Cherpunov smoked a cigarette. He knocked the ash off into a seashell covered with a petrified foam of the most delicate pink color.

"This is a seashell from New Guinea," Cherpunov said.

"Well, good-by," the young woman said loudly, got up, and went out.

"Well now," Cherpunov said, following her with his eyes, and then he showed me a portrait on the wall. It showed a bearded man with an emaciated face. "Do you know who that is? One of the best of Russians. The explorer Miklukho-Maklai.* He was a great humanist. You probably don't understand what that word means. It doesn't matter. You'll learn later. He was a great scholar and he believed in the good will of people. He lived alone among cannibals on New Guinea. Without arms, dying of fever. But he knew how to do so much good to those wild men and how to show such patience with them that when our corvette, the *Emerald,* came to take him back to Russia, crowds of savages wept on the shore, held out their arms toward the ship, and cried: 'Maklai, Maklai.' So, remember: with goodness, anything can be achieved."

The woman walked into the dining room and stood at the door. She was wearing a little black hat. She pulled a glove onto her left hand.

"By the way, what is poetry?" Cherpunov asked unexpectedly. "If you please, don't try to answer. It can't be defined. This seashell comes from the island where Maklai lived. If you look at it for a long time, it will suddenly occur to you that somehow in the morning a beam of sunshine fell on this seashell, and has stayed on it for all eternity."

The woman sat down on a chair near the door and began to pull off her gloves.

I stared at the seashell. In a minute it seemed to me as if I had actually fallen asleep and I could see the slow progress of the sunshine through transparent masses of ocean water and the flash of pink-colored light.

"If you'll hold the shell to your ear," Cherpunov was saying somewhere in the distance, "you'll hear a humming. I can't explain to you why this happens. Nobody can explain it to you. It is a mystery. Everything that man can't understand is called a mystery."

The woman took off her hat and laid it on her knees.

"Take it, and listen," Cherpunov offered.

I put the shell to my ear and I could hear a sleepy noise, as if far, far away waves were running up on a shore. The woman held out her hand:

"Give it to me. I haven't heard it for a long time."

* N. N. Miklukho-Maklai (1847–1887) was a famous Russian explorer best known for his travels in New Guinea where he became an expert on the Papuans.

I gave her the shell. She held it to her ear, smiled, and half-opened her mouth in such a way that I could see her small, very white, wet teeth.

"What's the matter with you, Masha? Aren't you going to Kirkheim's?" Cherpunov asked suddenly.

The woman stood up.

"I changed my mind. It's boring to go to Kirkheim's alone. Excuse me if I've bothered you."

She went out of the dining room.

"Well, anyway," Cherpunov said, "let us continue our conversation, young man. There are some black boxes there in the corner. Bring me the top box. But carry it carefully."

I put the box on the table in front of Cherpunov. It felt very light.

Cherpunov slowly opened the cover. I was looking over his shoulder, and I jumped in spite of myself. An enormous butterfly, bigger than a maple leaf, lay on a piece of black silk in the box, and glittered like a rainbow.

"Don't look that way!" Cherpunov said crossly. "You must look like this."

He took me by the crown of the head and started to turn it first to the right, then to the left. Each time the butterfly showed different colors, now white, now gold, now purple, now blue. It seemed that its wings were burning with some magic fire but didn't burn up.

"It's the rarest butterfly from the island of Borneo!" Cherpunov announced with pride, and he closed the cover of the box.

Then Cherpunov showed me an astral globe, some old maps with the winds shown on them, and a stuffed hummingbird with a beak as long as a little awl.

"Well, enough for today," Cherpunov said. "You're tired. You may come and see me on Sundays."

"Are you always home?"

"Yes. I'm already an old man, too old to wander and travel around, my friend. So I do my traveling on walls and tables." He pointed to the bookshelves and to the dead hummingbird.

"Have you traveled a great deal?" I asked timidly.

"No less than Miklukho-Maklai."

The young woman walked into the vestibule, where I was struggling into my coat, and not finding the sleeves. She wore a short, tight jacket, a hat, and gloves. A dark little veil was lowered over her eyes. This made them seem blue.

"Where do you live?" she asked.

I told her.

"That means the Kreshchatik is on your way. Let's go together."

We walked out. Cherpunov stood at the door and looked after us. Then he said loudly:

"Masha, I urge you to be careful. And come back quickly."

"I hear you," the woman answered, but she didn't look back.

We walked around the Nikolsky Fort, with bronze lion heads on its enormous gates, walked through Marinsky Park where I had once met the naval cadet, and turned into Institutskaya Street. The woman kept silent. I was afraid that she would ask me something, and that I would have to answer.

On Institutskaya Street, at last, she asked:

"What did you like best of all in our museum?"

"The butterfly," I answered, after a little pause, and I added: "Except that I'm sorry for the butterfly."

"Yes?" the woman said, surprised. "Why are you sorry for it?"

Up to this time, nobody had ever used the formal "you" in talking to me. She did, and this confused me all the more.

"It's very beautiful," I answered, "and almost nobody sees it."

"And what else did you like?"

On the Kreshchatik we stopped next to Kirkheim's candy store. The woman asked me:

"Are you allowed to drink cocoa in a candy store? And eat cakes?"

I didn't know whether I was allowed to or not, but I remembered that I had once been in Kirkheim's with Mama and my sister Galya and that we had actually drunk cocoa. So I answered that of course I was allowed to go to Kirkheim's.

"That's wonderful. Then let's go in."

We sat in the back of the store. The woman moved a vase of hydrangeas to the edge of the table, and ordered two cups of cocoa and a small cake.

"What class are you in?" she asked when they had brought us the cocoa.

"In the second."

"And how old are you?"

"I'm twelve."

"And I'm twenty-eight. At twelve, of course, it's possible to believe everything."

"What?" I asked.

"Do you have some kinds of favorite games and things you've made up?"

"Yes, I have."

"And Pyotr Pyotrovich has. But I haven't. So you should include me in your games. We would play well together."

"At what?" I asked. The conversation was becoming interesting.

"At what? Well, at Cinderella, or running away from the evil king. Or we could think up a new game. It would be called 'The Butterfly from the Island of Borneo'!"

"Yes!" I said, taking fire. "We would go looking in an enchanted forest for a well with living water."

"In great danger of our lives, of course?"

"Naturally, in terrible danger!"

"We would carry this water in our hands," she said, and she turned up her little veil. "When one of us would get tired, he would carefully pour the water into the palm of the other one."

"And when we pour the water," I pointed out, "one or two drops absolutely must fall on the ground, and in those spots . . ."

"In those places," she interrupted, "bushes will grow with big white flowers. And then what will happen? What do you think?"

"We'll sprinkle the water on the butterfly, and it will live again."

"And be turned into a beautiful girl?" the woman asked, and she laughed. "Well, it's time to go. They're probably waiting for you at home."

We went out. She went with me to the corner of Fundukleyev-skaya Street, and from there turned back. I looked after her. She crossed the Kreshchatik, also looking back, and she waved a little hand in a black glove.

I didn't tell anyone at home, even Mama, that I had been at Kirkheim's. Mama was very surprised that I didn't eat anything at dinner. I kept stubbornly quiet. I was thinking about that woman, but I didn't understand anything.

The next day I asked one of the older students who she was.

"Do you mean you really were at Cherpunov's?" he asked.

"I was there."

"And you saw his museum?"

"I saw it."

"You were lucky," the upperclassman said. "That was his wife. He is thirty-five years older than she is."

I didn't go to Cherpunov's the following Sunday because he had become ill in the middle of the week and had stopped coming to school. And suddenly, several days later, Mama asked me at tea in the evening if I had seen a young woman at Cherpunov's.

"I saw her," I said, and I blushed.

"Well, that means it's the truth," Mama said, turning to my

father. "And people say he was so good to her! She lived like a princess in a golden cage."

My father made no answer.

"Kostik," Mama said, "you've already drunk your tea. Go to your room; it will soon be time to go to bed."

She sent me away so that she could talk with my father about Cherpunov. But I didn't try to listen, although I wanted very much to know what had happened.

I soon learned about it at school. His wife had left Cherpunov, and gone off to Peterburg. The old man had become ill with grief, and wouldn't let anyone in to see him.

"It's just what he deserved!" said one schoolboy, Littauer. "Never marry a young woman!"

We were bothered by what he said. We had liked the old man Cherpunov. So at the next lesson, when the French teacher Sermout came into the room, we took our revenge on Littauer.

"Littauer!" the whole class yelled in a loud chorus. "Ittauer! Tauer! Auer! Er!"

Then at once everyone was quiet.

Sermout flared up and, failing as always to understand what was happening, cried out:

"Littauer, get out of this classroom!" And he gave Littauer a bad mark for conduct.

We didn't see Cherpunov again. He never came back to the *gymnasium*. I met him on the street a year later. He was yellowed, swollen, moving with a heavy cane. He stopped me, asked how my studies were going, and said:

"Do you remember the butterfly? From the island of Borneo? Well, I don't have that butterfly any more."

I was silent. Cherpunov looked at me attentively.

"I gave it to the university. It and all my collection of butterflies. Well, keep in good health. I am glad to have run into you."

Cherpunov soon died. I thought for a long time about him and about his young wife. An incomprehensible grief overwhelmed me when I thought of her little veil, and how, when she crossed the Kreshchatik, she had smiled and waved her hand.

When I was in the senior class, the teacher of psychology, telling us about the creative power of imagination, asked unexpectedly:

"Do you remember Cherpunov and his waters from various rivers and seas?"

"Why not?" we answered. "We remember him perfectly."

"Well, I can tell you that there was nothing in those bottles except the most ordinary water. You may ask, why did Cherpunov fool you? He supposed quite correctly that in this way he could give a spur to the development of your imagination. Cherpunov valued this very highly. He pointed out to me several times that man is distinguished from the animals chiefly by his capacity for imagination. Imagination creates art. It pushes out the boundaries of the world and of consciousness, and it gives to life that special quality which we call poetry."

THE FIRST COMMANDMENT

Our teacher of religion, a priest from the cathedral named Tregubov, had a different-colored cassock for each day of the week. They were gray, blue, lilac, black, brown, green, and the color of raw silk. You could tell what day it was—Thursday or Saturday— by the color of his cassock.

As soon as Tregubov started teaching us in our third year, he broke an old tradition in the teaching of the Scriptures. All students in all *gymnasiums* usually received top marks in this subject. This was perhaps to be explained by the fact that the teachers, being priests, were required to show the spirit of charity and not to cause distress to their students. Perhaps another explanation is that neither the teachers nor the students approached the subject seriously.

Tregubov shattered our disdain for the Scriptures with one blow.

"Altukhov," he said, "read the First Commandment."

" 'I am the Lord thy God and thou shalt have no other gods before me.' " Altukhov blurted the sentence out in a drone of syllables, and grinned. It was impossible to find fault with his answer.

"Sit down!" Tregubov said, and he gave Altukhov a 1,* the worst

* Before 1917, marks were given in Russian schools on a basis of 1 to 5, the latter figure being a perfect score. A 3 was generally considered a passing grade.

possible mark. "Borimovich, now you read the First Commandment."

Borimovich, turning pale with terror, read it just as accurately
as Altukhov, and also received a 1.

Tregubov called on us all in alphabetical order. We all read the
First Commandment accurately, and Tregubov, smiling with malig-
nant joy, gave us each the same mark. We didn't understand it.
His whole book, from the first name to the last, was covered with
1's. This was a threat of great misfortune for us all.

When he had marked down the last 1, Tregubov stroked his
beard with his scented hands, and declared:

"You are behaving disrespectfully to the marks of punctuation.
This is why you have all got the mark you deserved. You are in-
attentive to the text of God, and as light-minded as lambs. After
the first six words, there stands a comma. What does that mean?
It means that there you should make a short stop, in other words
a pause, so as to give meaning to the final phrase. Yet you all spit
the sacred words out in one breath, like peas bouncing off a wall.
Shame!"

He spoke softly, looking at us out of his narrow, scornful eyes.
His academician's golden cross shone on his silk cassock.

Before Tregubov, we had had a priest named Zlatoverkhovnikov,
who was senile and deaf, and lisped. With him everything had been
simpler. You could recite any kind of nonsense, so long as it was
fast and delivered in a monotone. This would make Zlatoverkhovnikov begin to drowse in the second or third minute, and finally he
would fall fast asleep. Then we could busy ourselves with what
we liked, provided it didn't wake the old man.

In the back rows we used to play *chemin de fer* and cook little
smoked fish on matches. Nearer the front of the room we read *The
Adventures of the Famous American Detective, Nick Carter*. The
old priest would breathe heavily, and the class would quietly have
its fun until finally, two minutes before the bell, we had to wake
up Zlatoverkhovnikov. We did this by dropping a pile of books
on the floor, or the whole class would sneeze together, on command.

After him Tregubov appeared among us like Yahveh, the
avenging lord of hosts. In fact he looked like Yahveh on the dome
of the church—a huge man, with a broad beard and angry eyebrows.

Tregubov was feared not only by the students but also by the
teachers. He was a monarchist, a member of the Government Council, and an opponent of freethinking. He was on a par with the

Metropolitan of Kiev, and he used to strike the shabby village priests dumb with fear when they had to appear before him to get a dressing-down for unworthy behavior.

Tregubov loved to take part in the religious-philosophical disputes which were fashionable at that time. He spoke smoothly and sweetly in public, spreading an aroma of eau de cologne. We hated him just as coldly as he hated us. But we learned his church texts by heart and for life.

We would use any device to run away from the Scriptures. By far the best refuge was the Roman Catholic course in the same subject. This was given at the same time as ours, but in another room. When we could make our way there, and only there, we felt safe. It was as if this were territory ruled by the Apostolic Church and the Pope of Rome, Leo XIII. Tregubov lost all his power on the threshold of this ordinary dusty classroom. The canon-priest Olendsky was the ruler here.

He was a tall, stout man, with a white head and with black spots on his hands. He was never in the least surprised when an embarrassed Orthodox student showed up at the door of his room.

"Are you a fugitive?" Olendsky would ask severely.

"No, Pan Canon, I just wanted to sit for a little while in your class."

"Sit for a little while? Ah, you good-for-nothing!" Olendsky would start to shake with laughter. "Come here!"

The student would walk up to Olendsky. The priest would tap him on the head with his snuffbox. This gesture represented absolution and the forgiveness of sins.

"Be seated!" Olendsky would then say. "Over there, in the corner, behind Khorzhevsky's back" (Khorzhevsky was a very tall student, a Pole) "so nobody can see you from the corridor and drag you back to the flames of Hell. Sit and read the paper. Good!"

Olendsky would pull his copy of *The Thought of Kiev*, folded in four, from the pocket of his soutane and hand it to the fugitive.

"Thank you, Pan Canon!" the student would say.

"Don't thank me, but God," was always Olendsky's answer. "I am only the poor tool in His hand. He has led you out of the house of captivity, like the Jews out of the land of Egypt."

Tregubov knew, of course, that Olendsky was hiding us in his classes. But even Tregubov was flustered by Olendsky. In any encounter with Tregubov, the goodhearted priest would become elegantly polite and venomous. And the dignity of a priest of the Orthodox Church would not permit Tregubov to start a quarrel with Olendsky. So we profited from this as best we could. In the end, we spent so much time on the Roman Catholic Scriptures that we knew them better than many of the Poles.

"Stanishevsky, Tadeus," the canon-priest said. "Recite the Magnificat."

Stanishevsky, Tadeus, stood up, straightened his belt, cleared his throat, swallowed his saliva loudly, looked first at the window and then at the ceiling, and at last confessed:

"I've forgotten it, Pan Canon."

"Forgotten it? But you don't forget to come to church every time Panna Gzhibovskaya is there. Sit down! Who knows the Magnificat? Well? Who? Oh, Blessed Virgin of the Virgins, the Queen of the Apostles! What is this? Everyone is silent. Whoever knows the Magnificat, let him raise his hand."

The Poles did not raise a hand. But sometimes it happened that one of the Orthodox students would raise his hand, some unhappy fugitive from Tregubov.

"Well," Olendsky would say, exhausted, "then recite the Magnificat, even if it's you. And if God doesn't punish them after this" —the priest would point to the Poles—"it will only be because of His great charity."

Then the fugitive stood up and recited the Magnificat smoothly.

"Come here!" Olendsky said.

The fugitive walked up to him. Olendsky took a handful of little candies, like coffee beans, from a pocket of his cassock, and poured them into the fugitive's palm. Then Olendsky took a pinch of snuff, calmed down quickly, and began to tell his favorite story of how he had celebrated a requiem Mass in Warsaw over Chopin's heart which had been soldered into a silver urn.

After his lessons Olendsky walked back to his home in a church building. He stopped children on the street and stroked their foreheads with his fingers. He was well known in Kiev—the big priest with the laughing eyes.

Studying the Scriptures and contact with church affairs were a constant torture for us. The only thing we liked about them was the Lenten holiday. We were released for a week so that we could fast and attend services, confess our sins and receive the Eucharist. We chose churches in the outskirts for this—the priests in these churches did not follow very closely whether a fasting student appeared at all the services during the Lenten holidays.

These holidays nearly always fell in March, the damp and foggy month. The snow was already starting to darken. And more and more often you could see through a break in the clouds the blue sky of approaching spring. The jackdaws screamed on the bare poplars. Melted water stood in dove-colored spots on the ice of the Dnieper, and in the markets they were already selling bunches of pussy willows covered with furry little catkins.

We dreamed about ways of annoying Tregubov. But he was invulnerable. Only once did we avenge ourselves on him for all his torture and his terror. But this vengeance was merciless.

In our fourth year in the *gymnasium*, we found out from older students that Tregubov was afraid of rats. We took a ginger-colored rat into his class one day and let it go under the desks just as Tregubov was telling a story from the New Testament.

The student Zhdanovich screamed and jumped up on his desk.

"What is the matter?" Tregubov asked threateningly.

"It's a rat, little father!" Zhdanovich answered, trembling.

We all jumped up from our places. The frightened rat dashed toward Tregubov's feet. At that, Father Tregubov jumped out of his chair with unusual nimbleness and pulled his cassock up above his knees. Under it we could see his striped breeches and his soft slippers with tabs on them.

We started to throw books at the rat. It began to squeal and ran up to the blackboard. Father Tregubov hurriedly jumped from his chair to his table.

"Open the door!" he roared from the table in his archdeacon's voice. "The door! Let it out in the corridor!"

We all pretended to be afraid of the rat, so that we couldn't open the door. Then Father Tregubov roared so loudly that the glass rattled in the windows:

"Platon Fedorovich! Come here!"

And he threw the class record book at the rat with all his strength.

The alarmed supervisor Platon Fedorovich opened the door. The proctor Kasimir looked over his shoulder. Behind him was the inspector Bodyansky. Frowning in order to repress his smile, Bodyansky began to organize the expulsion of the rat.

Father Tregubov did not get down from the table. He simply let down his cassock. He stood there in front of us like his own monument, twice life-size.

When the rat had finally been driven out, Tregubov got down from the table with Bodyansky's help. Someone obligingly handed him his record book and Father Tregubov, reassuming his usual magnificent manner, walked out of the classroom.

Somewhat too late it occurred to Tregubov that the rat had not appeared in the classroom without help. He demanded an inquiry. It led nowhere. The whole *gymnasium* rejoiced, and the inspector Bodyansky told us:

"Never gloat over human weakness! It's better to examine your own. Or I might notice some of you gentlemen with broken school insignia on your caps. For that I will mercilessly inflict the 'without dinner' penalty."

I must now break the proper course of this narrative and jump forward in order to relate how we finally did get rid of Tregubov. It was in our eighth year. I was then living alone, without a family, and I had rented a room on Wild Alley from an infantry lieutenant named Romuald Kozlovsky. He lived with his quiet, gentlehearted mother, the aged Panna Kozlovskaya.

It was in the autumn of 1910, dank and dreary, with all the tree branches sheathed in ice, a leaden sky, and the rustle of leaves which had died but not yet fallen from the trees. I often had headaches on such days. Then I wouldn't go to school but would stay in my little room on Wild Alley, lying down, with my head wrapped up, trying not to groan so as not to alarm Panna Kozlovskaya.

I felt warmer; the pain in my head gradually went away. Then I began to read, without getting up, the little yellow books of the "Universal Library." The fire crackled in the stove. It was quiet in the little apartment. A timid snowflake would occasionally dash against the windowpane. With the ache gone, my head felt very light and fresh and everything seemed good to me—the warm-gray color of the sky, and the smoke from the burning logs, and the snow clinging to the window.

It was on a day like this that Panna Kozlovskaya opened the door at the postman's ring, took the paper, and ran into my room.

"Kostik," she said, "Count Tolstóy is in trouble."

I jumped up, snatched the paper from her (it smelled of kerosene), and began to read the first dispatches about Tolstoy's flight from his home.

Panna Kozlovskaya watched me in terror and kept repeating: "God, save him! God, protect him!"

I got dressed at once, put on my overcoat, and went out on the street. It seemed to me that everything in the city ought to have been suddenly transformed at the moment when the stunning news arrived. But everything was as it had been. Horsecarts were going by loaded with firewood, the ancient Kiev trolley clattered on, governesses were walking up and down with little children.

I couldn't stand it and I went to school. Newspapers were spread out on all the desks. Our classroom teacher, Suboch, who taught Latin, was late for class, something which never happened with him. Finally he came in, sat down in his chair, took off his pince-nez, and sat there for a long time, looking out of the window with his nearsighted, screwed-up eyes. It was as if he were waiting for something. Then he said to me:

"Go along, my dear boy, to the editorial office of *The Thought of Kiev*. They'll have the latest dispatches there. Find out. We'll wait for you."

This was unprecedented in the history of our class. But every one accepted it at once as something perfectly natural. I got up and went out. In the corridor Platon Fedorovich caught me.

"Where are you going?" he asked threateningly, and he blocked my way.

I told him. Platon Fedorovich nodded his head and quickly stepped back against the wall to let me pass.

When I came back, I looked through the glass in the top half of the door before going in. Suboch was reading aloud. Everyone was sitting motionless. I opened the door, and I heard the familiar words:

"It was starting to grow dark. Low in the west Venus, clear and silver, was already shining its gentle light from behind the birch trees, while high in the east the somber Arcturus was pouring out red flames. Levin caught and then lost the Great Bear over his head. The woodcock had already stopped flying . . ."

For two or three days life at school went on somehow. And then on an equally raw morning there were extra editions of the papers with black borders, confused people on the streets, crowds of students around the university. They stood there silently. All of them were wearing black crape bands around the sleeves of their overcoats. A stranger pinned a black band around the sleeve of my gray coat.

I went to the *gymnasium*. Cossack mounted patrols were slowly riding along the pavements. Little knots of policemen stood in the courtyards. I met two of my classmates on the way; everyone was wearing a black armband like mine. In the cloakroom we unfastened the bands from our overcoats and put them on our jacket sleeves. It was extraordinarily quiet in the school. Even the little ones were making no noise.

It happened that our first class that day was on the Scriptures. Tregubov walked in too quickly, not as he usually did, crossed himself in front of the icon, and sat down at his table.

The student on duty that day, Matusevich, walked up and stood next to Tregubov. Tregubov looked at him somberly, but said nothing.

"Yesterday, at six o'clock in the morning, at the station of Astopovo," Matusevich said, trying to control his emotion and talking loudly, "the greatest writer of our country, and perhaps of the whole world, Leo Nikolayevich Tolstoy, died."

The desk lids made a noise. The whole class stood up. In the deep silence we could hear the clop-clop of horses—the patrols were going by on the street.

Tregubov leaned over his table, pressed his fat fingers against its edge, and sat motionless.

"Stand up, Father," Matusevich said to him in a very quiet voice.

Slowly and heavily, Tregubov stood up. His neck was crimson. He stood there, with his eyes down. Several minutes went by. They seemed hours to us. Then everyone sat down again, slowly and quietly. Tregubov picked up his class record book and walked out of the room. At the door he stopped and said:

"You have forced me to honor the memory of an apostate, a man divorced from the Church. We will not talk about whether or not he was a great writer. I have committed a crime against my order, and I shall have to answer for it before God and the highest ecclesiastical authorities. But from this day on, I shall no longer be the teacher in your class. Good-by. And may God bring you to your senses."

We were all silent. Tregubov walked out.

For the next lesson on the Scriptures we had, instead of Tregubov, a young priest with the face of the poet Nadson, a man who loved philosophy and literature. We fell in love with him at once for his delicacy and his youth, and our friendship with him lasted until we had finished the *gymnasium*.

THE LINDEN BLOSSOMS

I had never before seen such ancient trees. At night their tops were lost in the sky. If a breeze started to blow them, the stars would move like fireflies among the branches. In the daytime it was dark under the linden trees, but up above, in the green freshness, were the noise and the quarrels, the chirping and the fluttering, of a motley population of birds.

"Just you wait," Uncle Kolya used to say. "Soon all these lindens will be in blossom, and then . . ."

He would never finish saying what would happen when the lindens blossomed. But we knew for ourselves that then the old Ryovna park would be transformed into a place of such miracles as happen only in fairy tales.

Our whole family went back a second time, after school was over, to spend the summer at Ryovna in the Bryansk forests. My father came, too, for his vacation. The bankrupt owner of the estate rented out for the summer two or three wooden cottages in the park. It was a long way from any town, or railroad station, and almost no one went there for the summer except Uncle Kolya and us.

To give a sense of the charm of this place its topography must be described. The park of linden trees was overgrown with little nut trees and impenetrable buckthorn. Moss-covered benches in the middle of clumps of lilac. Quiet paths. They had names—"The Temple of Diana," "The Path of Sighs," "Nightingale Ravine." Then clearings in blazing sun, with pine trees and wild flowers, and then once again the canopy of majestic and—it seemed to us— thousand-year-old linden trees.

The park sloped down to the Ryovna River. Behind it, thick forest shouldered its way to the top of the hill. Here was the only dirt road on the estate. You could go along it as far as a decrepit chapel with an icon of Tikhon of Zadonsk, but beyond the chapel the road petered out in the dry grass.

No one, not even the most venturesome of the inhabitants of the estate, Volodya Rumyantsev, who was a student of the Peterburg Forestry Institute, would walk farther than the chapel all by himself. The thick of the forest marched right up to the little log chapel. A smell of moldiness and ferns came out of the woods. Owls flew out of it at twilight.

Once at night we heard faraway cries coming out of these woods. It was a peddler who had tried to go on foot from the Svensky Monastery to a fair at Trubchevsk. A forest warden found him and brought him to Ryovna. The peddler, a thin little man with blue eyes, was weeping and crossing himself.

We boys walked into these woods once, with Volodya Rumyantsev, taking a compass with us. We found bottomless ravines choked to their tops with blackberries and wild hops. We could hear water trickling down below but we couldn't get down to it. We found a little stream in the woods with water so transparent that it looked like glass. From the bank we could see clouds of little minnows swimming near its bottom.

Finally we found a rotting cross near a spring. A tin cup was hanging on its crossbeam. Morning-glories had grown around the cup and bound it tight to the cross. We tore the vines away, and drank spring water from the cup. It tasted of rust.

There were cranes in the sky above us, and orioles, and hawks. Blue-bottomed clouds floated over us. We looked up at them—from up there it would be possible to look down on this whole mysterious wooded region. Woodpeckers were busily at work on dry branches above us, and occasionally cones would drop on our heads.

Volodya Rumyantsev asserted that there was a small monastery hidden in the woods, built by Raskolniks but abandoned by them.* Wild bees had taken it over, he said, and we could collect the honey. But we never found it. We climbed up pine trees to look around over this green ocean for a planked roof with a crooked, eight-pointed cross which would be the monastery. There was a warm little breeze high up in the pine trees; our hands stuck to the resiny branches. Black-eyed squirrels jumped around us. The young green cones smelled like turpentine. But no matter how carefully we looked out from the pine trees, as if from lighthouses, shading our eyes with our hands, we saw nothing but the woods and the drifting clouds. They made our heads spin.

The clouds seemed much closer from the high pine trees than

* Raskolniks are religious dissenters against the Orthodox Church whose heresy dates from the seventeenth century. Many of them were sent to Siberia.

from the ground. They made you want to step up on to their snow-white masses. There was a light rippling of the sky higher than the clouds. Volodya Rumyantsev said that these were also clouds, but such high ones that they were not made of water vapor but of crystals of ice. Little plumes hung down from them in the cold, remote heights.

There was one other mysterious place at Ryovna besides the woods—this was the river. It flowed beside weeping willows, divided into two arms to flow around an island, and in many places the floating flowers of yellow water lilies filled it from shore to shore.

A wooden dam crossed the river at the island, on which there was an abandoned sawmill. Sawdust was piled high, next to empty sheds. On hot days there was an overpowering smell of moldering wood around the old sawmill.

It had once been powered by a water wheel. This was all broken now, covered with shaggy cobwebs, both the wheel and the wooden-toothed gearing. Sulphur-yellow mushrooms were growing on them. Above the dam were some water holes where enormous pike lived. The holes were called abatements. The water in them was dark, and moved in slow circles.

With Uncle Kolya we fastened dozens of fishhooks and spoons in these water holes. Besides the pike, there were big perch, almost blue. We fished for them from the wet planks of the dam, and sometimes the perch would pull the rods out of our hands and drag them down into the water. The bamboo rods would plunge down into the depths like golden arrows. They would usually come to the surface again below the dam, where we would get them, with the perch, from a boat.

What else was there at Ryovna? An old columned house which had been built, according to tradition, by Rastrelli.* There were nests of swallows on its pediment. A bright light filled the empty rooms, the stairways, and the corridors. It came in through windows of convex glass. When anyone walked through the drawing room, the furniture creaked. The chandeliers made a thin tinkle.

Nobody lived in the house. It was only on family holidays, on the name day of Maria (for there were two in our family, Mama and Aunt Marusya, Uncle Kolya's wife) that we opened the big drawing room with its special balconies for musicians, ventilated it, and organized a ball.

---

* Bartolomeo Rastrelli (1700-1771) was a great Baroque architect, of Italian origin, who designed many famous buildings in Russia including the Winter Palace in St. Petersburg and the St. Andrew Church in Kiev.

We put little round lanterns on the porch and late in the evening we set off rockets in the park. They would shoot up through the foliage of the trees and explode in many-colored flaming balls. The balls floated slowly upward, lighting the old house with their reddish glow. When the rockets went out, the summer night surged back into the park with its distant croaking of frogs, its shimmer of stars, and the fragrance of the blossoming lindens.

Uncle Kolya's comrades, artillery officers, came out to these parties from Bryansk. Even the Moscow tenor Askochensky came once, and he organized a concert in the old drawing room.

"Oh, if only you would return to me," Askochensky sang, *"where we were so happy together! You would hear a murmur in the branches, and know it as the sound of a broken heart."*

It seemed to me that the words of this song had been written for our park. It had heard many declarations of love, and had seen the pale faces of many lovers, and many tears of separation.

"When a sad sound troubles your sleep," Askochensky sang, leaning on the piano where Aunt Marusya was accompanying him, sometimes tucking her hair back into place, *"or when you hear a stormy noise in bad weather, you will know that I am sobbing somewhere, unconsolable . . ."*

After the ball there was always a supper at Uncle Kolya's cottage. The round shades over the candles were covered with dead night moths and butterflies. Wine was poured for us students as well as for the grownups. It gave us courage.

Once after we had drunk some wine we decided that each of us would run around the entire park in the dark. To prevent cheating, each of us had to deposit something on a bench in Nightingale Ravine. Uncle Kolya promised to check in the morning on whether or not we had honestly fulfilled this condition.

The first one to run was Aunt Marusya's brother, a medical school student named Pavel Tennov. We all called him Pavlia. He was long-legged, snub-nosed, had a curly beard, and looked like Chekhov. Pavlia was extraordinarily trusting and goodhearted, so we were always playing tricks on him.

Pavlia was supposed to leave an empty wine bottle on the bench in Nightingale Ravine. It was my turn to go right after him. I plunged down a tangled path. Dew-covered twigs slapped my face. It seemed to me someone was racing to catch up with me. So I stopped and listened. Someone was moving in the bushes. I ran out farther and came out into a clearing. Beyond it the moon was shining, and in front of it was Nightingale Ravine, black in its darkness. I plunged into it with all my strength, as if diving into dark water. A bittern hooted mournfully beyond the shining river behind me.

I stopped at the bench. The air was full of the smell of linden flowers; it filled the whole night up to the stars. Everything was still, and it was impossible to believe that not far away, on the brightly lighted veranda, there were the noises of happy people.

We had earlier agreed to make Pavlia lose. I took the bottle he had left on the bench and threw it into the river. The bottle turned and shimmered in the moonlight. Circles of moonlight moved across the water to the shores.

I ran farther, above the ravine. Here there was a strong smell of dampness. Then I ran back panting along a wide path through the lindens. Lights shone in front of me.

"Kostik!" I heard Aunt Marusya's frightened voice. "Is it you?"

"Yes," I answered, running up to her.

"What kind of nonsense are you all up to!" Aunt Marusya said. She was standing on the path, wrapped up in a light silk scarf. "Mama is terribly worried. Which one of you thought this up? Gleb probably."

"No, it wasn't Gleb," I lied. "It was all of us together."

Aunt Marusya had guessed. Uncle Kolya's ward, Gleb Afanasiev, a student at the Bryansk *gymnasium*, had thought up the night race through the park. He was a mop-headed little boy with an inexhaustible imagination. Sly little sparks were always glittering in his gray eyes. Not a day went by when he didn't think up something. So whatever happened, Gleb was always blamed.

Uncle Kolya checked the things left on the bench the next morning. Pavlia's bottle wasn't there. We all started to tease him, saying that he had turned coward, had not run to the ravine, had turned back after throwing the bottle away on the path. But Pavlia guessed right away what had happened, and he threatened:

"Well, just wait, Gleb, you'll pay for this!"

Gleb held his tongue, but he didn't give me away.

That same day Pavlia caught Gleb in the bathhouse, ducked him several times, then tied his trousers into a tight knot and dropped them in the water. It took Gleb a long time to undo his trousers with his teeth. He made a sorry sight in his chewed-up trousers. This was too bad, on account of two sisters named Karelina, schoolgirls from Oryol, who were living with their mother in a cottage at Ryovna. The older sister, Lyuba, read all the time, hiding in the quietest corners of the park. Her cheeks were burning red, and her blond hair was always in disorder. We often found, near the benches on which she had been sitting, the black ribbons which Lyuba had lost from her braids.

The younger sister, Sasha, was capricious and laughing, and Gleb liked her a lot. It was unthinkable for him to show up in front of her in his crumpled trousers. I felt guilty about Gleb, and I asked Mama to iron his trousers. This gave him back at once his usual flippant appearance.

There had been nothing special about that night race through the park, but I remembered it for a long time. I remembered the waves of linden flowers brushing into my face, and the bittern's cry, and the whole night filled with stars and the sounds of happiness.

Sometimes that summer it seemed to me that there was no place left on all the earth for human grief.

But this idea was shaken for me soon after the party. I saw a barefoot boy in a ragged peasant's cloth coat standing next to the cottage. He had come to sell strawberries. He smelled of fruit and smoke. He was asking ten kopecks for a jugful of berries, but Mama gave him twenty kopecks and a piece of cake.

The little boy stood there with downcast eyes, rubbing one bare foot against the other. He put the cake inside his shirt, and said nothing.

"Whose little boy are you?" Mama asked him.

"Aniskin's," he answered shyly.

"Why don't you eat the cake?"

"It's for my mother," he said huskily, still not raising his eyes. "She isn't well. She was carrying firewood; she wrenched her stomach."

"And where's your father?"

"He's dead."

The little boy sniffed, turned around, and began to run. He looked back, frightened, and he was holding his hand inside his shirt so as not to lose the cake.

I couldn't forget that towheaded little boy for a long time and I was secretly critical of Mama. She had bought off her conscience for a piece of cake and twenty kopecks. I understood this very well. I knew that bitter injustice calls for something more than paltry charity. But how to fight injustice—and I was to meet it more and more often in life—I did not yet know.

We heard frequent quarrels over the tea table between my father and Uncle Kolya. They fought about the future of the Russian people. Uncle Kolya could prove that the happiness of any people depends on education. My father argued that only a revolution would bring happiness. Pavlia used to get in the arguments. He considered himself a *narodnik*,* a populist. He was almost expelled once from medical school for a speech he made at a students' meeting. Volodya Rumyantsev held his tongue, but later he told the rest of us boys that Uncle Kolya and my father and Pavlia all understood nothing at all about it.

"And do you understand it?" we asked him.

"Not in the slightest!" Volodya answered cheerfully. "Nor do I want to understand it. I love Russia, and that's all there is to it!"

Volodya Rumyantsev was the brother of Uncle Kolya's closest friend at the Bryansk arsenal, Captain Rumyantsev. Volodya was hard of hearing. There was always hay in his red beard, because he slept in the hay barn. He despised every kind of human comfort. He would put his folded student's overcoat under his head instead of a pillow. He dragged his feet when he walked, and he talked indistinctly. Under his overcoat he wore a faded blue Russian blouse, and he belted it with a black silk cord with tassels.

Volodya's hands were always burned by developers and fixatives —he was interested in photography. He was an enterprising man. He had worked out an arrangement with a Moscow lithographing firm, Sherer and Nabgolts, under which he traveled in the summers through out-of-the-way little towns and took pictures of their sights, and the printers published these on post cards which were sold in bookstalls at stations.

This occupation of Volodya's fascinated us. He would often disappear from Ryovna for several days and then come back and tell us that he had been in Yefremov, or Yeltse, or Lipetsk.

"'This is the way to live, gentlemen!" he said, sitting in the bathhouse and soaping his red head. "Day before yesterday I swam across the Oka, yesterday I was in Moksha, and today here in Ryovna."

He filled us with a love for provincial Russia. He knew it intimately—the fairs, the monasteries, the historical estates, the customs. He had traveled to Tarkhana, to Lermontov's birthplace, to Fet's estate near Kursk,† to the horse fair at Lebedyan, to the island of Valaam, and to the Kulikovsky battlefield.

Old ladies everywhere were friends of his, former teachers and officials. He used to stay with them. They fed him cabbage soup

* *Narodniks* were Russian revolutionaries in the nineteenth century who based their program on the peasantry, rejected Marxism, and sought political influence through individual acts of terrorism.

† Fet, pen name of Athanassy Shenshin (1820–1892), was a lyric poet with great influence on the Symbolists; he was also a reactionary and very wealthy landowner with a large property in the province of Kursk.

and little cakes filled with fish, and in gratitude Volodya taught the
old ladies' canaries to whistle a polka, or he gave his hostesses
superphosphate. They could spread a little in a geranium pot and
produce the most enormous blossoms to amaze their neighbors.

He took no part in the arguments about the fate of Russia but
he would move in when the conversation got around to Tambov
hams, or the frozen apples in Ryazan, or Volga sturgeon. No one
could compete with Volodya in knowledge of these things. Uncle
Kolya used to say jokingly that Volodya Rumyantsev was the only
man alive who knew how much sandals cost in Kineshma and the
price of a pound of chicken feathers in Kalyazin.

One day Volodya Rumyantsev went to Oryol and brought sad
news back to us. We were playing croquet beside the cottage. The
game appealed to all of us. Games dragged out sometimes after it
had grown dark, and lamps were carried out on to the croquet
ground. We quarreled at croquet more than anywhere else, especially with my older brother Borya. He was a good player, and
quickly became a "rover." Then he would knock our balls so far that
sometimes we couldn't even find them. This made us angry, and,
when he was aiming, we would chant: "The devil under your hand,
a toad in your mouth!" This tactic sometimes helped and Borya
would miss.

We also quarreled with Gleb. When Gleb played against Sasha
he always missed and lost on purpose, just to please her. But playing with Sasha and against us, he performed miracles of skill
and daring, and always won. All the inhabitants of the cottages
usually gathered for our croquet games. Even Uncle Kolya's two
dogs, Mordan and Chetvertak, ran up to watch the game, although
they then lay down cautiously under the pine trees so as not to get
hit by a ball.

On this morning it was just as noisy as always on the croquet
ground. Then we heard the sound of wheels; Uncle Kolya's spring-
less carriage was driving up to the cottage. Someone cried out:
"Volodya Rumyantsev has come!" No one paid any attention to this:
we were all used to Volodya's private departures and arrivals.

A minute later he appeared. He walked up to us in loose overalls
and boots. His face was all creased up, as if he were going to cry.
He was holding a newspaper in his hand.

"What's the matter?" Uncle Kolya asked him, frightened.

"Chekhov has died."

Volodya turned and walked back to the cottage. We ran after
him. Uncle Kolya took the paper from Volodya, read it, threw it on
the floor, and stalked off to his own room. Aunt Marusya went

anxiously after him. Pavlia took off his pince-nez and cleaned them for a long time with his handkerchief.

"Kostik," Mama said to me, "go down to the river and call your father. Let him interrupt his fishing for once."

She said this as if my father should already have known about Chekhov's death but with his usual flippancy had attached no significance to the news and had not grieved over it. I took offense for my father, but I went down to the river. Gleb Afanasiev walked with me. He became suddenly very serious.

"Yes, Kostik!" he said to me on the way, and he sighed deeply.

I told my father that Chekhov had died. My father suddenly grew pinched in the face, and all hunched over.

"Well, well," he said, in confusion, "how can it be? I never thought that I would outlive Chekhov . . ."

We walked back past the croquet ground. The mallets and balls lay scattered on the ground. The birds were making a racket in the linden trees, the sun shone through the leaves and made green spots on the grass.

I had already read Chekhov and I liked him very much. I walked away, and thought that such people as Chekhov should never die.

Two days later Volodya Rumyantsev went to Moscow to Chekhov's funeral. We accompanied him to the station at Sinezerki. He took a basket full of flowers to put on Chekhov's grave. They were common wild flowers which we picked in the marshes and in the woods. Mama packed them on a layer of wet moss and covered them with wet linen. We tried to pick as many country flowers as we could because we were sure that Chekhov loved these. We had a lot of Solomon's seal, pinks, and camomile. Aunt Marusya added some jasmine which she cut in the park.

The train left in the evening. We returned on foot from Sinezerki to Ryovna and we got home only at dawn. A young moon was hanging low over the woods, and its tender light shone in the pools of rain. It had rained not long before. The grass had a wet smell. A late cuckoo called in the park. Then the moon disappeared and the stars came out but an early morning fog soon blanketed them. The fog rustled for a long time, trickling down the bushes, until a calm sun came out and warmed the earth.

I WAS, OF COURSE, A LITTLE BOY

Inspector Bodyansky walked briskly up to us in our third-year classroom. He was wearing a new uniform coat. The inspector's eyes shone with cunning. We all stood up.

"On the occasion of the imperial manifesto on the granting of civil liberties to our people," Bodyansky said, "all classes in the *gymnasium* will be canceled for three days. I congratulate you! Put your books away and go on home. But I advise you not to make nuisances of yourselves under your parents' feet during these days."

We ran out of the school. It was an extraordinary autumn that year. The sun was still hot in October. The gardens, decked in dry gold, shed it on the paths, and went right on burning in all their beauty. We walked around in summer coats.

We poured out onto the street and saw crowds with red flags around the long buildings of the university. Speeches were being delivered under the columns of the university. Men yelled "Hurrah." Hats were thrown in the air.

We climbed along the fence of Nikolayevsky Square. We yelled "Hurrah," too, and we threw our caps in the air. Falling, they caught in the chestnut trees. We shook the chestnuts, and the leaves fell on us like rain. We roared with laughter and were delighted. Red ribbons were already pinned to our coats. The dark bronze figure of Nicholas I stood on his pedestal in the middle of the square, one foot thrust forward, looking haughtily at the disorder.

The crowd grew quiet, the red flags were dipped, and we heard the triumphal singing:

You fell a victim in the fatal conflict . . .

Everyone started to fall to his knees. We took off our caps, too, and sang the funeral march even though we didn't know all the words. Then the crowd stood up again and moved along the fence of Nikolayevsky Square. I saw my older brother Borya in the crowd and our tenant, the Montenegrin student Markovich.

"Go on home right away!" Borya told me. "And don't you dare go out on the street alone."

"I want to go with you," I said shyly.

"You'd get crushed to death. Go on home. Tomorrow you can see everything."

I wanted terribly to go along with this happy and triumphal crowd. But Borya had already disappeared.

A band started to play somewhere far in front of us, and I recognized the winged, ringing sounds of the "Marseillaise":

> Let us renounce the old world,
> Let us shake off its dust from our feet!

I climbed over the fence and joined the crowd. A girl in an astrakhan hat who must have been a student held out her hand to me and we walked along together. I could see nothing in front of me except people's backs. People were standing on the roofs and waving their hats to us.

When we were going by the opera house I heard the sound of horses running. I climbed up on a pedestal and saw a line of mounted police. They were moving backwards, giving way to the crowd. A fat police chief was moving backwards with them. He held his hand at salute and smiled condescendingly.

I jumped down from the pedestal and again I could see nothing. I could tell where we were going only from the signs on the stores. We went down Fundukleyevskaya Street past the Bergon Theater, then we turned on to the Kreshchatik and walked past Kirkheim's candy store. We passed Luteranskaya Street and Idzikovsky's bookstore.

"Where are we going?" I asked the girl in the astrakhan hat.

"To the town Duma. There's going to be a meeting there. We're all free now, as free as birds. Do you understand?"

"I understand," I answered.

"Where do you live?" she asked me suddenly.

"On Nikolsko-Botanicheskaya Street."

"Do your parents know that you're in the demonstration?"

"Everybody's in the demonstration now," I answered, trying to avoid talking about my parents.

We passed Balabukhi's dried fruit store and Nikolayevskaya Street and then we stopped. It was impossible to go any farther. The packed crowd stood right up to the Duma. The gilded archangel Michael, on the coat of arms of Kiev, shone on the roof of the Duma. Its broad balcony could just be seen. People without hats were standing on it. One of them began to speak, but nothing could be heard. I saw only how the wind blew his gray hair.

Someone grabbed me by the shoulder. I looked around. It was our Latin teacher, Suboch.

"Paustovsky, Konstantin," he said sternly, but his eyes were smiling, "you here! Go on home, at once."

"Don't be worried; he's with me," the girl said.

"Excuse me, mademoiselle, I didn't know," Suboch answered politely.

The crowd surged back and separated us from Suboch. The girl took me by the hand and we began to move toward the sidewalk.

"Take it easy, citizens!" a hoarse voice rasped out next to us.

It grew very quiet. The girl managed to get us both up on the sidewalk. She pressed me against the wall of a yellow building with a vaulted entranceway. I recognized the post office building.

I didn't understand why she was holding me so tightly and pressing me toward the entranceway. I could see nothing except people's backs and the swallows—they were floating over the crowd, shining in the sun, like pieces of paper. Somewhere in the distance a horn blew: *ti-ti-ta-ta! ti-ti-ta-ta!* Then again everything was still.

"Comrade soldiers!" a strained voice cried out, and immediately after this came a loud crackling, as if calico were being torn. Pieces of plaster fell down on us.

The pigeons darted away and the sky looked completely empty. Then there was a second crackling, and the crowd hurled itself at the wall.

The girl managed to push me inside the courtyard, and the last thing I saw on the Kreshchatik was a little student in an unbuttoned overcoat. He jumped over the window sill of Balabukhi's store, and held up a black revolver.

"What's happening?" I asked the girl.

"They're shooting! The soldiers are shooting."

"Why?"

She didn't answer me. We ran across the narrow, crowded courtyard. Behind us we could hear cries, shots, hoofbeats. It grew dark suddenly and the air was full of yellow smoke. My schoolbag made it hard for me to run. It was full of books.

We ran through courtyards to Proreznaya Street and climbed up to Golden Gate. Two first-aid ambulances clattered by us. White-faced people, breathing hard, ran past us. On Proreznaya Street a troop of Cossacks galloped by. A bareheaded officer rode in front. Someone whistled derisively after the Cossacks, but they didn't stop.

"God, what scoundrels!" the girl kept repeating. "What a trap!

Give us freedom with one hand, and with the other—shoot us down!"

We walked in a big circle, past the Cathedral of St. Vladimir, and came out on Nikolayevsky Square at the exact spot where a little while before I had hung on the fence, yelled "Hurrah," and waved my cap.

"Thank you," I said to the girl. "It's not far from here. I can get home myself."

The girl walked away. I kept close to the fence around the square and took off my cap—it was hurting my head. I had a terrible headache. I was frightened, too. An old man in a derby hat stopped me and asked what was the matter with me. I could give him no answer. The old man shook his head and walked on.

I pulled my cap back on and walked home to Nikolsko-Botanicheskaya Street. It was already growing dark. A purple sunset was reflected in the windows. By this time of day street lights were usually lighted, but for some reason no one had lighted them.

At the corner of our street I saw Mama. She was walking quickly toward me. She grabbed me by the shoulder, and then she suddenly cried out: "Where's Borya? Didn't you see Borya?"

"There." I pointed in the direction of the Kreshchatik.

"Go home!" Mama said, and she ran up the street.

I stood for a moment, watching her, and then I went home. Our street was just as deserted as always. Lights were already burning in the windows. I could see the reading lamp with the green shade in my father's room. Lisa, our maid, was standing at the open gate. She took my satchel from me, wiped my face with her handkerchief, and said:

"You good-for-nothing! People are out of their minds worrying about you! Come on, get washed."

I found only Galya and Dima at home. Galya was walking through the rooms, stumbling into the chairs, and repeating: "Where is everybody? Where is everybody?" Dima was sitting on the window sill and listening. He had not gone to the demonstration. He wanted to hear the rifles fire. He hoped that he might hear them if he sat on the window sill.

I washed. Lisa gave me some hot milk. I was sobbing all the time.

"Did you see the people who were killed?" Dima asked me.

"Ah ha!" I said, not thinking about anything.

"Don't be a nuisance!" Lisa said angrily. "You can see whom he's like!"

Mama came home at last with Borya. Borya was all dusty, and

without his cap. He was smiling in a funny way, as if he had been deafened. The student Markovich came back soon after Mama. He said he had seen a great many killed and wounded.

Mama closed the shutters on the windows and ordered Lisa not to open the door to anyone until she had found out who it was. Then Mama sent me off to bed. Before I lay down, I opened the shutters and looked out at the street. The street lamps were not yet burning. A strange gray light fell on the roofs. It was as quiet as if the city had died. A man on a horse clattered down a neighboring street, and then everything was still again.

I closed the shutters, undressed, and went to bed. I looked at the thick walls, and I thought that this two-storied house was like a fortress. No bullets could come through it. The green tongue of flame quivered in the lamp. I began to drowse. Through my sleep I heard the doorbell, hurried steps, and then my father's voice. He walked from corner to corner in the dining room, talking all the time.

The next morning Mama told me I was not to go any farther than our courtyard. I was unhappy about this, and decided not to go out of the house at all. I put on my overcoat, sat on the balcony, and began to learn some lines of Nekrassov which had been assigned to us. But I succeeded in memorizing only two lines: "It was late autumn. The rooks flew off. The woods were bare, and the fields were empty." Everything distracted me. A fire engine went by. Then Staff Captain Zadorozhny, a member of the Black Hundreds* and a scoundrel, walked out of the wing of our building. He was wearing a gray overcoat, and a sword belt, and a revolver hung at his side in a holster. His wife came out behind him on the porch, a woman as gaunt as an ironing board, tousled, with blue circles under her eyes. She was wearing a black Japanese kimono embroidered with peacocks.

Zadorozhny had recently come back from the Japanese war with two enormous trunks. They were full of pieces of silk, kimonos, fans, and even a curved Chinese sword. "The hero of Mukden!" my father called Zadorozhny scornfully.

"Georges," his wife squealed in a mincing voice, "don't forget that I shall be anxious."

"It's nothing, my friend!" Zadorozhny answered pompously, and he kissed her hand. "We'll just finish off all this nonsense."

And he walked away without looking back.

* Black Hundreds were reactionary gangs in Russian towns and cities, often financed by Tsarist police officials, which, from 1905 until 1917, organized pogroms against the Jews, the intelligentsia, and liberal groups.

The Japanese War had just ended and we children, like all the grownups, were grieved and indignant over it. We overheard adult conversations about the stupidity of the high command, about Kuropatkin's "mattress," Stessel's treachery, the surrender of Port Arthur, and the embezzlers in the commissariats. Autocratic Russia had come unraveled like a rotten piece of old cloth.

But we also heard grown-up talk about the bravery and the fortitude of Russian soldiers, about how things could not continue like this any longer, and about how the long patience of the Russian people must end sometime.

The most terrible blow for us was the disaster to the Russian fleet at Tsushima. Borya showed me once a piece of paper on which some pale, lilac-colored lines had been printed by a mimeographing machine. It was barely possible to read them.

"Is this a proclamation?" I asked. I had several times read proclamations pasted up on the walls of our school.

"No," Borya said, "these are verses."

I could read, with difficulty, the way they began:

> *Enough, enough, heroes of Tsushima!*
> *You are the last victims.*
> *It is drawing near, it is on the threshold,*
> *The freedom of our native land!*

Freedom! I could still only vaguely imagine what this was. I imagined it as in an allegorical picture which hung in my father's room. A young woman stood on a barricade with an angry but radiant face and bare, powerful breasts. She held up a red flag in one hand, and with the other she moved a smoking match up to a cannon. This was Freedom. Behind her were crowds of people in blue blouses with guns in their hands, distraught but happy women, little children, and even a young poet in a broken silk hat. All the people were singing with enthusiasm, probably the "Marseillaise."

> *To arms, citizens! The day of glory has arrived!*

They beat the drums, and blew the horns, Freedom marched triumphantly across the country, and loud popular cries greeted her appearance everywhere. A man walking behind Freedom looked very much like the student Markovich, just as dark-complexioned and with the same burning eyes. He held a pistol in his hand.

Once I looked through the window into Markovich's room, which fronted on our balcony, and saw him singing while he

cleaned a black steel automatic pistol. Little copper bullets were
lying on a medical textbook opened on the table.

Markovich noticed me, and immediately covered the pistol with
a newspaper.

The next morning Lisa took all the icons off the walls
and stacked them by the windows. The janitor Ignati drew a
large cross with chalk on the gate to our house. Then he closed
the gate and the wicket gate and we found ourselves as if in a fortress.

Mama told us that a Jewish pogrom had started in the city.
"On orders from Peterburg," she added. And Lisa told us in a
whisper that they had already looted a house in Vassilkovskaya
Street and that the pogrom was getting close to us.

Markovich went off with Borya. Markovich was wearing boots,
with a leather belt around his student's coat. Mama didn't want to
let Borya go, but my father shouted at her. Then she made the
cross over Borya, kissed him, and let him go. All the time, while
Borya was going down the stairs with Markovich, she kept asking
Markovich to look after him.

"Where have they gone?" I asked my father.

"To a students' volunteer brigade. To defend the Jews."

My father left shortly after them. Dima and I spent the whole
day in the courtyard. We heard shots about noon. Then the shots
became more frequent. A fire started on Vassilkovskaya Street.
Scraps of burning paper fell in our courtyard.

In the afternoon my father brought back a terrorized old Jewish
woman with her gray hair done up in a scarf. She was leading a
speechless little boy by the hand. She was the mother of a well-
known doctor.

Mama summoned Ignati, the janitor, went out to see him in the
kitchen, and gave him ten rubles. But Ignati gave the money back
to Mama and said:

"I've got the tailor Mendel with his whole family sitting in my
janitor's room. You'd do better to watch out that Zadorozhny's wife
doesn't see anything."

Just before evening a short fellow in a black visored cap came
up to our gate. A wet forelock stuck out from under his cap. The
whole bottom of his chin was covered with shells of sunflower seeds.
Behind this fellow marched a tall, clean-shaven old man in short
trousers, behind him a fidgety man with no hat and with swollen
eyelids, then a fat old market woman in a warm shawl, and behind
her several young people of an obviously thievish sort. We often

saw this market woman at the Galitsky Market. Now she was carrying a new, empty bag.

"Open up!" the young fellow yelled, and he hit the wicket gate
with a crowbar.

Ignati went out of his janitor's quarters.

"Any Jews here?" the young fellow asked him.

"The same kind as you," Ignati answered him lazily.

"Are you hiding any Jews?" the fellow shouted, and he shook
the gate. "We know all about them. Open up."

"Look. I'll ask Colonel Zadorozhny to come," Ignati threatened.
"He'll talk to you in his own way."

"And I spit on your Jerusalem colonels! We'll make sausage
out of your colonel!"

Then Madame Zadorozhnaya, who had heard this conversation
from her apartment, could control herself no longer. She swept
across the courtyard like an infuriated hen. The sleeves of her
black kimono flapped in the wind.

"You cad!" she screamed, and she spat through the wicket gate
into the fellow's face. "How do you dare insult an officer of the
Imperial army? You tramp! Vassily!" she called. "Come here,
quickly!"

A dumbfounded orderly scurried out of the colonel's quarters.
He picked up an ax in the courtyard and ran up to the gate. The
young fellow turned and ran down the street, looking back at the
orderly. His companions scattered after him. The orderly bran-
dished the ax at them.

"Well, that's something new!" Madame Zadorozhnaya said,
wrapping her kimono around her and walking back to her apartment. "Any boor can try to pass himself off as a true Russian! No,
excuse me! Just keep in mind, this sort of thing won't get you
anywhere!"

So it happened that the wife of a member of the Black Hundreds
drove the thugs away from our house. The grownups laughed for
a long time afterwards over this.

The young fellow stopped at the next house and began again
to hammer on the gate. Then Dima led me up to the garret over our
apartment. For a long time an enormous catapult had been hanging there for no purpose at all. A heavy rubber belt had been
nailed to the frame of a little broken window; it was an inheritance
from the little boys who had lived in the apartment before us.

I picked up a piece of hard yellow brick from the attic floor.
Dima put it in the catapult and held it tight. Then we both pulled
it back with all our strength, aiming it at the young fellow on the
street, and let it go.

The brick whistled through the leaves across the courtyard, hit the tall old man in the leg with a loud thump, and broke into little pieces. We had missed our target.

The old man sat down in surprise, then scrambled up again and started to run. The young fellow tore after him, his boots clattering on the street.

"Get another brick!" Dima yelled at me.

But I was late, and the fellow was hidden by the corner house.

"You didn't pull straight," Dima told me. "That's why we missed him. You pulled crooked."

Dima always liked to blame mistakes on others and then to quarrel about them later. Although we had missed, we were still proud of our catapult shot.

In the evening Lisa took some millet gruel to Ignati to help feed the family of Mendel the tailor. I went with her. The windows were curtained in the janitor's quarters. Ignati was sitting on a little table, playing very quietly on his accordion and singing the waltz, "On the Hills of Manchuria"—a remembrance of the Japanese War:

A frightening night, with only the wind riding on the hills . . .

Mendel's family was sleeping, but he was sitting next to a kerosene lamp, sewing a new coat with white thread.

"They chase you," he said, "to kill you, but you just go on sewing. There's no other way to live."

Lisa stood by the door and listened sadly to Ignati singing:

Only the moon shines on the heights
And lights up the graves of soldiers.

THE LITTLE RED LANTERN

I lit the little lantern with red glass. Inside it was a small kerosene lamp. It made a violet light in the close little boxroom and on the dusty junk which was piled on its shelves.

I began to develop films, taken by my father. He had a little camera and he loved to take pictures, but the rolls of film piled up for months in a drawer of his desk. There was always a big cleaning in our house before holidays, and Mama would clean out the rolls of film and give them to me, and I would develop them.

It was an entrancing job, because I could never guess what would show up on the films. Besides, it pleased me that nobody, not even Mama, could come into the boxroom while I was working there. I was cut off from the world. Familiar noises—the rattle of plates, the striking of clocks, the rasping voice of Lisa, our maid—could barely be heard in the boxroom.

A papier-mâché mask hung on the wall of the little room. It was a snub-nosed clown, with red cheeks puffed out in bumps. A little red tuft of oakum stuck out from under his white top hat, worn at an angle.

This mask used to come alive in the light from the little red lantern. The clown would watch the black basin in which the films lay in the developing fluid. He even winked at me. He smelled of paste. Sometimes everything grew still in our apartment—this happens even in the noisiest families. At such times I never felt quite like myself when I was eye to eye with this clown.

I gradually came to know his character. I knew that he was a man with a sense of humor, that there was nothing sacred to him in the whole world, and that in the long run he would take revenge on us for keeping him all his life in the boxroom. It even seemed to me that the clown broke his silence sometimes, and muttered something, or sang a little song:

> *Nonsense cooked jam*
> *On the fence one day.*

The hens ate the rooster
On this Sunday.

But I had only to open the door of the boxroom and let in the
bluish daytime light, and the clown would die immediately and
retreat behind his dust.

This time my father had brought me several rolls of film and
asked me to develop them. He had just come home from a trip to
Moscow. It was at the beginning of January in 1906. My father had
arrived in Moscow during the final days of the December uprising.
He told us about the barricades on the Presna, the brigades of
armed workers, the artillery fire. In spite of the failure of the
uprising, my father came home excited, his face still flushed by
the frost in Moscow. He was firmly convinced that a general uprising all over Russia and our long-awaited freedom were no longer
"beyond the mountains."

"Develop them carefully," my father said. "There are some
historical pictures of Moscow there. Only I don't remember which
rolls they're on."

The rolls all looked alike. My father never marked them. So they
had to be developed at random.

On the first roll there were no Moscow pictures. There were only
some pictures of a thin little man in a short jacket and a bow tie.
This man was standing next to a wall on which there hung a long
narrow painting.

For a long time I couldn't make anything out of the painting.
Then at last I could see a thin, hook-nosed face with enormous, sad
eyes. And there were a lot of bird feathers around the face.

My father came to the boxroom and asked me:

"Well, how's it going? Have you found the Moscow shots?"

"Not yet. There's only some kind of an old man with a painting
hanging on the wall."

"But that's Vrubel! Don't you remember him? Be careful, don't
overdevelop it."

"None of the painting came out. Only a face and some kind of
feathers."

"That's the way it should be," my father answered. "That's
'The Demon'."*

My father walked away. And then I remembered how my father
had told Mama one day, drinking tea in the morning, that Mikhail

* Vrubel's painting, like Rubinstein's opera, was based on Lermontov's
poem, which is about the love of a demon for a mortal. Both Alexander
Blok and Boris Pasternak also found inspiration in this poem.

Alexandrovich Vrubel had come to Kiev for several days and had asked my father to meet him at his hotel.

"I don't understand your liking Vrubel," Mama answered with displeasure. "Such decadence! I'm frightened of those obsessed painters."

But my father went to see Vrubel anyway, and he took me with him. We went into a hotel near Golden Gate and went up to the fifth floor. The corridor smelled of hotel mornings—eau de cologne and coffee. My father knocked at a narrow door. A thin little man in a rumpled jacket opened the door. His face, his hair, and his eyes were all the same color as his jacket—gray with yellowish spots. This was the artist Vrubel.

"What kind of a young character is this?" he asked, and he took my chin firmly in his hand. "Your son? A completely water-color boy."

He took my father by the hand and led him to the table.

I looked timidly around the room. It was a garret room. Several water colors were fastened by thumbtacks to the dark wallpaper.

Vrubel poured some cognac for my father and for himself, drank his down quickly, and began to pace up and down the room. His heels made a loud noise. I noticed that they were very high heels.

My father said something in praise of the pictures on the wall.

"Rubbish!" Vrubel said with a sigh.

He stopped walking up and down the room and sat down at the table.

"Somehow I keep whirling around like a squirrel," he said. "It bores me. Why don't we go to Lukyanovka, Georgi Maximovich?"

"To the Kirillovsky Church?"

"Yes. I'd like to see my own work. I've forgotten it completely."

My father agreed. The three of us rode to Lukyanovka in a hansom cab. The driver took us for a long time along the endless Lvovskaya Street, then along the equally endless Dorogozhitskaya Street. Vrubel and my father were smoking.

I kept watching Vrubel and I felt sorry for him. He kept twitching all over, his eyes shifted, he spoke indistinctly, he kept lighting cigarettes and throwing them away. My father spoke to him gently, as to a child.

We got out of the cab at the Fedorovsky Church and went on foot along the streets of Lukyanovka and through the parks. We came out on a ravine. The road wound down it in curves. There, at the bottom, we could see the little tower of the Kirillovsky Church.

"Let's sit down for a little," Vrubel suggested.

We sat on the ground beside the road. Dusty grass was growing all around us. A dull sky was turning blue over the Dnieper.

"It's bad, Georgi Maximovich," Vrubel said. He slapped his flaccid cheeks and laughed. "I'm bored with carrying around this disgusting envelop I'm in."

I only understood part of what Vrubel said, of course, and I wouldn't even remember this conversation, probably, if my father hadn't told Mama about it later, and Uncle Kolya and several friends, and if they had not all been sorry for Vrubel.

Vrubel looked silently at his own frescoes in the Kirillovsky Church. They looked sculptured out of blue, red, and yellow clay. I could not believe that this thin little man had painted such big paintings on the walls.

"Now, that's painting!" Vrubel exclaimed when we came out of the church.

I could see that my father accepted these words quite calmly and even agreed with Vrubel, although he never allowed either me or my brothers to say a single boastful word. So when he left us, on Reitarskaya Street, I told my father that I did not like Vrubel.

"Why not?" my father asked.

"He's a braggart."

"Little fool!" My father clapped me on the back. "Walk straighter. Don't hunch your shoulders."

"Why am I a little fool?" I asked. I felt insulted.

"First of all you must know," my father said, "that Vrubel is a remarkable artist. Some day you'll understand this yourself. And then you must know that he's a sick man. He is spiritually unbalanced. And one more thing you must know is the golden law: never judge anyone in a fit of temper. Otherwise you'll always find yourself in a stupid position. Now stop stooping over! I didn't say anything to offend you."

Now, although the film had been developed, it was hard to make anything out of the painting behind Vrubel's back. I knew only that it was "The Demon." It was much later, in the winter of 1911, that I saw the picture for the first time, in the Tretyakovsky Gallery. That winter Moscow was smoking in a hard, cold frost. Steam seeped through the swollen doors of the taverns. In the middle of the cozy snowbanks of Moscow, the boulevards covered with hoarfrost, the windows coated with ice, and the greenish gas-burning street lamps, this picture by Vrubel sparkled like a blue emerald, like a precious stone found on the highest mountain of the Caucasus. It came alive in the great hall of the gallery with the cold of what is beautiful, and with the immensity of human grief.

I stood for a long time in front of "The Demon." For the first time I understood that looking at such pictures not only gives the spectator pleasure but also drags up from the depths of consciousness ideas a man had never before suspected.

I remembered Lermontov. I pictured to myself how he had gone into the Tretyakovsky Gallery, given his coat to the doorkeeper in the vestibule, and then stood for a long time in front of "The Demon," looking at it with his gloomy eyes.

Then he wrote those bitter words about himself: "Like the flame of a falling star at night, I am not needed in the world." But, my God, how wrong he was! And how needed in the world is the momentary flash of a falling star! Because man does not live by bread alone.

Lermontov considered himself a captive of the world. He wasted the warmth of his spirit in the wasteland. But the wasteland blossomed after this, and was filled with his poetic strength, his anger, his grief, his understanding of happiness. And he has admitted this, bashfully: "From under the bush, the silver lily of the valley nods its head in friendly greeting." And who knows, maybe the sharp, cutting air of the high moutains, bedaubed with the blood of the demon, is filled with the very weak, very distant fragrance of this friendly woodland flower. And he, Lermontov, like the demon plunged into darkness, may have been simply a child who had not received from life what he had passionately sought for: freedom, justice, and love.

"Well, how about it?" my father asked me again through the closed door. "Have you got the Moscow snapshots yet?"

My father's voice brought me back to reality. I began to develop the next roll, and forgot about Vrubel. Some Moscow streets piled high with snow, and lined with little houses, appeared on the film. Low barricades were built across the streets, slantwise, out of boxes, boards, paving stones, and signboards. People were standing around the barricades in civilian clothes but with rifles and revolvers in their hands.

Then some bigger houses showed up, gutted by shellfire, the Gorbaty Bridge, the Zoological Gardens, all shrouded in smoke, and then some bullet-riddled tavern signs, an overturned trolley.

All of this was covered with a kind of wintry sediment, and there was nothing I could do about it. No developing fluid could eat away this sediment and communicate the clearness of the pictures. The sediment did express the circumstances of the uprising. It seemed as if gunpowder smoke were rising from the photographs.

Uprising! This word had an unusual sound in the Russia of those days, a kind of patriarchal Russia. I had read stories about uprisings in India, I knew about the Paris Commune, and about the Decembrist revolt, but the Moscow uprising seemed to me the greatest, and the most romantic.

I got out a map of Moscow. My father showed me all the places where there had been fighting and barricades—the Chisti Prudi, the Samoteka, Kudrinsky Square, Gruzini, Presna, and the Gorbaty Bridge. Ever since then these names have been filled for me with the special charm of places which have become historic. Everything connected with the uprising had meaning for me: the ragged Moscow winter, the cafés where the brigades assembled, the mixture of ancient Muscovy and a new epoch heralded by the uprising.

Cabdrivers in torn coats, knot-shaped biscuits hanging over the bakeries, traders selling hot little cakes, and next to these the whistle of bullets, rushing men, the steel of revolvers, red flags, the singing of "Varshavyanka":

Enemy whirlwinds blow over us
Dark forces wickedly whip us.

This was the poetry of the struggle, the smell of distant freedom still shrouded in mist like a winter dawn which has hardly broken. This was goodness, faith, and hope.

The whole immense Russian land followed the glow which came from the Presna and waited for the victory of the armed workers' brigades. This uprising was like a winter thunderstorm—a promise of new storms and new refreshing shocks.

Now I can write about that feeling of being on tiptoe which filled me then. But at the time I could only feel it, not explain it.

The next day I printed all the negatives and took them to my father. It was getting dark. A lamp was burning in his room. It lit up all the familiar things on his desk: a steel model of a locomotive, a little statue of Pushkin with his curly sideburns, and piles of satirical revolutionary magazines—many of which were coming out at that time. In the most prominent place on the desk was a post card with a portrait of Lieutenant Schmidt,* in a black cloak with buckles in the shape of lions' heads.

My father was lying on the couch, reading a paper. He looked at all the pictures, and said:

---

* Lieutenant Peter P. Schmidt (1867–1906) was organizer and leader of the revolutionary revolt in the Black Sea Fleet in 1905. After its defeat, he was tried and executed.

"Incredible country! Vrubel and an uprising! Everything all mixed up together, and it all leads to one thing."

"To what one thing?"

"It all leads to something better. You'll see a lot of interesting things, Kostik. That is, of course, if you grow up to be an interesting man yourself."

THE DESERTED CRIMEA

Two years later, when I was fourteen, Mama insisted that we should spend the summer for once not in Ryovna but in the Crimea. She chose the quietest of the little towns in the Crimea—Alushta.

We traveled through Odessa. The hotels there were all crowded so we had to stay at the Afonsky Monastery, near the station. The lay brothers—white-faced youths in cassocks with black lacquered belts—fed us cabbage soup with nettles and dried fish.

I was delighted with the soup, with the smart, white city, with the sparkling soda water, and with the port. Clouds of dove-colored swallows swirled over it and mingled with clouds of white sea gulls. I was meeting the sea again. It was much more inviting on these meadowed shores than in the Caucasus.

An ancient steamboat, the *Pushkin*, took us to Yalta. The sea was in a dead calm. The oak railings were so hot that you couldn't put your hand on them. The vibration of the propeller made everything tremble and tinkle in the ship's saloon. The sun came in through hatchways, portholes, and open doors. The abundance of southern sunshine staggered me. Everything sparkled that could possibly sparkle. Even the coarse oilcloth covers on the portholes blazed.

The Crimea came up out of the azure sea like a treasure island. Clouds lay on the tops of its lilac-colored mountains. The white city of Sevastopol swam slowly toward us. It greeted our ancient ship with a midday cannon salute and the blue crosses of St. Andrew's flags.

The *Pushkin* churned the water for a long time turning into the bay. Fountains of bubbles shot up from the bottom. The water hissed. We ran from side to side, so as not to miss anything. There was the Malakhov burial ground and the Brothers' Cemetery, there was the Count's Wharf, and the Constantinovsky Fort, pushed forward right into the breakers, and the rebel cruiser *Ochakov* surrounded by pontoons. A cutter from the naval ships went by us, leaving astern a wake of malachite green water.

I watched, captivated by everything around me. It meant that this town really existed, and was not only in books, this town where Nakhimov died, where the round cannon balls burst in the walls of the fort, where Leo Tolstoy served as an artilleryman, where Lieutenant Schmidt swore loyalty to the people.* Here it was, this town, on a blazing day, in the fleecy shade of its acacias.

The *Pushkin* got into Yalta in the evening. The first thing I saw was the cart of a swarthy peddler. A lantern was hanging over it on a pole. It lighted up downy peaches and big plums, covered with a bluish bloom.

We bought some peaches and went into the Jalita Hotel. Cheerful porters carried our things. I was so tired that I went to sleep as soon as I was in the hotel, hardly noticing the centipede lurking in the corner or the black cypress trees outside the window. I could still hear for a few moments the fountain in the middle of the courtyard singing in a thin voice. Then sleep picked me up and carried me, as in a boat, somewhere far away, to a wonderful country, a country like the mysterious Crimea.

After Yalta with its magnificent beach, Alushta seemed boring to me. We settled on the outskirts, beyond the Stakheyevsky beach. Stony earth, fragrant cypresses, the empty sea, and the distant Sudaksky Mountains—this was all that surrounded us at Alushta. There was nothing else there. But it was enough so that I gradually made my peace with Alushta and came to love it.

Galya and I often walked to a neighboring vineyard to buy sweet grapes. Cicadas sang in the grapevines. Little yellow flowers with heads like pins colored the ground. An old woman named Anna Petrovna would come out of a low house, her face so burned that her gray eyes seemed to be quite white. She would cut the grapes

* Admiral Pavel S. Nakhimov (1803–1855) commanded a squadron which destroyed the Turkish fleet in the Black Sea in 1853; he was later killed in the defense of Sevastopol. Count Leo Tolstoy (1828–1910) served in 1854 with the garrison at Sevastopol; he wrote *Sevastopol Stories* which appeared while the siege of the city was still continuing.

for us. Sometimes she sent her daughter Lena to us, a barefoot seventeen-year-old girl with sun-bleached hair braided in a wreath around her head and eyes as gray as her mother's.

The grownups called this girl "the mermaid." At twilight Lena would often walk past our cottage down to the sea to swim, and she would swim for a long time, and then come back singing with a towel on her shoulder.

Galya became friends with Lena and wormed everything out of her. In general Galya loved to cross-examine people in detail about the circumstances of their lives. She did this with the stubbornness of all nearsighted, inquisitive persons.

It turned out that Anna Petrovna had been a widow, a former librarian in Chernigov, that Lena had become ill with tuberculosis, and that the doctor had advised that she be brought here to the Crimea. So Anna Petrovna came to Alushta. Here she had married an old Ukrainian, the owner of a vineyard. The old man soon died, and now Anna Petrovna and Lena were left as the sole owners of this vineyard. In the winters Lena lived in Yalta and studied in the *gymnasium* there, but on Sundays she came back to her mother at Alushta. Lena's disease had completely disappeared.

Lena had been hoping, after she finished high school, to become a singer. Galya talked her out of this. In Galya's opinion, the only worthwhile occupation for women was teaching. Galya herself wanted to become a village teacher. I had been bored for a long time by all these ideas of Galya's, all the more because she talked too much about her future profession and proved to everybody, even when no one disagreed, that there was no better occupation in this world than to be a teacher.

Somehow it made me angry that Galya had talked Lena out of being a singer. I loved the theater. To spite Galya I told Lena enthusiastically about every single play I had ever seen—*The Bluebird, A Nest of Noblemen,* and *Madame Sans-Gêne.*

I exaggerated a great deal. I foresaw an entrancing future for Lena. It pleased me to think that this slim, sunburned girl, who could swim in the sea better than any sailor, might some day walk out on the stage in a fine dress with a train. On her breast a dark flower would move gently with her breathing. Even through her powder the sunburn of the seashore would still be apparent.

I overwhelmed Lena with my impetuous dreams. She listened to me, cocking her head to one side as if her braids were pulling it back, and she blushed a little. Sometimes she would ask:

"Well, admit it, you've made this all up, haven't you? Isn't that so? I won't be angry."

She always called me by the formal "you" although she was three years older than I was. In those times people used the familiar form of the pronoun only when they felt very close to each other.

I couldn't admit what she asked me to, because I believed in all sincerity what I made up. This habit of mine was to be the cause of many of my misfortunes. Most surprising of all is the fact that in all my life I have never met anyone who wanted to understand, let alone approve, this habit.

But Lena believed me. She wanted to believe everything I thought up for her. If I didn't show up with Galya at the vineyard for two or three days, she would bring the grapes to us herself, and she would say, in an embarrassed way, to Mama: "Anna Petrovna sent you these as a present," and then, having waited for the right moment, she would whisper to me:

"For God's sake, this is a swinish trick! Why didn't you come?"

My father soon left Alushta. He had to go to Peterburg on business. Then Borya left, to take his examinations for the Kiev Polytechnical Institute. For some reason, Mama was deeply upset by my father's leaving, and she paid no attention to us. She was glad when we spent whole days at the seashore and didn't bother her.

I wandered for whole days up to my waist in the water, catching crabs under stones. It ended up with my catching cold somehow, when I was swimming in the late evening, and it turned into pneumonia. To cap the bad luck, on the first night when I was running a high fever, I was bitten by a poisonous lizard.

August went by. Classes would soon start again. We had to go back to Kiev. My sickness upset all the plans. In the end, Mama sent Galya and Dima back, and stayed with me.

I was very sick, and for a long time. I couldn't sleep at night. It was hard for me to breathe. I tried to breathe very carefully, and I looked sadly at the white walls of my room. Centipedes crawled out of the cracks in the walls. A lamp was burning on the table. The shadows of the medicine bottles looked like prehistoric monsters—they sniffed at the ceiling, stretching out their long necks.

I turned my head and looked at the black window. The lamp was reflected in it. Beyond the reflection was the drone of the sea.

A night moth beat against the glass. It wanted to fly away from the heavy medicinal smells of the room. Mama was sleeping in the next room. I called her, asked for something to drink, and asked her to let out the moth. Mama let the moth go, and I grew quiet.

But then I saw, I don't know how, that the moth lighted on the dry grass outside the window and, having sat there awhile, came back and flew into the room again, as big now as an owl. It came to rest on my chest. I felt the moth as heavy as a stone, and I knew it was going to crush my heart. I called Mama again and I asked her to get rid of the moth. Mama pressed her lips close together, and she took off a tight, hot compress and covered me with blankets.

I lost count of the nights, filled with rumblings I couldn't understand and with the dry heat of the bedclothes.

Lena came once in the daytime. I didn't realize at first that it was she. She was wearing a brown uniform dress, a black apron, and little black slippers. Her light hair was carefully braided and it hung down both sides of her sunburned face onto her breast. Lena had come to say good-by before going off to Yalta. When Mama walked out of the room, Lena put her hand on my forehead. Her hand was as cold as an icicle. The end of her braid fell into my face. I could smell the warm fresh scent of her hair.

Mama came back in. Lena took her hand away quickly, and Mama said that Lena had brought me some wonderful grapes.

"We don't have any better ones now, unfortunately," Lena answered. While she said this, she looked not at Mama but at me, as if she wanted to say something important to me.

Then she left. I heard her running down the stairs. No one was living in the house except for us, so every sound could be easily heard.

I began to get better from that day on. The doctor said that after I got out of bed I would have to stay in Alushta for at least two months, until November. I needed to grow stronger, and to rest. Then Mama decided to summon Lisa from Kiev to look after me and to feed me. Mama herself was in a hurry to get back to Kiev—I didn't know why. Lisa came in a week's time, and the next day Mama drove off in a carriage to Simferopol.

Lisa spent all her time gasping, with her mouth open. She had never seen the sea before, or cypresses, or vineyards—Mama had hired Lisa in Ryovna, in the Bryansk forests.

I had already begun to stand up, but I wasn't yet allowed to go out. I stayed all day in the glassed-in terrace under the not very warm autumn sun, and read. I had found *Tristan and Isolde* in a cupboard. I read this amazing legend several times, and each time I finished it, I became more unhappy.

Then I decided to write something like *Tristan and Isolde* myself and I spent several days making up a story. But I couldn't get

any farther on paper than a description of the waves of the sea
breaking against a rocky shore.

At the end of September, the doctor finally allowed me to go
outside. I wandered alone through a deserted Alushta. I loved to
walk on the wharf when the surf was heavy. The waves drove up
under the flooring which was full of holes. Streams of water came
up through the chinks.

I walked over to Anna Petrovna's. She poured me some coffee,
and told me I must definitely come back on Sunday, for that was
the day when Lena would come home from Yalta. All the time after
that I was thinking how I would meet Lena.

I remember that Sunday as clearly as if it had been yesterday
because two events took place on that day.

I knew that Lena was coming from Yalta on the morning cutter.
I went down to the wharf. But as soon as the cutter appeared
around the cape, I hid behind a boarded-up kiosk. It sold post
cards with views of the Crimea. I sat there on a stone during all the
time the cutter was coming up to the wharf. Lena got off it, and,
after having looked for someone on the wharf, walked slowly
home.

I was afraid that she would notice me. This would have been
terrible. She looked around several times, then came back to the
wharf and stood for a while in front of a wooden pillar which
carried notices and advertisements. She looked as if she were reading the notices, although they were all torn and hung down in
ribbons.

I watched her furtively. She was wearing a warm white scarf
on her head. She had grown paler and thinner in Yalta. She stood
next to the pillar with her eyes cast down, although she would
have had to raise them if she had really been reading the notices.
Then she went away.

I waited a little and then went home. I was ashamed of my
cowardice.

I didn't know whether to go to Lena's now or not. I ate nothing
at dinner. Lisa threatened to send a telegram to Mama. Lisa could
hardly read or write, and I laughed at her threat.

After dinner I made up my mind at last, put on my coat, and
went out. Lisa yelled after me to button up my coat, but I didn't
listen to her.

I walked up to the vineyard. It was already quite purple. I
opened the little gate. At that moment a door slammed in the white
house, and I saw Lena. She ran to meet me, with nothing over her
dress.

This was a good day. I stopped being shy, and I told her about Ryovna, about my geography teacher Cherpunov, and about my Aunt Nadya. Lena kept quietly filling my plate with grapes, then with greengage plums. Finally she said:

"Why did you come in an unbuttoned coat in weather as cold as this? For whom are you playing the dandy?"

"You ran out yourself in just your dress," I answered.

"Because . . ."—she said, and then she was silent—"because I haven't just had pneumonia."

Her face flushed underneath the sunburn. Anna Petrovna looked at Lena from underneath her spectacles and shook her head:

"Lena, don't forget that you're already seventeen."

She said it as if Lena were already a completely grown-up woman and, besides, was being stupid.

Anna Petrovna and Lena accompanied me home, and came in to see how I lived. Lisa blushed as red as a beet, but calmed down quickly and complained to Anna Petrovna that I paid no attention to her and always walked around with my coat unbuttoned. Anna Petrovna said that Lisa should turn to her for anything she needed. Lisa was overjoyed. She had no acquaintances in Alushta. Once in a long while she would go walking with me, and collect herbs to be spread out in her room. She spent all her free time in guessing the future with playing cards.

Lisa had red cheeks and bulging, kind eyes, and she was an exceedingly trusting person. She believed any kind of nonsense that was told her.

Anna Petrovna and Lena went home. I was bored. A long evening stretched ahead. I wanted to go back to the vineyard again, but I knew this was impossible.

I decided to work on my story, lit the lamp, and sat down at the table. Instead of the story, I wrote some verses. I've forgotten them now. I can remember only one line:

> *O, pick the flowers with drooping stems . . .*

I liked my verses. I was in a mood to write for a long time but Lisa came in and said: "What have you thought up now—ruining your eyes! It was time to sleep long ago," and she turned out the lamp. I was angry, I told her that I was already grown up, and I called her an idiot. Lisa went into her own room, crying from my insult, and she said in a hoarse voice:

"I'll go off tomorrow to Kiev on foot—you can do as you like here alone."

I said nothing. Then Lisa said that tomorrow she would send Mama a telegram about my behavior. She had a passion for frightening me with telegrams. She muttered something for a long time in her room, and then she sighed:

"Well, God be with you. Sleep. What a wind has started to blow outside!"

A round wall clock hung over my head. I woke up every time it struck two o'clock at night. This time it happened again, and for a long time I couldn't understand what had taken place. A purple light moved across the wall. The window looked out on the sea. Beyond it the wind blew monotonously. I sat on the bed and looked out the window. A red glow was rocking on the sea. It lit up the low clouds and the turbulent water.

I began to dress hurriedly.

"Lisa" I yelled. "There's a fire at sea!"

Lisa stirred, jumped up, and began to dress, too.

"But what can burn on the water?" she asked.

"I don't know."

"Then why are you getting up?" Lisa asked. Half awake, she didn't understand what was going on.

"I'm going down on the shore."

"I, too."

We went out. The wind came around the corner of the house and held me with its tight coldness. The glow was rising now straight into the sky. At the gate stood the janitor, a Tartar.

"A boat is burning up," he said. "What can be done about it, ah!"

We ran down to the beach. A bell was being rung near the wharf, apparently at the lifesaving station. Clusters of people were standing on the beach. I lost Lisa almost at once in the darkness.

Fishermen in high boots and oilskin raincoats were dragging a boat along the shingle to the sea. You could hear hurried voices: "Passenger ship," "Two miles from shore," "Hold back the stern, listen, don't let it roll." The wet fishermen jumped into the boat, and grabbed the oars. It rose on a wave, and slipped out into the sea.

Someone took me by the elbow. I turned around. Lena was standing next to me. The glow made it just possible to see her. I looked at her serious face. We stood quietly at the edge of the beach. A white flare went up from the sea. A second followed it.

"Help is on the way," Lena said. "If it hadn't been for Mama, I'd have gone with the fishermen in that boat. I would certainly have gone."

She was silent for a moment, and then she asked:

"When are you leaving?"

My heart stopped beating—so unexpectedly had she used the intimate form of the pronoun "you."

"Probably in a week."

"That means I'll see you again. I'll try to come earlier."

"I'll be waiting," I answered, and it seemed to me that with those terrifying words I had fallen off a cliff.

Lena led me gently away from the edge of the beach.

"What shall we do?" she asked in a low voice. "Mama is frightened. She's somewhere here, near the wharf. You're not angry at me?"

"For what?"

She did not answer.

"Lena!" Anna Petrovna called out of the darkness. "Where are you? Let's go home!"

"I'm leaving tomorrow on the early mail coach," Lena whispered. "Don't think of seeing me off. Good-by."

She squeezed my hand and walked away. I watched her go. For a few seconds—no more—I could see the white scarf wound around her head.

The glow over the sea grew dim. The green light of a searchlight lay on the water. The mine layer *Stremitelny* was coming up to help. I found Lisa and we went home.

I wanted to lie down and go to sleep as quickly as I could so as not to think about the wonderful and good thing that had just taken place between Lena and me.

In the morning, when there was only a little smoke where the glow had been, I walked down to the wharf and learned that a steamship had burned at sea. People said that a bomb had exploded inside the ship but that the captain had succeeded in beaching the ship on some rocks along the shore.

After I had learned this news, I walked for a long way along the road to Yalta. Only an hour before, the mail coach had driven along here with Lena. I sat for a long time on a little wall over the sea, with my hands inside the sleeves of my overcoat.

I thought about Lena, and my heart felt heavy in me. I remembered the smell of her hair, the warmth of her light breathing, her uneasy eyes, and her thin eyebrows. I didn't understand what was wrong with me. A terrifying grief filled me, and I cried. I wanted only one thing in the world—to see her all the time, to hear only her voice, to be near her.

I had just about decided to walk to Yalta on foot, but at that moment a wagon clattered up around a turn in the road. I dried my eyes quickly, turned around, and began to stare at the sea. But the tears came again, and I couldn't see anything except a blue, sharp shimmer. A strong chill went through me, and I couldn't keep my body from shaking all over.

An old man in a straw hat, driving the wagon, stopped his horse and said:

"Get in, friend, and I'll drive you to Alushta."

I climbed in the wagon. The old man looked at me and asked:

"You're not by any chance from the orphans' home?"

"No, I'm a *gymnasium* student," I answered.

The last few days at Alushta were extraordinarily melancholy and good. This is the way last days always are in places which one is sorry to leave. A fog swept in from the sea. The grass next to our cottage grew wet from it. The sun shone through the fog. Lisa stoked the stove with yellow acacia wood. The leaves were falling. But they were not golden, as they were at home in Kiev, but silver, with lilac-colored veins.

The waves rolled quietly out of the fog, broke against the shore, and quietly rolled back into the fog. Dead sea horses were strewn on the shingle of the beach. The mountains, Chatir-Dag and Bobugan-Yaila, disappeared in the clouds. Flocks of sheep came down from the hills. Wild sheep dogs ran after the flocks, looking suspiciously from side to side.

It was so still with the fog and the autumn that from my balcony I could hear voices down in the town below. Braziers glowed in small inns on the market place, and you could smell burned fat and roasted gray mullet.

Lisa and I were supposed to leave on Monday morning. Lisa had already hired a carriage to Simferopol. I expected Lena on Saturday, but she didn't come. I walked past the vineyard several times, but couldn't see anyone. Nor was she there on Sunday morning. I walked to the mail-coach station. It was empty.

I returned home, anxious. Lisa gave me an envelop.

"Some little boy brought it," she said. "It's probably from Anna Petrovna, asking you to come and say good-by. You'd better go. They are nice people."

I went out in the garden, tore open the envelop, and pulled out a piece of paper. On it was written: "Come at six o'clock to the three plane trees. Lena."

I got to the three plane trees not at six but at five o'clock. It was a deserted place. Three plane trees stood in a rocky ravine near the bed of a dried-up stream. Everything around them was faded. There were only a few withered tulip trees. At some time there must have been a garden here. A wooden bridge had been thrown across the stream. Under one of the plane trees stood a wicker bench with rusted iron legs.

Although I came before the appointed time, I found Lena there. She was sitting on the bench, squeezing her hands between her knees. Her scarf had fallen from her head on to her shoulders.

Lena turned around when I came up to the bench.

"You won't understand," she said, and she took my hand. "No, don't pay any attention . . . I'm always talking nonsense."

Lena stood up and smiled in a guilty way. She let her head fall forward and looked up at me distrustfully.

"Mama says I am mad. Well, what of it! Good-by!"

She took me by the shoulders and kissed me on the lips, then she moved away, and said: "And now go! And don't look back! I beg you. Go!"

There were tears in her eyes, but only one flowed down her cheek, leaving a thin wet mark.

And I went away. But I couldn't resist looking back. Lena was standing there, leaning against the trunk of the plane tree, with her head thrown back as if her braids were pulling it, and watching me.

"Go!" she screamed, and her voice had changed terribly. "This is all foolishness!"

I went away. The sky had already grown dark. The sun was setting behind Kastel Mountain. The wind whistled down from Yaila and rattled the dry leaves.

I did not imagine then that everything was finished, absolutely everything. It was much later that I understood that life had taken away from me, for some unknown reason, what might have been happiness.

The next day Lisa and I went to Simferopol. It was raining in the woods beyond Chatir-Dag. Rain beat against the train windows all the way to Kiev. At home it was as if no one noticed my arrival. Something bad had happened in our family. But I didn't yet know just what it was.

I was even glad that no one paid me any attention. I was thinking all the time about Lena, but I couldn't make up my mind to write her.

The next time after that autumn that I was in the Crimea was in 1921 when everything that had happened between me and Lena had become a memory, stirring not pain but only wonderings. Who doesn't have them? Are they even worth talking about?

DISASTER

Everything changed all at once after the Crimea. My father quarreled with the head of the Southern-Western Railroad and gave up his job. All our prosperity collapsed at the same time.

We moved from Nikolsko-Botanicheskaya Street to Basement Street where, as if it were a joke, we settled into a basement apartment.

We lived only because Mama was selling our things. More and more frequently silent men in sheepskin hats would show up in our chilly, dark apartment. Their sharp eyes would wander around our furniture, our pictures, the china on the table, then they would talk quietly and persuasively with Mama, and then they would leave. And in a couple of hours a cart would drive into the courtyard and take away a cupboard, or a table, or a pier glass and a rug.

In the mornings we would find a Tartar in a black quilted skullcap in the kitchen. We called him "Shurum-burum." Squatting on his heels, he would be examining in the light my father's trousers, his jackets, or some bedsheets.

Shurum-burum would bargain for a long time, walk out, come back again, and Mama would get angry until, finally, Shurumburum would clap his hands, take a thick wallet out of his pocket, and after delicately spitting on his fingers, count out his torn money.

My father was almost never home. He went out in the morning and came back late, when we were already asleep. None of us knew where he spent the days. Obviously, he was looking for work.

Mama aged suddenly. Her gray lock of hair fell more and more often from her forehead down into her face—Mama had begun to fix her hair very carelessly.

Borya left us to settle in furnished rooms near the station, allegedly because it was nearer the Polytechnical Institute. Actually he left because he couldn't get along with our father, considered him to blame for the unhappiness in our family, and didn't want to live in the gloomy world of Basement Street. Borya was earning money by giving lessons but he couldn't help us. Dima also gave lessons or, as we used to say then, was a tutor. Only I was still too young to teach others, and Galya was so nearsighted that she could do nothing except help Mama around the apartment. We had to let Lisa go.

One day in the morning a lean, creaky old man came in with the janitor. He was a bailiff and because of some sort of debts of my father's he made an inventory of almost everything we had left. My father had concealed these debts from Mama, but now they had come to light. After this my father took the first position offered him, a very bad post at a sugar factory near Kiev, and went away.

We remained alone. Unhappiness had come into the family. It was breaking up. I realized this. It was especially hard after the Crimea, after my short and unhappy love for Lena, after my happy, easy childhood.

Uncle Kolya sent Mama money from Bryansk once every month. Every time she received the money, Mama would weep with shame.

Once I saw her in the *gymnasium* director's waiting room. I ran toward her but she turned away, and I realized that she didn't want me to have noticed her. I couldn't guess why she had come to see the director but I did not ask her about anything. Several days later our new director, Tereshchenko, who had succeeded Bessmertny and who was short, round, and bald, with a head that looked as if it had been buttered, stopped me in the corridor and said:

"Please tell your mother that the pedagogical council has approved her request and released your brother and you from payment of tuition fees. But don't forget that we can do this only for good students. So I advise you to apply yourself."

This was the first humiliation I was to experience. At home I said to Mama: "They've released Dima and me from paying. Why did you go to the director?"

"What else could I do?" Mama asked me quietly. "Take you out of school?"

"I would have earned the money myself."

For the first time I saw fright on Mama's face, as if she had been struck.

"Don't be angry," she said, and she dropped her head. She was sitting at the table, sewing. "How could I force you to go to work?"

She was crying.

"If you only knew how badly I feel for all of you, and especially for you! How did your father dare to behave so thoughtlessly, and to be so careless! How could he do it!"

For some time Mama had been calling my father "he" or "your father." She went on crying, leaning over the old dress she was sewing. Little bits of cloth and pieces of white thread were strewn on the floor.

Mama sold nearly everything. It was damp and empty in the apartment. A dim light came through the windows. Through them we could see boots, shoes, high galoshes walking by. The sound of the footsteps, muffled by the winter dirt on the pavement, made it impossible to concentrate, and irritated us. It was as if all these strangers were walking through our apartment, inflicting the cold on us, without even thinking it necessary to glance at us.

In the middle of the winter Mama received a letter from Uncle Kolya which greatly upset her. That evening, when we were all sitting at the round table where the only lamp stood and where each of us did whatever concerned him, Mama told us that Uncle Kolya was insisting on my coming to him for a time in Bryansk. He would have me admitted to the *gymnasium* there, and this was absolutely essential until my father could get a better position and rejoin his family.

Galya looked at Mama with fright in her face. Dima said nothing.

"Your father will not return to us," Mama said sternly. "He has other attachments. It was because of this that he ran up those debts and left us in poverty. And I do not wish him to return. I don't want to hear anything about it, not a single word."

Mama was silent for a long time. Her lips were pressed very tight together.

"Well, all right," she said at last. "That's not worth talking about. What shall we do with Kostik?"

"It's very simple," Dima said, without looking at Mama. For Dima everything was always simple. "I'll finish the *gymnasium* this year and go to the Moscow Technological Institute. We'll sell everything. You, Mama, will move to Moscow with Galya, and you'll live with me. We'll make out. And meanwhile Kostik will live with Uncle Kolya."

"But what do you mean?" Galya asked in consternation. "Just how will he live there? Why should we all break up?"

I sat there, with my head down, feverishly drawing flowers and scrolls on a piece of paper. For some time, whenever I felt miserable, I had had the habit of drawing intricate scrolls on whatever was under my hand.

"Stop drawing!" Mama said. "I don't understand what you're smiling about! What do you think of this?"

"I'm not smiling," I muttered, but I could feel a strained smile on my face. "It's just . . ."

I broke off, and continued to draw. I couldn't stop.

"Kostik, my darling," Mama said suddenly in a very low voice, "why are you silent?"

"Good . . ." I answered. "I'll go . . . if it's necessary . . ."

"This way will be the best of all," Dima said.

"Yes . . . it will be all right . . . of course," I agreed, in order not to be silent.

Everything collapsed at that moment. In front of me I could see only a scalding loneliness and my own uselessness. I wanted to tell Mama that she didn't have to send me to Bryansk, that I could give lessons as well as Dima, and even help her out, that this was very bitter for me and that I couldn't escape the idea that I was being thrown out of the family. But my throat hurt so much and there was such a cramp in my jaw that I could say nothing and I kept quiet.

For an instant the thought went through my head of going off the next day to my father. But the idea disappeared at once, and was replaced by the thought that I was now completely alone. Finally I mustered all my strength, with difficulty, and repeated, stammering, that I was willing and even glad to go to Bryansk and that my head ached and that I was going to bed.

I went into the cold little room which I shared with Dima, undressed quickly and lay down, pulled the blanket over my head, bit my lip, and lay there almost all night long. Mama came in and called to me, but I pretended to be asleep. She spread my overcoat over my blanket, and went out.

Arrangements with Bryansk stretched out into December. It was hard for me to leave my school, my comrades, begin a new and, as I knew, unhappy life. I wrote my father that I was moving to Bryansk but for a long time I got no answer. It came two days before my departure.

Coming home from school, I usually walked through the empty square behind the Opera Theater. I always walked back with two schoolmates, Stanishevsky and Matusevich. One day we passed a young woman on the square—not tall, in a heavy veil. She walked by us, stopped, and looked after us. The next day we met the same woman at the same place. She came straight up to us and asked me:

"Excuse me, aren't you the son of Georgi Maximovich?"

"Yes, I am his son."

"I need to talk with you."

"Please," I answered, and I blushed.

Stanishevsky and Matusevich walked away. They acted as if the incident didn't interest them in the slightest, and never even looked back.

"Georgi Maximovich," the woman said hurriedly, digging into her handbag, "asked me to give you a letter. You understand, he wanted it to go directly to you . . . Excuse me for saying that . . . I could not refuse him. I recognized you right away. You look like your father. Here is the letter."

She held it out to me.

"Are you going away?" she asked.

"Yes, in a few days."

"Well . . . I'm sorry. Everything might have been different."

"Do you see Papa?"

She silently nodded her head.

"Kiss him for me," I said suddenly. "He is very good."

I had wanted to say that she should love him very much and take pity on him, but all I could say was those four words: "He is very good."

"Yes?" she said, and suddenly she laughed, opening her mouth a little. I could see her small, very white, wet teeth. "Thank you."

She pressed my hand and walked quickly away. A bracelet tinkled on her wrist. Even now I do not know what her name was. I never succeeded in finding out. Only Mama knew, and she took the secret of this name to the grave with her.

The strange lady reminded me in voice, in laughter, and by her bracelet, of the woman I had met at old Cherpunov's house. Maybe, if it hadn't been for her heavy veil, I might have recognized her, the butterfly from the island of Borneo. Even now the idea sometimes bothers me that she might have been the same young woman who treated me to cocoa in Kirkheim's candy store.

My father's letter was short. He wrote me to accept my fate with courage and with dignity.

"Perhaps," he wrote, "life will turn its bright side toward us again, and then I will be able to help you. I still believe that you will achieve everything in life I have not been able to, and will become a real man. Remember my one piece of advice (I've never bored you with my advice): don't judge anyone in a fit of temper, including me, before you know all the circumstances and have acquired enough experience to understand a good deal that you now, naturally, cannot understand. Keep in good health, write me, and don't worry."

Mama and Galya took me to the station. The train left in the morning. Dima could not miss his classes at school. When he left for school he had kissed me, but he didn't say anything. Mama and Galya were silent, too. Mama felt cold and kept her hands in her muff. Galya stuck close to her. In the last year her vision had grown worse. She was confused by the crowd and frightened by the locomotive whistles. Mama made the sign of the cross over me, kissed me with cold thin lips, led me to one side by my sleeve, and said:

"I know that this is hard for you and that you're angry. But remember that you're the one whom I want to protect from this poverty and this torture. It's only because of this that I insisted on your going to Uncle Kolya."

I answered that I understood everything quite well and that I wasn't at all angry. I spoke fair words, but there was cold in my heart and I wished only that the train would leave quickly and end this agonizing farewell.

It must have been that the real parting with Mama had come earlier, on that night when she spread my overcoat over me for the last time. The train pulled out but I could not see Mama, nor Galya, because a heavy cloud of steam from the locomotive blocked out the platform and everyone standing on it.

There was cold in my heart, the same kind of cold as in the compartment, filled with the thin light of winter. The wind blew shrilly at the window. Despondency flowed over the snow-covered plains. A ground wind blew at night. I wanted to sleep, but sleep did not come to me. I watched the tongue of flame in the lantern. The wind blew it from side to side, trying to extinguish it. I made a bet with myself—that if it were not blown out this would mean something good would happen in my life. The flame fought stubbornly with the wind all night, and was still burning in the morning. This made me feel better.

When we got into Bryansk, in the morning, the frost was so heavy that the air was full of the squeaking of boots. The cold clung to the earth like tenacious smoke. The purplish light of a frozen sun filled the sky.

They sent horses for me. A sheepskin coat, a hood, and mittens were in the sleigh for me. I wrapped myself up. The horses started off at a full gallop. We drove through shining snow dust—at first along the dike, then on the Desna. The little bells on the harness rang furiously. Up in the hills the old town with its shaggy designs of frost and icicles twinkled like a toy made out of gold foil.

The sleigh stopped next to a wooden house on the side of a hill. I walked up on the porch. A door opened. Aunt Marusya grabbed me by the sleeve, pulled me into the dining room where reflected sunbeams were dancing up to the ceiling, and forced me to drink a full glass of red wine. My lips were white with frost. I couldn't speak.

Everything was ringing and happy in Uncle Kolya's house. As always happens in such situations, memory has pushed everything unpleasant to one side. It is as if the bad piece had been cut out of the cloth and its good parts woven back together—the autumn in the Crimea and this Russian winter full of ringing voices.

I tried not to think about what had just happened in Kiev. I preferred to remember Alushta, the three plane trees, and Lena. I even tried to write a letter to her in Yalta, but I did not decide to send it. It seemed to me a very stupid letter. But I could not write a more intelligent one, no matter how hard I worked on it.

ARTILLERYMEN

The artillery officers of the Bryansk arsenal called Uncle Kolya "Colonel Vershinin." He even looked like the Vershinin of Chekhov's *Three Sisters*—a black-bearded man with dark, lively eyes. At least we all imagined Vershinin to have looked like that.

Just like Vershinin, Uncle Kolya loved to talk about the wonderful future, and he believed in it, and he was gentle and bubbling over with life. He differed from Vershinin in being a good metallurgist and the author of numerous articles about the properties of various metals. He translated these articles himself into French— which he knew perfectly—and published them in the Paris magazine *Revue de Metallurgie*. These articles were also published in Russia, but much less often than in France. When I moved to Bryansk, Uncle Kolya was working happily on the production of Damascus steel.

Uncle Kolya's hunger for life was amazing. It seemed as if there were nothing that didn't interest him. He subscribed to almost all the literary magazines, played the piano excellently, knew astronomy and philosophy, and was an inexhaustible and witty conversationalist.

Uncle Kolya's closest friend was the bearded captain Rumyantsev. In appearance he resembled Fet; he was red-haired, short of vision, and goodhearted. In spite of his military rank he behaved and looked like a civilian. Even the Bryansk schoolboys teased him about his unmilitary bearing.

Rumyantsev was not even easy to see. He was always enveloped in a cloud of tobacco smoke, and his shyness made him seek the darkest corner in the drawing room. He would sit there in front of a chessboard, absorbed in solving a chess problem. If he succeeded he would burst into laughter and rub his hands together.

Rumyantsev rarely took part in general conversation. He would just cough and watch with his screwed-up eyes. But as soon as talk turned to politics—the Duma or strikes—he would come alive and speak out with the most extreme opinions. He was not married. His three sisters lived with him, all of them short, with bobbed hair, and wearing pince-nez. They all smoked and wore severe black skirts with gray blouses, and just as if they had made an agreement about it pinned their watches with safety pins at exactly the same place on their bosoms.

The sisters were always hiding people in Rumyantsev's apartment: various students, old men in loose capes, and severe women like themselves. Uncle Kolya warned me never to mention who was living at Rumyantsev's to anyone.

Besides Rumyantsev and his sisters, a frequent visitor to Uncle Kolya's was Staff Captain Ivanov, a very clean man with white hands, a meticulously pointed light beard, and a delicate voice. In typical bachelor fashion, Ivanov became a member of the family at Uncle Kolya's. It was hard for him to spend an evening without dropping in to sit and talk. He blushed each time he took off his overcoat and unbelted his sword in the vestibule, and said that he had dropped in just for a word or to get Uncle Kolya's advice on some matter. Then of course he would sit there until the middle of the night.

I was grateful to Ivanov for breaking me of the habit of being embarrassed over simple things. I met him once at the market. He was buying potatoes and cabbage.

"Help me carry this to the cab," he asked me. "My Pyotr [Pyotr was Ivanov's orderly] has caught a cold. I've got to do everything for myself."

While I was helping him carry a heavy bag of cabbages to the cab, we met a young woman who taught us German in the Bryansk *gymnasium*. In answer to my bow, she sniffed and turned away. I blushed.

"It's foolish to be bothered by that," Ivanov said. "You're not doing anything vulgar. I have a trick for handling that kind of situation—look people straight in the eyes. It works very well."

We sat in the cab, surrounded by vegetables, and drove down the main street, Bolkhovskaya Street. We met many acquaintances. We even ran into the head of the arsenal, General Sarandinak, driving in a carriage with two horses. Friends started to laugh when they saw us, but Ivanov looked them straight in the eyes. It was they who grew embarrassed under his gaze; they stopped laughing, and in the end even nodded to us politely. Sarandinak stopped his carriage and offered to send his own orderly to Ivanov. But Ivanov refused politely, pointing out that he could handle this simple task very well. The general raised his eyebrows and gently prodded his driver in the back with his sword in a black scabbard, and the general's gray horses trotted on.

"So you see," Ivanov told me, "it never pays to try to duck when you run into prejudices."

I knew that Ivanov was right, of course, but I still felt uncomfortable when people looked at me with laughing eyes. It was a bad habit. Sometimes I would catch myself being afraid of behaving differently from others, and ashamed of my poverty, trying to hide it from my comrades.

Mama reacted to the change in our life as if it were the most enormous tragedy. She tried as hard as she could to hide it from her acquaintances. Everybody knew that my father had abandoned his family, but Mama always answered all her friends' questions by saying that he had gone away for a short time and that everything was fine with us. She used to patch and mend our clothing all night long in terror that "people might notice" the signs of our poverty. Her courage betrayed Mama. Her timidity was passed on to us.

When the cabdriver was going up the hill to Ivanov's house the cabbages spilled. Heads of cabbage scattered all over the road, bouncing against each other. Some little boys started to whistle. The cabdriver stopped. We got out and began to pick up the cabbages.

I must have turned completely red with shame because Ivanov, looking at me, offered: "Let me do it myself. It would be better if you went along home."

If I had been ashamed before to pick up cabbages with people looking on, after these words I blushed to the point of tears. I gathered up the last cabbages in a frenzy and gave a heavy box on the ears to a boy named Samokhin, the son of a Bryansk merchant, who had been dancing on the sidewalk and teasing me:

> *The schoolboy has come to grief,*
> *Look, he's lost a cabbage leaf!*

Young Samokhin, howling and in tears, took flight into his own courtyard. When I looked at Ivanov's cunning eyes, I was convinced that he had spilled the cabbages on purpose.

From this day on I began even to show off. I went out on the street every day with a wooden shovel and cleared the snow, I split firewood, stoked the fires, and not only did not run away from menial work but asked for it. And the Samokhin boy continued for a long time, whenever he saw me, to hide behind his gate and yell out at me: "Blue beef!" *Gymnasium* students were called this because of our blue caps. But his teasing no longer made the slightest impression on me.

Ivanov's lessons in living were reinforced by Lieutenant Colonel Kuzmin-Karavayev, a narrow-chested man with firm gray eyes. He had started the first consumers' co-operative in Bryansk and opened a grocery store on Bolkhovskaya Street. He delivered purchases himself, and sold behind the counter in the crowded store.

This undertaking of Karavayev's raised a commotion among the Bryansk merchants. The elders in the merchants' association sent complaints about Karavayev to Peterburg, to the Chief Artillery Administration. But the intelligentsia and the workers of the arsenal stood behind him like a stone wall. The complaints achieved nothing. The grocery store flourished and grew richer day by day.

All of us took turns helping Karavayev in the store and he took me on as a regular helper. I spent almost all my free time there, opening good-smelling boxes of groceries, and weighing out salt, flour, and sugar. Karavayev, who wore the kind of rough apron worn by blacksmiths with a smart jacket on top of it, worked very fast, joked with the customers, and told me many interesting things about the places where the goods came from.

He sold goods collected from all over the country—tobacco from Feodosia, Georgian wine, Astrakhan caviar, lace from Vologodsk, chinawear from Maltsevska, Sareptsky mustard, and printed calico from Ivanovo-Voznesensk. The store smelled of her-

ring brine and soap and over everything was the wonderful smell
of the fresh bast matting heaped up in the back room.

In the evenings Karavayev would close up the store behind its
iron bars and we would drink strong tea together. The tea kettle
jiggled on the iron stove. Karavayev cut the sugar loaf with a flat
Japanese bayonet. Blue sparks flew up from the sugar. I got honey
cakes, called *zhamki,* out of a wooden box. Some of our friends
would always come to drink tea with us, and to sit and talk—
sometimes Ivanov, sometimes the Rumyantsev sisters, sometimes
Aunt Marusya. Ivanov would sit on an empty box, without taking
off his overcoat or his gloves, and start to prove to Karavayev that
Russia had not yet developed to the level of consumers' co-
operatives. Karavayev would cough his choking cough, and wave
Ivanov's arguments away.

Aunt Marusya always brought homemade cookies or patties
with her. The Rumyantsev sisters drank their tea out of the saucer,
with their pince-nez gleaming. They called Karavayev Don Quixote
and said that his bother with the store was a petty business and
that what Russia needed was not co-operatives but a great explosion.

Then Ivanov would begin to polish his spurs and to sing *"Mal-
brough s'en va-t-en guerre."* The Rumyantsev sisters would call
him a reactionary, and go away.

Early in the spring the grocery store burned down. It was crude
and open arson—the door into the store had been broken and
kerosene poured over the goods. The whole town knew that it was
the work of the Bryansk merchants but the official investigation
stretched out endlessly and got nowhere. Karavayev's face grew
still more pinched, he began to cough still more, and he said:

"Finita la commedia! Only an explosion can remake our country.
Hang all Russia up on the rack, and then we'll start making sense."

The losses from the fire were enormous. The members of the
co-operative covered them with great difficulty—the workers of the
arsenal and Karavayev's comrades, the artillerymen. The most surprising thing of all was that Staff Captain Ivanov took on himself
the lion's share of the losses. He was a thrifty man and had saved
several thousand rubles in his years of service at the arsenal. He
gave almost all of it to Karavayev.

I lived through the winter and the summer in this friendly
family of artillerymen. But the bitter taste of what I had lived
through in Kiev did not go away. I thought constantly about Mama
and my father, and I was sometimes ashamed to be living in a

warm and hospitable house where the mood was always equable and happy. I pictured to myself the cold Kiev basement, the empty table with crusts of bread, Mama's anxious face, Dima exhausted from his tutoring.

Mama wrote seldom, and Galya and Dima not at all. Sometimes it seemed to me that Mama did not write to me simply because she had no money for stamps. Something had to be done to help her, but I did not know what.

I could not get used to the Bryansk *gymnasium*. All the boys in my class were much older than I. I thought of my Kiev school more and more often with real regret and I wondered how I could return there.

In the end I wrote a letter to my classroom teacher, the Latinist Suboch. I told him frankly everything that had happened to me and I asked if I could come back. I received an answer quickly.

"For the new academic year, that is to say, in the autumn," Suboch wrote, "you are already enrolled back in the First *Gymnasium*, in my class, and you will be freed of any payment. As regards the material side of things, I can offer you several excellent tutoring jobs. They will make it possible for you to live modestly but independently and without feeling yourself a burden to anyone. Don't be grieved over what you have gone through—*tempora mutantur et nos mutamur in illis*—we must hope that we change for the better."

I read this businesslike letter, and a spasm gripped me in the throat. I understood the affection in it, and I also understood that from this minute, not hoping for anything from anyone, I was starting to build my own life.

This awareness was terrifying, although at that time I was already sixteen years old.

THE GREAT TRAGEDIAN KEAN

The walls of Bryansk were covered with yellow posters announcing the arrival of the actor Orlenev, on tour. The posters were printed on thin, rough paper. It was soaked through with paste. So the goats tore these posters down and chewed them up. Shreds of yellow paper with the words "genius . . . dissipation" hung out of the mouths of these ruminants. It was only on a few of the posters which had been left whole that one could read that Orlenev was coming to Bryansk to play the role of the English tragedian Kean in the play *Kean, or Genius and Dissipation*.*

Uncle Kolya bought tickets well in advance. For several days we talked of nothing at home except Orlenev. The performances were to be in the summer theater in the municipal park. This was an old wooden theater covered with peeling red paint. Posters had been stuck up on its walls for years and their rain-faded paper hung down in rags.

The theater was always boarded up. Bats would fly out from under its roof at twilight and swoop down the paths through the park. The girls in their white dresses would run in fright—there was a superstition that bats fastened on to anything that was white and that it was impossible to tear them loose.

The disused theater was a mysterious place. I was sure there were still dried-up flowers, boxes of grease paint, ribbons, and yellowed music scores in the empty theater and the actors' dressing rooms. They would have been left over from the days when a touring light opera company had played in the theater.

Young ladies with red cheeks and blue eyes had once run across those squeaking boards from their dressing rooms to the stage, holding up their velvet trains. Guitars had throbbed seductively under the fingers of insolent lovers, and the words of cruel love songs had wrenched the hearts of the simple townfolk:

* This play, by the elder Alexander Dumas, described the famous English Shakespearean actor Edmund Kean (1787–1833), whose heavy drinking led to his loss of mind.

I dreamed of the day which will never return,
And the man who won't come back . . .

This theater had seen everything: young gypsies with voices to
rend your heart, ruined gentry smelling of the sweat of their
horses—they had just galloped sixty miles to get to the concert of
some Nina Zagornaya, cavalry officers with black sideburns, merchants in brown dress coats, frightened brides in rose-colored
dresses as magnificent as spume from a waterfall.

My thoughts of the theater were linked to July nights, when
heat lightning flashed under the tops of the linden trees, when one's
head felt giddy, when there was nothing to be frightened of and
nothing to be sorry for in the songs of dissolute women or in fleeting love. When the whole world—eternal happiness or a lighthearted flirtation—could be found in one glance from a sweetheart's eyes. One glance under the sound of bells, or under the
whooping of a drunken coachman. One glance like a flash of
summer lightning in these heavy evenings filled with the fragrance
of the linden trees and the distant humming of the Bryansk forests
—pathless and impassable and turning the heart away from melancholy and betrayal.

The walls of the theater held the echoes of silenced voices and
the memories of reckless living, of abductions and duels, of stifled
sobs and burning hearts. It seemed as if the theater had died a long
time ago and been taken over by the cobwebs, as if no one would
ever play in it again.

But they opened it, cleaned it up, aired it, swept the carpeted
aisles, beat the dust out of the velvet upholstery of the seats, and
turned it from gray to cherry-red. A chandelier hung from the
ceiling. At first its ancient crystals sparkled uncertainly and dimly
but then, trembling with the first notes of the orchestra, they shot
out dozens of many-colored little stars.

Elderly ushers in white cotton gloves appeared at the doors.
There were the smells of perfume, of the freshness of the park, of
candy. There was the muffled humming of voices, the jingling of
spurs, the scrape of chairs, laughter, the rustling of programs—a
lyre with a garland of oak leaves was printed on their covers.

"Orlenev, Orlenev, Orlenev!" could be heard from all sides of
the theater.

Uncle Kolya sat in his box in his natty uniform with a black
velvet collar. Aunt Marusya was surrounded with an ashy brilliance: it came from her new dress, as gray as smoke, from her
hair, and her excited gray eyes—it had been a long time since she
had been in a theater.

Staff Captain Ivanov walked calmly down the aisle. Tiny spurs clinked on his sharp-pointed boots. Even Captain Rumyantsev had combed his red spade beard and dressed in evening clothes. He kept taking a handkerchief out of his back pocket and wiping his red face. The three Rumyantsev sisters sat in a row and their cheeks were flushed with excitement.

My two old friends from Ryovna showed up at the performance —Volodya Rumyantsev and Pavlia Tennov. Volodya sat in the gallery, even though there was a place for him in the orchestra— he was quarreling with his sisters. Pavlia Tennov sat with his crossed legs stuck out in front of him and with a condescending look on his face. He, who had studied in Peterburg, was not the man to be impressed by this performance!

In the box Aunt Marusya took me by the hand, straightened a wrinkle in my collar, examined my hair closely, and smoothed it.

"Well, now, everything's fine."

I looked at myself in the dim little mirror hanging at the back of the box. I was very pale and so childishly thin that it looked as if I might break apart.

The curtain rose, and the performance started.

I had seen good actors in Kiev, but here a short man with a sad, sharp-featured face performed a miracle on the stage in front of me. Every word opened wide the sick and beautiful soul of the great Kean. "They have wounded the deer with an arrow!" he cried out in his ringing voice, and with this one cry he transformed all the inescapable sorrow over his fate into compassion.

I was shaking all over when the play called for the actors to start a scandal in the auditorium itself. I couldn't hold back my tears when they lowered the curtain and the weeping old director, an Englishman, came out to the footlights and announced in a trembling voice that the performance could not go on because "the sun that shines over England, the great tragedian Kean, has gone out of his mind."

Aunt Marusya turned toward me, tapped me on the arm, and wanted to say something, probably something funny, but instead of this she gave a little shriek and stood up. Uncle Kolya turned around, too, and then stood up.

The whole theater was rocking with applause.

I turned around. There behind my back stood my father, just as tired as ever, with his old, tender, sad smile, but completely gray. Everything whirled in front of my eyes, then suddenly stopped, and became quiet and dark. My father grabbed me.

I hardly remember—or rather, I don't remember at all—what

happened after that. I recovered consciousness on a small divan in the back of the box. My collar had been unbuttoned. There was water on my chin, and Aunt Marusya was rubbing my temples with eau de cologne. My father raised me by the shoulders, sat down beside me, and kissed me.

"Sit for a while, don't move," he said. "It will go away quickly. Did you really not get my telegram?"

While the exhausted Orlenev was coming out to make his bows and receive the flowers flying toward the stage, my father told us quickly that he had got a new position at a factory making railroad cars at Bezhitsa. The village of Bezhitsa was only a few miles from Bryansk. He had just arrived, had found nobody at Uncle Kolya's home, and had followed us to the theater.

"How is Mama?" I asked.

"Mama?" my father repeated. "By the way, I've brought you a letter from her. Mama doesn't want to live in Bezhitsa. She is going to Moscow with Dima and she's thinking of settling there for good. She'll take Galya with her, of course."

"Did she say anything about me?"

My father thought for a moment.

"No, I don't think so. I saw very little of her. She probably wrote you everything. Read it."

He handed me the letter. The applause was still thundering around us. I read the letter quickly. It was short and dry. Mama wrote me that I should stay with Uncle Kolya until life got better for us. At the moment Mama could tell me nothing reassuring. She was getting ready to go to Moscow in a month's time, in July. I should stay in Bryansk for the summer, but if I wanted to I could live with my father in Bezhitsa. But everything would be better and simpler if I spent the summer in Bryansk. "On the way from Kiev to Moscow," Mama wrote, "we won't be able to stop over in Bryansk, unfortunately, but I'll send a telegram, so you can come to the station where we can see each other and talk over everything."

When I had finished reading the letter, Aunt Marusya, laughing, said to my father: "We won't give him up now to anybody. Not even to you, Georgi Maximovich."

"We won't give him for anything." Uncle Kolya said. "But we'll talk about this together, Georgi."

"Let's talk about it," my father agreed.

We walked through the municipal park to our carriage. Glowing lanterns hung among the trees. A military band was playing a march on an outdoor stage, as if rejoicing that the performance was over and that the trombones and the bugles could roar out again with all their strength.

We sat in the carriage. The horses pawed the ground and then started down the steep hill.

I was disheartened by Mama's letter. It left everything just as unclear as before. Obviously Mama had not made peace with my father. I couldn't understand why Mama wrote so coldly to me. Had she really started to forget me? Was I really not needed by anybody?

My father was talking eagerly with Uncle Kolya. Why didn't he ask me about anything? I could have told him many sad things. Maybe I would have cried and then everything would have felt better.

Everyone loved me in Uncle Kolya's home—he and Aunt Marusya and even all of his friends, but still I felt a heavy lump all the time in my heart. I had to hide my sorrow in order not to offend Uncle Kolya and Aunt Marusya.

I remembered what Suboch had written me: that I could soon stop being a burden to anyone. Something tightened inside me. Now it was all clear. It meant I *was* a burden to everyone. My father had his own life. Who knows, maybe he wasn't going to live alone in Bezhitsa.

And Mama? Why was Mama giving me up so easily? It must be because of Galya. Galya was going blind, and the doctors couldn't do anything for her. Mama was in despair about this. Galya's strange fate dominated all her thoughts. It must be that nothing was left in Mama's heart except this terrible sorrow for Galya.

A dusty moon hung over the town. The tin roofs looked wet in the moonlight. Aunt Marusya leaned toward me.

"Give me the letter, if I may read it."

I handed it to her.

She folded it into a narrow strip, slipped it slantwise under one of her kid gloves, and fastened the mother-of-pearl button over it.

My head ached. It was so bad that tears came to my eyes.

"What's the matter with you?" Aunt Marusya asked.

"My head aches terribly."

"You poor boy, everything has collapsed on you at once!"

At home they put me to bed. I lay there and listened to the conversation in the dining room, and to my father's voice. I was waiting for him to come in and say good night to me.

Fresh air drifted in the window and befogged my head. Drowsing, I heard Orlenev cry out in the next room in his desperate voice:

"They have wounded the deer with an arrow!" Then far away, at the very edge of the night, soft music was being played. It moved still farther away and grew softer, as if it were looking back at me and nodding its head.

Then Aunt Marusya said: "You have a weak boy there. Too much emotion for him." "Who has me?" I asked. "Go to sleep," Aunt Marusya's voice said, "I'm not going away from you. You pour yourself some tea." The teaspoons began to whirl faster and faster in the tea glasses. My head whirled with them and I began to fall. I fell for a long time and while I was falling I forgot everything.

I lay there in a fever for several days, with pain in my head. During this time my father went to Bezhitsa. As soon as I got well, Uncle Kolya and I went to see him.

Bezhitsa turned out to be a damp, boring little settlement. The ground was piled high with spongy slag from the factory's furnaces. Crooked birch trees grew in the backyards. The factory smoked. My father was living in an apartment in a wooden house which smelled of coal smoke. The furnishings were shabby. There was no one living in the apartment except my father.

We found him reading the encyclopedia. He was very glad to see us.

"I realize," he said to Uncle Kolya, "that it would be quite impossible for Kostik to live here: it would be boring, and unsettling, and very lonely. I myself am not going to stick it for long."

"And what are you thinking of doing?" Uncle Kolya asked him sternly.

"I'll go somewhere. Life hasn't worked out for me in general. It's all the same to me now. I'm to blame for it."

I looked at my father. He was no longer at all like what he had been in 1905, or long, long ago in Gorodishche, or in Gelendzhik, or in the artist Vrubel's hotel room. It was as if that other man had really been he, while this was his double—a failure.

ALONE ON THE BIG ROAD

At last came the days which brought the first signs of autumn.

There was an old apple orchard on the steep slope of a ravine behind Uncle Kolya's house. The hollow trunks of the apple trees and the curving fence around them were all covered with lichen. Almost no one ever went into the garden besides myself. I would go there with a notebook, lie down on the ground, and write poetry. As far as I can remember now, it was bad poetry. Everything in it was drowned in a dim sort of sadness.

Ants ran fussily along the lines of the poems, dragging a dried-up wasp. Dead twigs fell from the trees on to my notebook. A sky which was transparent in spite of its thickness glittered over the garden. The wind piled the clouds up over the Desna. I started to count them, got to two hundred, and then gave up. I was dazzled by them.

Autumn was announcing its arrival by the dry leaves scattered on the bench and by the little green caterpillar lowering itself on a thread straight onto my head. I was sorry to see summer go. Uncle Kolya had spent it in Bryansk. During the summer I had visited him often at the arsenal, either in his laboratory or in the machine shops. I loved to watch the steam hammer work. It was here that I heard Staff Captain Ivanov's story about the famous blacksmith in the Obukhovsky factory. He could handle a two-ton steam hammer so gently that he could crack a walnut on the bottom of a glass which had been turned upside down, without breaking the glass.

I loved the arsenal, its low-lying buildings built in the time of Catherine the Great, its courtyards overgrown with grass and filled with iron castings, the lilac along the walls of the workshops, the boilers of old steam engines shining with oily copper, the smell of alcohol in the laboratory, the bearded blacksmiths and foundry workers, and the fountain of bluish artesian water which came up out of the ground near the arsenal wall.

I had to say good-by to all of this, to Bryansk, to Uncle Kolya's comfortable home, and maybe say good-by for a long time.

That autumn I went back to Kiev. This was decided at a short family council at the Bryansk railroad station when Mama was on her way to Moscow with Galya and Dima. I went to the station with Uncle Kolya and Aunt Marusya to see Mama.

She had grown old and she talked to Uncle Kolya in a guilty voice, as if she were trying to justify something to him.

Galya was almost completely blind. In addition, she had begun to hear badly. She was wearing thick, double-lensed glasses. When someone addressed her, she looked around for a long time, trying to guess who was talking, and then she would answer irrelevantly. Dima was sullen and quiet.

Mama embraced me, then examined me from head to toe, and remarked that I looked much better than I had in Kiev. There was resentment in her voice.

I said I wanted to go back to Kiev and that I had been reinstated in the First *Gymnasium*. I would live with Borya and earn my living by tutoring.

Mama turned away and answered that she wanted very much to take me with her to Moscow but that this was impossible now. She had no idea herself how she was going to organize her life there.

Galya kept repeating:

"Kostik, where are you? Ah, here you are! I don't see you at all."

Aunt Marusya began to say, very quickly, that it was senseless to let me go back to Kiev, that maybe she understood nothing and had no right to mix in our family affairs but . . .

She stopped, noticing a warning look on Uncle Kolya's face. Mama made no answer. She was looking out of the train window at the platform. Her eyes grew dark with anger.

"At last!" Mama said. "Better late than never."

My father was walking along the platform. He had just arrived on a workers' train from Bezhitsa. He was wearing an old jacket, shiny with age. He came into the compartment. Just at that moment the station bell rang twice.

We all began to say good-by. My father kissed Mama's hand and said:

"Marusya, I'll be responsible for Kostik. Every month I'll send him enough to live on and for everything he needs."

"May God grant that you do! Don't forget even this, I beg of you."

Dima said good-by coldly to his father, and Galya, just like a blind person, stretched out her hand to him and tried to feel his face. My father turned so pale that even his eyes grew white.

We heard the third signal. We got out on the platform. Mama

said out of the window that she would surely come to see me in Kiev in the winter. The train started.

My father stood there, holding his hat, watching the racing wheels of the train. He didn't want to come back to Uncle Kolya's house, saying he had to catch the first train back to Bezhitsa where an urgent job was waiting for him.

We rode back to the house in a carriage. Uncle Kolya and Aunt Marusya were quiet on the way. Aunt Marusya was biting a little handkerchief. Then she looked at Uncle Kolya and said:

"No, I still don't understand. How this can be possible!"

Uncle Kolya frowned and motioned toward me with his eyes. Aunt Marusya said nothing more.

I was ashamed for all our family troubles, which were spoiling life not only for ourselves. I dreamed of how quickly I could get away to Kiev and forget all this disorder and unpleasantness. It would be better to be all alone than to live in this tangle of mutual resentment which exhausted and puzzled me.

I was waiting for August, when I would go to Kiev. It came at last. Rain was falling on the day I left, and the wind blew. The cars of the Moscow-Kiev train were lashed by the rain. My father didn't come to see me off, although he had promised to.

Uncle Kolya tried to make little jokes at the station. Aunt Marusya shoved an envelop into the pocket of my overcoat and said: "Read it on the way."

When the train started, she turned around. Uncle Kolya took her by the elbow and turned her back, face to the train. Aunt Marusya smiled to me, and turned around again.

The raindrops raced down the glass of the windows. Nothing could be seen through them. I opened the window and leaned out.

Uncle Kolya and Aunt Marusya were standing on the platform watching the train go by. Steam fell toward the ground. Far behind the train I could see a strip of blue sky. The sun was already shining there.

This seemed to me a good sign. I took the envelop out of my pocket. In it there was money, and a note.

"Take care of yourself. You are going out alone on the big road, so don't forget that you have an uncle and an aunt left in the provinces. They love you dearly and are always ready to help."

WILD ALLEY

Borya lived in a boarding house named Progress, on dirty Zhilyanskaya Street near the railroad station. He met me affably and protectingly.

"Good fellow," he said, "to decide to live on your own! Move in with me for a while. Then we'll find you some place better. It won't be worth while for you to live here."

"Why not?"

"You'll see."

I saw quickly enough. As soon as Borya had gone off to the Polytechnical Institute a puffy man with a face like a head of sour cabbage walked into the room. A dusty student's coat and green trousers with bags at the knees hung on him. His bulging, empty eyes slowly surveyed the room, the shelf where food was kept, and me.

"Count Pototsky!" the puffball introduced himself. "Your brother's closest friend. Former student at the Polytechnical Institute. No longer one because of an incurable disease."

"What's wrong with you?" I asked sympathetically.

"My disease defies description," Count Pototsky said, and he took a handful of Borya's cigarettes from a box on the table. "I suffer indescribably. Thanks to the disease, I failed Professor Paton's examinations for three years in a row. Do you know Paton?"

"No."

"A beast!" Count Pototsky said, and he picked up a sausage from the table and put it in his pocket. "The oppressor of all who are thirsty for success. The medicine for my disease is ordinary creosote. But my parents have held up the sending of money and, naturally, my funds on hand have run too low to let me go to the drugstore for the above-mentioned creosote. Would it be possible for you to think it over by tomorrow?"

"Think what over?" I asked, not understanding.

"Well, all right," Count Pototsky smiled cheerfully. "I'm tired of playing the clown! I wanted to ask Borya for three rubles, but I'm late. Perhaps you might find the sum?"

"Yes, of course!" I took my money hurriedly out of my pocket. "You need three rubles?"

"Ah, young man!" Pototsky sighed in distress. "If a lout asks you for a loan, he exaggerates what he needs, but an honest man understates it. If I had been, God forbid, a lout, I would have asked you for twenty rubles. But I'm asking for only three! You may ask: where is the truth? The truth, as always, is in the middle. Twenty minus three equals seventeen. Let's divide seventeen in two and we get eight and a half. A certain rounding of the figure will make it nine rubles. Simple and easy."

I held out to him ten rubles instead of nine. He took it in the strangest way. I didn't even see him take it. It was as if the money had melted in the air.

While Count Pototsky and I were talking, a door kept creaking in the room. But as soon as the money disappeared into the air the door flew open and a little woman in a peignoir flew into the room. The slippers on her feet slapped with every step. They were too big for her.

"Why?" she cried in a passionate voice. "Why give money to this barbarian? Give it to me!" she demanded through her teeth and she grabbed Count Pototsky by his jacket.

The sleeve of the jacket ripped.

The count tore free and escaped into the corridor. The woman threw herself after him. Her slippers made sounds like pistol fire.

"Give it to me!" she screamed. "At least three rubles! Or just two!"

But the count had descended the staircase with incredible speed and disappeared into the street. The woman in the peignoir leaned against the wall and began to sob in an unnatural, unpleasant voice.

Boarders began to look out of all the other rooms. This made it possible for me to see them all at once. The first to look out was a pimply young man in a lilac-colored shirt who was buttoning a pink celluloid collar to it.

"Madame Gumenyuk," he called out imperiously, "please take measures!"

The owner of the Progress boarding house, Madame Gumenyuk, came out into the corridor. She was a very big woman with affectionate, languid eyes. She walked up to the woman in the peignoir and said to her suddenly, in a very clear, vicious voice:

"March back to your room! Without any more scandal! And wait there for the police! I give you my sacred word as a woman!"

The woman in the peignoir walked calmly back into her own room. The corridor was full of noise for a long time, and of discussion of what had happened with Count Pototsky.

When Borya came back, I told him about everything. Borya said that I had got out of it pretty cheaply and he warned me never in the future to be caught by such tricks. Count Pototsky was not a count at all, nor even a former student, but a court attendant who had been discharged for drunkenness.

"They're all afraid of me," Borya pointed out. "But with a character like yours it would be best to avoid them. Only riffraff live here."

"Why do you live here?"

"I'm used to it. They don't bother me."

After a month Borya found me a room with board at the house of an old lady who was a friend of Mama's, Panna Kozlovskaya, in Wild Alley. I received some money from my father and I figured that even if he didn't send me any more I had enough to live on for three months without tutoring.

Nobody lived in Panna Kozlovskaya's apartment except herself and her son, an infantry lieutenant named Romuald. It was crowded with furniture, and its floors were slippery with bad paint. The windows looked out on a park where the trees had been cut down. There were only two or three trees left. In the winters they made a skating rink in this park. Little fir trees were stuck in snowdrifts at the edge of the rink. They turned yellow quickly. The rink was a cheap one, for little boys from Glubochitsa and Lvovskaya Streets. It did not even have a band, but a gramophone with an enormous lilac-colored horn played there.

Wild Alley was really wild. It didn't lead anywhere. It petered out in vacant lots which were covered with snow and piles of ashes. The ashes burned with a biting smoke. Fumes were always blowing off the vacant lots.

I decorated my little room with portraits of Byron, Lermontov, and Victor Hugo. In the evenings I lit a kitchen lamp which illuminated only the table and Hugo's portrait. The bearded writer sat there holding his head sadly in a hand which stuck out of a round starched cuff, and looked at me. It was as if he were saying: "Well, well, young man, what are you going to do now?"

I was entranced at that time by Hugo's *Les Misérables*. I liked old Hugo's stormy excursions into history even more than the story of the novel.

I read a great deal that winter. I found it hard to get used to solitude. Books helped me forget that I was alone. I often thought of our life on Nikolsko-Botanicheskaya Street, of Lena, of the cheerful artillerymen, of the fireworks in the old park at Ryovna, and of Bryansk. Everywhere I had been surrounded by many good-natured people. Now there were no people at all around me. Something in the lamp used to hum, and the noise made my loneliness worse.

But a month went by and then another and I got over the hump. I began to notice that the more unattractive reality looked, the more strongly I could feel all the good that was hidden in it.

I worked out in my head that good and bad exist together. What is good often shines brighter through layers of lies, poverty, and suffering. Often at the end of a bad day gray clouds will suddenly let through on a slant the light of the setting sun.

I looked for what was good in everything around me. And often, of course, I found it. It could shine out unexpectedly like Cinderella's crystal slipper from under her ragged gray dress, as an attentive and caressing look from her eyes might shine out somewhere on the street. "This is I," that look said. "Don't you really recognize me? Right now I'm turned into a pauper, but I will only have to throw away the rags to become a princess again. Life is full of the unexpected. Don't be afraid. Believe in this."

Vague ideas like this overwhelmed me during that winter.

I was at the beginning of the road to life, but it seemed to me that I already knew the whole road. I read Fet's poems. They seemed to fit what I thought was awaiting me:

From the kingdom of storms, from the kingdom of ice and snow,
How fresh and clean your May leaps out!

I used to read these lines out loud. Panna Kozlovskaya listened behind her wall. Lieutenant Romuald always came home late and sometimes didn't spend the night at home at all. Panna Kozlovskaya was bored, and the sound of any man's voice made her happy.

THE AUTUMN BATTLE

After my return from Bryansk, both teachers and students greeted me at the *gymnasium* just as affably as Borya. Even the priest Tregubov produced some appropriate and edifying words for the occasion about the return of the prodigal son.

Suboch questioned me in the most detailed way about how I had organized my life, and promised to get me tutoring assignments in a month's time. Inspector Bodyansky made that extraordinary noise with his nose—it was a little like a snore—with which he used to frighten all young "swarmers," and said:

"You are guilty, but you deserve indulgence. Go back to your class and sin no more!"

But I was destined to sin again.

Every class in our high school was divided into two groups, the first and the second. The first section was considered to be aristocratic, the second democratic. The first section was made up primarily of blockheads—the sons of generals, of landowners, of important officials, and of financiers. In our second section were the children of the intelligentsia, of middle-class officials, of Jews, and of Poles. It was clear that the division was made deliberately, and on orders from on high.

The enmity between the first and second sections never died down. It was usually expressed in mutual contempt. But once a year, in the autumn, it produced a traditional battle between the first and second sections of all the classes. Only the swarmers and the *gymnasium* boys in their final year did not take part in this battle. The latter already thought of themselves as grownups, almost university students, and they would have lost face by fighting. And there were also some autumns when no battle at all took place.

The day of the battle changed from year to year. This was done to confuse our vigilant supervisors. But there were certain signs which let them know that the great day was approaching. They would start to grow nervous, trying with all their cunning to prevent the battle: sometimes after the first lesson they would release whichever class was suspected of being the instigators of the fight; sometimes they would send two or three classes off on an excursion to the art museum; sometimes they would close all the entrances to the park where the battle usually took place.

But not even the most ingenious devices saved them. The fight always started on the appointed day, and always during the main recess.

Some high school boys were "released from the battle." They were the sick ones, those with no physical strength, and those who felt an aversion not only to fighting but even to the usual rows which students have with each other. They were all released freely: they wouldn't have been of any use in any case. I was released for the last of these reasons.

The nonparticipants were required to wear no sashes during the battle. By an iron rule of *gymnasium* fighting, nobody might touch a boy who was not wearing a sash. The boys who were released always preferred to watch the fighting from the classroom windows instead of going out—you could see much better from there.

The battle always began with a sudden and ominous silence in the *gymnasium* buildings. The corridors were emptied in a wink of the eye. All the boys streamed out into the park.

Then a hollow, threatening rumble started. It always made the inspector Bodyansky turn pale and cross himself. Hundreds of chestnuts, whistling like buckshot, flew through the clouds of dust raised by the ranks of boys falling on each other.

All the proctors—Kasimir, Maxim Cold Water, and several others—ran at a trot into the park. Behind them, elbowing each other, went the frightened supervisors. Doors slammed. The corridors were filled with the excited voices of teachers. Inspector Bodyansky, pulling on his coat and his hat with its cockade as he ran, tore down the stairs, hurrying to the scene of the battle.

Once the priest Olendsky hurried down to the park right after Bodyansky. We leaned out of the windows, eager to watch how Olendsky would hold his crucifix over his head and challenge the enemy camps to make peace. But instead of this Olendsky rolled up the sleeves of his soutane and began to pick up fighting boys and throw them to one side. He did this with extraordinary skill. The boys tumbled away from him like tennis balls. Olendsky must have been remembering his childhood. Puffing a little, the priest came back from the park into the teachers' room. Judging by his flushed and happy face, his part in the battle, even as a peacemaker, must have given him great satisfaction.

As soon as the battle started, all the spare exits from the park were quickly opened. This was a military trick. It made it possible for the guards and the supervisors, after they had separated struggling schoolboys, to drive them in groups toward these exits.

"It's started in the First *Gymnasium!*" little boys shouted on the street outside.

It was hard to be sure from the windows just what was happening and what was starting. Dust swirled up and coated the branches of the trees. Cries could be heard, and a dull hammering, as if a herd of elephants had turned against each other in the park, stamping their feet.

Then a soaring shout of victory, rising above all the other noise, resounded through the empty corridors, climbed, ascended, turned into a roar like thunder. This meant that the second section had triumphed, and that the first section was in flight. There is not an instance in my memory when the first section won the battle.

Almost always in the front ranks of the conquerors was a high school boy with a perky, turned-up nose—the future writer Mikhail Bulgakov.* He tore into the fighting at the most dangerous places. Victory always followed him, and crowned him with a golden wreath of his own disordered hair. The blockheads of the first section were afraid of Bulgakov and tried to discredit him. After one battle they spread the story that he had used an illegal weapon— a metal belt buckle. But nobody ever believed this slander, even Inspector Bodyansky.

This one time I took part in the battle, because I had to square accounts with a boy named Khavin, the son of a broker on the Kiev exchange. He was a tall, straggling boy who tried slyly to use the word "sacramental" in almost every sentence, in spite of the fact that he spoke with a burr. Sitting in the theater, he would blow languid kisses through the air to girls he knew. He was driven to school in his own carriage and he was filled with scorn for us, the sons of middle-class fathers.

It was all on account of Panna Kozlovskaya. The old lady could hardly see, and she was afraid to go out on the streets alone. So I took her to church almost every Sunday. Panna Kozlovskaya was embarrassed at bothering me, never tired of apologizing for it, and blushed like a young girl in her confusion over it.

Usually I held her arm, so that she wouldn't bump into people. Sometimes Lieutenant Romuald would take my place, but this happened seldom. I suspected that the lieutenant was ashamed of his

* A. F. Bulgakov (1891–1940), Soviet playwright and novelist, was best known for his play *The Days of the Turbins*. He was born in Kiev and graduated from the medical school of Kiev University.

old mother, her old-fashioned coat, and her helplessness. In any case, the lieutenant was nearly always "devilishly busy" on Sunday mornings.

One Sunday I was taking Panna Kozlovskaya to a church on Mikhailovskaya Street. Khavin met us. He raised his eyebrows and looked at me, frowning. His face expressed a scornful bewilderment. Then he slowly looked Panna Kozlovskaya over from head to feet, smiled, snapped his fingers loudly, whistled, and walked on.

When the battle began, I walked out into the park. Khavin was standing on one side. He was not wearing a sash; he had been "released." I was also "released" and was also without a sash. But I walked up to Khavin and slapped his face hard.

Khavin squeaked in a funny way. The supervisor Shponka grabbed me by the arm. The next day Inspector Bodyansky summoned me to his office.

"What's this all about?" Bodyansky asked. "I could understand it if you had been fighting in the regular way, like all our Hottentots. But, begging your pardon, just to slap a man in the face? What for?"

"I had a reason. I've never been a fighter in my life, Pavel Petrovich. You know that."

"So, so. You're running a risk that in the second half-year you may not be released from tuition fees. Why did you hit him?"

I shut up, and did not want to tell why I had hit Khavin.

"It was worth it. You can believe me or not, Pavel Petrovich, but I'm not going to say any more."

"I believe you," Bodyansky said. "You may go. And let's allow this little incident to sink into oblivion."

After every battle Bodyansky had to make unpleasant explanations to the guardians of our educational district and to the parents of the battered blockheads.

"This is what happens when people don't have a Tsar inside their heads," Bodyansky would tell us angrily. "But you still read your crazy Ibsens and your Andreyevs! The education of our youth! The future pillars of society! Zulus and troglodytes!"

LIVING LANGUAGES

Latin was the only dead language we studied in high school. It was a major subject. It was taught by our classroom teacher, Vladimir Faddeyevich Suboch, who looked like a thin, rangy cat with light whiskers. He was a good man and we liked him although he sometimes gave us sudden and impetuous assignments which were disastrous for our entire Latin class.

Bodyansky also followed very closely our progress in Latin, and he loved to repeat: "The pronunciation of Latin is the greatest phenomenon in all language study."

Greek was not obligatory. Only a few studied it. The teacher was an elderly Czech named Pospeshil who was dusted all over with tobacco ash. He used to walk slowly along the corridors on sick, swollen legs, and was always late to class. Among the living languages we studied French and German. These lessons were boring.

The Frenchman, Sermout, had only one arm. He wore a pointed red beard in the style of King Henry IV. Under one arm he carried large colored oleographs which he hung up on the walls. These prints showed the happy life of rural people of some unknown nationality at different seasons of the year. In the spring these people plowed the earth in straw hats with many-colored ribbons, while their red-cheeked wives, laced up in tight bodices, fed some yellow chickens. In the summer they made hay and danced around the haystacks, waving wreaths of roses. In the autumn they threshed grain around their toy cabins, and in the winter, obviously for lack of anything else to do, they skated on a frozen river.

But even these pictures of farmers were much more interesting than some of the others which showed uninteresting, too-geometrical rooms with a few pieces of furniture and a cat playing with a ball of wool.

Sermout spread out the prints, took a pointer in his good hand, pointed to the farmers dancing with their sickles or to the cat, and asked, in a loud voice, in French:

"What do we see in this interesting picture?"

We answered in a chorus, and in French, that we could clearly see in this picture some peasants or a quite small kitten playing with the thread of a nice old lady.

This endless game with pictures lasted for two long years until one day the inspector led into our room not Sermout but a new teacher, Monsieur Govasse. Monsieur Govasse had only just arrived in Russia. He did not speak a word of Russian. His first teaching assignment in this mysterious country happened to be with our class.

Monsieur Govasse came from Brittany. He was a very short, fat man with such a good disposition that he never even took the trouble to get angry with us. The inspector introduced him to us, and walked out. Then Régamé, a French pupil, stood up and told Monsieur Govasse politely and in a magnificent Parisian accent that it was the custom in Russia to pray before each lesson. Monsieur Govasse accepted this with a superior smile, obviously thinking that every country has its own peculiar customs.

Then it was the turn of Littauer, another pupil. He was a Jew but he knew the Orthodox service perfectly. He walked over and stood in front of the icon, crossed himself with a flourish, and began the "prayer before the class": "We pray to Thee, O gracious Lord, send us the blessing of your holy spirit, enriching and strengthening our spiritual resources." He recited this prayer five times, then he recited another, and after this, he ran through the Credo, Our Father, and began to recite the prayer of Efrem Sirin.

Monsieur Govasse stood there with his head politely lowered, understanding nothing.

"O Lord, master of my life!" Littauer went on. "Save me from the spirit of sloth, despondency, the desire to dominate, and empty talk."

We repeated the words of each prayer in a chorus and kept looking at the clock. There were only ten minutes left before the end of the class. We were all afraid that Littauer would run out of prayers before the ten minutes were up. But Littauer did not let us down. He recited the Symbol of Faith a second time and wound up the class with a triumphal recital of the prayer, "O Lord, save your people."

The bell rang, and Monsieur Govasse, shrugging his shoulders a little, went off to the teachers' room. His black jacket was shining in the sunlight as it swam glossily down the corridor.

We collapsed in laughter, hiding behind the raised lids of our desks, but in a minute the inspector Bodyansky walked into the room, sighing deeply, and shouted at us:

"Buffoons! Now you stoop to blasphemy, you good-for-nothings! Who organized this prayer meeting? Probably you, Littauer?"

"What are you saying?" Littauer asked as he stood up. "You know I am Jewish, Pavel Petrovich."

"Oy, oy, oy!" Bodyansky said. "Jewish! An interesting excuse! As if I believed that your hand would wither if you crossed yourself! Collect your books and go home at once. On the way you can ponder over the unhappy fact that you now have a second failing mark in conduct."

Under Monsieur Govasse we sank into the debris of irregular French verbs and conjugations. A magnificent language was transformed into a tangled set of rules. We floundered among mysterious accents, all those *accents aigus* and *accents graves* and *accents circonflex*. Gradually the living language of Flaubert and Hugo became for us something quite divorced from what Monsieur Govasse was teaching us.

But the older we grew the more we loved French literature and we tried to read French writers in the original. To do this we learned the language by ourselves or with the help of private tutors, washing our hands of our phlegmatic Breton. He went right on conjugating and declining and looking out of the window at the cold white snow falling from a Russian sky. And nothing was to be seen in Monsieur Govasse's eyes except a longing for the warmth of a fireplace.

We tried to talk to him about Balzac and Dumas, about Hugo and Daudet, but Monsieur Govasse either kept silent or told us that this literature was for grownups, not for little Russian boys who did not yet know the difference between the future and the conditional tenses.

It became known in the course of time that Monsieur Govasse had a small stone house and an old mother in a little town in Brittany, and that Monsieur Govasse had come to Russia solely in order to earn a round sum of money in a few years so that he could return to his home where his mother bred rabbits. Monsieur Govasse planned to grow mushrooms for sale in Paris—this promised to be a profitable business. So Monsieur Govasse was not in the slightest interested in Russia, nor in French literature.

Monsieur Govasse really talked with us only once. It was in the spring. He had been getting ready to go home to Brittany for the summer vacation; this explained his good disposition. He made some bad jokes and told us that man had been created to live without strong emotions. This was why it was necessary to obey rules and to be content with little.

Then he told us how he had caught lobsters with his grandfather when he was a little boy. He sighed, and grew thoughtful. The chestnut trees were in blossom outside the windows. Spring was wandering down the corridor in a light breeze, blowing into our faces with its young girl's breath. Monsieur Govasse looked at spring, and shook his head sadly—life had thrown him into the foreign world as the wind blows a fat ladybug off a green leaf. And all because he was not rich and was forced to pay for a quiet future by his boring job.

"Yes," Monsieur Govasse said, "that's the way life is! Let us be patient. Let's not rebel against fate, or against God. Patience pays off. Isn't that so?"

No one answered him, because at that time we were all convinced that patience was a kind of idiocy.

Many years later I told my friend the writer Arkadii Gaidar how Monsieur Sermout had taught us French with colored oleographs. Gaidar was delighted, because he had learned French in the same way. Memories began to sweep through Gaidar. For several days on end he talked to me only about Sermout's method.

We were living then near Ryazan, and we used to walk a good deal, fishing in the lakes.

"What do we see in this picture?" Gaidar asked me suddenly in French during our wanderings one day, and he answered it himself: "We see an inhospitable village, being approached by two travelers. We see farmers who are not willing to trade these travelers three eggs for a handful of tobacco."

When we were going back to Moscow on the deserted little railroad line from Tuma to Vladimir, Gaidar woke me in the night and asked: "What do we see in this interesting picture?"

I couldn't see anything because the candle in the lantern was flickering badly, sending shadows racing across the compartment.

"We see," Gaidar explained, "a railroad thief who is now taking a pair of warm Russian boots out of the basket of a respectable old woman."

With these words, Gaidar—an enormous, good-natured man— jumped out of his upper berth, grabbed the collar of a nimble young man wearing a checked cap, took the boots away from him, and said:

"Get out of here! And don't let me ever catch sight of you again!"

The frightened thief jumped out onto the platform between the cars and dove headfirst from the moving train. This was, I suppose, the only practical application in history of Monsieur Sermout's method.

Our German lessons were more interesting than the French. This was not because Oscar Fedorovich Johanson was a model teacher, but because we sometimes concerned ourselves in his classes with things that were far from the German language. Most often of all, Oscar Fedorovich would set us to copying the score of his opera, *The Spirit of Tokay Wine*.

Johanson was an elderly, nervous Viennese. He always came to class with a wooden chair leg. When disorder reached an intolerable level, Johanson would pick up the chair leg and begin to hit his desk with all his strength. It restored order quickly.

Johanson both knew and loved music. He had started out to be a composer but some unhappy chapter in his life had made this impossible, and with disgust he became a teacher. He required from us only the most minimal knowledge of the German language. Whenever one of us would fail to answer a question, Johanson would look at him for a long time over his pince-nez, sigh deeply, and put down a mediocre but passing mark.

Once, when I was already in my sixth year, Johanson lost the manuscript of his opera in a trolley. This was the only copy. He put an advertisement in the papers, but no one returned the opera. For a whole week Johanson did not even come to school, and when he did come we hardly recognized him. He had grown gray, and his yellow neck was wrapped up in a yellow muffler. There was a deep silence that day in Johanson's class.

"Well, well, young men," Johanson said to us, "everything is finished! This opera was the work of my whole life. I became younger while I was writing it. Every page lifted years from me. Yes! That is how it was! For it was the music of happiness. That was what I was writing about. Where is happiness? Everywhere! In the noise the forest makes. In the leaves of an oak tree, in the smell of wine barrels. In the voices of women, and birds. Everywhere. I dreamed of being a wandering singer, without this teacher's uniform. I envied the gypsies. I would have sung at village weddings, and in the homes of foresters. I would have sung for lovers and single people, for heroes and poets, for the disappointed and for those who have not lost their faith in what is good. All this was in my opera. All of it! I thought that I might die in peace if I could only see it produced in Vienna. Perhaps, I thought, my friend, the poet Peter Altenberg, would come and sit like a bear in his upholstered seat, and tears would come into his eyes. That would be the highest reward for me. And perhaps that music might even have been heard by the one person who never believed in me . . ."

Johanson went on talking, looking at his thin fingers. It was as if he were drunk with grief. He always talked a little elegantly and theatrically, but this time we didn't notice it. We sat there with downcast eyes.

During recess after the lesson Suboch came up to us.

"I wanted to warn you," he said when we were all around him, "to treat Oscar Fedorovich with special care today. But then I thought that you would guess it without any help from me."

On that same day, in every class in the school, the challenge was given: "Find that opera! Find it whatever it costs!" Who started it, I don't know. It went from mouth to mouth. We assembled in little groups and planned our search. We walked around like conspirators. Impatience was bubbling up in each of our hearts.

The search began. We cross-examined the conductors of all the trolleys. We ransacked the markets. We burrowed in the stores of old paper merchants. And finally the opera was found in Lukyanovsky market. A pupil in the eighth class saw it on the counter of a lard merchant. The merchant complained that the paper wasn't any good for wrapping—the inked lines came off on the lard and purchasers complained. This was the reason why there were only three pages missing.

The manuscript was returned to Johanson during his eighth-year class. We did not see this take place. We only saw how he walked down the corridor afterward, surrounded by pupils. He was without his pince-nez. He walked unsteadily, stumbling. The eighth-year pupils were holding him up. Inspector Bodyansky was standing in the doorway of the teachers' room, smiling and nodding his head. He threw his arms around Johanson, and they kissed each other.

For a few days there was complete confusion in the *gymnasium*. Johanson distributed the score of the opera together with clean sheets of music paper. We made several copies of the entire opera.

This was toward the end of winter, and in the spring I received a piece of cardboard through the mail. On it was written that Oscar Fedorovich Johanson requested the honor of my presence at a performance of selections from his opera which would take place at the apartment of one of my classmates.

I went to the apartment, on Bibikovsky Boulevard, on the evening of the performance. The wide staircase in my friend's house was brightly lighted. Two large rooms were full of people. They were mostly pupils from our *gymnasium*, but there were some girls from the Marinskaya *Gymnasium* and some gray-haired musicians and some actors.

Johanson was not yet there. I stood at the entrance to one of the rooms and watched the brightly lighted stairway. Finally Oscar Fedorovich appeared and bounded up the stairs—he looked thin, much younger, in an elegant black evening coat. He walked quickly into the main room and everyone applauded.

The music began right away. A quartet played, accompanied by a piano. And it really was music about happiness, and about the suffering of lovers like the anguish of Tristan and Isolde. I can't begin to describe the melodious quality of the music, or its strength.

When the music had finished and most of the guests had gone home, after congratulating Johanson, those of us who had stayed were invited into the dining room. It was late at night when we accompanied Johanson home. On the way he walked into the telegraph office and sent a telegram to Vienna. When he came out, he was a little sad, and he said that he had waited for this day too long. And when you wait too long, then happiness turns into a kind of sorrow.

"MESSRS. GYMNASIUM *PUPILS"*

Who could know what would come of us "Messrs. *Gymnasium* pupils," as Bodyansky called us? What would come of these young boys in faded caps, always ready for any kind of prank, joke, or fight? What, for example, would come of Bulgakov? Nobody could have known.

Bulgakov was older than I, but I remember very well his impetuous liveliness, his merciless tongue which everyone feared, and the sense of determination and strength which could be felt in every word he spoke.

Bulgakov was full of tricks, jokes, and mystification. He transformed school customs we had learned by heart into a world of improbable events and persons. Any colorless supervisor like Shponka, once he had been involved in Bulgakov's imagination, grew to the dimensions of a Tartarin de Tarascon. He would begin to live a second, mysterious life, no longer as Shponka with a puffy, alcoholic nose, but as the hero of uproarious, miraculous happenings. By the tricks he thought up, Bulgakov moved the people around him from their real world out to the very edge of another world of almost fantastic exaggeration.

I did not meet Bulgakov again, after the *gymnasium,* until 1924, when he was already a writer. He always wrote honestly about Kiev. In his play, *The Days of the Turbins,* I could recognize the vestibule of our *gymnasium* and the proctor Maxim Cold Water —an honest, boring old man. Behind the scenes of the theater I could hear the rustling of our Kiev chestnut trees in autumn.

Several young fellows studied at almost the same time with me who later became well-known writers, actors, and playwrights. Kiev was always a city with a passion for the theater.

Was it an accident that this *gymnasium* produced in a short time so many people who were attracted to art and literature? I think not. (It was not for nothing that Suboch used to tell us, when we were "accidentally" late for class: "There is nothing accidental in life except death." Having uttered this maxim, Suboch would give the late pupil a bad mark for conduct.)

It was, of course, no accident. The reasons are so numerous and so hard to define that we are too lazy to search for them and we prefer to think that everything happened by some happy accident.

We forget about those teachers who nurtured our love for culture, about the magnificent Kiev theaters, about our attraction to philosophy and poetry, about the fact that Chekhov and Tolstoy, Serov and Levitan, Scriabin and Komissarzhevsky were still alive when we were boys.* We forget about the 1905 revolution, about the students' meetings which we schoolboys schemed to get into, about the quarrels of our elders, about the fact that Kiev was always a city with a great tradition of revolution.

We forgot how avidly we read Plekhanov, Chernishevsky, and the illegal pamphlets printed on crumbly gray paper with slogans: "Workers of the world, unite!" or "Land and Freedom." We read Herzen and Kropotkin, the Communist Manifesto, and the novels of the revolutionary Kravchinsky. In the newspaper *The Thought of Kiev* we liked the articles which were signed by "Homo Novus."

---

* V. A. Serov (1865–1911) was a neo-realistic artist and portrait painter. I. I. Levitan (1861–1900) was an Impressionist painter famed for his landscapes. Alexander N. Scriabin (1871–1915) was a famous Russian pianist and composer. Theodore Komissarzhevsky (1882–1954) was a Russian theatrical producer and director, one of the most famous pupils of Stanislavsky.

It was much later that I learned that this was Lunacharsky's pseudonym.*

But even this disorderly reading bore its fruit.

We forget about Idzikovsky's famous bookstore on the Kreshchatik, about the symphony concerts, about the parks of Kiev, about the autumns with their shining, crackling leaves, about the solemn, noble Latin which kept us company through all our school years. We forget about the Dnieper, about the soft foggy winters, the rich and tender Ukraine circling the city with fields of buckwheat, thatched roofs, and gardens full of bees.

It is hard to measure the influence of these things, so different and sometimes so remotely connected with each other, on our youthful consciousness. But it was there. It gave a special poetic structure to all our thoughts and all our feelings.

We were carried away by poetry and literature. But an understanding of Russian literature, in all its classical clarity and depth, came to us later than our understanding of the lighter literature of the West. We were young, and Western writing attracted us by its elegance, its calm, and the perfection of its design. The cold and gloomy Mérimée was easier for us than the tortured Dostoievsky. Everything in Mérimée or Flaubert was as clear as a summer morning, while Dostoievsky came on us like a thunderstorm with all its terror and a desire to hide under any sheltering roof. And Dickens knew no doubts. Nor Hugo. Nor Balzac.

It may well be that the cheap little yellow books of the "Universal Library" were to blame for our passion for Western literature. In those days they flooded the bookstores. For twenty kopecks one could read *Mount Oriole* or *Eugénie Grandet* or *The Wild Duck* or *La Chartreuse de Parme*. We read them all avidly.

At one time I was especially attracted by French poets—Verlaine, Leconte de Lisle, and Théophile Gautier. We read them in the original and in translations. The French language, sometimes so light that you couldn't catch it, like a distant fragrance, sometimes as hard as metal, sounded in their poems like sorcery.

* G. V. Plekhanov (1857–1918) was the founder of Russian philosophic Marxism, a friend and colleague of Lenin until 1914, an opponent of the Bolshevik Revolution. N. G. Chernishevsky (1828–1889), writer and political leader, was closer to Herzen and to the *narodniks* than to Marx in his political views, but he is now regarded as a major revolutionary by the Soviets. Prince Peter Kropotkin (1842–1921) was a leading theorist of anarchism. S. M. Kravchinsky (1852–1895), better known under his pen name of Stepniak, was also in the revolutionary movement, supporting terrorist action, until he was obliged to leave Russia in 1880. A. V. Lunacharsky (1875–1933), who was born in Kiev, was a leading Soviet educational theorist and administrator from 1917 until his death.

This poetry captured us not only by its melody and its vague-ness, like springtime smoke, but also by its pictures of the poets themselves, and of Paris. This poetry was only one of many alluring things connected with Paris. Slate roofs, the ring of boulevards, rain, lights, the Pantheon, the rose-colored night sky over the Seine, and—finally—these poems. This was how Paris took shape in our naïve imaginations. It was as unthinkable without the poetry as without barricades, or kisses.

But it was not long before I realized that the attraction of French poetry for me was cold and glittering, while right beside it was the gold mine of living, pure Russian poetry. We grew up, and little by little the powerful literature of Russia, perhaps the greatest in the world, possessed our hearts, and pushed back into second, if respectable, place the literature of the West.

We were attracted to painting as well as literature. The names of prize winners and of famous men who had studied in our *gymnasium* were written in golden letters on a marble plaque in the assembly hall. Among them was the artist Ge.* The dark tone and the moralizing of his pictures kept us from appreciating him, even though he was an older schoolmate. The new taste for Im-pressionism was just beginning in our time.

My classmate Shmukler was preparing to be an artist. He studied painting with the Kiev Impressionist, Manevich. I liked Manevich's pictures very much—little houses and courtyards in small towns, painted thickly, almost with a house-painter's strokes.

I often visited Shmukler's apartment. It was what was called an artistic home. His father, who was widely known in the city as a doctor uninterested in money, had dreamed in his youth of be-coming an opera singer. For some reason, this never worked out. But his passion for opera was still the most important thing in Dr. Shmukler's life.

Everything in his apartment was operatic, not only the owner, a powerful, clean-shaven, loud-spoken man, but the piano, the hand-written scores spread out on it, the flower vases, the posters, the portraits of famous singers, and the mother-of-pearl opera glasses. Even the noise, which was never stilled in the doctor's home, was operatic. Shouts at the children and angry quarrels blended with trills and runs, recitatives, *moderato*, *allegro* and *forte*, with duets and trios, with men's, women's and children's arias all interrupting one another, and there was a kind of melody

* N. N. Ge (1831–1894) was a painter, a precursor of the Impressionists, who was much influenced by Tolstoy's religious views.

hidden in all this noise. Voices from the Shmuklers' apartment always sounded loud and free, like *bel canto*, and carried up and down the main staircase of their building.

I went there often, but I preferred the little room of another of my classmates, a Pole named Fitsovsky. Like me, he lived alone. He was a sturdy boy, with a light-brown lock of hair falling over his forehead, always incredibly steady. He treated all problems as if they were unimportant details.

He had his own eccentricities which irritated his teachers. For instance, he could converse with the boy at the next desk, a merry fellow named Stanishevsky, in the most beautiful Russian but in such a way that not one word could be understood. He did this by a simple method. Fitsovsky put the accent on the wrong syllable in every word, and spoke quickly.

Fitsovsky induced me to learn the international language, Esperanto. This colorless language, dreamed up by a Warsaw dentist named Zamengof, had only one virtue: it was easy. It was not a language, but a weightless husk unlike any other language in the world. A good many newspapers were printed in it in different countries. What interested me in these papers was the addresses of people who wanted to exchange letters in Esperanto.

I began, following Fitsovsky's example, to write back and forth with people in England, France, Canada, and even Uruguay. I sent them post cards with views of Kiev, and in exchange I got post cards with pictures of Glasgow, Edinburgh, Paris, Montevideo, and Quebec. I began gradually to make distinctions among my correspondents. I began to ask them to send me portraits of writers and illustrated magazines. This is how I got my beautiful portrait of Byron, sent me by a young English doctor from Manchester, and my portrait of Victor Hugo. This was sent to me by a young French woman from Orléans. She was a very curious correspondent, who wrote me a mass of questions: Was it true that Russian priests wore clothes made out of gold leaf, and did all Russian officers speak only French?

Every week we used to organize drinking parties in Fitsovsky's room. The thing we did least at these parties was to drink: our money would suffice for only one bottle of brandy. But we played at being Lermontov's Hussars, we read poetry, we quarreled, we made speeches, and we sang.

We did this until dawn. Every sunrise, pouring into the smoke-filled room, looked to us like the dawn of a wonderful life waiting for us on the threshold. The spring sunrises were the best of all. In the clean morning air the birds sang, and our heads were full of romance.

This amazing life which was waiting for us on the threshold was inextricably connected with the theater. We were especially entranced that year with Russian plays, and with an actress named Polevitskaya. She played Lisa in *A Nest of Gentlefolk* and Nastasya in *The Idiot.*

We were allowed to go to the theater only with permission from the inspector Bodyansky. He would not give us more than one permission in a week. So we began to forge permissions. I signed them for Bodyansky, and I copied his handwriting so well that Bodyansky could only shake his head when the supervisors showed him permissions taken from the pupils. He could never distinguish the real from the false signatures, and he would say: "I'll tie these theatergoers up to a ram's horn! They need to learn Latin, not to hang around theater galleries. You're all counterfeiters, and not the sons of your respected parents."

We would wait for Polevitskaya after each performance at the actors' exit. She would walk out, tall, clear-eyed. She would smile at us, and get into her sleigh. The bells would ring. Their sound would carry down Nikolayevskaya Street and disappear in the snow at the end of it.

We would scatter to go home, and the snow would fall and fall. Our cheeks would be aflame. Our young and passionate happiness would race along with us on the slippery pavements, accompanying us, not letting us sleep for a long time. This happiness would move across the walls of my room, in the light of the night lantern. It would rain down to the earth in drifts of snow. It would sing all night, through warm sleep, an eternal song of love and sadness.

The sleigh runners whistled outside the window. Fast horses galloped past. Whom were they carrying, and where, on a night like this?

In Lieutenant Romuald's room, the guitar made a sound all by itself. The humming of its strings lasted for a long time. It grew thinner and thinner until it was like a silver hair, then like a silver cobweb. Then it was silent.

Thus the winter went by, in happy excitement, in the bustle of days when life is braided so tightly with poetry that it is impossible to tear one from the other. I was living then completely alone, earning money by tutoring. The money was enough for food and books, and at that time I had no sense, perhaps because of my youth, of any burden or any fear.

THE HOOK-NOSED KING

Whenever any high dignitary visited Kiev, it was obligatory to show him our *gymnasium*. It was one of the oldest in Russia. The officials were proud of the history of the school and also of its immense, uncomfortable building. The only adornment of the whole building was its assembly hall decorated with marble in two colors. It was always cold there, even in summer.

We liked the visits of important people because nearly every one of them requested the director to release the pupils from lessons for a day or two to commemorate his visit. The director always expressed thanks for the honor, and agreed. We would hurriedly pack our books in our bags and swarm out into the street.

But not all the visits of great men were carried off so smoothly. Sometimes there was trouble. One unfortunate experience occurred on the visit of Peter Karageorge, the King of Serbia. We knew that he had ascended the throne after a bloody palace revolt and that he had connived at the enslavement of the Balkan peoples by Austria.

Director Tereshchenko, whom we called "Butter Churn," was supposed to make a short welcoming speech to the king in French. Monsieur Govasse wrote the text of the greeting. He was very proud of it; this was the first time the high honor of writing a greeting to a king had fallen to his lot.

The director memorized the greeting. In this he had to compete with us, but Butter Churn was known for his bad memory. He was afraid he would forget it when he stood face to face with Peter Karageorge.

The director grew nervous. He insisted that our new inspector, Varsonify Nikolayevich Ivanov (Bodyansky had just been appointed director of the Third *Gymnasium*), give him the services of the best prompter among the pupils. We didn't like Butter Churn and refused to name our best prompter: let Butter Churn look after himself. The best prompter—and a Frenchman to boot—was Régamé, who was in our class. He listened imperturbably to the

inspector's request, along with the rest of us, and only smiled
politely.

In the end we gave in. We promised to supply a prompter but
only in exchange for correction of an unfair mark in mathematics
which had been given to a meek classmate named Borimovich.
Ivanov promised to raise his mark. An agreement was reached.
Régamé wrote out the text of the greeting on a crib. It began with
the words: "Sire, permettez à nous . . ." and went on. In Russian,
it came out something like: "Sire, allow us to greet you in the gray
walls of our famous *gymnasium*."

We all learned the welcome by heart. When the director walked
down the corridor, we would all chant it to his back in chorus from
our classroom, imitating his squeaky voice: "Sire, allow us to greet
you in the gray walls of our famous *gymnasium*." We were especially delighted with the "gray walls." Butter Churn pretended that
he heard nothing.

A holiday cleanliness sparkled all over the school on the day
of the king's arrival. The wide staircase was covered with red carpet. In spite of its being a sunny day, the chandeliers were lighted
in the assembly hall. We attended in our dress uniforms. Our class
was lined up in two ranks in the vestibule. Suboch stood sideways
with a little sword in the pocket of his dress coat. Only its thin
golden hilt shone above the pocket. Suboch smelled of perfume.
His pince-nez sparkled as if their lenses had been made of diamonds.

Butter Churn stood next to the marble columns. In our schoolboy slang Butter Churn was "releasing steam." He was chalk-
white. His medals trembled on his tight coat.

We could hear "Hurrahs" from the street, shouted by the soldiers
who were lined up in ranks outside. The "Hurrahs" came closer
to the school. A band was playing. The doors were flung wide.
Butter Churn looked helplessly at Régamé and moved up at a jog
trot to meet the king.

A little hook-nosed king with a gray mustache, wearing a light
blue overcoat with silver edging, came hopping quickly into the
vestibule. Behind his back everything was blue with uniforms and
glossy with top hats.

The hall porter, Vassily, a former wrestler in the circus, was
supposed to take the king's coat. But he grew confused, and instead
of helping him to take it off, he tried to help him on with it. The
king resisted. He even blushed. Finally he tore himself out of
Vassily's powerful clutch. An adjutant ran up to the king, pushed
Vassily away with a hand gloved in white kid, and obsequiously

took the king's coat. Vassily's eyes turned muddy, like a drunkard's. He stood there at attention, puffing; he had no inkling of what had happened.

"Sire!" Butter Churn said, bowing in front of the king, and he waved his left hand desperately behind his back. This meant that he had forgotten what came next.

Régamé began at once to prompt him. He did it like a virtuoso.

At first the king stared unhappily at the director's red bald spot. He was still breathing hard after his struggle with Vassily. Then the king heard the prompting, and he smiled. Somehow the director managed to finish his greeting, and, showing him a narrow passage between the ranks of schoolboys, invited His Highness to proceed into the assembly hall.

The king moved. His retinue moved after him, carelessly clanking their swords on the iron floor of the vestibule. Epaulets sparkled in our eyes. A step behind the king marched the belligerent-looking General Ivanov, commander of the Kiev military district. And behind the retinue were the Serbian ministers, taking off their top hats, smiling, all sugar and honey.

We had agreed on everything beforehand. As soon as the king began to march between the ranks of blue uniforms, we all shouted out amicably and with all our voices: "Swindler!" The Russian word for this sounds very much like "Zhivio!," the Serbian word "hurrah," which we had been ordered to shout.

We repeated it several times. The shout echoed in the "gray walls" of the *gymnasium*. The king, suspecting nothing, walked slowly on, clanking his spurs, nodding to us, and smiling.

Suboch turned white. General Ivanov, commander of the Kiev military district, managed without being noticed to shake his fist at us behind his back. The glove he held in it was shaking with indignation. Butter Churn, white with terror, minced after the king.

The king walked on, and we could hear the *gymnasium* choir singing the Serbian national anthem to him in solemn, pious voices. Suboch stared at us. But we stood there, erect and silent. Our faces showed nothing except the tender emotions aroused in us by this solemn moment. Suboch shrugged his shoulders, and turned away.

But the story with the king was not yet finished. When he marched back we shouted out, just as amicably and as deafeningly as before, "Hold him!" which also sounded a little like the Serbian "Hurrah." Again, the king understood nothing. He smiled graciously, and the ministers held their top hats with white silk lining elegantly in front of them as they filed past us.

But when the gray-bearded prime minister, Pashich, who was considered a liberal, passed us, we all shouted out the correct Serbian word clearly and distinctly: "Zhivio Pashich!"

Of course we overdid it. We had assigned Matusevich, who had a powerful bass voice (he later became a singer in the Kiev Opera), to shout "Hold him!" straight into the king's ear. The king shuddered all over, but collected himself and nodded politely to Matusevich.

After this meeting with the king, twelve high school pupils from our class, including myself, were given a formal dressing down by the director. For three days we were forbidden to go inside the school. The officials were clearly trying to cover up the whole incident, afraid of the publicity it might get.

I still don't understand the sense of our suspension. We had three wonderful, tranquil days in which to rest, to read, to walk beside the Dnieper, and to go to the theater.

It proved impossible, of course, to hush up the incident with the King of Serbia. The whole *gymnasium* envied us out of all measure, and not only ours, but the Second and the Third, and the trade school, all of them places where kings were never taken.

FROM EMPTY TO EMPTIER

I am distrustful to this day of all people with round, black little eyes like olives. My pupil, Marusa Kazanskaya, had such eyes. They looked mindlessly out on the world, and there was curiosity in them only when they saw a gallant Junker or a lyceum student in a coat with a beaver collar. A Junker had only to walk past the window and everything that had been learned by heart—chronology, geography, and the rules of syntax—flew out of Marusa's head with the speed of light.

I was her tutor. She cost me a lot, that chattering, sharp-nosed Marusa with her pinhead eyes! Suboch had got me the job. "A most respected family," he had told me, "but I warn you, the girl's talents are not dazzling."

The respected family consisted of Marusa, her father, a retired general, and her mother, a scraggy Frenchwoman. The general had the stature of a dwarf, but he wore a broad, thick beard. He was so small that he couldn't hang up his own coat. But he was a very clean, well-washed little general with puffy hands and watery eyes. His eyes filled with fury when he thought about his enemies—the generals who had risen higher in the service: Sukhomlinov, Dragomirov, Kuropatkin, and Rennenkampf. Kazansky had reached the rank of adjutant general, had commanded several military districts, and had taught strategy to Nicholas II.

"In strategy that young man was a downright dunderhead," the general used to say of the Tsar. It was his opinion that the last real Tsar had been Alexander III.

Kazansky had a wonderful military library. But I never once saw him take a single book out of the locked bookcases. He would spend all day reading *New Times*, and playing solitaire. A little Pomeranian with eyes as black as Marusa's would lie curled up on his lap. The Pomeranian was stupid and mean.

After every lesson Kazansky would accompany me as far as the Galitsky market. He loved these daily walks. Once on the street, the general would begin to gambol, chuckling and telling army stories.

Madame Kazanskaya and her husband called each other by childish nicknames. I have met many boring people in my life. But I have never seen a more boring person than Madame Kazanskaya. Blinking her little eyes like a toy dog, she would sew pinafores for Marusa all day, or paint violet irises on satin ribbons with oil paints. She used to give these ribbons as presents to her friends on birthdays. Nobody knew what they were for. Some people hung them on the wall or used them as table runners in the drawing room. Others tried to use them as bookmarks, but the ribbons were wide and wouldn't fit in a book. People with any taste hid the ribbons out of sight. But Madame Kazanskaya kept on painting new ones with idiotic stubbornness, and she would give them a second and a third time to the same acquaintances. Her own apartment was full of them. They stuck to your fingers, crackled, and could drive a nervous man to distraction.

The Kazansky's apartment was very high-ceilinged and full of light, but the light was always cold and raw. The sunshine which came in lost its light and its warmth, and lay on the floor like sheets of faded paper.

I couldn't guess what the Kazanskys were living for. They believed in God, and they believed the world had been created by God in precisely the way which would be most profitable for the Kazanskys. They saw God as a kind of governor general, on a world scale. He established order in the universe and took care of their well-ordered family.

Besides God, the Kazanskys had Marusa. They loved her with the sick affection of people who have had a child only when they were already old. They found her caprices not only charming but sacred. She had only to press her lips together and her papa, the general, would take off his spurs, walk around on tiptoe, and sigh deeply, while her mama would run to the kitchen to make Marusa's favorite dish—a sponge cake.

The principal subject of conversation between the parents was Marusa's marriage. The search for a husband never stopped. It became a kind of mania, a passion. Madame Kazanskaya's memory was like a bookkeeper's account book in which were entered the names of all the eligible young men in Kiev and southwest Russia.

Marusa was a pupil in Duchinskaya's Private School. This was a bourgeois school where marks were given in accordance with the wealth and the rank of the pupil's parents. But Marusa was so dumb that even General Kazansky's rank could not save her from getting 2's. When Marusa was called to the blackboard she stood there sullenly, pressing her lips together and plucking at the edge of her black pinafore.

Every 2 produced panic in the general's family. Marusa would lock herself in her room and declare a hunger strike. Madame Kazanskaya would start to cry and shake all over. The general would run from corner to corner shouting that tomorrow he would go to see the governor and have all this "Jewish gang" driven out.

The next day the general would put on his parade uniform with all his medals and drive off for an explanation from the director of the school, Duchinskaya, an imposing lady who perfectly understood the official dignity and power of the parent of each of her pupils. The affair would always end with Marusa's mark being changed to a 3 minus. Duchinskaya could not afford to lose a pupil from a general's family. This might have cast a shadow on her irreproachable institution. And the Kazansky family would calm down until the next 2 was given to Marusa.

I was convinced after the first lesson that it would make no sense at all to try to explain anything to Marusa. She could not understand a thing. So I took a daring step. I forced her to learn her textbooks by heart. Somehow she managed to do this. She memorized them page by page, the way children learn abracadabra in children's games.

I could have taught history, geography, and Russian grammar to a parrot with exactly the same success. It was poisonous work. I grew very tired of it. But I soon had my reward: for the first time Marusa was given a 3 plus.

When I rang at the Kazansky's door that evening, the general opened it himself. He was dancing and waving his arms. The Order of St. Anna bounced up and down on his chest. He helped me off with my old student's overcoat.

Marusa, in a new dress and with enormous ribbons in her hair, was waltzing with a chair in the drawing room. The piano was being played by Mademoiselle Marten, her French language tutor. The Pomeranian rushed around the room barking crazily. The door to the dining room opened and Madame Kazanskaya walked in in a dress with a train. Behind her back I could see a festively set table.

To celebrate Marusa's first 3 plus, they gave a delicious supper. Afterward, the general skillfully uncorked a bottle of champagne. Madame Kazanskaya watched carefully to see that he didn't spill any of it on the tablecloth. The general began to drink it like water. He turned red almost at once and waved his arms so that his shining little shirt cuffs popped out of his jacket sleeves.

"Yes!" the general said, and he shook his head sadly. "Every man must carry his own cross in this hellish life. And we'll carry it, we won't shirk. Women, my dear young man, don't understand us. They have chicken brains."

"My dove," Madame Kazanskaya said in terror, "what are you saying? I don't understand at all."

"I spit on it!" the general declared with force. "I spit on it three times! Drink up, young man. As our great poet said: 'What sort of a trick is this, Creator, to make me the father of a grown-up daughter!' "

"My little dove!" Madame Kazanskaya cried out, and the blue pouches under her eyes started to shake.

"My little muff," the general said unctuously and threateningly, "have you not forgotten that I am an adjutant general in the Russian army?"

He pounded his fist on the table and yelled in a shattering voice: "I ask you to listen when you're being spoken to! I have taught the Tsar-Emperor, and I do not wish to listen to comments by brainless fools! Stand up!"

It all ended when the general jumped up from the table, clutch-

ing his napkin, and started to dance. Then he fell into an armchair
and they revived him with spirits of valerian. He groaned, and
kicked his short legs.

I walked out of this revelry with Mademoiselle Marten. The
street lamps could just be seen. It was a foggy March evening.

"Ah!" Mademoiselle Marten said. "How tired I am! I just can't
go on with that foolish girl. Or stay any longer in that stupid home.
I refuse."

I envied Mademoiselle Marten—she could refuse to give lessons
to Marusa but I couldn't. The Kazanskys paid me thirty rubles a
month. This was incredibly high pay for a tutor.

It was just at this time that my father threw up his job at the
Bryansk factory and moved from Bezhitsa to Gorodishche, to my
grandfather's farm. He couldn't help me any more. And I lied to
Mama. I wrote her that I was earning fifty rubles a month and
that she did not need to send me any. As if she could have!

Mademoiselle Marten said good-by to me on the corner of
Bezakovskaya Street. Heavy snow was falling. An incandescent
lamp was humming over the entrance to a drugstore. Mademoiselle
Marten walked quickly up Bibikovsky Boulevard with her sliding
gait as if she were moving quickly on roller skates. She bent her
head down and protected it from the snow with her muff.

I stood there and looked after her. I had a strange feeling after
the champagne. My head was foggy and seemed to me full of
wonderful ideas, but then the wave of fog would disappear and
I would realize with dreadful clarity that nothing special had happened to my life. Tomorrow, just like today, I would go along this
street on which I knew every single sign, past the front yards, the
cabdrivers, the pillars carrying advertisements, and the policemen, to the Kazanskys' house. I would climb up the steps decorated
with yellow glazed tiles, I would ring at the painted oak door, and
the Pomeranian would start barking its head off, and I would walk
into the same vestibule with its mirror and its coat tree where, on
the same hook, the general's overcoat with its red lapels would be
hanging with all its buttons buttoned.

But when the wave of fog rolled back, I thought of the kinship
of solitary people like Mademoiselle Marten and Fitsovsky and
myself. It seemed to me we ought all to be friends and protect one
another so that we could conquer life together.

But where did I get the idea that Mademoiselle Marten was
a solitary person? I didn't know her at all. I had only heard that
her family came from the city of Grenoble, and I could see that
she had dark, slightly sullen eyes. That was all.

I turned at the corner and went to Fitsovsky's. He wasn't home.

I got the key from its regular hiding place and opened the door. It was cold in his room. I lit the lamp, stoked the iron stove, took a book of poems from the table, lay down on the oilcloth-covered couch, and began to read.

The fog rolled back into my head. "Slowly the autumn day descends," I read. A warm light appeared between the lines of the poem. It spread, and warmed my face. "The yellow leaf turns slowly, and the day is transparently fresh and the air is clean— the soul will not escape its invisible decay."

I turned the page. "Believe this—there is nothing unhappier in the whole country than my young generation."

I put the book aside. I lay and thought how the life that was waiting in front of me would probably be full of fascinating things, some happy, some sad.

Life was like this night, with light reflected weakly from the snowdrifts, the quiet of the parks, the glow of street lights. In its darkness the night was hiding all the good people who would some time be close to me, and that quiet dawn which would surely break across the earth. The night was hiding all the secrets, all the new friends, all the happiness of the future. How wonderful!

No, that poet was not right when he complained about the fate of my generation. We were not unfortunate. We believed and we loved. We didn't bury our talents in the ground. Of course, our souls would escape the invisible decay. No! No! We'll be living all our lives in amazing times. This is what I thought, lying on that oilcloth-covered couch. To hell with all the nauseating Kazanskys, the whole mean and respectable anthill!

When I came home to Wild Alley from Fitsovsky's, Panna Kozlovskaya gave me a telegram. It told me that my father was dying on the farm at Gorodishche near Belaya Tserkov. I left Kiev the next morning to go to Belaya Tserkov.

My father's death broke one of the threads which had tied me to my family. Then all the other threads began to break.

THE INN ON THE BRAGINKA

The old steamboat moved up the Dnieper, slapping its paddle-wheels. It was late at night. I couldn't sleep in the stifling cabin and went out on the deck.

A wind was blowing out of the black darkness, carrying drops of rain. An old man in a patched overcoat was standing next to the captain's bridge. A dim lantern threw light on his bristled face.

"Captain," the old man said, "can't you do a favor for an old man? Let me off on the shore here. It's less than a verst from here to my village. But from Teremtsov I'll have to walk all night. Be kind!"

"What are you doing, joking?" the captain asked. "You can't see your nose in front of your face, but I should put you ashore on the bank here and wreck the steamboat!"

"I haven't any reason to make jokes," the old man said. "But my village is just over the hills there." He pointed into the darkness. "Let me land here! Be a good fellow!"

"Terenty," the captain spoke to the helmsman, looking as if he had not heard the old man, "can you see anything?"

"I can't see my own sleeve," the helmsman growled morosely. "This damned darkness! I'm steering by sound."

"We'll run aground," the captain said with a sigh.

"Nothing will happen to your old tub," the old man muttered. "What's a captain for? You ought to be selling pears in Loev, not running a boat on the Dnieper! Well? Are you going to put me ashore or not?"

"Talk to me about it!"

"I am talking to you," the old man answered peevishly. "Who ever heard of taking passengers all the way to Teremtsov?"

"Why can't you understand," the captain yelled at him plaintively, "that you can't see a thing out there? Where am I going to land you? Just where?"

"Why, right here, across from the steep bank!" The old man

pointed again into the pitch-black darkness. "Right here! Let me stand next to the helmsman and I'll show him."

"Do you know what you can do?" the captain said. "You can go to hell with the devil's grandmother!"

"Aha!" the old man cried triumphantly. "It means you refuse? Is that it?"

"Yes! I refuse!"

"It means you don't care that I'm hurrying to my daughter's wedding? It makes no difference to you. You'd persecute an old man!"

"What's your daughter to me?"

"But maybe Andrei Gon means something to you?" the old man suddenly asked in a quiet, threatening voice. "Or haven't you met up with Andrei Gon yet? I have news for you, that Andrei Gon himself is coming to the wedding."

The captain was silent.

"Lost your tongue?" the old man asked maliciously. "You call your old tub *Hope*. Well, you won't have any hope of getting back in good condition if you don't land me on the bank here. Gon does good turns for me. We're brothers-in-law. Gon won't forget this."

"Don't start making threats!" the captain muttered.

"Sidor Petrovich," the helmsman wheezed, "you can see for yourself how stubborn the old man is. Come on, let's land him on the bank. There's no sense in getting mixed up with Gon."

"Well, the devil with you!" the captain said to the old man. "Stand up there with the helmsman, show him. Only look out and don't wreck the boat."

"Lord! Why, I know the Dnieper like my own barn! The boat, after all, belongs to the government!"

The old man walked up to the wheel and began to give commands: "Come over with your right hand! Sharper! Or else you'll swing too far. So. Still sharper!"

Willow branches began to scrape along the side. The steamboat scraped against the bottom, and stopped. Down below on the covered deck we could hear noise from the passengers who had been wakened by the bump.

A sailor lit a lantern on the bow. The steamboat was standing in flooded underbrush. It was about thirty paces to the shore. Black water was racing through the bushes.

"Well, there you are," the captain said to the old man. "Jump off. We've arrived."

"But where am I going to jump?" the old man asked in surprise. "It's over my head here. I could drown!"

"What's that to me? You asked for it yourself. Well!" the captain shouted. "Jump quickly, or I'll have the sailors throw you in the river."

"An interesting problem!" the old man muttered and he walked up to the bow of the steamboat.

He crossed himself, climbed over the railing, and jumped into the water. It came up to his shoulders. Swearing a blue streak, he began to flounder noisily toward the shore. The steamboat inched slowly backward and pulled out of the underbrush.

"Well, how's it going? You still alive?" the captain shouted.

"No thanks to you!" the old man answered from the shore. "Just the same, you'll still meet up with Andrei Gon."

The steamboat moved on up the river.

An elusive gang of bandits were wandering around Chernigovsky province and the whole Polessya that summer. They attacked estates, robbed the mails, and raided trains. The fastest and most daring of these *atamans** was Andrei Gon. Battalions of dragoons and frontier guards surrounded him in the woods and drove him into the impassable marshes of Polessya, but Andrei Gon squirmed out each time he wanted to, and the flames of the fires he set marched behind him through the dark nights.

Legend had already spun its web around him. People said that Andrei Gon was a protector of the poor, the wretched, and the orphaned, that he attacked only the owners of big estates, that he himself was either a *gymnasium* student from Chernigov or a village blacksmith. His name became a symbol of popular vengeance.

I was traveling that summer right into Andrei Gon's district, to a distant relative named Sevruk. He owned a small and modest farm called Iolcha in the Polessya. Borya had arranged the trip for me, since I didn't even know Sevruk.

"You'll get a rest at Iolcha," Borya told me. "The Sevruks are curious people, but they're very simple. They'll be glad to see you."

I agreed to go to Iolcha because I had no alternative. I had been promoted to the eighth class in *gymnasium*. I had just finished my examinations, and a fatiguing summer in Kiev awaited me. Uncle Kolya had taken Aunt Marusya to Kislovodsk. Mama was staying in Moscow. And I didn't want to go to Gorodishche because I could guess from Uncle Ilko's letters that things were not going well between him and Aunt Dosia. All family quarrels frightened

* Originally a Cossack rank, *ataman* is also the word used for any leader of a gang of bandits or freebooters.

me. I didn't want to watch them any longer, or to play any part in them.

In the evening of the second day, the steamboat came up to the low Polessya bank of the Dnieper. Clouds of mosquitoes were hanging in the air. A purple sun was sinking into the white mist over the river. Cold came out of the underbrush. A bonfire was burning. Some stringy saddle horses were standing next to the fire.

The Sevruks were waiting for me on the shore: a thin man in boots and a silk jacket, who was the owner of the farm, a short, young woman who was his wife, and a student who was her brother. They put me in a wagon. The Sevruks jumped onto the saddle horses and rode off, whooping, in a swinging trot.

They disappeared from sight quickly, and I was left alone with a morose driver. I jumped out of the wagon and walked along beside it on the sandy road. The grass on the sides of the road was growing in dark swamp water. The reflection of the sunset was slowly fading in this water. Wild ducks flew over us, beating their heavy wings in steady rhythm. Fog slid out of the bushes in gray rags which trailed down to the ground. Then suddenly hundreds of frogs started to croak and the wagon clattered onto a corduroy road. The farm, surrounded by palings, appeared. It was a strange, eight-cornered wooden house, with many verandas and outbuildings, standing in a clearing in the woods.

That night, while we were still sitting over a modest supper, a stoop-shouldered old man in a cap with a torn visor walked into the dining room. He took a long hunting rifle from his shoulder and leaned it against the wall. A skewbald pointer followed the old man, his toenails making a sharp noise on the floor, sat down at the threshold, and began to wag his tail against the floor. It made such a noise that the old man said:

"Quiet, Galas! Remember where you are!"

Galas stopped wagging his tail, yawned, and lay down.

"Well, what do you hear, Trofim?" Sevruk asked. Turning to me, he said: "This is our forester, our inspector."

"What do I hear?" Trofim sighed, and sat down at the table. "Always the same. At Lyadakh they've burned down a Pole's estate, and at Staroi Gutoi they beat Pan Kaputsinsky to death, may the kingdom of God be his. Although, to tell the truth, he was a wicked old scoundrel. They're killing everybody all around; you're the only ones they have mercy on. A strange business! Why doesn't he touch you, this Andrei Gon? Nobody knows. Maybe he's heard that the simple people trust you. Or maybe he just hasn't got around to you yet."

Marina Pavlovna, Sevruk's wife, laughed.

"That's the way Trofim always is," she remarked. "He's always surprised that we're still alive."

"And may you go on living in good health," Trofim said. "I'm not against it. Did you hear about the blind man's guide?"

"No," Marina Pavlovna said eagerly. "What about him?"

"What, indeed! They're going to bury him tomorrow. At Pogonny. You ought to go."

"We'll go," Marina Pavlovna said. "We'll certainly go."

"For that God will forgive you many sins," Trofim said with a sigh. "And take me with you. I haven't the strength to walk there."

Trofim looked out of the window and asked in a low voice: "No one else around?"

"Just our own people," Sevruk said. "Speak."

"Well," Trofim said mysteriously, "the masters have all got together at Leizer's inn on the Braginka."

"Who?" the student asked.

"Well, the masters, the old men of Mogilev."

"Wait a minute, Trofim," Sevruk said. "Let me explain to the others. They don't know anything about the old men of Mogilev."

Then I heard for the first time the amazing story of the famous Mogilev old men. This story turned time itself around and carried me back a hundred years, and maybe even farther, to the Middle Ages.

For a very long time, since the time of the Polish occupation of this part of Russia, a colony of beggars and blind men have collected at Mogilev on the Dnieper. These beggars—the people call them "the old men of Mogilev"—have always had their own elders and teachers—the masters. They teach those who have just been accepted into the group the complicated rules of their trade —the chanting of religious verses, and how to ask for alms—and they train them in the strict rules of the beggars' world.

Beggars were scattered all over the Polessya, White Russia, and the Ukraine, and the masters assembled every year in secret places, at inns, in the marshes, or at abandoned forest lodges, for the judging and the admission of new beggars into the society. The old men of Mogilev had their own language, which other people could not understand.

In times of trouble, in the years of popular uprisings, these beggars represented a really threatening power. They kept anger alive among the people. They supported it with their songs about the injustice of the Polish rulers and about the heavy burdens of the exploited village folk.

This story made Polessya, where I had just arrived, an entirely different place for me from what it had been before. In this region of swamps and stunted forests, of fog and emptiness, it seemed the flames of vengeance and insult still burned, as steady as the long sunsets of the district. Ever since then it has seemed to me that the coarse, heavy clothes worn by beggars smell not of bread and dust but of gunpowder and burning. It was then that I first began really to look at blind men and at beggars, and to understand that they make up a special race of men who are not only unhappy but also talented and with strong will power of their own.

"Why have they assembled at the inn on the Braginka?" Sevruk asked.

"That's their business," Trofim answered shortly. "The year doesn't go by that they don't get together. Have the frontier guards been sniffing around here?"

"No," Sevruk answered. "But I hear there were some yesterday at Komarina."

"Well, well!" Trofim stood up. "I thank you. I'll go out to the hayloft and get some sleep."

Trofim walked out, but not to the hayloft. He went back into the woods and returned in the morning.

Marina Pavlovna told me the story of the blind man's guide, a little boy. Two days before, the two had walked up to the estate of a rich landowner named Liubomirsky. They had been driven out of the courtyard. When the blind man went out of the gate, an Ingush watchman (many rich landowners used to recruit their own guards for their estates in those days from among the Ingushi, a people living in the Caucasus) turned a chained wolfhound loose to chase him.

The blind man stopped, but the little boy who led him took fright and began to run. The wolfhound caught him and killed him. The blind man was saved only because he had stood motionless. The dog had just sniffed at him, and gone away. The peasants picked up the murdered little boy and carried him to the village of Pogonny. Tomorrow they were going to bury him.

I liked the Sevruks. Marina Pavlovna was a magnificent rider and hunter. She was small but very strong, with a drawling voice. She walked quickly and easily, she talked about everything sharply, like a man, and she loved to read long historical novels like *The Fugitives in Novorossii* by Danilevsky.

Sevruk seemed a sick man. He was very thin and given to mocking. He made friends with none of his neighbors, preferring the company of simple peasants and field workers, and he kept busy on his medium-sized farm. Marina's brother, the student,

spent all day hunting. In his free time he would make shotgun
shells, split wood, and clean his double-barreled Belgian gun.

We all drove to Pogonny the next day. We took a ferry across
the deep, cold Braginka. The wind rustled in the willows on the
shores. Beyond the river a sandy road led up to the edge of a pine
forest. The swamp stretched out on the other side of the road. It
lost itself on the horizon in the dull light, shone in puddles of water,
turned yellow with islands of flowers, and made little noises in the
gray sedge.

I had never before seen such enormous swamps. A long way
from the road we could see in the middle of the green, luxuriant
quagmires a dark slanting cross—many years ago a hunter had
drowned there in the swamp.

Then we could hear the funeral bells ringing in Pogonny. The
carriage drove into an empty village with low huts covered with
rotting straw. Hens squawked as they flew out from under the
horses' feet. A crowd was milling around the wooden church. We
could see burning candles through its open doors. They lighted up
garlands of paper roses which had been hung on the icons.

We walked into the church. The crowd quietly parted to make
way for us. The little boy was lying in a narrow pine coffin with his
flax-colored hair carefully combed. In his bloodless hands, crossed
on his breast, he held a tall, thin candle. It flickered while it burned.
Wax dropped down on the boy's yellow fingers. A shaggy priest in a
black chasuble hurriedly swung the censer and read the prayers.

I looked at the little boy. He looked as if he were trying hard to
remember something, but couldn't think of it.

Sevruk touched my arm. I looked around. He pointed with his
eyes to one side of the coffin. I looked. There the old beggars stood
in a row.

They were all dressed in identical brown robes with wooden
staffs, shining with age, in their hands. Their gray heads were
raised. The beggars were looking up at the altar where there was a
picture of the God Jehovah in a gray beard. He looked amazingly
like these beggars. He had the same sunken, threatening eyes in the
same dry, dark face.

"Masters!" Sevruk whispered to me.

The beggars stood there motionless, without crossing themselves
and without bowing. There was an empty space all around them.
Behind the beggars I could see two little boys, blind men's guides,
with canvas bags on their backs. One of them was crying quietly,
wiping his nose on his sleeve. The other stood there, his head
lowered, laughing.

The women sighed. Sometimes the dull rumble of men's voices

carried in from the church porch. Then the priest would raise his head and begin to read the prayers more loudly. The rumble would die down.

At last the beggars moved all together toward the coffin, silently picked it up, and carried it out of the church. Behind them, the little boys led the blind men.

The coffin was lowered into the grave at the cemetery. There was water in the bottom of the grave. The priest read his last prayer, took off his chasuble, rolled it up and walked away, limping, out of the cemetery.

Two old field workers spat on their hands and picked up their shovels. Then a blind man with a face like a hawk walked up to the grave and said:

"Wait, people!"

The crowd grew quiet. The blind man punched his cane on the ground, bowed toward the coffin, then turned around, looked straight in front of himself with his white eyes, and recited in a singsong voice:

> *Under dry willows, by a little stream,*
> *God sat down to rest from his long travels.*
> *And all kinds of people came up to God,*
> *And brought him everything they had.*

The crowd drew closer to the blind man.

> *The old women brought him honey, and the brides necklaces.*
> *Old men brought him black bread, and old women icons.*
> *And one young girl came with periwinkles*
> *And laid them at his feet, but then ran away*
> *And hid. So God laughed*
> *And asked: "Who will bring me his heart?*
> *Who does not begrudge me his heart as a present?"*

A young woman in a white scarf uttered a quiet little shriek. The blind man was silent, then he turned toward the woman, and went on:

> *And then a young fellow put into his hands*
> *His heart—it was fluttering like a pigeon.*
> *God looked at it, and the heart beat, and the blood*
> *Clotted, and turned as black as the soil.*
> *It turned black with tears, and eternal insults,*
> *Because the young lad was a wanderer across the world,*
> *Leading a blind man, and had never known happiness.*

The beggar held his arm out in front of him.

> *God stood up and held out this weak little heart.*
> *He stood up all-powerful, and cursed injustice.*
> *And black clouds rolled over the earth,*
> *The woods trembled under the great thunder,*
> *And God's voice rang out to be heard by all:*

The blind man suddenly smiled, happily.

> *"I will carry this heart to my throne in Heaven,*
> *This rich present from the race of people,*
> *So that all good souls will bow down before it!"*

The blind man stopped, was silent for a moment, and then sang in his strong, dull voice:

> *This orphan's heart was more valuable than diamonds,*
> *More beautiful than flowers, brighter than lights in the sky,*
> *Because it was given by a lovely young boy*
> *To all-powerful God, as his modest gift.*

The blind man stopped. The women in the crowd rubbed their eyes with the corners of dark handkerchiefs.

"Give, people," the blind man said, "for peace to the soul of the innocent murdered boy, Vassily."

He held out his old cap. Copper coins were thrown into it. Men began to shovel dirt into the grave.

We walked slowly back to the church, where the horses were waiting for us. Marina Pavlovna walked in front. We were silent all the way back. Only Trofim said:

"People have been living for a thousand years, and they still haven't learned what goodness is. Strange business!"

After the funeral alarm gripped the Sevruks' farm. The doors were all closed with steel locks at night. Every evening Sevruk and the student went out and walked around the property. They took rifles with them.

One night we saw a fire in the woods. It burned until dawn. In the morning Trofim told us that an unknown man had spent the night close to the fire.

"It must have been one of Gon's men," he added. "They roam around like wolves."

The next day a barefoot fellow walked onto the farm in black soldier's trousers with faded red stripes on them. He was carrying his boots on his back. The boy's face was peeling from sunburn. His eyes were sullen and bold.

The fellow asked for a drink. Marina Pavlovna gave him a jug of milk and a loaf of bread. The boy drank the milk thirstily and said:

"You're brave gentlemen. You're not afraid to live in a place like this."

"Nobody bothers us," Marina Pavlovna answered him.

"Why not?" the fellow asked, laughing.

"We don't do anything bad to anybody."

"Others may know better about that," the fellow answered cryptically, and he went away.

This was why Marina Pavlovna was reluctant to let Sevruk go the next day to a neighboring village to buy some goods and some gunpowder. Sevruk took me along with him. We were supposed to return in the evening of the same day.

I loved this trip through deserted country. The road wound through the swamps, along sandy hills overgrown with little pine trees. The sand dropped off the wheels in tiny trickles. Grass snakes crossed the road in front of us. It was terribly hot, and we could see the hot air hanging over the swamps.

In one little village we could see goats wandering around the Jewish houses. A wooden star of David was fastened up over the entrance to the synagogue. On the village square, littered with hay dust, unsaddled dragoons' horses were tethered. The dragoons, red with the heat, were lying on the ground. Their uniforms were unbuttoned. They were singing lazily:

> *Soldiers, bravo, little fellows,*
> *Where are all your wives?*
> *All our wives are cannon fodder,*
> *That's where all our wives are.*

Their officer was sitting on a porch, drinking muddy kvass made out of bread.

We went into the stores, which were all vaulted. It was dark and cool inside them. Pigeons ate grain out of the scales. The Jewish traders in shiny black coats complained that there was no point in trading because all the profit went to the district police officer. They told us that two days before Andrei Gon had raided a neighboring estate and driven away four good horses.

We drank tea in one of the stores. It tasted of kerosene. They put pink Lenten sugar in the tea.

We were late. When we left the village, Sevruk began to whip the horses. But they grew tired in the sand, and could only walk. Clouds of flies hung over the horses' cruppers. The horses' thin tails whistled ceaselessly.

A thunderstorm was coming up from the south. The swamp grew black. The wind started to blow. It shook the leaves, and carried the smell of water with it. Lightning flashed. The whole earth rumbled somewhere far away.

"We'll have to turn off to the inn on the Braginka," Sevruk said. "We'll spend the night there. We wasted too much time in the village."

We turned onto a wood road which we could hardly see. It began to grow dark. The woods grew thinner. A freshness blew into our faces and we drove up to a dark inn.

It stood on the bank of the Braginka, under some willow trees. Behind the inn, the bank was overgrown with nettles and high umbrellalike flowers of poison hemlock. From under this fragrant growth you could hear a frightened clucking—this was obviously where the chickens had taken refuge from the approaching storm.

A stout, elderly Jew walked out on the curved porch—this was Leiser, the owner of the inn. He was wearing boots. His wide trousers, like a gypsy's, were held up by a red belt. Leiser smiled sweetly at us, and closed his eyes.

"What guests!" he said, and he shook his head. "It would be easier to find a diamond in the forest than to entice such pleasant guests to come here. Do me a favor, come right away into our clean house."

In spite of his sweet smile, Leiser was looking at us carefully from under his swollen red eyelids.

"I know, Leiser," Sevruk told him, "that the masters are living in your inn. Don't be upset. They don't concern us at all. It's none of our business who spends the night in your inn."

"What can I do?" Leiser said, and he sighed deeply. "All around are woods and swamp. Can I pick and choose my lodgers? Sometimes I'm afraid of them myself, Pan Sevruk."

We walked into a clean room. The scraped ground crunched under our feet. The room was warped out of shape, and everything in it was curved. A bloated, white-haired old woman was sitting on the bed, propped up by pink cushions.

"My mother," Leiser explained. "She has dropsy. Dvoira!" he cried out. "Set up the samovar!"

A little woman with a sad face—Leiser's wife—looked out from behind a curtain and greeted us. The windows were closed because of the storm. Flies swarmed against the glass. A fly-specked portrait of General Kuropatkin hung on the wall. Leiser brought in some hay and spread it for us on the ground. He covered it with a tarpaulin.

We sat down at the table and began to drink tea. At that moment there was a clap of thunder so heavy that it made the blue plates jump on the table. The downpour made a loud, steady drumming on the roof of the inn. A gray darkness poured down in streams beyond the windows. Dull lightning flashes broke through it continually.

The cloudburst drowned out the humming of the samovar. We ate rolls with our tea; tea had not tasted so good to me for a long time. I loved this inn, and the backwoods, the noise of the rain, and the rumbling of the thunder in the woods. The voices of the beggars could just barely be heard through the wall.

I was tired from the jolting of the wagon and from the long hot day, so right after tea I lay down on the hay spread on the ground. I slept all night soaked in perspiration. The smell of kerosene hung in layers around us. The night light flickered. The old lady groaned. Sevruk sat up on the hay next to me.

"It would be better to lie outside in the wagon," he said. "I'll have a heart attack from this stuffiness."

We walked out carefully. The wagon was standing under a shed. We took out some hay, lay down on it, and covered ourselves with the tarpaulin. The storm had passed. Wet stars were shining over the woods. Drops of water were still falling from the roof. The smell of wet weeds drifted into the shed. A door squeaked. Someone came out of the inn. Sevruk whispered to me:

"Keep quiet. That must be the masters."

Someone sat down on a log next to the shed and began to strike a flint to make flame. Then we could smell *makhorka,* cheap tobacco.

"As soon as it gets light, we'll wander on," said a rasping voice. "Or else they'll have us in a bag."

"Simple," a hoarse voice answered. "We've been living at Leiser's. The archangels will take care of us."

"Nothing to be seen from here," said a third voice, quite a young one, anxiously. "Maybe everything was too wet from the rain."

"For Gon's men there is no such thing as wetness, nor trouble," the rasping voice answered.

"It'll be," the hoarse voice said. "They will avenge our wrong. We'll see God's punishment. They haven't seen it yet."

The beggars were silent for a little.

"Petro," the rasping voice asked, "are all the people ready?"

"All of them," the young one answered.

"Then let them all leave the inn. And without bothering Leiser.

His business is separate. He's had his kopecks. Are those travelers sleeping?"

"They're sleeping. What shall we do with them?"

The voices grew quiet again. I stirred a little. Sevruk touched me on the arm. A few more men came out of the inn.

"I'm going to Chernobuil, and then I'll go to Ovruch with Kuzma," a familiar voice said. "Maybe I'll find a boy to guide me at Chernobuil. The people are starving there." This was the blind man who had sung over the grave of the dead boy at Pogonny. My heart was thumping.

It seemed to me then that a long time went by before I heard a quiet exclamation:

"It's burning!"

The beggars all began to stir.

"Well, brothers," the hoarse voice said, "let us pray to God, and then be on our way."

" 'Our Father, who art in Heaven,' " the beggars chanted in low voices, " 'blessed be thy name . . . thy kingdom come . . .' "

The beggars all stood up then and walked away.

"What were they talking about?" I asked Sevruk.

"I don't know," he answered. "Let's go and have a smoke away from the hay." He stood up and walked out of the shed.

"What's this?" he said in surprise, standing in the darkness. "Come over here."

I hurried to him. Beyond the black Braginka, beyond the willow saplings on its farther bank, the sky was red and full of smoke. Tall showers of sparks seemed to be shooting up from clumps of bushes. The glow of flames was dully reflected in the river.

"What's burning?" Sevruk asked.

"Liubomirsky's is burning," Leiser answered out of the darkness.

We had not noticed his coming up to us.

"Pan Sevruk," he said in an imploring voice, "have pity on yourself and on a poor innkeeper. Let me harness your horses, and you drive away with God. It's bad for you to stay here."

"Why?"

"The dragoons may come here from the village. Or the frontier guards. They can't do anything to the innkeeper. He had no eyes and no ears."

"We didn't see anything either," Sevruk said.

"Pan Sevruk!" Leiser pleaded. "I pray you by your own Orthodox God. Please go away. I don't want your money. Peace is worth more to me. You can see what's happening all around."

"Well, all right, all right," Sevruk agreed. "You're a man with weak nerves, Leiser. Harness the horses."

Leiser had the wagon ready quickly. We drove away.

The road ran along the bank of the Braginka. Sevruk didn't drive, but let the reins hang loose, and the horses went as they wished. The flames were growing higher. Wet branches slapped into our faces.

"Now it's clear," Sevruk said quietly. "They set fire to Liubomirsky's."

"Who did?"

"I don't know. It must have been because of the little boy. But you and I did not spend the night at the inn, and we've seen nothing. All right?"

"All right," I agreed.

A low but distinct whistle came from across the river. Sevruk stopped the horses. The whistle was repeated. The wagon was in thick undergrowth and we couldn't be seen from any direction.

"Hey, innkeeper!" a man called out in a low voice from the other bank. "Ferry me over!"

No one answered. We kept listening.

There was a splash. The man had obviously dived into the water and was swimming. Soon we could see him through the bushes. He was in the middle of the river which was dimly lighted by the glow from the fire. The river was carrying him downstream fast.

He got out on the bank not far from us. We could hear the water dripping off him.

"Well, just you wait, Leiser," the man said as he walked into the woods. "You'll pay me yet for this crossing."

When we could no longer hear the man's footsteps, we drove on.

"Did you recognize him?" Sevruk asked me in a barely audible voice.

"Who?" I didn't understand.

"Did you recognize the man?"

"No."

"That was the fellow who came to the house. Drank milk. It sounded like his voice. Now everything's clear. The masters must have complained to Gon. This was one of Gon's men. It was he who set the fire. That's what I think. Leiser ferried him across to the other side. But remember, you and I didn't see a thing, and we don't know anything."

Sevruk carefully lighted a cigarette, covering the match with the skirt of his raincoat. The glow from the fire was now filling the sky. The river roared through the flooded underbrush, the axles squeaked. Then a cold fog blew out of the swamps. We got back to the farm, wet and cold, while it was still early morning.

The days went by anxiously after this incident. They delighted me. I liked the steady expectation of danger, the low-voiced conversations, and the rumors which Trofim brought of Andrei Gon's sudden appearance first here, then there.

I liked the cold Braginka, the bandits' underbrush, the puzzling horseshoe marks on the road which had not been there the night before. I even wanted, I might as well confess, to have Andrei Gon descend on Sevruk's farm, but without arson or murder.

Instead of Andrei Gon, the dragoons came. They rode up to the gate of the farm about twilight. An officer in dusty boots walked up to the veranda where we were drinking tea, excused himself, and asked:

"Are you Gospodin Sevruk?"

"I am," Sevruk answered. "What can I do for you?"

The officer turned to his soldiers.

"Hey, Marchenko!" he shouted. "Bring him here!"

Two dragoons led a barefoot fellow out from behind the horses. His hands were tied behind his back. He was wearing black soldier's trousers with faded red stripes.

"Do you know this fellow?" the officer asked.

All of us were silent.

"Look at him closer."

"No," Marina Pavlovna said, and she turned white. "I've never seen this man."

The man shuddered, and dropped his eyes.

"And you?" the officer asked Sevruk.

"No, I don't know him."

"So, brother," the officer said, turning to the man, "you were lying all the time when you said you came from here and that you worked on the Sevruks' farm, weren't you? Now it's all up with you."

"Good," the man said. "Take me away! The might is yours, but not the right."

Marina Pavlovna jumped up and went into the house.

"No more talk out of you!" the officer said. "Out the gate, march!"

The dragoons rode off. Marina Pavlovna cried for a long time.

"And he was looking at me so hard," she said through her tears.

"Why didn't I guess? I should have said that I knew him and that he worked for us."

"How could you guess a thing like that?" Trofim said in distress. "If he could have given some kind of sign. But that man burned down Liubomirsky's to the foundations. He burned it famously. For the murder of the young boy."

Soon after this I went back to Kiev.

Polessya has stayed in my memory as a sad and somewhat puzzling region. It would go on growing buttercups, and hairgrass, its alders and its willows would go on rustling in the wind, but it seemed to me that its church bells would never summon its speechless field workers on the eve of a joyous people's holiday. This was how I thought then. But fortunately, things worked out quite differently.

SLEEP IN MY GRANDMOTHER'S GARDEN

My grandmother, Vikentiya Ivanovna, lived in Cherkasy with my aunt Yefrosinya Grigorievna. My grandfather had been dead for a long time, and my aunt Yefrosinya Grigorievna died of heart failure during the summer when I went to Polessya. So my grandmother then moved to Kiev, to live with one of her daughters, my aunt Vera, who had married an important Kiev businessman.

Aunt Vera had her own home on the outskirts of the city, in Lukyanovka. She set Grandmother up in a little cottage in the garden of her home. After her independent life in Cherkasy, Grandmother felt herself a boarder in a strange house at Aunt Vera's. She used to cry about this quietly, but she was glad that she could live in her own little house and cook for herself. In this at least she could be independent and not obligated to her rich daughter.

It was lonely there for Grandmother, and she talked me into moving out of Panna Kozlovskaya's and into her little house. It had four small rooms. Grandmother lived in one, an old cellist named Gattenberger in another, the third was mine, and the fourth was called a hothouse although it was always cold. The floor there was always covered with pots of flowers.

When I got back from Polessya in the middle of the summer, the city was empty. Everyone had moved to summer cottages outside Kiev. Borya had gone to Yekaterinoslav to get practical engineering experience. My grandmother, Vikentiya Ivanovna, and Gattenberger were the only ones living at Lukyanovka.

Grandmother had grown much older, she stooped more, and her old strictness had disappeared, but she had not changed her habits. She got up at dawn, and immediately opened her window wide. Then she made coffee on a spirit lamp. When she had drunk it, she went out into the garden and, sitting in a wicker chair, read her favorite books—the endless romances of Krashevsky or stories by Korolenko or Eliza Ozheshko. She often fell asleep over her reading—white-haired, dressed all in black, her thin hands lying on the arms of her chair.

Butterflies lighted on her hands and her black hat. Ripe plums plopped down noisily from the trees. A light breeze blew through the garden, blowing the shadows of leaves along the path. The clear, hot sun of Kiev summertime stood high in the sky over Grandmother. And I thought that sometime Grandmother would go to sleep forever in the warmth and freshness of that garden.

I made friends with Grandmother. I liked her best of all my relatives. She paid me back in the same coin. She had raised five daughters and three sons and yet in her old age lived all alone. She also had, in fact, no family. Our mutual attachment grew out of the loneliness each of us felt.

Grandmother was prodigal with both caresses and melancholy. In spite of the difference in age we had a lot in common. She loved poetry, books, trees, the sky, and her own thoughts. She never forced me to do anything.

Her only weakness was her use of a cure she had invented herself, whenever I caught the slightest cold. She called it "spiritus." It was a beastly medicine. She mixed up all the spirits she knew—wine, wood alcohol, liquid ammonia—and added turpentine to the mixture. The result was a purple liquid as pungent as nitric acid. Grandmother would rub this spiritus on my chest and back. She believed deeply in its curative power. A smell that gripped your throat would spread through the little house. Gattenberger would immediately light a fat cigar. Its blue smoke would fill his room with pleasant fog.

Grandmother fell asleep most often in the garden when Gattenberger began to play his cello in his room. He was a handsome old
man with a wavy white beard and clear gray eyes. He used to play
a piece he had written himself called "The Death of Hamlet." The
cello fairly sobbed. Chords as resonant as if they were being
played under the vaults of Elsinore mounted to the solemn climax:

> *Let four captains*
> *Bear Hamlet, like a soldier, to the stage.*

When I listened to this music, I could imagine myself in the
great hall at Elsinore. I could see the narrow Gothic rays of sunlight, I could hear the fanfare of trumpets, and I could see the
huge—tall and light—banners over Hamlet's body. They dropped
to the ground, and rustled. The stream had long since carried
Ophelia's bouquet down to the sea. Waves far from the shore
buffeted the wreath of rosemary and rue, the final symbol of her
bitter love. The cello sang about this, too.

Grandmother would wake up, and say: "My God, can't he play
something happy?"

Then Gattenberger, to please Grandmother, would play her
favorite pastoral from *The Queen of Spades:* "My darling little
friend, my beloved little shepherd."

Music tired Grandmother. She rested from it in the evenings
when Gattenberger went off with his cello to the concerts in the
Merchants' Park.

I used to go often to these concerts. The orchestra played in a
white wooden bandstand while the audience sat under the open
sky. Large flower beds of stock and nicotiana smelled strong and
sweet in the twilight. They were watered before every concert.
Floodlights played on the musicians, the listeners sat in the dark.
The women's dresses were dimly white, the trees rustled, sometimes summer lightning flashed over our heads.

Best of all I liked the cloudy, raw evenings when almost no one
came to the park. It seemed to me then that the orchestra was playing for me alone, and for a young woman with the brim of her hat
pulled down. I ran into her at nearly all the concerts. She used to
stare at me. I followed her furtively. I caught her glance only once
and it seemed to me her eyes were shining with sly little lights in
them.

My long Kiev summer was filled with dreams about this
woman. They made the summer anything but boring. It was filled
with the thin-voiced sound of summer rains. They poured down
out of a high sky, drumming on the greenery of the parks. Crystal
drops, falling from the clouds, filled my room with their rapid

sound. It seemed to me a true miracle that ordinary water falling off a roof into a green tub could sing like this.

"These blind rains all summer long!" Grandmother said. "But they're good for the harvest."

Just beyond the smoke of these "blind rains" and the radiance of the rainbow somewhere near them lived my unknown young lady. I was grateful to her for having changed everything by her sudden appearance in my world. Even the pavements of yellow brick, covered with little puddles, now seemed to me as wonderful and marvelous as something in Andersen's fairy tales. Grass grew between the bricks, and ants wallowed in the little puddles. When I was in the mood to invent a world out of such material, everything seemed miraculous to me, even the Kiev sidewalks. Even now I don't know what to call this mood. It was compounded of unnoticed things. There was not a trace of exaltation in it. On the contrary, it brought peace and quiet. But even the simplest worry could end this mood.

It was a state of mind that demanded expression. And it was in that hot summer with its "blind rains" that I first began to write. I hid this from Grandmother. When she showed surprise that I sat in my room writing for hours on end, I told her I was getting ready for my school work in literature and preparing abstracts of what I studied.

On days when there were no concerts in the Merchants' Park I would go out on the Dnieper or into the outskirts of the city to a private park called "Good-by to Grief." It belonged to a Kiev patron of the arts named Kulzhenko. For two or three cigarettes the watchman would let me into the park which was completely empty and overgrown with weeds. Duckweed choked the ponds. Jackdaws made a racket in the trees. Rotting benches sagged when I sat on them.

I ran into an old artist in the park. He was sitting under a big cloth umbrella, making sketches. He looked at me even from a distance so angrily that I never dared go near him. I went instead into the most remote corner of the park where there was a deserted house. Here I sat on the terrace steps and read.

Sparrows played behind my back. I would look up often from my book, into the depths of the park. A smoky light fell through the trees. I waited. I was sure that it was precisely here, in this park, that I would meet my unknown lady. But she never came, and I would go home by the longest possible route—by trolley across Priorka and Podol, then by the Kreshchatik and Proreznaya Street.

On the way I stopped in at the Idzikovsky bookstore on the

Kreshchatik. In summer it was empty there. Young men with damp mustaches, pale from the stifling atmosphere, Idzikovsky's salesmen, would exchange my books. I borrowed books both for myself and for Grandmother. In my mood that summer I wanted to read only poetry. For Grandmother I took love stories by Shpilhagen or Boleslav Prus.

I would go home to Lukyanovka tired and happy. My face was burned by the sun and the fresh air. Grandmother would wait for me. The small round table in her room would be covered with a tablecloth. Supper would be ready on it.

I told Grandmother about "Good-by to Grief." She would nod her head. Sometimes she would say that she had been lonesome all by herself through the long day. But she never scolded me for staying away so long.

"Youth," Grandmother said, "has its own laws. It's none of my business to get mixed up with them."

Then I would go to my own room, undress, and lie on my narrow cot. The lamp lit up the crooked apple branches outside the window. Through my first uneven sleep I could feel the night, its darkness and its boundless quiet. I loved the nights, even though I was frightened by the idea that far above Lukyanovka, above our little house, were Sagittarius and Aquarius, the Gemini, Orion, and Virgo.

I wrote a short story into which I put all of this summer in Kiev: the cellist Gattenberger, the unknown lady in the Merchants' Park, "Good-by to Grief," the nights, and a dreamy, slightly ridiculous young *gymnasium* pupil.

I tortured myself for a long time over this story. The words lost their hardness, and became sort of quilted. The sheer weight of beauty overwhelmed me. At times I was close to real despair.

A magazine was being published then in Kiev with the strange name, *The Knight*. Its editor was the well-known Kiev writer and art lover, Yevgeni Kuzmin. I hesitated for a long time, but in the end I took my story to him.

The editorial office was in Kuzmin's apartment. A polite little student let me in and showed me into Kuzmin's office. A spotted bulldog was sitting on the rug, drooling and looking at me out of enormous eyes. It was stifling. I could smell the smoke from aromatic candles. White masks of Greek gods and goddesses hung on the walls. Books with leather bindings were lying all around in big piles.

I waited. The books crackled. Then Kuzmin walked in—a very tall, very thin man with white fingers. Silver signet rings glittered on them. When he talked with me, he cocked his head respectfully. I was blushing, and I didn't know how to get out of there quickly enough. The story already seemed to me worthless, and I, a tongue-tied fool.

Kuzmin leafed through my manuscript with limp fingers, and underlined something with a sharp fingernail.

"My magazine," he said, "must be a forum for young talent. I will be very glad if we have found another colleague. I'll read your story and send you a post card about it."

"If it isn't too much trouble, please send me your answer in a sealed letter."

Kuzmin smiled in a knowing way, and nodded his head.

I walked out. Sighing deeply, I ran down the stairs and out on to the street. Janitors were sprinkling the pavement. Water was gurgling out of the hoses. Little sprinkles hit my face. I felt better.

I jumped on a trolley while it was moving, just to get away from the district as quickly as I could. The passengers all looked at me in amusement. I jumped off the trolley, and walked along on foot. Dust was heavy over the Senny market place. Identically round clouds were floating over Lvovskaya Street. There was a faint smell of horse manure. A white horse was pulling a wagon loaded with coal. A man black with coal dust was walking beside it and shouting:

"Coallll, anybody need coallll?"

I remembered suddenly that my story, filled with beautiful and obscure thoughts about life, was lying on the table in Kuzmin's stifling office. I felt ashamed. I swore never to write another story.

"It's all not like that, not like that!" I repeated. "But maybe, even if it's bad, it is like that?"

I didn't know anything. I was completely confused.

I turned on Glubochits toward Podol. Shoemakers were hammering on the soles of old shoes, and little fountains of dust were rising from the old leather. Little boys were shooting at sparrows with slingshots. Flour was being moved in carts, and it dripped out on to the street from the bags which were full of holes. In the courtyards women were hanging out laundry of many colors.

It was a windy day. The wind blew dust over Podol. High on the hill over the city was the Cathedral of St. Andrew with its silver cupola, the work of Rastrelli. I went into a tavern and drank some sour wine. It did not make me feel any better.

By evening I returned home with a bad headache. Grandmother immediately rubbed me with spiritus and sent me to bed.

Gattenberger was playing in his room on the sly. He was no

longer playing "The Death of Hamlet" but selections from a new
piece of his called "Banquet During the Plague." Gattenberger
had worked very hard on this piece, and he often played parts of it
to Grandmother and me. Grandmother was still astonished by
Gattenberger's gloomy fantasies.

"First death, now plague!" she complained. "I don't understand
it. I think music should make people happy."

At this moment Gattenberger was playing his favorite part:

> *Unhappy groans resounded strong and loud*
> *Along the banks of streams and little brooks*
> *Which used to run in happy peace and calm*
> *Through that wild paradise, your native land.*

"There it is! That's the real thing!" I mumbled to myself.
"Through that wild paradise, your native land."

Wild paradise! These words hit me like a health-giving wind.
I would have to achieve, to work, to live my poetry. I could guess
how long and how hard this road would be. But somehow the
thought made me feel calmer.

Two days later, a post card came from Kuzmin. He had not
granted my request that he answer me in a sealed envelope.
Kuzmin wrote that he had read my story and would print it in the
next issue of his magazine.

Grandmother, of course, read the post card. She even cried a
little.

"Your father, Georgi Maximovich," she said, "used to laugh at
me. But he was a good man. I'm sorry that he didn't live to see
this."

Grandmother made the sign of the cross over me and kissed
me.

"Well now, work hard and be happy. It's clear that God has
taken pity on me and brought me this happiness in the end."

She was happier about my first story than I was. When the
next number of *The Knight* came out, she even baked a special
cake and organized a celebration. She wore her black silk dress.
Formerly she used to wear it only at Easter. The same bunch of
artificial heliotrope was pinned to her breast. But it no longer made
her grow younger, as it had formerly. Only her black eyes were
laughing when she looked at me.

Wasps got stuck in the jam jar. And Gattenberger, as if he had
guessed what was going on in her room, played the Venyavsky
mazurka and beat time to it with his foot.

"GOLDEN LATIN"

Our Latin teacher Suboch stared at me out of his round eyes. His mustaches were bristling.

"And in the eighth class, too!" Suboch said. "The devil knows what you're up to! I ought to give you a failing mark for conduct. Then you'd sing a different song!"

Suboch was right. The trick or, as we called it, the "psychological experiment" which we had just performed in our Latin class could only be described in the words "the devil knows what."

Pictures had once hung in our classroom. They had been taken down long ago, but six big steel spikes were left in the walls where they had hung. These spikes gave us a good idea, and the class carried it out with great skill and complete success.

Suboch was a most impetuous man. He used to fly into class like a meteor. The flaps of his coat would sail in the wind. His pince-nez would glitter. The class record book would whistle through the air in an arc and fall on to the table. Dust would rise like a whirlwind behind the teacher's back. The class stood up, slamming the desk lids, and then sat down with just as much noise. The glass in the doors rattled. The sparrows fled from the poplar trees outside the windows and flew into the depths of the park.

This was Suboch's usual way of arriving. He would stop for a moment, take a dog-eared notebook out of his pocket, hold it close to his nearsighted eyes, and stand stock-still, holding a pencil in his hand. He would be looking in the notebook for the name of his first victim.

So one morning six of the smallest and lightest pupils in the class, including myself, were hung up on those spikes by our belts. The spikes hurt where they pressed against our waists. It took our breath away.

Suboch flew into the room. At that moment all the other pupils stood on their heads between the desks, their legs waving in the air.

Suboch had gained his full momentum, and couldn't stop. He threw his record book onto the table, and at that moment the whole class returned to its initial position and sat down at the desks. The six of us unfastened our belts, fell to the floor, and also sat down in our places.

An ominous silence followed. Everything was completely in order. We sat there looking innocent, as if nothing had happened.

Suboch started to rage. But we denied everything out of hand. We insisted quietly but stubbornly that nothing had happened, that there had been nobody hanging on the wall, and that the class had been sitting properly in its places. We even managed to hint that perhaps Suboch was suffering from hallucinations.

Suboch lost all control. He called up the six pupils he had seen hanging from the spikes and examined us suspiciously from all sides. There was not a trace of plaster on our coats. Suboch shrugged his shoulders. He looked at the spikes, and examined the floor for evidence. There was none. An expression of terror came over his face: Suboch was a very nervous man.

He told a pupil to go out and summon Platon Fedorovich, the corridor supervisor. They came back together.

"Did you notice anything at the beginning of my class?" Suboch asked him.

"No," Platon Fedorovich answered.

"Any noise or racket?"

"The class always stands up and sits down with a certain noise," Platon Fedorovich answered cautiously, and he looked at Suboch curiously.

"Thank you," Suboch said. "It seemed to me that something strange happened in the class."

Platon Fedorovich looked at Suboch expectantly.

"Just what kind of thing?" he asked ingratiatingly.

"Nothing!" Suboch snapped, suddenly angry. "Excuse me for having bothered you."

Platon Fedorovich threw up his hands, and walked out.

"Sit there quietly," Suboch told us, and he picked up his class record book. "I'll return in a minute."

He walked out and came back in a few minutes with the inspector, Varsonify Nikolayevich, whom we all called "Varsapont."

Varsapont looked at us closely, then walked over to the wall, stood on a desk, and pulled at one of the spikes. The spike came out of the wall without any effort.

"So-o-o!" he said mysteriously, and he pushed the spike back in. The whole class was watching him.

"So-o-o!" Varsapont repeated. "What can this mean?"

"So-o-o!" he repeated a third time, and then he walked out.

Suboch sat quietly at the table for a long time, staring at the record book, and thinking. Then he jumped up and flew out of the class. The doors rattled. The sparrows swarmed out of the poplar trees. A wind blew between the desks, ruffling the pages of our textbooks. We sat there until the end of the class, trying not to make any noise. We were alarmed at the success of our "psychological experiment" and we were afraid that maybe we had done some real harm to Suboch's mind.

But it all ended more simply. Rumors about the "psychological experiment" swept through the school and produced the most envious admiration for us. But the pupils of a younger class decided to repeat the experiment with one of their teachers. As is well known, acts of genius are successful only once. The attempt to imitate it ended in disaster.

Suboch learned the whole story and flew into a rage. He delivered himself of an accusing speech which was fully up to the standards of Cicero's great oration against Cataline. But he surprised us by one thing in his oration. He did not rebuke us for having deceived him, but because we had dared to behave so unworthily in a class devoted to "golden Latin," a class in the most magnificent language of the whole world.

"The Latin language!" he exclaimed. "The language of Horace and Ovid! Of Titus Livius and Lucretius! Marcus Aurelius and Julius Caesar! Pushkin and Dante, Goethe and Shakespeare held this language in reverence! And they not only revered it, they also knew it, and vastly better, by the way, than you do. Golden Latin! Every word in this language can be cast in gold. And not a grain of valuable metal would be lost, because there is no verbal dust in the Latin language. It is pure ingots. And you? What do you do? You ridicule it! You permit yourselves to turn your work on this language into a circus. Your heads are crammed full of cheap ideas! Rubbish! Anecdotes! Football! Smoking! Scoffing! Moving pictures! Every kind of balderdash! You should be ashamed of yourselves!"

Suboch was fairly thundering. We were crushed by the weight of these accusations and by this picture of our worthlessness. But we were insulted, too. For most of us knew Latin very well.

An armistice was soon arranged. And with it there started a great triumph for "golden Latin."

We really worked on the language, trying to expunge our guilt toward Suboch. For we were friendly toward him, and we really liked him. And the memorable day finally arrived when Suboch was required to give every single pupil he called on a perfect mark, a 5.

"A lucky concatenation of circumstances!" Suboch said, and he smiled into his mustache.

But the next day, no matter how hard Suboch nagged at us and drove us into sight reading, he was forced again to give everyone a 5. Suboch beamed. But his happiness was tinctured by a certain nervousness. This was an unprecedented phenomenon in his experience. He was, again, witnessing a miracle.

After the third class in which every single pupil got a perfect mark, Suboch became very gloomy. It was clear that he was frightened. Our spectacular knowledge of Latin was becoming something of a scandal. The whole school was talking about it. Ugly rumors started. Evil tongues accused Suboch of connivance with his pupils, and of trying to build his reputation as a Latin teacher.

"It looks," Suboch told us in a hesitant voice, "as if I shall have to give 4's to three or four of you. What do you think?"

We were so insulted we couldn't answer. It seemed to us that Suboch would be happy now only if one of us should flunk. Maybe he was sorry now that he had made his inspiring oration on "golden Latin."

But we couldn't pretend not to know the Latin we knew very well. Not one of us would agree to fail on purpose just to shut the mouths of scandalmongers. We were all delighted by this game.

It ended with Suboch giving in to general disbelief in us and organizing a public examination. He invited to a special session of his class the deputy trustee of our educational district, the director, the inspector Varsapont, and the Catholic priest Olendsky.

Suboch harried us with all the cunning he possessed. He tried as hard as he could to confuse us and trip us up. But we fought back with courage, and the examination was a spectacular success.

The director shouted with laughter and threw up his hands. Varsapont rumpled his hair. The deputy trustee smiled patronizingly. Father Olendsky just shook his white head and said:

"Oh, what polyglots! Oh, what paragons! Oh, what sly fellows!"

After the examination, of course, we all went limp. We couldn't have stood the tension any longer. Again 3's and 4's began to show up in our marks. But Suboch had his reputation as the greatest Latin teacher. Nothing could touch that now.

TEACHERS OF THE HUMANITIES

An elegant old man with blue eyes and a clean white beard, our Russian literature teacher, Shulgin, had one unusual characteristic: he couldn't tolerate a foolish remark. He had only to hear one to go into a shattering fury. He would turn purple, pick up the textbooks and tear them into shreds, or clasping his hands together he would shake them in front of the frightened pupils with such force that his round stiff cuffs knocked against each other. And he would shout:

"You! Yes, you! Go away! I beg of you! Get out of here!"

These attacks always ended in complete exhaustion. It was, of course, a kind of disease. We knew this, as did all the teachers and the supervisors. When the attack dragged on, Platon Fedorovich would come into the room on tiptoes, put his arm around Shulgin's shoulders, and lead him away to the teachers' room. There he revived him with spirits of valerian.

Generally Shulgin was a gentle, meek old man. Russian literature, as he taught it, was simple and unclouded. He gave out marks completely at random. Pupils in the younger classes had only to bother him with a little whining to get their marks raised from 2's to 3's or from 3's to 4's.

One day we were writing compositions in Shulgin's class on the tired subject, "Feminine Types in Turgenev's Work," when an ink-stained pupil named Gudim suddenly yelled out in an affected, insolent voice:

"The parrots have flown out on the boulevard!"

This was one of the foolish remarks which was certain to drive Shulgin into a rage. His attack started immediately. He grabbed Gudim by the shoulders and shook him so violently that his head was beating against the wall. Then Shulgin pulled the pupil's uniform so hard that the gilt buttons flew off and rolled on the floor.

Matusevich took him by the arm. One of us ran out in the corridor to get Platon Fedorovich. Shulgin sat down at a desk, put his head down, and began to sob. Many of us, who couldn't stand this sight, hid behind the lids of our desks.

The frightened inspector and Platon Fedorovich came in and led Shulgin away. Silence gripped the class. Then Stanishevsky stood up in his place. He was very pale. He walked slowly up to Gudim and said to him:

"You bastard! Get out of our class, right away! Otherwise— we'll kill you! Go on!"

Gudim smiled a little crookedly and did not budge. Stanishevsky grabbed him by the collar, pulled him to his feet, and threw him on the floor. Gudim jumped up. The class kept silent.

"Well, go on!" Stanishevsky repeated.

Gudim walked unsteadily to the door. He stopped on the threshold. He wanted to say something, but forty cold, hostile eyes were staring at him. Gudim dropped his head between his shoulders and walked out.

He never came back to our class. He could not have—the laws of adolescent morality were merciless laws. There was no getting around them. His parents took him out of school and sent him to Valker's trade school, an asylum for hooligans and ignoramuses.

Shulgin collapsed after this incident. He was sick for a long time, and after he recovered he didn't return. The doctors forbade him to take up his teaching again. We would run into him sometimes on Nikolayevsky Square. He would be sitting there, leaning his chin on his cane, warming himself in the sunshine. We always bowed to Shulgin but he only looked at us in a frightened way and never acknowledged our bows.

We were not lucky with our Russian literature teachers. Shulgin was followed by a tall, conceited man with a pale, hypocritical face, named Trostyansky. He believed that all Russian writers could be divided into those who had been loyal, and thus deserved study, and the seditious ones, including all the intelligentsia who had strayed from the right path. He spoke about the latter pityingly, as wasted talents.

Trostyansky irritated us. In the compositions we had to write for him we subverted his gods and exalted the seditious. Trostyansky would smile politely, prove to us in a quiet voice how wrong we were, and give us 2's.

Trostyansky was succeeded by Selikhanovich, a teacher of psychology and Russian literature. He looked like the poet Brusov. He always wore a black, tightly buttoned civilian jacket.

This was a gentle, talented man. He "cleaned" Russian literature for us, the way an experienced restorer cleans an old painting.

He removed from it the dust and the dirt of petty, erroneous judgments about writers, the indifference and the banal words of boring books we had used for cramming. And he showed it to us with such a magnificence of color, such depth of thought, and such enormous truth that many of us, already young men, were thunderstruck.

We learned a great deal from Selikhanovich. It was not only Russian literature that he opened to us. He showed us the Renaissance, and European nineteenth-century philosophy, and Andersen's fairy tales, and the poetry of the great national classic, *The Campaign of Igor*. Until then we had only carelessly memorized its Old Slavonic text.

Selikhanovich had a rare gift for clear and exciting exposition. The most complicated philosophical ideas became understandable and structured in his telling of them. Philosophers, writers, scholars, poets, whose names had stuck in our memories only for their dead dates and for dusty phrases about their "services to humanity," were transformed into real people. They existed in Selikhanovich's own imagination as vital parts of the epochs in which they lived.

In our classes on Gogol, Selikhanovich spread out in front of us the Rome of his days—its map, its hills and ruins, its artists, its carnivals, the very smell of the Roman earth and the blue of the Roman sky. Long files of famous people who had lived or worked in Rome marched in front of us, brought back to life by magic. These magic powers were simple, and available to everyone. They were called knowledge, the spirit of love, and imagination.

We moved from one epoch to another, and from one interesting place to another no less interesting. We traveled everywhere when we were studying with Selikhanovich—through the outskirts of Tula, in the Cossack villages on the borders of Dagestan, under the freezing rains of the autumn Pushkin spent at Boldino, through the damp houses and the endless prisons of Dickens' England, the markets of Paris, the ruined monastery on the island of Majorca where Chopin lay sick, and the deserted Tamana where the sea winds rustled the dry cornstalks.

We studied the lives of those men to whom we were indebted for what we knew about our country and the world and for what we could feel of beauty, the lives of Pushkin, Lermontov, Tolstoy, Herzen, Ryleyev, Chekhov, Dickens, Balzac, and many of the finest people of all humanity. This filled us with pride and with consciousness of the strength of the human spirit and of art.

Along the way Selikhanovich also taught us some curious things, including politeness and even thoughtfulness. Sometimes he asked us riddles.

"Several men are sitting in a room," he told us once. "All the chairs are occupied. A lady walks in. Her eyes show that she has been crying. What should a polite man do?"

We answered that a polite man should, of course, offer her a chair at once.

"And what should a man do who is not only polite but is also thoughtful?" Selikhanovich asked.

We couldn't guess the answer.

"He should give her a chair with its back to the light," Selikhanovich said, "so that her eyes will not be noticed."

Selikhanovich surprised me once when he was talking about my desire to become a writer and he asked me:

"Do you have enough endurance?"

I had never suspected that this might be a factor in literary work. Afterward I became convinced that Selikhanovich had been right.

Once he stopped me in the corridor and said: "Come tomorrow to the lecture by Balmont.* You must. You want to be a prose writer, and this means that you must understand poetry."

I went to Balmont's lecture. It was called "Poetry as Magic." It was hot and stifling in the hall of the Merchants' Assembly. Two bronze candlesticks were burning on a little table covered by a green velvet cloth. Balmont walked in, dressed in a frock coat with an elegant silk necktie. There was a daisy in his buttonhole. His thin yellow hair fell over his collar. His gray eyes looked out mysteriously and even haughtily over our heads. Balmont was no longer a young man.

He spoke in a slow voice. He stopped after every sentence and listened to it, as a man listens to the sound of piano strings after the pedal has been released.

After the intermission Balmont read his own poetry. It seemed to me that all the melody of the Russian language was in these verses.

> *Tender cuckoos singing in deep woods*
> *Sound an entreaty sad and strange.*
> *How happy and how sad in spring—*
> *How good the world in its fresh color!*

* Konstantin Balmont (1867–1943), son of a noble landowner of Scottish origin, became a Decadent poet with great popularity especially on lecture platforms before provincial audiences. After 1918 he was an *émigré*, living in France.

He lifted his reddish beard high while he was reciting. The lines rolled in waves over the audience.

Like quiet distant footsteps grows a murmur out the window
A whisper I can't understand—the whispering of drops of rain.

Balmont finished. The lampshades shook in the roar of applause. Balmont raised his hand. Everyone was silent again.

"I will read you Edgar Poe's 'The Raven,' " he said. "But first I want to tell you how destiny somehow manages to be kind to us poets. When Edgar Poe died and they buried him in Baltimore, his relatives put on his grave a stone slab of extraordinary weight. Those pious Quakers obviously feared that the poet's rebellious soul might escape from his tomb and climb out to trouble the peace of mind of businesslike Americans. But look, when they placed the stone on Edgar's grave, it split. And this broken stone lies over him to this day, and in its cracks little pansies grow every spring. This was the name, by the way, which Edgar called his beautiful wife, Virginia, who died so young."

Balmont began to read "The Raven." The tragic, magnificent poem came alive in the hall. Outside the windows was no longer Kiev, nor the lights hanging in blue chains along the Kreshchatik; there was nothing. Only the wind howled dolefully across the snow-covered plain. And the iron word "Nevermore" fell heavily into the emptiness of the night like the striking of tower clocks.

"Nevermore!" It was something one's consciousness couldn't cope with. Was it really never? Would Virginia never return to earth, and would she never knock again, playfully and carefully, on the heavy door? Would youth, love, and happiness never come back? "Never, nevermore!" the raven croaked, and a man shuddered with loneliness in his shabby chair and looked with his sick child's eyes at the cold emptiness. And this little man rejected by everyone was Edgar Allan Poe, the great American poet.

I have remained grateful to Selikhanovich all my life for having developed my love for poetry. This has opened for me the richness of language. Words renew themselves in poetry, acquire new strengths. When the poets' vast world of imagery enters into one's consciousness, it is as if a veil has been removed from one's eyes.

While Selikhanovich revealed literature and philosophy to us, old Klyachin gave us the history of Western Europe. He was a thin man with an enormous Adam's apple, who never shaved and always wore his frock coat unbuttoned. His eyes were frowning and unseeing. He spoke hoarsely and harshly, in scraps of sentences. He threw words around like hunks of clay. Out of them he made for us living statues of Danton, Babeuf, Marat, Bonaparte, Louis-Philippe, Gambetta.

He choked with indignation when he talked about the 9th Thermidor or the treachery of Thiers. He grew so excited that he would light a cigarette and then, remembering where he was, stub it out immediately on the nearest desk. Klyachin was an authority on the French Revolution. The very existence of such a teacher in a *gymnasium* of those days was a mystery. Sometimes his talk rose to such eloquence that it was as if he were talking from the tribune of the Convention and not in a classroom. He was a living anachronism, and at the same time the best man of all our teachers.

Sometimes it seemed that he was the last old *montagnard* who had miraculously outlived his time by a century and settled down in Kiev. He had escaped the guillotine and death in the jungles of Guiana, and he had not lost a single drop of his fierce enthusiasm.

Once in a while Klyachin would grow tired. Then he would tell us about Paris at the time of the Revolution—about its streets and its houses, how lanterns burned then in the streets, how the women dressed, what songs the people sang, and how the newspapers looked. Many of us, after Klyachin's classes, would have liked to step back a hundred years in time so that we might witness the great things he told us about.

THE SHOOTING IN THE THEATER

The parquet floor in the assembly hall was so highly polished that you could see reflected in it, as in a lake, the blue ranks of boys in full-dress uniforms with shining buttons, and the chandeliers which had been lighted in the middle of the day. There was a low rumbling in the room. Suddenly it stopped.

A short colonel with light-colored bulging eyes walked into the hall, jangling his spurs. He stopped and looked steadily at us. The trumpets sounded their brassy voices. We stood there without a quiver.

Following the colonel, who was Nicholas II, came a very tall, dried-up woman in a white, hard dress and with an enormous hat on her head, which she was nodding. Ostrich feathers dropped down from the brim of her hat. The woman's face was dead, beautiful, and evil. She was the Tsarina.

In Indian file behind her walked their daughters with thin, bloodless lips, all dressed in the same kind of white, hard dresses. These dresses didn't bend. There was not a crease in them and they looked as if they were made of stiff white cardboard.

Behind the girls, who were the grand duchesses, swam an enormous lady, rustling loudly in a violet dress with black lace, wearing gold pince-nez, with a silk ribbon over her shoulder—the governess of the Tsar's daughters, Fräulein Narishkina. The fat bulged over her tight silks. She kept wiping her face with a lace handkerchief.

This was the opening of the solemn celebration of the centenary of our *gymnasium*.

Nicholas was hidden from us by his retinue. We could see only the carefully plastered hair around the bald spots of the ministers, scarlet ribbons, white trousers with gold stripes and with foot-straps going around patent leather shoes, the wide trousers worn by generals, and silver sashes.

Ndelsky, who was the best orator in the *gymnasium,* read the Tsar a poem of welcome he had written himself. He diligently rasped it out in a wooden voice. He addressed the Tsar as "thee" and "thou."

Then the retinue parted in the middle and Nicholas walked toward us along a broad passageway. He stopped, stroked his light brown mustache, and said slowly, burring his consonants:

"How do you do, gentlemen?"

We answered as we had been instructed, not loudly but distinctly:

"We wish good health to Your Imperial Majesty!"

I was the last one in the row because I was the smallest in the graduating class. Nicholas came up to me. A slight tic made his cheek twitch. He looked at me absent-mindedly, smiled with one eye as he always did, and asked me:

"What is your name?"

I told him.

"Aren't you a Ukrainian?" Nicholas asked.

"Yes, Your Highness," I answered.

Nicholas slid his bored glance over me and moved on to my neighbor. He greeted all of us. He asked each one what his name was.

After he had finished the round, the concert started. Nicholas listened to it standing up. So we all stood. Everything about him showed that Nicholas was bored by the celebration and that he had no intention of wasting time on a *gymnasium* concert. He kept plucking impatiently at the glove he had taken off his right hand.

The concert dragged on. The *gymnasium* orchestra played "Glory, glory to our Russian Tsar." Then someone recited "The Prophet Oleg" and the choir sang a cantata. It was all very boring and unnecessary. The ministers were yawning behind the Tsar's back. It was awkward to look at those who were playing in the concert— they were all shaking with fear.

While it was going on, we looked at the ministers and the Tsar's retinue. We were amazed at the difference between the Tsar and his courtiers. Nicholas, who was plain and even clumsy-looking, was simply lost in his vast entourage. They sparkled and glittered with gold and silver, the tops of their varnished boots, their epaulets, their sword knots, their sabers, their spurs, and their medals. Even when the courtiers all stood motionless we could still hear a dim sound coming from their regalia and weapons.

Nicholas listened to the concert with a face of stone, and then he walked out of the *gymnasium*. He was not happy. He had his own score to settle with our *gymnasium*. Two days before this ceremony, our former pupil Bagrov had shot his minister Stolypin in the Opera Theater and mortally wounded him. But I have more to tell about this later.

To honor our centenary it had been decided to give the *gymnasium* the better-sounding title of a lyceum. The imperial decree had been drawn up. But after the shooting in the theater this was awkward—how could the rights and privileges of a lyceum be given to a *gymnasium* which had produced a political criminal! So instead they simply renamed it "Emperor Alexander's *Gymnasium*" in honor of Alexander I, adding a new coat of arms with the monogram "A" and a crown.

The letters on the new coat of arms, "EAG," gave the boys in all the other schools of Kiev new material with which to ridicule us. Fights about it were not uncommon. But we in the graduating class decided not to change the old coat of arms on our uniforms. The school officials objected, but we pointed out that we could not afford to buy new buttons and buckles. The officials gave in finally. There was no point in feuding with the graduating class.

There were many different ceremonies to honor Nicholas' visit to Kiev. The ugly bronze statue of Alexander II was unveiled, and the even uglier plaster monuments to Saints Olga, Kyril, and

Mefodia. Military exercises were held in the outskirts of Kiev. Church parades and solemn spectacles were arranged to bless, to unveil, or to organize all kinds of things. Flags flew on all the houses for a whole week.

On the race course, after the trotting races, they had a parade of all the *gymnasiums* of Kiev. We all marched by Nicholas in a great cloud of dust. The setting sun was in our eyes. We could not see a thing and mixed up our ranks. A military band was blaring away in full strength.

Our *gymnasium* distinguished itself by forgetting to reply to the Tsar's greeting. A full general galloped up to us and swore at us for a long time, reining in his horse in temper. The reddish-brown horse laid its ears back and danced in front of us.

There was a special performance in the Opera Theater to honor Nicholas. They assembled the graduating classes, both boys and girls, of all the *gymnasiums* in Kiev. Our class was included.

We were led up to the gallery by the dark service stairway. The gallery was then locked so that we could not get down to the lower sections of the theater. Friendly but insolent police officers stood at the doors. They winked at each other, and let the pretty girls go through. I was sitting in the back row, and I saw nothing. It was terribly hot. The ceiling of the theater was just above my head.

It was only during the intermission that I could get up from my place and go up to the railing. I leaned over and looked down at the theater. It seemed filled with a light mist, with many-colored diamonds shining through it. The Tsar's box was empty. Nicholas had moved back into the little room behind it, with all his family. Ministers and courtiers were standing in a crowd next to the railing which separated the audience from the orchestra.

I watched the audience and listened to the blurred sound of voices. The musicians in black evening clothes sat in their places but they did not tune their instruments as they usually did.

Suddenly there was a sharp crack. The musicians jumped up from their chairs. The crack was repeated. I had no idea that these were shots. A girl standing next to me cried out:

"Look! He sat right down on the floor!"

"Who?"

"Stolypin. There. Next to the railing by the orchestra."

I looked where she was pointing. It was unusually quiet in the theater. A tall man with a round black beard and with a ribbon over his shoulder was sitting on the floor next to the railing. He was feeling for the railing with his hands as if he wanted to grab it and stand up. Around Stolypin there was only empty space.

A young man in evening clothes was walking along the aisle from Stolypin to the exit door. I could not see his face at that distance. But I did notice that he was walking quite calmly, not hurrying.

Someone gave a long-drawn cry. A roaring started. An officer jumped out of a box and grabbed the young man by the arm. A crowd immediately swirled around them.

"Clear the gallery!" a police officer said behind me. They drove us quickly into the corridor. The doors were locked again behind us.

We stood there, understanding nothing. A dull roaring filtered through to us from the theater. Then it died down, and the orchestra played "God, Save the Tsar."

"He killed Stolypin," Fitsovsky whispered to me.

"No talking! File out of the theater at once!" the police officer shouted.

We walked down the same dark stairway to the brightly lighted square. It was deserted. Lines of mounted police had pushed the crowds standing around the theater back into the side streets, and they were pushing them still farther away. The horses were prancing nervously. The rolling sound of horse's hoofs could be heard all over the square.

Someone blew a little horn. An ambulance clattered up to the theater at full speed. Orderlies jumped out of it with a stretcher and ran into the theater.

We were walking slowly away from the square. We wanted to see what would happen next. The police hurried us along, but they all looked so worried that we didn't listen to them.

We saw Stolypin carried out on the stretcher. They put him in the ambulance and it moved off along Vladimirskaya Street. Mounted police rode along beside it.

I went home to Lukyanovka and told Grandmother and Gattenberger about the murder of Stolypin. Grandmother said that it was wrong to shoot in a theater because innocent people might get hurt. Gattenberger got very excited, puffed at his cigar, then commented that the scoundrel Stolypin had had to be killed some time, and went into the city to learn more news.

He came back late in the night and told us that Malaya Vladimirskaya Street, where Stolypin was lying in a hospital, had been covered thick with hay, and that the Black Hundreds were calling for a pogrom of all the Jews.

"That was all we needed!" Grandmother exclaimed angrily.

But Gattenberger said that while the Tsar was still in Kiev there would be no pogrom.

The next morning Grandmother asked me:

"Are you going into the city again?"

"Yes. To the *gymnasium.*"

"Why?"

"There's going to be a rehearsal of our meeting with the Tsar."

"It would be better to get sick and not go," Grandmother advised me. "It's all so stupid. Hasn't the Tsar really anything better to do than just show off in front of the people?"

I said that obviously this was how it was.

"Well, then, don't go," Grandmother said. "It's all on account of this Nicholas that people are wandering around town, not thinking of anything. They're wasting their time on bagatelles, on nonsense, as if God will lengthen their lives to give them back the time they're wasting. Stay here. Maybe you can have a headache! Sit in the garden and read, and I'll bake you some *strutsel* [this was what Grandmother called apple pie in Polish]. I don't understand how people can throw their time away without any sense, stupidly, when the days are like this outdoors!"

I listened to Grandmother and did not go to the rehearsal. The days were really wonderful then. The leaves on the apple trees had turned pink and begun to dry up. Some of them were curled into little cylinders and wound around with spiderwebs. Red and white asters were blooming along the edges of the paths. Yellow butterflies were flying among the trees. They lighted in little clusters on anything warmed by the sun—the stone veranda steps or a tin watering can forgotten in the garden.

The sun moved slowly over my head toward the tops of the nut trees; it looked as if it had been squeezed smaller by the autumn.

I read in the garden, sitting in Grandmother's wicker chair. From time to time I heard music far away, somewhere in the city. Then I put down my book and began to look at the path. It had been cut through heavy grass, and along its steep sides a small moss was growing which looked like green velvet. Something very delicate looked white in the middle of this moss. It was the flowers of wood anemones which had blown into our garden from nobody knows where and were blossoming a second time.

A white duck flew into the courtyard. When it saw me it quacked angrily and went back where it had come from. Obviously I bothered it. Sparrows were sitting on the roof, washing themselves and occasionally craning their heads out to see if there were anything interesting below. The sparrows were waiting. Then Grandmother came out on the veranda and threw a handful of bread crumbs onto the path. The sparrows swooped down from the roof and bounced like gray rubber balls along the ground.

"Kostik," Grandmother called to me, "come in to dinner."

She was standing on the veranda steps. I got up and walked toward her. Out of her room came the smell of apple pie.

"As if this weren't a real royal holiday!" Grandmother said, looking at the garden. "People just think up all kinds of stupidity for themselves with this Nicholas II!"

In the garden it was a real holiday of light and of clear, warm air.

RAZGULYAI

For the Christmas holidays I went to visit Mama in Moscow. The snow was falling so heavily when we went through Bryansk that nothing could be seen out of the train windows. I could only imagine to myself the little town far beyond the falling snow, the shimmering carpets of snow along its streets, and Uncle Kolya's home with its glassed-in porch.

This was my first trip to Moscow. I was excited at the thought of seeing Mama, and of traveling from our southern provincial city of Kiev to the capital in the north.

The train moved deeper with every hour into the white plains, slowly nearing the very edge of the gray sky. There I could see only haze. I imagined that somewhere there on the horizon daytime would merge into eternal polar night.

I was a little afraid of the Moscow winter. I had no warm overcoat, only mittens and a hood. It was so cold that the bells rang with a special clarity at the stations. Felt boots crunched in the snow. A fellow passenger gave me some ham made out of bear meat; it smelled of resin from pine trees.

In the night, beyond Sukhinicha, the train got stuck in snowdrifts. The wind whistled through the tin ventilators. Conductors carrying lanterns hurried through the cars, white and shaggy with snow like bears coming out of their lairs. Each one of them slammed the door behind him with all his strength. I woke up every time.

In the morning I walked out on the platform of the car. The grainy air bit into my face. In the fields the wind was blowing little ridges of snow next to the ditches. It was hard to open the door. The storm had died down. The cars were standing up to their buffers in magnificent snow. You could have jumped into it over your head. A little bluebird was sitting on the roof of the train, twisting its head and cheeping. You couldn't tell where the white sky ran into the white landscape. It was so quiet that I could hear the water leaking out of the locomotive.

Dima met me at the Bryansk station in Moscow. He had a stubborn little mustache on his upper lip. He was wearing the uniform of a student at the Technological Institute.

I was very cold, and we went into the station buffet to drink tea. The Moscow station amazed me—wooden, low, like a huge tavern. An orange sun lit up the counter with its nickel dish covers, the tables with blue palm trees, the steam from the teapots, the muslin curtains. Beyond the layers of frost on the windowpanes cabdrivers were shouting. We drank our tea with broken loaf sugar. They gave us crunchy cakes covered with flour.

Then we went out on the street. Steam was rising from shaggy horses. The cabdrivers' patched peasant coats, with tin numbers, rippled in front of us. Swallows were darting over the manure-covered snow.

"Where do you want to go, your excellencies?" the cabdrivers yelled as they slapped their reins against the horses.

One of them was in front of the others. He pulled back a shabby piece of wolfskin, and we sat down in a narrow sleigh. Hay was strewn under our feet. I looked around in wonder. Was this really Moscow?

"To Razgulyai," Dima told the driver. "But take us through the Kremlin."

"That I'll do!" the driver said. "It's all the same to us. Here or at the Kremlin, this old homespun coat won't keep me warm."

Right outside the station, in Dorogomilova, we were swallowed up in a chaos of sledges, bells, steam beating into our faces from the horses' mouths, tavern signs, policemen with frozen mustaches and the sound of church bells rocking in the air.

We drove over the Borodinsky Bridge. A dark glow could be seen in the windows of houses across the river; it was the reflection of the setting sun. According to the round clocks at street crossings, it was only two o'clock in the afternoon. It was all strange, overpowering, and good.

"Well," Dima asked me, "how do you like Moscow?"

"A lot."

"Just wait. There are wonderful things to show you."

Beyond Arbat Square we turned into a narrow street. At its end, on a hill, I could see fortress walls and towers, the green roofs of palaces and the gray bulk of cathedrals. All of this was wrapped in a reddish evening smoke.

"What is that?" I asked Dima, completely confused.

"Don't you really recognize it? That's the Kremlin."

I sighed convulsively. I wasn't prepared for this meeting with the Kremlin. It stood up above the great city like a massive fortress constructed of rose-colored stone, gold, and silence.

So this was the Kremlin. Russia, the history of my people. "It would be a proud man who didn't take off his hat in front of the Kremlin's holy gates."

My eyes filled with tears.

We drove into the Kremlin through the Borovitsky Gate. I saw the Tsar-bell, the Tsar-cannon, and the Ivan Veliki belltower rising into the evening sky. The driver took off his hat. Dima and I took off our caps and the sleigh drove on under the Spassky tower. A lamp flickered in the dark tunnel. Chimes were sounding carelessly and magnificently over our heads.

"But what's that?" I asked Dima and I grabbed his arm when we had driven out of the Spassky Gate. Fantastic domes like many-colored burdock seed pods could be seen running down the slope to the river.

"Don't you really know?" Dima answered, and he laughed. "That's St. Basil's Cathedral."

Bonfires were burning on the Red Square. Passers-by and cab-drivers were warming themselves around them. Smoke hung over the square. On the wall right next to us I saw an advertisement of the Moscow Art Theater with a picture of a flying wild duck, and other posters with the words in heavy type: "Emile Verhaeren."

"What's that?" I asked Dima again.

"Verhaeren is in Moscow right now," he answered, and he laughed when he looked at me. I must have looked dumbfounded. "Just wait, you'll still see lots of wonders."

While we were driving to Razgulyai it grew dark. The sleigh stopped outside a two-storied house with thick walls. We went up a curving staircase. Dima rang, and Mama opened the door. Galya was standing behind Mama, sticking out her head and trying to see me in the dark vestibule.

Mama embraced me and burst into tears. She had turned completely white since I had last seen her.

"My God!" Mama said, "you're already completely grown up. And how like your father you are! God, how like him!"

Galya had become almost completely blind. She led me to the lamp in the room and examined me for a long time. I could guess from her tense face that she couldn't see me, although she kept saying that I hadn't changed at all.

The furniture in the room was strange to me and poor. But I saw some things I had known since childhood—Mama's box, an old bronze alarm clock, and a photograph of my father, taken when he was still young. The photograph hung on the wall over Mama's bed.

Mama was upset because the dinner wasn't ready yet, and she went out to the kitchen. Galya started to ask me, as she always did, about unimportant things—what the weather was like in Kiev, why my train had been late, and whether Grandmother Vikentiya Ivanovna still drank coffee in the mornings. Dima was silent.

It seemed to me that so much that was hard and meaningful had happened to our lives over these years that I didn't know what to talk about. Then I realized that it wasn't necessary to talk about anything difficult or important. Our lives had taken us far apart during these two years. The ten days for which I had come to Moscow would not be long enough to tell everything.

So I didn't tell about my short story. I hid this from Mama and Galya and Dima.

I thought about Grandmother, and about my little room in Lukyanovka, with a little homesickness. My real life, probably, had stayed there. Here were only strange things—Dima's institute, and this gloomy old two-room apartment, and Galya's uninteresting questions. Only Mama's eyes were the same as they had always been. But she grew upset now over the little things to which she had paid no attention before.

I was waiting for Mama to talk about the future with me, but she kept silent about that. Then after dinner she asked casually:

"Well, what are you thinking of doing when you've finished the *gymnasium?*"

"I want to go to the university," I answered.

Then Mama took some gray theater tickets, with the picture of the wild duck on them, out of her box, and handed them to me.

"They're for you."

They were tickets to the Moscow Art Theater for *The Living Corpse* and *The Three Sisters*. It turned out that Mama had stood

in line outside the ticket office through an entire cold winter night
to get these tickets. I was passionately happy and I kissed Mama,
but she just smiled and said it had been very interesting to stand
all night in a crowd of students and it had been a long while since
she had had such a good time.

The Three Sisters was playing the night I arrived. So Dima and
I got ready to go to the theater right after dinner. We rode in a cold
tramway as far as Theater Square. Blue electric sparks showered
down from the wires. Theater Square was filled with shining snow
crystals. They hung in the air and you could see them clearly
around the street lamps. The Muir and Merilize store threw a great
shaft of light out on the pavement. A Christmas tree was lighted
up in its display window, and chains of gold and silver paper hung
down from it to the floor.

We walked through Theater Square to Kamergersky Lane and
went into a plain-looking theater. The floors were covered with
gray cloth. People moved around without making any noise. Warm
air was blowing out of the heat registers. The big brown curtain
with its wild duck was fluttering slightly. Everything was severe
looking and yet very gay.

My cheeks were so flushed and my eyes, probably, so shining
that people sitting next to us smiled when they looked at me.
Dina said: "Pull yourself together. Otherwise, you won't hear anything or see anything."

I felt sorry for the people who were so unhappy in the Chekhov
play. But I didn't lose the feeling of freshness and gaiety. Both the
freshness and the gaiety were products of great art.

Everything unattractive and unhappy that I had seen on Razgulyai now seemed temporary to me, and not very important. Poverty, insults, failure might well exist, but nobody could extinguish
this light that was coming now from the mysterious world of art.
Nobody could take this richness away from me. And nobody had
any power over it except myself. This was the mood in which I
lived in Moscow for ten days. Mama kept looking at me and saying
that I looked surprisingly like my father.

"It's clear to me," she said one day, "that you're not likely to be
a positive sort of person." She was quiet for a moment, and then
she added: "No, of course, you won't be much support in life. Not
even for yourself. Not with your interests! With your fantasies!
With your lighthearted relation to things!"

I said nothing. Mama put her arms around me, and kissed me.

"Well, God be with you! I would like you to be happy. All the
rest is unimportant."

"I'm happy the way I am," I answered her. "Please, don't worry about me. I've lived alone for two years. I'll survive."

Mama was wearing glasses then. She had broken the frame and they were held together by tape. Mama took off her glasses, looked at the tape for a long time, and then looked carefully at me.

"How cold and formal our family has become!" she said with a sigh. "And so secretive. That's what comes from being poor. Here you've come to see us and haven't told us anything about yourself. And I don't say anything, but keep postponing it. We must have a talk."

"Well, all right. Only don't you worry."

"Galya is blind," Mama said, and she was quiet for a while. "And now she's started to grow deaf. She couldn't live a week without me. You don't know how much I have to do for her. All the strength I have left is for Galya. Only God knows how much I love you—you and Dima and Borya, but I can't do everything."

I answered that I understood everything perfectly and that I would soon be able to help her and Galya. As soon as I finished the *gymnasium*. I no longer thought, as I had formerly, of ever returning to Mama. But I was sorry for her and I loved her and I didn't want her to suffer by worrying about me. So I calmed her and set off with a light heart for the Tretyakovsky Gallery.

I felt like a guest in my own family. The contrast was too great between the frosty city of Moscow, blanketed by snow and the winter sky, with its theaters, its museums, its church bells, and this pinched and cheerless life in two cold rooms on Razgulyai.

I saw, without understanding, that Dima was completely satisfied with his life, with his institute, with the profession he had chosen which was utterly alien to me. I also noticed without understanding it that Dima's room had almost no books in it except for a few textbooks and some mimeographed lectures.

The whole day went by for Galya, because of her blindness, in a careful bustle about unimportant things. She groped her way through everything. Time had stopped for her three years before, when she had begun to lose her sight. She lived now only in memories, little ones and all the same. The circle of these memories kept shrinking—Galya had begun to forget a great deal.

Sometimes she would sit quietly with her hands on her knees. Occasionally in the evenings Mama would find time to read to her, usually Goncharov or Turgenev. After the reading Galya would question Mama about what she had just heard, trying to fasten down in her memory the detailed sequence of events in the novels. Mama would patiently answer all her questions.

I went out to the Tretyakovsky Gallery. There were almost no visitors there. It was as if the quiet winter had moved the gallery out of the capital into the suburbs—there were no city sounds to be heard. Old men, the custodians of the famous pictures, drowsed on their chairs.

I stood for a long time next to Nesterov's picture, "St. Bartholomew's Vision." Its thin little birch trees were as white as candles. Every blade of grass stretched trustingly up toward the sky. My heart beat faster when I looked at this moving and undemanding beauty.

A stout, white-haired lady dressed in black was sitting on a divan in front of the picture. She was looking at it through a lorgnette. Next to her was a girl with reddish-brown braids. I stood to one side so as not to block their view of the picture. The white-haired lady turned toward me and asked:

"What do you think, Kostik, is it like the hill at Ryovna behind the park, or not?"

I was startled and embarrassed. The lady smiled when she looked at me.

"Youth is so unobservant nowadays!" she said. "Have you really forgotten the Karelins? At Ryovna? Me, and Lyuba, and Sasha? It's true, that was some years ago."

I blushed, and greeted them. Now I recognized the white-haired lady—Maria Trofimovna Karelina. But I didn't recognize Lyuba right away. She had grown, and she was no longer wearing black ribbons in her hair.

"Sit down," Maria Trofimovna said to me. "How you've grown! Tell us what brings you here. And let's remember Ryovna together. Ah, what a place, what a place! This summer we simply must go back."

I told them about myself. Maria Trofimovna told me that she was still living in Oryol with Sasha. Lyuba had finished the *gymnasium* and had enrolled in the Moscow School of Painting and Sculpture. Maria Trofimovna and Sasha had come to Moscow to visit Lyuba over the winter holidays.

"And where is Sasha?" I asked.

"She stayed at the hotel. She has a sore throat."

Lyuba was looking at me from the side, with her head at an angle. We all went out together. I accompanied them as far as the Loskutnaya Hotel. They invited me in to get warm and drink coffee.

It was dark from the heavy curtains and drapes in their big room. Sasha greeted me as an old friend and asked right away about Gleb Afanasiev. As far as I knew, he was still studying in the Bryansk *gymnasium*.

Sasha's throat had a bow tied around it, like a cat's. She took me by the hand: "Come on. I'll show you Lyuba's pictures."

She dragged me into the next room. But Lyuba siezed me by the other hand and stopped us.

"That's stupid!" she said, and she blushed. "Look at them later. We will see you again, won't we?"

"I don't know," I answered hesitantly.

"He'll greet the New Year with us!" Sasha cried. "At Lyuba's. At her studio on Kislovka. Oh, what a Bohemian life she has there, if you only knew, Kostik! The knights of canvas and the palette. One artist is right out of a French novel. You absolutely must fall in love with her. She walks around in a black silk dress. And perfume! What perfume! 'Grief of tuberoses'."

"Oh, ye gods!" Lyuba said. "What an intolerable chatterbox you are! It's clear why your throat is always sore."

"I have a throat like a nightingale's." Sasha made her face look languorous. "It can't stand the Russian winter."

"No, really, you will come, won't you?" Lyuba asked me. "On New Year's Eve?"

"I'm going to celebrate it at home. It's an old family custom with us."

"Then greet the New Year at home," Maria Trofimovna advised me firmly, "and come over to Lyuba's later. They'll be making fools of themselves until morning."

I agreed. Then we drank coffee. Sasha put four pieces of sugar in my glass. Coffee as sweet as that cannot be drunk. Maria Trofimovna grew angry. Lyuba sat there, with her eyes lowered.

"Why are you sitting there like a princess in a fairy tale?" Sasha asked her. "Kostik, it's true, isn't it, that Lyuba has become a beauty? Look at her. Not like her younger sister—the slut and the ugly duckling."

Lyuba flushed, stood up, and moved her cup aside.

"Stop it, once and for all! You magpie!"

I looked at Lyuba. There was a blue flame burning in her eyes. She really was very good-looking.

I left. At home I told Mama that I had met the Karelins and that they had invited me for New Year's Eve. Mama was delighted.

"Of course you'll go! Or else it will probably get boring for you here in Moscow. They are very nice people, and highly intelligent."

The measure of a person in Mama's eyes was intelligence. If Mama respected someone she would always say: "That's a highly intelligent person."

There were two days left before New Year's. They were wonderful days, covered with hoarfrost and gray with fog. I went alone to the rink at the Zoological Gardens and skated there. The ice was hard and black, not at all like ice in Kiev. Men were sweeping the rink with huge brooms.

I raced after a bearded man in a black caracul hat. I caught up to him. He reminded me of the artist I had met at the farm near Smela where I had gone with Aunt Nadya.

Mama promised to go with me to Aunt Nadya's grave in the Vagansky Cemetery, but we never got there. She told me that porcelain roses were still lying on the grave. They had faded, but had not been broken.

For some reason I kept remembering the long ago in that snowy, December Moscow—Alushta, Lena, and how she had cried out to me: "Go! This is all foolishness!" All these years I had been planning to write to her, but I never wrote. By now I was convinced that she had forgotten me.

I thought of Lena, and I was staggered at the thought of how many people walk out of one's life and never return. It had happened with Lena, and Aunt Nadya, and my grandfather the bee-keeper, and my father, and Uncle Yusia, and many others. It was strange and sad, and, in spite of my eighteen years, it seemed to me that I had already lived through a great deal. I had loved all these people. Each one of them, in leaving, had taken a piece of my love with them. This must have left me poorer.

This was how I thought then, but these ideas were in no way connected with the surprising love for life which grew in me from year to year. Many people left me for a long time or for good, and so my meeting with the Karelins—I had forgotten about them completely—seemed to me significant, as if there were some hidden design behind it.

I greeted the New Year at home. Mama baked a cake. Dima bought some snacks, some wine, and cookies. At eleven Dima went out somewhere. Mama told me he had gone to get his fiancée. Her name was Margarite. Mama said she was a remarkable girl and that she could not wish for a better wife for Dima.

In order not to disappoint Mama I smiled cheerfully although I didn't like the name of Dima's fiancée or the fact that her father was a government official.

I helped Mama set the New Year's table. The room smelled of

burned hair: Galya, curling her hair by touch, had burned a long
lock of it. She was distressed about it, but I did my best to cheer
her up. We lit the candles. Mama put the bronze alarm clock on
the table and I set it for twelve o'clock.

I got out the presents I had brought from Kiev: gray cloth for
a dress for Mama, slippers for Galya, a big case of drawing instruments for Dima. I had asked Borya for it. It was a remarkable case.
Mama was overjoyed by the presents. She even had a little color
in her cheeks.

Several minutes before the New Year, Dima came in with a
tall, pale girl with a long, crestfallen face. Her lilac dress with a
yellow sash didn't fit her properly. A lace handkerchief was fastened to its front. She blushed all the time, and took cookies from
the bowl with a fork.

Galya started a conversation with her at once on the raising
of children. The girl answered without any spark, and kept looking at Dima. Dima smiled in a very controlled way.

The alarm clock went off with a desperate clatter, interrupting
one of Galya's opinions. We all drank wine out of one goblet, and
congratulated each other on the new year. Mama was clearly trying very hard to make Margarite like us. But she jealously watched
how Margarite looked at Dima, as if she were trying to measure
how much love there was in every look.

I chattered away and tried as hard as I could to show that I
was happy, but I also kept looking at my watch on the sly. Mama
drank down her wine, grew cheerful, and started to tell Margarite
about Easter at Grandmother's in Cherkasy and about how well
and how happily we used to live in Kiev. It was a little as if she
didn't believe herself that all this had really happened. "Isn't it
true, Kostik?" she kept asking me. Every time I told her that, yes,
it had been just like that.

At half past one I excused myself and left. Mama went with
me as far as the vestibule. She asked me in a conspiratorial voice
if I liked Margarite. I realized how useless it would be to tell the
truth. It would have resulted in nothing but added disappointment.
So I told her that Margarite was a delightful girl and that I was
very glad for Dima.

"Well, please God, please God!" Mama whispered. "It looks to
me as if Margarite gets along well with Galya."

I went out on Basmannaya Street, stopped and breathed in the
cold air. Lights were burning in the houses. I hired a cab and
drove to Kislovka. The driver swore at his horses all the way.

Sasha opened the door for me at Kislovka. An elegant new bow

was tied around her neck. Some girls ran out into the vestibule,
and a handsome older man in a student's jacket. For some reason,
Lyuba was not to be seen. The girls, laughing, started to undo
my hood and to pull off my coat, and the old man sang in a youthful voice:

> On a mountain, in the evening,
> Three goddesses began to quarrel.

"His eyes! His eyes!" the girls cried out. Sasha covered my eyes
with the palms of her hands. My head was whirling from the
smell of the girls' hair, their perfume, and Sasha's firm little fingers
pressing against my eyes.

They took me by the hand and led me in. I could feel it when
when the door opened—heat struck me in the face. The noise died
down and a woman's voice said imperiously:

"Swear!"

"Swear what?" I asked.

"That for this whole night you will forget about everything
except happiness."

Sasha's fingers were hurting my eyes.

"I swear it!" I answered.

"And now take an oath!"

"To whom?"

"To the one who has been chosen queen of our festival."

"Swear it," Sasha whispered in my ear.

The tickling was making me squirm.

"I take the oath."

"As a symbol of obedience you will now kiss the queen's hand.
That is the knightly custom," said a voice which was holding back
laughter. "Sasha, take your paws away!"

Sasha released me. I saw a brightly lighted room with a lot of
pictures in it. A thin man in a short velvet coat was lying on the
piano in the pose of Vrubel's "The Demon." His hands were folded
under his head. He looked at me with sad eyes.

A snub-nosed young fellow played a chord. The girls fell back
and I saw Lyuba. She was sitting in an armchair on top of a round
table. Her white silk dress hung lightly on her and fell over the
table. Her bare arms were hanging down. In her right hand Lyuba
was holding a fan made of ostrich feathers. She looked at me, trying not to smile.

I walked up and kissed her hand. The old man in the student's
jacket gave me a goblet of ice-cold champagne. I drank it in one
gulp.

Lyuba stood up. I helped her get down from the table. She held the edge of her long dress, curtsied to me, and asked:

"We didn't frighten you with our foolishness? Why did he give you iced champagne? Drink something warmer. I think there's some mulled wine left."

I was pushed down into a chair at a table and urged to eat, but they forgot about this right away and laughingly moved me and the table into a corner of the room to clear a space for dancing. The young fellow played a waltz.

Vrubel's "Demon" jumped down from the piano and started to dance with Lyuba. She moved lightly through the room, leaning far backwards, covering her face with her black fan. Every time she danced by me, she smiled at me through the fan. She was holding up the train of her dress.

The old man was dancing with the woman whom Sasha had called the heroine of a French novel. The heroine had a sinister kind of laugh. Sasha dragged me away from the table to dance with her. She was so thin that it seemed she might wilt away at any moment.

"But don't dance with Lyuba," Sasha told me.

"Why not?"

"She's a proud woman!"

After the dance, Vrubel's "Demon" started to drink out of all the opened bottles, and quickly became drunk.

"I'm thirsting for summer!" he shouted. "Down with icicles! Up with rain!"

No one paid any attention to him and he disappeared. The old man sat down at the piano and sang in a voice that tugged at the heartstrings:

My distant friend, understand my sobbing!

When he had finished, we suddenly heard the sound of rain. It was pouring somewhere close to us, a heavy, fresh rain. Everyone was frightened into silence, then we dashed down the corridor to the bathroom. Vrubel's "Demon" was standing in the bathtub in his overcoat and galoshes, under a black umbrella, and the shower was pouring water down on him.

"It's gold! Gold is falling from heaven!" he shouted.

We turned off the shower and dragged Vrubel's "Demon" out of the bathtub.

I talked, too, and recited some poetry, and laughed, in the general confusion. I came to myself only when Lyuba turned out the chandelier, and the room was filled with the blue, hazy light of dawn. Everyone grew quiet. The blue light mixed with the light from the lamp on a table. Faces looked dull and beautiful.

"The nicest time of all is after a muddled night," the old man in the student's jacket said. "Now we can drink our wine calmly. And talk about different things. I love the dawn. It rinses the soul."

Vrubel's "Demon" had not yet sobered up.

"No rinsing!" he shouted. "I don't want to hear anyone gargle with his soul. Dostoievsky! All light consists of seven colors. I bow down before them. And on all the rest I spit!"

Then everyone was quiet for a long time in a light drowsiness. Lyuba was sitting next to me.

"Everything is whirling in front of my eyes," she said. "And everything is so blue . . . and I don't want to sleep at all."

"Catharsis!" the old man said, importantly. "The cleansing of the soul after tragedy."

"I don't know," Lyuba answered.

She grew thoughtful. The morning light was reflected in her eyes.

"You're tired," I said.

"No. I feel simply wonderful."

"Is it true that you're going to Ryovna this summer?"

"Yes," Lyuba answered. "And will you come?"

"I'll come. If Uncle Kolya's there."

"But why 'if'?" Lyuba asked slyly.

Soon we stood up and began to say good-by. I was the last to go. I had to take Sasha back to her hotel; she had been drinking very hot tea and was waiting for her throat to cool.

Fashionable women and young men, probably actors, were throwing snowballs on the street. Confetti was scattered over the snow. The sun was up, dissolving the night fog with its shaggy light.

After this noisy night I felt ashamed to go back to Razgulyai, to our poor apartment smelling of kerosene. But I thought about this for only a moment. Then everything started ringing in my heart, as if the snow and the sunshine and Lyuba's hand, which had pressed mine for a moment when we said good-by, as if all this life had suddenly been transformed into the quiet playing of an orchestra.

The next day I left Moscow. Mama, hunched over in a warm dress, went to the station with me. Dima was going to the theater with Margarite. And Galya kept fussing over whether or not I would miss my train.

On the platform Mama said to me:

"Don't be angry. I think I told you that you are like your father. I know only that you're good."

The train pulled out. It was evening. I watched the lights of Moscow for a long time. One of them, perhaps, was a light in Lyuba's room.

A STORY ABOUT NOTHING

The thaw started in February. Kiev began to be fogbound. A warm wind would sometimes blow the fog away. At Lukyanovka there was a smell of melting snow and of bark—the wind brought this from beyond the Dnieper, from the Chernigov woods which were already darkening with spring.

The rooftops dripped, icicles sparkled, and sometimes at night the wind blew the clouds away, puddles froze over, and the stars gleamed in the sky. They could be seen only in the outskirts where we lived. There was so much light from windows and street lamps in the city that nobody there even suspected the existence of the stars.

It was warm and comfortable in Grandmother's little house on those raw February evenings. We had electric lamps. There was a clatter sometimes in the empty gardens from the wind blowing through the shutters.

I wrote another story, about Polessya and the old men of Mogilev. I kept tinkering with it and the more I tinkered the more the story "got tired"—it became limp and gutted. But still I finished it and took it to the editorial office of the magazine *Flames*. This office was on Fundukleyevskaya Street, in a small room on a court-yard. A cheerful, chubby man was cutting sausage on a pile of galley proofs, preparing to drink tea. He was not in the least surprised by the appearance in his office of a young *gymnasist* with a story.

He took it, glanced casually at its ending, and said that he liked the story but it would have to wait for the editor.

"Have you signed the story with your right name?" the chubby man asked me.

"Yes."

"That's a mistake. Our magazine is on the left politically. And you're still in the *gymnasium*. There might be difficulties. Think up a pseudonym."

I agreed humbly, crossed out my name, and wrote in "Balagin" instead.

"That's better!" the chubby man said.

A thin sallow-faced man with a tangled beard and sunken, piercing eyes walked into the room from the street. He took a long time, swearing and coughing, taking off his high galoshes and unwinding a long muffler.

"There's the editor." The chubby man stopped pulling the skin off the sausage and pointed with his knife to the man who had just come in.

The editor walked to his desk without looking at me, sat down, held out his arm in front of him, and said in a hollow, frightening voice:

"Give it to me!"

I put my manuscript in his outstretched hand.

"Are you aware," the editor asked, "that unaccepted manuscripts are not returned?"

"I know."

"Excellent!" the editor mumbled. "Come back in an hour. I'll tell you then."

The chubby man nodded to me and smiled.

I walked out disheartened, walked for a long time along the Kreshchatik, went into the library, and ran into Fitsovsky. He had just borrowed a volume of Ibsen. He began to attack me because I had read little Ibsen, and he declared that *Ghosts* was the greatest of all works of art.

We walked out together. It was still too early to go back to the editorial office. We walked into a dark courtyard to smoke: on the street we might be seen by one of our teachers or supervisors. Smoking was strictly forbidden for us.

Fitsovsky walked back to the editorial office with me and decided to wait at the gate. He wanted to know what would happen. I asked him to go away. I was scared. What if they didn't take the story? What would Fitsovsky think of me?

I walked in. The editor looked at me searchingly for a while, without saying anything. I was silent, too, and I could feel the perspiration pouring down my face. Obviously, I was blushing profusely.

"May I have my manuscript back?" I asked.

"Manuscript?" the editor asked, and then he started to cough with laughter. "If you please. Just as you like. You can take it and throw it in the stove. But as a matter of fact, I'd like to print this story. Just imagine, I like it very much."

"Excuse me, I didn't know," I muttered.

"Hotheaded youth! Once you start along the writer's path, please remember, you must store up patience. Come back for your honorarium on Wednesday," he went on in an icy voice. "And bring us everything you write."

I darted out of the office. Fitsovsky was standing in the gateway. He had not left.

"Well, how about it?" he asked me nervously. "Did they take it?"

"They took it."

"Come home with me!" Fitsovsky cried out. "I've got a bottle of wine and some pickled apples. We'll celebrate!"

The two of us drank his bottle of wine. I went home very late. The trolleys had all stopped. I walked through empty streets. The street lamps were not burning. If I had met a beggar I would probably have given him my overcoat or done something equally wild. But I didn't meet anyone except a wet, white dog. It was sitting next to a fence, holding up one paw. I searched my pockets, but found nothing. Then I petted it. The dog at once attached itself to me.

All the way home I talked to the dog. In answer it jumped up and bit at the sleeves of my overcoat.

"Just listen!" I said, and I stopped. The dog cocked one ear. Out of the gardens was coming a little rustling, as if last year's leaves were stirring.

"Do you understand what that means?" I asked the dog. "That's spring. And then there'll be summer. And I'll go away from here. And maybe I'll see a girl—the most wonderful girl in the world."

The dog jumped up again, snapping at my sleeves, and we walked on.

There was not a light to be seen in any house. The city was asleep. It seemed to me that all its inhabitants should wake up at once and pour out onto the streets, to see this somber overcast of clouds and to hear the snow melting and crunching and the water slowly dripping out of old snowdrifts. It was wrong to sleep on such a wonderful night.

I don't remember how I got home. Grandmother was asleep. The dog followed me politely into my room. A cold supper was on the table. I fed the dog bread and meat, and fixed it a corner near the stove. It fell asleep immediately. Sometimes, without waking up, it wagged its tail in gratitude.

The next morning Grandmother saw the dog, but she did not object. She felt sorry for it, named it Kado, began to feed it, and the dog and Grandmother became good friends.

Spring drew nearer with every day. And so did our final examinations. Studying for them meant reviewing everything we had learned in the *gymnasium*. This was hard, especially in spring.

Easter came. At the end of the Easter holiday, Uncle Kolya came from Bryansk for several days to visit Grandmother. A bed was fixed for him in my room. My Aunt Vera, who lived with her family in the big house on the street, was angry at Uncle Kolya for staying with me. But Uncle Kolya managed to laugh it off.

In the evenings we would lie on our beds and talk and laugh. When Grandmother heard us, she would get up, dress, and come in and sit with us until late in the night.

Once we had to go to an obligatory formal supper at Aunt Vera's. She had assembled a group of what Grandmother called "various creatures and monsters." One of them who irritated me most was the well-known eye doctor, Dumitrashko, a very short little man with a squeaky voice, a wavy beard, and golden curls which tumbled down on the collar of his black coat. As soon as he appeared, the air was filled with poison. He would wave his flabby little arms and begin to slander the intelligentsia. Aunt Vera's husband, a pimply businessman who looked like a Moldavian, yessed him continually.

Then inevitably a retired general named Piotukh appeared with the three old maids who were his daughters. The general talked chiefly about the price of firewood—he traded in firewood on the side.

Aunt Vera tried hard to carry on formal conversation, but she didn't succeed very well. She began nearly every sentence with her favorite words, "Keep in mind."

"Keep in mind," she would say, "that Madame Bashinskaya wears only lilac-colored dresses." "Keep in mind that this pie is made out of our own apples."

To entertain her guests, Aunt Vera made her daughter Nadya play the piano and sing. Nadya was frightened of the drilling eyes of the general's three old maids. She played without confidence and sang in a thin, trembling, unhappy voice a song which was then fashionable called "The Swans":

The backwater sleeps, the water is as quiet as a mirror . . .

Her music teacher, a German woman who was always a silent guest at these parties, watched Nadya closely. This German woman had a big and unusually thin nose. When she was under strong lamplight you could see right through it. Her hair was stacked in scallops on top of her head.

After the supper Uncle Kolya and I went back to Grandmother's house.

"Phoo-oo!" Uncle Kolya said, puffing. "How disgusting!"

To forget the evening and to change our mood, Uncle Kolya called Gattenberger down to Grandmother's room and organized a concert. Accompanied by the cello, he sang Polish peasant songs for Grandmother:

> *Ah, you, the Vistula River,*
> *As blue as a flower.*
> *You run away to foreign lands*
> *It's a long road.*

Grandmother listened, clasping her hands on her knees. Her head shook quietly, and her eyes filled with tears. Poland was far away, far away! Grandmother knew that she would never again see the Niemen, or the Vistula, or Warsaw. She was already finding it hard to get around, and she had even stopped going to church.

On the day he left Uncle Kolya told me that he was going back to Ryovna for the summer and he made me promise that I would come, too. I didn't need to be asked very hard. I accepted happily.

From the moment I knew I was going back to Ryovna everything was changed for me. I even believed that I would pass my final examinations successfully. All I had to do was wait, and the expectation of happy days is sometimes nicer than the days themselves. But I learned about that later. At this point I did not suspect this strange truth about human life.

CERTIFICATE OF MATURITY

Final examinations began at the end of May and lasted for a whole
month. All the other classes had already been released for the
summer vacation. We were the only ones to walk through the
empty, cool *gymnasium.* It seemed to be resting after the winter
hurly-burly. The sound of our footsteps echoed through all the
floors.

The windows had been opened in the assembly hall where the
examinations were held. Dandelion seeds floated on the sunshine
into the room, like white, glittering sparks.

We had to take the examinations in our uniforms. The silver
lace on their stiff collars made our necks sore. We used to sit under
the chestnut trees in the park outside with our uniforms unbuttoned while we waited for each examination to begin.

The examinations frightened us. And we were all unhappy at
leaving the *gymnasium.* We had grown used to it. The future
loomed up unclear and hard, chiefly because we were inevitably
separating from each other. Our loyal, happy family was being
destroyed.

A meeting was organized in the park before the first examination. All the *gymnasists* in our class were there except the Jews,
who were not supposed even to know about the meeting. It was
agreed there that the best Russian and Polish pupils in the class
would all take care to get no better than a 4 on at least one subject,
so that none of us would win a gold medal. We were determined
to give all the gold medals to the Jewish boys. Without them, they
would not be admitted to the university.

We all swore to keep this decision a secret. To the honor of
our class it was never mentioned, either then or later when we
were students at the university. I break the oath now because
almost none of my comrades in the *gymnasium* are still among
the living. The majority of them perished during one or the other
of the two great wars which my generation has lived through. Only
a few of us survived them.

There was a second meeting. At this one we worked out which of us should help write compositions for some girls of the Marinskaya *Gymnasium.* I don't know why, but they took their written examination in Russian literature together with us.

Stanishevsky carried on negotiations with the girls. He brought us a list of the names of those who needed help. There were six names on the list. I was supposed to help a girl named Bogushevich. I did not know her and had never seen her.

We wrote our compositions in the assembly hall. Each of us sat at a separate small table, the boys on the left and the girls on the right. Monitors walked up and down a broad aisle between us. They kept a sharp watch to see that we did not exchange notes, blotters, or any other suspicious objects.

All six of the girls on Stanishevsky's list were sitting next to the aisle. I tried to guess which one was Bogushevich. Her name suggested a plump Ukrainian, and one of the girls was plump, with heavy braids down her back. I decided she must be Bogushevich.

The director walked in. We stood up. The director opened a thick envelop with a tearing sound, took out a paper with the theme of the composition chosen by the district educational officers, took a piece of chalk, and carefully wrote out on the blackboard: "True education combines moral with intellectual development."

A murmur of alarm swept through the room—it was a deadly subject. I had no time to lose. I began at once to write an outline of an essay for Bogushevich on a thin piece of paper.

We were allowed to smoke during final examinations. To do this we went out one by one to a smoking room at the end of the corridor. The monitor there was the decrepit old watchman Kasimir, the same one who had led me into the beginners' class the first day I went to the *gymnasium.*

On my way to the smoking room I twisted my outline into a thin cylinder and slipped this into the mouthpiece of a cigarette. I smoked the cigarette, and left the butt on a window sill we had agreed on. Kasimir didn't notice anything. He sat there in his chair, chewing at a sandwich.

This was the end of my assignment. Littauer followed me into the smoking room. He left his cigarette butt on the window, took the crib out of mine, and walked back down the aisle to his place, dropping it on Bogushevich's table as he passed it. Stanishevsky, Régamé, and two others followed him. Their work required sharp eyes and clever fingers.

I had already started to write my own composition when Lit-

tauer came back. I watched him; I wanted to see how and to whom
he would give the crib. But he did it so quickly that I could see
nothing. I knew it had been done, and Bogushevich saved, only
because one of the girls suddenly began to write feverishly. It
wasn't the plump girl with heavy braids, but a different one. I
could see only her thin back, striped with shadows from the
white curtain at the window, and some reddish curls around her
neck.

We had four hours to write our compositions. Most of us finished much earlier. Only the girls were still sitting in torture at
their tables. We went out into the park. There were so many birds
singing in the trees that it seemed they had assembled here from
all over Kiev.

A quarrel almost started between Littauer and Stanishevsky.
Littauer began it by saying that our help to the girls had been
stupidly organized. Stanishevsky flew into a rage. He had been
glowing with pride in the success of his operation, and he was
expecting praise, not criticism.

"What was the matter with it?" he asked Littauer in a bullying
tone which promised nothing good.

"Well, there wasn't any point in our knowing the names of the
girls we were writing for. Six girls—six cribs. Any girl could have
used any crib. Why did I have to know I was writing for Bogushevich, or for Yavorskaya? It was all the same to me. It only complicated the whole business when we had to drop the cribs."

"My God!" Stanishevsky shook his head in sorrow. "You really
are a downright cretin! There's no flight of fantasy in you. Listen,
I did it that way on purpose."

"But why?"

"It seemed to me more interesting," Stanishevsky answered
momentously. "Perhaps a flaming love affair may develop out of
this between a damsel and her rescuer. Have you thought about
that?"

"No."

"Well, you're just a dunderhead!" Stanishevsky said sharply.
"And now, let's go to François's. The ice cream is there."

We squandered our meager resources after each examination
by going to François's café and eating as many as five portions
of ice cream.

The hardest examination for me was in trigonometry. But I
passed it. It lasted into the evening. We waited until the inspector
had given out our marks and then, happy that no one had failed,
we streamed noisily out onto the street.

Stanishevsky ripped the back off his textbook and threw it into the air with all his strength. The pages floated down on to the street all around us. This delighted us. Each of us in turn did the same with his textbook. In a minute the street was white with paper. A policeman whistled at us and we ran.

We turned on to Fundukleyevskaya Street, then into the narrow Nesterovskaya Street. Gradually our numbers dwindled until there were only five of us left: Stanishevsky, Fitsovsky, Shmukler, Khorozhevsky, and me. We walked to the Galitsky Market where there were a lot of small taverns and eating places. We all decided to get drunk because we felt that examinations were finished with. Only Latin was left, and none of us was frightened of this.

We joked and laughed. The devil was happy inside us, as the old-fashioned saying goes. Passers-by looked at us. We went into a tavern. The smell of beer rose from the floor. Compartments had been built along the walls and decorated with pink wallpaper. They were called "private rooms." We took one, and ordered vodka and beef Stroganov.

The proprietor carefully closed the faded curtain but we made so much noise that from time to time someone would open it and look into our "private room." Each time, we offered the visitor a drink. They all drank with us, and congratulated us on our success.

It was already late in the evening when the proprietor came into our "private room" and, motioning with his eyes toward the curtain, said in a low voice:

"A spy outside the door."

"What kind of spy?" Stanishevsky asked.

"From the Criminal Investigation. You must all go out the back door into the courtyard. From there you can get out on to Bulvarno-Kudryavskaya Street."

We did not attach much importance to what he said, but we all filed out the back door into a dark, smelly courtyard. Ducking our heads to miss the clotheslines, we walked past trash barrels and woodsheds until we came out on the street. No one followed us. We walked through the gate on to a dimly lighted pavement. There stood a round-shouldered man wearing a derby hat, obviously waiting for us.

"Good evening!" he said in an ominous voice, and he raised his hat. "Have you enjoyed yourselves, gentlemen?"

We made no answer, and walked up Bulvarno-Kudryavskaya Street. The man in the bowler hat walked behind us.

"The milk isn't dry on your lips yet," he said with malice in his voice, "and you go sneaking through courtyards!"

Stanishevsky stopped. The man in the derby hat also stopped and he put his hand in the pocket of his long jacket.

"What do you want?" Stanishevsky asked. "Get the hell away from here!"

"And frequenting taverns," the man went on. "While you're still enrolled in the Imperial *Gymnasium!* For frequenting taverns, the punishment is expulsion with a wolf's ticket. Or don't you know about that?"

"Let's go!" Stanishevsky said to us. "It's stupid listening to a fool."

We went on. The man in the derby hat walked after us.

"I'm not the fool," he said. "It's you who are fools. I studied at the *gymnasium* myself."

"That's clear," Shmukler remarked.

"What's clear?" the man cried out hysterically. "I was thrown out of the *gymnasium* with a wolf's ticket for drinking. Am I asking to join your drinking party? No! I can organize my own. But I'll see to it that you get wolf's tickets. You've thrown away your examinations. You'll never make the university now. Did you talk against the government in that tavern? You did. Did you ridicule the Tsar's family? You did. Why should I protect you? I spit on it. I'm not a man to be trifled with. And I'm going to turn you over to the Secret Political Police if it's the last thing I do."

We turned down an empty street to the Svyatoslavsky *yar*. We thought the agent might be scared to follow us there. But he followed stubbornly behind us.

"Couldn't the five of us manage him?" Stanishevsky asked quietly.

We stopped. The agent took a revolver out of his pocket. He showed it to us, and laughed.

We led him through the streets for a long time, avoiding the intersections where there might be policemen. Fitsovsky suggested dividing up and disappearing one by one. Then the agent would have to follow first four of us, then three, then two, and finally, just one. Instead of five, he would be able to have only one of us arrested. But none of us agreed with Fitsovsky. This was no solution for comrades.

We made loud fun of the agent. Each of us contributed to a biography of him which we invented. It was imaginative and insulting. The agent grew hoarse with anger. He was also obviously getting tired, but he stuck to us with an insane obstinacy.

It was already growing light in the east. It was time to act. We made a plan and then circled through little alleys toward the house where Stanishevsky lived. A high stone wall, half again as high as a man, ran along the street here, with a small projection about halfway up. At a signal, each of us jumped up to this projection and scrambled over the wall. What we had learned about gymnastics made it easy for us.

There was a pile of broken bricks in the yard behind the wall, and they soon showered down on the agent, hitting him in the back. He screamed, ran into the middle of the street, and started firing. It did him no good. We tore through the yard into a second courtyard, ran upstairs to the fourth floor where Stanishevsky lived, and in a very few minutes we were all undressed and lying on couches and sofas and listening to what was going on in the street.

Stanishevsky's father, a lawyer with white bristles on his face, walked up and down in a dressing gown. He was in the same fighting mood we were, but he kept imploring us to lie still, not to make any noise, and not to look out of the windows. At first we heard someone shaking the gate frantically, and swearing at the janitor. Then we could hear the voices of the agent and of policemen inside the courtyard. Fortunately, it was a courtyard which opened on to another and the janitor declared that the *gymnasists* must have escaped through the adjoining courtyard. The agent and the police went away noisily.

We fell into deep sleep and didn't wake up until noon. We sent a scout out on to the street—Stanishevsky's sister. She reported that there was nothing suspicious, and we all went home. Strange as it may seem now, we had narrowly escaped a terrible danger: absolutely certain expulsion with wolf's tickets two days before our graduation from the *gymnasium*. It would have meant the end of any career for all of us.

At last the great day arrived when, at a table covered with green felt in the assembly hall, the director gave each of us his diploma and congratulated us on our graduation from the *gymnasium*.

The next day we had our traditional graduation ball. The girls who had taken their examination in Russian literature with us were invited. The school was all lighted up. Colored Chinese lanterns hung in the park outside. An orchestra was playing.

Before the ball Suboch made us a speech:

"In the fourth year, I could barely stand you. In the fifth, I began to teach you something, although there was very little chance of making real people out of you. In the sixth year I became friends with you. In the seventh, I fell in love with you, and now in the eighth I have begun even to be proud of you. I'm an unlucky father. I have too many children—no fewer than forty of you. And every few years, I have to change my children. Some leave, and others come. The result is that I have forty times as many disappointments as ordinary parents have. And forty times as much bother. This is why I haven't been equally attentive, perhaps, to all of you.

"It makes me sad to part with you. I have tried to make good people out of you. You on your side have given meaning to my life. I have grown young with you. I hereby forgive you now and forever all your stupid tricks and even your autumn battles with the first section. I forgive everything. There is, of course, no generosity in this. But I want to challenge you to become generous-minded people.

"Heine said that there are more fools on this earth than there are people. He was, of course, exaggerating. But what does this mean, really? It means that every day we meet people whose existence brings no happiness or usefulness, to themselves or to those around them. Always be afraid of being useless. Whoever you are, remember the wise counsel: let no day pass without having written something. Work! For what is talent, after all? It's work, work, work. Love your work, and may you always be sorry to put it down. May the roads you travel be happy ones! And think kindly sometimes of your teachers whose hair has turned white in their fights with you!"

We threw ourselves on him, and he kissed each one of us.

"And now," Suboch said, "a few words in Latin!"

He waved his arms and began to sing:

> *Gaudeamus igitur juvenes dum sumus!*

We joined in our first real student's song.

Then the ball started. Stanishevsky was in charge. He instructed each of his knightly cribbers to ask the girl he had rescued to waltz with him. He had introduced me to a thin girl with happy eyes, Olya Bogushevich. She was wearing a white dress. She looked at the floor while she thanked me for my help, and she turned white with embarrassment. I told her it had been nothing at all. We danced. Then I brought her some ice cream from the buffet.

After the ball we took the girls home. Olya Bogushevich lived in Lipka. I walked there with her under a warm canopy of leaves. Her white dress seemed too fancy even for this June night. We were already friends when we said good night.

Then I went back to Fitsovsky's where some of us spent the rest of the night. We had pooled our funds for a supper with wine, and we had invited Suboch, Selikhanovich, and Johanson. Johanson sang Schubert songs, and Suboch accompanied him by clinking bottles like a virtuoso.

We made a lot of noise, and, when we broke up, the sun had already risen but there was a long, cold shadow on the streets. We hugged each other in farewell, and then each of us went his own way with a strange feeling of grief and happiness.

A SUMMER NIGHT

And there again were the familiar leaves of the nut trees outside the window. Drops of rain sparkled on them. Again the sun shining on the rain-drenched park, and the noise of water running over the dam. Again Ryovna, but no Lyuba.

The Karelins' cottage was closed and empty. A stray black dog had taken up quarters on its porch. When anyone approached, he would jump up, yelping, and disappear into the bushes, his tail between his legs. He would lie there for a long time, waiting for the danger to pass.

Sasha had caught diphtheria, and the Karelins were coming, perhaps at the end of the summer, and perhaps they wouldn't come at all. No one knew for sure.

And the summer turned out to be stormy and changeable, because—according to Uncle Kolya—of sunspots. A drouth followed the spring rains. Sometimes a hot wind, bringing dry haze with it, would crumple up a quiet day. The water turned dark in the river. The tops of the pine trees began to shake and to make a little rustling. Dust piled up on the roads, swirled along them to the edge of the world, and followed everyone who moved.

"A waterless summer," said the peasants.

Dry leaves appeared on the linden trees. The river dropped day by day. Every morning there was less dew. And in the daytime you could hear dry seed pods rattling in the grass. The hot fields were covered with white burdock.

"What a storm there will be after such heat!" everyone said.

And the storm came at last. It developed slowly and Gleb Afanasiev and I watched it from early in the morning. It was so stifling at the bathhouse on the river that everything turned dark before our eyes. We lay in the lukewarm water for a long time.

The sky seemed filled with smoke. Enormous black puffs moved behind it, like petrified cotton. These were the storm clouds seen through the smoke. Dead silence stood all around us. The frogs and the birds grew silent, fish stopped splashing. Even the leaves stopped quivering, as if frightened by the storm. Mordan crawled under the cottage and lay there quietly and wouldn't come out. Only people went on making noises and calling to each other, but even people didn't feel like themselves.

At twilight the smoke disappeared, and a great cloud as dead as night itself filled half the sky. There were lightning flashes, but no thunder. A dull moon rose in the east. It moved all alone toward the big cloud, abandoned by everything else—not one star was to be seen around it. Each flash of lightning made the moon turn pale.

Then at last the earth seemed to give a fresh, long-drawn-out sigh. The first thunder roared through the woods and moved far away to the south through the grain rustling in the wind. It vanished, still rumbling, and then a new peal followed it and also moved off to the south, shaking the earth.

"The rain god," Gleb Afanasiev said, "is rolling around in heaven."

Moving yellow whirlwinds began to be seen in the cloud. Its edge drooped down to the earth. Lightning ran and danced in the black caverns of the sky. Someone struck the bell in the village belltower twice, hurriedly, and repeated this several times. This was the signal to all the peasants to put out the fires in their huts. We closed all the doors, and windows, and the dampers in the stoves, and the shutters, and sat down on the porch to wait.

An ominous roaring as wide as the whole earth started far beyond the park. Aunt Marusya couldn't stand it, and went into the house. The roaring came toward us as if the ocean were advancing, washing everything before it. This was the wind.

Then everything began to howl and whistle. The century-old linden trees creaked. A yellow haze moved over the ground. An incredible white light caught flame in this haze and then we heard such a crash that it seemed the cottage was being hammered into the earth. A ball of yellow flame moved up to the tops of the trees, crackled and smoked and then exploded with a dry noise like a long-range artillery shell.

"If it would only rain quickly!" Aunt Marusya kept repeating. "If it would only rain quickly!"

Finally the downpour started. Gray streams poured down on the disheveled park. The cloudburst roared as it picked up strength. Under its reassuring sound we went off to our rooms and fell into deep sleep.

During the night I was wakened by the barking of dogs, the snorting of horses, hurried steps downstairs, laughter, and the clatter of dishes. Gleb was also awake. The downpour had moved on but lightning was still flashing constantly.

"Kostik," Gleb said, "my prophetic heart tells me someone has arrived. But who is it? Let's listen and find out."

We lay there quietly for some minutes. Then Gleb jumped out of bed and began to get dressed in the dark.

"It is!" he said. "I hear the quiet sound of the divine Sasha talking. It's the Karelins! Get up!"

I began to get dressed, too. I could hear Aunt Marusya say downstairs:

"Yes, Kostik's here. A long time. And Gleb is here. We must wake them up."

"Let them sleep," Maria Trofimovna answered. "Tomorrow they'll have time to chatter. I don't understand myself how we managed to get here. We waited out the storm for two hours in Ryabchevka. It's lucky the road is a good one."

"Well, let's go down," Gleb said.

"You go first."

"Aha!" Gleb declared. "It means you're excited, young man!"

"Why should I be excited?"

"Then let's go together!"

We went downstairs. The lamps were lit. Aunt Marusya was fixing tea on the table. Soaked suitcases stood next to the wall.

Maria Trofimovna was sitting at the table. Sasha ran to greet us, and kissed both Gleb and me. She was frighteningly thin, but her eyes were shining as they always did. We kissed Maria Trofimovna's hand respectfully.

"Oh, how sunburned you are!" Maria Trofimovna said, and she stroked my cheek.

Lyuba was on her knees with her back to us, looking for something in a basket. She did not look around but continued her search.

"Lyuba," Maria Trofimovna called to her, "what's the matter, haven't you noticed? Kostik is here. And Gleb."

"Right away," Lyuba answered, and she slowly stood up. "I can't find the lemon, Mama."

"Well, God will take care of the lemon."

Lyuba turned around, straightened her hair, and held out her hand to me. She just glanced at me, and then looked away.

"Sit down," Aunt Marusya said. "The tea is getting cold."

We sat down at the table. Uncle Kolya was not in the room. I could hear him shake hands with someone on the porch, and the other man snorted, splashed water on his face, and then said, slurring his words:

"For God's sake, don't bother. Thank you."

"Who's that?" I asked Sasha.

She took me by the shoulder and whispered into my ear: "Lenka Mikhelson. Lyuba's schoolmate. Artist. Prodigy. Ass!"

"Who?" I repeated.

"A donkey!" Sasha said again. "You'll see for yourself. I hate him."

"Sasha!" Maria Trofimovna said. "Stop whispering!"

Lyuba looked at Sasha angrily, and then looked down at the table.

Uncle Kolya came in from the porch. A tall young fellow in glasses, with a long face and big teeth, followed him, still drying his hands. He shook hands with Gleb and me, looking at us indifferently. In spite of his nearsightedness and his awkwardness, it was clear that he came, as Mama loved to say, "from a good family." He held himself politely and without embarrassment, but it was also clear, of course, that he was a prodigy and a city boy.

He sat down at the table, took a glass of tea from Aunt Marusya, thanked her, and said:

"What a pastoral life!"

Gleb snorted. Aunt Marusya looked at Gleb and me with a worried expression, and Sasha said:

"Lenya, for God's sake, take some jam instead. It's strawberry."

Uncle Kolya also looked severely at Gleb, but then he smiled.

After tea, we helped the Karelins take their things to their cottage. The park was rustling, shaking itself all over from the rain. Roosters were crowing in the village. Dawn was breaking over the hilltops.

The Karelins started right away to unpack and get themselves organized. The sun came up, gilding the railing of the porch and spreading an extraordinary cleanness and freshness all around us. Lenya Mikhelson was drawing something with his cane in the sandy little road around the Karelins' cottage.

"What a morning!" Gleb said to me when we had carried over the last suitcase and Maria Trofimovna had told us she needed nothing more. "Let's go for a swim."

We picked up our shaggy towels and went off to the bathhouse. Drawn on the sandy road next to the Karelins' cottage we saw a profile very much like Lyuba's, with the sun drawn over it, and the words: "O light-weaving sunshine!"

Gleb was angry: "Decadent! Calf's love! Mother's poet!"

He walked on, swinging his towel. Then, without looking at me, he said:

"As for you, Kostik, chuck it, don't think about it. Seriously, chuck it! It's not worth spoiling the summer because of it. Well, who'll get there first?"

He ran, and I ran after him. Frogs jumped out of our way in the wet grass. The white ball of the sun climbed higher and higher. The clean-scrubbed sky grew clearer and clearer.

It seemed to me that the bitterness in my heart went away while we were running to the bathhouse. I panted, got red in the face, my heart was pounding, and I was thinking: am I really going to torture myself because of Lyuba, because of a supercilious girl, when a morning like this is on fire around me, with a long summer day stretching out before me?

Uncle Kolya came into the bathhouse. We swam and we dove and we made such waves in the river that we could see the water lilies rise and fall far out near the dam. And I almost forgot that I had just lived through my first betrayal. My only wish was to show Lyuba that I was not in the slightest disappointed by her, and that my life was full of such interesting things that to suffer through any foolish love affair, with sighs and veiled confessions, would be simply funny.

"And in the long run isn't this true?" I thought. "How is my feeling for Lyuba better than this sunshine?" It was already falling through the greenery onto the dark water. "How is it better than the wonderful smell of these unmowed fields? How is it better than even that green beetle sliding hurriedly along the planked wall of the bathhouse?"

It was easy to find consolation. Obviously, because everything around me was so full of wonder and beauty.

Gleb climbed up to the roof of the bathhouse, stretched out his arms to the sun, and cried out solemnly and nasally: "O light-weaving sunshine!" and jumped into the water.

"Ah, you cynics!" Uncle Kolya said. "Get out. After tea we'll go on an expedition."

"Where?" I asked.

"Down the river, behind Melovaya Hill."

I climbed out of the water. It was pleasant walking along the
dry warm planks, leaving wet footprints on them. The footprints
disappeared while you watched them. The towels smelled salty
like the sea. The sun warmed our chests and our wet heads, and
all we wanted to do was to laugh and chatter about interesting
things, or else race back to the cottage.

This we did. Mordan and Chetvertak raced with us, barking
and springing up and trying to snatch our towels away from us.
We tore past the Karelins' cottage in a cloud of laughter and barking, and plumped ourselves down on our own porch, frightening
Aunt Marusya.

After tea we all walked along the river. Gleb and I had made
our own map of the river and thought up names for every bend,
every backwater, every cliff, and every pleasant place along it.
We were lashed by twigs and the high grass. Our shirts turned
yellow with flower pollen. The banks of the river smelled of warm
grass and sand. Gleb announced with a profound air:

"I cannot tolerate melancholy."

This was how we lived all summer.

Soon the hot days were followed by others. A storm broke over
the park, dropping its clouds down to the tops of the trees. The
clouds caught in them, then moved away, leaving wet rags of mist
on the branches. The trees swung in the wind and groaned. The
leaves of the water lilies in the river stood on end. Rain hammered
on the roof. It made sounds upstairs as if we were living inside a
drum.

Everyone cursed the bad days except Uncle Kolya, Gleb, and
me. We put on raincoats and walked out on the dam to check the
lines we had put out the day before. Actually this wasn't why we
went. We went to breathe in the fresh raw storm until it hurt. The
wind blew with such strength that it could paste to your face a
wet leaf blown from a tree. Our raincoats grew stiff. We shouted to
each other.

We got to the very heart of the storm and rested, turning our
backs to it.

"Wonderful!" Uncle Kolya yelled. "Absolutely marvelous! Don't
let it blow you away."

"What a pastoral life!" Gleb yelled back, slurring the words. He
was still making fun of Lenya Mikhelson.

We surveyed our kingdom. The old willow trees were shaking
their tops furiously. They were fighting the wind with their last
strength. Rotten branches cracked and splintered. Disheveled

crows rode with the wind. They were screaming, but nothing could
be heard. We could only see their open beaks.

Behind the high dam there was one place where the wind never
came. We crept there through the storm. Nettles beat against our
faces, but didn't burn. Here, behind a beam, was where Uncle
Kolya hid his fishing rods. We got them out, like thieves. Our hands
were trembling. What if Aunt Marusya knew about this! She
thought we were madmen anyway.

We cast our lines. The storm howled above our heads within an
arm's reach. But everything was still below us.

"There's not a chance that they'll bite," Gleb said. "The fish are
not half-witted, like us."

He said this on purpose, to reassure the fish. He desperately
wanted them to bite. And actually a miracle took place—our floats
sank slowly into the cold water.

"Pull!" Uncle Kolya yelled to us.

We started to pull out strong tin-colored fish. The storm grew
worse. Rain scudded over the water with frightening speed. But we
noticed nothing.

"You're not cold?" Uncle Kolya yelled at us.

"No! It's wonderful!"

"You mean, you want some more?"

"Of course!"

The storm lasted for five days. It stopped in the night, and no one
noticed it. I woke up in the morning to the twittering of birds. The
park was drowned in mist. The sun was breaking through it. It
was obvious that there must be a clear sky above the mist, because
the mist was blue.

Uncle Kolya set up the samovar on the porch. Smoke rose from
it. A beam of sunshine broke through the leaves and lighted green
and golden sparks among the linden trees. No artist could ever
have captured this sight, and least of all, of course, Lenya Mikhelson. In his pictures the sky was always orange, the trees were
blue, and people's faces were greenish, like unripe melons. It was
all imagined, probably, like my feelings for Lyuba. By now I was
completely cured of them. Perhaps what helped me most to free
myself was that long summer storm.

I watched the sunshine strike deeper and deeper through the
leaves. First it lighted up a single yellowing leaf, then a tomtit
sitting on a twig sideways to the ground, then a raindrop. It
shook and trembled, almost ready to drop.

"Kostik, Gleb, did you hear?" Uncle Kolya was asking under our
window.

"What?"

"Cranes!"

We listened. Through the bluish mist we could hear strange sounds, just as if someone in the sky were pouring water.

A SMALL DOSE OF POISON

The village pharmacist sometimes used to come to visit Uncle Kolya. He was called Lazar Borisovich. He was a rather curious man in our opinion. He always wore a student's jacket. Round pince-nez, on a black cord, barely hung on to his broad nose. He was a short, thickset man, bearded up to his eyes, and very sarcastic.

Lazar Borisovich came from Vitebsk and had studied once at the University of Kharkov, but had not taken his degree. He was living now in the village apothecary shop with his sister, who was a hunchback. It was our guess that the pharmacist was mixed up with the revolutionary movement.

He used to carry with him pamphlets by Plekhanov with many passages underlined in blue or red pencil and with the margins filled with question marks and exclamation marks. On Sundays he would disappear with these pamphlets into the far end of the park, spread his jacket on the grass, lie on it and read, crossing one leg over the other and swinging his heavy boot.

Once I went to his apothecary shop to get some powders for Aunt Marusya. She had started to suffer from headaches. I liked this shop. It was a clean, old peasant cottage with mats on the floor and a potted geranium, porcelain phials on the shelves, and the smell of herbs. Lazar Borisovich used to collect them in the fields, dry them, and make infusions out of them.

I have never known such a squeaky house. Every floor board squeaked in its own way. Besides, everything else squeaked: the chairs, a wooden couch, the shelves, and the counter on which Lazar Borisovich wrote his prescriptions. Every movement in the store produced such a variety of squeaks that it seemed as if some unseen fiddlers in the shop were drawing their bows across dried-out, tightened strings.

Lazar Borisovich was quite at home with all these squeaks and he understood their most delicate nuances.

"Manya!" he would cry out to his sister. "What's the matter with you, can't you hear? Vaska's going into the kitchen. There's fish there!"

Vaska was the pharmacist's shabby black cat.

Sometimes the pharmacist would tell his customers:

"I beg you, please don't sit on that couch. Otherwise you will start such music that it will drive us all out of our minds."

Lazar Borisovich would point out, while he pounded a powder in his mortar, that—thank God—the drugstore squeaked less in raw weather than when it was dry. Suddenly the mortar would grate. The customer would jump, and Lazar Borisovich would say enthusiastically:

"Ah ha! You have nerves, I see. I congratulate you!"

On this occasion Lazar Borisovich was pounding the powders for Aunt Marusya, making noises to set your teeth on edge, and he said:

"The Greek philosopher Socrates was poisoned by hemlock. Yes. And that same hemlock grows here, in the marsh near the mill, a whole woods full of it. I warn you—it's a white flower like an umbrella. There is poison in its roots. Yes. But, by the way, that poison is good if it is taken in small doses. I think every man should put a small dose of poison in his food sometimes if he wants to come to his senses."

"Do you believe in homeopathy?" I asked him.

"In psychic matters—yes," Lazar Borisovich declared firmly. "Don't you understand why? Well, let's test it on you. Let's make an experiment."

I agreed. I was curious to see what kind of experiment it would be.

"I also know," Lazar Borisovich said, "that youth has its own rights, especially when a young man has just finished the *gymnasium* and is enrolling in the university. Then there's a merry-go-round in your head. But just the same, you must be thinking."

"About what?"

"As if you didn't have enough to think about!" Lazar Borisovich exclaimed angrily. "Look, you're starting out to live. What will you be, if I may ask? And how do you propose to exist? Will you really be able to just have a good time, make jokes, and duck all the hard questions? Life is no vacation, young man. No! I will make you a prediction: we are on the eve of great events. Yes! I assure you of this. I know Nikolai Grigorievich laughs at me, but we'll still see which of us is right. So, I'm interested in knowing, what will you be?"

"I would like . . ." I began.

"Stop!" Lazar Borisovich cried out. "What are you saying? That you would like to be an engineer, or a doctor, or a scholar, or something like that? This has no importance at all."

"Then what is important?"

"Jus-tice!" he shouted. "You must be with the people. And for the people. You can be what you like, even a dentist, but you must fight for a good life for people. No?"

"But why are you telling me all this?"

"Why? Just in general! Without any reason! You're a pleasant young fellow, but you don't like to think things over. I've noticed this for a long time. So, do me a favor, think things over!"

"I am going to be a writer," I said, and I blushed.

"A writer?" Lazar Borisovich adjusted his pince-nez and stared at me with threatening surprise. "Ho-ho! It's not much just wanting to be a writer. Perhaps I too would like to be Leo Nikolayevich Tolstoy."

"But I've already written . . . and been published."

"In that case," Lazar Borisovich said firmly, "be so good as to wait a minute. I'll wrap up these powders, and then I'll go along with you and we'll clear this up."

He was clearly very excited, and, while he was wrapping up the powders, he dropped his pince-nez twice.

We went out and walked across the fields to the river, and from there into the park. The sun was dropping toward the woods on the other side of the river. Lazar Borisovich plucked at the tops of the wormwood plants, rubbed them together, then sniffed his fingers, and said:

"This is a big thing to do, but it requires a real knowledge of life. Yes? And you have very little, not to say that you have none at all. A writer! He needs to know so much that it's frightening just to think about it. He should understand everything. He must work like an ox, and never worry about fame. Yes! That's how it is! I can tell you one thing—you must go into huts, into fairs, into factories, into beggars' night lodgings. All around, everywhere—to theaters, to hospitals, down in mines, and in prisons. Yes! Everywhere. So that life will impregnate you like . . . like spirits of valerian. So that it produces a real infusion. Then you can pass it on to people like a life-giving balm. But also only in specific doses. Yes!"

He went on talking for a long time about the writer's profession. We left each other at the edge of the park.

"You're wrong in thinking that I'm just a lazybones, or a good-for-nothing," I said.

"Oy, no!" Lazar Borisovich exclaimed, and he grabbed my hand. "I'm glad about this. You'll see. But agree with me that I was a little right, and that now you have something to think over. After my small dose of poison. No?"

He looked into my eyes without letting go my hand. Then he sighed and walked away. He walked through the fields, a short and shaggy man, and he kept plucking off the tops of the wormwood. Then he took a big penknife out of his pocket, squatted on his heels, and began to dig some medicinal herb out of the ground.

The pharmacist's experiment worked. I realized that I knew practically nothing and that I hadn't even thought about many important things. I took the advice of this curious man and soon went out to people, to that school of life which no books and no abstract reflection can replace.

This was a hard task, but a real one.

Youth had its way. I did not wonder whether or not I had the strength to go through this school. I was convinced that I had.

That evening we all climbed up Melovaya Hill—a steep cliff over the river, covered with young pine trees. From there the enormous warm autumn night opened up around us. We sat on the edge of the cliff. The water was gurgling over the dam below. Birds were fluttering in the branches, preparing for the night. Heat lightning played over the woods. Then we could see some clouds as thin as smoke.

"What are you thinking about, Kostik?" Gleb asked me.

"Just thinking—in general . . ."

I was thinking that I would never believe anyone who might try to tell me that this life, with its love, its striving for the truth and for happiness, with its summer lightning and the distant noise of water in the night, did not make sense. Every one of us should struggle to affirm this life, everywhere and always—to the end of his days.

1946

Restless Youth

"Here Lives Nobody"

ON PROFESSOR GILYAROV'S DOOR WAS A BRASS PLATE WITH THE inscription: "Here lives nobody."

Gilyarov lectured on the history of philosophy to the students of Kiev University. Gray, unshaven, in a baggy, shiny jacket dusted with tobacco ashes, he would hurry up to the rostrum, hold on to its edge with his knotty hands, and start to speak—in a dull voice, inarticulately, almost reluctantly.

The gardens of Kiev would be burning in gold outside the windows of the auditorium. Autumn in Kiev was always a protracted season. The southern summer stored up in the city parks and gardens so much sunshine, so much green, so much of the smell of flowers, that it was always sorry to abandon such wealth and make way for autumn. So almost every year, summer threw the calendar into confusion and delayed its departure.

As soon as Gilyarov began to speak, we students stopped noticing anything around us. We followed the professor's hardly audible mumbling, transfixed by the miracle of human thought. Gilyarov revealed it to us slowly, almost angrily. Great epochs shouted to each other in his lectures. He built in us the feeling that it was impossible to chop the flow of human thought into hunks, and that it was almost impossible to tell the point where philosophy stops and poetry begins, or where poetry blurs into the ordinary life of human beings.

Sometimes Gilyarov would pull from the bulging pocket of his jacket a book of poetry with an owl—the bird of wisdom—on its cover and read a few lines jerkily, nailing down his philosopher's point:

If our sun today forgot
Its path and lost its way—
A whole new world would be conjured up
By some madman the very next day.

Occasionally the bristles on his cheeks would stand out and his screwed-up eyes would start to laugh. This happened whenever Gilyarov talked to us about learning to know ourselves. This kind of talk gave me my belief in the boundless power of human intelligence.

Gilyarov used to shout at us. He commanded us not to bury our potential in the ground. We must work on ourselves like the devil, to develop everything that was in us. We should learn to work like an accomplished orchestra conductor, who forces the most stubborn player under him to play all his notes, and who brings every instrument to its fullest possible expression.

"Man," Gilyarov said, "must reflect upon, enrich, and beautify life."

Gilyarov's idealism was colored with bitterness, and with a constant regret over its gradual decay. Among many of Gilyarov's phrases, I remember one about "the evening glow of idealism and its deathbed ideas." This old professor, who looked a good deal like Emile Zola, was full of scorn for the prosperous citizens and the educated liberals of those times. This was the reason for the brass plate on his door, with its reminder of the insignificance of man. We all realized, of course, that Gilyarov had put up the plate to annoy his decorous neighbors.

Gilyarov was always talking about enriching man's life. But we didn't know how to go about it. I concluded fairly early that in order to enrich life one must express oneself as fully as possible in some kind of living relations with people. But how? In what? The surest way still seemed to me to be in writing. This was how I started thinking about it as the only road to life for me.

This was when my grown-up life began, often hard, less ofteⱕ happy, but always restless and so changing that it is easy to become confused when I try to remember it.

My youth had begun in my last years at the *gymnasium* and it ended with the First World War. Maybe it ended sooner than it should have. But enough wars, revolutions, experiences, hopes, labor, and happiness have fallen to the lot of my generation to have satisfied several generations of our ancestors.

During the time, roughly, that it takes Jupiter to complete an orbit around the sun we have lived through so much that just thinking about it wrings one's heart. And those who come after us will envy us for having shared in and watched great turning points in the fate of man.

The university was the focus of all progressive thinking in the city. At first it made me shy, like most of the first-year students, and I was thrown into confusion by meeting older students, especially the "perpetual students." These bearded people in their shabby, unbuttoned coats looked on us beginners as thoughtless puppy dogs.

Besides, it took me a long time to get used to the fact that we were not required to attend lectures and that there was no penalty for spending the time reading at home or simply wandering around the city. I grew used to the university gradually, and I came to love it. But it was not the lectures or the professors I loved (there were not many with any talent) but student life itself.

The lectures went on, in their own way, in the classrooms, while the turbulent and noisy life of the students went on, also in its own way, quite independently in the long, dark corridors. This was where daylong arguments took place, where meetings gathered, where groups and fractions of groups were formed. I found out here for the first time about the violent contradictions between the Bolsheviks, the Mensheviks, and the Social Revolutionaries, about the Jewish Bundists, and the Armenian Dashnaks, the Ukrainian nationalists and the Poale Zion party. But members of all these parties would unite against their one common enemy— members of the pogrom-minded Academic Union. Quarrels with them led quite often to physical fighting, especially when the boys from the Caucasus were involved.

In the boiling-up of all these passions there could be felt the approach of some kind of new era. It seemed strange that a few steps away, behind the doors of an auditorium, gray-haired and respected professors were lecturing in quiet boredom about the trading customs of the Hanseatic League or comparative philology.

In those years before the First World War many people felt the storm coming, but they could not predict the violence it was to unleash across the earth. It was as hard to breathe, in Russia and outside, as it is before a big thunderstorm. But the storm had not yet broken, and this comforted people of little vision. There were alarm signals in the morning haze around Kiev—strikes of factory workers, arrests and exile, hundreds of proclamations—these were the first lightning flashes of the distant storm. But it took very sharp hearing to detect the rumbling of the storm itself. This is why its first deafening crash, in the summer of 1914 when the war began, stunned everyone.

When we left the *gymnasium* we lost each other almost at once, in spite of our oaths that we would never let this happen. The war rolled over us, and then came the Revolution, and since then I have hardly seen one of my school fellows. The cheerful Stanishevsky disappeared somewhere, and the home-grown philosopher Fitsovsky, the discreet Shmukler, the sluggish Matusevich, and Bulgakov who was as quick as a bird.

I was living then in Kiev. Mama was still in Moscow with Galya and Dima. My oldest brother, Borya, still lived in Kiev but we almost never saw each other. He had married a short, plump woman who wore a lavender Japanese kimono with cranes embroidered on it. Borya spent all day designing concrete bridges. His dark room, with wallpaper covering its oak walls, smelled of paste. Your feet stuck to its painted floor. A photograph of the world-famous beauty, Lina Cavalieri, was thumbtacked to one wall.

Borya did not approve of my attraction to philosophy and literature. "You ought to build yourself a road through life," he told me. "You're a dreamer. Just like Papa. Just to amuse people— that's not serious business."

He really believed that literature was written simply to amuse people. I didn't want to argue with him. I wanted to hide my passion for literature from all hostile eyes. So I stopped going to see Borya.

I was living with Grandmother in Lukyanovka, in the green outskirts of Kiev, in the same little cottage deep in the garden. My room was filled with pots of fuchsias. I did nothing but read until I was exhausted. In the evenings I would go out in the garden to rest from reading. There I could find sharp autumn air and the sky full of stars shining through the leafless branches.

At first Grandmother was cross at me and called me back to the house, but then she grew used to it and left me in peace. She only commented that I was spending my time senselessly and that it would all end in galloping consumption. But what could Grandmother do with my new friends? What could she object to in Pushkin or Heine, Fet or Leconte de Lisle, Dickens or Lermontov?

In the end, she washed her hands of me. She would light her lamp with its pink glass shade shaped like a big tulip and settle down to her endless reading of Polish novels by Krashevsky. And I remembered the poet's lines: "in heaven, like a gentle summons, a star twinkles its golden eyelashes." The earth seemed to me a treasure house of just such valuables as those golden eyelashes of the stars. I knew that life would bring me many wonderful things, meetings, loves and sadnesses, joys and shocks, and that the greatest good luck of my youth was in this foreknowledge. Whether it would come true, the future would show.

And now, as actors used to say in old-fashioned theaters when they walked out in front of the audience before the play began: "We will present various incidents of real life to you, and we will try to make you reflect upon them, to make you cry and laugh."

THE UNPRECEDENTED AUTUMN

I traveled from Kiev to Moscow in the heating compartment of a railroad car. It was crowded with three passengers in it—an elderly land surveyor, a young woman in a white shawl, and myself.

The woman sat on the cold iron stove while the land surveyor and I took turns sitting on the floor—there was not room for us both to sit at the same time. Little pieces of coal crunched under our feet. It quickly turned the woman's shawl gray. Out of the jammed window—also gray, with long streaks left by raindrops— nothing could be seen clearly. I can only remember, somewhere around Sukhinicha, a huge, bloody sunset covering the whole sky.

The land surveyor looked at the sunset and said that there, near the frontier, probably they were already fighting Germans. The woman put her handkerchief to her face and cried; she was going to her husband in Tver and she did not know if she would find him there or if he had already been moved up to a front-line position.

I was going to say good-by to my brother Dima, who had been drafted into the army. I had not been called because of my near-sightedness. Besides, I was the youngest son in the family and a student, and the law in those days released both youngest sons and students from military service.

It was almost impossible to move out of the heating compartment on to the platform between the cars. Mobilized soldiers lay in long rows on the roof, and hung in clusters on the buffers and on the steps of the car. Stations greeted us with the long-drawn-out wailing of women, the howl of accordions, whistles, and singing. As soon as the heavy train stopped, it seemed to freeze to the rails. It took two engines to get it moving again, and then only with a heavy jerk.

Russia itself was beginning to move. The war, like a subterranean tremor, had shaken us loose from our foundations. Church bells were ringing in thousands of villages, announcing mobilization. Thousands of peasant horses were bringing soldiers to the railroads from the darkest corners of the country. The enemy was invading the country from the west but a huge wave of people was rolling to meet him from the east. The whole country was being transformed into a military camp. Life was being transformed. All that was customary and routine disappeared overnight.

The whole way to Moscow, the three of us ate only one hard roll with raisins and drank a bottle of muddy water.

This was probably why the air of Moscow seemed to me fresh and fragrant on the morning when I got out of the train onto the raw platform of the Bryansk station. The summer of 1914 was coming to an end—a threatening, frightening summer of war, and there was already a cool, sweetish smell of autumn in the Moscow air, the smell of wilted leaves and stagnant ponds.

Mama was living then right next to just such a pond on Bolshaya Pressnya Street. The windows of her apartment looked out on the zoo. You could see the red brick walls of the Pressnya homes which had been destroyed by shelling in the December, 1905, uprising, and empty paths through the zoo, and a big pond with black water in it. Wherever the sun hit it, the water in the pond had the greenish color of slime.

I had never seen an apartment so like the people who lived in it and the life they led. It was empty, almost without furniture except for the kitchen tables and a few creaky chairs. The shade from dark old trees fell into the rooms and made the apartment always cold and gloomy. The gray, sticky oilcloth on the tables was cold, too.

Mama had developed a weakness for oilcloth. It replaced the tablecloths she had formerly used, and served as a persistent reminder of poverty, of the fact that Mama was striving as hard as she could to keep some kind of order and cleanliness in her home. Without this, she couldn't have gone on living.

I found only Mama and Galya at home. Dima had gone off to a rifle range at Gravornovo to teach reserve soldiers how to shoot. Mama's face had grown more wrinkled and yellower in the two years since I had last seen her, but her thin lips were pressed together as firmly as ever, as if Mama still wanted to show everyone around her that she would never give up to the intrigues of her petty enemies, and would emerge victorious from all her difficulties.

And Galya was still wandering aimlessly around the rooms, as always, bumping into chairs, asking me meaningless questions— how much did a ticket from Kiev to Moscow cost now, and were there still porters at the stations or had they all been driven off to war?

Mama seemed to me calmer than she had been before. I didn't expect this. I couldn't understand where she got her calm when any day Dima might be sent off to the front. But Mama told me herself what she was thinking.

"Things are much easier for us now, Kostik," she said. "Dima is an ensign, an officer. He gets good pay. Now I'm not frightened that tomorrow there won't be money enough to pay the rent."

She looked at me anxiously, and added: "Not everyone gets killed in war. I'm certain they'll leave Dima in a rear-line job. He stands very well with his superiors."

I agreed with her that it was quite true that everyone did not get killed in war. It was impossible to take this shaky reassurance from her. When I looked at Mama, I could understand how hard daily life can be for defenseless people, and how desperately they fear being homeless and starving. But it bothered me that she was happy over this shabby blessing for the family at the cost of her son's safety. Maybe she didn't realize what his danger was. She just tried not to think about it.

Dima came back sunburned and very sure of himself. He took off his new sword with its golden hilt and hung it up in the vestibule. In the evenings, when the electric lights were on, the hilt glittered as the only stylish object in Mama's squalid apartment.

Mama had been in a hurry to tell me that Dima's marriage with Margarite had been called off since Margarite had turned out to be, in Mama's expression, "a very unpleasant character." I made no comment.

Several days later, Dima was assigned to the Navaginsky infantry regiment. He packed and left so quickly that Mama had no chance to think about it. She did not cry until the second day after he had left.

Dima's detachment left from the Brest station. It was a windy, drab day, an ordinary day filled with yellow dust under a low sky. On days like this, it always seems, nothing extraordinary can ever happen. Our parting with Dima was like the day. He was in charge of getting his detachment on the train. He talked with us in fits and starts, and said good-by in a hurry when the train had already begun to move. He ran after his car and jumped on to its steps but at that moment another train blocked him from our sight. By the time the other train had passed, Dima could no longer be seen.

After his departure, I transferred from Kiev to Moscow University. Mama rented out Dima's room to a civil engineer of the Moscow trolley lines named Zakharov. I still don't understand what attracted Zakharov to our apartment. He had studied in Belgium, lived in Brussels for many years, and returned to Russia not long before the war. He was a cheerful bachelor with a clipped, graying beard. He wore loose-fitting foreign suits and conspicuous glasses. He covered the table in his room with books. I did not find a single technical book among them; most of them were memoirs, novels, or collections of the magazine *Znanye*.* In his room I saw for the first time French editions of Verhaeren, Maeterlinck, and Rodenbach.

This was the summer when everyone was admiring Belgium—the little country which had taken the first blow of the German army. People sang songs everywhere about the defenders of besieged Liège. Belgium was smashed to smithereens in two or three days. The halo of martyrdom hung over the country. The Gothic lacework of its cathedrals and town halls was destroyed and ground into dust under the feet of German soldiers and the wheels of German cannon.

I read Verhaeren, Maeterlinck, and Rodenbach, trying to find in these Belgian books an explanation of the bravery of their country. But I could not find it in the complicated poems of Verhaeren, describing the old world as a great evil, nor in the lifeless novels of Rodenbach, as brittle as flowers under the ice, nor in Maeterlinck's plays, which seemed to me as if they had been written in his sleep.

I ran into Zakharov once on Tverskoi Boulevard. He took me by the arm and began to talk about the war, the destruction of culture, and Belgium. He talked with a slight French accent.

Those were magnificent autumn days in Moscow. The trees were dropping their gilded leaves on the cannon barrels which stood with ammunition cases in gray ranks along the Moscow boulevards waiting to be shipped to the front. A transparent, incredibly deep, blue sky stretched over the city in the radiance of the end-of-summer sun. And the leaves fell and fell, filling the roofs, the pavements and the streets, rustling under the janitors' brooms and

* *Znanye* (*Knowledge*) was an important literary annual which Gorky began to edit in 1902 and which favored writers of peasant or proletarian origin.

under the feet of pedestrians, as if trying to remind people that the forgotten earth still existed around them and that perhaps, thanks to this earth, thanks to the weak shimmer of September cobwebs, thanks to the clearness of the dry, cold horizons, thanks to the smell of the yellow broom, thanks to all these delights of an unusually beautiful Russia, thanks to its trees, its cottages, its straw burning with milky smoke, the blue mist over its rivers, its past and its future—thanks to all this, honest people all over the world by some gigantic effort could stop this war.

I realized, of course, that one could not hope for this, and that all these ideas were, as Borya loved to say, "pure Don Quixote," and that those who had drawn the sword against our people and our culture might well perish by this sword but would never sheathe it of their own free will.

The war kept coming closer at its own remorseless pace. It seemed as if smoke from its fires were already darkening the Moscow sky. We found out later that this had indeed been smoke but only from forest fires—the woods and dry marshes near Tver were burning.

In the mornings I woke up in my room—I slept on the floor— and looked out of the window. Leaves would be flying in the sky and rocking gently down to the ground. The window frame kept me from following each one to see just where it landed. I could not free myself from the thought that this slow, unending falling of the leaves might be the last one in my life. And it always looked to me as if the leaves were floating from west to east, away from the war.

I am not ashamed now to admit having had these ideas—I was very young. Everything around me was filled to the brim with a kind of lyric power which came, probably, out of myself. But I thought then that it was the essence of life.

"So, my friend," Zakharov said to me, "isn't it time for you to stop wandering around the outskirts of Moscow in your foggy condition? In just one week, Maria Grigorievna tells me, you've managed to get to both Arkhangelskoe and Ostankino."

"Yes, I was in both places," I admitted. "What's this foggy condition you're talking about?"

Zakharov laughed. "You're behaving as if the world existed solely to fill you with interesting ideas."

"Well, and what of it?" I asked sharply. I was beginning to get angry. Why was everybody accusing me of having a casual, little-boy's relation to life?

"It's just that you've been reading modern poetry until you're belching with it," Zakharov said conciliatingly, and he repeated smugly: "Until you're belching with it."

"Judging by your books, you also prefer artistic literature to trolley cars," I told him.

"The fact is," Zakharov explained, "that Belgium is a great country for trolleys. And for mystical poetry. I was sent abroad before I'd finished the *gymnasium*. I ended up in Belgium, liked it there, and finished the engineering institute in Liège. But that's not the trouble. The trouble is the war. Just look there, if you please."

Marching music was coming from the direction of Strastnoi Square, and a drawn-out, deafening "Hurrah" roared down the street. Reserve battalions were being formed to be sent to the front.

"I was just up there, on the square," Zakharov added. "I'd forgotten a lot about Russia. Not my fault. For example, I walked right up to the front ranks to get a look at the soldiers. You know, they smell of bread. An amazing smell! You smell it, and for some reason you believe that nobody can ever defeat the Russian people."

"And Belgium?" I asked.

"What about Belgium? I don't understand you."

I laughed and said the first thing that came into my head:

"Why did the Belgians fight so desperately against the Germans?"

"Oo-la-la!" Zakharov sang out. "A little people lives on the memory of its great past. I respect them for it. Take Maeterlinck. A mystical poet with cloudy eyes and cloudy ideas. The old Catholic God simply annoys him. God is too crude for a refined character like Maeterlinck. So he exchanges God for this world, which is, of course, somewhat more modern and more poetic. It makes a stronger poison than religion. That's all it is. But besides this, Maeterlinck is a citizen. With a citizen's education. A citizen's tradition. As a citizen, he picks up his rifle in his mystical fingers and shoots it just as well as any of the King's sharpshooters. The poet's dim ideas are nobody else's business. But the citizen's shooting is everybody's business. That's why nobody interferes with his poetry. That's the way Belgium is. It's a good country. The wind from the sea blows right across it, and it's full of happy people. They know how to work, by the way. What else do you want to know about Belgium? Nothing at the moment? Well, let's leave Belgium alone, and talk about things that are more important for you."

What was more important for me turned out to be this: Zakharov offered to fix me up on the Moscow trolley lines as a driver. The fact was, he explained, that most of the drivers and conductors had been conscripted into the army. But you couldn't leave an enormous city without trolleys in time of war. So they were starting to hire new drivers and conductors.

I was taken aback. The switch from Maeterlinck to trolley driver had been too sudden.

I had been thinking about writing ever since I left the *gymnasium*. All the changes in my life seemed to me a kind of preparatory school for this. I had to start living, without being fastidious about how I lived; this was the only way to acquire experience, to create that storeroom from which I would later take ideas, subjects, images, words, in whole handfuls. I also realized that now I could not leave Mama. I had to stay with her and help her. The pay would help. So I agreed.

When I told Mama and Galya that I was going to be a trolley driver, Mama only sighed and commented that she had never been ashamed of any kind of work and that she had tried to teach us to feel the same way. Galya became very worried—wouldn't the electric current kill me?

"I read somewhere," she said in a frightened voice, "about an elephant in a circus. They burned him up with current from a trolley line. Could that be so, or not?"

I answered her that it was all nonsense.

I didn't feel like sitting at home, so I went out to a tavern on Kudrinskaya Street. It was smoking with steam.

A mechanical organ in the tavern was grinding out a popular song, filled with cymbals and kettledrums:

> *The daring troika dashes along*
> *On the ice of Mother Volga in the winter . . .*

An old man with a turned-up collar was writing something at the next table, constantly dipping his pen in the ink and then removing little hairs from it.

I wanted to write someone close to me, some friend, about myself, and about the fact that life had turned around again and was making me a trolley car driver, but then I remembered that there was absolutely nobody for me to write to.

> *The coachman was silent, and the whip*
> *Dangled from his lowered hand . . .*

the machine went on grinding, and in answer to it the empty glasses jangled on the tables

THE COPPER LINE

I was hired as a trolley driver at the Miusski trolley yard. But I didn't work long as a driver. I was quickly transferred to being a conductor.

The Miusski yard was on Lesnaya Street, in buildings of red brick turned black with soot. Ever since then I have disliked Lesnaya Street. It still seems to me the dirtiest and stupidest street in Moscow.

My memories of it are all mixed up with the screeching of the trolley cars as they pulled out at dawn through the iron gates of the yard, with the heavy conductor's bag which cut into my shoulder, and with the acid smell of copper. Our hands were always green from copper coins, especially if we were working on "the copper line."

The copper line, sometimes called the B line, ran along Moscow's outer ring of wide streets which is known as the Sadovy ring. Conductors did not like this line, and preferred to work on "the silver line," also called the A line, which ran along the inner ring of boulevards. The copper line served the big, crowded railroad stations on the dusty edges of the city. Its cars pulled trailers in which passengers were allowed to carry heavy goods with them. Most of these passengers came from outside Moscow—handicraft artisans, truck gardeners, and women selling milk. They paid in copper coins, hiding their silver away and taking it most unwillingly from their pockets or their purses. This is why it was called the copper line.

The A line was much smarter, serving more theaters and stores. Its cars pulled no trailers, and the passengers were a different type, more educated people and more officials. These paid usually in silver or paper money.

The leaves of the trees along the boulevards made a rustling noise which could be heard through the open windows of the A-line trolleys. The trolleys circled slowly around Moscow—past the tired Gogol and the quiet Pushkin, past Trubnoi market where the sound of birds has never stopped, past the towers of the Kremlin and the gold-domed bulk of the Church of the Redeemer and the hunchbacked bridges over the lazy Moscow River.

We took the trolleys out early in the morning and got back to the yard at one o'clock in the night, and sometimes later. I had to turn over my earnings before I could drag myself home through the dark city with my empty bag on my shoulder. The nickel plate with my conductor's number shone on my jacket in the green light of the gas street lamps. At that time there were electric street lamps only on the big streets.

At first I wasted a lot of time each night in counting my small change but then an older conductor named Babayev—my inspector —taught me how to avoid this. Then I returned to the yard with nothing but bigger paper bills and a little silver. The device was simple. Two hours before getting back to the yard we would start to hand out small change shamelessly, giving change for a ruble only in copper coins and for three rubles only in silver coins. Sometimes the passengers swore at us. When they did, we never argued with them, so as to keep our trolleys as peaceful as we could. This was Babayev's worldly wisdom.

"Every passenger nowadays," Babayev said, "has weak nerves. We must be indulgent. You must treat the passengers with compassion, and even carry some of them free. For example, I know right away, as soon as a man gets into the trolley, when he wants to travel without a ticket. By the expression on his face. You can see the man has to go somewhere, but he's trying to hide from you—it means he hasn't a kopeck in his pocket. So never offer him a ticket. Just act as if you had already given him one, with the correct little tear in it. In every walk of life one must be indulgent, and this is especially true for us conductors. Our business is with the whole city of Moscow. And in Moscow people's sorrows are like sand in the sea."

Babayev taught me all the guileless tricks of the conductor's trade—how to tear the tickets, which color on the tickets corresponded with each day of the week (to keep passengers from traveling today with yesterday's ticket), how to turn in the trolley to the supervisor at the yard, in what parts of the city passengers were most likely to jump on or off while the trolley was moving, thus requiring special readiness to stop the trolley in case of an accident.

Babayev taught me for ten days. Then I took a conductor's examination. The hardest part of it was the test of our knowledge of Moscow. We had to know all the squares, streets, and alleys of the city, all the theaters, railroad stations, churches, and markets. And we had to know not only their names, but how to get to them. In this respect Moscow cabdrivers were the only people who could compete with conductors.

I owe my knowledge of Moscow to my work as a conductor. A caustic old man in a very full-skirted coat examined us. He sipped at a glass of cold tea and gently asked:

"What's the shortest way, chum, for me to get from Marina Grove to Khamovniki? Eh? You don't know? And by the way, how do you suppose Khamovniki got its name?"

The old man picked on us ferociously. Half the conductors failed his examination. When they did, they went to complain to the chief engineer, Polivanov, a magnificently barbered, exceptionally courteous man. Cocking his gray head, he would answer that a knowledge of Moscow was one of the foundations of the conductor's trade.

"A conductor," he would say, "is not just an animated machine for handing out tickets but also a guide to Moscow. It is a big city. The oldest resident doesn't know all parts of it. Just imagine what confusion it would be for passengers, especially those from the provinces, if there was no one to help them find their way around this wilderness of blind alleys, gates, and churches."

I soon became convinced that Polivanov was right.

I was assigned to line Number 8—an accursed railroad station line which was considered even worse than the B line. It connected the Brest station and Kalanchevskaya Square with three other stations—the Nikolayevsk, the Yaroslavl, and the Kazan. It ran through Sukharevsky Square.

It sometimes happened that, as conductors said, a trolley would "fall under the train," from the Troitsko-Sergievskaya Monastery. An army of pilgrims would jam into the trolley. They were headed for various Moscow churches, they did not know the city, they were as stupid as hens, and afraid of everything. Day after day it was the same story: some of the God-fearing old ladies wanted to go to one church, some to another, others to a third, and none of them had the names of the churches quite right. We had to explain patiently to each of them how to get there, after which each old pilgrim would pull out of a pocket in a petticoat a handkerchief with coins tied up in its corners. One corner would have kopecks, another half-kopecks, a third five-kopeck pieces. The pilgrims would take a long time untying the knots with their teeth and counting out the fare carefully. In their hurry they would often make mistakes and untie the wrong corner. Then they would tie it up again with their teeth and start working on another.

It was a disaster for the conductors. We were supposed to have sold our tickets before Krasnaya Vorota, but the old women held us up, we had no chance to sell them tickets, and at Krasnaya Vorota some eagle-eyed controller would be sure to catch us and fine us for working slowly.

One day Babayev took me to his home. He lived with his daughter in a ramshackle little house near the Paveletsky station. His daughter worked as a seamstress.

"Look, Sanya," Babayev cried out cheerfully from the doorway, "I've brought you a bridegroom."

Sanya made a noise behind a muslin curtain but did not come out.

Some cages covered with newspapers were hanging in the low room. Babayev took off the papers. Canaries started to flutter and sing in the cages.

"Canaries rest me after too many human beings," Babayev explained. "Passengers never spare conductors anything; they show themselves to us in their worst character. It's clear this is why we are so suspicious of people."

Babayev was right. I don't understand why but nowhere are people ruder than in trolley cars. Even courteous people seem to be infected with peevishness when they board a trolley. At first this surprised me, then it began to irritate me, and finally it became so depressing that I did little but wait for a chance to give up working on trolleys and return to my former relations with human beings.

Sanya, a rawboned girl, came in and greeted me silently, put a gramophone with a red horn on the table, started it, walked out and never came back. It played an aria from *Rigoletto*. The canaries stopped their own singing at once, and began to listen.

"I keep the gramophone for the canaries," Babayev explained. "I'm teaching them to sing. They're very imitative birds."

Babayev told me that canary fanciers in Moscow have their own tavern where they take their canaries on Sundays and organize contests. A regular public assembles to listen to these canary concerts. Chaliapin went there once, with the millionaire Mamontov. They were distinguished people, of course, but they knew very little about canary singing, you might even say they didn't understand a damn thing about it, or even the price of a canary. They wanted to pay enormous sums for two birds. But the canary owners refused to sell, although they apologized for it. There's no point in putting a canary into the hands of an inexperienced person. A lot of labor goes to training it, and it's easy to spoil it. Besides, a canary isn't a toy, it requires expert handling. So Chaliapin and Mamontov had to go away empty-handed. As a result, Chaliapin boomed out in his

bass voice "How the king went to war," so loudly—probably in spite
—that all the canary owners packed up their birds and took them
out of the tavern. A canary's a nervous character; if you frighten it,
it will stop singing altogether, and then it's not worth a kopeck.

That dry autumn ended in heavy rains. This was the worst of
all for conductors. Drafts in the cars, the sticky mud on the
floors, mixed with torn-off corners of the tickets, the fusty smell
of wet clothing, and streaming windows behind which slid the
rows of dark wooden little houses and the rain-lashed signs of
wholesale warehouses.

On days like these everything got on a conductor's nerves,
especially the passengers' foolish habits of sticking their old, limp
tickets to the windows and drawing foolish big-nosed faces on the
glass with their fingers. A trolley car would become like a be-
draggled dormitory filled with quarreling residents. It was as if
Moscow had shrunk into itself, hidden under black umbrellas and
turned-up coat collars. The streets grew empty. Only in Sukharevsky
Square was there always noise and the rolling movement of great
human waves, as at the sea.

The trolley made its way with difficulty through noisy crowds of
buyers, sellers and traders on Sukharevsky Square. Gramophones
blared out next to the very wheels of the trolley, with a gypsy voice
singing: *"Hurry, horses, the snow is fluffy, a night of frost is all
around us!"* Her voice was smothered by the kerosene stoves sending their blue flames slowly up toward the sky; their roaring
drowned out all other sounds.

Broken mandolins jangled. Rubber devils with red-dyed cheeks
released the air blown into them with a screeching cry: "Go away,
go away!" Pancakes sizzled in enormous frying pans. The smell
was a mixture of manure, mutton, hay, and carpenters' supplies.
Hoarse people clapped each other furiously on the shoulders.
Wagons clattered by. Horses' sweaty muzzles stretched over the
platform of the trolley, breathing out heavy steam.

Chinese magicians squatted on the street, crying out in falsetto
voices: "Foo, foo, magic, magic!" Cracked-voiced church bells rang,
and a sobbing woman's voice cried out from under the black gates
of the Sukharev Tower: "Put your pale hand on my withered
breast."

Pickpockets were everywhere, holding old trousers over their
arms as if trying to sell them. They had quick, shifty eyes. Police
whistles blew like nightingales. Pigeons, released by little boys
from inside their shirts, flew up into the dirty sky.

It is impossible to describe this gigantic Moscow market which stretched from Samoteka almost to the Krasny Gate. You could buy everything there, from a three-wheeled velocipede or icons to a Siamese rooster, from Tambov ham to stewed cloudberries. Everything was full of wormholes, damaged, rusted, or slightly smelly.

This market was an all-Russian gathering of beggars, tramps, crooks, thieves, swindlers, people of poor and shifty lives. In the very air of Sukharevsky market, it seemed, dreams of easy money were mixed with pieces of meat jelly made out of calves' feet.

Here was an incredible mixture of people of all times and all conditions—from a God's fool with downcast eyes, clanking his rusty ascetic's chains and trying to ride the trolley without a ticket, to a goat-bearded poet in a green velvet hat, from Tolstoyans plodding angrily on red bare feet through the Sukharevsky mud to corseted ladies holding up their heavy skirts as they picked their way through that same mud.

A passenger in a black hat, a tightly buttoned overcoat, and brown kid gloves, got on my trolley one warm rainy day at Yekaterinsky Square. His long, well-groomed face showed a stony indifference to the Moscow slush, to the wrangling in the trolley, to me, and to the whole world. But he was a very polite man; when I gave him his ticket, he even tipped his hat and thanked me. The passengers were shocked by this, and began to look with unfriendly curiosity at this strange character. When he got off at Krasny Gate the whole trolley broke out into laughter at him. They called him the "actor from the burned-out theater" and "Von Baron." The passenger had interested me, too, with his haughty and at the same time shy look, a mixture of refinement and a sort of provincial pomposity.

Several days later I took an evening off and went to a Futurist concert by Igor Severyanin* at the Polytechnical Museum. What was my surprise, as old-fashioned writers used to write, when my passenger walked out on the stage in a black evening coat, leaned against the wall and waited for a long time, with lowered eyes, until the young girls' shrieks of delight and the applause could die down!

Flowers were thrown at his feet—dark roses. But he went on standing there motionless, without picking up a single flower. Then he took a step forward, the hall grew quiet, and the slightly burred

* Igor Severyanin, pen name of I. V. Lotarev (1887–1942), was a Futurist poet with considerable popularity on the periphery of the intelligentsia and the middle class. After 1917 he was an *émigré*, living abroad.

singing of his fashionable verses began. His magic was in finding melody in poetry composed of words which made no sense. Language existed for him solely as a kind of music. He required nothing else. All human thought was reduced to the gleaming of bugles, the rustling of scented silks, ostrich feather fans, and the foam on champagne.

It was savage and strange to hear these words in days when thousands of Russian peasants were lying in rain-filled trenches, beating back the German armies with rifle fire. Here was this former realist poet from Cheropovets, named Lotarev, who had become this same "genius" Igor Severyanin, rolling his r's in the French manner, singing verses about the boudoir of some grieving Nelly. Then he suddenly changed, and began to sing mincing songs about the war, and how, when the last Russian officer had fallen, his turn would come, and then "your loving, your one and only, Severyanin, I will lead you to Berlin."

Life is so powerful that it can redeem even the falsest people if there is a drop of poetry in them. And there was more than a drop in Severyanin. In later years he began to drop the trumpery; his voice started to sound almost human. The clean air of our steppes began to creep into his verses, "the wind over the waving grain fields," and his sophistication was sometimes replaced by a true lyric simplicity.

I could only rarely take an evening off. I spent every day and part of every night in exhausting work, always on my feet, grinding my teeth, hurrying, and like all conductors I got terribly tired. When we couldn't stand it any longer, we would ask the trolley dispatchers to transfer us for a day or two to the steam trolley which ran from the Savolovsky railroad station to the Petrovsko-Rasumovsky Agricultural Academy. This was the lightest and, in conductors' language, the most "suburban" line in Moscow.

A little steam engine which looked like a samovar was hidden, with its funnel, in a steel box. It gave itself away only by its childish whistle and its puffs of steam. It pulled four suburban cars. They were lighted at night by candles, since there was no electricity in the steam trolley.

I worked on this line during the autumn. When I had given out the tickets, I could sit on the open platform between two cars and sink mindlessly into the beauty of the autumn moving past the trolley. The dampness of leaves which have lasted too long poured out of the woods of birch and pine. Then the woods ended, and the academy's magnificent park stretched out in front of us in all the colors of autumn. Great lindens and maple trees stood in their lemon paleness, like sentinels of some marvelous, peaceful country. Autumn had been shaped here, in all the variety and pattern of its colors, by human wills and talents, for this park had been planted by some of our most famous botanists, masters of landscape gardening.

A love of nature was a passion which had possessed me since childhood. Sometimes it became so powerful that it frightened people close to me. When in the autumn I used to return to the *gymnasium* in Kiev from the Bryansk forests or from the Crimea, I was filled with bitter sorrow for the dying year. I lost weight, and couldn't sleep at nights. I tried to hide my condition from people around me. I had long before become convinced that it would only bewilder them. This was my "lack of seriousness," which my family and friends feared was deeply rooted in me and would keep me from real life.

How could I have explained to them that my awareness of nature was something larger than just surprise at its perfection, that my feeling was not just a vague love for nature but a recognition of it as something indispensable to any man wanting to work in the full measure of his strength? People usually go to nature as to a vacation. But I felt that a life in nature should be the constant vocation of every man.

In the autumn of 1914 I felt this attraction to nature especially sharply. The war was a war against nature, too, not here in Moscow, but in the west in Poland, and this made my love of nature all the stronger.

I would watch the smoke filter into the yellow woods from the steam trolley's smokestack. In the evenings the bluish glow of Moscow showed weakly through the smoke. Looking at those woods around Moscow stirred thoughts of Russia, of Chekhov, of Levitan, of the Russian spirit, of the forces within the people, their past and their future which ought to be, and of course will be, surprising and wonderful.

TO ONE SIDE OF THE WAR

Now that almost a half century has passed since the First World War I remember those quite recent times as if they were long, long ago, shrouded in the mists of the distant past. It is as if a thundering, stormy century lay between two eras of history. Everything has been mixed up. Everything has shifted, as if from a sudden blow. Nowadays we laugh over what seemed important to us earlier. We forgive ourselves our former thoughtlessness and our inability to cope with the complications of life, with social relationships, with ourselves. Now we look back at everything before 1917 as we look back at our childhood, even though people of my generation were already over twenty.

The 1914 war did not flood through our consciousness as completely as what has happened since then. A life was going on in Russia at that time which had nothing to do with the war. The auditorium of the Polytechnical Museum was crowded with people when the Futurists put on a show with Igor Severyanin. Rabindranath Tagore had captured people's minds. The Moscow Art Theater was desperately looking for a new Hamlet. Literary circles continued to exist in Moscow, and writers in these circles talked very little about the war. Religious philosophy, the search for God, symbolism, the challenge to a rebirth of Hellenic philosophy—these went right on, along with progressive revolutionary thinking, and competed with each other for men's minds.

I had come from the middle-class intelligentsia. My father had been a statistician. Like the majority of statisticians of that time, my father had been a liberal. From my earliest childhood I heard from my father and his friends generous-spirited words about freedom, the inevitability of revolution, and the misfortunes of the people.

Talk like this went on chiefly over tea, and each time Mama would motion at us children with her eyes and say to my father:

"Georgi, you're being carried away, as always."

I imagined the people—many millions of suffering, unfortunate people—to be the peasants. About workers I had heard little.

The word "proletariat" was pronounced rarely in our circle. Sometimes people spoke about "artisans" or about "factory workers" and this made me think of the suburbs of Kiev, crowded barracks, and strikes. Every time I heard the words "proletariat" and "working class" it seemed to me for some reason that they existed in Russia only in smoky Petrograd, in enormous factories like the Putilov or Obukhovsky works.

These naïve, childish conceptions and my passionate attraction to literature explain why, until the February Revolution, I knew nothing useful about the revolutionary movement among the workers. By the word "revolutionary," I understood at that time something desperately brave, inflexible, and selfless. It would be wrong to say that the revolutionary movement had left my childhood completely untouched. I had been a witness of the events of 1905, I knew the story of the December uprising in Moscow, what had taken place on the Kazan road, the mutiny of the *Potemkin* and the *Ochakov*, and I had been an admirer of Lieutenant Schmidt. But I had been attracted mainly by the romantic side of revolutionary activities—underground tunnels, illegal printshops, dynamite, bombs, flight from exile, incendiary speeches.

I saw for a long time the inner meaning of events as something very dim which might have been defined as "the struggle for freedom." It was with notions like these that I lived right up to the 1914 war. It was only at the start of that war that I began, slowly and with difficulty, to become aware of the social forces which were working in Russia.

In 1914 Moscow was very far from the front. Almost the only reminders of the war were the wounded men wandering around the city in their brown hospital gowns, and the mourning the women wore.

One day I attended one of the literary circles. Some writers had gathered in an old house on an alley near Gruzin. I sat in the back row and I never even stood up until the end of the evening. I was afraid I would be noticed and asked to leave, and I felt like a passenger without a ticket, although there were several other young fellows just like myself sitting near me. They seemed to be quite at ease, and this only made me more embarrassed.

My face was flushed—this was the first time I had ever seen writers so close. I couldn't escape from the idea that, although they were dressed in ordinary clothes and speaking the same words as we, mere mortals, there was still an enormous gap separating them from us. This distance was called talent, the free possession of ideas, images, and words, everything that seemed almost wizardry to me at that time. I looked at every writer there as if he were the direct heir of Turgenev, Chekhov, Tolstoy, as if he were the guardian of the tradition of Russian poetry and prose. At that time I could not understand Pushkin's words that every now and then writers and poets are the lowest "of all the people of the lowest world." I could make no distinction between a writer and everything he wrote about.

This was why I looked with equal excitement at Alexei Tolstoy, with his beard cut like a coachman's, and at the tousled Ivan Shmelev, who looked like a land surveyor, at the quiet Zaitsev, and at the icy Bunin, reading his story "Psalms" in a hollow voice.* I had hoped to see Maxim Gorky in this circle but he wasn't there. I did not suspect then that some twenty years later I would know him as a wise comrade and teacher.

An elderly man, probably tubercular, who looked as if he were made entirely out of wrinkles, was sitting next to me. He coughed into a dark handkerchief, and his eyes were shining—it was clear that he was running a fever. He followed every word that drifted down to us from the platform where the writers were sitting, and he would turn to me and say:

"Ah, but Russia is wonderful! Ah, how wonderful!"

We walked out together. He lived beyond the Presnensky Gates, so we walked along together.

A gray moon hung among the bare branches. Frozen leaves crunched under our feet. Light from windows fell on my companion's round caracul hat. He turned out to be a typesetter from Sitin's printing shop. His name was Elissei Sverchkov.

"I grew up in the provinces," he told me, stopping every few minutes to cough. "In the town of Kashin. As long as I can remember my heart has been in writing, but I know my own weakness at it. Words don't come easily to me. I understand them correctly, I can use them by touch, by taste, I knew all their qualities, but I just can't arrange them. There are a lot of ideas in every word, and the writer's job is to put a word next to another in such a way, young man, that it does the job it has to do in the reader's heart. Here is where talent comes to the rescue. Illumination! A real writer doesn't seek, he doesn't choose—he picks the word he needs

---

* Alexei Tolstoy (1882–1945) was an *émigré* writer, after having served as a propagandist for General Denikin's White army. In 1923 he returned to the Soviet Union, becoming later an extremely successful fellow-traveling novelist and playwright. Ivan Shmelev (1875–1950), who wrote realistic stories about the lower middle class, also became an *émigré*. So did Boris Zaitsev (1881–   ), a disciple of Chekhov. Ivan Bunin (1870–1953) emigrated to France in 1918 and remained an enemy of the Soviet Union until his death. He was an outstanding writer and lyric poet; in 1933 he became the only Russian writer until Pasternak ever to receive the Nobel prize.

just as a typesetter, without even looking, picks the letter he needs from the type tray. And once he has it in its place, the devil himself couldn't make him give it back. Otherwise his miraculous construction would crumble."

"And have you tried to write?" I asked the typesetter.

"I've tried and tried. And I'm still trying. But what good is it? I have formed a habit—on holidays I go to the Tretyakovsky Gallery, or to the Rumyantsev. I pick a picture I like and I look at it, I pretend that I'm a part of what is depicted in the painting. Let's take, for example, Savrasov's 'The Rooks Have Flown.'* Or Levitan's 'March.' All my childhood is in Savrasov's picture. The slushy Russian spring, with puddles, a cold little wind, and a low sky, and wet fences and clouds. Now Levitan's 'March'—that's a different spring, but also very much ours, very Russian, with the drip of melting snow, with the sky blue over the woods, when, you know, the water drops off the icicles drop by drop, and with every drop the light of the sun is falling off the roof. I can see it perfectly. So I look at the picture, and then I go home, and I try to express everything I've seen in a notebook, as if I were painting with words, just as a painter uses umber or sienna or cobalt. So that a man who had never seen that picture could imagine it to himself in all its details, with complete clarity. So that he could smell the manure, begging your pardon, and hear the rooks. I have written hundreds of such descriptions. I showed them recently to a writer—I won't tell you his name. I was all of a tremble, I was even sorry for myself. He read them through, and said: 'It's all done in a literary way, and completely correct, but what's it for? I'd rather look at pictures in nature than to get them through your descriptions of them. Brother,' he said to me, 'what made you want to compete with Savrasov or Levitan or Korovin? After all, they weren't sewed together with old thread.' I argue with him. 'My idea,' I tell him, 'is to work with words until they act on a man just as paint on a painter's canvas.' But he says: 'Well, only the devil knows what that means!' So I leave him with this 'only the devil knows.' One thing I understand: words don't come easily to me. And I'm sorry! I could have created something big; I feel it in me."

I accompanied the typesetter home. He lived at the back of a narrow courtyard which was filled with broken, twisted iron beds: a bed factory backed on to the same courtyard. Sverchkov invited me to come in with him, and then added as an afterthought:

"I live among beds, but I sleep on a wooden trestle bed. These

---

* A. K. Savrasov (1830–1897) was one of the founders of realistic landscape painting in Russia.

beds are all old, scrapped. They're cleaning them up now for soldiers' hospitals. Because of the war. I don't understand this war. It happened because of a lack of friendliness. If we, ordinary people like us, had only been able to agree, we could have said one word, no, and the whole bloody business would have stopped. This is what I dream about—who could have taught us friendliness? Is it possible that there isn't such a person somewhere in the world?"

Sverchkov knocked on a little window. No one answered but instead we heard a woman's angry crying.

"She doesn't understand!" Sverchkov said, with a sigh. "The weaker sex. I've got, maybe, a year to live. But no, she doesn't understand. You'll have to excuse me, young man."

I said good-by and left. There was such a quiet on Bolshaya Pressnya that I could hear the night watchmen yawning. The white and blue tiles shone dead under the lanterns in front of Chichkin's and Blandov's milk stores. Since Chichkin's store on one corner was faced with white tiles, Blandov's on the other corner had to have blue, in order to take away his neighbor's trade.

Everyone was asleep at home. Even Zakharov's room was dark. I lay down on the floor. Faint light from street lamps fell into the room.

I lay there and thought about the sick typesetter from Kashin. My thoughts did not bring me sorrow but, on the contrary, a kind of peace. What talents there were around the country! Who could guess how many talented people there were in the towns and villages of Russia! Tens or hundreds of thousands? How many minds, imaginations, and gifted hands they had to celebrate, to enrich, to glorify their country!

The typesetter, of course, was right. Miracles can be performed with the Russian language. There is nothing in life or in our consciousness which can't be expressed in a Russian word. The sound of music, the shine of paints, the play of light, the noise and the shadow of gardens, the unclearness of sleep, the heavy rumble of thunder, children's whispering, and the rustle of sand at the sea—there are no sounds, colors, images, or ideas, complicated or simple, for which an exact expression cannot be found in our language.

It is easy to think like this on city nights when train whistles can be heard from freight stations or railroad yards, or sometimes a cab clattering over cobblestoned streets.

I stood up, walked to the window, and looked for a long time at the Zoological Gardens. Deep and quiet, they seemed an im-

mense black island in the middle of the faintly lighted blocks of
Moscow. I turned around, and noticed something shining on the
table. It must be a note from Mama. I lighted a match and read
the slanting lines of a telegram from Kiev:

Assigned engineers regiment leaving for west will send my front-
line address later and will write as often as possible dont worry I
kiss you Galya and Kostik

Borya

So! So Borya had gone, too. I suddenly felt unbearably ashamed
of myself. What could I pride myself on compared to him? My
cloudy passion for literature? Without having yet written a single
decent line, I considered myself already among the elite. I had
laughed at his room, his concrete bridges, his worldly philosophy.
And just what was funny about any of it? In any case, he was
honorable. He worked like an ox, never told untruths, and didn't
duck his responsibilities. And if he preferred Henryk Sienkiewicz
to Chekhov, was this a mortal sin? It was clear that I, dead set
against all prejudices, had succumbed to the most petty kind of
prejudice myself.

I lit a second match, read the telegram again, and thought:
why didn't Mama wait up for me, instead of just leaving the telegram on the table? Why? Perhaps because she knew how I had
felt about Borya, and it would be hard for her to see my face at
such a difficult moment.

I dressed and went into Mama's room. She wasn't sleeping. We
sat there, and I stroked her dry, white hair and didn't know how to
comfort her. She was crying quietly, so as not to wake Galya.

Then I realized how cruel and unjust youth can be, even when
it is full of big thoughts.

Mama did not fall asleep until just before dawn. I went back
to my own room, put on my conductor's uniform, took my empty
bag, and carefully walked out of the house. A gray light poured
down the stairs from the unwashed windows. Old cats were snoring
on the steps.

Two-wheeled ambulances, with the red cross on green tarpaulins, were being driven along Gruzin to the freight station of
the Brest railroad. Dry, shriveled-up lilac leaves were blowing out
of the Zoological Gardens on to the street. Heavy morning raindrops were splashing loudly on these dusty leaves and on the tarpaulin tops of the ambulances.

THE OLD MAN
WITH THE HUNDRED-RUBLE BILL

It was first pointed out a long time ago that people whose lives are spent in constant motion—locomotive engineers, sailors, fliers, chauffeurs—tend to be a little superstitious. We conductors on the Moscow trolleys were superstitious, too.

We were afraid most of all of an old man with a hundred-ruble bill, called a "Katerinka." It carried an elegant, engraved portrait of Catherine II in a tight satin bodice.

To be fair about it, the old man was pleasant enough—clean, courteous, even cultivated. A carefully folded copy of *The Russian Gazette*, a paper read by liberal professors, was always sticking out of the pocket of his overcoat. He would get on a trolley and hand the conductor his hundred-ruble note with a courteous smile. Of course, we never had change. But the old fellow never insisted on it. He would politely get off at the next stop, and wait for the next trolley.

The incident would be repeated. So, changing from trolley to trolley, the old man would ride to his office, day after day and month after month, without ever paying his fare. There was no point in getting angry at him.

The hundred-ruble note was always the same one. We who were conductors on line 8 had long known its number by heart—123715. We sometimes discomfited the old boy by saying:

"Show your Katerinka No. 123715 and get off the trolley."

He never took offense. He would always show the bill politely and then just as politely leave the trolley, hurrying a little so as not to bother anyone.

He was an incredibly stubborn free-rider. The fiercest conductors were helpless against him. But we really hated him not because of his hundred-ruble bill but because, as was confirmed by old conductors who had known him over the years, he always brought bad luck with him.

I had four bad experiences while I worked on the trolleys. At first, I was a driver. I was assigned to the B-ring route, a devilish job. These trolleys pulled trailers which were attached in such a way that it was practically impossible to start the trolley without giving the trailer a sharp jerk and without hearing, in reply, the shouted profanities of the passengers.

One day a white truck belonging to Chichkin's milk concern drove on to the trolley tracks on Smolensk Boulevard. The chauffeur was just barely moving; he was clearly afraid of spilling his milk. So I had to go just as slowly behind him, and fell behind schedule. My trolley was greeted at every stop by a thick crowd of angry passengers.

Soon another B line trolley caught up to me, and then a third, and finally a fourth. All of us were impatiently and deafeningly clattering our signals; at that time trolleys had no bells, but electric rattles. The whole line became heavily jammed. And the chauffeur in front of me poked along timidly on the trolley tracks and refused to turn off.

We followed him all along the Kudrinskaya, then the Tverskaya, the Mala Dmitrovka, and the Karetny Ryad. I clattered my signal desperately, I stuck out my tongue at him, I swore, but the chauffeur only blew tobacco smoke out of his window at me. The oaths of other drivers behind me filled the air. They rolled up to me from the last trolley in a great wave which then surged back again down the line of trolleys.

In despair, I decided to act. At the entrance to the Samoteka I turned off my motor, pretended that my brake wouldn't work, and hit the back of Chichkin's truck and its impudent chauffeur with a deafening crash. Something exploded. The truck settled down on one side. White smoke poured out of it. Its mustached chauffeur jumped out on to the street, pulled a police whistle out of his pocket, and began to blow it furiously. This was a complete surprise to me. I could see a police officer and a policeman running up to the trolley, holding on to their hats.

The next day I was transferred from driver to conductor.

This was not the end of my misadventures. I was soon fined for sitting on the back platform while my trolley was going through Theater Square. Conductors were always supposed to stand there, because it was the busiest place in Moscow with passengers always jumping on and off.

Some of us younger conductors thought up a scheme, which seemed very successful at first, for getting a breather in the middle of a busy day. We would arrange with the driver to start the route two or three minutes earlier than scheduled, without "keeping the interval" as trolley workers called it. Then the driver would go at full speed until he had caught up to the trolley in front of him. We were happy now. The trolley in front of us picked up all the passengers and we followed along empty. It was quiet inside the trolley, and I could even read a newspaper.

The scheme seemed to us irreproachable. But of course, as often happens, we overdid it, and sometimes rode through Moscow three or four times in a row without a load. Our revenue was considerably less than that of other conductors. The management began to suspect something wrong. In the end they discovered what we were doing, and fined us heavily.

These misfortunes took place without help from the old man with the hundred-ruble bill. But one day he sat down in my trolley and the sight of him seemed to me more evil and suspicious than ever—the old man was beaming with liking for me, the conductor. Perhaps this was why I overlooked him, and let him ride free not to the first stop, but to the second. When he got off, the driver, a taciturn and moody man, noisily opened the front door of the trolley and shouted down the car to me:

"Now you'd better watch out, conductor! Some kind of bad luck is sure to hit you!"

And he slammed the door shut again just as loudly.

I expected something bad all day long, but nothing happened. So I calmed down. At midnight we left the Yaroslavl railroad station on our last trip. There were several passengers in the trolley, and nothing presaged misfortune. I even began lightheartedly to hum a popular song to myself: "Tell me, little birdie, can you change my money for me?"

A fat man in a top hat and an overcoat with a rolled collar got on the trolley at Orlikov Lane. Everything about him was in the grand manner—his slightly puffed cheeks, an aroma of cigars, his white foreign muffler, and his cane with a silver head. He walked the entire length of the trolley with the gait of a gouty man and sat down heavily near the exit. I walked up to him.

"I ride free!" the gentleman said abruptly, looking not at me but at the window on which reflections of nighttime lights were racing by.

"Where's your ticket?" I answered, just as abruptly.

The gentleman lifted his heavy eyelids and looked at me with immense scorn.

"You ought to recognize me, my boy," he said irritatedly. "I am the mayor of the city, Briansky."

"Unfortunately, it's not written on your face," I answered rudely, "that you're mayor of the city. Show me your ticket!"

The mayor flew into a rage. He flatly refused to show his credentials. I stopped the trolley and asked him to leave. The mayor dug in his heels. Then, as might have been expected, the other passengers cheerfully joined in the dispute.

"What kind of a mayor is he?" a laughing voice said from the depths of the trolley. "A mayor rides only in his own carriage. Everybody knows that. We've seen mayors like this before."

"It's none of your business," the gentleman in the top hat shouted back.

"My dear fellows!" said a frightened old lady with a bag of apples. "What a loud voice he has! Rich people are always stingy. They hate to waste five kopecks on a ticket. That's how they get their capital—save enough quarter-kopecks and you'll have a ruble."

"But maybe he's really broke," a young fellow in a cap said laughing. "In that case, I'll pay for him. Here, conductor! And give him the change so he can buy something to eat."

It ended only when the enraged mayor jumped out of the trolley, slamming the door so hard that the glass rattled. For this he received some additional remarks from the driver about his insolence, his top hat, and his fat, ugly mug.

Two days later the head of the Miusski trolley yards summoned me. He was a heavily bearded, red-haired, humorous man, and he said in a loud voice:

"Conductor number two hundred and seventeen! Accept this second reprimand with a warning. Sign here. So! And light a candle to the Iberian Virgin in gratitude that you've got nothing worse. What a thing to do—throw the mayor out of your trolley, and at night, too, and on Meshchanskaya Street!"

He insisted that I describe to him the whole incident with the mayor in great detail. I did so, and I reminded him, among other things, of the old man with the hundred-ruble bill and the belief of all the conductors that the old man brought bad luck.

"I've heard about that damned old fool," the head of the yards said. "How will we ever catch a swindler like him?"

All the conductors on line 8 dreamed of catching him. Every one had his own plan. I had one, too. I described it to the head of the yards. He just laughed.

But in the morning I was given, against my receipt, a hundred rubles in the smallest paper bills. I waited for the old man for three days. On the fourth day, at last, he showed up.

Suspecting nothing, cheerful and happy, he climbed up into the trolley and held out his Katerinka to me. I took it, turned it over, looked at it against the light, and put it away in my bag. The old man's jaw dropped open in surprise.

Then I patiently counted out ninety-nine rubles and ninety-five kopecks, checked the change twice, and handed it to the old man. It was frightening just to look at him. His face had turned dark. There was so much yellow evil in his eyes that I would not have liked to meet him in an empty alley. But he took the change, without saying anything, put it in his coat pocket without counting it, and walked to the exit.

"Where are you going?" I said to him politely. "After all, you've got a ticket now, at last. You can ride as far as you like."

"You scoundrel!" the old man said in a squeaky voice, and he opened the door to the front platform, and got off at the first stop. He did this probably out of old habit.

When the trolley started again, he struck its side with his heavy cane with all his strength and shouted again:

"You scoundrel! Swindler! I'll show you!"

I never met him again. People told me that some of the conductors saw him after this incident walking cheerfully from his home to his office. The neatly folded copy of *The Russian Gazette* was still sticking out of the pocket of his overcoat.

The hundred-ruble bill number 123715 was put up as a trophy on the bulletin board at the trolley yards where official orders were posted. It stayed there for several days. Other conductors looked at it, recognized it, and laughed. And I won the reputation of being a resourceful fellow. Only this saved me from being fired when I deliberately transported twenty-four armed men without tickets and ran afoul of the inspector.

This was at night. Some soldiers climbed into the trolley at the Yaroslavl railroad station in battle uniform—with cartridge cases, rifles, and leather belts tight around their new greatcoats. These were reserve soldiers, bearded, weathered men who had been dropped down in a city they neither knew nor understood. They were going to the Brest station, and from there to the front. Three soldiers were accompanied by their wives, wrapped to the eyes in warm shawls. Each held tightly to her husband's sleeve, and said nothing. The soldiers were all silent, too.

I committed two violations of the rules—I transported soldiers with their wives without payment, and besides I had let armed men into the trolley, which was strictly forbidden. The inspector boarded the trolley at Yekaterinsky Square.

"Save yourself the bother," I told him. "The soldiers haven't got any tickets."

"Are you carrying them for the King of Denmark?" the inspector asked me calmly.

"Yes. For the King of Denmark."

"Good luck!" the inspector said. He wrote down my number, and jumped off the trolley while it was moving.

A little later the red-bearded head of the trolley yards summoned me again. He looked at me for a long time, frowned, thought for a while, and then addressed me very formally:

"You just can't work with passengers. That's clear. You've already picked up, by God, three reprimands."

"Well, what then? Discharge me."

"You'll get discharged soon enough. But why? I'm transferring you to night work with ambulance trolleys. You'll be taking wounded from the railroad stations to the hospitals. You're a student, aren't you?"

I agreed. This new work seemed to me much more ennobling than the exhausting squabbles with passengers, tickets, and making change. So I felt easier as I turned in my conductor's bag and walked home. I walked along Gruzin. The wind twisted the tongues of flame in the gas street lamps. The night air, with its slight taste of gas, seemed to me to promise a change in my life, new travel, new experiences.

LEFORTOVO NIGHTS

Sparkling with arc lights and looking as if it had been melted down by their chalky, hissing light, the Brest railroad station was at that time Moscow's chief military station. Echelons of troops were dispatched from here to the front. At night, long hospital trains smelling of chloroform moved stealthily up to its half-dark platforms and began to unload the wounded.

Every night, about two o'clock, when life had died in the city, we trolley operators moved white hospital cars up to the station. Inside the cars spring beds had been hung instead of seats.

We had to do a lot of waiting. We would smoke near the trolley cars. Women in shawls would come up to us and shyly ask us when we were going to load the wounded. These words—"to load the wounded"—which meant to drag living men who had been badly wounded into the cars like dead freight, were one of the absurdities produced by the war.

"Wait," we told them. The women would sigh, walk away along the pavement, stop in the shadows, and silently watch the heavy station door.

These women came to the station just on the chance that they might find among the wounded a husband, a brother, a son, or else the fellow soldier of a relative who could tell them about his fate. All of us conductors, who were men of different ages, characters, and opinions, feared one thing more than anything else: that one of these women would find her mutilated man in our presence.

When the orderlies appeared at the station doors carrying stretchers, the women would swarm around them, looking in a frenzy at the dark faces of the wounded and giving them strings of hard rolls, apples, and handfuls of cheap, loose cigarettes. Some of the women would cry. The wounded men tried not to groan, and quieted the women with special words that could be understood. These are the words a simple Russian hoards within himself for an evil day, and uses only to people as simple as he is.

The wounded were carried into the trolley cars, and we began our tedious trip through nighttime Moscow. The drivers drove slowly and carefully. We usually moved the wounded to the chief military hospital in Lefortovo. Ever since then, the memory of Lefortovo has been fixed for me in cold autumn nights. Many years have passed, but I still seem to feel that nights are always like that in Lefortovo, and the dull rows of windows in the military hospital just the same. I can't lose this impression because I have never gone back to Lefortovo since then, and I have never seen the hospital or the vast square in front of it in daytime.

At Lefortovo we helped the orderlies carry the badly wounded into the wards and the barracks scattered through the park around the main building. A little stream which smelled of chlorine could be heard at the bottom of a ravine in the park. We carried the wounded very slowly, so we often had to stay at Lefortovo until dawn.

Sometimes we transported wounded Austrians. In those days Austria was jokingly called "the empire of scraps" and the Austrian army "the gypsy bazaar." The many different races of this army gave the impression of a crowd of dark-faced, incredibly thin people in blue greatcoats and faded caps with tin cockades and the letters "F" and "J" printed slantingly across them. These were the initials of the Austrian Emperor, Franz Josef.

We questioned these prisoners, and were astonished: who wasn't in this army! There were Czechs, Germans, Italians, Tyroleans, Poles, Bosnians, Serbs, Croatians, Montenegrins, Hungarians, gypsies, Hertzogovinians, and Slovaks . . . I had not even known of the existence of some of these peoples although I had been graduated from the *gymnasium* with a 5 in geography.

One night they brought to my trolley car, together with our wounded, an Austrian as long and thin as a pole, wearing gray puttees. He had been wounded in the throat, and he lay there wheezing and rolling his yellow eyes. When I walked by, he raised his dark hand. I thought he wanted something to drink, and I bent down to his unshaved, dried-out face, and heard a faint whisper. It seemed to me the Austrian was speaking in Russian, and I started back. Then he repeated, with difficulty:

"I'm a Slav! They got me in the big-big battle . . . my brother."

He closed his eyes. Obviously he had said something in these words which was terribly important to him and which I could not understand. Obviously he had been waiting a long time for a chance to say them. Then I wondered for a long time what this dying man with the blood-caked bandage around his throat had meant. Why hadn't he complained, or asked for something to drink, or taken out of his shirt his regimental number on its steel chain with the address of his relatives, as all wounded Austrians used to do? Clearly he had wanted to tell me that power breaks even straw, and that it was not his fault that he had taken up arms against his brothers. This idea was linked in his feverish consciousness with memories of the bloody battle into which he had been driven straight from his village by the Germans. From a village where ancient nut trees grew, throwing wide shadows, and where a bear danced to a street organ on holidays in the market square.

When we began to take out the wounded at Lefortovo and walked up to a red-headed soldier from Vologda, he told us: "Take the Austrian. Look, he's suffering. We can wait."

We lifted the Austrian. He was heavy, and on the way he started to groan quietly. "Oh-oh-oh," he said slowly, "Mother Mary! Oh-oh-oh, Mother Mary!"

When we got him to the barracks at the bottom of the trampled-down park, he was already dead. The army surgeon there told us to take him to the mortuary. This was a shed with a door as wide as a gate, standing partly open. We carried the Austrian in, took him off the stretcher, and placed him on the straw already covered with many bodies. There was no one around. A yellow electric light was burning near the ceiling. Trying not to look around me, I took the Austrian's regimental badge from under his open collar—it was a little book of two sheets of white oxidized metal. The name of the soldier, his number, and the address of his relatives were written on it.

I read it, and wrote down: "Jovann Petrich, 38719, Vesseli Dubnyak (Bosnia)."

When I got home I wrote a post card (for some reason I wrote it in block letters) about Jovann Petrich's death and sent it to Bosnia, to the village of Vesseli Dubnyak, to the family named Petrich.

While I was writing the post card, I imagined I could see a little white house, so low that its windows were close to the ground. I could see the burdocks growing under the windows, and a hawk circling over the house in a hot sky. I could see a woman taking a child from her dark breast and looking with gloomy eyes at the fields around her where the wind was blowing the dust. Maybe this wind had blown all the way from the field where her Jovann was lying, but the wind couldn't talk and would never tell her anything. And no letters came.

"They got me in the big-big battle . . . my brother"—I remembered his broken whisper. Who was to blame that the Germans, in their green uniforms, had come and taken Jovann from the garden in which he had grown up? He had been an obedient, good man—this was clear from his round, gray eyes, the eyes of a little boy in the face of a grown man.

Ah, those Lefortovo nights! Nights of war, of suffering, and of wondering about man's road through this tortuous, hard life. These were the nights when I really grew up. With every day, worthless parts of my earlier conception of reality shriveled up and blew away. I began to see life as something hard and demanding, requiring constant work to clean it of its dirt, pus and deceit, and I began to see its magnificence and its simplicity.

MEDICAL ORDERLY

In October, 1914, I got my discharge from the Moscow trolley lines and became an orderly on a hospital train operating in the rear of the armies. I couldn't stand just sitting in Moscow. All my thoughts were in the west, in the wet fields of Poland where Russia's destiny was being decided. I was looking for a chance to be closer to the war and finally to pull myself out of the despondency which had long since overwhelmed my family.

Almost all the orderlies on this rear-echelon hospital train were student volunteers. We wore soldiers' uniforms but we were allowed to keep our students' caps. This often saved us from the rudeness and arrogance of military commandants.

Each one of us orderlies had his own passenger car equipped for forty wounded men. It was considered a question of honor to keep the car shipshape, so clean that the senior doctor, Pokrovsky, who was a member of the Duma, would only smile into his light-brown imperial beard and say nothing when he inspected the train after each trip.

I was frightened on my first trip. I didn't know if I could manage to take care of forty wounded men. There were few nurses on the train. So we, simple orderlies, were required not only to wash all the wounded and give them food and drink, but also to watch their temperatures and the condition of their bandages, and to give them their medicine at the right times.

My first trip showed that the hardest task of all was to feed the wounded men. The car with the kitchen was a long way from me. I had to carry two full pails of hot soup or boiling water through forty-eight doors. Those orderlies whose cars were closer to the kitchen had to open and close only ten or fifteen doors. We considered them lucky and we envied them, getting only a little ill-spirited satisfaction out of the fact that, when we had to carry our pails through their cars so many times, they sometimes spilled. And the lucky ones had to get down on the floor with a rag, constantly cleaning up after us.

The first time, those forty-eight doors drove me to despair. There were the usual kind of doors, opening in, and there were sliding doors, leading to the platforms between the cars. Each door had to be opened and closed, which meant putting the full pails down each time and trying not to spill them. The train went at high speed. It bucked and swerved at all the switches, and this is probably why I still dislike the sudden lurching of a railroad car when it passes over a switch.

Besides, we had to hurry, to keep the soup or the tea from getting cold, especially in winter when the cutting wind blew across the icy open platforms between the cars, as if tormenting us, and it would have been easy to slip and fall under the wheels of the train. Add to this the fact that at least twelve trips a day were needed (for bread and for dishes, for tea, for soup, then back with the dirty dishes and the pails and everything else) and it becomes clear why we cursed the designer, already long and peacefully dead, who had first thought of putting six, and sometimes eight, doors in every passenger car. We gave thanks to heaven when eating time for the wounded coincided with a stop at a station. Then we could get out and run with our pails along the hard ground and not on the unsteady floor of the cars.

Many of the wounded could not feed themselves. We had to feed them and help them drink. In the mornings we washed them, and after this we scrubbed the floors with a solution of carbolic acid.

Only in the evenings, after supper, were we able to rest a little, and even then we had to start our eternal battle with the candles in the tin lanterns on the sides of the cars. They either went out, or became bent, or suddenly started to blaze like torches. And on the platforms between the cars our candles were always being stolen by the brakeman from the train crew—a big-nosed, short-legged fellow named Vasya, whose larceny won him the nickname "Candle Snout."

Of course, not a single one of us could have coped with his job at all if it hadn't been possible to enlist in every car a helper from among those soldiers who were only slightly wounded.

But in the long run, these difficulties were not important. My first trip scared me not because of these routine problems. There was something much more complicated that all orderlies thought about in secret. This was how we could manage to look into the eyes of forty shattered men, especially when we, as students, had been freed from military service. We were afraid of sneers and of the just indignation of men who had taken on their own shoulders all the burden and the danger of the war while we, young and most of us healthy people, went on living in safety, having made no sacrifice at all.

At the start of my trip I had simply no time to talk with any of the wounded or to listen to them. But at night, finally, things grew quiet. I sat by myself a little while, smoked, and looked out of the window. We were at some station, and its lanterns threw stripes of light into the car. Then the night and the twinkling lights of lost little villages closed over the window again above the noise of the train wheels.

"Orderly!" a hoarse, insistent voice yelled out of the car. "Orderly!"

I got up and walked into the car. A wounded man with a brown, puffy face had called me.

"Were you sleeping, you enema-giver?" he asked me in a quiet, unmocking voice. "You're not supposed to sleep, according to the rules. Give me something to drink. Or I'll be suffering here all night with my parched throat."

"Everyone's supposed to sleep," a man with a thinnish beard and a dry face said conciliatingly from the next cot. He spoke in a high-pitched, little boy's voice. "For some, eternal sleep, for others, only short snatches."

"What the hell are you, a monk, or what?" the puffy-faced man asked him cheerfully.

"Eh-eh-eh, you country fellow," the dry-faced man said laughing. "The monastery hasn't been built yet in which I could be a monk. I'd need a special monastery, conforming to my view of life."

"Shut up! What a nut you are!" a third man with a bandaged face said angrily. His little eyes shone in the white bandages like a polecat's.

"Well, we're laughing at each other," the dry-faced man said, "but we don't understand what life is all about. What it amounts to."

"Well, tell us then, don't be stingy," the puffy-faced man said roughly. "Tell us what it's all about, or tell us about ducks."

"That I can do," the dry-faced man said willingly, and then he was silent for a moment. "An old man who was pretty famous once lived on this Russian land. Count Tolstoy. He wrote so many books that people say his right arm shriveled up a little from it. His arm got sick, in other words, and he kept it always tied up in a sash. This made it easier for him, as if his arm had healed."

"That's true," the bandaged man said. "I saw it myself, in a picture of him."

"Just lose something, your arm or your leg, there's nothing worse," the puffy-faced man agreed, raising himself on his cot with difficulty, and he said to me: "You sit down, orderly. I woke you up, so sit with us for a while, and listen."

"It's wrong, too, to wake up a man without any reason," a sleepy voice said from the depths of the car. "It makes the blood turn sour."

"You shut up!" the puffy-faced man cried out. "Give people a chance to talk."

"Yes-s," the dry-faced man said, and he pressed his thin lips together. "The old man was all dried up, but they called him Leo. And maybe that was a good name for him. Because they say he had a strength that was like a lion's. In ideas, of course, in his thinking. Well, in our settlement, there used to live a house painter called Koler. He had a curious encounter with this Count Tolstoy. Or not an encounter, really, but a simple conversation. This painter Koler was sitting one day at a little station God knows where, or maybe it was somewhere in the suburbs below Moscow, and he sat there all day long, waiting for a train, and all around him there was nothing but the summer, and dust, and the dull station, without any people. And this Count Tolstoy shows up at the same station, and he's also waiting for a train.

"Well, of course, they start talking about where they're going. Koler says: 'I'm headed for the city of Odessa, in the south, because I'm bored with doing painting work around here.' 'And why is that?' Tolstoy asks him. 'Because,' Koler answers, 'they paint houses around here in dark colors, and there in bright colors. And that's much happier. There you paint a house with ordinary paint, but clean and well-strained paint, and that house will stand there between the sky and the sea like a shining stone. And it becomes lighter, as if the inhabitants of paradise had built it with fingers of air.' 'But there is no paradise,' Tolstoy tells Koler, and he laughs, but it's a bitter kind of laugh. 'I know there isn't," Koler answers. 'I just used it as a word in conversation. And where might you be going, if it isn't a secret?' 'And what if it is a secret?' Tolstoy asks him. 'If it's a secret, then I beg your pardon. I'm a clumsy man.' Then the old man grabbed him by the shoulders, patted him on the back and said: 'Sure, it's clear you're clumsy. But you ought to be proud of it! For you're an artist at living, and you understand it excellently. Go on living now, just the way you've been living, to make people happier. There's truth in that. As for me, I'm looking all over Russia for the quietest little secluded monastery, a refuge, where I can live and finish my last book without a lot of distracting bothers.' 'And what might such a book be about?' Koler asks him; "please forgive again my lack of courtesy.' 'It's about everything in this world that's good and that I've managed to see in this world,' the old man answers him. 'That's hard work,' Koler observes in answering him. 'Since the choice is so big. Take just good colors —there are dozens of them. So how are you going to write about all that's good in life?' 'I'll write as much of it as I can. At first I'll write about how an old man lives in a hut by a river, and goes out every morning onto the threshold to watch the yellow buntings bathing in the dew. And thinks: "Today I'll go into the woods to pick some red bilberries, and maybe I'll get a basket full, and maybe I won't but I'll just lie down under a pine tree and go to sleep forever. Because of my extreme old age. But it's all the same, one way or the other, no matter what happens, it's all to the good, whether I've got a little longer to live on this earth or, on the other hand, I make room for younger men. I myself have lived a long time and enjoyed it, so now let others live and be happy in my place." ' 'Well, no,' Koler says. 'I don't understand that kind of talk. Happiness comes when the shavings fly out from under the plane or, let's say, when the paint goes on as smooth as a reflection in water. I find the big happiness in work. And your words, Leo Nikolayevich, don't add up for me.' "

"That's right!" the man with the bandaged face said eagerly. "The whole world stands on work. And the man who works is the foundation of all the world. Finish your job, and then you can love. Either the dew, or the yellow bunting. Whichever you like."

"Tolstoy worked more than any of us," the sleepy voice said from the depths of the car. "I've read a lot of him."

"Correct!" the puffy-faced man suddenly cried out. "For instance, I can take a hunk of dirt before sowing, feel it, smell it, and understand how the seed is going to feel in that earth, how much moisture there is in it, and whether it will be enough for the whole plant to drink."

"What is there to shout about?" the sleepy voice asked again. "That Koler of yours, maybe he got it all mixed up. Painters are known to talk twaddle mostly. I'm sorry for one thing, that Leo Tolstoy never wrote that book about all that's good in this world. We'd have read it!"

"Orderly!" the puffy-faced man called out suddenly in his former demanding voice. "Raise the curtain. It's already morning outside. Let's see what's outside the window. It'll soon be our Kostroma."

The wounded men were all silent. I raised the heavy cotton curtain and saw outside the window the autumn of north Russia.

It was hazily gold all the way to the horizon with birch woods, pastures, and innumerable winding rivers. The train hurtled along, wrapping the track watchmen's little cabins in steam. I had never seen such an autumn before, such clear skies, the air so fragile, or such silver brilliance from the filaments of spider webs, from the ravines overgrown by red sorrel, from the ponds where the sandy bottom could be seen through the water, from the radiance of misty distances, and the tender banks of clouds filling the blue sky in the wet morning.

I was looking at it so hard that at first I didn't feel a pressure on my back. The puffy-faced man had put on my shoulder a hand which might have been cast in iron, pulled himself up, and was looking out of the window.

"Ekh, my darling little brother!" he said in a singing sort of voice. "I could walk this land barefoot, and drink tea in every peasant's hut. That's the bad luck. Because I haven't got anything to walk on any more."

I looked down and saw under his hospital robe the tightly bandaged stumps where his legs had been amputated.

The train was running smoothly through some dew-covered hills. The locomotive suddenly blew its whistle, as happily as if it were the bearer of good and long-awaited news.

"Ekh," the puffy-faced man added. "We're rushing straight toward the tears of wife and mother. But you can never turn back! It can't be done. Never try it, little brother!"

RUSSIA IN THE SNOWDRIFTS

Our hospital train made several trips from Moscow to various cities of central Russia. We went to Yaroslavl, Ivanovo-Voznesensk, Arzamas, Kazan, Simbirsk, Saratov, Tambov, and several other towns. For some reason I remember little of these places. My memory is much clearer of some little station like Bazarni Sizgan, or of different villages, especially one hut in a settlement covered with snow. I don't even know which province it was in—Kazan, or Tambov, or Penzensk.

I can still see that hut, and the tall old man with the raw sheepskin coat thrown over his hunched shoulders. He came out of its low door and, holding on to it with his hands, looked for a long time at the long train with the red cross painted on the side of each car. The wind was blowing snow down from the eaves on to the old man's shaggy head.

It was winter. Russia was lying in the snowdrifts.

When we were carrying wounded, I noticed nothing around me—there was no time to. But during our trips back every orderly was alone in his scrubbed and empty car, and there was as much time as you wanted to look out of the window, to read, and to rest.

My memories of these trips back are of heavy snow, its whiteness filling the car with color, and the lowering dove-gray sky. I kept remembering a line I had read somewhere: "The country which is silent, all in white like a bride, is dressed in its shroud." And this line and the snow were all mixed up in my mind with the three-cornered scarfs and the dresses of the nurses when they inspected the train in the mornings.

Bazarni Sizgan. I remember that station because of a completely unimportant happening. We stopped there all night on a siding. There was a blizzard. In the morning the train was filled with snow. I went to the station buffet to buy hard rolls, with the orderly in the next car, a goodhearted lout named Nikolasha Rudnyev, a student at the Petrovsk Agricultural Academy.

As always happens after a blizzard, the air was piercingly clean and strong. The buffet was empty. A hydrangea plant, yellowed by the cold, was standing on a long table covered with oilcloth. A poster hung by the door, showing a mountain goat on the snow-covered mountains of the Caucasus. Under the goat was written: "Drink Saradjev Brandy." There was a smell of burned onions and coffee.

A snub-nosed girl in an apron over a short fur-trimmed jacket was sitting sadly at a little table and looking at a young fellow with a sallow complexion. The boy had a long neck which looked transparent, worn almost red by the collar of his peasant's coat. A few flax-colored hairs fell across his forehead. His feet in their thawing boots crossed under the table, he was drinking tea out of an earthenware cup. He was breaking big pieces off a hunk of rye bread, and then picking the crumbs up from the table and putting them in his mouth.

We bought our hard rolls, sat down at a table, and ordered tea.

The samovar was boiling on a wooden shelf. The snub-nosed girl brought the tea to us, with wilted little pieces of lemon. She pointed to the boy in the peasant's coat, and said:

"I always feed him. I pay for it myself, not the buffet. He lives on charity. On the trains, begging in the cars."

The boy drank his tea, turned his cup over, stood up, made the sign of the cross in front of the advertisement for Saradjev brandy, drew himself up unnaturally, and with his eyes fixed on the wide station window began to sing. He was singing, obviously, to thank the tenderhearted girl. He sang in a high, doleful voice, but this young boy's song was for me the best expression of old village Russia. I remember only a few words of his song.

> They buried her
> In the damp pine woods
> In the damp pine woods
> Under a log
> Under a log
> Of an old oak tree . . .

I automatically looked where the boy was staring. A snow-covered road ran down a ravine between clumps of trees sheathed in hoarfrost. Beyond the ravine, beyond the thatched roofs of some barns, smoke from peasants' stoves hung like threads in the shy, murky sky. There was sorrow in the boy's eyes, grief for the slanting hut he didn't have, for the wide bench along its wall, for the broken window covered with paper, for the smell of hot black bread.

I thought to myself: how little a man needs to be happy when he isn't happy, and how much he needs as soon as he gets that little bit!

Since then I have lived a good deal in peasants' huts and I have come to love them for the dull shine of their wooden walls, their smell of ashes, and their plainness. A peasant's hut is very much like other familiar things: spring water, or baskets made of bast, or the plain blossoms of potato plants.

Real human character cannot exist without a feeling for one's country—something special, dear, and beloved in all its little details. It is an unselfish feeling, and it sharpens our interest in everything. Alexander Blok* wrote in the long-ago hard years:

> Russia, beggared Russia,
> To me your gray huts

* Alexander Blok (1880–1921) is considered by many the greatest Russian poet of the twentieth century. A Symbolist, he is best known for a poem called "The Twelve."

To me your windlike songs
Are like the tears of first love . . .

Blok was right, of course. Especially in his comparison. Because there is nothing more human than the tears of love, nothing which moves one's heart so strongly and so sweetly. And there is nothing more loathsome than a man who is indifferent to his country and its past, its present and its future, to its language, its life, its woods and its fields, its villages and its people, whether they are geniuses or village shoemakers.

It was in these years of my service on the hospital train that I first became aware of myself as Russian to the last drop of my blood. It was as if I opened myself to a flood of people, soldiers, workers, peasants, artisans. It gave me great confidence. Not even the war could cast a frightening shadow on this confidence. "Great is the God of the Russian land," Nikolasha Rudnyev loved to say. "Great is the genius of the Russian people. The future—is with us."

I agreed with Rudnyev. In these years I saw Russia in its soldiers, its peasants, its villages with their skimpy resources and their abundant grief. For the first time I was seeing many Russian towns and factory settlements, and their general features all blended in my consciousness, leaving behind them a love for the essence of our country they were so full of.

I remember Arzamas for its wicker baskets full of firm red apples, and for a similar abundance of red church domes which looked just like the apples. The town seemed to have been sewed together by artists with golden thread.

Nizhni Novgorod hit you in the face with its Volga wind, smelling like old matting. Here was the city of Russian enterprise, wholesale warehouses, boxes, pickling, a bustling trans-shipping wharf into the history of Russia.

In Kazan, the monument to Derzhavin was covered with snow. I went to the opera there, tired out, and fell asleep in the gallery during *Snow Maiden*, remembering in my sleep the last words of the opera I heard: "Are the doors really closed for girls, the entrances all forbidden?"

I slept until the middle of the night. A watchman found me and took me to the police station. It had a smell of sealing wax, and the fat police chief wrote out an official record of my "impermissible sleep inside a theater." I walked back to the station. Snow was blowing into my face from the Volga, and I felt sorry for the frozen Derzhavin staring into the dark with his brass-hard eyes.

I was in Simbirsk on a winter night, too. The whole deserted town was sheathed in hoarfrost. Its parks seemed to have been made out of tin. From the Stari Venetz I looked at the Volga in the night, but I could see nothing except a frozen colorless haze. At that time I didn't know that Simbirsk was the town where Lenin had been born. Now, of course, I sometimes feel I must have seen the wooden house in which he lived. It seems that way, perhaps, because there were so many such warm little houses in Simbirsk, throwing light through their windows onto the narrow sidewalks in the evenings.

All I knew then about the town was that Goncharov had lived there—that sluggish man with a fabulous command over the Russian language, the language which lives so lightly, warmly, and strongly in his books.

Saratov seemed to me too correctly constructed, and even boring. The city produced an impression of prosperity and order. This was strong in the bigger streets, but later I wandered down some side streets and alleys where little boys were sliding down the hills on toboggans in a flurry of dry snow. I slid with them. I liked lying flat on the toboggan and rushing past the little houses with geraniums standing in their windows. I envied the people who lived in those little houses, because I had been inside one of them. A little boy took me to the house of a lady named Sofia Tikhonovna to drink hot milk. Her house had windowpanes next to its front door and the pale sunshine lay on the clean floor in neat quadrangles. Another door opened into a room with velvet curtains at the windows. A wall clock with an enormous pendulum struck the time so loudly that I had to raise my voice to talk with the shy old lady, Sofia Tikhonovna. A pile of copies of *Niva* bound in blue paper stood on a table near a window covered with a lace tablecloth. There were also some flowers which had dried out a long time ago. Among some photographs and water colors on the wall was a yellowing poster for Maxim Gorky's *Children of the Sun*.

"My son's an actor," Sofia Tikhonovna told me. "In a Peterburg theater. Once a year, every summer, he comes to see me, for a week on his way to the Caucasus and another week on his way back."

I tried to picture this life to myself, a life filled with waiting for her son. It must have been a bitter life, but the old lady carried it off lightly and without a sigh. Every object was cleaned, cared for, and loved only because it might be useful to her son during those two weeks in the long year. Either he would just glance at it, or he would say suddenly: "By the way, Mama, what's happened to that brass night lamp, or that Crimean stone from Simeiz which I brought you five years ago?"

The brass night lamp, polished with tooth powder, would be standing in its usual place. And the Crimean stone was lying on top of the copies of *Niva*—that aquatic stone known to half of Russia with its inscription: "Greetings from the Crimea" and its painting in crude oil colors of a cypress tree and, behind it, an azure sea with a white sail on it.

There were a great many towns. Spring came at last, to gladden the provincial wasteland and the sewage-filled streams with its fragrant leaves, a little sticky to the touch of fingers. Spring found us in Kursk, which seemed filled to the rooftops with masses of flowering branches. The famous Kursk nightingales sang in the wet woods. The lazy, cold little Tuskor River flowed between low banks covered with yellow flowers.

Kursk was a strange city. Many people love it, even those who have never been there, because Kursk is the promise of the south. When the houses and church towers on its hills first appear through the dusty, thick windows of the Moscow-Sevastopol express train, the passengers know that in one more day through those same windows they will be seeing almond blossoms in the early morning fog. The clear luminescence of the horizon is enough to make you guess the nearness of the south.

Spring blossomed over Russia. It blossomed over Vladimir on the Klyasma, over Tambov, over Tver, all places where we took the wounded. With each new trip we noticed that the wounded men became less talkative, harder. And the whole country was silent, as if it were wondering how to ward off the blow that was coming.

Soon our whole unit was transferred from the rear to the front lines. We set off on our first trip to the west, to Brest-Litovsk, to the battlefields.

THE BUGLER AND THE TORN-UP PAPER

Once in the battle area, our hospital train was made up chiefly of boxcars. It had only four passenger cars, one of which was fixed up as an operating room. They made me medical orderly in this car, and from then on I was alone much of the time. Nobody was allowed to enter this car except doctors and nurses.

For days on end I scrubbed the white walls of the car with turpentine, washed the floors, sterilized bandages and gauze, and listened to our "apothecary," Romanin, a student of the Moscow Commercial Institute, singing to amuse himself behind the partition which fenced him and his drugs off from the rest of the car.

Romanin's repertoire was extensive. When he was in a playful mood, he would sing:

> I'd like to marry a dandy man
> Who'd swagger around in a handsome shirt
> Who'd swagger around in a handsome shirt
> Twirling a little cane.

But when Romanin was filled with sadder thoughts he would give out in a sobbing voice:

> Ah, why did you ever kiss me
> And start this fever in my heart . . . ?

After any run-in with the senior surgeon, Pokrovsky, over some mix-up with his drugs, Romanin would be plunged in gloom, and he would then sing the ominous hymn of the anarchists:

> At the sound of the tocsin, mid the cannon's roar,
> Arise, brothers, to the call of Ravasholle.

Romanin had the bad habit of sitting for hours hidden among his drugs and not answering when I called him through the partition. So I flinched and swore every time the silence in his dispensary was shattered by a sudden, desperate howl:

He was a little paunchy,
Paunchy, paunchy,
And also a little bald on top,
But what difference did it make?

It was to the accompaniment of songs like these that the train pulled its empty cars from Moscow to Brest across the plains of White Russia which were limp with spring rain.

I left the operating car at night to sleep in the orderlies' car. My neighbors in my compartment were Romanin, Nikolasha Rudnyev, and a silent Pole named Hugo Lyakhman. His chief interest was in shining his boots several times a day to an incredibly high polish.

It was a period of relative quiet at the front, so we stayed for a long time at Brest—a flat city set in sad fields. Across these fields spring was moving with a kind of melancholy. Only dandelions blossomed on the sides of the ditches. The sunlight seemed whitish, the sky was covered with mist nearly all the time.

The war was right next to us, but we could see it only in the abundance of soldiers and officers around the Brest railroad station, and in the long troop trains which jammed the dirty sidings. There was no aviation in those days. The sound of artillery did not reach Brest. The fighting was far away, near Kielce.

We waited impatiently to be sent to the front. We were already tired of waiting. It seemed to us that the train wheels had rusted away and the train had become tightly stuck to the rails. Our youth and our ardor made us forget that our staying at Brest meant that there were no wounded, no mutilated men. Only Romanin realized this, and said:

"You've gone off to war as if it were the Moscow Art Theater. The curtain doesn't go up for a while, so you stamp your feet. Blockheads!"

After statements like this, our orderlies' car always grew quiet. But arguments would flare up again quickly—typical students' arguments, noisy, endless, and always based on good motives even when the participants held completely different points of view. We argued most of all about Germany, and about the incredible stupidity and insolence of the Prussian army. The twirled-up ends of Wilhelm II's mustache—the dream of all drill masters and pimps—were the symbol of Germany at that time. It had no relation with the fact that Schiller and Heine, Richard Wagner and the wonderful young writer Heinrich Mann, lived in the same country.

But at long last the inevitable occurred. The train slowly started off. I jumped off while it was moving and climbed back into the operating car—while the train was going there was no way of getting from our orderlies' car to the operating car. I opened the door, sat on the platform for several hours swinging my legs, staring at the Polish fields and woods, trying to see traces of the war which was so close.

But there were none to be seen. Villages went by with morning-glories covering the fences on which earthenware pitchers had been placed upside down, just as at home in the Ukraine. Arrogant storks stood in their enormous nests on the roofs of cottages. The air was golden and pale, like the hair of the children anxiously waving their hands at the passing train.

The face of a Polish girl carrying pails of water on a yoke over her shoulders seemed to me just as golden and pale. She put her pails down on the ground, shielded her eyes with the palm of her hand, and looked for a long time at the cars rumbling slowly past her, and then she brushed back a lock of hair which had fallen across her face and picked up her pails again.

Tall black crucifixes stood at road crossings. Old women sat around them with their knitting, pasturing goats on long tethers. I saw candles burning in a little chapel, but I could see no one inside it. And the fields shone with the same pale gold, and little rivers flowed through them slowly pouring their golden, pale water over their sandy bottoms.

"Where can the war be?" I asked myself. The train went past the fortress of Ivangorod. Far beyond the Vistula we could see its green earthworks, and the high stumps of the black poplars which had been cut down during the siege.

And then suddenly I saw: hurriedly dug trenches, filled with water, stretched in rows across the swampy low land from the railroad tracks to the very horizon. The train was moving along a high dike. The engine whistled, the brakes screeched, and we stopped—for some reason the bridge across the Vistula was closed.

In the silence which followed we could hear a bugler inside the fortress blowing some kind of military signal.

The orderlies all tumbled out of the cars.

"We're stopping here for a whole hour," Romanin yelled to me. "Come along!"

We ran along the steep slope, moving down toward the trenches, and I began to notice in the grass, which had obviously grown up after the battle, an enormous number of scraps of paper and of crumpled tin cans. They had been opened, obviously, in a hurry, perhaps with bayonets. The edges of the cans were covered with rust, which looked like dried blood.

I couldn't understand how so much torn paper had accumulated
on a field of battle. There were pieces of letters, newspapers, post
cards, books, documents, photographs, all obliterated and soaked
with sweat. Soldiers' caps were scattered around, trampled in the
mud. An Austrian cap with a torn visor was hanging on a burned
bush. Rags of soldiers' coarse cotton underwear were dangling, as
if they had been hung there to dry, on a twisted barbed-wire
entanglement.

Barbed wire lay in piles of rust.

"It looks as if water isn't the only thing," Romanin remarked
casually, "that can rust iron."

"What else can?"

"Blood can rust, too," Romanin answered, reluctantly.

There were soldiers' boots, and buttons, and cartridges, steel
cartridge clips, crumpled-up cigarette boxes, red silk ribbons,
soaked tobacco labels, gray machine-gun straps, nails, little icons,
belts, the soles of boots, tobacco pouches with a cross sewed on
them, the wrappings of packages, dirty bandages tied up with
string, Austrian bayonets, broken wooden spoons, steel shell casings, flasks, and broken glass.

This was the rubbish of war, everything a man leaves on the
field of death, everything he had taken care of so long while he
was still alive and had now thrown away, abandoned to sun, wind,
and rain. I thought to myself that grown men had fought and died
here, but that they had treated their soldiers' property, which each
had carried with him and feared to part with, like children.

A dead horse was lying near a shell hole, its bones picked clean
by carrion crows, its long, yellow teeth opened as if in a smile.
The shell hole was black with fat tadpoles, as round as rubber balls.

It was very quiet. You could hear field mice rustling in the rubbish. And then the bugler's notes sang out again sadly from the
fortress.

The sound reminded me of my childhood belief that war was
something magnificent. All the falsehoods about war inculcated in
me—and not only in me—from my earliest years were in those
soaring notes. The noise of banners, the singing of horns, the impetuous clatter of horses' hoofs, the whistle of bullets in the cold
air, stirring feelings of danger, the glitter of swords, the steely
bristling of bayonets . . .

My father had owned Gneditch's *History of Art* in three heavy
volumes. I used to love to look at their reproductions of the pictures
of the battle painters Mateiko, Villevalde, Meissonier, Gros. There
were pictures of battles near Preisish-Eilay and Fère-Champenoise,
of Hussar attacks, the Uhlans' lances, the round smoke of cannon

fire, and generals with copper spyglasses in their hands standing next to maps spread out on drums. Of course I knew that war was not really like those pictures. But the picture of this splendid colorful kind of warfare was deep in my brain, and it hung on stubbornly.

Now I was looking not at war itself, but at its aftermath, its dirt, its evil, and its litter. It was not what I had expected. But I kept silent, and said nothing to Romanin.

The engine whistled, and puffed out two balls of steam on both sides of the track. We had to return. We walked quietly back to the train. On the platform of our car Romanin looked at me and said:

"You've got to get used to it, young fellow. Get used to it! It will get worse."

I flared up and answered Romanin with a curse. It was the first and the last in all our front-line friendship.

RAIN IN THE CARPATHIAN FOOTHILLS

On this trip we were going from Brest to Kielce but there seemed no chance of our getting through to that faraway Polish city. We were constantly held up along the way. We stood for more than a week at a junction called Skarzhisky.

Many of the junctions were amazing places in those times, built at points where railroads crossed each other, far from any population. A big station with a buffet, bright incandescent lights, dozens of tracks, a grimy roundhouse, the little wooden houses of the railroad workers surrounded by acacia, and just beyond the station— empty fields. Crows soared in the wind, and wherever you looked there was no dwelling, no hut, no ribbon of smoke, only a boring road leading to the edge of the earth.

This is what Skarzhisky was like; skylarks chirped within a hundred steps of the big station and a narrow road lost itself in the waving fields.

The stone walls of an uncompleted church stood not far from the station. Who had started to build it in this empty spot? Who needed it there? There was no one to answer these questions. Swifts skimmed over the stone walls of the church. A stone staircase without a railing led up to the gallery. Grass, waving in the wind, grew on the steps.

Having cleaned up everything in the operating car, I took a book by Rabindranath Tagore and walked over to the church. I read there, sitting on the wall above the fields. As sometimes happened, my own thoughts replaced those of Tagore, and this did not bother me at all.

Some children of Polish railroad workers had followed me in single file into the church. Dogs followed the children, and soon the church had become a children's playground. The children were quiet, even seeming a little frightened, with very attentive eyes. In the depths of their eyes a trusting smile seemed always ready to break out.

I tried to talk to them in Polish, but they simply looked at each other in embarrassment—they couldn't understand me. I was talking in that frightful Polish-Russian-Ukrainian jargon which we in Kiev used to think was the Polish language.

By and by Romanin, Nikolasha Rudnyev, and a nurse, Elena Petrovna Sveshnikova, started to go to the church with me. Everyone called the nurse Lelya. She was a capricious girl with a somewhat sirupy voice and a face as pale as if it were masking some hidden emotion. We had become friends when we were still on the rear-echelon train, when Lelya had noticed, during a night inspection, that I had fallen asleep when I wasn't supposed to, had started to waken me, and had dropped on my face some tallow from the candle with which she was making her inspection of the cars. I had jumped up, blinded by the burning tallow. Then Lelya bandaged me, crying from fright and shame and laughing through her tears over her stupidity and my sorry appearance.

One day Lelya came to the church, tiptoed up behind me, took the book by Rabindranath Tagore out of my hands, and threw it far away. The book sailed for quite a while, dropping its pages, and then fell into the grass. I looked around and saw Lelya's eyes black with anger.

"You're drunk enough," she said, "with all that misty philosophy."

I stayed silent. Lelya also was quiet for a minute, and then she said:

"What's that on the horizon? Way over there."

"The spurs of the Carpathian Mountains."

"Are you angry at me?" she asked. "If so, I'll find your book for you."

"No, you don't have to."

"Well then, good! Let's go to the bridge instead."

We walked up to the railroad bridge over a little river with banks thickly grown with willow trees. We stood there for a long time looking at the spurs of the Carpathians. They lay heavily in the distance, like clouds. A guard walked up to us, and also stood and looked.

"No matter how hard you try," he said at last, "you can't get used to strange country. The rain isn't the same. And the grass looks familiar, but it isn't ours."

"Is this really so bad?" Lelya asked him.

"No, it's not bad, little sister," the soldier answered sadly. "As ground, it's all right, even if it's like land ploughed in autumn, somehow. As if it were sleeping in the daytime."

Lelya laughed, and grew silent. The guard sighed, and walked on.

"It's forbidden to stand here," he said in an uncertain voice as he walked away. "Even if you're on our side, nobody's allowed to stand here."

Lelya was the cause of the greatest humiliation of my life. I had been sent back from Brest to Moscow for medical supplies. The doctors, the nurses, and the orderlies all gave me a lot of letters and errands. In those days everyone tried to send letters by friends taking such trips in order to evade the military censorship.

Lelya gave me her gold watch and asked me to give it to her uncle in Moscow, a professor. The gold wristwatch embarrassed Lelya; it was, of course, hardly the right thing to wear on a hospital train. Lelya gave me, besides, a letter to her uncle. She wrote a lot of nice things about me in the letter and asked the professor to put me up, if I needed a bed.

In Moscow I looked for the respected professor's apartment, and rang the bell. No one opened the door for a long time. Then a dissatisfied woman's voice asked me from behind the closed door who I was and what I wanted. An elderly maid with a squinting eye opened the door. Behind her stood a tall, imposing old lady as magnificent as a statue, in a snow-white starched headdress and a black old woman's necktie—the professor's wife. Her gray hair was pinned up in an arrogant roll and shone as brightly as her pincenez. She stood there, guarding the door to the dining room, where the professor's family was drinking morning coffee, clinking spoons against cups.

I handed the watch in a little box, together with the letter, to the professor's wife.

"Wait here," she said, and she walked back to the dining room, looking meaningfully at the maid. The latter began at once to dust a polished little table in the vestibule which had been wiped already and was shining brightly.

"Who rang?" a rasping old man's voice asked in the dining room. "What does he want?"

"Just imagine," the professor's wife answered, rustling paper (obviously, she had opened the package). "Lelya is behaving just as extravagantly at war as she always did. She's sent us her gold watch. By some kind of a soldier. What carelessness! Just like her mother!"

"Uhuu!" the professor mooed. His mouth was evidently full of food. "He could easily have pocketed it."

"In general, I just don't understand Lelya," his wife went on. "Here she writes and asks us to take him in. Why? Where would we put him up? Pasha is already sleeping in the kitchen."

"That's the last straw," the professor mooed again. "Give him a ruble and send him away. It's high time Lelya realized that the one thing I cannot stand is strange people."

"A ruble doesn't seem right, though," the professor's wife said. "What do you think, Pyotr Petrovich?"

"Well then, give him two rubles."

I opened the door out on to the staircase, went out, and slammed the door so hard that something fell and broke with a loud crash inside the professor's apartment. I stopped on the landing.

The door was opened at once on its little chain. Behind the maid, who was holding the door, stood the entire professor's family—his haughty wife, a student with a horse's face, and the old professor with a crumpled napkin tucked into the collar of his shirt. There were spots of egg yolk on the napkin.

"Why are you making a row?" the maid cried through the chink. "And you're a soldier from the front! Defender of the fatherland!"

"Tell your masters," I said, "that they're a bunch of cattle."

There in their vestibule began a confused scramble. The student moved up to the door and took hold of the chain, but the professor's wife shoved him back.

"Genya, leave it alone," she cried. "He'll kill you. They're used to killing everyone at the front."

Then the old professor shoved himself forward. His clean-washed beard was shaking with indignation. He yelled through the chink in the door, cupping his hands around his mouth:

"Hooligan! I'll turn you over to the police."

"Ah, you!" I told him. "The light of science!"

The professor's wife pulled the old man back, and slammed the door.

All my life since then, a distrust of the so-called "high priests of science" has stayed with me, a distrust of all the pseudo learned, of those who pride themselves on their scholarship but in real life are Philistines and vulgar people. There are many kinds of vulgarity which we don't recognize. Even such an expert on vulgarity as Chekhov could not manage to describe all its manifestations.

Oh, those professors' families, with their idolizing of foolish family customs, their overemphasis on their own probity, their excessive politeness, their pedantic fathers engaged in counting the number of hairs on a worm, their smooth language, their standoffish wives and their overfastidiousness, their secret reckoning of the scientific successes and failures of other scholars! And those professors' apartments with their disciplined servants and their intolerable boredom, regulated once for always and the same unto death.

I didn't tell Lelya about the incident.

She and I chattered a lot, argued, and went on walks in the evenings to a little café where we drank coffee and ate homemade cakes and watched the old proprietress sewing red flowers on to a tablecloth. We were living without any consciousness of the war. If it had not been for the guard at the bridge, it might have seemed that we had gone on a vacation deep into the Polish rear. There was no link that I could find between the war and Lelya's young-girl paleness or Tagore's judgments on the cleansing of the human spirit of all evil.

Quiet sunsets spread themselves over the fields and over the Carpathians. In their smoldering depths a day died with each sunset, a day filled with thoughts and happinesses. Boys and girls, such as we were, do much more thinking than more mature people, and are, of course, much happier, even at war.

But one day the sun went down in a lead-colored sky that looked like the dregs of wine. That night rain drummed on the roofs of the cars. In the morning we left Skarzhisky for Kielce. The foothills of the Carpathians moved toward us. A damp air from the beech forests blew in through the windows. Clouds were tied to the tops of the mountains, first covering, then revealing, the crucifixes set up along the tracks.

Suddenly a single cannon sounded lazily and weightily in the haze. It seemed to me the train changed its speed. Then a second shot was heard, a third—and everything grew quiet again.

"Romanin!" I yelled through the partition. "Did you hear?"

"I heard it," Romanin answered. "And I'm surprised."

"Why?"

"Come in here. I'll tell you."

I went into the dispensary. Its clean crowdedness always pleased me. It smelled of dried raspberries. Romanin was weighing out powders in little mother-of-pearl cups on a small scales.

"Sit down," he said. "You can smoke, the devil with you! I'll smoke myself. Well, I'm surprised, and I don't understand just why, I'll admit."

"But just the same, why?"

"Well, it isn't worth understanding. Just look around. Everything sparkles here, everything's in its place. Every phial is in its wooden holder. It's cosy, isn't it? I sit here all day, even when I don't have to. I read. I look out of the window. I sometimes even sleep in this armchair."

He ran his eyes over the rows of porcelain bottles and sighed.

"And all of this will be blown to hell by the first stray shell that hits it. Here's what I find surprising: the nearer you come to danger, the more you love these fragile phials, so light they might be made of air, these books, the cleanliness, the quiet, or a cigarette."

"That shell won't fall on us," I said. "It just won't fall."

Black sidings sped past us outside the window, intersecting each other. We were approaching Kielce.

Light rain was falling on the shell-riddled roofs of the station warehouses. We had to wait three days for the wounded in Kielce. The chief surgeon gave permission to Lelya, Romanin, and myself to travel up to the village of Khentsin, a front-line position. An artillery regiment was fighting there. Lelya's cousin was in the regiment.

We went in a two-wheeled ambulance cart late in the morning. The rain never stopped, and never let up. The city was wrapped in acid locomotive smoke. Red water stood in deep pits, from which clay was scooped. Red bubbles burst on its surface.

We rode by a brick factory shattered by artillery fire. Women and children, with empty kettles, were digging in the piles of broken bricks, as if they were looking for something. A single-tracked front-line road stretched out in front of us. It was like a little river of mud.

Soldiers were walking in the fields beside the road, holding up the skirts of their overcoats. They were dragging coils of barbed wire on poles. A primitive ambulance which had lost a wheel was standing in a ditch beside the road. Soldiers were crowding around it. They took turns climbing into the ambulance to have a smoke protected from the rain.

The soldiers waited their turn without complaining, then climbed into the ambulance, rolled a cigarette out of cheap *makhorka* tobacco and damp newspaper, lighted it, and drew in the acrid smoke with deep enjoyment. They waited, hunched over, their hands stuck up the sleeves of their overcoats, and they spat only when they looked at the west. A raw wind was blowing in gusts from that direction, lashing the boughs of the trees and driving the clouds.

"What a place they've found for smoking," our driver, a small, dark soldier with his collar turned up, said scornfully. "What tobacco won't make a man do!"

"Why is it a bad place?" Romanin asked. "They can get cover from the rain."

"Why, the Germans shoot up this little hunk of road regularly," the soldier answered. "Once every hour, and sometimes more often, they drop two or three shells on it. As a warning. The German makes war by his watch. He fights accurately, the devil take his soul! So I always take care to drive past here after they've fired."

"And how about it, does it work?"

"Sometimes," the soldier answered calmly. "Most times, I manage to get through. Only it doesn't pay to try every day. It depends on luck."

The soldiers around the ambulance began to stir. Some of them quickly squatted on their heels, others ran to a little ravine near the road. But those who were smoking inside the ambulance did not climb out but went right on inhaling, burning their fingers and spitting.

"They've finished their smoking, those German gunners," the driver yelled, laughing, to the soldiers. "Maybe the Germans will let you finish yours."

Then something exploded with a rasping screech, a sharp thunder sounded, and the earth shot up in a fountain of clods and mud.

"Go on," the driver yelled at his horses. "You pestilence! There's room for you in the butcher shop, if you're no good for real work."

But the horses did not increase their speed. A second shell fell behind us on the edge of the road. For the first time I heard the whistling rustle of shell splinters.

A very young volunteer ran up to our wagon. His face had not yet had time to get hardened by wind or sun. It was clear that he

was a boy from an educated, city family. He grabbed the back of
the wagon and asked, in a hesitant but very polite voice:

"Can you tell me, please, if they will soon stop firing?"

The driver grunted at the unexpected question, and stopped his
horses.

"Now why don't you ask the Germans?" he said with icy humor.
"Get down on your knees to them. You're an educated man, that's
clear. Maybe they'll do a favor for you out of respect. Well, that will
be fine. I can see this is the first time for you. Sit in the ambulance.
But don't get on that hay, with your dirty boots. I didn't put it there
for that, may you get ulcers on your heart."

The volunteer jumped hurriedly into the ambulance and looked
guiltily at us. He could turn his head only with difficulty, as if it
were bolted on to him. A third shell fell behind us, farther away
than the second.

"Well, that's all," the driver said. "Now you can smoke. The
German has finished his timetable and has gone off to drink coffee."

The soldiers who had run away collected again around the
ambulance. But they no longer stood there uncomplaining. We
could hear them quarreling.

"What are you doing, you pockmarked devil? You smoking a
second one? What for? Get out of here. Or we'll throw you out."

"Don't grab, you beard! Listen, brother, we've handled bigger
men than you."

We went on. Maybe it was because we had just been in danger,
but the rain seemed warmer and the smell of wet grass came up
from the fields. A clear stretch of sky appeared on the horizon.

The road wound between high poplars. We had entered the
foothills of the Carpathians. The rain hung on them like untidy
strings of oakum. Clear streams of rain water ran along the stone
sides of the road. The road glistened. Steam rose from the wet
horses. Far in the distance we could see a city shattered like a
toy, through the blue smoke of clouds and rain. The wind blew the
sound of church bells toward us.

"That's Khentsin," the driver said. "Where do you want to go?
To the searchlight regiment, or the artillery?"

"The artillery."

The ambulance stopped next to a two-story house. There were
no windows in its front, only a narrow door and above it a black
crucifix on the wall.

The crucifixion of Christ followed us all the time we were in
Poland. Some of the crucifixes were made with such anatomical
detail, including the drops of blood oozing out of Jesus' thin side,

that they repelled you. Romanin declared that he was bored by these dead men hanging at all the road crossings and wished he were home, on the Sakmara River, where for a hundred miles around there were only the wooded slopes of the Urals, with rivers full of fish, and his father's pasture. Romanin's father, a former village doctor, had outlived his generation on a pension in a little country place on the banks of the Sakmara.

Artillery officers met us. They poured us tea and gave us their folding cots. We were soaked. The tea and the warmth made us sleepy. I fell asleep at once.

The roar of cannon woke me up in the middle of the night. An artillery duel was going on around us. A candle flickered in the next room, where officers were arguing around a table. They had taken off their blouses and were playing cards in their undershirts.

The glass rattled in the windows, and every explosion made the church bell ring over our heads. Rain was pouring down. Outside the windows the fog was so opaque that it was frightening to look at it.

I started to smoke. Romanin turned over on his cot.

"Yes-s," he said, "rivers of blood all because of criminals and idiots."

"Who?" I asked.

"Idiots," Romanin repeated. "All these bombastic Wilhelms and foolish Nicholases. And the grasping businessmen. Some are cretins, the others are black rascals. But that doesn't make it any easier for us."

"Listen," Lelya said quietly—it seemed she wasn't asleep— "drop the talking. Otherwise I'll start screaming."

We were silent. The rain continued. I was hungry, but it would be a long time before morning.

I dozed off. Through my sleep I watched Lelya get up, walk over to the window, look for a long time into the darkness where something was blazing, then sigh, straighten the overcoat which was slipping off me, and sit down at the little table next to her cot. She sat there for a long time without moving, as if she were dead, squeezing her hands between her knees.

BY THE MUDDY SAN RIVER

A scorching sun beat down on the sparse pine woods beyond the San River. Single pine trees, tall and thin, bending over with the weight of their crowns, stood in the middle of stumps and bushes. The crimson sunlight slipped along their trunks, fell on the sand around them, and was reflected, shimmering, in the swift water of the San. The plains, bluish with evening mist, started at the edge of the woods. The bitter almond smell of marsh flowers blew out of the plains.

This was Galicia.

They held our train at the frontier station next to an old wooden bridge over the San. Troop trains came to meet us there.

I crossed the frontier for the first time. On the other bank of the river was Austria. I had a feeling that on the other side everything should be completely different, not like our side—not only the people, the villages and the towns, but even the sky and the trees.

This was how I had imagined "abroad" when I was a little boy. The foolish idea stayed with me until I was already grown up.

But for the time being, everything was just the way it was on our side of the frontier. The same dry chicory grew on both sides of the path. Your foot sank into the sand just the way it did in Russia, and even the water in the San was muddy although I had expected it to flow in a clear, ringing current.

We crossed a bridge over the San at night, and entered Galicia. In the morning we stopped at the little town of Melets. I got no chance to see it. Fighting was going on in front of us, near Dembitsa, and they sent us there immediately. I only managed to see from the window some cheerful green hills, tiled roofs, walls overgrown with hops, and roads as white as chalk, lined with poplar trees.

Then we could hear the heavy, unrelenting cannon fire and we could see dark dust covering the whole horizon to the south. Maybe it wasn't dust, but the smoke of burning villages. Fleeing carts passed the train at a trot, going north to a ford where they could cross the San. Tired infantry units moved by us separately. The earth shook more and more distinctly. The windows rattled in the train.

The train stopped at last in a wide glen. Yellow clouds of shrapnel fire blazed up continually in the leafy woods around the edges of the glen. Mounted soldiers were galloping past the train. A field battery hidden in some underbrush near by roared out deafeningly. Our chief surgeon, Pokrovsky, ordered us to raise two big Red Cross flags over the train.

After this they moved us a little farther forward, up to a demolished signalman's hut. Dozens of wounded men, roughly bandaged, were lying on the dusty grass around it.

We began immediately to load the wounded into the boxcars. The train was already full, but the wounded kept on coming. We put them in the corridors, on the buffers, in our own car. The entire train was now grumbling in a long-drawn-out, many-voiced groan.

The fighting was obviously getting closer, but we didn't see it. I caught just a glimpse of broken glass in the window of a car, and I heard the biting rattle of stray bullets on the rails.

One of our orderlies was wounded in the shoulder. Romanin was knocked off his feet by a hot blast of air. But these things went on outside our consciousness. We were all possessed by one thought: "Load the wounded as fast as possible. Faster."

A sweaty officer galloped up to the train and called Pokrovsky. His shoulder straps were covered with such a thick layer of dust that the star on them could not be seen.

"Faster!" the officer yelled in an angry voice. "Get your train to the devil's mother out of here. In a quarter of an hour it'll be too late. At double speed! And right away!"

The officer swung the whip which was clenched in his fist, and pointed to the north. The horse under him pranced as if it were possessed.

"We can still take some wounded on the roof," Pokrovsky cried to the officer.

"Take them while you're moving," the officer yelled back, spurring his horse and galloping up to the engine. The train started at once. Several wounded men managed to grab the handrails, and orderlies pulled them up onto the platforms.

It was only then that I noticed that twilight had fallen. The fire of explosions could be seen more clearly, and the dust on the horizon took on an ominous crimson color.

Then bullets began to strike the sides of the cars, but this only lasted for a few minutes. The train picked up speed. When it slowed down again, at last, we imagined that we had escaped from the pocket in which we had been caught.

The train had taken on several hundred wounded men, their bandages soaked with blood and slipping off their wounds, their faces black with pain and thirst. All of them had to be bandaged again. And we had to move those who were badly wounded and needed surgical care quickly.

Work began at once, and at that moment time itself stopped. We ceased to notice it. Every quarter of an hour, I mopped up the blood on the linoleum-covered floor of the operating car and washed out the hardened bandages. Then I would be called to the operating table where without knowing clearly what I was doing I would hold the leg of a wounded man and try not to look while Pokrovsky cut, with a little steel saw, a bone that looked like white sugar. Suddenly the leg would feel heavy in my hands and through the fog in my consciousness I would realize that the operation was finished, and take the amputated leg over to a metal box, to be buried later at our next stop.

Everything smelled of blood, tincture of valerian, and hot alcohol. Instruments were constantly being boiled on alcohol lamps. Ever since then the blue flame of a spirit lamp has been linked in my memory with unbearable suffering covering men's faces with a gray, dead sweat.

Some of the wounded cried out loud; others, biting their lips, gritted their teeth and swore. The fortitude of one man amazed even the imperturbable Pokrovsky. His pelvic bone was broken. He was suffering inhuman pain, but he walked into the operating car alone, without an orderly, hanging on to the wall. While the bone was being set, he asked only for permission to smoke, "to make it lighter." He never groaned, didn't cry out once, and kept trying to comfort Pokrovsky and Lelya, who was helping the surgeon take out pieces of shell splinter and make a deep and complicated dressing of the wound.

"It's nothing," he said. "I can stand it. I can even stand it quite well. Don't you worry, sister."

Only his eyes gave away the pain he was feeling. They faded minute by minute, with a yellow film covering them.

"How does it happen you're the only one who can take this?" Pokrovsky asked him angrily.

"We come from Vologda," the wounded man answered. "My mother gave me birth, Your Excellency, in a damp pine forest. She delivered me herself. And washed me with water from a little pond.

At home, Your Excellency, don't forget, we're all like this. A wounded animal cries, of course. But it isn't fitting for a man to cry."

I can no longer remember how much time it took for these uninterrupted operations and dressings. The train was stopped at stations for the more complicated operations. I remember only that sometimes I lit the bright electric lights (the car had a generator in it) and sometimes I put them out, because the sun, it seemed, was shining through the windows. But it never seemed to me to shine for more than an hour or so before I had to light the white, blinding lights again.

Once Pokrovsky took me by the arm, led me to the window, and forced me to drink a glass of some brown, sticky liquid.

"Hold out," he told me. "It'll soon be over. We can't relieve a single one of us."

And I held out, only changing my blood-soaked gown from time to time.

The wounded came and came and came. We stopped even trying to tell them apart by their faces. It seemed they all had the same unshaven, greenish face, the same eyes white and round with pain, the same often helpless breathing, and the same prehensile steel fingers—they would sink them into our arms while we held them during the dressing of their wounds. All of us had bruises and abrasions on our arms.

I went out just once, to smoke for a minute at some unknown Polish station. It was evening. It had just rained. Little pools shone on the station platform. Thunderclouds hung in the greenish sky like a bunch of gigantic grapes, barely lighted by the pink color of the sunset.

A crowd of women and children stood around the train. The women were wiping their eyes with the corners of their shawls. "Why are they crying?" I wondered, having no clue to the answer, and then I suddenly heard the quiet groan which was coming from the cars.

The whole train was groaning a long, tired, unbroken groan. No heart born of a human mother could stand this inarticulate plea for help, for compassion, without crying. For every wounded man became a child again, and it was no wonder that in the middle of their feverish nights and their exhausting pain they called for their mothers. But there were no mothers. And no one could replace them, even the most devoted nurses. Compassion seemed to flow out of the nurses' warm and skillful hands, gently touching a mutilated body, or an infected wound, or tousled hair.

We got to Lublin at dawn of some day I don't remember. They gave us three days of leave. I walked along the station path to the water tower and washed myself for a long time under the strong, foamy water from its pipe. I washed for a long time because I must have dozed off while I was washing. This transient sleep was full of the smell of water and of Marseilles soap.

Then I changed my clothes and walked back to the station. It had a little garden with lilac growing next to its high walls. Some kind of flowers in the flower beds were nodding in their violet and white chintz dresses.

I sat on a wooden bench, leaned back, and looked at the town. It was perched on a high green hill, surrounded by fields and washed by the morning sun.

The sun was radiant in a clean, blue sky. The sound of silver church bells floated down from the town. It was Good Friday.

I fell asleep. The sunshine struck against my eyes but I felt nothing. My head was in the shadow of an umbrella. Right next to me on the bench sat a little old man in a starched, yellowed collar. He had opened his umbrella and held it so that it would shade me from the sun.

I did not know how long he had sat there. I woke up when the sun was already high in the sky. The old man stood up, lifted his hat, said "Excuse me" in Polish, and walked away.

Who was he? An old teacher, or a railroad clerk? Or a church organist? Whoever he was, I felt grateful to him because in days of war he had not forgotten how to do a simple human favor. He had appeared as a goodhearted old spirit out of the shady streets of Lublin. Out of those streets where retired petty officials lived out their clean, scanty lives, where a man's last happiness was a bed of nasturtiums next to a fence, or a box of cigarettes made of fragrant Crimean tobacco. The children had flown away into the world, the wife had died a long time ago, and all the old magazines had already been read through many times. Everything had gone. There was left only a quiet wisdom, and the smoke of a cigarette, and the distant sound of church bells from the town, which rang in exactly the same way on holidays and at funerals.

SPRING BY THE WIEPRZ RIVER

In wartime quiet is especially wonderful.

Lublin was full of quiet. The noisy life of war went on outside
the town, and the military trains went by the Lublin station almost
without stopping. The station smelled of cheap *makhorka* tobacco,
it clanged with mess tins, it clamored with the sound of boots and
the rattle of rifles. But one had only to walk out on the wide street
into the town to hear the silence and to smell the lilacs growing all
around one. A man could take off his cap, wipe from his forehead
the red streak left by its tight cap-band, sigh, and say to himself:
"What kind of crazy hysteria this is! There's no war, and probably
never was one."

The man might raise his head and see swifts darting over the
rooftops. Light clouds would pile up out of the blue distance and
float over into another blue distance without subtracting a single
ray of sunshine from the world. Beams of sunlight would be
falling through the heart-shaped leaves of lilac, dropping on the
cracks in the pavement, warming them in a weak, springtime way.

A brass band played opera selections in the municipal gardens.
The sound of the band was carried a long way in the silence which
hung over the town. Somewhere in a bystreet leading down to the
river between little fences with narrow gates you could hear some
familiar melody:

He's far away, your lover, in a foreign land . . .

Forged iron lanterns hung over the little gates. Lilac was
blossoming behind the fences. And from morning to evening the
silver church bells rang and rang.

Easter found us in Lublin. The holy days came right on top
of the commotion and the dust of the fighting we had gone
through. But even in our clean-swept, clean-scrubbed train we were
still finding pieces of blood-soaked cotton wadding on a brake
handle, or the ends of cigarettes, chewed to pulp in someone's
pain and then dropped on the floor of one of the boxcars.

We went to the Easter night service in the Bernardine Church. It was all very theatrical: the lace on the acolytes, mountains of lilac around the wooden images of the boy Jesus dressed in blue brocade, gray-haired priests singing Latin chants through their noses, and the ominous rolling sound of organ music.

Only one thing could be seen in the eyes of the praying women: the frenzied hope for a miracle, the enormous faith that this plump little Christ Child or maybe the pale woman with thick eyelashes, the mother of the God at her breast, would fix things so that there would be no more war in the world, no more exhausting labor, and no more poverty, and that at last, perhaps, it might be possible to raise one's back from the washtubs full of dirty clothes and smile at the sun reflected in the soapy water.

Religion was a sweet self-deception for these people. It was a world of fruitless wondering for tired people. They could see no other way out, and therefore they believed with such fanaticism, in spite of all honest thinking, in spite of all the experience of their lives, that justice was embodied in the image of that sickly wandering beggar out of Galilee, in the image of God. But somehow this God, who was invented by men, had plunged humanity into a terrible and bloody chaos, kept silent, and done nothing about the ways in which the world was moving.

But for some reason they still believed in him, although the inactivity of this God had lasted for centuries. Their thirst for happiness was so great that people tried to carry over the poetry of happiness into religion, into the peals of church organs, the smoke of incense, and the solemn incantations of these services.

On the first day of Easter, Romanin, Lelya, and I walked far outside the town to the banks of the Wieprz. The river was pouring clear water through fields filled with wheat. Reeds formed dark walls in its depths. Small gulls flew back and forth over the reeds.

It was pleasant walking along the hard country road through a strange country without knowing where the road would take us. Wild flowers bloomed on both sides. The snowy tips of clouds towered in the sky before our eyes. And nobody—neither then on the Wieprz nor later in the course of my whole life—has been able to explain to me where the sudden feelings of happiness come from at times when nothing extraordinary is taking place.

I was really happy then.

On the bank of the Wieprz there was a little hut with a thatched roof. A fishing net was hung over its wattled fence. Brown gulls were sitting on it, pecking at the dried seaweed in the net. They were frightened by us, and they flew off with great cries

which woke up a sleeping baby. He had been sleeping in a basket
under a window on the earth mound which surrounds peasants'
huts.

The baby started to cry. A young peasant woman came out of
the hut, dressed in a striped skirt. She saw us and stopped short,
holding her hands against her breasts.

An old hound crawled out from under a broken trough, walked
up to the hut, and barked at us. Convinced that everything was all
right, it sat down and watched us out of old yellow eyes, while it
began to hunt for fleas.

"Go away, Sivwi!" the woman said quietly, and she took the
baby to her breast. She turned toward us, and her face showed such
a heartfelt smile that we automatically smiled back at her, but
we couldn't say anything, and we stood there quietly.

The woman offered us milk, shyly. We thanked her, and went
into the hut.

Everything in it was made of wood, not only the walls, the floor,
the table, the shelves and the bed, but also the plates, the comb on
the window sill, the saltcellar, and the lamp in front of the icon.
There was a wooden fork on the window sill, too. All these wooden
objects created an impression of poverty and of cleanliness.

Lelya took the baby, and the woman went down into the cellar
and brought back a misted pitcher of milk. She wiped the table
with a towel, leaning over it, and sunlight fell on her golden hair.
I looked at her wavy, thin hair. She felt my glance and lifted her
green, embarrassed eyes. And from this and some other signs, I
knew that in this hut there lived a quiet kind of happiness.

For some reason I thought about this while I was looking at
the ceiling. A little chandelier with tiny wax candles was hanging
there. It was wound around with dried flowers. Instead of candlesticks it had big red thistle blossoms to which the candles were
fastened.

"What is that?" I asked the woman. "What a wonderful thing!"

"That's just for fun," she said, embarrassed. "You can't light it.
My husband made it, so it would be more cheerful here in the hut.
He's a basketmaker. He weaves baskets out of reeds, and he makes
stools, and a little while ago he made a little parasol for Pan
Yavorsky."

Romanin didn't know what a parasol was, and he was very
surprised when we explained to him that it was just an ordinary
umbrella.

At that moment the door opened and a tall, young peasant stood
on the threshold. A white leather singlet, sewed with green thread,

was hung over his shoulders. He was very thin, and he smiled just as shyly as the woman in the hut.

"Here is Stass, my husband," the woman said. "But he's not like other husbands."

Stass bowed silently, put his bundle of bast down in a corner, sat down at the table, and looked at each of us in turn with a smile on his face.

Larks were singing outside the open window. You could see them, fluttering their wings, soar straight up from the green wheat and disappear into the blue sky.

Stass looked out of the window, and laughed.

"Our helpers," he said, "the larks."

"Why your helpers?" Lelya asked.

"They make people happy while they're working," Stass answered, still laughing pleasantly. "I've never seen it myself, but people say that there's one lark with a golden beak. He's their leader."

"Stass!" the woman said reproachfully. "Who ever dreamed of anything like that?"

"People say," Stass answered, "that maybe the larks will save us from the war, as they did under King Yanko Liuti."

"There's no need to tell people fairy tales," the woman warned him.

Stass made no answer. All he did was to smile just as indulgently, pressing his fingers against the table.

"Well, what of it?" he said after a while. "Whoever doesn't want to believe it doesn't have to. But whoever does believe it, maybe he'll find it easier to live in this world. King Yanko Liuti went off to war against a neighboring country, and in that country there lived only serfs who ploughed their land and planted grain. They stood up against Yanko's knights with their pitchforks, dressed only in their white working clothes. But those knights had suits of armor made from copper, and they blew their copper horns, and their swords were sharpened on both sides and they could kill an ox with one blow. It was an unfair war, so unfair that the earth refused to take the blood that flowed onto it. That blood ran across the fields as if they were glass, into the rivers. The serfs died by hundreds, their huts were burned down, their wives lost their minds from grief. But there was an old hunchbacked musician who lived among them. He used to play at weddings on a violin he had made himself. And this old hunchback said: 'There are different birds on this earth, including birds of paradise, but best of all are our larks. Because it's the peasants' bird. He sings for the sowing, and that makes the crops grow thicker and richer. He sings for the ploughing, so it will be easier to plough, and for the reapers, to make their scythes whistle and their hearts rejoice. Now these larks have a leader, a young bird and the smallest of them all, but with a golden beak. We must send to ask him to help us. He won't allow the serfs to die a black death. He'll save you all, brothers, and your wives, and your children, and your green fields.' So the serfs sent messengers to this lark."

"What kind of messengers?" the woman asked suddenly.

"All kinds. Sparrows, swallows, and even a bald-headed wood-pecker, the one who bored through the wooden cross on the church at Liubartov. And then" —Stass looked at us with cunning eyes— "thousands of larks flew into the kingdom of the serfs, sat on the rooftops and said to the women: 'Look here, mothers and wives, sisters and lovers. What would you give to have this war finished and over with?' 'We'll give everything,' the women cried out. 'Take everything, to the last crumbs of our bread.' 'Well,' said the larks, 'in that case take out today to the common pasture outside your villages all the old threads that are kept in all your drawers and closets.' The women did just what they had been told to do. And in the middle of the night thousands of larks swooped down on the common pastures, picked up piles of these threads, and flew off with them toward the troops of King Yanko Liuti. They began to wind them around his troops, to tie them in knots, and to ensnare the soldiers the way a spider catches a fly. At first the knights broke the threads, but the larks just tied them tighter until the knights fell down on the ground, unable to move hand or foot, or even to spit out the wool that gathered in their mouths. Then the serfs took the shields away from the knights, broke their swords, piled the knights up on wagons and carted them to the frontier of their country and dumped them across the river into a ravine, like trash one carts to the dump. Even King Yanko Liuti swallowed so much wool from the threads that he first turned green and then choked to death, which was a blessing to all good people."

Stass stopped, and was silent.

"That's why we, Pans," he said, smiling, "ought to go looking for the lark with the golden beak."

It was evening when we left Stass's hut. The woman came with us to show us the main road to Lublin. Stass stayed at home. He stood in the open door of the hut and looked after us, with smoke spiraling up from his pipe.

The woman was carrying her baby in her arms, and she told us that Stass was not at all like other men, and that we shouldn't be offended by anything he had said.

We said good-by to her at the crossroads. The sun was setting over the Wieprz. Replacing the sun, a silver sickle of a moon rose in the sky over the quiet woods and fields.

The woman held out her hand to me. I don't know why, but I leaned over and kissed that roughened hand, which smelled of bread. "Thank you," she said simply and she looked at me out of her quiet eyes. "Be sure to come back to see us. I'll bake cakes for you, and Stass will catch you fish in the Wieprz."

We promised to come back, but the next day they sent our train to Sedlets and from there to Warsaw, and I never saw Stass again or the woman with the baby. I regretted this, deeply, for a long time. I don't know why. Perhaps because I had never had in my life, nor had any of my contemporaries, such simple happiness as this Polish peasant woman had.

THE GREAT SWINDLER

During one of our stops at Brest a smart lieutenant wearing rather foppish, rimless pince-nez limped up to Pokrovsky, the head surgeon on our train. His name was Sokolovsky, and his story was a quite ordinary one: he had been wounded and was now released from the hospital for three months of convalescence. Since he had no relatives and nowhere to go, he asked to be taken on as a simple orderly for these three months. He felt in good shape, except for his slight limp.

All of Sokolovsky's documents were in order. Our chief agreed to take him on, and brought him into the car where we orderlies lived.

As students, we didn't like officers, so we were on our guard. If he had been noncommissioned, we would have accepted him, but a lieutenant seemed to us the embodiment of what we didn't like in regular officers.

From the moment of Sokolovsky's arrival in our car, a series of miracles began to happen.

"You live miserably, you monks!" Sokolovsky announced in a loud voice. "You don't know how to wash a floor. Go bring me a pail of hot water and a pail of cold water, and I'll show you educated fellows how to scrub a floor. Well, get going! Two pails of water and no back talk."

Nobody made a move. All of us were looking quietly at Sokolovsky.

"Too proud?" Sokolovsky asked, laughing. "I'm proud myself. But just the same I'll show you, by the devil's grandmother."

He took off his tunic, with a St. George's Cross on it, and walked off to the kitchen in his snow-white shirt and his sky-blue braces. He came back with his two pails of water. Shouting at us to pick up our feet, he diligently proceeded to wash the floor in our car so clean that we were forced to admit, reluctantly, that in this at least he was our master.

But then other things happened which were quite beyond our understanding.

Sokolovsky took down from the wall the guitar which belonged to the orderly Lyakhman, struck a few chords, and then sang a mournful Georgian song. He followed it with an Armenian song, then with Ukrainian, Hebrew, Polish, Finnish, Latvian ones, and he wound up this unexpected concert with a virtuoso's execution of "A Pair of Bay Horses" with authentic gypsy howling.

It turned out that Sokolovsky was at home in many languages and that he knew his way around all of Russia. There didn't seem to be a city where he hadn't been, and where he didn't know all the more or less important people.

His curious talents led us to treat him with even greater reserve, especially after he manufactured a prescription with Dr. Pokrovsky's signature and his medical stamp, used it to get a bottle of pure alcohol at a Brest drugstore, and drank it in the course of a single night.

"Take care, my friends," said Grekov, the taciturn orderly who was also a Moscow student. "Fate has sent us a very mysterious character. We should be on our guard against all kinds of bad luck. We really ought to find out what he was before the war."

That same day Romanin asked Sokolovsky bluntly about this. Sokolovsky screwed up his handsome, impudent eyes. He looked challengingly at Romanin for a long time, and then he said, with a quiet threat in his voice:

"So that's how it is! You're interested in who I was. Well, I was a cantor in a synagogue. That's one thing. And I swallowed flaming sausages in a circus. That's two. I was a court photographer. Three.

And I've also been Prince Sandro Shervashidze of Abkhasia, by the
way. Is that enough for you? Or still too little? Then I won't hide
from you that I've also been a gynecologist, and that I used to sing
in the gypsy chorus at the Yar Restaurant in Moscow. Any more
questions?"

No one spoke. Sokolovsky laughed good-naturedly and threw his
arm around Romanin's shoulders, saying:

"Ah, you simple fellow! Really, I was just a traveling salesman.
That explains everything about me. But I might have been a
student like you."

Sokolovsky was clearly making fun of us. He always tried to
seem cheerful, but some evil in him made him turn so pale sometimes that a little scar on his lip became transparent.

The miracles continued. At whatever game Sokolovsky played,
"tossed-up fool" or Polish faro, he always won. He soon confessed
that he knew all the tricks of a cardsharp and he gave us a long
lecture on cheating at cards with historical references and illustra-
tions of how each trick is done.

Sokolovsky could cut a pack of cards with two fingers and say:
"There are nineteen cards here. I humbly ask you to count
them."

We would count the cards. There were always precisely the
number Sokolovsky named. It was incomprehensible, and like
everything that passes the limits of our experience, unpleasant and
a little tiresome. Dealing with Sokolovsky made our heads ache.

His devilry reached the point where he would put a box of
matches or a cigarette case on a cot and force us to look at it
steadily until it disappeared in front of our eyes, as if it had
vanished into thin air. All this time Sokolovsky would be sitting
there with his hands stuffed into his trouser pockets. Then
Sokolovsky would take the box of matches or the cigarette case out
of the pocket of one of the orderlies.

"It's simple nonsense," Sokolovsky would say. "I urge you not
to get excited over it. It's as simple as an orange. The explanation
is that untrained human eyes notice only slow movements. And
there is a kind of speed which the human eye can't follow. It took
me ten years of practice to be able to move so quickly. Ten years!
And it wasn't like your sweating over histology, or Roman law. Not
at all. For this is just vaudeville. It's nothing but nonsense."

The front was quiet at that time. There were almost no
wounded, but there were a lot of sick men, especially epileptics. In
those days, few people used the word "epilepsy." For the most
part, the disease was called by its popular name, "falling sickness,"

Epileptics were not allowed to be transported with other wounded men. So they were always assembled separately in field hospitals and sent back to the rear in special detachments. This involved long and unpleasant work. The field hospitals always tried to get rid of their epileptics as quickly as they could, by faking. They would bandage their arms or their legs, sometimes they would even put epileptics in splints or casts, to get them on our hospital train as wounded men. Then they would have seizures which could produce epidemic psychosis in a boxcar full of wounded men.

This was why our doctors did their best to sort out the epileptics while the men were being loaded, and send them back to the field hospitals. They seldom succeeded. The epileptics had no outward signs of their disease.

Sokolovsky came to the doctors' help. He asked permission from Pokrovsky to accompany one of the medical inspections of the train while it was still standing at the station where we had taken on the wounded. Pokrovsky laughed but agreed—he was also intrigued by this extraordinary orderly.

It was a history-making inspection round. Sokolovsky went into a boxcar with the doctors, looked over the wounded very quickly, and then said to a bearded peasant with a bandaged arm:

"Hey, farmer, come over here."

The soldier stood up from his cot and walked up to him.

"Well, now, look at me," Sokolovsky ordered, and his heavy eyes started to bore through the confused soldier. "Now don't turn the pupils of your eyes away. It won't do you any good."

Sokolovsky then moved up close to the soldier and asked him, quietly so that the other wounded could not hear, and very trustingly and sympathetically:

"Falling sickness?"

The soldier shuddered and drew back.

"Yes, that's just it, Your Excellency," he answered in a pleading whisper. "But it's not my fault . . ."

"Then get out of this car!"

In one inspection, Sokolovsky turned up seven epileptics. They were sent back to the hospital. From that point on, the hospital authorities were scared to sneak their epileptics on to our train.

"You must have," they told us, "either a soothsayer or a swindler in that man, the devil knows which! How in hell can he guess like that?"

But Sokolovsky answered all the doctors' questions with only a courteous smile.

"There's no answer I can give you. Please believe that I don't understand myself how I do it."

Most of the orderlies and doctors treated Sokolovsky with good-natured curiosity. They were amused by this curious, undoubtedly talented, but empty man. Others, including Romanin and myself, were irritated by our contact with Sokolovsky. His endless buffoonery, his boasting, the commotion he caused, and his cold cynicism all repelled us.

Most surprising of all was the occasional glimmer, deep in his eyes, of an almost doglike hunger for sympathy, for pity. Where do such people come from, from what backgrounds, and what are the circumstances that shape them?

I never saw Sokolovsky sad. This was when I firmly decided for myself that a capacity to feel sadness is one of the true characteristics of a real man. A man who has no feelings of sadness is just as miserable as a man who does not know what happiness is, or who has no sense of humor. The absence of any one of these capacities is proof of some incurable limitation of the human spirit.

I didn't trust Sokolovsky, although he told me once that all his life he had wanted to do good for people but that he hadn't been stupid enough to succeed in this.

The uneasy atmosphere on the train, especially in our orderlies' car, which had begun with Sokolovsky's appearance, could not continue for long. Its end came unexpectedly.

One day we had pulled in to Kielce. That evening, the senior surgeon gave some of us passes to go out into the city. Kielce was dark and empty. We went into a café. It had bright lights, a smell of chocolate, and two chattering waitresses. The wet night, blocked off from us by dark windowpanes, did not seem as dismal as it was on the street.

We sat there quietly drinking coffee. A lieutenant of engineers was fast asleep at another table. The steam of the coffee, the smell of vanilla, the sweet candy-store warmth, and the insinuating half-whispering of the waitresses had worn him out.

Then the glass door to the street opened noisily, and Sokolovsky walked in. He was without an overcoat. He was wearing a new Hussar officer's uniform. Silver epaulets glittered on his shoulders. A cavalryman's saber was dragging behind him, clanking on the red brick floor of the restaurant.

We looked at Sokolovsky quietly and without understanding. He walked slowly up to us. His face was twisted in an unnatural smile, and the whites of his eyes were bloodshot. He stopped, and stared straight at Romanin.

"I didn't know you were a Hussar officer, Sokolovsky," Romanin said. "Sit down with us."

"Stand up!" Sokolovsky yelled in a wild voice. "Why don't you salute an officer? Salute, you scoundrels!"

"Chuck the foolishness," Romanin said uneasily. "You're drunk."

"Quiet!" Sokolovsky roared, and he drew his saber from its scabbard. "I'll butcher you like puppy dogs. Educated men! I'll show you who Sokolovsky is!"

He slammed the saber down on our table with a loud crash. The table broke, cups fell on the floor. The girls started to scream. The lieutenant of engineers woke up and ran out. In a frenzy, Sokolovsky swung the saber at Romanin, but the orderly Grekov struck him on the back with all his strength. Sokolovsky fell across the broken table and dropped the saber.

We got out of the place quickly and made our way through a courtyard and back to the train standing on the tracks. We went to Pokrovsky right away, and told him what had happened. Pokrovsky ordered that the orderlies' car be locked for the night and that Sokolovsky not be admitted if he showed up, and he said he would report the incident in the morning to the military commandant of the station.

I spent the night in the operating car. I had to sterilize bandages before we could load wounded the next day.

During the night, someone started to fool with the door, trying to open its lock with a knife. But I checked the lock; it would be impossible to open it without a key. The man tried for a long time, then started to knock on the window. I walked over and looked out. Sokolovsky was standing there, without a cap and with a soldier's overcoat thrown around his shoulders.

"Let me spend the night here," he said. "Hide me, student."

"No," I answered. "I won't let you in."

"If I only had a revolver," Sokolovsky said and he laughed crookedly, "I'd solder some metal onto you, Friar. I'd send you to join your unmentionable female ancestors. You're not going to let me in?"

"No."

Sokolovsky came closer to the window.

"Some day, God willing, we'll meet again. Remember me well, Friar. So that you'll recognize me right away, and have a little time for praying before I let your living blood run out onto the ground."

"Romanin!" I called, even though I knew that Romanin wasn't in his dispensary. "Come here."

Sokolovsky spat on the windowpane, backed away, and disappeared in the darkness. I turned out the light, got out a revolver which we kept hidden in a closet, and sat there for a long time waiting for an attack.

But Sokolovsky never showed up again. He disappeared. But on the fifth or sixth day, while the train was standing at the Rado station, a cheerful peasant boy walked up, gave the man on duty a package wrapped in oilcloth, and went away again. On the package was written: "To the nurses of Front-line Hospital Train No. 217."

The man on duty gave it to the senior nurse. There was a note under the oilcloth which said: "Earrings for all the sisters. To help them keep happy memories of Lieutenant Sokolovsky."

They opened the package. It was filled with little black cases, each one of which contained a pair of diamond earrings, lying on pink velvet. There were exactly as many cases as there were nurses on the train. Pokrovsky ordered that they be turned over at once to the commandant of the station.

Three days later we read a story in a little Brest newspaper about an unusually bold burglary of a jewelry store in Vilna. The same day the commandant came up to Pokrovsky and asked him:

"Did a man who called himself Lieutenant Sokolovsky work for you as an orderly?"

"Yes, he worked here."

"Where is he now?"

"I don't know."

"You ought to be interested in knowing."

"Why?"

"Because that was quite a bird you had."

"I'm not a hunter," Pokrovsky said, laughing.

"You should have been!" the commandant said cryptically, and he went away, without having explained who Sokolovsky was.

At first we spent a lot of time guessing, but then we forgot all about Sokolovsky.

Nearly two years later I accidentally found out. I was working then at the Novorossisk Factory in the Don Basin, in the smoky town of Yuzovka. A former Social Revolutionary named Grinko was working as draftsman in our shop, a white-faced, tubercular man who walked around in a soft hat and treated everything with open irony.

I was living in a cheap room at the Great Britain Hotel. It was in that musty room that Grinko once told me how he had been tried in Yekaterinoslav for membership in the Social Revolutionary party and sentenced to a five-year term in Siberia.

On the way from Kharkov to Siberia, a handcuffed young man, wearing frameless pince-nez, had been led into the railroad car transporting prisoners. The car was full of petty thieves, riffraff. When the man in irons walked in and said the one word "Well!" the riffraff at once stopped what they were doing, cleared a section of the crowded car for him, and began to fawn on him in every possible way.

The draftsman remembered that even the escorting police officers treated the young man with a certain respect, and granted him special favors. The man invited Grinko into his special section of the car, telling him that he, too, was an educated man, that he could speak several languages, and that he was especially fond of music.

Grinko told him about his misadventures. The man listened attentively, leaned over, and said in a low voice:

"I will set you free."

"How?"

"No joking. It's stupid to get sent to Siberia on such a foolish charge as yours. In two years of exile, you'd rot to death."

The man then cross-examined him in great detail about all the circumstances of his case. The draftsman told me that he had not believed for a moment that this criminal could help him. It all seemed arrant boasting.

But somewhere in Penzensky province, at some unknown junction, a police officer boarded the train with telegraphic instructions sent in pursuit of the train from Yekaterinoslav to take Grinko off the train and hold him in the prison at Narovchat until further instructions. So they took him off, and the young man in handcuffs simply waved good-by to him and told him in the future to "be more careful on the turns."

The draftsman was kept only a short time in the godforsaken prison in Narovchat. Notification soon arrived that the Yekaterinoslav court had judged Grinko's case in his absence and that Grinko had been acquitted for lack of evidence against him. The head of the prison congratulated him and let him go. Grinko went home to Yekaterinoslav, but was arrested at the station there and convicted of having escaped. It was only then that he realized that the whole complicated business of his release with forged court documents had been arranged by the handcuffed man.

"He was a famous swindler," the draftsman told me, "the chief of a powerful organization of counterfeiters and crooks. It was clear that he had given instructions about my case to one of his agents, probably in Kursk, by bribing one of his guards. It was all done so cleverly and skillfully that I, like a fool, thought it was the real thing, and so got caught a second time."

"Tell me," I asked him, "did the young man have any distinguishing mark on him?"

"He had a scar on his lip. His name was Sokolovsky."

Then I told the draftsman about the mysterious orderly named Sokolovsky.

"That's the same man," he said. "He was just hiding when he was on the train with you. A very good place to hide."

"Why did he do it under his right name?"

"Because there are thousands of Sokolovskys. And besides, people who live desperate lives often want to play with fire and tempt their fate."

Over many years I have become convinced that every encounter with other men, even with men like Sokolovsky, leaves its traces. From some of his remarks it was possible to guess that from early childhood he had been raised on a good deal of injustice. Embittered by it, he had devoted all his talent to seeking revenge, of any kind, for his humiliating life.

THE OCEAN-GOING STEAMSHIP PORTUGAL

The summer of 1915 was hot and dry. Out of the windows of the train we could see brown curtains of dust hanging over the fields of Poland. The army was falling back.

The dust of defeat, bitter and smelling of burned houses, lay heavy on everything—the soldiers' faces, the grain in the fields, weapons, horses, and our train. The red freight cars had turned gray.

We stopped nowhere now for more than three or four hours. The train was in constant motion. The wounded came and came and came.

Once we picked up casualties on the right bank of the Vistula, in the suburb of Warsaw called Praga. Fighting was going on in the part of the city behind the Mokotov barrier. Low-burning fires were reflected in the river. Smoke and fog hung over the houses. Volleys could be heard across the river. They sounded as if someone were ripping dry cloth in jerks.

The wind was blowing from the east. It filled Praga with freshness at night. But the daytime closeness hung on in the cars, especially in the operating car where the windows were always kept tightly shut and where we could never scrub away the smell of surgical dressings.

At that time we were transporting the wounded from Poland to Gomel. As soon as the train moved into the Polessya, everything grew fresher. The damp woods and the slow-flowing rivers of White Russia seemed as refreshing as paradise to us. The wounded men came alive; lifting their heads from their cots, they would stare out at the rustling pine forests or at the sky turning green in the evening.

The train had been used so hard, by the middle of the summer, that it was ordered to Odessa, to be repaired in the railroad workshops there. We went through Kiev, the city of my childhood. I saw it at dawn from the siding at the station. The sun was already gilding the pyramid-shaped poplar trees and shining back from the windows of the high houses built of Kiev's yellow brick.

I could remember its streets in the mornings, just after they had been washed. I could remember the housewives carrying hot rolls and bottles of cold milk in their shopping bags. But for some reason nothing pulled me out into the freshness of those streets—Kiev had already receded into the unrecoverable past.

It made good sense that the past should be unrecoverable. I became convinced of this later after I had made two or three attempts to relive what had already been lived through. "Nothing in life ever is repeated," my father used to love to say, "except our mistakes." And the fact that nothing in life can ever be lived a second time was one of the reasons for the deep satisfaction in being alive.

The undulating Ukraine, warmed by the sun, poured past the windows beyond Kiev. All day long the air twinkled and sparkled in the crystal-clear distance. I assured Romanin that the brilliance on the horizon was the reflection, in very high levels of the atmosphere, of sunlight falling on the sea and being refracted in it.

For once Romanin raised no objection, and did not laugh at me. Instead he declaimed in a loud voice from his dispensary:

> Here it is, the sea! Burning in turquoise
> And glittering with pearly foam.
> Heavy and troubled, it runs along
> The wet sand bars, wave upon wave.

I woke up outside Odessa. The train was standing at a small station. I jumped down from the platform onto the tracks. Little cockleshells crackled under my feet.

I saw a small station building with a white-tiled roof. High corn was growing next to a white wall. The wind fluttered its long leaves. The air over the tiled roof and the corn was the most magnificent of dark blues.

"Now this really looks like refraction from the sea," Romanin said to me out of the window.

There was the smell of wormwood. This was when that sharp, astringent smell was first linked in my imagination with nearness to the Black Sea. The link has grown so strong since then that even in the north when I come across the smell of wormwood I instinctively listen for the distant roaring of the sea. Sometimes I have thought I heard it, too, but of course it wasn't the sea I was hearing, but a pine forest.

I was delighted that in a few hours I would see the sea. From my childhood its joyous foaming vastness had filled my heart.

They moved us up to the Odessa warehouses for unloading. The sea was not visible. Only the big Odessa station shone in the distance. But everything around me seemed filled with the sea, even the puddles of oil along the tracks. They were shot through with the dark blue of the sea. Old pieces of metal scattered on the ground were covered with a sea rust. This, anyway, was what I thought then.

We orderlies were moved into an old third-class passenger car, where we settled ourselves quickly. A shunting engine began to nudge it back and forth along the sidings until it stopped next to a little slope of empty garden where it was left all the time we were in Odessa.

The location pleased us all. In the mornings we washed at a water tower right next to our car. The heavy shadows of acacia trees ran across our windows. Behind the garden was a noisy little market, and a little beyond that began the Odessa suburb of Moldavanka, a hangout of thieves, receivers of stolen goods, small traders, and many other characters with devious and dubious occupations.

The doctors and nurses were lodged in a country house at Little Fountain, near Odessa. We went to see them there nearly every day.

I never did see the sea on the day of our arrival. But the next day I got up very early, washed in the saltish water from the tower, and went to the market to drink milk and get something to eat.

Red from the heat and from shouting, traders were sitting on little stools, with their sleeves rolled up. All day long they swore at each other, called to the customers, or ridiculed the public. They swore at each other in screeching voices, they invited customers ingratiatingly, even coquettishly, and they made fun of them in the most friendly tones possible, forgetting for the moment their disputes with each other.

"Little boy!" they yelled at me. "Here's some warm milk. Here's milk with foam on it. Remember, your darling mother ordered you to drink unskimmed milk!"

Others called out their wares in gloomy voices: "A pocket full for a kopeck! For one miserable little kopeck!"

Best of all was the row of fish merchants. I stood for a long time around the cold zinc counters covered with fish scales and strewn with rock salt. Flat halibut with blue bony growths along their backs looked up at the sky out of dim eyes. Mackerel thrashed about in wet baskets, like blue mercury. Brown perch slowly opened their mouths and quietly moved them, as if they were tasting the morning freshness of the market. Bullheads lay in mountains, black, gray, and brick-colored. A specially ingratiating group of traders sat around a basket filled with insignificant minnows. Housewives bought these only for their cats.

"Here is something for your cats! Young ladies or young women, here is something for your kittens!" they called out in wheedling voices.

Apricots and cherries were piled in great heaps on carts. The owners of this wealth—German colonists from Lustdorf and Libenthal—snored in the warm dust under their carts, while on top of them were the boys they had hired to sell their produce, little Jewish boys from the Hebrew *cheder*. With their eyes closed, rocking back and forth as if in prayer, they would sing out in whining voices:

"Ai-i, good people, kindly gentlefolk. Ai-i, cherries, ai-i, sweet apricots, good cherries! Ai-i, five kopecks a pound. Ai-i, five kopecks! We're losing money at that price. Ai-i, good people, come and buy! Ai-i, buy for your good health!"

The roadway was covered with cherry stones and little pieces of the red pulp of the fruit, and with apricot stones.

I bought some gray bread with raisins and walked to the far end of the market, to an eating place where round samovars were standing on heavy tables, reflecting the unbearable Black Sea sun, and Ukrainian sausages were sizzling in great frying pans.

I sat down at a table covered with a homemade tablecloth. The inscription had been sewed on it in little crosses: "Little Raichka, don't forget Ovidiopol where you were born." In the middle of the table, some peonies stood in a blue vase of cracked enamel.

I ate a pan of fried sausages, began to drink hot, sweet tea, and decided that life in Odessa was wonderful.

It was about then that a lean man, wearing a nautical cap
with a flapping lacquered visor, walked up to me. Yellow sideburns stuck out like a wildcat's on both sides of his gray face.

"Tell me, young man," he asked in the confidential voice of a
conspirator, "you don't happen to be, excuse me, an orderly?"

"Yes, I'm an orderly."

"From the train that came in yesterday for repairs?"

"Yes, from that train," I answered, and I looked with surprise
at this omniscient stranger in the nautical cap.

"Then I'm very glad to meet you!" he exclaimed, lifting his cap
with both hands and then replacing it on his bald head. "Aristarkh
Lipogon, former captain in the coasting trade. Born to be a sailor."

"What are you bothering the young man for?" yelled the flushed
woman who had poured my tea. "What kind of nonsense are you
telling him?"

"Aunt Raya," the born sailor answered her very politely, "just
what bitchy business of yours is it to mix into other people's
affairs? You're just trying to take a piece of bread out of my mouth.
You're well fed and fat, that's clear, and I'm as hungry as an empty
box. Do you understand?"

Aunt Raya grumbled a little bit more, and then was silent.

"I can offer you co-operation," Lipogon said to me. "I will not
shirk any service which might possibly help you, or possibly your
doctors who are living in Buikhovsky's luxurious country house at
Little Fountain. I can execute anything quickly and cheaply."

"Well, for example," I asked, "what is 'anything'?"

"I can find and purchase anything you like, with delivery to
your railroad car. Tobacco from Constantinople, without wrappers.
It's not tobacco, it's curled-up gold. Greek vodka. Oranges from
Messina, of incredible fragrance and flavor. Or fresh canned goods,
bullheads in tomato sauce, made today, fresh from our Odessa
factory. By the second day they've already begun to lose that God-
given taste. I recommend them highly. I am widely acquainted in
the city. Ask anybody about me, and if he's an upstanding man,
he'll tell you unconditionally: 'Lipogon can do anything. He has
twenty legs, forty arms, and a hundred eyes.'"

"But you've only got one tongue, you convict!" Aunt Raya said
from her heart. "You've only got one tongue, but you flap it enough
for seven."

I told Lipogon that I didn't need anything. But perhaps the
doctors or the nurses might need something. I would ask them.

"And by the way," Lipogon said, "I plan to visit Buikhovsky's
country house this evening. I am very glad to have made your
acquaintance, young man."

Again he lifted his battered cap from his bald head with both hands and put it back again, and then he walked away, shaking the tails of his jacket and cheerfully singing:

> *The young midshipman*
> *With the light-brown hair*
> *Sailed away from lovely Odessa . . .*

"There," Aunt Raya told me, "you have before you an example, young man, of where fantasy can lead a man."

"How fantasy?" I asked in surprise.

"He used to live like a good man," Aunt Raya said sorrowfully. "He sailed his little boat, carried watermelons from Kherson to Odessa, had a fine suit of clothes and an extra twenty-kopeck piece to jingle in his pocket, and enough to eat every day. But no. The man couldn't put up with it! I know him well, we've been friends since childhood, we grew up next door to each other in Ovidiopol. He just couldn't live like everybody else. The gray boredom of existence, he'd tell me, makes my heart hurt, Raichka. I want to live, Raichka, he'd say, like people in novels, with tears and flowers and music and luxurious love. I must take some risks, he'd say, either neck or nothing!"

"You said it!" her neighboring trader said with a sigh, spreading her blue eggplants along her stall. "But he lost his neck, and got nothing."

"But what did he do?" I asked.

"He got married," Aunt Raya answered. "But you just listen to how he got married. We had a kind of Rumanian orchestra here in Odessa. They weren't really Rumanians, but all kinds of people. Some from the Caucasus, some from Kishenev, and some from Moldavia like us. And this orchestra had a cymbals player named Tamara. She was a good-looking woman, it's true, a striking woman. Well, he married her. Maybe he was a little dazzled by it all—the bugles and the velvets and the cymbals and the waltzing. I'll give her, he'd tell me, the kind of life that will make anyone else die of jealousy."

"You said it! He certainly made her a life!" the eggplant merchant said with a sigh.

"But the man really did work for that woman," Aunt Raya said grudgingly. "And he's still working. As soon as he was married, he began to chase the kopecks. Started carrying contraband on his boat. They caught him, of course, and took away his license. He bought his way out of jail. He was really on the streets, but he still managed to fix up an apartment for her. Apartment? More a

cakebox with pink ribbons. A real box with paper lace in it. He
went off with his boat and started doing little jobs, a real jobber.
He's lost respectability, of course, with other people. But he won't
give up his fantasy. Goes right on telling lies. He hides his poverty
from Tamara. She's a lazy woman, maybe a little bit crazy. She
isn't interested in anything. Leans all day long on the window sill
reading tattered books and listening to the gramophone. She puts
on 'The night was breathing' or 'Yesterday I saw you in my sleep,'
and reads. It's all the same to her, it might as well be Turkish
Delight. Her hair is always in a mess. But that a man has cheapened
himself for her, become riffraff for her, this she doesn't want to
see. So she reads love stories. I spit on her."

Aunt Raya spat from her heart.

"He'll earn himself a term in prison, I assure you of that, young
man!"

I went home to our railroad car and was getting ready to go
down to the sea when they sent us to the railroad workshops to
help the workers scrape the old paint off the cars. We worked until
evening.

Then I washed and went to Little Fountain, to the country
house. There at last, from a cliff, I saw the sea. A hazy evening was
flowing into a blue expanse of water. The waves made barely more
noise than the gulls. The first star came alight just under a cloud
which looked like the wing of a silver bird.

The lighthouses were not blinking. The outline of a ship was
dark against the horizon. This was the Turkish cruiser *Medzhidie*
which had been shelled by our coastal artillery and run aground
on the rocks. They had not yet pulled it off. The cruiser slowly
merged into the twilight and soon disappeared in it completely.

I ran down a steep path to the sea. Dry acacia bushes were
growing on the hard ground. Big seaworn pebbles slipped under
my feet. Stiff broom spread its dark branches all around, with
yellow flowers that could be seen even in the dark. There was a
smell of heated mussel shells and broiled mackerel—the nurses
were cooking near the house on an open fire.

I went down to the sea, stripped, and walked into the warm,
fresh water up to my neck. The reflections of the stars swam
around me in the water like little jellyfish. I tried not to stir, so
as not to shatter them into dozens of rocking sparks. You had to
wait a long time for them to reform into reflections of the stars.

All through my body I could feel the careful but powerful
breathing of the sea. Its rippling was barely noticeable. The sea
began just below my eyes, at the level of my chin. My heart

pounded with the thought that there was nothing between me and the endless ocean distances stretching out from here to the Bosphorus, to the shores of Greece and Egypt, to the Adriatic and the Atlantic, that here before my eyes began the great oceans of the world.

Far away in the direction of the Dniester estuary, machine-gun firing bounced and echoed along the shore. The war was here, too, in places which seemed to have been created for true and happy living, made for sailors, gardeners, winegrowers and artists, for children and lovers, carefree childhood, productive maturity, for old age like a clear September.

The nurses called to me from the shore. I came out of the water, dressed, and went up to the house. Lipogon was standing there, on a terrace covered by an awning instead of a roof, without his hat, talking ingratiatingly to the nurses. As a start, he had sold them a cloth bag full of Greek olives.

I went back to the city with Lipogon.

"I can guess," Lipogon told me in the trolley car, "that you're a great lover of the sea."

I agreed.

"Then you oughtn't to be working in a hospital train, in those converted boxcars, but on a hospital ship. Right now we have the *Portugal,* a hospital ship, here in Odessa. A former French ship."

"Well," I answered cautiously, "I'd be glad to transfer to a ship like that."

"It can be done," Lipogon said casually. "You're in luck. A junior doctor there is a friend of mine. I supply him with smuggled tobacco. Come down at one o'clock tomorrow to the Quarantine Wharf. I'll meet you there, next to the *Portugal.* I won't charge you anything. You can treat me to a meal, and we'll be quits."

He was silent for a moment.

"There'll come a time," he said, leaning toward me so the sound of the trolley wouldn't drown out his voice, "when I'll tell you about myself. People tell lies about me. For me, life is like a novel, with the next installment in the next issue of the magazine. I have a secret life. My fate's been all fouled up, of course. But maybe I'm better than all your good people. It's only that I haven't had many successes, and that cuts down the scope of my activity."

The dark night poured through the windows of the unlighted trolley in jerky gusts of wind. In those days, lights were forbidden at night in all port cities.

"If I'd had my own way," Lipogon said, "I'd have sailed around the world. It would have been better than life, more a picture by Aivazovsky."

The next day I got to the Quarantine Wharf not at one o'clock but at ten in the morning. A white ocean-going steamship, with two red crosses on its sides, seemed to be dissolving in the dry brilliance of the sunshine at the breakwater. I could read the golden French letters on the stern of the ship—PORTUGAL—MARSEILLES.

There was something unreal about the whiteness of the ship, the lightness of its masts, its rigging and its bridges, the shine of its brass, the diamondlike cleanliness of its searchlights and the freshness of its decks, as if the ship had come from some holiday world, as if it had been made out of hardened light.

It was a passenger ship of the French line, Messageries Maritimes. Before the war, it had sailed between Marseilles and Madagascar, Syria and Arabia, and then for some reason it came in to the Black Sea. It had been trapped here by the war with Turkey, and by agreement with the French government it had been turned over to us for use as a hospital ship. It had been repainted white.

Young nurses were walking on the deck of the *Portugal* in gray summer dresses, and sailors all in white. I was afraid I might be seen ahead of time, so I went away and wandered around the port until one o'clock.

I went back to the *Portugal* exactly at one. Lipogon was standing at the ship's ladder, talking with a young naval doctor. The doctor had black, laughing eyes and his red neck was a little squeezed by the white collar of his tunic. He shook my hand quickly and said to Lipogon:

"So, good-by, skipper! After this trip, bring me some more tobacco."

"That I'll do!" Lipogon exclaimed with affected good nature. He raised his hand to the visor of his cap, and walked away.

The doctor took me by the elbow and led me to his cabin. He held me tightly, as if he were afraid I might slip on the polished deck and fall and, God forbid, break some instrument or glass door. I didn't like this very much, but I kept quiet and did not break his grip on me.

"In general," the doctor said in his cabin, which was filled with fresh sunshine and the smell of good tobacco, "I need one orderly to work in the dressing station. You're a student? Excellent. Have you your papers?"

"Yes."

"May I see them?"

I showed him my papers. He glanced at them and returned them to me.

"Consider everything agreed," he said. "Come aboard the day after tomorrow. We'll finish some formalities then, and you can stay on the ship. It's possible we may make a trip soon."

I felt in a fog. I couldn't believe that I might be sailing on this ocean-going ship. My childhood dreams were coming true. I would miss the train, of course, and my comrades, but my thirst for the sea overcame everything.

The doctor led me back to the ship's ladder. A short old man was standing there, as fidgety as a monkey, dressed in a naval uniform which was not Russian. I guessed from the number of gold stripes on his sleeves that this must be the highest-ranking officer of the ship.

"Our captain, Monsieur Bayard," the young doctor warned me in a low voice.

He bowed to the captain, and said to him in French:

"Here is our newest orderly, Captain. A student from Moscow."

I bowed, too.

"It's beyond understanding, mon Dieu!" Monsieur Bayard exclaimed in French, and he lifted both hands to the sky. "University students, instead of studying, will feed Russian peasants their gruel with little spoons! Nobody tends to his own business in this incredible country. Nobody!"

The captain grabbed me by the shoulder with a strong brown paw, turned me around, and looked into my eyes.

"O-o-o!" he said. "Yes, yes. Everyone has been through this. Now I understand you. Dreams, dreams! No!" he exclaimed suddenly. "The sea—here's where it really is, my friend!" He took off his cap with its gold braid and pointed to his gray, close-cropped head.

"Here are all the magic nights at the Equator! All the Bengal sunsets! The smell of cinnamon and all that nonsense! In the head! You have a bad disease, young man, but I don't know any cure for it. So I am glad to see you on board."

He turned around quickly and ran along the deck to the captain's bridge. The doctor looked at him with an amused but respectful smile.

"That's the kind of captain we have," he said. "A magnificent Gascon. So, until the day after tomorrow."

The next day I treated Lipogon to a dinner at the Dardanelles Restaurant on Stepovaya Street. Properly speaking, it wasn't a restaurant but a cookshop swarming with flies.

Romanin and Nikolashka Rudnyev came with me. They were both disappointed about my leaving the train and, strange as it may seem, did not envy me in the slightest. On the contrary, they seemed to disapprove of the step I was taking.

Dinner at the Dardanelles ended with a row. We had been served lamb stew. We had eaten it, but Lipogon immediately called over the lazy waiter who was serving us, and told him:

"Call the boss over here."

"Why?"

"It's none of your business."

The sleepy proprietor—an obese man with a green face—came reluctantly out of a back room.

"What's the matter?" he asked in a hoarse voice. "If you don't like it, well, my restaurant isn't the London Hotel. You can go there if you're so finicky."

"The matter is," Lipogon answered in an ugly tone, "that you, Gospodin Kamenyuk, are serving your customers rotten lamb. And so you may be sending us to eat in Heaven."

"You think so?" Gospodin Kamenyuk asked ironically. "Ai-ai-ai! So it's rotten, is it? I'll have you know—my lamb is top grade."

"And I tell you, it's spoiled."

"Then why did you eat it?" Kamenyuk asked with the same irony, which promised nothing good. "You've eaten it all but the bones. You've even polished your plates with bread. Don't take me for a fool. I'm not a puppy!"

"Ah, so! So your lamb is not rotten?" Lipogon exclaimed with a kind of delight in his voice. "Then may I humbly request you to serve us four more portions of this delicious ragout."

It was clear that this request did not please Kamenyuk.

"We're all out of lamb," he said, his face turning white. "There's no more left. Understand? And I'll serve you nothing more."

"Then I'll have no choice," Lipogon said sadly, "but to go out to the police officer, Gospodin Skulsky, and put this affair into the hands of the law. So, in the event of any trouble, don't blame me, Gospodin Kamenyuk."

Kamenyuk hit the palm of his hand against our table with all his strength.

"This is my last word: get out of here without any more fuss. I don't need your money." Turning to Lipogon: "I hope you choke on that money, you worm!"

We were so taken aback by the unexpected course of events that we had no chance to interfere. I still took out the money and put it on the table, but I'm not sure that it all found its way into

Gospodin Kamenyuk's pocket, because Gospodin Kamenyuk angrily pushed the money toward Lipogon, and the latter picked it up and pushed it back at Gospodin Kamenyuk with a magnificent disdain. I noticed that the number of bills was already considerably smaller than it had been before Lipogon picked them up.

"Why did you bother making that stupid row?" I asked Lipogon, who was still furious, when we got out to the street.

"Because," Lipogon answered, "you're students. The wind blows through your pockets. And Kamenyuk gets fat on tainted meat."

"But that lamb wasn't spoiled at all!"

"Today no, but tomorrow yes," Lipogon answered coolly. "You saw how he crumpled up when I asked for second servings. Because he thought—the son of a bitch—that maybe it was true that the lamb was rotten. Then I would have material evidence for the police. So it was better to throw us out than to run any risks."

Back in our car we spent a lot of time discussing this incident. Then in the evening we went to the country house at Little Fountain where I had to say good-by to the doctors and the nurses.

Everyone there was thunderstruck by my decision. Some envied me, others couldn't understand it. Only Lelya said nothing, just bit her lips and did not even look at me.

We were sitting on the dark terrace. The surf was thundering below us.

Lelya squeezed my arm until it hurt, and said:

"Come on!"

We went out into the dark garden and began to go down to the sea. Lelya was silent but she held tightly to my hand, just as people lead a naughty little boy to punishment. Lelya didn't stop until we had come right up to the sea. She was breathing hard.

"You dreamer!" she said. "Adventurer! Little boy! Tomorrow, you go down to that shiny, stupid ship, and you resign. Do you hear me?"

"Why?"

"What do you mean—why? My God! Don't you really understand anything? Because it isn't the way to treat your comrades. Because only the devil knows what it is! Of course, it would be much more pleasant to twiddle your thumbs in that floating parlor, with its proper curtains and its coldhearted dolls for nurses, than to work in the dirt and the blood of our beaten-up boxcars. Even Romanin and Rudnyev and all your comrades are ashamed of you. As if you hadn't noticed it! Of course, nobody will tell you this. But I'll tell you. Because for me it isn't all the same. . . . Because I want to think well of you. . . . And anyway, don't ask me about what you already know."

"But I'm not asking you about anything."

"That's just the trouble! Well, how about it? I'm waiting."

A storm was rising in my heart. In some of this, Lelya was right, of course. But how could I miss this fabulous chance, lose what I had waited for so long, from the first years of my life?

"No," I said. "I can't resign now. And it's not at all the way you think it is. You don't have to talk about it with such hatred."

"Well then, good-by!" Lelya said hollowly. She turned and walked off into the darkness along the white edge of the surf.

I called to her. She did not answer. I ran after her. She stopped, and said in a cold voice:

"Don't come after me. That's stupid! And repulsive. Good-by. Give my greetings to your new friend, that—what's his name?— Lipogon."

She laughed. I waited. I could hear her walk farther, stop, throw some stones into the sea, and then, clearly mocking me, start to sing.

I turned around, climbed up the bank and, without going into the house, walked back on foot to Odessa. It was a very dark night. The wind rustled in the gardens. Patrols stopped me twice to check my papers.

I went over in my mind, hour by hour, what had happened. I suddenly realized with terror that I myself didn't know if what I had done was good or bad. I couldn't make up my mind.

"What is this?" I asked myself. "A weak spirit? Or some kind of illness? Or simple unwillingness to think about myself and my life? Or cowardice?"

First it seemed to me that Lelya was completely right. Then, on the other hand, I began to think that what she had said was really hypocrisy and sham. But then why hadn't Romanin or Rudnyev looked me in the eyes? What was bothering them? Had they really decided that I was a coward? Why? And who imagined that work on a hospital ship would turn out to be a happy lark? No, I wasn't going to give it up. I wouldn't quit. To hell with them all!

I lost my way, of course, and didn't get back to our car until everyone else was asleep. This pleased me.

In the morning I went down to the Quarantine Wharf, but where the *Portugal* had been the day before there was now a steel barge loaded with coal.

A man who was sitting on the barge, cleaning fish, told me that the *Portugal* had left during the night and sailed off to Trebizond.

"But how can that be?" I asked in dismay. "It was supposed to leave in a few days."

"It happens," the man with the fish answered indifferently. "They got an urgent call. Immediate. A military question, my friend. But it'll come back. Don't you worry."

I was ashamed to go back to our car and to my old comrades. But I had to.

"What are you going to do now?" Romanin asked me carelessly.

"Wait until the *Portugal* comes back."

"Well then, wait. It's your decision, of course."

I went out on the trolley car to Lustdorf. I felt awkward staying at the railroad car.

I spent the whole day at the edge of the sea in Lustdorf, a boring little colony of German farmers. I didn't eat. In the evening I bought a couple of dozen apricots.

I decided to go back to Odessa on the last trolley, but the trolley didn't come. So then I went on foot. It was about twenty kilometers back to the city.

Again it was night, and windy. Again the gardens rustled all along the road, and acacia seeds beat into my face. It seemed to me that I was all alone in the world. I would have given a great deal right then to see Mama, to have her stroke my hair and say: "Ah, how incorrigible you are, Kostik!"

I sat down to rest next to the forged iron gates of a big country place. A deep recess for a statue had been built into the stone wall, but there was no statue in it. I climbed into the empty niche, sat down, hugging my knees with my arms, and stayed there for a long time. Then I fell asleep.

I woke up when a *gymnasium* student got off his bicycle next to the niche in which I was sitting and looked at me in sheer delight.

"Good morning to you!" he said. "You look just like the sculptor Antokolsky's statue of Mephistopheles."

"There is no such statue!" I answered angrily, even though I knew perfectly well that the statue does exist, and I jumped down to the ground and walked back to the city.

The road ran between stone fences. I looked at them—they seemed familiar. What was this? Was it really Little Fountain? In the distance I could already see the iron lamp in front of the gate to the house where the doctors and the nurses lived. I had completely forgotten that the road to Lustdorf ran close to Little Fountain.

I stopped at the gate, opened it, and looked into the garden. It ran down to the white, quiet sea.

It was a cloudy morning, without any wind. A few drops of rain had fallen on my face and on the pebbles, gray with drying salt,

along the road. I could see black wet spots on the pebbles which
dried while I watched them.

"Everyone must still be asleep," I thought. I wanted to see Lelya.
Again, just as in the nighttime not long before, a feeling of loneliness was strong in me. Did they know here that I had not gone
away, that the *Portugal* had sailed without me? Probably not.

I walked cautiously into the garden. A familiar green bench
stood there behind some high box trees. I sat down on it. I could
not be seen from the terrace or the garden. I told myself that I
would rest for a little while and then go away unnoticed.

Some more drops of rain fell. Gulls were crying over the sea.

I lifted my head. Someone was walking quickly from the house
to the gate. I looked through a chink in the box, and saw Lelya.
She was hatless, in a raincoat, and her face was whiter than I had
ever seen it. She was walking very quickly, almost running.

I stood up from the bench, parted the bushes, and walked to
meet her. Lelya saw me, screamed, fell on her knees and, leaning
on one arm, began to sink down on the gray gravel of the path.
Her eyes were closed. I ran up to her, grabbed her shoulder, but
couldn't lift her. She groaned quietly, and then said in a whisper:

"Oh, God! He's alive. Oh, God!"

"I missed the *Portugal*," I told her thoughtlessly, not knowing
how to calm her.

"Help me," she said and she raised her tear-streaked face. "Give
me your hand."

She stood up with difficulty.

"Don't you really know?"

"No," I answered, completely confused.

"Let's move away from here. Anywhere."

We walked into the overgrown garden of the next house where
no one was living. There Lelya sank exhausted on a bench.

"My God!" she said and she looked at me with her eyes full of
tears. "You're stupid, stupid. Look—read this."

She pulled out of her pocket a small gray paper; it was an extra
edition of the newspaper *Odessa News*. I opened it and saw the
black headlines:

"Latest monstrous barbarity of the Germans. Hospital ship
Portugal sunk by torpedo from German submarine on its way to
Sevastopol. Not a single person saved of ship's entire command
and personnel."

I dropped the newspaper and took Lelya by the shoulders. She
was crying now like a little girl, not ashamed, not holding herself
back, the abundant tears of relief.

"God!" she said through her tears. "Why am I crying like this? What nonsense! Please don't think that I've fallen in love with you. I was simply scared."

"I'm not thinking anything," I answered and I stroked her damp hair.

"Is that true?" Lelya asked, lifting her eyes to mine and smiling. "Give me my purse, please. I've a handkerchief there. I was running into the city to find out if—maybe not everyone was lost."

ON THE ROAD OF DEFEAT

A month before our trip to Odessa, Romanin and I had sent a request to Moscow to be transferred from the hospital train to a field medical unit. We wanted to be closer to the war.

Romanin had his own reasons for this. He told me in confidence that he was writing feature stories about the war for a radical newspaper in Vyatsk and that the train was furnishing him with too little material. He showed me some of his pieces which had been printed. I liked the precision and the simplicity of their style.

Romanin persuaded me to write some pieces for the same paper. I wrote only one, which was my first feature story. It was called "Blue Overcoats" and it was published. I wrote about the capture of many thousands of prisoners in the Austrian fortress of Przemysl. We had seen these prisoners in Brest. That article was not the place, though, to write about one particularly strange happening which astonished me and all the other orderlies.

The prisoners were being led through Brest. Thousands of Austrian soldiers and officers—a slow stream of dull blue overcoats—were wearily dragging their broken boots through the streets of the town. Sometimes the stream would stop, and the unshaven men would wait with downcast eyes, looking at the ground. Then they would move on again, their shoulders hunched under the weight of their unknown destiny.

Suddenly an orderly, Hugo Lyakhman, grabbed my arm.

"Look!" he yelled. "Over there! That Austrian soldier. Look at him!"

I looked, and I felt a chill go through my body. There, walking toward me at a tired but even pace, was I myself, in the uniform of an Austrian soldier. I had heard a lot about doubles, but I had never before encountered one. Here was my exact double walking toward me. He was like me to the tiniest detail, including a little birthmark on the right temple.

"How the devil can it be!" Romanin said. "This is really frightening."

Then a curious incident took place. The soldier convoying the prisoners looked at me, then at the Austrian, went up to him and took him by the arm, pointing me out to him. The Austrian looked, stumbled, and then stood still. And the whole crowd of prisoners stopped with him.

We looked each other directly in the eyes, probably not for very long but for what seemed to me an hour. Excited talk ran down the rows of prisoners. I could see surprise in the Austrian's dark eyes. Then it changed for a moment to terror, but he conquered this quickly, and suddenly gave me a shy, sad smile and waved a very white hand at me in greeting.

"Forward, march!" the soldier yelled out finally.

The blue overcoats swayed and then moved on. The Austrian turned around several times and waved his hand. I waved back. So we met and parted, and never saw each other again.

There was a lot of talk in the train about this incident. Everyone agreed that the Austrian soldier must have been a Ukrainian, and since I was part Ukrainian our strange resemblance became less incredible.

I have wandered from my story. A few days after the sinking of the *Portugal,* Romanin and I got a telegram from Moscow saying we were both being transferred to the same field medical detachment and instructing us to proceed to Moscow at once, and from there to our new unit, organized by the Union of Cities.*

After my scrape with the *Portugal* I would have been glad to stay with the train, so this new assignment did not altogether please me. But I couldn't get out of it. One consolation was that I would be working with Romanin.

* The Union of Cities had been organized in August, 1914, by Russian municipalities and wealthy citizens to operate ambulances, hospital trains, and rear-area hospitals; later it took over many supply functions for the army. Although distrusted by the Tsarist government, it became essential to the Russian war effort.

We were given a noisy farewell at the station in Odessa. Someone decided to hire for the occasion, with Lipogon's help, a small Jewish orchestra. Old men in dusty coats stood imperturbably on the platform, playing waltzes and cakewalks, and, after the third signal bell, they played the march, "Grief for the Fatherland." Hundreds of passengers, as well as hundreds of those seeing them off, shouted their delight at this magnificent farewell.

In the end Lelya threw her arms around me, kissed me, made me promise to write, and whispered to me that she wanted to transfer to a field unit or a field hospital, too, and that we would probably run into her soon in Poland.

The train started. Lipogon lifted his cap over his head and held it there until the train had disappeared. The violins sobbed. I leaned out of the window and for a long time I could see Lelya's white scarf which she was waving after the train.

And just as always, when one part of my life has ended and another started, grief began to fill my heart. Grief, and regret for what was over, for the people left behind. I knew only one thing: that it was right for me to live as I had lived for the last year, with a constant change of place and people. It was right for me to live this way as long as I wanted to devote my life to literature.

Nothing had changed in Moscow: the apartment with its kitchen smells impregnated in the walls, Galya endlessly worrying about something, and Mama quiet, her lips pressed tight together as before.

I was given a uniform in Moscow, an overcoat with strange silver shoulder straps with a single star, and I presented myself to a man named Chemodanov who was in charge of all medical units in the field. Romanin had gone off earlier, leaving me a note in which he wrote that Chemodanov was a good man, an expert on music, author of many articles on musical questions. I remembered what Captain Bayard of the *Portugal* had said about nobody attending to his own business in this incomprehensible country. I thought the captain had a fairly strange notion of what was a man's own business; in time of war, everybody's business ought to be the defense of Russia. I was sure of this.

Chemodanov—a tall, black-haired, very polite man in a field jacket—greeted me easily, but with a trace of distrust.

"I'm afraid," he said, "you'll find things difficult in your new detachment."

"Why?"

"You're a shy man. And in this situation, that's a liability."

There was no protest I could make to this.

My detachment was somewhere near Lublin. I could find out its
exact location only in Brest. So I went off to Brest. I traveled in an
upholstered car filled with officers. I was embarrassed by my new
uniform, by its shoulder straps with a single little star, and by my
sword with its glittering hilt. A captain who was my neighbor in
the compartment noticed this, asked me who and what I was, and
gave me some worldly advice.

"Son," he said, "just salute as often as you can, and say only
two things: 'May I?' to your seniors, and 'Please' to your juniors.
This will save you from any trouble."

But that captain turned out to be wrong. The very next day I
went into the dining car to eat. All the tables were filled except for
one free place at a table where a heavy, gray-haired general was
sitting. I walked up, bowed slightly, and said:

"May I?"

The general was chewing roast beef. He mumbled some kind of
answer. His mouth was so full of meat that I couldn't be sure what
he had said, but it seemed to me it was "Please."

So I sat down. The general, when he had chewed his roast beef,
looked at me for a long time through sharp, round eyes. Then he
asked me:

"What kind of clothing are you wearing, young man? What
kind of uniform is it?"

"It's what they gave me, Your Excellency," I answered.

"Who gave it to you?" the general shouted in a frightening
voice.

The whole car was now quiet.

"The Union of Cities, Your Excellency."

"Mother of the Blessed Virgin!" the general thundered. "I have
the honor to be a member of the staff of the commander-in-chief,
but I never suspected anything like this. Anarchy in the Russian
army! Anarchy, breakdown, and debauchery!"

He got up and stalked out of the car, snorting loudly. I could
then see for the first time the imperial monogram on his shoulder
straps.

Dozens of laughing officers were now looking me over.

"Well, you've done yourself a bad turn!" a tall cavalry captain
told me from the next table. "Do you know who he was?"

"No."

"General Yanushkevich, on the staff of the commander-in-chief,
the Grand Duke Nikolai Nikolaievich. His right hand. My advice
is to go back to your car and not to stick your nose out of it until
you get to Brest. You might not survive a second time."

I found what they called the Medical Units Base in Brest—a little house hung with wild grapes. It was almost empty. There was only one old nurse who was waiting for Gronsky, the chief of the units. It turned out that I would have to wait for him too. He was the only one who would know where my unit was stationed.

The nurse was a Pole, who spoke with an accent, and she kept on saying, with sighs: "He's such a flighty man, Pan Gronsky. He flies in, makes a great racket, kisses us all, and flies away again. You never know what it's all about. Ah, Mother of God! I'm just withering away here to no good purpose, thanks to that feather-brain."

I had already heard about Gronsky from Chemodanov. He had been an actor in the Polish Comic Theater in Warsaw. He was a gallant and courageous man, with many virtues, but frivolous in the highest degree. Because of this, and his short stature, he was called "the little knight."

"You'll see for yourself," Chemodanov had told me. "It's as if he had jumped out of the pages of a Sienkiewicz novel."

I washed after my trip, drank coffee with the old nurse Panna Yadviga, and lay down on a folding cot. I wasn't sleepy. I found a tattered book on the window sill, Sarcey's *The Siege of Paris,* and started to read it. Outside the window the wind was rustling the grape leaves.

Suddenly an automobile stopped outside the house and raced its motor deafeningly. Someone stamped out of it, jingled his spurs on the steps, and threw open the door. I saw a little man in uniform with exultant, gray eyes, a nose as enormous as Cyrano de Bergerac's, and fluffy, light-brown mustaches.

"My child!" he cried out in a high-pitched voice, and he hurled himself toward my folding cot. I barely managed to stand up.

"My child! I am happy beyond measure! We have been waiting for you like manna from heaven. Romanin has been pining away for you."

He embraced me tightly and kissed me three times. There was the faintest fragrance of violets in his mustaches.

"Just wait!" he shouted at me, and he ran to the window, leaned out, and called down: "Panna Yadviga! Good morning! Good news. I've lined up the most wonderful unit for you. They all stutter, and butter wouldn't melt in their mouths. What? I'm deceiving you?"

Gronsky raised his arms to the heavens:

"I swear before Pan God and his only son Jesus! I'll take you there tomorrow morning in this limping Ford. All three of us will go."

He turned away from the window, and called out:

"Artemenko! Come here!"

An orderly assigned to the base walked into the room, his boots squeaking.

"Let me look at your open, honest face," Gronsky said.

Artemenko turned his glance away shamefacedly.

"Where are those five cans of condensed milk? The ones that were under my cot?"

"I have no idea," Artemenko shouted at him.

"You son of a bitch!" Gronsky said. "Let this be the last time. Otherwise—a trial, the disciplinary battalion, a sobbing wife, unhappy children. Get out of my sight!"

Artemenko dashed toward the door.

"Stop!" Gronsky yelled in a loud voice. "Bring me a box out of the automobile. And don't break it, you rascal!"

Artemenko dashed out of the room.

"My child! My son!" Gronsky said, as he took me by the shoulders, shook me, and stared into my eyes. "If you only knew how sorry I am for every lad who lands up in this madhouse, this bedlam, this burning pigsty, this nest of lice, this hellish meatgrinder, this devil's sabbath that's called war. But put your hopes in me. I will stand by you."

Artemenko dragged a plywood box into the room. Gronsky kicked the top of the box with his polished boot. The top flew off, but so did the sole of his boot.

"I humbly offer you," Gronsky said politely but sadly, and he pointed to the box. Chocolate bars were packed tightly in it, covered with waxed paper.

Gronsky sat down on the cot, took off his boot, and looked at it for a long time, frowning.

"Amazing!" he said with inexpressible sorrow, and he shook his head. "And frightening! It's the third time this week I've torn the sole off. Artemenko? Where are you hiding?"

"I'm here," Artemenko snapped, standing right next to him.

"Take my boot to that pockmarked rascal, that virtuoso of shoemaking, Jacob Kur. Tell him to have it fixed in an hour. If he doesn't I'll hop over there in one boot and I'll chop his rotten little hut to ribbons with my sword. I'll make him dance."

Artemenko took the boot and darted out of the room.

"Well, how are you?" Gronsky asked me. "That old turkey, Panna Yadviga—may God give her a hundred kicks in the croup! —hasn't pecked a hole in your head yet, has she? Where can I send her, since she bats her eyes and falls into a swoon whenever she hears strong language? They certainly sent me a fine nurse! Come on, let's have some tea with brandy. No? And in the evening we'll go over to the officers' mess. There'll be a concert there. We'll be off at dawn tomorrow. That is, of course, if that great nobleman, Pan Zvonkovoi, my chauffeur, manages to fix his motor."

"What's wrong with it?"

"It was shot up. At Lyubaryov, at the railroad crossing. God knows where all those bullets came from! A-a-ah! You're reading Sarcey? A remarkable book. But I prefer Zola. I like analytical writers best of all. For example, Balzac. But I love poetry."

Gronsky took a small volume out of the pocket of his field jacket, tossed it in the air, and said with genuine pathos in his voice:

"*Eugene Onegin!* I cannot part with this. Never! Let the world fall to pieces, but these words will go on living in their own immortal glory."

Pan Gronsky had already made my head whirl. He looked me carefully in the face, and began to fret.

"My son! Lie down, and sleep until the concert. I'll wake you up."

I lay down willingly. Gronsky stamped downstairs. I heard him washing under the faucet, snorting and whistling the "Marseillaise." I could hear Panna Yadviga sigh and call on the Mother of God. Then Gronsky said:

"Although I'm only a worm compared to him, I'll still bust that adjutant in the nose. I'll go as far as shooting him. Sealed and delivered."

Then I fell asleep.

I was wakened by a noise which sounded as if a tightened cord had been snapped in the room. It was already deep twilight and the high, dark-green sky spread out beyond the open window.

I lay there and listened. Panna Yadviga was praying out loud, then again came the sound of the broken cord. A reddish light appeared in the sky, and I heard the quiet throbbing of motors somewhere in the depths of the evening.

"Get up!" Gronsky yelled at me. "There's a Zeppelin over Brest!"

I jumped up and went out on the balcony. Gronsky and Artemenko were both standing there, staring at the sky.

"There he is!" Gronsky showed me. "Don't you see him? A hand's breadth to the left of the Great Bear."

I looked hard, and I could see a long, dark shadow slipping lightly and quickly across the sky. Rifle fire cracked out steadily quite near us. Shrapnel exploded over our house with yellow flame.

"Not bad!" Gronsky said. "If it goes on like this, our own bullets will be falling down on our heads. The German dropped two bombs and is going home. The show's over. Let's go. Tea, by the way, is ready."

After tea, Gronsky and I went to the officers' mess. It was in a long wooden shed whose windows looked out on a garden. Fresh air floated in from the garden.

I wanted desperately to sleep. Through my drowsing I heard a rumbling bass voice:

> At twelve o'clock at night,
> The drummer gets up from his grave . . .

I opened my eyes. A tall, clean-shaven officer with his hair parted in the middle was singing.

"He's a famous singer," Gronsky told me, and he gave his name, but I had dozed off again without hearing it. I slept through the whole concert.

We left in the morning. The great nobleman, Pan Zvonkovoi, turned out to be a snub-nosed, goodhearted mechanic from Penza. When he listened to Gronsky's conversation, he just grinned and shook his head in admiration, saying: "Well, well!"

I remember quicksands, wide shell-pocked roads, villagers who were frightened to death. Up to their hubs in the sand, the wagons of the fleeing peasants came toward us. We left Panna Yadviga in one of the smaller villages.

Toward evening we finally reached the village Vuishnitsa where Romanin's unit was stationed. The yellow and black flag of a communications commandant was flying over a house built of planks. The dust raised by the wagons and the cattle hung in a heavy cloud, and slowly settled back on the ground.

Some old Jews with armbands—they were serving as emergency military police—were running from house to house, driving the inhabitants out to dig trenches around the village. There was a hollow, repeated roaring in the distance. An artillery duel was going on.

Everything was frightening, suffocating, and disorderly. Dozens of fires were burning through the village. The fleeing Polish peasants were sitting and lying side by side in their carts drawn up around the fires. Little babies, their faces turning blue, squirmed in the arms of exhausted, bareheaded women. Dogs barked. Drivers swore as they tried to make a road through this human jumble. They struck people with their whips and drove their wheels over the peasants' piles of goods and chattels, and linen, shawls, and shirts dragged along behind the wagons. Crying women would snatch them out from under the wheels and carry them to the fires. But the things were already covered with tar, ripped, and black with dirt.

Very ancient-looking Jews in reddish wigs were dragging junk out of their scraggy houses—feather beds, china, old sewing machines, greenish copper basins—and tying them up in sheets and blankets. But I didn't see a single cart or a single wagon which could have hauled the stuff away.

We found Romanin's detachment at an old inn near the exit from the village. The earth had been tramped down around the inn, and four enormous iron kettles were boiling there on iron tripods.

Soldiers were messing around the kettles. Romanin was shouting hoarsely at an officer who was gray with dust.

"Yes, you can go to hell!" Romanin was yelling. He noticed Gronsky and me, waved to us, and turned again to the officer. "One of your cows is dying every thirty minutes. You're turning them loose on the roads. So what are you being so stingy for?"

"I must have a statement," the officer said dolefully. "For every cow we lose we must draw up a statement. Imagine how happy I'd be to be court-martialed because of you."

"Well then, let's go and draw up a statement, the devil with you!" Romanin said, taking the officer by the elbow and leading him into the inn. He looked around, smiled at me, and yelled out: "I'll be right with you. As soon as I finish dealing with this cow captain."

We walked into the inn. It was empty, and it smelled of cold smoke. Cockroaches raced in a frenzy along the walls when they saw us.

"Have a smoke," Romanin told me, "because you'll have to go to work right away. You can see what's happening. And I'll go and butter up this cattle captain."

I sat down on a broken bench, lit a cigarette, and listened. Women were crying outside the window and asking the soldiers something, the cows were mooing heartrendingly, and the rumbling in the distance grew more and more frequent.

Little streams of sand shot up through the cracks in the floor after every explosion and fell back onto a hunk of black bread standing on the table. I moved the bread.

Three voices were now shouting behind the partition: Romanin was droning something, the officer was mournfully quarreling with him, and Gronsky was calling out something in a singing, exasperated tenor.

"Give me the two cows and here's your statement!" Romanin yelled. "And get out of here! I have nothing to feed these people. They're peo-ple! Children are dying like flies, and you're interested in calligraphy. You ought to be ashamed of yourself, Captain!"

Then everything was quiet behind the partition. Romanin came out.

"Well, wonderful," he said in a hoarse voice, and he embraced me. "You got here just in time. I almost killed that fool. I got two cows away from him. Take some orderlies—you'll have to kill one cow right away and cut up its carcass and put it in the kettles. We haven't time to wait for it to cool. These people haven't eaten in two days."

Romanin lifted the dirty curtain at the window and looked out at the village pasture outside.

"What can be done?" he said. "I haven't slept, I think, for five days. Well, that's unimportant. Get to work, and we'll talk later, we'll find the time somehow."

Even though Gronsky had told me on the way that some medical detachments, including ours, had been ordered to take care of the feeding and doctoring of Polish peasants, since Poland had begun to evacuate its towns and villages and to get out of the war, I still had no idea of how this was done.

"Don't ask anybody about anything," Romanin told me. "Just do whatever you think is necessary. To hell with your manners and delicate feelings now! They'll do you no good, and you'll be paying for them with dozens of human lives."

Romanin assigned two orderlies to me. By the light of the fires in the courtyard of the inn they killed a mangy cow. Its dry horns stuck in the ground. Blood flowed out into little pools, not mixing with the dust. The three of us cut up the carcass. The rolled-up sleeves of my new shirt were soaked with blood.

We cut up the meat and hung it on the fence so that it would dry out a little. The dust was growing thicker. The flames of the fires were orange spots in the dust. The old glass in the windows of the inn shook and danced and jangled.

Gronsky walked into the courtyard.

"Good-by, my son," he said, taking me by my bloody sleeve and hugging me. "I'm off to the third detachment; things are bad there."

"What's that rumbling?" I asked. "More wagons?"

"That isn't wagons," Gronsky answered. "That's the artillery retreating. Well, good-by. May God give you success. Don't slow up feeding these people. That's dangerous, my child."

He embraced me again, turned around, and walked out of the courtyard. His head was hanging. It seemed as if he had a yoke around his neck.

Then we stuffed the meat into the kettles. A dirty, gray foam formed on the broth. We scooped it off onto the ground with big skimmers. Thin dogs, piling up on each other, licked up the fat and the dirt.

The food was ready in the middle of the night and we began to serve it to the refugees. Hundreds of shaking hands were held out to the orderlies, holding cups, old plates, glasses, and basins. Women, after they had got their food, tried to kiss the orderlies' hands.

The crying, which couldn't be distinguished from laughter (and maybe it really was laughter with all these hungry people smelling the hot beef), hung heavy over the crowd. They drank and ate on the spot, scorching themselves and mooing like the cattle.

In ten minutes the kettles were empty. Romanin ordered us to fill them again. We cut up the second cow, and dressed it, and again the dust settled in a black film over the fresh meat, and clouds of night flies appeared from somewhere. The children cried again, and the wagons clattered past, and men went on swearing. And again there was a rumbling in the distance, no longer as far away as in the evening, but significantly nearer.

By dawn we had fed a second lot of the fleeing peasants. Dawn broke crimson and foggy, and there was a smell of burning. Black columns of smoke stood against the horizon. The orderlies said this was burning grain.

A Cossack patrol galloped through the little village. They rode up to the square in front of the synagogue, went into two or three houses, and then galloped away. Smoke began to pour out of the houses. Flames stretched up toward the sky, and people shouted.

Sparks fell on the sleeping children. The peasants' junk started to burn. Women grabbed their children and, dropping everything else, ran to the outskirts of the village. Their men followed them.

We cleared out of the place through smoke and the smell of burning. The horses were snorting and prancing. The orderlies hid their heads in the turned-up collars of their coats.

"Go to Pishchats and to Terespol," Romanin told us. "I'll ride ahead and look for quarters. But you go along with the ambulances. Pick only country roads, leave the big roads alone. They're all jammed. If I'm not in Pishchats, go straight on to Terespol. Well, good-by."

We embraced each other, and Romanin said:

"You wouldn't have got this on the *Portugal*."

He clapped me on the shoulder, hopped a little on one leg next to his horse, holding on to the pommel, then swung himself heavily into the saddle, and rode off at a trot along the side of the road.

We walked all day along little roads. I checked the map often. The smoke of fires surrounded us now on all sides. It formed into heavy wreaths and floated off to the east.

It seemed to me that the only peaceful sound I heard that day was the rustling of willow leaves when we stopped to water the horses at a shallow river.

We caught up to the fleeing peasants. The wagons and the artillery caught up to us. More and more often we heard the word "Mackensen," the name of the field marshal commanding the German army, which was advancing behind us.

We stopped twice to bury our dead beside the road. The first time it was a child. He lay on a checked shawl—obviously, the mother had taken it off to give him. Someone put a sprig of winter cress, pulled up with its root, on the child's breast.

The second time it was a young peasant woman with light, wide-open eyes. She was looking quietly into the sky where a yellow sun was shining through the smoke. A bee had got caught in the woman's hair and was angrily buzzing. It must have been caught there a long time; it couldn't find its way out.

When we had already ridden fairly far beyond the fresh graves, a lanky orderly, a meek man named Spolokh, said to me:

"Well, we've buried the woman, Your Excellency. It's my guess that she was the mother of that little child."

"Why?"

"She was lying there without any shawl on her head. And her shawl had been wrapped around the child. So it seems to me she must have been his mother."

"War is mother to some, and the devil is mother to others," a stocky orderly named Gladishev said suddenly.

I rode for a while, and it made me very tired. Sand gritted in my teeth. I wasn't thinking about anything then. Well, if you like, not about anything except the fact that I had just buried two people and that I didn't even know their names. I remembered the woman's arms, covered with golden, hardly visible, little hairs, and the clean, bulging forehead of the child.

Who would have thought that death would come like that into their lives, into their little village, where the periwinkles had not yet blossomed, where there might still be the smell of hot bread, death driving them out of their house in a hurry and in tears, killing them in strange places, in the quicksand, along the road, where the steel rims of cart wheels would screech a hand's breadth away from their faces, now asleep forever?

"Your Excellency!" Spolokh said to me.

"What's the matter with you?"

"You should stop what you're doing, this remembering. I advise you against it. You'd better listen to me. I've been in the war for a whole year."

"What gave you the idea that I was remembering anything?"

"How could I not see it? Don't you know how clear it is on your face?"

It was hard to believe that only yesterday I had been in Brest, drinking coffee at a table with the old nurse and Gronsky, sleeping on a soft cot, breathing the fresh night air.

We got to Pishchats in the evening—the sand slowed us up. There was no Romanin there.

Piles of old junk and torn-up books lay on the street. I picked up a few books, looked at them, and threw them back—they were written in some kind of incomprehensible ancient Hebrew alphabet.

There were no people left in the little village. Cowering cats poked about from courtyard to courtyard.

We stopped to rest in a building where there had been a barber's shop. A sign hung over the rattling glass-paned door with a bell on it: it showed a black-haired, red-cheeked youth, wrapped up in a snow-white towel, sitting in an armchair, his boots with high women's heels stretched out in front of him. Half of his face was covered with soap. An enormous razor, held by no human hands, hung threateningly in the air over the young fellow's cheeks. The fellow was smiling carelessly. On the sign was written: "Viennese hairdresser. Isaac Moses and his grandson."

All the floors in the barbershop were shaky. At every step one took, the broken pier glass covered with dried soapsuds shook and rattled. There was a smell of eau de cologne. Some thick tattered magazines, *Ogonyok* and *World-wide Panorama* and *Argus,* were lying on a little bamboo table. Sleepy flies drummed against the window.

We made ourselves some tea. I didn't want to sleep. I wanted to sit in the barber's chair, leaning back against the worn velvet headrest and closing my eyes to think. About what? About the noise the sea makes, and about how cicadas crackle in the dry mountains. About an autumn evening in Alushta when the big yellow leaves are floating down from the plane trees. About a happy girl running to meet someone. About poetry. And God knows about what else, so long as it was far from the war.

But we had to be on our way. Again the pungent smell of horses' sweat, the yelling, the screeching of wheels, the hard saddle, and sand and more sand.

Now the long plumes of smoke no longer stretched out behind us. There was a crimson glow instead, and then the stars were shining quietly. But still an iron thundering rolled across the earth, the barren thunder of war, the voice of the Krupp cannons which had been built to rip human bodies to pieces.

I dozed again, and through my sleep I seemed to see falling stars, first here and then there, cutting through the canopy of heaven. It was as if heaven were sending its messengers to the earth, to find out what was being done by these descendants of Leibnitz and Humboldt and Herschel, great Germans all of them.

It was day when we arrived, at last, at Terespol.

TWO THOUSAND VOLUMES

In Terespol I found Romanin in the house of the village priest. The dark wooden house stood in a garden which was a wilderness of celandine and nettles. In places, crimson hollyhocks stood up through the tall weeds.

The priest had not left Terespol with the fleeing peasants. He met me, with Romanin, on the steps of his house. He was a tall, thin man with lively eyes. His brown boots showed underneath his shabby soutane.

The priest gave me his blessing, as was the custom in those days, and said:

"My home is open to everyone. Like the house of God. Come in, my son. Make yourself at home."

The priest's voice was pitched very high, like a little boy's.

We walked into the house. Our footsteps made the glass shake in the windows. The priest opened a door into a dark, low-ceilinged room. Hundreds of books were standing on wooden shelves along its walls.

"I don't want to see the Germans," the priest said suddenly. He raised his big hands above his head, as if he were warding off the prospect. "May the Virgin Mary protect me from them! I don't want to lay eyes on a single Prussian. May the loathsome night be cursed when each one of them was conceived in some dirty bed under the portrait of Chancellor Bismarck!"

Romanin nudged me, but I didn't understand what he wanted to warn me about.

"Bismarck looked down goggle-eyed at the conception of every German now alive," the priest said with disgust, "and thought to himself each time: '*Ach, mein Gott!* One more brave soldier for the Fatherland. *Ach, mein Gott,* how good you are to send Germany so many red-haired fellows!'"

The priest walked slowly along the shelves, running his hands over the bindings of the books. It was as if he were counting them. Then he turned around suddenly.

"As long as I've lived," he said in Polish, "I've been collecting these books. Two thousand volumes on history. I wanted to save them, but where would I get wagons enough for them? And so, you see, I've stayed with them. You can take out any book and look at it. But I see you're very tired. Rest."

The priest patted me on the shoulder with his dry hand and walked out, rustling his soutane.

"Pretty good?" Romanin asked. "We've become friends. What hasn't he got here! That shelf there is all about Suvarov. And that one—about Napoleon. And up above, the Middle Ages and the works of the Church Fathers."

I picked out at random a thick book in a crackling cover. It was Carlyle's *History of the French Revolution.*

"We'll move to Brest at dawn tomorrow," Romanin said. "Everything's going to the devil. All these books, too, and their crazy owner. Go and get washed; you look like a Negro. There's a little bathhouse in the garden. It was heated a while ago."

I went out to the bathhouse. Nettles were growing up to the roof of its leaning frame. The boiler was full of warm, muddy water. I put some pieces of rotten wood from the fence under it, and lit them. Dampness drifted through the broken window; evening was approaching.

I undressed, and was amazed at the weight of my dusty clothes and boots. Then I sat on the bench for a long time, waiting for the water to heat. I lit a cigarette, and let my mind go blank. It felt good to be alone for a little while, and it was good to breathe the fresh air coming in from the garden. A cloud of midges swarmed in a pale shaft of sunlight. Some white umbrella-shaped flowers were blooming above the window sill.

It was so quiet that I could hear our horses snorting where they were tethered to the trees in the garden. Then a slow rumbling rolled up from a great distance, passed over the bathhouse, and died away somewhere in the west.

A gray cat jumped up to the window sill, looked at me, and mewed. Then he walked around all the walls of the bathhouse and examined my boots. It was quiet and dark inside them. The cat mewed again, but questioningly this time, and began to rub up against my legs. I could barely hear his soft fur crackling.

I petted him. The cat purred with satisfaction.

"You can dig in here in the rear," I told the cat. "Nobody will touch you. Men in steel helmets won't hunt you down to kill you for unknown reasons. How about changing places with me?"

The cat looked as if he hadn't heard me. He walked calmly out of the bathhouse without even looking around.

"You swine!" I said after him. "You're a pig and an egoist."

I very much wanted him to come back. I needed some kind of living being who could not understand what war was, and who might think the world was just as fine a place as it had been a month or a year ago. For the nettles were still growing in the garden, the sun still shone over the village, it was still possible for him to drowse in an old armchair and quiver his whiskers whenever something mysterious moved in the dusty books.

Fatigue scrambled my thoughts. I wanted to sort them out, to think out, once and for all, what had been smarting in my heart for a long time. I wanted to think about kindness, and a warm shoulder, a shoulder one could hold to tightly.

"Mama!" I said to myself in a low voice, but then I thought of Mama's dry, tight-pressed lips and her anxious face. No, she couldn't help me. But who could then? There was no one. Maybe sometime in the future, if there was going to be a future, I'd find someone with a big and tender heart. . . . But I had lost Lelya, too, and no longer saw her.

The heavy thunder rolled over the bathhouse again. Jackdaws flew out of the elm trees around the church with frenzied cawings. Romanin came up to the window.

"What happened to you? Did you fall asleep?" he asked. "Pan Priest has found some cherry jam."

"I guess I must have dozed off," I admitted.

"Young man," Romanin said, "I'm not pleased with you. What have you been thinking about here? Get washed in a hurry, and come and have some tea."

An old man in a rough smock—the sexton of the church—put out the tea in the room with books in it. He put a gray tablecloth on a round table, and on it glasses and a sugar bowl made of dull, gray glass. Only the cherry jam stood out with its clear, pomegranate-colored sirup.

We got out our provisions: canned meat, some biscuits, and some cranberry juice. We had nothing else.

The gray cat came in. His name was Velzevul.

We invited the priest to the table. Before sitting down, he murmured a short prayer. We stood while we listened to it.

"You are polite young men," the priest said, and he smiled.

"May the blessings of God be on you," he said as he sat down. "May the Blessed Virgin watch over your every step. You don't believe in her, of course. But she is real. And may she turn her gaze on you, and turn away the hand of your enemy."

The priest pushed away a cup and turned to the sexton who was sitting, drinking tea at the edge of the table.

"Yanosh," he said, "you go and open the church, and we'll have services all night and all tomorrow."

"Yes, Pan Priest," the sexton agreed in a low voice, and he started to stand up. "All night and all tomorrow."

"We will celebrate the great litany for the downtrodden."

"Yes, Pan Priest," the sexton said again, very low. "The litany for the downtrodden."

"And then we will celebrate a Mass to Pan God to ask him to help Poland to rise again like a phoenix from the ashes."

"Yes, Pan Priest," the sexton agreed hollowly, "like a phoenix from the ashes."

"Amen!" the priest said.

"Amen!" the sexton muttered, and he lowered his tousled gray head.

Romanin and I felt awkward listening to the incantations of the priest and the mumbling of his janitor. The priest must have sensed this, for he got up quietly and walked out. The sexton limped after him.

I lay down on the couch which was covered with black oilcloth, pulled my overcoat over me, and was swallowed up in a buzzing darkness.

I woke up suddenly, without any reason. It was obviously late night. Something began to sound, and then it grew quiet, in the pitch-dark garden outside the open window. I looked at the window: there was neither moon nor stars. The sky must have been covered by clouds.

A deep silence was all around me. But I had the feeling that I had been wakened by some kind of sound. I lay and waited. I was sure the sound would come again. I wanted to smoke, but I delayed lighting the match, simply to avoid breaking the safe darkness of the night.

I waited. Expecting the unknown sound began to frighten me. I lay there for several minutes, then suddenly turned over and sat up. The overcoat slithered to the floor noisily.

The noise had come—a strange, long-drawn-out, clattering, exhausting sound like an old man crying. What was it? It died away and then started again, and I recognized the slow pealing of the church bells. The priest was holding his service in the middle of the night, celebrating the great litany for the downtrodden.

I stretched out my hand for the box of cigarettes on the chair, but just then a whistling started over the roof of the house, a crimson flame followed it, there was a loud explosion, and then for a long time I heard a strange kind of rattling, as if small stones were being poured down on a cobblestoned street.

Romanin jumped up and lit a candle. The whistling passed over us again. Again an explosion sounded outside the window, lighting up the whole garden.

"They're shelling us!" Romanin shouted. "Get dressed. Saddle the horses. I'll get the wagon harnessed."

I was already dressed. I walked out into the garden with an electric flashlight. The horses stood there pointing their ears and drawing tight the ropes with which they were tied to the trees. The wakened orderlies were shouting to each other. A glow started to spread at the edge of the village. It helped us get ready quickly.

We were in a hurry. Infantrymen were already thronging in confusion through the village.

When we rode by the church, its doors were partly open. Inside it, candles were smoking. It was obvious that the sexton had lit all his reserve supply. I could see a big crucifix over the altar.

The priest was standing in his lace cape on the church porch, holding a black cross high above his head. In the light of the fires around us I could see the brown boots underneath his garments. The sexton was standing behind him.

When we had ridden up to the church porch, the priest made the sign of the cross in the air over us and said loudly:

"May the Blessed Virgin of Virgins, the lily of Heaven, the mother of all sufferers, protect you!"

The glow from the fires fell on the priest's clothing and on his face. The flames flickered and made it seem that the priest was smiling.

We rode out to the edge of town. The shooting died down. There was a smell of dust raised by the horses, and of marsh water. Behind us we heard again the clattering sound of the church bells.

"He must be a little out of his head," Romanin said.

I made no answer, but turned up the collar of my coat and lit a cigarette. A chill went through me. All I could think of was how to get warm.

THE VILLAGE OF KOBRIN

From Brest we went out to the village of Kobrin. Pan Gronsky went with us in his scratched and battered Ford.

Brest was on fire. The fortifications had been blown up. The sky behind us was filled with pink smoke.

Outside of Brest we came across two children who had lost their mother. They were standing on the side of the road, holding on to each other, a very little boy in a student's overcoat and a thin little girl about twelve. The boy had pulled the visor of his cap down over his eyes to hide his tears. The little girl was clinging tight to the boy with both arms around his shoulders.

We put them in our wagon and covered them with old coats. A biting rain was falling.

We reached Kobrin in the evening. The soil, as black as coal, had been kneaded in the wake of the retreating army. Slanting houses with their rotten roofs pulled down over their eyes stood up to their thresholds in the mud.

Horses were neighing in the darkness, lamps flickered dimly, broken wagon wheels screeched, and the rain poured off the roofs in noisy torrents.

It was in Kobrin that we watched the evacuation from the village of a Hebrew holy man, a so-called "*tsadik.*" Gronsky told us there were several such *tsadiks* in western Russia and in Poland. They always lived in small villages. Hundreds of people used to come to them from all over the country for advice on how to live. The whole population of these little villages used to live on the money spent by these visitors.

A crowd of disheveled women was huddled around a flat-roofed wooden house. A closed carriage, drawn by four mangy horses, was standing in front of the door. I had never seen such an ancient carriage. Some dragoons were standing, smoking, around it. They were apparently the convoy for the *tsadik* along the road.

Suddenly the crowd started to shout, and to surge toward the door. The door opened, and an enormous, tall Jew with black bristles on his face walked out carrying in his arms, as if he were a little child, a completely withered-up old man with a snow-white beard, wrapped up in a bright blue quilt. Behind the *tsadik* streamed some old women in cloaks and some young men in caps and long coats.

They placed the *tsadik* in the carriage, the old women and the young men climbed in, too, the cavalry sergeant major called to his men to get in their saddles, and the carriage moved off, jouncing, in the mud. A crowd of women ran after it.

"Do you know," Gronsky said, "that a *tsadik* never leaves his house during his lifetime? And they feed him with spoons. On my word of honor!"

We were billeted in Kobrin in a damp old synagogue. Only one man was sitting there in the dark, muttering something between a prayer and a curse. We lit some lamps and saw an ancient Jew with sadly laughing eyes.

"Oi-oi-oi!" he said to us. "What happiness you've brought with you for us poor people, my dear soldiers!"

We were sullenly quiet. The orderlies dragged some sheet iron in from the courtyard, we made a fire on it, and started to boil water for tea. The children we had picked up outside Brest sat quietly watching the fire.

Gronsky walked into the synagogue, tightening his belt, and said:

"My friends, unharness the wagon. To hell with it! I'm not going to move an inch until dawn. The army will be pouring through this little village. It'll grind us to powder. Feed these children something."

He looked at the children for a long time, and the light from the fire shone in his light eyes. Then he talked to the little girl in Polish. Her answers were hardly audible, and she never raised her eyes.

"When will this all end?" Gronsky asked unexpectedly. "When will we get our fingers around the throats of those who brewed up this bloody mess?"

Gronsky swore profusely.

We were all silent. Then the old Jew stood up. He walked over to Gronsky, bowed to him, and asked:

"My dear Pan, is it possible that you don't know who profits from this unhappiness?"

"Not I, and not you, old man!" Gronsky answered. "And not these children, and not all these people."

Sparks flew past the windows; they were from field kitchens which were passing the synagogue.

"Go out to the soup kettles," Gronsky said. "All of you go. Get something to eat."

We walked out to the field kitchens. The little boy went with us. The orderly Spolokh held on to his hand tightly.

The hungry crowd of refugees was straining toward the kettles. Soldiers were holding them back. Torches flared in the dark, lighting up, it seemed, nothing but eyes, the bulging, glassy eyes of people who could see nothing except those uncovered, steaming kettles. The crowd was even more violent here than in Vuishnitsa.

"Let me go!" someone cried out desperately.

The crowd seemed to give a jerk. It wrenched the little boy from Spolokh's hand. The boy stumbled and fell under the feet of hundreds of people who were lunging toward the soup kettles. He didn't even have a chance to cry out.

Men tore the food basins from each other's hands. Women hurriedly stuffed pieces of gray stewed pork into the mouths of children in their arms. Spolokh and I shoved toward the boy, but the crowd shoved us back. I couldn't yell. A cramp caught me in the throat. I pulled out my revolver and waved it in the air. The crowd gave way. The boy was lying in the dirt. Tears were still wet on his pale, dead cheek.

We lifted him up and carried him back to the synagogue.

"Well," Spolokh said, and he started to swear. "Well, God grant us a little strength, and we'll make them pay for this."

We put the little boy down on an overcoat inside the synagogue. The girl saw him and stood up. She was shivering so hard that we could hear her teeth clicking.

"Mama!" she said quietly, and she ran toward the door. "Mama, my mama!" she cried, and she dashed out into the street.

The wagons were clattering by.

"Mama!" she called desperately outside the window.

We stood there numbed, until Gronsky yelled out:

"Bring her back! Fast: To hell with all of you!"

Romanin and the orderlies rushed out onto the street. I ran with them. There was no sign of the little girl.

I untethered my horse, jumped on him, and rode into the jam of wagons. I slashed at the cart horses with my whip, cutting a path through them. I galloped along the sidewalk, and then turned back. I stopped soldiers and asked them if they hadn't seen a little girl in a gray coat, but they didn't even answer me.

Hovels were burning on the outskirts of the village. The glow bounced back and forth on the puddles in the road, and made still worse the confusion of carts, wagons, guns, horses, trucks—all the disorderly mess of a retreat at night.

I went back to the synagogue. The girl wasn't there. The little boy was lying on the overcoat, pressing his pale cheek against the wet cloth. He looked as if he were asleep.

There was nobody in the damp, dark building. The fire had died down, and only the aged Jew was sitting near the little boy and muttering his half-prayer, half-curse.

"Where are our men?" I asked him.

"How would I know?" he answered, and he sighed. "Everyone wanted the hot soup."

"Pan," he said to me quietly and politely, "I am a harness maker. My name is Iosif Shifrin. I don't know how to talk well, but what I say lies on my heart. Pan! We Jews know from our prophets how God can take revenge on man. But where is he, that God? Why hasn't he scorched with flame those who dreamed up all this misery? Why hasn't he gouged their eyes out?"

"God is God!" I said rudely. "You talk like a stupid man."

The old man smiled sadly.

"Listen," he said, and he touched the sleeve of my coat, "you listen to me, you educated and intelligent man."

He was quiet for a little. The glow hung motionless outside the windows of the synagogue.

"Here I sit and I think. I don't know as well as you do who is to blame for all this. I didn't even go to school at the *cheder*. But I'm not yet entirely blind, and I can see a few things. And so I ask you, Pan, who will have to pay for this? Who will pay, and pay dearly, for this little boy? Or are you the kind of good man who has compassion and forgiveness for all those who gave us this present, this war? My God, when will people at last get together, and make a decent life for themselves?"

He raised his hands toward the ceiling of the synagogue and cried out in a piercing voice, closing his eyes and swaying backward and forward:

"I cannot see who will give us our revenge! Where is the man who will dry the tears of the poor and give the mothers milk, so their children don't need to suckle at dry breasts? Where is the man who will sow grain on this earth for the hungry? Who will take gold away from the rich and give it to the poor? For those who stain the hands of men with blood and who rob the poor will be accursed to the end of time. They will have no children, and no grandchildren. Let their seed rot, and their own spit kill them like poison. Let air turn gray for them, and water become boiling oil! Let the blood of a child poison the bread of the rich, and let that bread kill them so that they die in torture like dogs!"

The old man was shouting, holding up his arms. He waved them, his hands clenched into fists. His voice thundered, and filled the whole synagogue.

I could not stay there. I walked out of the synagogue, and lit a cigarette, leaning against the wall. The rain was cold, and the fog clung closer and closer to the earth. They seemed to be trying to make me confront my own thoughts about the war. One thing was clear for me: we had to put an end to this, no matter what it cost. We had to expend all our strength and all our heart's blood so that justice and peace might triumph across a desecrated and impoverished earth.

TREACHERY

In Kobrin we were ordered to move north. We went, almost without stopping, until we got to the little village of Pruzhana near the Belovezhskaya forest.

Along the way we passed endless untilled fields overgrown with wild mustard. Brest, which had been blown up, was still smoking in the southwest. In the fields around Pruzhana we saw cannon with shattered barrels, and we stopped.

Some soldiers in mud-caked overcoats were sitting around the guns. Some were smoking, others were fixing their packs, still others sat there doing nothing, looking at us dully. I walked up to them.

"What's this?" I asked a bearded soldier, and I pointed to one of the broken cannon. The soldier was leaning against the wheel of the gun carriage, smoking. He looked at me glancingly, and made no answer.

"What's this all about?" I asked again.

"So I'm supposed to report to you!" the soldier growled. "What kind of an officer are you? Can't you see what it is? It's a cannon."

"Why is its barrel broken?"

The soldier turned away and waved his hand. The tearful voice of a young soldier without a cap answered for him. His shaved head shone like a glass ball.

"Well, what are you worrying about, young man?" he said sadly. "There's no rest from all of you. Go jump in a pond."

"What's he asking about?" another soldier with a greenish face interrupted. He was squatting on his heels, scraping the dirt off a dried rusk with a little stick. "What's eating him? Can't he imagine what's wrong with the cannon? Treachery—that's what's wrong."

"Treachery!" the bearded soldier repeated in a hoarse voice, and he made himself a cigarette. He clenched his dark fist and shook it at the east, where the wind was blowing in the thin broom.

"Treachery, curse their god, their mothers and their hearts! Now the artillery retreats before the transport carts. There's no ammunition. And what there is explodes inside the muzzles. And there aren't even cartridges to shoot back. What are we supposed to do? Fight the Germans off with sticks?"

"Treachery," several hollow voices said. "It's nothing else but treachery."

Our wagons started up. I drove away.

This was the first time I heard at the front that black word— "treachery." But it was soon being repeated all through the army, all over the country. Some said it in a whisper, some in full, hoarse voices. Everyone said it, from transport soldiers to generals. Even wounded men, when they answered the question: "How were you wounded?" replied sullenly: "By treachery."

The name of the Minister of War, Sukhomlin, was heard more and more often. There was talk of the enormous bribes he had received from big industrialists who were supplying the army with defective shells. The rumors quickly spread wider and higher; people began to accuse the Empress, Alice the Hessian, of being in charge of German espionage inside Russia.

Anger grew. There were still no shells. The army rolled back toward the east, unable to hold the enemy.

We marched across the southern part of Grodnensky province, feeding refugee peasants, directing them toward the rear, collecting the sick and distributing them among the hospitals.

Heavy rains started. The roads were covered with yellow, foaming puddles. The rain seemed as yellow as horses' urine. Overcoats never dried out; a reek of dogs clung to them. The wind steadily blew the leaves along the roads and whipped the branches like birch trees.

The places we went through—Pruzhana, Ruzhana, Slonim— had been picked as bare as bones by the retreating troops. There was nothing left in the little shops except bluing and wallpaper paste. "The Polish infantry has cleaned us out," the frightened Jewish merchants complained.

Romanin and I talked together less and less. His face, above the strap of his cap which he kept fastened constantly under his chin because of the wind, seemed to me harder and more angular.

Pan Gronsky went off somewhere in his beaten-up Ford and got us supplies. He showed up rarely—disheveled, unslept, with crumpled cheeks. His fluffy mustaches grew out and covered his mouth completely, which gave him the look of an old man. Every time he came, he would take me by the elbow, lead me to one side, and tell me in a confidential whisper:

"Never mind! Don't be disturbed, my boy! As soon as this devil's war is finished with, we'll go to Petrograd and we'll throw that oaf with his Hessian degenerates off his throne, we'll feed them to the dogs and the pigs. And Poland will arise again. May God protect her! You can't defeat a nation which has produced men like Mickiewicz, Chopin, Slovatsky.* It can't be done! All the best men of Poland will gather around their fame like soldiers around a bonfire. And they will swear to make Poland great again."

Every time he told me the same thing, even in the same words, like a man possessed. I didn't know whether this was because he was tired or sick. Gronsky's eyes burned feverishly, and he would hold my elbow so tightly that it was hard not to cry out from the pain. I remembered that insane people are said to develop great strength in their hands.

I told Romanin about my misgivings. He looked at me sharply, and said in an ugly way:

"Well, and do you know the difference between insane and normal men? You don't? Then to hell with you and your suspicions! I spit on them. Maybe I'm mad myself."

I had never seen Romanin in such an evil mood.

"Why don't you tie up the wild beast inside you?" I asked him, trying to seem completely calm.

He smiled a crooked smile, took me by the shoulder, and pulled me toward him, then immediately turned away and walked out.

This was in Slonim, in a little shop where kerosene had been sold recently. The floor was covered with sheet metal, and kerosene stood on it in puddles. There was nowhere to sit. I leaned against the wall, smoked a cigarette, and then followed Romanin outside.

The detachment was already leaving. Rain was pouring off the tarpaulin raincoats. Tousled crows flapped down and sat on the rotting edges of the roofs and opened their beaks to caw, but no caws came out—the crows must have realized that there was no point. You can't caw for dry weather.

* Yulii Slovatsky (1809–1849) was a Polish Romantic poet who was driven into exile after the uprising of 1830–31.

IN THE MARSHY WOODS

Monotonous marshy woods stretched out beyond Slonim. A good many young aspen trees grew there. They stood in thin gray rows and the rain fell on them in thin gray streaks. The sky would clear only in the afternoons. It was green, and cold. A sharp wind harried scraps of dirty clouds.

Romanin was riding in front, and I behind. I saw a young White Russian peasant come out of the woods. He took off his cap, grabbed Romanin's stirrup, and walked along beside the horse, humbly asking for something. Tears were shining in his eyes.

Romanin stopped, and called me.

"A refugee is giving birth," he said, without looking at me, "here in the woods. This man's wife. All the others left, and he's stayed alone with her. It seems the birth is hard."

"She's being tortured, my Pan," the peasant said in a singing voice, and he wiped his eyes with his cap.

Romanin was quiet for a minute.

"Deliver the baby," he said, still without looking at me, and he fussed with his horse's bridle. "None of us knows how to do it. Any more than you do. But still, in a business like this, intelligent hands are best."

I could hear ridicule in his voice. I felt the blood drain out of my face.

"All right," I said, controlling myself.

"We'll wait for you in Baranovichi." Romanin held out to me his wet hand. "Do you want an orderly, too?"

"I don't need any orderly."

I took a bag with medicines and the simplest surgical instruments—we had no others—and turned off on a path into the woods. The peasant, whose name was Vassil, ran along beside me, hanging on to my stirrup. Mud from the horse's hoofs splattered in his face. The horse was running at a fast trot.

I tried not to think about what might happen in a few minutes in those woods. I didn't look at the refugee, and I kept quiet. I felt terrible. I had never in my life even been near a woman in labor. Suddenly I heard a wailing cry, and I pulled up my horse. Someone was yelling not far from us.

"Faster, Pan!" Vassil said in despair.

I spurred on my horse. He broke through a thicket. Vassil let go the stirrup, and fell behind me.

The horse carried me into a little clearing. A fire was dying in the middle of it. Beside the fire sat a little boy about ten years old in a black cap pulled down over his ears. He was rocking back and forth, with his arms around his knees, quietly and monotonously repeating: "Oy, Zosia! Oy, Zosia! Oy, Zosia!"

Smoke from the dying fire filled the clearing. It was caught by the low branches of the little nut trees, so that it was hard to see anything.

I jumped off my horse. A farm wagon was standing on the other side of the fire, with a woman sitting on it, hanging on to its edge by her hands. I saw only her black, distorted face with enormous white eyes. She was howling, with her mouth wide open, through lacerated lips, sometimes leaning forward, and then bending way back, howling steadily, raucously, like a wild animal.

A shaggy dog had crept under the wagon, where it lay licking its lips.

My heart turned to ice. The cold rose into my head, and my fright disappeared at once.

"The fire!" I yelled at the little boy. "Get it going, fast."

He jumped up, stumbled, fell, and then darted off into the woods for some dry brush. Vassil ran up. I hadn't the least idea what to do. I could only guess about it darkly.

First of all I took off my overcoat and washed my hands. Vassil poured the water for me, out of a pitcher, and his hands were shaking so badly that he poured most of the water right past my hands. The little boy brought some dry wood and started the fire going again. It was beginning to grow dark.

"Take the little boy away," I told Vassil. "He doesn't need to watch this."

"But he's her brother," Vassil answered hurriedly. "There's a spring in the woods back there; maybe he could bring some water."

"Yes, water, water!" I repeated convulsively. "And a clean towel, or some old rags."

"Zosia has two clean shirts," Vassil mumbled helpfully. "You run for some water, Mikholaichik, and I'll get the shirts. I'll get them."

I had one more moment of real hesitation, just as I was pulling my field jacket off over my head. Everything grew dark, and I stopped. I wanted to quiet myself, and to collect my thoughts. What thoughts? About what? I had no thoughts—nothing but despair.

At last I decided, pulled off the jacket, rolled up the sleeves of my shirt, took a flashlight out of my pocket, and handed it to Vassil.

"Give me some light."

I walked up to the wagon. I must have been deafened by emotion. I could no longer hear the woman's cries, and I tried not to look at her.

I saw something pink and small. I put out my hands quickly and carefully, took hold of it, and pulled it toward me with all my strength. I didn't know if this was the way to do it, or not. I was doing everything as if through sleep. I did not know then nor can I remember now whether the baby came out quickly. I remember only the feel of little shoulders. It must have been his shoulders. I pressed the palms of my hands around them and once more pulled toward myself, carefully but strongly.

"Pan!" Vassil cried out, and he grabbed me. "Pan!"

I stood there and staggered. Something warm and wet was lying in my hands. And suddenly this incredible thing sneezed.

I did everything that needed to be done after this calmly, although my head was beginning to swim. Vassil and I washed the baby, then wrapped him up tightly in the shirts and some old rags. I held the swaddled baby in my hands, and was frightened that I might drop him. Vassil was holding his own sleeve tight in his teeth, shaking his head from side to side, and crying.

I shouted at him, walked up to the woman and carefully laid the baby down by her side. She smiled all over her face when she looked at him, and she just touched him with a thin, dark hand. This was her first child.

"My little dear one," she said, and her voice was barely audible. "My light. My unlucky little son."

Tears were pouring out of her open eyes. Unexpectedly the woman grabbed my hand and pressed her hot dry lips against it. I didn't pull my hand away, for fear of disturbing her. My hand was wet with her tears.

The baby squirmed, and began to squeak a little, like a kitten. Then I took my hand away, the woman took the child, and shyly pulled out her breast.

Vassil had stopped crying, and only kept wiping his eyes with his sleeve. The little boy was squatting on his heels by the fire and looking happily at him. Far away in the woods we could hear some bursts of machine-gun firing.

I washed my hands, put on my overcoat, sat down by the fire, gave Vassil a cigarette, and lit one myself. Seldom in my life has a cigarette brought me such satisfaction as on that gloomy evening.

But the calm didn't last long. The woman worried me. I got up and walked back to the wagon. In the dancing light of the fire, her face looked inflamed. She seemed to be asleep, lying on her side and holding the baby tight against her breast. The dark shadow of her eyelashes fell on her cheek.

I really saw the woman then for the first time, and I was astonished at the happy and moving expression on her face. At that time I didn't know that the faces of almost all women become beautiful and calm, if only for a short time, immediately after labor. This beauty of maternity must have inspired the great artists of the Renaissance—Raphael, Leonardo, and Botticelli—when they painted their Madonnas.

I carefully picked up the woman's dry hand, and felt for her pulse. It was there, weak but regular.

Without opening her eyes, the woman took my hand again and caressed it gently, sleepily. But this was not in thanks, as it had been the first time. Now in her stroking of my hand she was trying to reassure me. It was as if she were saying: "Don't worry. I'm all right now. You take a rest."

I had never dreamed, while I was riding along that shell-pocked road an hour earlier with an empty heart, that anyone would touch me so gently. Every day of the war dragged on like a night without shelter. And I would never have believed that a smile of heartfelt gentleness would so quickly and so fleetingly shine on me in the dreary loneliness of that night.

Short rumblings rolled one after the other across the dark horizon beyond the woods. They seemed to be racing after each other.

"Pan," Vassil said to me, "the German is coming up. Where can we go?"

An unnatural calm possessed me; I was incapable of rational thinking.

"Don't worry," I told him. "We'll stay right here for another two or three hours. It would hurt her to be jounced now on that wagon."

"But the Pan won't leave us?"

"No, I won't leave you."

Vassil was reassured, and he and the little boy began to boil a thin soupy *kasha*.

I knew it was dangerous to stay in the woods. Judging by the

sounds of the firing, the Germans were already close. Maybe there
had been another breakthrough, and, as always happened in such
cases, the front might crumple up, disappear, melt away without
a trace. But I just didn't want to go away from that clearing.

I sat next to the wagon and watched the fire. Nothing erases
time so quickly as watching a fire at night. I watched each little
twig disintegrate, I followed each spark flying up from the dry
brushwood, I stared at each gray, glowing piece of ash.

The woman was breathing quietly and evenly. "No," I said
to myself, "you won't escape from the war, no matter how much
you want to. You're not alone in the world."

I looked at my watch. Two hours had gone by while I was
staring at the fire.

"It's time to get ready," I told Vassil.

We ate the soupy *kasha*. Zosia woke up and Vassil fed her. She
ate little and slowly, looking all the time at her child. Vassil
bothered her, trying to make her eat his *kasha*. She carefully pushed
him away:

"I don't need it now."

There was still a long time before dawn. Vassil harnessed the
horses. We fixed Zosia as comfortably as we could, covering her
with two old jackets, and the wagon began to move carefully out of
the woods onto the road. It was empty there, with the wind blowing.
The pine trees sighed mournfully. The glare of artillery firing had
died down. I rode in front, and lighted the road occasionally with
my flashlight so that Vassil could drive around the holes and bumps.

Romanin had told me that the old barracks of the Baranovichi
garrison were only a few kilometers away. I was hoping that I
might find some retreating field hospital at those barracks and be
able to fix Zosia up there until she was in good shape again.

We were in luck. There was a field hospital in the wooden
barracks of the camp. It was already packing up and getting ready
to evacuate. But we got there in time.

I went up to the senior surgeon. He was sitting in an empty
hut, drinking tea out of a tin cup. He was an unshaved old man
with eyes as red as a rabbit's. He took off his glasses and listened
to me quietly, twisting the string on the sleeve of his doctor's
gown—it had dropped into his tea and become soaked.

"That means you delivered the child?" he asked, and he looked
at me suspiciously.

"Yes, I did."

"Just delivered it any old way?"

"There was nothing to do," I answered, trying to justify myself.

"Sometimes it works out that way, that there's nothing to do," the doctor agreed. He dipped a piece of sugar in his tea, and then put it in his mouth. "The baby, it's clear, came out by himself. So don't put on too many airs, Lieutenant."

"I am not putting on any airs."

"That's wrong, too. In your place, I'd be proud of myself. Want some tea? What's next, after tea? Next we'll have soup made of cat meat. We're leaving right away. Meanwhile, put your refugee in the theater. Tell the nurse on duty that I ordered it."

"In what theater?" I asked, surprised.

"In the Imperial Opera Theater in Petrograd," the doctor answered, crossly. "Don't be so stupid! Here in this camp there's a summer theater. Or rather, was one. For the gentlemen officers. Take her there."

We carried Zosia to a decaying barracks which had been the camp theater. The nurse on duty had disappeared somewhere. We put Zosia down ourselves on a folding cot.

There was a stage at one end of the barracks. Its torn canvas curtain had a landscape painted crudely on it—the cliffs of Divo and Monakh at Simeiz in the Crimea. It was hard to imagine why those cliffs, and a sea as clear as laundry bluing, and the black crowns of cypress trees had been painted on a curtain here.

"Where's the mother?" a woman's voice asked behind a wall.

I whirled away from the cot toward the dark wall. I had recognized Lelya's voice.

She walked in quickly. The lock of hair still stuck out as it always had from under her nurse's cap. Coming in from the daylight, she couldn't see the woman lying on the cot in the dark barracks, or us, the two men standing beside her.

"Who brought her here?" Lelya asked.

"He did, the Pan Lieutenant," Vassil muttered, pointing at me with his cap.

Lelya turned toward me.

"You?" she asked.

I came out of the dark corner and walked up to her.

"Yes, I did," I answered. "I did, Lelya."

She turned white, moved back a step, sat down on an empty cot, and stared at me with frightened eyes.

"God," she whispered. "How are you? What are you standing there for? Like a statue?"

She held out her hand to me, without standing up. I bent down to kiss her hand, but Lelya pulled me toward her and kissed me on the lips.

"At last," she said. "It must be that you and I were born under a lucky star."

UNDER THE LUCKY STAR

The field hospital was not supposed to be evacuated until evening. I was afraid I wouldn't catch up to my unit, and I told Lelya that I would have to leave right away.

"Wait," she asked me. "If only for an hour. That won't make any difference. Just wait, and I'll be back right away."

She walked out of the barracks. Zosia asked me:

"Who is that Pan lady? Is she your fiancée?"

"Yes," I answered. What else could I tell her? Simplehearted people need answers they can understand.

"Keep quiet, Zosia!" Vassil shouted at her, frightened. "How can you talk to the Pan Lieutenant like that? God will punish you!"

Ten minutes later an orderly came in and told me the senior surgeon wanted to see me in his hut. He greeted me angrily.

"Just what are you finagling here, young man?" he asked, and the thick lenses of his glasses glittered at me.

"What do you mean, finagling?"

"I can find, begging your pardon, no other word for it. Actually, you're nothing but a civilian here! Your unit belongs to the Union of Cities. A civilian organization. Don't you realize that at the front you are under the command of military authorities?"

"It's sort of like that," I said.

"Not sort of like that!" the doctor yelled at me, turning crimson and coughing with indignation. "It's exactly like that. I must request you to behave in a proper manner. Otherwise I'll have you arrested. Sort of like that!" he imitated me, puffing out his cheeks.

"Yes, sir," I answered, "But I don't understand."

"Well, understand me now. I am offering to attach you to this hospital on special assignment. The necessary written instructions will be prepared. And they will be handed to you when you need them. As an explanatory document for your superiors. Who is in charge of you now?"

"The director of my unit is named Gronsky."

"Gronsky—Gavronsky—Pshiperdonsky!" the doctor said.

I kept silent.

"Ah, you, now your feelings are hurt!" The doctor shook his head reproachfully. "Stay with us a few days. After what happened with that childbirth, I would have been glad to take you on anyway. But in general, young man, don't be embarrassed. I am well informed about everything. I was young once myself. And I've suffered, too. And I hate old men who forget what it was to be young. I don't know why, but we don't make enough of love."

The doctor sighed loudly. The conversation had made my head spin. I could guess that Lelya had mixed into this.

"There are not enough men in my unit," I said. "You will understand that I can't desert . . ."

"Yes," the doctor sighed again. "Desert! Of course! You express yourself bombastically, young man, but I understand you. It's a rough situation. Well, all right! You're going to Baranovichi, and we're going to Baranovichi. We're leaving not this evening, but in two hours. We're empty. We turned over our last wounded yesterday to a hospital train. You come with us to Baranovichi, and that's all! And we'll take your new mother, too. We'll keep her under observation."

I agreed. The old man clapped me on the shoulder.

"Permit me to give you an old man's advice. Cherish love as the most valuable thing in the world. Treat love badly just once, and the next time you'll find it's no good to you. Yes-s-s! It'll turn out to be no good to you at all. Well, on your way! Glad to have met you."

I walked out of the barracks and saw Lelya. She was sitting not far away on a bench under a slanting wooden mushroom, the kind of shelter put up in army camps for men on sentinel duty.

I walked up to her. Lelya leaned forward and covered her face with her hands.

"No, no, no!" she said quickly, without taking her hands away, and she shook her head. "What a fantastic fool I am! I hate myself! Go away, please."

"I'm staying," I said. "We're going to Baranovichi together."

Lelya took her hands away from her face and stood up. I could see the marks of her fingers on her cheeks.

"Come on," she said, taking me by the hand, and we walked down the road. We walked as far as the first milestone, and then turned back. The wind was blowing, ruffling the puddles. Clouds were piling up from the west again, weighing down the wet horizon. We walked back and forth, holding hands, saying little. Lelya simply told me that after Odessa she had gone back to Moscow and had succeeded in getting transferred to a field hospital on the western front.

She didn't explain why she had done this. But everything was clear, and neither she nor I wanted to talk about it. We both knew that any words, even the wisest and tenderest, would sound wrong, and that we couldn't yet express that aching feeling of closeness which had now been born in both of us.

The hospital was evacuated at two o'clock. The first-aid wagons filed out one after the other. Vassil followed them in his wagon. The shaggy dog, tied to the wagon, ran along eagerly behind it.

I rode beside the field ambulance. Lelya and an older nurse in gold-rimmed glasses were riding in it. Sometimes I fell back and rode alongside Vassil's wagon, to find out how Zosia was. She nodded to me politely, and told me everything was fine. But Vassil was gloomy; he must have been wondering what would happen to him now. Would he find his friends from his village, or would he have to languish alone among strange people in White Russia?

About twenty versts short of Baranovichi, a group of armed soldiers was standing by the road with an officer riding a mud-caked horse. The officer held up his hand. The convoy stopped.

The officer rode up to the senior surgeon, saluted, and began to report something to him. The doctor watched him sullenly, biting his mustache. There was something ominous about this conversation between the officer and the doctor. We were all on guard.

But it quickly turned out that there were a good many sick refugees in a nearby village—you could see it from the road— and the officer was asking, on behalf of the chief of staff of the army corps that a part of the medical personnel be sent to this village to give first aid to the refugees.

The doctor agreed. Three wagons were taken out of the convoy.

"You're coming with us," Lelya said to me. "Taking care of refugees is your job. By evening we'll catch up to the hospital in Baranovichi."

"Let's go."

We turned off on a side road. The hospital convoy went on. Vassil stood for a long time beside the road, looking at us. He seemed to be wondering whether to come with us. But then he picked up the reins, and shouted to his horse, and the wagon rumbled off on the road to Baranovichi.

About a kilometer from the road we found some soldiers with rifles and a machine gun in a clump of bushes.

"Are the Germans really so close?" the elderly nurse in the gold-rimmed glasses asked fearfully. "Do ask them, please."

I rode over to the soldiers.

"Keep on going!" a soldier with corporal's stripes answered me; he didn't even look at me. "You're allowed to pass. But we're not permitted to talk to anybody. And nobody's allowed to stop here."

We rode on. The outskirts of the village were right ahead of us. It was raining. The wretched little village looked like a spread-out pile of manure.

"It looks as if they're waiting for the Germans here," I said to Lelya.

I looked to the west, where the Germans would come from, and saw a line of outposts across a pasture leading down to a ravine. Soldiers were sitting or lying in a long chain, each one fairly far from the next one. Well, that was that.

"But it's not against the Germans," said the orderly who was driving. "This is something else. Look over there."

He pointed to the east. There soldiers could be seen, too.

"The whole village is surrounded!" the orderly said excitedly. "It's got a ring around it. I feel something isn't right, sisters."

"What isn't right?"

"I haven't any idea. But it's bad that we've wormed our way in here. Nothing but bad."

The orderly turned out to be right. We rode into a deserted village. An empty two-wheeled Red Cross cart, part of a mobile brigade which was strange to us, was standing in the outskirts, and from its driver we learned the staggering news that we were in a trap.

There was smallpox in the village. An army was on the march all around it, temporarily dragging with it thousands of fugitives from villages along its march. The smallpox might break out in the army. So the mobile brigade had been sent to the village, which had been cut off so that no one could leave it. The order was to fire on anyone trying to get out.

The officer who had stopped us on the road had said nothing about smallpox.

The first feeling we had was one of indignation. Not because we had been caught in a trap, but because we had been brought to the village by deceit even though not one of us, of course, would have refused to help as a volunteer.

"It's impenetrable stupidity," Lelya said irritably. "If they hadn't fooled us, we could have brought what we needed to handle smallpox. And now we haven't anything. Even vaccines!"

"I'm not so sure, whether it was stupidity or not," the driver said.

"What kind of nonsense is this?" the nurse in the gold-rimmed glasses, Vera Sevastyanovna, said angrily.

"The devil only knows," the driver muttered. "The officers have their reasons for everything. They're always smarter than we are."

We couldn't set up a base in the peasants' huts—they were full of sick people. There was one empty shed on the common village pasture. The strange mobile brigade had already established itself there. We carried over to it our medicines and our supplies. A doctor, a nurse, and two orderlies were established there, but we found only the nurse, an eyebrowless creature with a sulky face. It was hard to get more than a few words out of her.

"Well, to the devil's mother with the mobile brigade," our orderly said. "It must be a fraternity of undertakers!"

As we unpacked our drugs in the shed, the doctor of the mobile brigade walked in. He was a young, flabby man, with dark bristles on his face and swollen eyelids.

"Greetings, and welcome, please!" he said when he saw us. It looked as if the meeting was an unpleasant surprise to him. "Do you realize where you've ended up?"

"With smallpox," I answered.

"Precisely! And do you know what smallpox is, young man? Have you seen it with your own eyes?"

"No, I've never seen it."

"May I have the honor of congratulating all of you? Do you have any vaccines? No? Welcome, if you please. What do you propose to do here? Play the gramophone? Listen to music?"

We were despondently silent.

"As far as I'm concerned," the doctor went on, "I've had enough. I've no intention of going on playing the fool."

"How can you talk like that!" Lelya said indignantly.

"Mademoiselle!" The doctor's face was twisted with evil. "Don't fly into a tantrum! It becomes you very well. In anger, you look simply delightful, but that's all! I repeat, that's all! It's straight bluff! It's just thoughtless, pleasant sounds. We and you are caught in a trap. How did Pushkin say it? 'Ah, you're caught, little bird, stay still, you won't escape this net.' Something like that, wasn't it?"

"You're playing the clown, doctor," Lelya said with disgust in her voice. "It's simply revolting."

"Laugh, clown," the doctor sang, and then he laughed. "And just what else is there for me to do? Perhaps you can tell me how to get out of this damned fix we're in?"

"He's drunk!" Vera Sevastyanovna said.

"Greetings, if you please, I'm drunk!" the doctor answered calmly, not in the least offended. "Do you have any morphine?"

"Very little. But we have a lot of camphor."

"If we had any morphine, I'd put them all to sleep. And that would make an end to it!"

"We've had enough of this foolish nonsense," I said rudely. "Turn over to us whatever you have. We'll do the work ourselves."

"If you please! Just do me the favor! I welcome you with all my heart!" the doctor cried out theatrically. "I will give you all my vaccines. Vaccinate the sick. Because they are all sick. This will be a remarkable medical experiment."

"Do you want to know something?" I said, and I walked up to him. "Shut your mouth, or I'll throw you out of here, even if you are a captain. There are no laws here any longer."

"You're absolutely correct," the doctor agreed. "There are no laws any more. Like in a city of the plague. Take the vaccines! Go to work! I want to sleep. I haven't slept for two days. That's something else you should take into consideration, my fine young idealists."

He went to a corner of the shed, lay down on some straw, and pulled an overcoat over himself, already half-asleep.

"Let him sleep, God be with him!" Vera Sevastyanovna said conciliatingly. "Sister, give us your vaccines."

"Write me out a receipt," the nurse answered. It was clear she had been paying no attention at all to our conversation with the doctor.

I wrote out a receipt, and the nurse gave us the vaccines.

"Well?" Lelya asked me in a whisper.

"Well what?" I answered. "It's a simple business. You stay here, while I start inspecting the huts with the orderly. I'll find out what's there."

"No! I won't let you go alone. Not because I can't get along without you"—she blushed a little—"no! It's just that it won't be so frightening if we're all together."

The four of us went out together—Vera Sevastyanovna, Lelya, the orderly, and I. A gray rain was soaking the field. Potato stalks stood in the gardens like black, broken bones. It was already autumn. Our feet slipped in the sticky clay, mixed with manure and old straw. There was not a single ribbon of smoke rising from the peasants' huts, yet everything around us smelled of smoke, like the stench of burned feathers. At the edge of the village was a great heap of half-burned rags, and the smell was coming from it.

"That's where they've tried to burn all the junk of the sick people," the orderly commented. "That's called disinfection," he added with a laugh, and then he was silent.

There were no dogs and no chickens in the village. In one

shed a hungry cow was mooing. It was mooing slowly, swallowing its spit.

"Yes," Vera Sevastyanovna said suddenly. "It's like Dante's Inferno."

We entered the first hut. On the threshold, Lelya tied a gauze bandage around the mouth of each of us. I opened the door, and a warm wave struck me in the face.

The windows in the hut were curtained. For a minute it was impossible to make out anything. I could hear only a monotonous child's voice saying the same words over and over again: "Oy, Granddad, untie my hands.—Oy, Granddad, untie my hands."

"Don't touch anything!" Vera Sevastyanovna ordered. "Make some light, please."

I lit my flashlight. At first we could see only a broken wooden bed, covered with a pile of clothes. Someone's legs, wrapped in old rags, hung down from the stove. But nobody was to be seen.

"Who's alive in here?" the orderly asked.

"I don't rightly know myself," an old voice answered from the stove, "whether I'm alive, or dead."

I turned my light on the stove. An old man was sitting there in a brown robe, with a ragged beard that looked as if it had been plucked.

"For you people to have come into the hut, for this I thank you," he said. "Help me, little soldiers, for I can't pull him out by myself."

"Who?"

"Why, he's lying on me here, my daughter's husband. Since yesterday evening. At first he was hot, like a stove, but now it's not pleasant even to touch him—he's grown very cold."

"My God!" Lelya said, very low. "And what is that?"

The pile of rags on the bed heaved and the child's voice said again: "Oy, Granddad, I can't stand it any longer. Untie my hands."

"Everything's finished there on the stove," Vera Sevastyanovna said. "Let's have your light here."

I pointed the flashlight at the bed, and we saw two eyes. They were enormous black eyes, shining with fever, with crimson spots on the cheeks below them. A little girl about ten years old was lying under the rags. I carefully threw the rags off her. The little girl shuddered, bent over, and held out her hands, which were tied together with a torn towel.

The shirt fell away from her chest and I saw smallpox for the first time—flaming crimson spots with black points which looked like dried tar. The spots seemed pasted on to the girl's greenish skin.

The little girl moved her head. Her dark hair fell forward. A rumpled red ribbon fell out of it.

The orderly brought in some cold water from the barn. He was upset at seeing how the sick had had their hands tied so they couldn't scratch their sores.

"Oh, what torture that must be!" he said in a low voice. "What can people do to deserve such treatment?"

Lelya gave the little girl a drink. I held up the girl's head. I could feel the dry fever in the thin back of her neck even through my leather gloves.

"Give me some camphor!" Vera Sevastyanovna said. The hut smelled of ether. After the camphor, we gave the little girl morphine. Lelya wiped her face with spirits of vinegar.

"Well, how about it?" the orderly said to me. "Let's take out the dead one."

Lelya put her hand on my arm, but released it at once. Her eyes were entreating me not to go near the dead man, but she said:

"Just remember . . . Well, all right, all right!"

The dead man was lying on a coarse cloth. We picked it up by holding on to the corners of the cloth, trying not to touch the corpse. We dropped him anyway, but only on the threshold.

"Put him in the shed," the old man advised us. "There are a couple there already."

The door of the shed was propped open by pitchforks. Inside an old woman and a girl about five were lying face down on the earth floor.

"Oh, war, war!" the orderly said. "If we could only push the generals and the politicians into this filth—nose first! The sons of bitches!"

We went back to the hut. We had to ventilate it, but it had already grown cold outside, like just before the first snow.

"We ought to heat the stove," the orderly said. "But they've burned up everything already. There's not a log left."

He went outside and I could hear him, puffing, wrench a board off the roof. We opened the door, and lit the stove.

"Granddad," Vera Sevastyanovna said, "get down. We'll give you a vaccination."

"What for?" the old man answered indifferently. "No, I won't live through this. I'll die of hunger, anyway. It would be an evil thing to waste your medicine on me."

But we vaccinated him, ventilated the hut, and promised the old man to send him some bread.

The farther we went, the worse it got. We worked, biting our lips and not looking at each other. The orderly muttered obscenities about everybody's mother in a low voice but no one paid any attention to him.

"This is all useless," Vera Sevastyanovna said at last. "We won't be able to save anyone. There never were any vaccinations here. And of course that clown, the doctor from the mobile brigade, was absolutely right."

"But what do you mean?" Lelya asked. "What can we do?"

"Not get infected ourselves. That's all."

"But how about the sick people?"

"Morphine," Vera Sevastyanovna said curtly. "So they'll suffer less."

The orderly spat, and swore a long oath.

We returned to our shed, where Vera Sevastyanovna vaccinated each of us.

A dark, agonizing time began for us.

We walked from hut to hut, injecting morphine, giving the dying water to drink, watching with silent despair as the few who had been given a respite by the disease grew sick themselves. We stacked up the corpses in the sheds. The doctor from the mobile brigade ordered that these sheds be burned. He took care of this himself, and each time it revived his spirits. The orderlies piled hay around the sheds and lit it. They burned slowly, but with great heat, and they gave off a heavy smoke.

Our shed was soon permeated by carbolic acid. Our hands were so burned by the carbolic that we couldn't wash them; water made them hurt unbearably.

At nighttime it was easier. We lay on the straw in a row, covered with overcoats and felt cloths. By the middle of the night we had warmed ourselves up, but we slept badly.

The doctor would talk in a low voice about his family in Berdyansk, about his wife, who was a thrifty housekeeper, and about his son, who was the quickest-witted boy in all the world. But nobody listened to him. Each of us thought about himself.

I lay between Lelya and a quiet, freckled orderly, a Pole named Sirokomlya. He cried often in the night. We knew that people cried at the front only about loved ones who had been lost forever. But we were all silent, and none of us tried to comfort him. His tears were useless. They didn't ease his sorrow but only made it worse.

Lelya, too, cried quietly sometimes in the night, holding tight to my hand. I could guess that she was crying only from the slight shivering of her body. Then I would carefully stroke her hair

and her wet cheeks. In answer she would press her burning face
to the palm of my hand and begin to cry harder. Vera
Sevastyanovna said to her once:

"Lelya, stop it. Don't weaken yourself."

The words worked. Lelya calmed down.

Lelya was always pulling back on top of me the overcoat which
would slip off. We never talked together at night. We lay there
quietly and listened to the rustling of the straw under the eaves.

Sometimes the roar of distant artillery fire would float up to
our shed. Then everyone would lift his head and listen. If the front
would only catch up to us quickly!

I don't remember what night it was that Lelya said to me, very
quietly:

"If I die, don't burn me in a shed."

Her whole body shuddered.

"Nonsense!" I answered. I took her hand, and I could feel my
own heart shrink. Her hand was as cold as ice. I felt her forehead;
it was burning hot.

"Yes," Lelya said sadly. "Yes . . . I noticed it yesterday. Only
don't leave me alone, my dear one . . ."

I wakened Vera Sevastyanovna and the doctor. The orderlies
also woke up. Lanterns were lighted. Lelya turned away from their
light.

For a long time everyone was silent. Then Vera Sevastyanovna
said:

"We must scrub, disinfect, and heat the hut next door. It's
empty."

The orderlies went out, talking to each other and sighing. The
doctor led me aside, and muttered to me:

"I will do everything that's in my power. Do you understand?
Everything!"

I quietly pressed his hand. Lelya called me.

"Good-by," she said, looking at me with a strange, quiet smile.
"Even if it wasn't for long, it was wonderful for me . . . very. But
there wasn't any way to talk about it . . ."

"I'll be with you," I answered. "I won't go away from you,
Lelya."

She closed her eyes, and just as she had before, when she was
sitting on the bench at the barracks, shook her head.

No matter how I prod my memory, I can't recall now in detail
what happened then. I can remember only in snatches.

I remember the cold hut, with Lelya sitting on the cot. Vera
Sevastyanovna undressed her, and I helped.

Lelya was sitting with her eyes closed, breathing heavily. For the first time I saw her naked girl's body, and it seemed to me priceless and tender. It was crazy to think that those long, flowing legs, those thin arms, those disturbing little breasts, had already been touched by death. Everything was dear to me in her feverishly helpless body, from the little hair on the back of her neck to the birthmark on her dark hip.

We put her to bed. She opened her eyes, and said distinctly: "Leave my clothes here. Don't take them away!"

Vera Sevastyanovna and I stayed with her all the time. By night, Lelya seemed to have lost consciousness. She hardly tossed at all, lying so still that sometimes I grew frightened and leaned over her to hear her breathing.

The night dragged slowly on. There were no signs by which one could know if it would soon be morning, no cocks crowing, no tramp of passers-by, no stars in the heavy sky. At dawn, Vera Sevastyanovna went back to the shed to rest for an hour.

When at last it began to grow vaguely blue outside the window, Lelya opened her eyes and called me. I leaned over her. She pushed me away weakly, and looked at my face for a long time with such tenderness, such sadness and care, that I couldn't control myself, my throat contracted, and I cried—for the first time in the long years since my half-forgotten childhood.

"Don't, my dear little brother," Lelya said. Her own eyes were full of tears, but she didn't cry. "Put a pitcher on the table . . . with water. There . . . in the shed . . . there's some cranberry extract. Bring it to me . . . I'd like to drink . . . something sour . . ."

I stood up.

"Also . . ." Lelya said, "I also want . . . my only joy, you mustn't cry. I've forgotten everyone, even my mother . . . only you . . ."

I ran to the door, brought some water back to Lelya, and quickly ran out of the hut. When I came back from the shed with the cranberry extract, Lelya was sleeping quietly and her face, with its half-opened mouth, struck me with its unnatural pale beauty.

I was late with the extract. Lelya, without waiting for me, had drunk the water. She had spilled some of it on the floor next to her cot.

I don't remember how long I sat next to her, guarding her sleep. A muddy light was already filling the window when I noticed that Lelya was not breathing. I grabbed her hand. It was cold. I couldn't find any pulse at all.

I ran to the shed to get Vera Sevastyanovna. The doctor, too, jumped up and ran back to the hut with us where Lelya was lying.

Lelya had died. Vera Sevastyanovna found a box of morphine under her dress on the table. It was empty. Lelya had sent me for the cranberry extract in order to take a fatal dose of morphine.

"Well, what of it?" the doctor muttered. "She deserved an easy death."

Vera Sevastyanovna said nothing.

I sat on the floor next to the cot, hiding my head in the turned-up collar of my overcoat, and I don't remember how long I sat there. Then I stood up, walked over to Lelya, lifted her head, and kissed her eyes, her hair, and her cold lips.

Vera Sevastyanovna pulled me away and ordered me to rinse my mouth immediately with disinfectant, and to wash my hands.

We dug a deep grave on a little hillock beyond the village, next to an old willow tree. You could see the willow from a long distance away. The orderlies made a coffin out of old black boards. I took a simple silver ring from Lelya's finger and hid it in my knapsack.

Lelya was even more beautiful in her coffin than she had been just before she died. While we were filling in the grave, we could hear rifle shots. There were not many of them, and they were repeated after regular intervals of time. This was the day when we learned that the guard around the village had been removed. They had gone away without warning us. Maybe these shots had been a signal, but we didn't understand it.

We left the village at once. Everything was empty all around us.

When we had gone about a half a verst, I stopped and turned my horse around. Just behind, in a thin mist, in the gloomy light of an autumn day, I could see the little cross over Lelya's grave under the spreading willow tree. It was all that was left of her girl's heart, her hair, her laughter, her love, and her tears.

Vera Sevastyanovna looked at me.

"Drive on," I told her. "I'll catch up to you."

"Your word of honor?"

"Go on!"

The wagon started. I sat there on my horse, and looked at the village. It seemed to me that if I should move even the slightest bit it would tear the last thread of life, I would fall from the horse, and everything would be over.

The wagon stopped several times, and waited for me, then it disappeared behind a copse of trees.

I rode back to the grave, sank down on my knees, and pressed my forehead against the cold earth. Under the heavy layer of wet dirt a young woman was lying, a girl who had been born under a lucky star.

What was I to do? Stroke this clay with my hand, this clay that lay against her face? Dig up the grave, to see her face again, and kiss her eyes? What was I to do?

Someone gripped me firmly by the shoulder. I looked around. The orderly Sirokomlya was standing behind me. He was holding a gray horse by the bridle. It was the horse of the doctor from the mobile brigade.

"Let's go!" Sirokomlya said, and he looked at me embarrassedly out of his light eyes. "You mustn't act like this."

For a long time I couldn't get my foot in the stirrup. Then Sirokomlya held it for me, I sat in the saddle, and rode slowly away from the grave through the cold, lead-colored rain.

THE BULLDOG

I did not find my detachment in Baranovichi. It had already moved on farther to Nesvizh, the military commandant told me.

I didn't want to go back to the hospital even for a short time. It was hard to meet people. I spent the night outside the town, in a railroad signalman's station on the way to Minsk, and in the morning I rode off toward Nesvizh. I didn't hurry my horse. He walked along, stopping sometimes as if to think things over, or simply to rest. Having rested, he would go on, swinging his head.

It was a fresh autumn day, without rain but with gray clouds. They hung low over the land.

I got to some little place while it was still daylight. I don't remember its name. I decided to stay there until the next morning. The retreat was slowing up, and our detachment could not have gone farther than Nesvizh. I was certain that I could catch up with it the next day.

The buildings were crowded into a hollow on the shore of a big pond. At one end of the village water was running through an old millrace; you could hear its sound everywhere in the village.

Dark willow trees leaned over the pond; they looked as if they were just about to lose their balance and fall into the deep water.

I asked some old Jewish women where I could spend the night. They pointed out an ancient inn, a wooden building full of chinks and smelling of kerosene and herring. The innkeeper, a little Jew with a shock of reddish-brown hair, told me that he had a place, of course, to spend the night, in a little room like a closet, but that an artillery officer had already settled himself in it and that it might be crowded.

He led me into a closet as narrow as a grave. The officer was not there, but he had set up his folding cot. There was just room for another cot, but the space between them was so narrow that you couldn't sit on the edge of either one.

"Well, you can spend the night here," the innkeeper said. "It's quiet, and we have no bedbugs, thank God! We can fix you an omelet or, if the Pan wants, some hot milk."

"How about the officer?" I asked. "Will he agree?"

"Oh, my God!" the innkeeper exclaimed. "That makes me laugh. Dvoira, do you hear what he's asking? Why, he isn't an officer. He's an angel from God."

I put my horse in the stable, fed him, and walked around the village. I didn't feel like talking or listening, to others. Every word, spoken or heard, widened the gulf between Lelya and myself. I was afraid my hurt would be blunted, deadened. I was guarding it, as the last thing left me from my love.

The only thing that did not irritate me, and which I did not want to hide from, was poetry. It came back to me from I don't know where and for reasons I didn't understand, out of the depths of memory, and its comforting language was not importunate, and did not disturb the hurt in me.

I walked down to the pond, sat on the bank under a willow tree, and listened to the water roaring along the rotten old millrace. Toward evening the clouds were covered by a feeble yellow film of light. Somewhere beyond the edges of the world a stingy sun was shining. The yellow sky was reflected in the water. It was dark and damp under the willow trees.

Somehow I remembered lines I had read a long time before:

> On my night journey, an old miller
> Opened his house to me, under black willows . . .

There was nothing remarkable in these words. But they had a magical healing power for me. The loneliness of a night journey moved inside me like a great quieting.

But then I had to hold my head in my hands—a faraway dear voice repeated the same words to me from a great distance, out of some dank, weather-beaten space. It was deep twilight there now over the deserted grave. There lay the girl from whom I should never have parted for an hour. I heard the words clearly: "There is no name for you, spring, no name for you, my faraway one." These had been her favorite lines. I repeated them to myself, and my voice sounded to me like Lelya's, which no one would ever hear again. Not I, nor anyone else.

I got up, and walked across the field behind the little village.

Twilight filled all the air between the sky and the brown fields. It was already hard to see the path, but I walked on and on. A dim glow appeared in the direction of Luninets. To the north a white star shone over a solitary, dark hut.

"Lucky star!" I thought. "She believed in it up to the last days before her death."

It was already dark when I went back to the inn. A cot had been fixed up for me in the little room. The artillery officer, a man with a dark face and faded eyebrows, was lying in the other cot. He was reading a book by the light of a candle.

When I walked in a hoarse growling could be heard from under the officer's cot.

"Quiet, Mars!" the officer shouted, sitting up and holding out his hand to me. "I'm Lieutenant Vishnyakov. Glad to meet my neighbor. Think we can manage somehow to sleep here till morning?"

He said this in an uncertain tone of voice.

"Dvoira!" the innkeeper called behind the wall. "Fix something for the gentlemen; maybe they want something to eat."

I did not want to eat. I drank some tea and lay down at once. My neighbor proved to be a silent man. This reassured me. An enormous yellow bulldog crept out from under his cot, came up to me, and looked attentively at my face for a long time.

"He's asking for sugar," the officer said. "Don't give him any. He has the habit of begging. It's no fun having a dog at the front. But I hate to get rid of him. He's a wonderful watchdog."

I petted the bulldog. He took my hand in his teeth, held it for a moment to frighten me, and then let it go. He was obviously a friendly dog.

I lay there for a long time with my eyes closed. Ever since I was a child I have loved to lie like that, pretending to be asleep and imagining all kinds of adventures and travels around the world. But now I wanted neither to imagine things nor to travel with my eyes closed. I only wanted to remember.

And I remembered all that I had lived through with Lelya and I felt sad that we had lived next to each other for so long but been so distant from each other. Only at Odessa, at Little Fountain, had everything become clear, both for me and for her. Or no, perhaps it was earlier, when we sat in the poor Polish hut next to the Wieprz River and listened to the fairy story about the lark with the golden beak. No, it must have been still earlier, in Khentsin, when the rain poured down and Lelya sat all night at the table next to my bed.

Then I remembered Romanin. What had happened to him? Why had he become so gruff with me? It must have been my fault. I remembered that my compliant ways had always irritated him— he called it slackness—and my inclination to see the best sometimes even in unpleasant people—he called this spinelessness. To him I seemed the "enervated intellectual," and this was all the more insulting to me because it was only in relation to me that Romanin was so prejudiced and unjust. "I swear," I told myself, "I'm not like that at all." But how could I prove it to him?

The clatter of iron-rimmed wheels woke me in the night. Artillery was rolling through the little village. Then I drowsed, maybe I fell asleep.

I was wakened by a terrifying, troubled howling in the little room. For the first second, I thought it was the bulldog howling. The cot next to me was shaking and bouncing. I lit a candle, The officer was roaring and wailing. He vomited, and a yellow foam trickled out of his mouth.

It was an epileptic attack, the "falling sickness." I had seen many such attacks in the hospital train, and I knew what to do. I had to get a spoon into his mouth and hold his tongue with it, so that he could neither bite it or choke himself to death.

A glass with cold tea stood on the window sill. There was a spoon in it. I grabbed it, and tried to push it into the officer's mouth, but it was so crowded and he was thrashing and flailing so hard that I couldn't manage to get it in his mouth.

I was holding him firmly by the shoulders when I felt a sharp pain in the back of my neck. Something very heavy was hanging on my back. Still understanding nothing, I raised my head to break away from this weight, and then I felt clearly the sharp teeth which were deep in my neck.

The bulldog had quietly hurled himself on me from behind, defending his master. Obviously, he thought I was choking him.

The bulldog made a swallowing motion with his clenched jaws. It stretched the skin on my neck, and I realized that I would lose consciousness in a few seconds. With a last effort of will, I made myself reach for the revolver under my pillow, and I fired backwards at the level of my ear.

I didn't hear the shot. I heard only the crash of a falling body, and I looked around. The bulldog was lying on the floor. Blood was pouring out of his shattered muzzle. Then he twitched convulsively, and went limp.

"They're fighting!" the innkeeper was yelling beyond the wall. "They're fighting, people."

"Quiet!" I yelled back at him. "Come in here! I need help."

The innkeeper came in in his underwear, holding a thick candle in a silver candlestick. His eyes were white with fear.

"Hold him," I told the innkeeper. "I'll put the spoon in his mouth, or he'll bite his tongue off. It's the falling sickness."

The innkeeper grabbed the officer by the shoulders and pressed him down. I forced the spoon into his mouth, and turned it edgewise. The officer bit the spoon so hard that his jaws creaked.

"Pan, you have blood on your back," the innkeeper told me.

"It's the dog. He jumped on me. I shot him."

"Oy, what is the world coming to!" the innkeeper cried out. "What have people done to each other!"

The officer sank down a little in the bed and grew quieter. The attack was ending.

"He'll sleep now for several hours," I said. "The dog needs to be taken away."

The innkeeper took the dog out and buried him in the garden. Dvoira came in—a thin woman with a good, humble face. I got a first-aid packet out of my knapsack, and Dvoira washed and bandaged the wound on my neck. I told the innkeeper that I didn't want to see the officer again and that I was leaving as soon as it grew light.

"That's right," the innkeeper agreed. "It would be unhappy for him, and uncomfortable for you, even though nobody's to blame in this. Come in our room. Dvoira, heat the samovar. Drink some tea for the road."

While I was drinking watery tea in the innkeeper's quarters, Dvoira said:

"Just think! One more minute, and he would have killed you. It makes me shake all over just to think of it."

My neck was hurting. It was hard to turn my head.

"Life is no longer life," the innkeeper said, and he sighed. "And a kopeck's no longer a kopeck, but just rubbish. You should have come here in peace time. Every day had its own order, and its own satisfaction. I'd open the inn early, and good people would drive

up in their wagons, some going to the market, some to the mill. I
know them all, for fifty versts around. They'd come into the inn,
and they'd eat and drink, some of them tea and some of them
vodka. And it was good to watch people eat the simple food, bread,
or onions, or sausage and tomatoes. And there would be good talk.
About prices, about the crops and the milling, about potatoes and
hay. And I don't know what else! About everything in the world, I
guess. It rested your soul to listen to it, and I never drove myself
for money. Just enough to pay off the district police officer. And I
had just one idea—to give my children an education. Well, they're
getting it all right, that education, they're soldiers in the army.
Everything's been ground to dust, all our life."

It was beginning to grow light. A thick fog hung over the
ground. The trees looked bigger in the fog than they really were.
The mist promised a clear day.

I said good-by to the innkeeper. He asked me to leave a note
for the officer. I wrote: "Excuse me. I was forced to shoot your dog."

When I had ridden away from the little village the sun came
out. Everything was shining with dew. Rusty groves of trees were
lighted by the early sun. From a distance it looked as if they were
rotting with some dark fever. A surprisingly fresh air stood over
the earth, as if it had been locked up for a long time and only this
morning released for the first time to float where it wanted to.

I stopped my horse, took the little silver ring out of my pack,
and put it on my little finger. It felt very warm.

I caught up with my detachment in the village of Zamirya, near
Nesvizh.

THE PUTRID WINTER

All was quiet on the front in October. Our detachment had stopped in Zamirya, next to the railroad from Baranovichi to Minsk. It was to stay there all winter.

I have never seen anything more dismal than that village. Low-roofed, dirty peasant huts, flat, bare fields, and not a single tree. Muddy transport carts filled this gloomy landscape, thin, shaggy horses, and transport soldiers who had by this time completely lost any kind of military appearance. Their shabby sheepskin hats, made of artificial lambskin, were torn, their earflaps twisted like broken birds' wings; their quilted jackets were greasy with lard; their overcoats were tied together with string. Nearly every transport soldier had a chewed cigarette of cheap tobacco stuck to his lip.

Late autumn was dark, with no sunshine. The windows in our little hut were always misted. Water streamed down them, and through them nothing could be seen.

The carts sank deep in the mud. Wind blew along the roads. Sticky clay from the streets was tramped in on men's boots. This made it uncomfortable inside the huts, and it bothered Romanin and me. We cleaned and scrubbed our own hut, and let no one in except on business.

When I got back to the unit, Romanin embraced me as if there had never been any misunderstanding between us. Clearly, it had been the result of being tired. He turned around to hide his eyes, and then he told me that I was a downright swine and that he had turned gray from missing me. He pointed to a gray lock of hair. It had always been there but now, it was true, it had grown bigger and whiter.

I told Romanin about Lelya's death. He sat at the table, blew his nose for a long time, and his eyes turned red. I tried not to look at him. Then he went out and came back very drunk, but quiet. This had never happened with him before.

I missed Gronsky. He had become ill, with some psychic disorder, they said, and had been shipped off to Minsk. They had sent us a new director in his place, the well-known lawyer and leader of the Cadet party, Kedrin. He was a short old man with a gray imperial beard and thick eyeglasses. In his gray frock coat, he looked like a large, intelligent rat. This was why we all called him "Most Honored Rat."

He talked boringly but politely, was incredibly naïve in military matters, knew nothing of the countryside or of real life, busied himself with political calculations and "analysis of the existing situation," and in general stood out in Zamirya, in the rapidly disintegrating army, like a white crow.

There were few refugees left. The greater part of them had been settled in neighboring villages. We had no work to do, and Romanin set about building a bathhouse in Zamirya. Most of the people who had nothing to do were gradually drawn into the construction of the bathhouse. It became a major undertaking. Experts, engineers, military specialists on baths and heating, came from Minsk and even from Moscow. Romanin quarreled with them all, became embroiled with them, even succeeded in driving some of them away.

The louse-infected rear waited for that bathhouse as if it were a gift from God. Soldiers regarded Romanin as their father and benefactor. Even the transport troops saluted him, and obeyed every order he gave.

On the question of the bathhouse Kedrin delivered wide-ranging speeches at evening tea, very skillfully constructed pronouncements rising sometimes even to generalizations. The business of bathing was explained not only in philosophical terms but also as one of the vital links in the progressive policy of the Cadet party which in the long run would bring happiness to our tortured Mother Russia.

Kedrin's speeches glittered with names and with quotations. He cited Tugan-Baranovsky, Struve, even Lassalle. Speeches like his would not have sounded out of place, as Romanin said, even from the tribune of the Duma. But in general they furnished us with abundant material for jokes at the expense of the aged Cadet. Kedrin took all these jokes in earnest, and each time was deeply offended by them.

Romanin used to send me to Nesvizh, or to Mir, or Slutsk and Minsk, to get materials for the bathhouse.

One day a red-bearded man with a coat slung over his shoulders appeared at our hut. His sheepskin hat managed by some miracle to balance on the back of his neck. His eyes were laughing. His voice was loud but pleasant. He claimed to be a specialist on baths and disinfection chambers. No one knew his name. We all called him "Red Beard."

He burst into our hut, settled down in it, and from that point on gave the whole bathhouse question a new aspect. He started conversations on the construction of the Roman baths, recollections of the Sandunovsky baths in Moscow, of the hot baths in Tiflis, and of how wonderfully Pushkin described them, then continued on Pushkin's prose, and on prose in general—Red Beard considered prose to be "the god of the arts"—and went on about whose prose was better, Pushkin's or Lermontov's, about the plot for *War and Peace*, which he said had been tossed off by Lermontov and fell into the hands of Leo Tolstoy, about Tolstoy's funeral at Yasnaya Polyana, about Anna Karenina, about Levin's hunting woodcock, about hunting in general, and about Chekhov's *The Seagull*. It turned out in the end that Red Beard had been in Chekhov's house at Yalta, that he had produced Chekhov's plays in provincial theaters, and that he had never had the slightest thing to do with the construction of bathhouses.

We never did manage to clear up his profession. He answered direct questions by quoting Maximilian Voloshin* whose verses, according to him, clearly expressed the character of his life:

> *Exiles, wanderers, and poets,*
> *Men thirsty for life, but powerless to be.*
> *For the bird—his nest, for the beast—his dark ravine,*
> *For us a crooked staff, and sacred poverty.*

Two days after Red Beard's appearance we could no longer imagine how we had been able to survive at all in that cursed Zamirya without him. Red Beard paid no attention at all to Kedrin. When the latter would launch one of his dull speeches, preventing general conversation, Red Beard would say with a goodhearted smile:

"Old man! Wait a bit! We'll call on you later."

Sometimes, especially at night, the conversation turned to vital things. We talked about revolution. Romanin was inclined toward the Social Revolutionary party, Kedrin spun his professorial threads around the Cadet program, and Red Beard said that a workers' revolution would dispatch both Romanin and Kedrin straight to the devil's mother. The name of Lenin and the word "Internationale" began to be repeated more and more often.

* Maximilian Voloshin (1877–1932) was a Symbolist poet whose work was filled with a kind of mystical patriotism.

When Red Beard talked, we were all silent. It seemed as if we could already hear the noise of crowds of people, the noise of revolution sweeping across Russia like an ocean breaking down the dikes.

Even Kedrin never interrupted Red Beard. Instead, he would polish his glasses with trembling fingers, blow his nose as if it were an instrument, and shrug his shoulders. This was Kedrin's way of expressing great indignation, like his way of pronouncing the word "pl-ee-ee-ze." He could manage to say it both arrogantly and defiantly at the same time. But then the wind usually went right out of him, and he would go off to bed, muttering to himself while he carefully hung up his uniform.

But once, when a nurse nicknamed "Raspberry" came to visit us from a neighboring medical detachment, Kedrin was unmasked as a desperate woman-chaser. He found in his trunk a bottle of Coty perfume from Paris and gave it to the nurse, who rolled her eyes skittishly and giggled with stupid delight. Kedrin minced around her, rubbing his hands together, until Red Beard shouted at him:

"Old man! Grow up! We'll call on you later."

After the February Revolution, Kedrin served for a time as commissar of the Provisional Government on the western front. It is easy to imagine how many toothless, nauseating speeches he must have given then. If the soldiers didn't murder him, it was just Kedrin's good luck.

I did a lot of traveling that winter through little towns and villages. Sometimes I went on horseback, sometimes by train.

White Russia looked at that time like an old painting hanging in the buffet of some little station near the front. Traces of the past were still visible everywhere, but they were only an envelop, out of which the contents were spilling fast.

I saw the palaces of the Polish aristocrats—the one belonging to Prince Radziwell in Nesvizh was one of the richest of them— their farms, their Jewish villages with their picturesque crowding and poverty, old synagogues and Gothic churches which here, among these stunted bogs, looked like tourists from abroad. I saw striped milestones left from the times of Nicholas I.

But the aristocrats were gone already, with their luxurious and reckless way of life, their humble "serfs" and their half-baked rabbi-philosophers, threatening Days of Judgment in the synagogues, and the rotting Polish banners of the time of the first uprising draped around the altars of the churches. It was true that the old Jews in Nesvizh could still tell stories about Radziwell's expensive pleasures, about the thousands of his "serfs" lining the entire road from the Russian frontier to Nesvizh holding flaming torches to welcome his mistress, the adventuress Miss Kingston, about the hunts, the feasts, the petty tyranny, the swaggering arrogance, the stupid haughtiness which were considered in those times the passport to status as a noble Pan. But people were already talking about these things with hostile words.

And now, during these years, this life and the muddy memories it left behind it were wiped clean away by the war itself. The war trampled over it, drove it into its final grave, drowned it under hoarse oaths and the lazy thunder of cannon firing in the winter, as if to clear men's throats. But in all the muddleheadedness and the confusion of war, some features of a new transitional time began to stand out sharply, and people felt anxious in their hearts, as if they were waiting for a slowly approaching thunderstorm.

The winter was a putrid one. Snow fell and grew soggy. And the weeks followed each other soggily. The fields were covered with a dirty porridge of snow. The damp wind blew stubbornly out of Poland, stirring the overripe straw on the roofs of the peasant huts of White Russia.

I loved my trips because I could be alone. After what had happened in the autumn I could not get rid of my feeling of alienation or my memories. Everyday life chopped up and soiled my thinking about Lelya. I was beginning to forget how her voice sounded, and this frightened me.

With a stubbornness which I couldn't understand, I treated myself roughly on these trips: I was soaked to the skin and frozen to the bone, I slept in old sheds, and sometimes right on the ground, I ate almost nothing, and I smoked acid-tasting cigarettes one after the other.

The slightest thing could give me an internal shudder, sad thoughts, and confusion. It was like this, for example, in Molodechno. I spent the night in an empty, unheated third-class railroad car on a siding. I woke up at dawn. Everyone knows those tight, chilly dawns which put an end to nights just as tight and cold. The winter belongs to night, and the days exist in winter like unwelcome boarders, trying to be seen as little as possible.

I lay on a wooden shelf under my overcoat, and warmed up a little. A bugle player was playing along the tracks. Some troop train must have been standing at the station. His notes were whining and jangling. Everything inside me shuddered, and I suddenly understood, listening to the whine of that bugle, all the helplessness of the world to which I belonged, all my corrupted, uncomfortable, lonely life. I remembered Mama, and my brothers fighting somewhere on a neighboring front, and Lelya, and I remembered how the heart grows hardened without caring for someone, and without kindness.

What was the reason for the helplessness of persons like me? I wanted to understand it. Obviously, it came from the fact that we had gone straight into life from our books, our misty poetry, our fine ideas, and from the fact that the people were moving ahead of us with complete indifference, not even noticing us. It must be that we were not the sons and helpers the people needed.

At the beginning of December I was coming back to Zamirya on horseback from a routine trip. I lost my way, and rode out on to a road near our front-line positions.

A gloomy wind was blowing. The road was covered with ice. My horse was moving at a walk, trying not to slip. It soon grew so dark that I couldn't see the bushes by the side of the road.

Somewhere in front of me I could hear a distant rumbling. The horse quivered a little, and started to prance. I listened, and I recognized the familiar sound of army transport. Although it was still far away, I turned my horse onto the side of the road—we all knew how transport troops drove, without looking at anything in their way.

Suddenly I heard a thin whistle. A shell fell on the road in front of me with a weak explosion. Then another, and a third. The Germans were firing on the road—that was clear. In the intervals between the explosions I could hear clearly that the transport train was now coming toward me at a gallop. The usual panic had started there, beyond any doubt.

One shell dropped right next to me. I did not notice it. But something happened to my left leg. It felt as if something soft had been wadded into it.

I quickly put my hand into my boot and my fingers felt something wet and warm. When I raised my hand, I felt a pain in my leg as if it had been splintered, and I grabbed the pommel of my saddle, but I couldn't hold on to it, and I fell onto the road. I must have fallen on my wounded leg, because I lost consciousness for a moment.

When I came to, the frantic rumbling of the transport train was right on top of me. I held on to the stirrup and yelled at my horse. Snorting and picking his way carefully, he pulled me off the road and into the ditch beside it.

I lay there, holding on to the stirrup, and two paces from my face a supply train roared by me with yells, whistles, and all the clatter of frightened horses and grating wagon wheels. It seemed to me it would never end.

Then everything was quiet. The horse poked me with his nose and neighed apprehensively. I wasted five minutes trying to get my flashlight out of my pocket and light it. After that I don't remember anything. Apparently, I lost consciousness again, but the flashlight was lying next to me, shining its light into the darkness.

Some signal corps soldiers who were traveling to Nesvizh in a two-wheeled cart found me by its light, managed somehow to bandage me, and took me to a field hospital in Nesvizh. I stayed for a month in the hospital there. The wound was slight, and the bone was not damaged. I was alone in the hospital; there were no other wounded.

Romanin came often to see me. His bathhouse was finally finished, and Romanin was beaming.

The "Most Honored Rat," Kedrin, came twice to see me. He told me angrily about Rasputin, and about "the disintegration of the imperial family" and his gray imperial beard quivered with terror and indignation.

It was at this time that Nicholas II visited the western front. He "visited" Zamirya, too. Orders were given to clean up the village before his arrival. This was done chiefly by cutting spruce trees in the forest and using them to camouflage the shabbiest of the peasants' huts.

I read a lot in the hospital. Everyone was interested then in Scandinavian writers—Ibsen, Strindberg, Hamsun, Bang. I read a lot of Ibsen, that great manual laborer of the human soul. Then I ran across Muratov's *Images of Italy* and I grew giddy with the bitter air of Italian museums and cathedrals. In my imagination I saw the high hills of Perugia rising above blue fog and lightly illumined by the sun. I started to read Leonid Andreyev's *The Life of a Man,* but I put this book aside for the simple, clean *Steppe* of Chekhov.

I began to be homesick for Russia. Most often of all I remembered the Bryansk forests as the happiest, most blessed corner of the earth. I remembered the wooded ravines, the rivers and the felled timber, the growths of young pine and birch, the crimson fireweed and the white blossoms of wild flowers. That was the golden country, the land of easy breathing, of quiet. I wanted that quiet to the point of tears. But who could give it to me?

I soon began to get around with crutches, and I was allowed to walk out in the village. I used to go and rest in the shop of a watchmaker whom I knew. Clocks ticked quietly all around him, a pelargonium was blossoming in his window, and the watch-maker, looking into his black magnifying glass, would tell me all the local news.

They gave me newspapers and magazines, most often *Ogonyok*. I looked at the battle drawings of the artist Svarog, and at dozens of photographs of officers who had fallen at the front. The papers were full of veiled references to Nicholas and Alice, Rasputin and Goremikin.* The black shadow of a crow's wing had fallen across Russia.

Romanin often sent me small presents—sugar, sausage, or cheese.

Once when I had nothing else to do I began to look at a crumpled old newspaper in which cheese had been wrapped. The paper was covered with spots of fat. In the list of those who had fallen at the front there was printed: "Killed on the Galician front, Lieutenant of Engineers Boris Georgievich Paustovsky" and a little lower: "Killed in fighting near Riga, Ensign Vadim Georgievich Paustovsky."

These were my two brothers. They had fallen on the same day.

In spite of the fact that I was still weak, the senior surgeon of the hospital released me. I was given an ambulance to take me to Zamirya. In the evening I left Zamirya for Moscow, to see Mama.

A SAD FUSS

Mama had become quite shriveled and seemed even shorter in height than before. But her face still had its old expression of humiliation and of some pent-up grief which no one could possibly understand.

It had been a month since the death of my brothers when I arrived. Mama cried seldom. In general, she was not given to tears.

* I. L. Goremikin (1839–1917), a reactionary Tsarist official and or-ganizer of anti-Jewish pogroms, was President of the Council of Ministers when Rasputin rose to power.

My sister Galya began to shudder whenever she talked about our brothers, but only when Mama wasn't present. When Mama was there, she controlled herself.

By this time I had already witnessed human grief, and I had noticed that people almost always try somehow to lighten it. This is easiest for those older people who believe in life after death and in the ascent of a dead person's soul into a heavenly paradise.

What can lighten grief? Memories, friends, nature, the knowledge that a man has left a good reputation behind him, care for near ones who survive.

But Mama's and Galya's grief was dry, and buttoned-up. They had to go on living. Mama had to live for Galya's sake, and Galya so that Mama could take care of her.

I did not know how to help. I myself was deeply grieved by this double death occurring at the same time. We brothers had had little in common. We were all very different. But this only strengthened my sorrow for them, who were no longer living.

Relief came quite by accident. I asked Galya what she and Mama knew about the circumstances of her brothers' deaths. It turned out they knew nothing.

"Then you must find out."

"How?" Galya asked.

"Write to the regiments they served in. Find their comrades, find those who were with them on the day they died. Ask for all their letters, diaries, documents, to be sent to you, everything they left."

I never suspected what these words could accomplish. A goal for living had been found. It was a task to be done. Galya told Mama about it, and the next day there began a feverish, stubborn, indomitable activity.

Galya and Mama wrote letters to the army. They searched for Dima's and Borya's fellow soldiers, even those still in hospital or released from the army. They learned the names of all the men who had served under them. They sent their questions literally everywhere.

Besides, Mama began to try to collect her pensions.

Answers started to arrive. Mama and Galya spent nearly all their time studying them, comparing facts to work out clearly the circumstances of their deaths, repeating questions about places in the reports which were not clear. It turned out that Dima had kept a diary, a few pages of disconnected notes. Deciphering this filled whole days.

A great many persons were involved in this correspondence.

Every one of them referred, if only glancingly, to the circumstances of his own life. So there developed a set of remote acquaint-
anceships, all dedicated to the memory of my brothers. The lives
of these new friends sincerely interested Mama and Galya. Mama's
old habit of instructing people, as she put it, in "honorable and
intelligent behavior" led her to write them long letters full of advice, persuasion, and examples from her own life.

There was something touching and painful to me in watching
this old, unhappy woman, who had learned so little from her own
life, teaching others how to live. But this is the way grief is gradually dissipated in the lives of others, in feverish activity, in a bitter
kind of fuss and bother. I was glad of it, although I realized that
it could not go on indefinitely. What would happen then?

My aunt in Kiev, Vera Grigorievna, owned a small, wooded
country place called Kopan, on the Pripyati River. Aunt Vera had
been distressed for a long time because the place was abandoned,
and because no one took care of it. She had proposed several times
that Mama and Galya might move to Kopan, but Mama never
agreed because of her need to live with Galya and Dima in Moscow.

Now Aunt Vera invited them again to Kopan, and Mama willingly accepted. They decided to go early in the spring. Mama grew
calmer, and even a little more cheerful, as soon as the decision had
been made. A gleam of hope had appeared.

Mama was making plans of how she would put the place in
order and make it prosper by insignificant expenditures of the
kind that "Aunt Vera, of course, with her carelessness, would never
think of."

Mama was not in the slightest worried about me. Once I overheard a conversation between her and Galya.

"Why do you worry less about Kostik than about us?" Galya
asked.

"He has another life," Mama answered her. "He has traveled a
great deal, seen a lot, and met different kinds of people. And he
has his own interests, of course. Eternal wanderer! Just like his
father."

This praise had, of course, its share of reproach. My father's
"passion for changing the scene," in Mama's opinion, had led to
the impoverishment and the disintegration of our family.

Duty was the only thing that was real to Mama. Duty alone,
and nothing else. She found all her happiness in fulfillment of her
responsibilities, while my father, in Mama's expression, had "taken
life in handfuls," which was possible, of course, only for a hopeless
egoist. Such was Mama's philosophy of life in her old age.

The Union of Cities gave me a two-month leave of absence for convalescence after my wound. I was supposed to return to the unit in March. Meanwhile I was offered a job connected with the dispatch of medicines and supplies from Moscow to the front. It gave me extra income, so I accepted it. I needed money to finance Mama's trip to Kopan.

The job consisted of hiring draymen, taking them to the warehouses, picking up medical and other supplies, transporting them to the freight stations, and shipping them off to the various field units of the Union of Cities.

I walked every morning to Warsaw Square. Here was the carters' exchange of Moscow. The rules were very strict. It was impossible to deal with any drayman individually. You could get badly beaten up for trying. The draymen stood in a crowd in the middle of the square. They were enormous, bearded peasants, wearing aprons on top of their sheepskin coats, loud, profane, and full of wit.

You had to make your way to the draymen through flocks of fat pigeons. As soon as a customer appeared, the senior drayman would take off his hat, into which all the drivers would throw their brass numbers, and the old man would walk up to the customer, shaking the hat. The customer would pick out as many numbers as he needed carters. But before this lottery there would always go on the most violent bargaining, even though the prices for loading and unloading had been established and known for decades.

In a month of this work I got to know almost all of Moscow's freight stations, and the majority of its warehouses and depots. They were all parts of an enormous but little-known world which lived by its own rules. You got the impression that everyone stole —the managers of the warehouses, the guards, the porters, the drivers, and especially the men who weighed the goods at the freight stations. The drivers stole quite openly, and when they were caught they resorted to counterattack: they would start a fight in a cloud of staggering profanity. There were few who wanted to tangle physically with these raging peasants bound to each other by a common corruption.

They stole literally everything, even old nails and worn-out matting. This went on openly, where it could be seen. About what was being stolen in higher circles, one could only guess.

Everything that was dubious, mean, or greedy had been inflated to hysterical proportions by the example of Rasputin. People talked about him everywhere. This horsethief from Tobolsk, this peasant with lascivious eyes, was ruling the country, sitting on the throne of Russia.

"How are we any worse than Grisha Rasputin?" the draymen would cackle, and they would whistle at a woman passing by. "Fall to, fellows! Eat your fill, while there's still something to eat. Grigori Yefimovich Rasputin will stand up for us. We know how to play the hypocrite, too, as well as he knows how to steal horses at a fair!"

This band of thieves had one inflexible and sacred rule—divide. They shared their loot with anyone who joined them in the act, giving away a share of what they stole.

And the warehouses! I saw enormous cellars filled with things for the army: sheepskin hats which fell to pieces in your hands, shoddy overcoats made of cotton to look like real linen, caps with broken visors which had lost their shape, boots with soles of scorched leather, coarse underclothes which would draw blood because of the number of prickly substitutes for textiles woven into them. All of these things were sewed up in smelly, new bast matting and shipped off to the front. It sometimes seemed as if the matting was the only honest goods in this mass of rotten and defective products.

I was so eager to get back to my detachment that it was hard to wait for the end of my leave. At a distance, the front became close and dear to me. I felt that there, at the front, was all that was healthy and honorable in Russia, while here everything was rotting away.

That winter in Moscow was a match for thoughts like these. It had frequent thaws, the snow was always dirty, the streets were sheathed in frozen rain. The ponds melted in the Zoological Gardens. At one of them some kind of water bird kept screeching piercingly, as if asking: "What's this all about? My God, what's this all about?" I could hear it in my apartment.

I was busy only during the first half of each day. I went home early, ate a meager dinner, and closed myself in my little room. Mama and Galya would sew, getting ready for their trip. The sewing machine would hum into the middle of the night. The floor was covered with scraps and little threads.

I sat by myself and wrote. I wrote about the war, and about my generation. I was convinced that my generation would reshape the face of the world.

There was a great deal that was restless and visionary in my generation. I was confident that these qualities would not allow us to live inglorious lives and quit without having accomplished anything except, as Romanin liked to say, "having smoked up the whole universe." But in spite of this confidence, I could see more and more clearly that alongside my generation of intellectuals, people who considered themselves outside any class and saw themselves as "the salt of the earth," a separate, strenuous life which I did not understand was being lived by an enormous sector of the people, millions of men and women, who called themselves "our brother workers."

They had a genuine strength for living, an intolerance, and a sober truthfulness which they had won by dint of their own hard toil. This truthfulness could not be smothered by the most beautiful and melodious poetry, or darkened by the misty philosophy of Bergson which was so popular at that time. You could feel its presence everywhere, as a stubborn, strained look in men's eyes. And it became increasingly clear to me that without having defined my relation to the working class, to its struggle and to its despair, it would be impossible to live and to work in Russia.

I began to write a story about a young man of my times. I wrote it slowly, over a long time. It traveled with me through all the years of the Revolution and the civil war and ripened for a long time. In the end I published it under the title *Romantics,* but this was much later, in the 1930's.

Then I wrote several poems, and sent them to an important poet. I did not expect him to answer me, but he did. He sent me a post card, on which was written in a strong handwriting: "You are living like a voice off stage." This sentence filled the whole post card.

At this time I was living a double life—one that was real and one that I dreamed up. This book is written about the real life. The life I invented went on independently of the real one and added to it everything that was not there and could not be there, everything that seemed to me entrancing and beautiful. The life I invented went on in wanderings, in meetings with unusual people, in surprising happenings. It was wreathed in the smoke of love. It was in reality a long, coherent dream.

It is easy now to smile condescendingly at my condition then. It's the easiest thing of all to do. We all grow wise with experience, and we think we have the right to such smiles. This at any rate is what sober people believe who consider that they alone are concerned with what is serious and important.

But on an honest count they don't have the right to that smile. They don't have the right to laugh at the young dreams which plant the first seeds of poetry in many hearts. There was something clean in those dreams. There was nobility in them. These qualities were reflected in those who dreamed them all through their lives.

Everyone who has had these traits in his youth will agree with me that he has been the possessor of inexhaustible riches. He has possessed the world. There have been no frontiers for him, in time or space. He can breathe the mushroom-scented air of the taiga, and in the next minute the air of Paris boulevards after their lights have gone out. He can talk with Hugo and Lermontov, with Peter the Great and Garibaldi. He can offer his love at the feet of a seventeen-year-old schoolgirl in a brown uniform, her braids shaking with emotion, just as if she were Isolde. He can live in the tropical forests of New Guinea with Miklukho-Maklai, or with Pushkin in Erzerum. He can take part in the French Revolution, and cut the first roads through the forests of Florida. He can sit in prison with the father of Little Dorrit, and take Byron's ashes back to England.

For a man who has lived in this second world of his own imagination, there are no frontiers. I'd like to see the skeptic who would not agree that this second world enriches a man and influences his ideas and his actions as long as he lives.

I wrote about this. I wrote on the wide window sill because I had no table. I stopped often, to look out of the window and watch the branches of the linden trees, covered with frozen snow, in the Zoological Gardens. And I heard the bird on the pond crying sadly and without any answer: "What's this all about? My God, what's this all about?"

A letter from the Union of Cities arrived when my writing was in full swing. It was a summons from the chief executive of the organization, the well-known Cadet party leader Shchepkin.

The next morning I went to see him. The Union of Cities was located in a big building next to the Moscow Art Theater. I was met by a little gray man, pleasant enough in appearance but with a squeamish expression on his face.

"Well, my dear young man," he said, "I must communicate some most unpleasant news to you."

He was quoting the phrase from Gogol's *The Inspector General* and obviously this greatly pleased him, because he coughed, waved his puffy hands in the air, and repeated:

"Some most unpleasant news! During your stay in our hospital unit in Zamirya, did the Tsar come there?"

"Yes," I said, "that's true."

"Yes," Shchepkin went on, "and something else happened. To be precise, one of the staff of the detachment described this visit in highly satirical language. In a letter to a friend, forgetting in his youthful immaturity that there exists a military censorship. Did this also happen?"

"It happened," I answered. When I was in the hospital in

Nesvizh I had heard a great deal about Nicholas' visit and I had
written about it to a school friend in Kiev.

"And it also happened," Shchepkin went on, "that the military
censors opened this letter. Since the signature on it was illegible,
and the envelop carried nothing but the stamp of your detachment,
the censor decided to turn the affair over to us, so that we might
find the writer of the letter and, once discovered, refuse to let him
return to the front. Is this your letter?"

Shchepkin held out a piece of paper.

"It's mine."

"You're getting off cheap," Shchepkin said. "Even though we
are losing a good worker in you, according to the record, I must
request you to turn in your documents immediately and accept your
discharge."

I had been so eager to get back to the unit that this was a cruel
and stunning blow for me. What was I to do now?

I didn't return home, but went to the Tretyakovsky Gallery instead. It was empty. The guards were drowsing in their corners. A
warm breeze blew out of the registers of the stoves.

I sat down in front of Flavitsky's picture "The Princess Tara-
kanova." I looked at it for a long time, more than an hour. I looked
at it because the woman in the picture looked like Lelya.

I did not want to go home. Now I realized once and for all that
I had no home.

THE SUBURB CHECHELEVKA

Mama and Galya went off to Kiev in February. I stayed in Moscow,
hoping to find a job.

It was just at this time that my uncle, Nikolai Grigorievich,
the artillery engineer, was transferred from Bryansk to Moscow
and attached to the French military mission. The mission had been
sent to Russia to arrange for the manufacture of French high-
explosive grenades. Aunt Marusya had come to Moscow with him.

They were given a government-owned apartment in a little house on First Meshchanskaya Street.

The members of the mission—French artillerymen—dined often at Uncle Kolya's. I was invited to one of these dinners and I watched the Frenchmen with curiosity. Their blue uniforms gave off a smell of perfume. Almost all the officers brought Aunt Marusya flowers and were very gallant. But behind all the gallantry and the extremely courteous conversation was hidden something of Dumas's musketeers.

This "something" usually became clearer after Russian vodka. There would be an upsurge of noise, of wit, and of rolling laughter, and then the officers would begin to sing in chorus a song about a stationmaster. This was a favorite song of passengers on French railroads, and it had been composed exclusively to reduce all stationmasters to raving lunacy.

When the stationmaster walked out on the platform the passengers stood next to the open windows of the train and began to sing this little song in time with the wheels—at first slowly, and then faster and faster. Then all at once, like Chinese puppets, they would bow to the stationmaster out of the windows. The song had a chorus which consisted of a single line: "C'est le cocu, le chef de gare."

The officers acted out this song. The best of them all was an elderly colonel with a yellow beard who played the part of the infuriated stationmaster.

Sometimes the officers quarreled, and then Uncle Kolya's low-ceilinged dining room would begin to smell of gunpowder, and it seemed as if swords might soon be drawn. Eyes flashed, little mustaches twitched, sharp phrases interrupted each other, until the colonel lifted his hand in its round cuff. Then everyone would subside.

According to Uncle Kolya, these officers were good engineers. The colonel was considered to be France's outstanding scholar in the field of metallurgy, and he had written many scientific books.

Uncle Kolya was connected with many metallurgical factories. I asked him to get me a job as a worker in one of them. He was not a bit astonished by the request, and he arranged for me to become an inspector of shells at the Bryansk factory in Yekaterinoslav. Before this, I was supposed to study inspection methods at a Moscow factory, and at the same time learn something about the hydraulic presses on which shell casings were then made.

I did this at the Gustave List factory on the Sofiiskaya Embankment. The studying started with learning to read blueprints—

sheets of blue paper with cloudy pictures of parts of the hydraulic presses. Reading those blueprints could make a man blind. Besides this, I was taught how to use exact measuring instruments on shell casings and fuses.

I used to come back from the factory to a completely empty apartment. Mama had sold all the shabby furniture. Only a folding bed and a chair were left. I loved this emptiness. Nobody kept me from reading late in the night, smoking, and thinking. I thought all the time about the books I was determined to write. Later on I wrote quite different books, but this is not the point.

I left before long. I got on the wrong train by mistake, and had to change at Rzhava, beyond Kursk. I stayed there several hours, waiting for the right train which was following us.

I didn't mind. It was good to sit in the third-class waiting room, reading the timetable, listening to the warning bells and the clatter of the telegraph key, and walking out on the platform when the express trains roared by without stopping, making the little station dance.

I wandered through the fields around the station. Spring was already beginning here. The snow had settled, and was as porous as pumice stone. Jackdaws circled in clouds. And I wanted, as I have often wanted since then, to walk off across the fresh spring fields and never come back again.

In Yekaterinoslav, I rented a corner in the suburb of Chechelevka, not from the Bryansk factory. All the money I had was twelve rubles. The corner was in the kitchen of a lathe operator, a widower, who lived with his only daughter Glasha, a girl about twenty-five years old who had tuberculosis.

Besides myself, a riveter from the Bryansk factory also lived in the kitchen, a tall man with wild eyes. I never heard him say a word. He never answered questions, because he was completely deaf. Every evening, when he came back from work, he would bring with him a bottle of muddy Yekaterinoslav *"bouza"*— an intoxicating liquor made of millet. He would drink it, and then fall down, completely dressed, on his torn mattress on the floor and sleep like a dead man until the first morning whistle.

The lathe operator had black mustaches. He, too, was a laconic man, deeply indifferent to us, his boarders. But once he said to me:

"You look like a student. I wish you'd give me some literature to read. Something to clear my brains."

I didn't have any literature. But after thinking for a while quietly, he went on:

"If Glasha were in good health, I'd marry her off. To you. There'll be some future for you. I can see—you write all night. And then you wouldn't have to roll around on the floor under the sink. That faucet leaks and dribbles; it never lets you really sleep."

He said this in a bored voice, simply "for conversation," and he didn't believe himself that anything might come of it.

In the evening I heard Glasha talking to him behind their door:

"What do you mean, creeping up on all the boarders with your stupid conversation? Why do you try to foist me off on all of them? I don't sit here like a sponger. I do all the housework."

"You goose," her father answered, without irritation, almost caressingly. "You're a dunce, that's what you are! It's your happiness I worry about. It's no life for you to sit in this closet staring at the wallpaper."

"My luck was left in the other world," Glasha said, and she began to cry. "What you had me for, you don't know yourself. You don't even wonder about it. My life will be over in the spring."

The father walked away angrily. Glasha, cried out, came into the kitchen and asked me if I didn't have something to read, about love which was faithful unto death. Her face was heavily powdered. With the powder on top of her usual paleness, her face looked like a cheap cardboard mask. She smelled of candy-flavored eau de cologne.

I told her I had no books about love, faithful unto death or not.

"Oh, you roomers!" Glasha said. "I'm bored with all of you."

She locked herself in her room and put on the gramophone a record of songs by the clowns Bim and Bom:

> *Lucretia in the pawn shop*
> *Was boiling up some dumplings.*
> *And Monna Giovanna*
> *Washed a hen in perfume.*

Often in the night Glasha would cough for a long time, gasping for breath, and say into space:

"Oh, God, if only some good man would come along and shoot me like a dog."

I was sorry for her. I found Victor Hugo's *Toilers of the Sea* in the free library in Chechelevka, a story about the sailor Jilliat who was faithful in his love unto death. Glasha read it with extraordinary speed, in a single evening.

I was lying on my mattress, reading. The riveter was asleep, grinding his teeth. Suddenly the door to Glasha's room opened and the Hugo novel flew through the air, dropping pages as it went, onto the floor next to my mattress.

"Take it!" Glasha yelled. "Take the dirty book away, it's poison! Let your Frenchman choke on his book! It's all lies! He lies, like a dog! There never was anything like that, and couldn't be. If there were people like that on this earth, would I be living the way I am? I would carry a man like that in my arms."

"There are people like that," I said. "Don't scream."

"Ah, you tell me not to scream? Tell me something new, please. What do you want me to do? Sing 'They all say I'm a little flighty'? Or dance a jig? I hate you!" She threw the gramophone off the table. "I hate you! I wish I had never laid eyes on you. May you burn in the fires of hell!"

She ripped a piece of wallpaper off the wall. Dust flew out from behind it. The riveter jumped up and began to wash at the faucet. He must have thought he had just heard the first morning whistle.

At this moment the lathe operator came in. He grabbed Glasha by the arms, but she went right on, her teeth clenched and her face all white with burning eyes, tearing strip after strip of paper off the walls, making the room black and bare as if someone had turned it inside out.

Outside the window a delicate spring dawn was just beginning to turn the sky blue.

It all ended with Glasha's throat full of blood, and in the morning they took her to the factory hospital. The lathe operator got drunk. And the riveter went on drinking his *bouza* and sleeping, completely indifferent to the destruction of the apartment and the fate of its owner. Soon after Glasha's death the riveter moved somewhere else and the apartment became as empty as death itself.

One evening, when I was alone, reading on my mattress as was my custom, someone knocked quietly but insistently on the door. I opened it. A worker in our factory, a quiet, humorous man named Bugayenko, was standing there. For once, it was clear, he was a little embarrassed.

"I've come to see you," he said. "We ought to spend some time together."

He looked at the bare, black walls, and sighed.

"You've been unlucky. You ended up boarding with a good-for-nothing man. You ought to change your lodgings."

"I'm not going to stay here long, in Yekaterinoslav," I answered. "It's not worth it."

"He's an empty man," Bugayenko went on. "Walked away from life, from his comrades, drowned himself in vodka. People like him are just a nuisance to the proletariat. But our people in general are strong."

"I know," I agreed. "Your people are outstanding."

"That's what I wanted to chat with you about. We've been watching you for a long time. But it looks as if you hadn't noticed."

"What for?" I asked, taken aback.

"Making up our minds," Bugayenko answered, and he laughed. "Nowadays we have to look people over very carefully. To see if they can be trusted."

"Well, why?" I asked.

Bugayenko sat down, smoked a thick cigarette, and little by little, as if talking to himself, told me he had been looking me over for a long time before he had decided that I was a man, in his opinion, who was, although still far from the revolutionary movement, nevertheless a man with possibilities. And this was his problem: they wanted to put out a leaflet against despotism but they had nobody to write it. It would be best if I, obviously a literary man, would write it for them and they, the workers, could correct it and then put it "into circulation."

I agreed. I wrote the leaflet, and I put into it all the pathos of which I was capable. The ghost of Victor Hugo leaned over me while I was writing it. But Bugayenko rejected it completely.

"It's not written for us," he said. "The words aren't wrong, it's written beautifully, all polished. But beauty, you know, sometimes softens what shouldn't be softened, and brings a kind of relaxation. Everything's all right in its place. But in things like this what we need is clarity. So that it's all simple and clear even to the least literate of the illiterate. So a man will read it and get angry and be ready to do something. So his fist clenches all by itself. I realize it may be harder than to write beautifully. Try it again."

After this I struggled with the leaflet through several evenings before I succeeded in making it simple and clear. They duplicated it on a hectograph, stapled it together, and distributed it around the factory. I was very proud of it, but to my regret, I could not tell anyone that I was its author. I wanted to keep one copy for myself, but Bugayenko took it away from me and warned me that I was a bad conspirator. But he was satisfied with the leaflet, and he smiled into his short-clipped mustache and said:

"Ah, you know, we have some fine fellows in our Zaporozhsky district."

At the factory I was busy checking shell casings. They were piled in stacks on long tables of unplaned boards. I examined the inside of each casing with a little electric lamp to see if there were

blisters or overburning on its sides. Then I measured the diameter
of each casing with a calipers. On those which I rejected, I made a
cross with chalk. The wastage was large. Elderly workers hauled
the rejected casings on wagons back to the smelters.

A circular saw was set up right next to the place where I worked.
It cut metal with an unbearable screeching noise. This noise made
your skin turn cold and produced madness in your heart. The noise
cut its way into your brain like a drill.

I grew deaf and blind, and, if I could have done it, I would
have destroyed that saw. It would be hard to imagine a greater
mockery of a man, his nerves, his brain, and his heart. When the
saw was not working it was even worse: we were all waiting
nervously for the noise to start. Just the waiting could produce
nausea. Then the saw would start up again triumphantly, grinding
its steel teeth into the metal and throwing up fountains of hot
sparks.

I was responsible not to the factory administration but to
Captain Velyaminov, who had been sent from Petrograd to represent the artillery command at the Bryansk factory. Once every
three or four days I had to go to him and report on my work.

For a long time I couldn't guess whom he resembled, but
finally I remembered: it was the Decembrist leader Yakubovich.
Velyaminov had the same dry face, dark mustache, and the same
black bandage around his forehead.

He lived on Bolshoi Prospect. From the window of his room
the Dnieper and its gardens could be seen. Buds were already swell-
ing in the gardens. Over the treetops, as always in early spring,
there was a hardly noticeable greenish smoke.

Velyaminov's room was filled with blueprints, books, and a
lot of other things which had no relation to his specialty—artillery.
He enjoyed photography, and regional studies. His window sills
were crowded with measuring glasses, bottles of developing fluid,
frames for making prints. There was always the sour smell of
fixative.

Photographs lay on a torn tablecloth on a round table holding
a philodendron plant. They were views of provincial towns—
Porkhov, Gdov, Valda, Loyev, Rosslavl, and many others. Velyaminov had turned up something curious in each town. With a cigarette smoking in his mouth, he would tell me patronizingly but with
obvious pleasure about each of his finds. Sometimes it was a
wooden gate dating from the time of Peter the Great, sometimes
just an intricately carved banister on a balcony, sometimes a row
of shops, or a watchtower out of Gogol.

Velyaminov spent one after another of his vacations in forgotten little places far from the capital. He would photograph the paintings in crumbling old landowners' mansions, exceptional stoves, old sculpture hoarded in rooms or gardens, and he would show these photographs to his friends in Petrograd who were art lovers. He told me proudly how he had managed to track down the grave of Pushkin's nurse, Arina Rodionovna, in the village of Suida near Luga, and a bust by the famous sculptor Kozlovsky, and two pictures by the French artist Poussin in an abandoned house near Chereptsov.

I sat for long times at Velyaminov's looking at his photographs. He poured me tea out of a thermos bottle and gave me little sandwiches of smoked sausage. It was very warm in his crowded room. I was always reluctant to go back to Chechelevka, to my desolate kitchen where cockroaches, transparent from hunger, ran races up and down the walls.

One day Velyaminov said to me:

"You've had enough moping here in Chechelevka, and going deaf from that saw. I'll send you to Taganrog. It's a splendid town. But on the way you should go to Yuzovka to the Novorossisk factory and fix up the wastage of shell casings there. Spend two or three weeks on it. Do you agree?"

I agreed, of course.

Velyaminov gave me my pay, and money for the trip, promising to come to Taganrog to see me in the summer, and we parted.

Back in Chechelevka I spent almost the whole night without sleeping. We never turned out the light; it was all that saved us from the cockroaches. In the darkness they tumbled off the walls and crawled over our hands and faces.

I lay there, and a crazy thought came into my head—to go five or six days late to Yuzovka, and spend the time going to Sevastopol instead. Velyaminov would never know about it.

I had been in Sevastopol when I was a little boy, when the whole family was going from Kiev to Alushta, and I had never been able to forget the town. I often dreamed of it, filled with reflections of the sea, small, picturesque, smelling of seaweed and the smoke from steamships.

Water dripped out of the faucet, the cockroaches drank out of little puddles on the floor, a drunk yelled out on the street: "Shoot me, Judas! Stab me in the heart!" but I noticed nothing. I was already breathing in the air from gardens filled with flowering almond trees.

❀

❀   ❀

JUST ONE DAY . . .

At the ticket office in Yekaterinoslav they asked me for a permit to go to Sevastopol. I had no permit, and I had to take a ticket to Bakhchisarai. I was sure I could manage somehow to get from Bakhchisarai to Sevastopol.

The aged cashier even sympathized with me.

"Strict rules!" he sighed. "And all because of what happened to the *Empress Maria.*"

The tragic destruction of the most powerful battleship of the Black Sea Fleet, the *Empress Maria,* was a great mystery. People were talking about it all around the world. Standing at anchor in Southern Bay at Sevastopol, without any apparent reason, the battleship had exploded and turned turtle.

Not long before the explosion the ship had been inspected by "visitors of the highest rank." Among them had been some retainers of the Empress Alexandra Fedorovna. Probably one of them had left some small bombs, the size of a champagne cork, with clockwork mechanisms, in vulnerable places. For this incident was not unique. Military transports, bringing arms to Europe, were often blown up or burned by such small bombs. Sometimes they were thrown into the bunkers of the ships while they were being loaded with coal.

I stood for a long time next to the window of the platform on the train. It was a warm, dark, southern night. At the stops, I opened the outer door and listened. A little rustling came out of the blackness. It must have been the drying out of the ground, still soaked from the winter's snowdrifts.

I grew restless at each stop, and happy over each milestone we passed as it receded smoothly behind us in the dim light falling from the windows of the cars. In those days there was no electricity on trains. They burned candles. In the dark cars it was good to speculate about your future, all that was entrancing and different lying ahead of you. The second world I have been writing about came alive then with extraordinary power. One could plunge right into it, with no pangs of conscience. For it was impossible to work on the train anyway, or to read, and there was a lot of time for imagining. That is, of course, if there were no importunate fellow passengers to bother you.

Fortunately, I had none. A young sailor in a black overcoat stood beside me on the platform. He kept beginning a song, breaking it off, and starting all over again. The only words I remember are:

> *Jankoya was the place*
> *Where it happened once* . . .

so I never found out what happened at Jankoya, a little station through which our train passed as night came on. After Jankoya I kept looking into the blackness, trying to see the outline of the Crimean Mountains, but all I could see was the lights of Simferopol.

The windows were brightly lighted in the station buffet at Simferopol. Branches of almond stood in vases on a long table which held silver buckets for serving champagne. A dark young sailor was sitting with his elbows on the table, smoking. When the train started to move again, he walked calmly out of the restaurant and pulled himself neatly up on the platform of the last car.

The conductor put out the candles. The ancient land opened up before me in the dark blue dawn: the mountain tops lit by the rising sun, transparent little streams gurgling along over their pebbles, plane trees, and the magic luminescence of the sky in the distance toward which the train was rolling, leaving behind it a long cloud of the softest pink smoke.

I got out at Bakhchisarai. The conductor told me that a local train would go to Sevastopol at night and that it would be the best way of getting there. I had only to give the policeman three rubles.

So I had the whole day to spend in Bakhchisarai. It was a crowded little town, paved with worn flagstones. Water could be heard dropping from fountains. Women collected it in copper kettles. As the water filled them, it changed its sound from a very high note to a low one. This music of the water and the copper kettles fascinated me. It seemed to be happening in one of the imaginary countries I had made up for myself. It occurred to me that maybe I hadn't invented them, and that there might actually be such countries in the world where everything really existed that I thought I had dreamed about.

Everything was new to me here, and especially the fountains. They were not at all like fountains I had seen before, where water spouted out of the beak of a bronze heron or the jaws of a dolphin. Here the fountains were flat stones set into hollow walls, and the water poured in lazy streams out of openings in these stones. The famous Fountain of Tears in the palace of the khans was not like any ordinary fountain. Its slow drops fell like tears from one shell into another, making hardly any sound at all.

I walked into a crowded coffee house. It had been set up in a decrepit, glassed-in terrace which jingled and danced whenever a bullock cart went by. Pigeons were walking around among the rickety tables and cooing loudly.

Outside the windows was a gorge, a yellow hollow of stone and prickly shrubs. The road to the cave dwellers' town, Chufut-Kale, led along this gorge.

"What a life!" I thought as I sat on the terrace. Fuchsias in vases were dropping their black and red blossoms on the tablecloths. I was greedy for new impressions. And now I was getting them.

It is true, there was more sorrow than joy in these quick changes in my life. But unconquerable youth still stood over all my misfortunes, just as the sea stands behind its blue waves, and this softened the feeling of failure and loss.

I paid for my coffee, and walked to Chufut-Kale.

I did not know what a cave dwellers' city was until I saw the sheer yellow cliffs moth-eaten like honeycombs with a multitude of windows. I climbed up along a winding path and suddenly found myself in such antiquity that it seemed unreal. Deep paths had been hacked into the limestone, yellow with lichen. Heavy wheels had once bitten ruts into them. Low entrances led into the houses of the cliff dwellers. Lizards ran around the altar in a tiny underground basilica.

Who had hewed out this town? There was no one to explain it to me; there was not a person anywhere around.

Carpets of tiny, lilac-colored flowers covered all the open spots of stony ground between the cliffs. The flowers were very formally shaped, each with five little petals, but it would have taken a magnifying glass to see them properly.

A skinny bay horse was grazing on the cliffs. She stopped often and dozed, twitching her skin when wasps lighted on her.

I climbed up on a cliff and sat there, resting my arms against it. The stone was warm under my hands. In front of me there stretched the most magnificent semicircle of mountains just as flat as Chufut-Kale. I was alone in this aerial wilderness. Far below me I could see sheep, looking like little balls of dirty wool. I could hear

clearly the baaing of their lambs. I did not want to move. I lay
on my back and dozed. The sky was shimmering with blue lights.
Sharp beams of different-colored flame broke through my eyelashes.
An eagle was circling in the heights, watching me and wondering
whether or not to light beside me.

Then I heard a thin trickling of water drops, turned around, and
noticed that a little stream, no bigger than a thread, was coming
out of a crack in the next cliff and falling in tiny drops, like beads.
I fell asleep.

When I woke up the sky was aflame, no longer with blue fire
but now with colors of ochre and red. Crimson clouds were
tossed around the sky in feathers, fans, great trunks, and mighty
mountain peaks and islands. The sun was setting. Its copper-colored
disk was pouring an ominous glow over all the hills.

This incredible evening light grew sharper and more violent
moment by moment. It burned up to its final incandescence, so
that it could then go out in a flash. This is what happened. The
sun went down, and immediately I could hear a cold wind in the
blackthorns all around me. I went down out of the hills. The
fountains in Bakhchisarai were louder than they had been in the
daytime.

I drank a cup of coffee in the same coffee house—I had just
enough money for that—and walked back to the station, hungry
but lighthearted and excited.

The train left at five o'clock in the morning. I did not buy a
ticket. I stood on the platform. A strapping policeman climbed up
behind me. He couldn't help seeing me, for I was the only passenger
who got on at Bakhchisarai.

"Your permit?" he said, smiling.

I handed him three rubles. He took the money, put his finger
to the visor of his blue cap, and walked away. I stayed on the platform.

I could not tear myself away from the window. When would
I see the sea at last? It was already growing light. The train rumbled
wherever the tracks had been cut into the side of the cliff, then it
moved on to lightly jingling bridges over the ravines. The car
swung sideways in a tight circle. It passed a slope covered with
yellow flowers. The curly branches of vineyards swept by us, then
we heard again the dull rumbling as we passed into the face of the
mountain. The broken cliff wall was so close to the side of the
cars that it was dangerous to put out your hand.

Suddenly, after a tunnel, the green water hit us in the face with
all its power, and there, darting and bending and vanishing into
the dry haze, was the broad expanse of Southern Bay.

Everything outside the window was motionless, but the train was moving, and this was why it seemed that the whole world outside was tossing and sounding and flashing—black schooners turned keel upwards on the shore, gray cruisers, long mine layers, buoys, flags, guard ships, masts, tiled roofs, nets, piles, acacia trees, and flashes of prickly fire on the shore—the reflection of the sun from old tin cans.

And then through the spurts of smoke appeared the amphitheater of the town itself, as if covered with a bronze film of fame and glory. Grinding its brakes, the train cut boldly into a wilderness of side streets, slopes, courtyards, staircases, and walls, and stopped at last beside a handsome station.

I have seen a great many towns in my life, but a better town than Sevastopol I do not know.

The Black Sea came up almost to the doorways of the houses. It filled the rooms with its noises, its breezes, and its smells. A little open trolley slid carefully down the hills, as if afraid of falling into the water. The noise of floating signal buoys was carried in from the roadstead outside the harbor.

At the market place, right next to the zinc-lined bins filled with flounder and pink fish, little waves splashed and slapped at the hulls of fishing boats. Surf, rolling in from the open sea, beat against the round fortifications. Armored warships were steaming out in the roadstead. Whistles blew, ships' bells rang, shouting to each other over the clang of the trolleys and the pealing of church bells. Passenger ships hooted impatiently, there was the rasping clang of anchor chains. The brassy notes of bugles floated in at sunset from the battleships where the ensign flags were being lowered for the night. These were followed by light waltzes being played along Primorsky Boulevard. It sounded as if it was not an orchestra playing, but the twilight itself singing, calming down the last splashing waves around the monument to sunken ships.

I walked through the town until I was exhausted, and all day long I kept finding new, picturesque corners. I liked especially the staircases which served as ladders between the upper and lower parts of the town. They were made of porous yellow sandstone. Houses stood on ledges to the side of these flights of steps. Hanging bridges, covered with plush, ran from the landings of the steps to the entrances to the houses. All the windows and balcony doors were open so that from the steps everything could be heard that was going on inside the houses: children laughing, the voices of women, the clatter of dishes, scales being practiced, singing, dogs barking, and the metallic cries of parrots. For some reason there were a great many parrots in Sevastopol at that time.

The town was darkened in the evenings. They were afraid of a sudden attack by the German fleet. But it was not a full blackout. Letters had been cut in the blinds which covered the windows of the stores, and the light from inside the stores illumined words like "Candy Store," "Mineral Waters," "Beer," and "Fruits," and threw a deadened, mysterious light into the streets.

Talkative women sold violets in big baskets on the pavement until late at night. Lanterns and candles stood on little tables next to them. The candle flames hardly quivered in the still night air. Crowds of officers and sailors filled the streets in the evening. Without the blackout, and without the searchlights probing in the distant sky, there would have been no thought of war.

Maritime towns must have looked like this during blockades at the beginning of the nineteenth century, when the military danger was not so great. Clumsy enemy gunboats stood off the shore then and fired their bronze cannon at forts overgrown with blackberries. It wasn't really war in those days. But the sensation of danger must have given people a nervous kind of enthusiasm, and produced that careless cheerfulness which has always been considered an indispensable trait in men of courage.

I sat through the dusk into the evening next to the 1854 bastions on Historic Boulevard. Southern Bay lay below me, and Korabelnaya Bay beyond it. Flowering almond trees were all around me. There is no other tree with such fresh and lovely blossoms. Each branch was covered with pink flowers, like a bride in her shining gown. Lights were not lighted in the town, and the twilight gradually muffled the town in an unsteady kind of smoke.

At the beginning this smoke was touched by the gold of the setting sun, then it began to take on a clear silver shade until the silver completely replaced the gold. But soon the silver, too, began to darken, losing its clearness, being covered gradually by a thick, impenetrable blue. When this blue had faded in its turn, it was night.

From Historic Boulevard, I walked to the station to try to buy a ticket and get on the train without a permit. The only train left in the night. The first porter I talked to agreed to get me a ticket without any permit.

"You have three hours before the train," he said, "and you're a young man. Why sit around the station? Go and take a walk, fall in love with our town."

I walked to the trolley, thinking of the goodness and open-heartedness of southern people, but a naval patrol came up to me at the trolley stop, two sailors with rifles and arm bands. They asked for my papers, which I showed.

"Where do you live?" one of the sailors asked me. "On what street?"

I admitted that I did not live in Sevastopol.

"That's clear!" the sailor said. "There's no reason why you should. But I'll have to take you to the warrant officer. And make no mistake about it, he's the kind that can see right through a man at one glance."

On the way, the sailor asked me, "How much did you give the porter?"

"Ten rubles."

"Here's your money," and the sailor handed me ten rubles.

I looked around, but it was dark and I couldn't see the porter, but I was sure that he was looking at my back with malicious joy.

The sailors took me to a small building somewhere near Nakhimovsky Prospect. A lean, hook-nosed warrant officer was sitting on the window sill in a vaulted room, next to a young girl in a short checked skirt. Two reddish-brown braids hung down onto her breast, and she was rebraiding them, swinging her leg. An old, worn slipper hung from her foot, hooked onto her big toe. Another warrant officer was sitting at a table, in field dress with his overcoat and cap on, and with a black revolver in a shiny holster.

The sailors reported about me, and walked out into the corridor. The warrant officer at the table took my papers, lit a cigarette, frowned from the smoke, and began to read them.

"Well, so," he mumbled at last, "the little bird hopped down the path with laughter, not seeing the dangers that might come after."

The girl laughed, and looked at me cheerfully, still waving her leg up and down.

"So that's how it is," the officer said. "Now tell me honestly who you are, what you are, why you came to Sevastopol, and why you want to slip away from us so secretly. Your papers are in order. But to hell with papers, in general."

I was embarrassed, but I told the officer just how it had happened.

"Aha!" he said, contentedly. "I understand. So you are a poetical, Bohemian sort of fellow?"

"Sasha," the hook-nosed man said from the window sill, "don't play the fool."

The officer with the revolver paid no attention to the hook-nosed man.

"If you can succeed in proving," he told me, "that you are a poet by nature, and that the muse of far places bewitched you, then perhaps we can come to some kind of arrangement."

I couldn't be sure if he was kidding me or talking seriously. But I decided to act as if I took him quite seriously.

"If Admiral Eberhardt knew your talents as a detective," the hook-nosed man said from the window sill, "you'd never get out of the barge, Sasha." The floating prison at Sevastopol was at that time called the "barge."

"A poet," the officer with the revolver said didactically, again paying no attention to the hook-nosed man's words, "must know poetry by heart. What can you offer us along this line?"

I did not understand him.

"Recite some verses to him," the girl explained. "He's a poet himself."

"Like 'God sent the crow a piece of cheese,' " the hook-nosed man suggested, laughing.

"No," I said, "if this is what you want, I'll recite a poem by Leconte de Lisle for you."

"That's the stuff!" the man with the revolver said with surprise. "Where did you come from? A clever fellow! No, better recite Blok's 'I will never forget'. But without any slips, if you want a permit."

"Stop making jokes, man," the hook-nosed man said, but the officer with the revolver again paid no attention to him.

I recited Blok's poem. It was one of my favorites. There was a silence. The sailors clattered their rifles in the corridor. They must have been astonished at what was going on.

"That's the end of the Punch and Judy show!" the man with the revolver said, with feigned disappointment. "Haven't you anybody in Sevastopol who could vouch for you?"

"No," I answered.

"I'll vouch for him, Sasha," the hook-nosed man said. "You've played the fool long enough. It was clear right away, what kind of a man he is. Write out his permit. I'll write out a guaranty for you tomorrow."

The warrant officer with the revolver laughed, and started to fill out a permit with great care. While he was writing, we all talked about poetry. The hook-nosed man liked Fofanov, and the girl liked Mirra Lokhvitskaya.* The girl told us, blushing, that if

* Konstantin Fofanov (1862-1911), a minor poet, was a member of the so-called Patrician school. Mirra Lokhvitskaya (1869-1905) was one of the best of women poets in Russia, with considerable influence later on Futurist poets.

there were time enough she would recite one of her own poems for us but it was too long.

"There!" The officer with the revolver handed me my papers and a permit, and sighed. "Too bad you're leaving. Otherwise, we could get together after work. We'd have plenty to talk about."

I thanked him, and said that Sevastopol was obviously a town of miracles. Nowhere else could my arrest have ended so unusually.

"My dear and slightly naïve young man," the officer with the revolver answered, "there are no miracles. Remember that spies and other dubious characters never deal openly with porters. That works out as a kind of aphorism, doesn't it?"

I walked out. The girl and the hook-nosed man offered to walk with me to the station. The officer with the revolver was clearly disappointed; it was evident that he, too, would have liked to walk through the streets of Sevastopol at night with the red-haired girl. On the way, she said to me:

"Come back and visit us. I live on Green Hill, at number 5. My name is Rita. Everybody there knows me. Oh, how sorry I am that you're going away! There are so few of us here in Sevastopol."

"Of us?"

"Yes, poets. Really only two, myself and a student from Kharkov."

The porter I already knew came up to me at the station. He was grinning broadly and happily.

"Well, look who's here," he said. "Fix everything up? It's better for you, and for me, too. Give me five rubles and I'll get you a ticket right away."

The smell of seaweed floated in through the open window of the car. The white streams of the searchlights poured out over the dark sea and disappeared without a trace. And I was terribly sorry to leave that town—a short and happy change for me after the last exhausting months.

THE GREAT BRITAIN HOTEL

I settled in Yuzovka in a cheap room in the Great Britain Hotel. This stinking den had been named in honor of the country of Hughes and Balfour, two Britishers who owned enormous factories and mines in the Don Basin.*

Not a trace is left now of the old Yuzovka. A handsome city has grown up in its place. But then it was a disorderly, dirty settlement, surrounded by hovels and mud huts. Different neighborhoods were called by words like "dog" and "filthy," and the gloomy humor of the names was the best proof of how wretched and miserable they were.

In a hollow next to the settlement smoked the Novorossisk Metallurgical Factory where I had been sent to improve the inspection of shell casings. The smoke came not only out of the factory chimneys, but out of all its buildings. The smoke was as yellow as fox fur, and it stank like burned milk.

An improbable crimson flame danced over the open hearths. Greasy soot dripped from the sky. Everything that was supposed to be white took on a dirty gray color, with yellow designs in it. The curtains, pillowcases, and sheets in the hotel were gray, all shirts were gray, even horses, cats, and dogs were gray instead of white.

It almost never rained in Yuzovka, and day and night a hot wind blew around rubbish, coal dust, and chicken feathers. All the streets and courtyards were littered with the shells of sunflower seeds. There were even more of them after holidays. The entire population ate sunflower seeds. It was unusual to see a local person without a few shells stuck to his chin. People ate them like virtuosos, especially the women gossiping around their wicket gates. They ate them with incredible speed, never putting the seeds in their mouths but flipping them in from a distance with their thumbnails.

---

* In 1870 a British subject named Hughes was given a concession by the Tsarist government to manufacture iron rails. The town which grew up around his factories, which were very profitable, was named for him.

The women also had a vulgarity of speech attainable only by Philistines in the south of Russia, an evil gossip compounded of impudence, dirt, and hatred. Each of these women was, of course, "the main one in her own yard." In spite of the slander and the chewing of sunflower seeds, they still had time to fight. As soon as two women had grabbed each other's hair with animal shrieks, a crowd would form around them and the fight would be turned into a gambling game: bets of two kopecks were placed on which one would win. Old drunkards of the neighborhood were always the bankers. They would hold the money in a torn cap.

The women were deliberately provoked to this fighting. Sometimes a fight would spread to include a whole street. Shirt-sleeved men would join in, using brass knuckles and lead-tipped whips, and cartilages would crack and blood would flow. Then a patrol of Cossacks would ride up at a trot from Novi Svet, where the administration of the mines and factories lived, and disperse the crowd with knouts.

It was hard to understand who had settled Yuzovka. The imperturbable hall porter in the hotel explained to me that it had been chiefly "illegals"—buyers of secondhand goods, small usurers, market traders, richer farmers, tavern keepers, all of them living off the surrounding workers' and miners' settlements.

Factories were smoking all around the town. Mines could be recognized on the horizon by the gray, dusty pyramids of their waste heaps.

The Great Britain Hotel deserves to be described, like some long-extinct fossil. Its walls had been painted the color of dirty meat. But this had bored the owner of the hotel who ordered them covered with the kind of decadent murals which were then fashionable—white and lilac-colored irises, and the coquettish heads of women looking out of water lilies. An ineradicable smell of cheap face powder, cooking fumes, and medicine filled the hotel. The electric lights burned dimly; it was impossible to read in their yellow glow. All the beds were broken, with deep troughs in them. The chambermaids "received guests" at any hour of the day or night.

Downstairs hollow-cheeked young men with their caps at an angle and wearing bow ties played billiards on tables which had been patched and repatched. Every evening someone broke someone else's head. They played for heavy stakes. They kept the money in a billiard pocket but they watched it like hawks for fear of its being stolen by the minor characters who hang around a billiard room.

The walls between the rooms were very thin. At night I heard sighs and groans and rude bargaining and sometimes a heart-chilling woman's cry. Then the hall porter would be called, they would smash in a door, and a distraught woman would rush out screaming, most often a chambermaid known to everyone in the hotel, and after her would come some dim fellow with his hair slicked down, bellowing and swinging backhand blows at everyone to right and left of him.

They would tie him up and lead him away, kicking him in the back, and tell him: "Cheating a girl again, you nuisance! How many times! Strangling would be too good for you!"

Her friends would run to the sobbing girl. Choking her tears, she would show them the money clenched in her fist—proof that she had been cheated. The girls would count the money together, ah and oh together, and say that all men deserved to be dipped in sulphuric acid.

A regular participant in these scandals was a short, gray-haired commercial traveler, representative of a ready-made clothing firm, Mandel & Company. He wore a loose cherry-colored suit, and yellow shoes with pointed toes. He always comforted the wronged girl.

"Musya," he said, "you should be more philosophical about it all. Take me as an example."

"You know where you can go," Musya answered through her tears. "And I hope you choke on your own advice. I know you and your philosophy."

But this never bothered the old man.

"The ancient Hellenes," he said, "realized that calm is the basic condition of all happiness. The basic condition! *Ultima ratio!* Do you understand? And just think, how much did he cheat you out of?"

"A ruble, the snake!" the girl answered, stopping her crying.

"Well, here's a ruble for you. Just dry your tears, wash your face, get dressed, be beautiful again as you were before, and bring a bottle of wine, some mineral water, and some biscuits to my room."

"You know where you can go!" the girl said angrily. "Is this just so you can get me for one ruble? You old rat, you!"

But the old man was never offended. He would go off down the corridor, his hands stuck in his pockets, singing a tango.

There was one man beloved by everyone in the hotel, who was called Uncle Grisha. He was a blurred, worn-out old man with a reddish-brown beard and blue child's eyes. He wore a silk jacket over his skin, pulled modestly tight around him, and he was always shuddering as if from cold but really from drunkenness.

People said that Uncle Grisha was the son of a senator from

Peterburg, that he had finished school, squandered an enormous
fortune in Paris, and then played the piano in a motion picture
theater (what was then called "illusions" in Russia) and was now
living on charity, occasionally earning a ruble or two at parties as
an exceptional guitar player and a singer of unhappy love songs.
Uncle Grisha was so unlucky that even the owner of the hotel, a
fat man in a derby hat and turned-up checked trousers, was sorry
for him and gave him work—heating water for tea in a boiler.
For this Uncle Grisha was allowed to live free in the little room
where the boiler was. This little room was a kind of club for the
hotel. It was there that the permanent boarders gathered to play
cards or dominos, to tell fortunes, and to discuss the day's events,
while the girls darned stockings, sewed, or ironed.

One day they organized a party in Uncle Grisha's room to
celebrate the birthday of Lyuba, the chambermaid on the third
floor where I lived. Four guests, including myself, were invited to
the party "out of respect"—an elderly woman dentist named Faina
Abramovna, a reporter from a Kharkov paper, a tall man who
walked on his heels, and a pharmaceutical student named Albert,
a freckled boy with very tender skin. He was always smiling in
a contemptuous way.

The old commercial traveler tried to crash the party, but the
girls wouldn't let him in. They were all dressed up, and Lyuba,
pale and silent, in a black dress, looked just like Queen Margo,
according to Albert. Excited, she would sometimes raise her long
eyelashes and look at us, and each time I was struck by the clear
brilliance of her eyes.

It was hard to believe that she was the same Lyuba who not
long before had been sobbing in the corridor at night, clutching
her torn batiste slip to her breasts and squeezing her thin, bare
knees together, denouncing at the top of her voice the dark, fat
boarder in Number 34, who was, according to her, a scoundrel
and a rascal.

Uncle Grisha had shaved and put on a pink shirt with detachable
cuffs fastened by copper buttons shaped like caterpillars.

We sat down at the table, which was covered with stale cold
cuts from the hotel restaurant, and with bottles of ashberry brandy.
A big bouquet of paper roses stood in the middle of the table.

Lyuba walked up to Uncle Grisha and stroked his thin hair.
Uncle Grisha took her hand, and pressed it. Then for a minute
Lyuba pressed his trembling head to her breast. She looked over
his head at the window, and her eyes were as calm and quiet
as always.

The blushing, happy girls forced us to eat. They looked sympathetically into our eyes, and said:

"But please, do eat, to good luck and good health for Lyuba. Don't be timid, please. It's all fresh, it's just come from the kitchen. The hell it has!"

Lyuba was sitting between Uncle Grisha and me.

"I'd like to ask you," she said to me, "what it is that you're writing. Every time I clean your room, there are pieces of paper all over. What are you writing about? About love?"

"Yes," I answered. "I'm writing about happy life, Lyuba."

"I might be interesting to you," she sighed. "Maybe you could write something good about me. A whole novel. And people would read it, and they would cry."

"Drink, Lyubka!" Musya yelled to her. "Drink, before grief gets you down."

Lyuba's eyes darkened.

"Listen," she said to me quietly. "Grief will never get me down."

"I just told you so," Musya answered. "I sympathize with you, Lyubka."

"And do you also write songs?" Lyuba asked me. "Don't pay any attention to that foolish Musya, by the way."

"No, I don't. I used to write poetry. And I know a lot of poems."

"Tender ones?"

"Yes, if you like."

"Recite them."

"Well, why not?" I answered. The ashberry brandy I had drunk was already making my heart flip. "I'll recite one for you. Today is your birthday."

"Really only one?" Lyuba asked, and she tugged a little at the silver ring on my little finger. "Whose is that ring?"

"Mine."

"That's not true. It's not yours."

Everyone was making a lot of noise. I thought for a minute: what could I recite that was clear and simple? "It's all the same," I thought, "whether she understands or not." And I began to recite, in a slightly singsong voice:

> No, it's not you I love so dearly.
> Not for me does your beauty shine.
> In you I love the suffering I have lived through,
> And the lost youth that once was mine.

The noise around the table died down.

> Sometimes when I glance at you,
> Taking the meaning of a look apart,
> I'm engaged in secret conversation,
> But it's not to you I'm talking from my heart.

I stopped.

"Well!" Lyuba said sharply. "When you start reciting like that, it tears my heart out."

> I'm talking with a friend of my young days
> In your features looking to find others,
> In your lips for lips that now are dumb,
> In your eyes for lights that time now smothers.

One of the girls drew in her breath noisily, and sobbed.

"It's better to sing Lermontov's poems than to recite them," Uncle Grisha said, tuning his guitar. He struck a soft chord, and then sang in a strong, pleasant tenor:

> I walk out on the road alone,
> The stony path shines through the fog . . .

"Join in!" he ordered, and the guitar began to talk again under his fingers. "Everyone join in!"

> The night is quiet, the wilderness worships God,
> And the stars talk to each other . . .

Everyone sang the last lines softly. Lyuba was sitting with her elbows on the table, resting her chin on her folded hands and singing while she looked out of the window. Uncle Grisha raised his head while he played, and there were tears shining on his cheeks.

The door suddenly swung open, and a dark, fat man with sugary, Eastern eyes, the boarder from Number 34, walked into the room.

"Lyubochka darling," he said ingratiatingly. "I've come for you. Come on out with me for a little while. I need terribly to talk to you."

"Talk?" Lyuba asked, and she turned around. "You need to talk with me? In your room?"

"Well, why not? It's a nice room."

Lyuba stood up.

"You know yourself what kind of a day I've had. So get out of here. I can't stand the sight of you, you scoundrel! Get out of here!"

"Lyuba!" Musya screamed, but it was already too late. Lyuba had picked up the brandy bottle and thrown it at the man with all her strength. It hit him on the head, and broke. He clapped his hands to his face, rubbing the blood mixed with brandy on his fat cheeks, rushed toward the corridor, stumbled on the threshold, and fell silently backward.

"I'll kill him!" Lyuba shrieked wildly. "I'll kill them all, like mad cats. All of them! Don't touch me! Don't try! I'll go to Siberia, I'll go to exile, but I'll get even with all of you, you snakes!"

She collapsed in a chair and laid her head on the table.

"Girls!" she said, with a quiet sadness in her voice. "My dear friends! Won't they ever give us a chance to live? Girls!" she screamed, and she shook all over. "It's as if I'd had a happy dream. Thank you, Uncle Grisha, thank you, my darling. Thank you all."

She choked on her tears and coughed. Uncle Grisha was standing next to her, shuddering, and swallowing hard. I took Lyuba by her shoulders. Even through her dress I could feel them burning hot.

I realized then that she needed to be told the big thing that is said to someone once in her life, to save it. But I couldn't say that big thing, about loving her, to save her. I couldn't say it no matter how much I wanted to. Maybe I should have lied, if I had been sure that it would make Lyuba feel better. I had already said my words long ago, there in White Russia, when Lelya, dying, had gently pushed me away and when the tears had stood in her eyes, without falling.

Besides, my words were not what Lyuba needed. Uncle Grisha should have said those words. But he couldn't, that drunken shuddering, weak old man who was living on the charity of others.

So I said nothing. I took Lyuba's hand and pressed it, and she looked at me quickly through eyelids drenched in tears, and she stroked my cheek with her hand. No matter how serious people may smirk, no matter what they say about sentimentality, I have carried that look of hers with me throughout my life, and I shall never forget it.

Hurried steps could be heard in the corridor, the jingle of spurs, loud voices. I looked around. The corridor was filled with a crowd of frightened boarders. A skinny police captain walked into the room, followed by some policemen. They took off their hats politely.

"If you please, young lady," the captain said sternly, but as if with some sympathy. Lyuba quickly stood up and walked out without looking at anyone. She didn't even turn around.

They carried the dark man away. The girls wept, hugging one another, and Uncle Grisha feverishly drank ashberry brandy, glass after glass, like water. Then the man who walked on his heels, who had been quiet all evening, went over to the door, closed it, and said:

"We were all witnesses. At the trial we must all say that this man attacked Lyuba with abuse and blows and that she hit him with the bottle in self-defense. And this old man"—he pointed at Uncle Grisha—"has got to be as sober as window glass at the trial. And testify just like the rest of us."

Then Uncle Grisha stood up. He looked steadily at the man and then said, very weightily:

"My dear sir! It's not your business to teach me good manners toward women. I absorbed them with my mother's milk. If destiny has led me to a fall, it gives nobody the right to insult me. I forgive you only because you have acted in a chivalrous way." And Uncle Grisha shook his hand warmly.

With that evening something changed sharply in me. I was no longer frightened by parts of life I had always stood apart from. I stopped treating people as remotely as I formerly had. From that time I realized that one must look for every flicker of humanity in people around one, no matter how hostile or uninteresting they may seem. For there is something in every heart which must respond to even the weakest challenge of what is good.

Soon after this incident with Lyuba, I moved from the Great Britain Hotel to the factory, where I could live in the draftsmen's room in the shell-casing shop. I was helped in this by the draftsman Grinko, a flabby, tubercular man, formerly a Social Revolutionary. He had come to my room once and been terrified by the stench of the hotel, so he persuaded me to move to the factory even though I was not going to stay much longer in Yuzovka.

Grinko was the only man working in the draftsmen's room. I came back from the shop late and spent the nights on a wooden couch. The life of the factory was so far from the suffocating life of the hotel that there seemed to be a hundred versts between them.

I walked over to the Bessemer shops every evening. I could watch for hours as the melted steel poured down from the gigantic rotary furnaces which looked like steel pears three stories high. Later every night I would walk over to see each pouring of iron at the open-hearth furnaces. It was a sinister sight. The iron ran into ditches in the ground, smoking with scarlet steam. Everything was in just two colors, black and red. In the glow of the liquid metal, the workers looked like fugitives from hell.

Sometimes I walked over to the rail mill. Enormous rollers, shaking and grinding, seized the white-hot pig iron and crumpled it in their cold metallic embrace, throwing out thick squared bars of iron. The bars moved quickly from one roller to another before they emerged as dark-red rails. The finished rails skidded past your legs on steel rollers, shining with hundreds of sparks.

Everything all around roared and shook and screeched, steam whistled out, iron smoked, scattered sparks, echoed, and jangled. Through the noise could be heard excited cries: "Watch out!" Workers moved ingots around quickly on steel wheelbarrows. If anyone in the way didn't move quickly enough, his clothes would begin to smolder. A crane swung other ingots overhead, holding them in the air in two steel tongs like a crab.

Grinko used to leave the drafting room late. He was a bachelor with nothing to pull him to his home. When he had left, I lay down on the wooden couch and read. It pleased me to hear the roar of the factory close by. My spirit was quiet in the knowledge that hundreds of people were keeping vigil all night so close to me.

I lay there and read and looked at the portrait of an old man hanging on the wall. This was Bessemer, the inventor of a new process for making steel. Then I fell asleep, and it seemed to me that I was sleeping in a train—through my sleep I could hear shaking and rumbling and ringing.

Sitting at his angled drawing board, long-legged, with his hair falling down to his neck, Grinko reminded me of a Gogol caricature. The resemblance was strengthened by the fact that Grinko wore a black hat and an old black raincoat with buckles shaped like lions' heads. Naval officers used to wear such raincoats.

Once I told him about our hospital train, and in return he told me how Sokolovsky had liberated him from prison. But I tried not to talk to Grinko about politics. I was embarrassed by the fact that a former Social Revolutionary had been given work in a military shop of a factory as a draftsman.

Grinko talked about everything with a contemptuous little smile, obviously bored, and only once in a while was there a short wicked gleam in his eyes. I noticed that the workers treated him with ridicule. Once when I was examining shell casings with an electric lamp I found a note inserted in a casing:

"Don't trust your neighbor in the drafting room. Burn this note."

I burned the note and began to watch the workers delivering the casings. But their faces were unreadable.

On the day before I left Yuzovka I found a proclamation, printed on a hectograph. On its corner were written the words: "Workers of the world, unite!" This was a Bolshevik proclamation, demanding the transformation of the imperialist war into a civil war.

I read the proclamation, and shoved it back in the same casing I had found it in. When I came back to the shop, after the dinner break, it was no longer there. The workers smiled when they looked at me, but no one said a word.

The train to Taganrog left in the evening. I said good-by to Grinko.

"You've been wrong to be afraid of me," he said, sitting sullenly at his little desk and not looking up at me. "It's true, I used to be a Social Revolutionary. But now I'm an anarchist."

He was silent for a while, and then he added dejectedly, as if not believing his own words:

"Anarchy—that's the only intelligent form of human society."

"Well," I said, "God help you!"

"Either you're an opportunist," Grinko said just as quietly as before but with hatred in his voice, "or you're a cynic. And I thought I was dealing with a progressive young man."

"It's written in my papers: 'Lower-middle-class citizen from the town of Vasilkov in Kiev province.' What do you want from me? In any case, I'm grateful to you for your hospitality, and for that reason I have no desire to quarrel with you."

"It looks as if you'll go a long way," Grinko said, already rude and not trying to hide it.

"Well, as far as you'll go, I won't be going. I can swear to that. Good-by."

I picked up my bag. Grinko went on sitting there just as sullen, looking at me out of his little eyes.

I went out.

I waited in the night for the train to Taganrog at the gloomy little buffet in the station at Yasinovata, and I thought that yet another small stage of my life had gone by, and had only added to my bitterness. But strange as it may seem, the bitter taste did not weaken but only strengthened my faith that wonderful days were coming, that the freedom of all the people lay ahead.

It would come, I told myself. It couldn't fail to come, if only because such enormous creative strength had been expended just in waiting for it and expecting it.

NOTEBOOKS AND MEMORY

Writers are often asked whether they keep notebooks or rely only on their memory.

The majority of writers keep notebooks, but seldom use them for their work. Notebooks figure chiefly in literature as an independent form of writing. This is why they are sometimes published like novels or short stories.

While we were still in the *gymnasium*, Shulgin, the Russian literature teacher, told us over and over again that "culture is memory." At first we didn't understand what he was talking about, but as we grew older we realized that this was true.

"We hold centuries in our memory," Shulgin used to say. "All the history of the world, all imagination, all human thought—this is preserved in memory, and forces our intelligence to work. If it were not for memory, we would live like blind moles."

For a writer, memory is nearly everything. For it not only hoards the material he has accumulated. It retains, like a magic sieve, what is valuable in it, the dust and trash fall out and are carried away by the wind, and the gold stays. Memory is essential, according to all the evidence, for the production of any work of art.

I have a reason for writing about notebooks. Some years ago I was given the notebook of a writer who was dead. When I began to read it I was convinced that these were not separate, short notes, such as are usually found in notebooks and diaries, but a rather careful description of an unnamed town by the sea. I will try below to reproduce this description as exactly as I can.

The farther I read in this notebook, the more clearly colors and smells of some place I had known came back to me. But I couldn't remember right away where this had been, or when. Impressions emerged from it as from mist, or an old dream which one tries to reassemble in pieces, the way a broken statue is put together again.

What was in these notes? First of all, an exact description of acacia trees and their blossoms.

"These flowers are touched with a yellow and pink bloom, and seem always the slightest bit dried.

"The shadow of the fleecy acacia leaves falls against a white wall and trembles even in breezes which cannot be felt. You have only to look at this living shadow to realize that you are in the south, and not far from the sea.

"When the flowers fall, the breeze carries little piles of them along the streets. They scud along the pavement with a noise like dry surf and pile up against garden fences and the walls of houses."

There was also in this notebook a description of the slopes which run downhill toward harbors. The descent to a port, the road to ships and the open sea, is not so easy to describe as one might think.

"The pavement leading down to harbors is always polished to a leaden shine by the hoofs of cart horses. Shoots of oats and wheat grow up between the stones. Winding walls, breast-high, are overgrown with flowering broom. It hangs over from above like an arrested waterfall of impenetrably woven twigs, leaves, thorns, and yellow flowers.

"Niches have been carved in places into this dusty green. Little coffee houses and stores are hidden in them. Soda water and *baklava*—a leafy Greek pastry made with honey—are sold in them.

"The front walls of the coffee houses are always made of glass. Through it can be seen people in faded shirts, gambling at cards.

"But this is not all. Old women sit here on low benches and sell roasted chestnuts. The corners of their braziers are filled with embers. There is a steady little crackling—this is the bursting of the chestnut shells.

"Go around a sharp turn and down below, as in a child's picture, the port lies like a toy. Its narrow piers are covered with grass, which has grown over the railway tracks. This is too bad, because otherwise we could see the red-rusted rails, and the daisies clinging to them with their white blossoms.

"Salt water stands, as in a glass, in the opening of every iron mooring gun. Lean over it and the smell will make your heart beat faster—it's the smell of the ocean and of wormwood, a smell which makes you lightheaded with its reminder of voyages that heal the heart and enrich the mind.

"Little greenish waves dance around the pilings.

"The sea gulls screech raucously and greedily when they see from the sky a school of unsuspecting little fish.

"The iron tower of the little signal beacon on the end of the breakwater makes a jangling noise from the beating of the waves against its base.

"Mysterious signs—circles and cones—hang from the flagpoles around the harbor.

"What do those black circles mean? A storm perhaps. Or maybe calm weather. Then the transparent air will seem to dissolve in the water of the sea. And the sea, drinking in this clearness, will become transparent itself, all the way to the bottom.

"No, it will probably be a storm. The black sails of the fishing boats are flapping warningly. The lights on the ships are moving rapidly in the twilight.

"The idea of a long sea voyage has already impressed itself on your mind. It will be hard to leave this comfortable town, where the breeze clatters the blue and green shutters on the walls and where thick books, probably bound volumes of *Niva* and *Around the World* and *Fatherland*, can be seen on the shelves of lighted rooms.

"But you can't sail away anyhow, because there are no steamships in the port. They are standing far beyond the breakwater.

"Are there really no steamships in the harbor? There is, of course, the tender. It is snuffling good-naturedly at its mooring. And there is the old schooner, the *Toiler of the Sea*. And there are two disarmed corvettes.

"They had been destined for scrap a long, long time ago but they are still in the harbor, dropping their heavy anchor chains into the water like outstretched arms. The corvettes are dreamy reminders of their own past when they sailed through the Straits of Magellan and their bows cut through the oily water of the Aegean Sea. In the dark it is hard to see their curved ram's-head bows, their bowsprits, and their funnels.

"In the daytime you can row out to one of the corvettes in a rowboat, give a package of Gypsy Ada cigarettes to the guard, and then sit on the deck in the shade of a funnel and read what you want, as long as you want to. Of course, what is best to read in a place like that is poetry, or travel books like *The Frigate Pallada* or the diary of Captain Cook. But you can choose whatever book is suggested to you by this deck whitened by age and the iron sides of the ship, covered to the water line with fringed seaweed.

"It is easy to watch the sea from the decks of these frigates. It does not sparkle with the azure, turquoise, sapphire, aquamarine, and other colors of the southern seas. It is greenish, and quiet. The clouds are its only decoration. They are like a medieval town with fortified towers, basilicas, triumphal arches, shining oriflammes of mounted knights and the distant outline of snow-covered mountains—Mont Blanc and Monte Rosa. Some extravagant artist painted this town in a whimsical mood. And the clouds shine, burning in the sunset, with all the half-colors of evening light, from blue to gold, and from purple to silver."

I read this note, and was tortured by something familiar about it. I looked for any place name which would help me recognize the town. Deep in my heart I even guessed what town it was, but I was not completely sure.

Aha! That's it! At last! "It is surprising that in the books of one of our most famous writers—a man born in this town—nothing is reflected of what has just been described, not the sea, nor the port, nor acacia, nor the black sails."

The solution lay in these words. Well, of course, all this was written about Taganrog, Chekhov's birthplace.

As soon as I had guessed it, all that I had read came alive, lost the film of strangeness that had covered it while I was reading, and took on sharp vividness and reality. Yes, this was Taganrog. This was the way I saw it in 1916, when I went there from Yuzovka and lived there until late in the autumn. I saw it like this because I was young and romantic, engrossed in poetry and books about the sea, and because I saw what I wanted to see. This is why, for a long time after I had grown up, I was afraid to go back to Taganrog, afraid of being disappointed and finding it quite different from the town as it first appeared to me. What can be done? With age we lose the happy faculty of exaggeration.

But in the autumn of 1952 I happened to be in Taganrog, quite by accident, and I convinced myself that I had been right when I was young. Taganrog was just as wonderful. It had not lost its charm, although it had acquired a different character. By now it had become a town of students, boys and girls, ringing shouts on the streets, bags of books, songs and arguments. Handsome new little towns, workers' settlements around new factories, had sprung up where there had been only plain outskirts in 1916. They closed a noisy ring around the old Taganrog.

But in Taganrog itself it was still empty, comfortable, and quiet. The fishermen's boats with their black sails left the shore and went out to sea so smoothly that it looked from the hills, where the bronze statue of Peter the Great stands, as if the wind were blowing black autumn leaves across the water.

In 1916 I lived in the Kumbaruli Hotel in Taganrog, which was spacious, empty, and cool. It had been built in those legendary times when Taganrog was the richest city on the Sea of Azov, the capital of Greek and Italian traders. Italian opera had prospered there; Garibaldi had lived there; this was where that balding dandy, Alexander I, had lived and died, surrounded by his courtly retinue.

The rooms in the Kumbaruli Hotel were so high that the ceilings were dark in the evenings; the lamps could not light them. The darkening frescoes on the walls showed a classical country with ruins, waterfalls, and languorous shepherdesses in red skirts. The shepherdesses, of course, were weaving garlands.

For the first two months I worked at the Nev-Vilda boiler factory. It belonged to a Belgian corporation. The factory stood on the steppe beyond the town.

When I arrived at the factory they were putting together its only hydraulic press for the production of shell casings. Belgian engineers wearing Panama hats and colored suspenders walked through the light, empty shops. They treated us, Russian workers, arrogantly and untrustingly. Their sour smiles, in any case, never left their faces.

What was really going on at the factory was an uninterrupted slowdown strike. Everyone worked so dejectly, so sluggishly, and so slowly that in two months we had barely got together enough plates for the press.

It was already cold, and there was not always enough bread. Prices soared, and we lived chiefly on soda water and hard biscuits. Boxes of these salty sea biscuits were acquired surreptitiously from the government commissary and divided up among the workers in our shop.

It was expensive to live in the hotel, and I soon rented a room from a noisy, free, and easy broker named Abrasha Flaks. Flaks was convinced that besides working at the factory I was writing stories about Jack the Ripper and the famous American detectives Nick Carter and Nat Pinkerton. Abrasha did not recognize any other kind of literature. His disorderly apartment was filled with dog-eared little books printed on wretched gray paper but with colorful jackets which pictured the miraculous crimes of the bandits and the no less miraculous exploits of the detectives.

I remember especially one cover which showed Nat Pinkerton after he had fallen into the clutches of a Negro murderer. The Negro was holding Pinkerton, his hands clutching his waist, over a bottomless pit, and Pinkerton was cold-bloodedly pointing two revolvers at the murderer. The moral of the picture was clear—if the Negro relaxed his grip and let Pinkerton fall, the detective would have time to fire two bullets into him. Obviously, it would pay neither the detective nor the Negro to kill the other. Abrasha Flaks was delighted with this cover.

He had a wife, a small, whining woman all in black ringlets, with a complaining voice and protruding eyes.

"Don't pay any attention to the fact that she's small," Abrasha told me confidentially, "but remember that she's as evil as a crazy cat. It would be better to drown in the sea than to live with someone like her."

Abrasha did not drown himself, but sought happy distractions on the side. I met him once on the wharf with a mincing, large-eyed girl. Red velvet poppies bobbed up and down on her hat. The girl was twirling on her shoulder a Japanese umbrella with a picture on it of a bathing Negress. Abrasha hired a boat and rowed out to sea with the girl. When the boat was some distance from the shore, the girl began to giggle and shriek.

The boatman Lagunov, a stern, unhappy man, used to say that Abrasha Flaks was a rogue and a woman chaser and that sometime he would have to pay for his dirty character. To rent a rowboat to a man like that was simply to pollute the sea.

Every time Madame Flaks learned about a new betrayal by Abrasha a violent row broke out at home. First of all Madame Flaks ran out to the courtyard in her housecoat, and cried out in a tragic voice, lifting her thin arms to the sky:

"Listen to me, honest women! All of you listen. He's mixed up again with that dirty, that scabby Lyuska. May I never go home again if I don't kill that viper and poison myself with acid! Give her to me! Let me at her!"

Then Madame Flaks would dash out into the street, obviously to buy the acid at the drugstore, or perhaps in search of Lyuska. Tenderhearted housekeepers from the courtyard caught up with her and led her home, sobbing, while they vied with each other in calming her:

"Don't get so excited, Madame Flaks, it will hurt your heart. Take pity on your poor woman's nerves! Every man has his failings."

"Bring me Mama!" Madame Flaks sobbed. "My gentle old Mama. From Telegraph Alley, house number five. And sister Berta. And Aunt Sofochka. And my darling little Boris. Let them pass a terrible verdict against him. And bring him to me, too, that rascal, or I don't know what I'll do with myself."

She began to thrash on the floor, flailing her legs and screeching. The women moaned, rushed about, poured spirits of valerian for her until there finally appeared a severe, fat old woman with a white mustache, her gentle old mama. Hardly in the vestibule, she shouted in a loud, bass voice:

"Keep quiet! What kind of a gypsy bazaar is this? Pour a pail of cold water on her!"

Madame Flaks grew quiet at once, and only groaned a little, like a wounded bird.

"I'm already fed up," the gentle old mama grumbled, "with taking care of this abnormal fool. Shut up, you epileptic! Stand up, wash your face, and don't let me hear another word out of you, you idiot."

The family court would assemble in an hour or two in the courtyard right under the window of my room. Everyone came, including sister Berta with the little darling, Boris. It was inexplicable and vile that this nasty family squabble had to be played out in front of people, in the courtyard, and judged in the presence of all the neighbors, guzzling with curiosity.

They would drag out a round table, covered with a knitted tablecloth, and some rickety chairs. Everyone sat down around the table. Abrasha would sit a little apart, with a beaten look, as the accused. The trial could not start at once. They had to wait for the rabbi. Meanwhile everyone was silent, looking reproachfully at Abrasha.

Abrasha always appeared at his trials looking torn to pieces, in a shirt without a collar, in suspenders, and with unlaced shoes. Perhaps he wanted to evoke pity, or perhaps Abrasha thought it was an expression of repentance, a substitute for the ancient custom of putting ashes on the head.

Then a goodhearted old rabbi would appear, blow his nose, sit down in a soft armchair, stroke his beard with his handkerchief for a long time, and then say: "The circus begins again," and the court examination would begin. It was carried on in Yiddish, but this did not prevent the numerous Russian spectators from sharing in all the troubles of this family drama.

It always ended in reconciliation. The rabbi would be taken into the apartment for refreshments, and after a while silence would be restored.

There was not much to do at the factory. I came home early, wrote a great deal, and read.

I joined the town library. The books which Chekhov had given to it were arranged on separate shelves. They were sometimes shown to readers, who were not allowed to borrow them. They were books by half-forgotten writers—Shcheglov, Potapenko, Ertel, Izmailov, Barantsevich, Muizhel—some of them autographed by the authors, some with notes by Chekhov. His notes were simple, relaxed, a little like doctors' prescriptions.

Life went by so quietly that I even established a kind of order

in it. I did my writing at home, and to read I went out to one of
the disarmed corvettes in the harbor, usually to the *Zaporozhets*.
I would hire a rowboat from Lagunov, row out to the ship, tie up
to the iron ship's ladder, and climb up to the top deck. I always
took some food with me, and the watchman and I would make tea
together. It seemed to me, and maybe it was really true, that I grew
more healthy from the sun and from light hunger—I was a little
hungry all the time.

I read and learned by heart all the poets whose books I took
from the library. It was the music in poetry which conquered me
then. All the singing richness of the Russian language showed
itself in this poetry. I could repeat my favorite lines almost without stopping. They changed from day to day; one favorite would
give way to another.

I was surrounded by a crowd of poets. I talked with them. My
head swam with their ideas and their images. I felt like a rich
man. Leconte de Lisle and Heine, Verhaeren and Robert Burns,
were talking with me. And they all told me the very best of which
they were capable.

I was firmly convinced that foreign poets sounded better in
Russian translation than in their own languages. I was especially
impressed then by the poems of Heredia. They seemed to fit the
Azov shores and their ragged capes, their plains, their feeling of
antiquity.

Poetry was as real for me as bread, as work in the factory, as
sunshine or air. It forced me to live in a constant state of tension,
in an unexpected and infinitely varied world. It swept me along,
as a foaming torrent carries a branch torn from a tree. I couldn't
resist it.

I saw everything around me through a transparent filter of
poetry. At first it seemed to me that my surroundings acquired from
my involvement with poetry something which was not really in
them, and shone with a greater brilliance. But that wasn't so.
Neither then nor now could I regret for a single moment my youthful surrender to poetry. Because I know that poetry is life carried
to its fullest expression, the discovery of the world in all its depth.

It was in Taganrog that I first really lived by the sea. Impressions did not slip away, but stayed with me and grew. This was
why I was particularly fond of poetry filled with images of life by
the sea. I tested it against all the things going on around me.

I often rowed far out to sea, usually in the evenings after work.
The sun was setting. I stopped the boat. Drops of water trickled
off the oars. The spectacle of sunset filled my memory with the
words: "The sun is a golden disk which comes out of the azure

wilderness and sinks slowly and radiantly into the lap of the surg-
ing waves. . . ." The precision of these words surprised me. The
golden disk of the sun actually did come out of the empty sky and
slowly sink into the light surge of the sea. There was nothing high-
flown or contrived about these words, but at the same time they
expressed an enormous solemnity. I could never manage to discover the exact point at which this solemnity developed out of the
poetic lines, to flow on freely and strongly through the rest of the
poem.

I loved the little steamship offices in the port, blue with tobacco
smoke, with timetables pinned on their walls. Most of the people
working in these offices were Greeks. I unconsciously applied to
them the meaning of the lines: "My searching glance so often met
the searching glances of Ulysses in the haze of steamship offices,
Agamemnons scoring billiards in a tavern." I believed that I too
would find my Ulysses among these people. And so it happened.
His name was Georgi Sirigos. He was a steamship agent, a dry man
with a brown face and sad black eyes. He carried a string of amber
beads in his thin hand.

Sirigos went out to the steamships in the roadstead in any
weather in his little boat. He was considered the greatest expert on
the Sea of Azov. He could tell by the color of the sky what the wind
would be tomorrow and whether the schools of herring would be
running in the mouth of the Don. He could name the direction of
the wind within one degree; no compass could define it more
exactly.

Sirigos had a beautiful daughter. She often came into her
father's office, sat on the window sill, and read with great concentration. When someone spoke to her, she didn't answer right
away but lifted her head as if she were waking up from a deep
sleep. Her blue eyes never smiled, and there was a smell of lavender
in her long black hair. She wore a pewter sailor's bracelet on her
thin wrist. She never talked with anyone.

Sometimes I saw her in the harbor. She would be sitting on the
breakwater, swinging her legs. The breaking waves splashed her
black dress. Like all Greek women, she loved to wear black. Most
of the sailors tried to court her, but she refused them all.

Sirigos and his daughter engrossed me for a long time, and who
knows how many romantic stories I made up with Sirigos, his
daughter and myself as their chief heroes?

A flashing beacon stood on some low rocks about a mile out to
sea from Taganrog. It was called Cherepakha. I went there often.
In calm weather I could tie my boat to its iron framework and

fish. Almost the only fish I caught were bullheads, with a look of great concentration on their snouts. It seemed almost as if they were not disappointed by their bad luck at being caught, but deeply preoccupied trying to figure out how it had happened.

The clear water poured between the rocks. Taganrog could be seen far away, the cupola of its cathedral, the lighthouse, and the rusty-brown slopes of its shore line.

Once I became so interested in fishing that I did not notice twilight coming on. I was sitting with my back to the open sea when I suddenly heard a roaring noise. I looked around. The wind was blowing in from the sea. A gray haze hung on the horizon. Lightning was flashing dimly in it. The water around me began to turn dark, with steel-colored ripples.

I untied my boat from Cherepakha and began to row toward Taganrog. The wind freshened so fast that within a couple of minutes waves were beginning to break over the sides of the boat. As often happens at sea, especially on the Azov Sea, the wind reversed itself, blowing away from Taganrog, and began to carry me out to sea. A little waterspout went up noisily right next to me.

It was rapidly getting dark. The Taganrog lighthouse was lighted. The lamp in this lighthouse was so fixed that it gave different-colored lights at different distances from the port. I no longer remember their order, but I think that inside the harbor itself the light showed red, farther out green, and really far away white.

I stared at it. It was a white light. That meant I was a long way from the harbor.

The wind was blowing fiercely. It came in gusts, changing sharply from side to side, turning around, and whistling evilly past my oars. The waves bounded against the bow, the rowboat flew into the darkness, and I could hear the sea throwing heavy buckets of water into its bottom.

My feet were already in water above my ankles. I had to bail it out. I dropped the oars and picked up the bailing bucket. But the waves swung the boat around at once, and I realized that the first big roller would fill the boat and sink it.

I grabbed the oars and began to row again with all my strength. My wet shirt stuck to my body and bothered me a lot. My hands were on fire; I must have broken the skin on them.

When I looked around again, the light was green. The harbor was closer. "A little bit more," I said to myself. "Just a little. The light will turn red right away. Then you'll be saved."

I lost all consciousness of time. It must have been about midnight. The heavy darkness roared and raged around me. I couldn't even see the foam on the rollers breaking over me.

I rowed, and groaned with exhaustion. Wet hair fell into my eyes, but I left it there; nothing was visible around me anyway, and I didn't dare stop rowing even for a second: the wind would blow the boat backwards.

I looked again, and swore: the lighthouse was now showing a white light! I was being carried rapidly out to sea, and it seemed there was nothing that could hold the little boat against that furious wind.

Then I dropped the oars and began to bail again. A strange indifference swept over me. I bailed water and suddenly started to think of Mama and Galya, a little bystreet in Lublin where I had picked lilacs for Lelya, the wet clouds over the road at Baranovichi, a warm woman's palm gently stroking my cheek, the bonfire in the synagogue at Kobrin. These memories flashed through my head without any links between them, grew confused, tumbled on top of each other. For a while I seemed to have grown deaf and blind.

When I next raised my head, the light from the lighthouse hung on the horizon itself. It looked like a drowning star. I started to row again, slowly, evenly, rigid with fear. I was amazed that I had not yet drowned. A wave struck me, and for a time I couldn't think of anything.

I looked around again, and saw the light was green. I was filled not with happiness but with a strange bitter feeling. I started to row with such strength that the oars bent. I rowed standing up, with all the weight of my body. I swore through my clenched teeth, and then I began to repeat stupidly over and over again the same words: "To hell with you! I won't give up!"

I was sure the night would never end.

Suddenly I heard a new and hellish roaring behind me, looked around, and saw the lighthouse shining red. I was right next to the harbor. It was the waves that were roaring, piling up on the breakwater, dropping back again and colliding with new waves following them. Columns of black water and foam flew up toward the sky. The greatest danger of all lay at the entrance to the harbor—what the sailors call the "devil's cauldron." I would have to get inside the harbor through a barrage of boiling, raging water.

Lights were burning on the ends of the breakwater. I turned my boat toward them. The feeling of danger left me. I figured by the lights where the waves would fling me, and began to row like mad. To feel better, I yelled. I have no idea what I yelled.

The boat tossed like a cork in a waterfall. It leaped into the air, its bow buffeted from all directions, its bottom cracking with the blows of the waves.

A clear white light shone right over my head. I couldn't guess, of course, that this was a searchlight and that I had been noticed from the breakwater.

Then I saw its black walls right next to me, and suddenly felt that the violence of the water was subsiding. The lights on the breakwater began to move backwards and unexpectedly I stopped being hurled and tossed around. I made out in front of me the high bowsprits of the familiar corvettes, the dancing reflection of lights. I heard a drawn-out cry:

"Hey, you in the rowboat! You in the rowboat!"

A lantern waved on the pier. I rowed toward it, found a stone stairway, and dropped the oars.

Port watchmen lifted me out of the boat and carried me to their guardhouse where I saw myself in the blinding electric light—tattered, soaked through, my arms blue and stained with blood.

"Your God's been good to you," a white-haired port inspector with ferocious eyebrows said to me. "Why did you go out to the open sea when the storm signals have been flying since two o'clock?"

"I never learned what the signals mean," I admitted.

"So that's how it was," he said, and he held out to me a silver cigar case. "Remember now, every man must learn to recognize storm signals. On the sea, and in his own life. If he wants to avoid disasters that can't be mended."

THE ART OF WHITEWASHING HUTS

I was transferred, at the end of the summer in 1916, from the Nev-Vilda factory to the Vaksov oil mill. The owner was a young and fairly stupid fellow whom people in Taganrog thought to be a millionaire. He always walked around in a dirty, crumpled silk suit, combed his disheveled reddish beard with his five fingers, and talked in an obscure and slipshod sort of way.

Eager to show his patriotic spirit, Vaskov was installing a hydraulic press in his oil mill and was beginning to make shell casings. But nothing ever came of all the bother. Vaskov's press produced nothing but terribly defective casings.

There was absolutely nothing to do at Vaskov's factory. I sent a request to Captain Velyaminov, my direct superior in Yekaterinoslav, to be released from this work. A week later I received an answer that my request had been granted.

I left my work at the factory without worrying because I had become acquainted at the Taganrog market with an old fisherman from Cape Petrushina named Mikola and arranged for him to take me on as his assistant. A lazy fellow who was driving out to "some kind of hellish farm" took me in his oxcart as far as Cape Petrushina. His wheels sank into the dust up to the axles, and the driver told me:

"It's the devil's own dust, may he disappear in it! But there's a trick, by the way, for avoiding it. A very old trick."

"What is it?"

"Soak the road with salt water. The salt firms up the dust like cement. Where I come from people pour salt water on the mud floors of their huts, and those floors are hard as rock. They do the same thing when they're threshing wheat to make the ground flat and even. That's the way it's done, Pan. Just imagine, everything has some use in this world."

He put me down near the road leading down to the spit of sand which was Cape Petrushina, and drove on farther, yelling lazily to his drowsing oxen:

"Get on there, you devil's slaves! May the cholera strike you dead!"

I could see below me a little sandy cape with a few blindingly white huts scattered on it. Thin pink fishing nets were drying on supports along the shore. Black fishing boats were tossing in the clear water. There was absolutely nothing else to be seen, if you don't count the indigo sky, the sea, the sun, and the yellow grass waving in the breeze.

When I walked down the steep slope I noticed two very small boys, whiteheaded and barefoot, and an equally whiteheaded little girl about eight years old. They were running toward me as hard as they could. The girl was running in front, looking back and crying to the little boys:

"Faster! It'll be too late to hide. Faster!"

Then all three disappeared, as if the earth had swallowed them. But when I walked past some high thistles, I could hear light breathing and a hurried whisper:

"Don't cry. The man will hear you. I'll take the splinter out."

The children were hiding in the thistles. When I had gone by they came out and followed me, but at a respectful distance. One little boy was limping; he must have stepped on a thorn.

I stopped and waved to the children. They came up to me slowly, embarrassed, lowering their eyes and sniffing. The little girl stood in front, with the little boys hiding behind her.

"How do you do?" I said to the little girl. "Where around here does Grandfather Mikola live?"

The girl began to tremble, raised her shining, deep, gray eyes, and smiled at me. All that was light and graceful in her sunburned little person was poured out in that smile: courtesy, pride, and confusion. The pride was because a mysterious man from the city had addressed his question first to her and not to the little boys.

"Come on, uncle!" she said boldly. She took me by the hand and, happy and flushing, led me to the last tiny hut, standing by the very edge of the water. On the thresholds as we passed, as if by command, women appeared, both old and young. They hurriedly straightened the shawls on their heads, greeted me cheerfully, and said deliberately:

"Natalka, where ever did you pick up such a fine guest? What a girl you are! And we were wondering whom she could be leading to us. We thought it must be the captain of the *Kerch*."

The *Kerch* was a little paddle-wheel steamboat which cruised back and forth between Rostov and Mariupol. When there was freight, the *Kerch* would occasionally stop at little fishing villages along the way. It was clear that the *Kerch* was a fairy-story boat for the children.

Natalka walked along proudly, paying no attention to the women's jokes. Only her crimson cheeks betrayed her pleasure. And the little boys, recognizing their insignificance, danced along behind in a deep and reverential silence.

So we came to Grandfather Mikola's hut. There Natalka handed me over to a withered-up old woman with searching eyes, Mikola's wife Yavdoka.

These were the good omens with which my life on Cape Petrushina began.

Grandfather Mikola had taken me on willingly as his assistant. All the young fishermen had been conscripted and gone off to war, and in his words there was "fabulously nobody left on the cape to work." The word "fabulously" was used by Mikola in different senses. It meant "completely" and "absolutely," and "a lot" and sometimes just "yes." In answer to any question, Grandfather Mikola often answered, "Fabulously!"

He took me on "for grub and without pay"; in other words, he committed himself to feeding me, and I renounced any financial share in the sale of the fish we caught. I ate so little that I proved to be an excellent assistant.

The fact that I refused pay and ate very little, although it was profitable to Mikola, bothered him a great deal. He often discussed the problem with his old lady, Yavdoka, and they agreed in the end, of course, that I must be a little touched in the head.

I occupied myself with the "science of fishing." It really was a science in its way, a complicated set of skills. It "fabulously" demanded a great deal of experience and some special knowledge which has never been written down. It is handed down by fishermen from generation to generation.

Grandfather Mikola initiated me into his science slowly, explaining the business of fishing by example and by incidents out of his own life. Gradually I learned all the kinds of fish to be found in the Azov Sea, their habits, and the chief underwater roads along which they swam. I learned a great number of the signs and all the winds (and there were many of them on the Azov Sea).

Every fisherman had his "place" in the sea where he let down his nets. It was necessary to locate this place with great precision. First of all Grandfather Mikola taught me how to orient myself by motionless objects on the shore. Fishermen called this "taking one's bearings."

"Look over there," Grandfather Mikola told me, "just when that dead tree on the slope is in line with the cross on the Taganrog Cathedral. That will be our line. We have to hold to it, going along fabulously as if we were following a string until that burial mound on the steppe near us is in line with the other burial mound farther away. Where those two lines cross is our 'place' and there we can let down our nets."

It was easy to take your bearings in calm weather, but in the wind I had to wrestle with the oars for a long time before I could get the clumsy fishing boat in the correct position.

We let down our nets at night and brought them back at dawn, whatever the weather. Only in very heavy storms did the fishermen not go out. But they never admitted even then that it was dangerous, explaining instead that the waves had "upset" the fish and that they wouldn't catch anything even if they went.

I watched many dawns over the sea. There were some that were warm and gentle. The dawn was born slowly in the quiet of the night. The sky grew blue tenderly in the east, the stars twinkled (they never went out all at once, but moved farther and farther away, growing smaller and paler, into the depths of the sky), and a thin mist curled over the transparent water.

By the time we had rowed out to our nets, the sun was already up. The shadow of the boat lay on the water. In the shadow the water took on a dark malachite color. It was so quiet that the noise made by the oars against the side of the boat boomed a long way across the sea, as if in a room.

The fishermen called dawns like this "angels' dawns."

But there were others which were chilly, gray, and raw. The wind would drive up reddish, turbulent waves, and a whitish haze would wreathe the horizon. There were black dawns, stormy, with the sky torn to tatters, and there were muddy green dawns which threw foam into your face. Dawns with a scarlet, inflamed sky and a cutting wind always brought bad luck. But these bad dawns were infrequent—it was still August, the stillest and warmest month on the Sea of Azov.

Grandfather Mikola sold his fish to a buyer—a sprightly, talkative old woman—but sometimes on Sundays he took it himself to the market in Taganrog. He was a quiet old man, who seemed even taciturn, not like the other old fishermen on the cape. His old woman Yavdoka was an ailing, gentle sort who held her tongue and sighed when her husband was around but loved to complain about his stinginess when he wasn't there.

They had a custom on the cape of whitewashing all the little huts at once. They did it often, especially before holidays and after rains. The fishermen would assemble in the early morning and do each hut in turn, beginning with the farthest one, which belonged to Grandfather Mikola.

These were cheerful days. The women in their turned-up skirts, with heavily sunburned legs, red-cheeked, with shining white teeth, noisy, shouted to each other, jingled their necklaces, made jokes, and looked up slyly from under their long eyelashes. The best of them all at whitewashing was Natalka's mother, Khristina, a thin, courteous woman with a coral necklace around her dark neck. Her husband was in the army and she went out herself to fish in a small boat with Natalka. With a simple rough brush Khristina could give a blue or green border to a window cleanly and exactly.

I remembered what the oxcart driver had told me about salt, and I advised the women to mix salt with the lime in their whitewash so that the walls would not smear and the whitewash would last longer. The idea won their strong approval. In gratitude Khristina painted enormous blue roses and cockerels on the stove in Grandfather Mikola's hut.

On Sundays I took the two little boys and Natalka out in the boat. We would anchor not far from the shore and fish for bullheads. We talked in whispers. Natalka whispered endlessly about everything that came into her head, all the news on the cape, about how people said, for example, that an old woman walked along the roads in the steppe looking at people out of steely eyes, and anyone she looked at was sure to have some relative killed in the war. And about how the thistles burned with red flames every night on the burial mounds ("I didn't see it myself, but that's what people say") and about how a sailor from Mariupol made a bet of three rubles that he could light a cigarette from those thistles.

"And did he light it?" the little boys asked timidly.

"Why, of course!" Natalka answered casually. "And he didn't even die. Sailors can do anything. And last night, there was lightning all night, only it wasn't really lightning but the spirits of men who've been killed at the front, trying to talk to us and look at us. Mama says that maybe our father's spirit will crackle over the sea some night, and then cry for us. But I comfort her, and I tell her that no bullet will ever hit our father because I buried my steel cross under the old stone woman of the steppe and turned around three times on one leg and said three times: 'Saint Mikola Mirlikiiski, guardian of all sailors, keep death away from my father.'"

"Do you think, maybe," Natalka asked me anxiously, "or does it sometimes seem to you, that I'm telling lies? Not a bit of it! May God punish me if I have lied even half a word." To prove it she

made a little sign of the cross and crossed her fingers. The frightened little boys clung to her, and they also covertly crossed their
fingers.

Once in October Grandfather Mikola brought me three letters
from Taganrog all at once, one from Mama, one from Romanin,
and a third letter addressed in a crude handwriting which I didn't
know. I couldn't make up my mind to open them for a long time.
Just as in Odessa, when I had decided to transfer to the hospital
ship, the *Portugal,* I felt myself to be a traitor. I had picked myself
a soft spot while the war was still going on and when the approach
of some unclear but imminent storm was clear to everyone.

"Of course," I told myself, "the easiest thing of all is to live here
on this cape, catching fish and getting sunburned and growing
strong, reading books as if nothing were happening and as if peace
and good will were ruling the world. But it's no real excuse to say
that I wasn't allowed to go back to the front, or that I need this
kind of experience for the big job I'm preparing for—for writing."

For some reason I remembered Polonsky's* words: "A writer,
if he is a wave in the ocean which is Russia, cannot help being
moved when the elements move." Polonsky, of course, was right.
If I wanted to be a writer, then I belonged in the thick of life and
of what was happening, and could not withdraw to this remote
quiet and satisfy myself with music, even that of the most magnificent poetry. Even before I read the letters, I decided to go back
to Moscow.

I walked down to the boat on the shore. It was pulled half out
of the water. I sat on the stern, opened the letters, and began to
read them.

Romanin wrote that the unit had been moved to Molodechno,
near Minsk, that there was little work, but that he was not planning
to quit because he predicted the coming of significant times (these
words were underlined in the letter) and that there were reasons
for him to stay with the army.

"As far as you are concerned," he wrote, "maybe now they would
send you back to the unit. Turn on pressure in Moscow, and come
on back. Gronsky has recovered and is with us again. He has
quieted down a lot. Kedrin's in Moscow, with the head office. All
he's doing there, as usual, is nonsense. How are you, and what are
you doing? The devil knows where you've crawled off to."

Mama wrote that she and Galya were very pleased with living

* Y. P. Polonsky (1819–1895) was a minor lyric poet in the Romantic
tradition of Lermontov.

at Kopan, very busy with the land and farming, and that it would
be nice if I would come and see them.

The third letter was from Lyuba, in Kharkov.

"I'm writing you to General Delivery, in Taganrog, just on the
chance. Maybe my letter will reach you. I learned from Faina
Abramovna that you are in Taganrog. They read your deposition
at my trial. Thank you, my darling. I was acquitted, given only a
month of religious repentance at the church, and you know yourself how bad a nun I'd make. Uncle Grisha died of delirium
tremens. Poor man, I'm so sorry I can hardly bear it. And they
buried him without me there. I'm in Kharkov now, working as
cashier in a motion picture theater. If I knew for certain where
you were, I'd come if only for a day, just to talk things over—I go
mad living alone, without anything to say to anybody. I remember
everything, and won't forget. If you're coming through Kharkov,
write me. I'll run down to the station day or night. I kiss you, and I
remain your Lyuba."

I decided to wait for the *Kerch,* to go to Mariupol, and then by
railroad to Moscow. I was putting off the day of my departure because I was sure I would never see this blessed place again. Besides,
the last days of October were so clear and warm that it was hard
to tear away from them, hard to lose a minute of this heavenly
autumn.

The clear days did not start out with all their glittering trans-
parence. They slowly burned away the morning haze and then
blazed with a heady, just faintly chilly light until the sun went
down. All sounds could be heard with exceptional clarity because
there was such a calm over the sea. Autumn, unlike summer, was
filled with slow sounds. The noise of dead plants crunched underfoot, the far-off whistle of a steamship, women talking in their
courtyards, all of these died away not quickly but with a confused
aftersound, such as follows the slow tolling of a church bell.

The autumn air seemed a capacious sounding box which was
trying to hold on to the little noises of each hour and each minute.
It was as if autumn itself was sorry to leave these places and these
people, and was listening intently to their life.

Two quite separate events strengthened my determination to
go away. The first took place in Taganrog. Fishermen who had
taken their fish to the market came back one day and reported dis-
orders in the town. Crowds of hungry women with children had
stormed the bakeries and food stores, and the Cossacks had refused
to fire on them.

The second happening was comparatively insignificant. I was

repairing Grandfather Mikola's nets when a lanky fisherman named Ivan Yegorovich sat down beside me. We smoked, and then he said:

"I've wanted to talk to you for a long time about something that involves all of us here. But I couldn't make up my mind. You're an educated man, maybe you see things differently from the rest of us, who are just fishermen. If so, excuse me."

"What's it all about?"

"It's just that it seems unfair somehow. All the young fishermen are in the army. Their wives, of course, are left here with their children. The women are thrashing around like fish on the ground, trying to live, to get enough to eat. They do the fishing themselves. Sometimes it's work that's too heavy for them. And you, a young man, and a strong one, come as an assistant to Grandfather Mikola. It would be better if you went—say—with Khristina in her boat. It would be more fair. People, you know, are a little surprised by it. For Grandfather Mikola needs your help, you know, only to put more rubles in his money box."

I could feel myself blushing. The man was right. How had I not guessed it myself! I told Ivan Yegorovich that I had not really thought about the matter, that I was going away, and that there was nothing to be done about it now.

"That's the way it is," Ivan Yegorovich agreed. "The people here are all well-disposed toward you. Stay with us on the cape."

"No, I can't possibly do that."

"Well, excuse me for bothering you." Ivan Yegorovich stood up. "It's a matter for you to decide, of course. Keep well."

After this conversation I lost all interest in Grandfather Mikola and his old woman Yavdoka and I decided to go to Taganrog the next day, but fortunately the *Kerch* showed up that evening. It was on its way to Mariupol.

The whole population of the cape assembled on the shore to greet the *Kerch*. Everyone parted with me kindly, wishing me good health and happiness and success. Everyone kissed me, after having first wiped his lips with the back of his hand.

Khristina and Natalka took me out to the *Kerch* in their fishing boat. They took the two little boys, too. I didn't tell Khristina about my conversation with Ivan Yegorovich. I was ashamed to admit how stupid I had been.

I climbed up to the deck of the *Kerch*, which was covered with baled hay, and walked to the railing. The little steamship produced a hoarse bass whistle completely unrelated to its shabby appearance and tiny size. The paddle wheel churned the green, foamy water. Natalka stood in her fishing boat. Her face was frowning unhappily, and she covered it with her sleeve. She was crying, and Khristina, kneeling beside her, was nuzzling against her and laughing.

The fishing boat and the shore behind it began to move away. The women were waving their white shawls and it looked as if a flock of gulls were hovering over one spot on the shore, uncertain whether to land on the sand. The weeping Natalka waved her faded blue shawl, too.

The steamship carried me away from the familiar shore. Again, as at so many turning points in my life, my heart felt heavy. And it was all the heavier because life was not working out well. There was no link at all between its separate parts. People who had unexpectedly walked into my life were disappearing from it just as unexpectedly, and perhaps forever.

I sent a telegram from Mariupol to Lyuba in Kharkov. Having sent it, I began to regret it, but it was too late.

The train got into Kharkov early on a chilly morning. Lyuba was waiting for me on the platform. She was wearing a short jacket, with a light shawl over her head. She was so cold even her lips were turning blue.

She hurried up to me. We kissed each other. Then she looked carefully into my eyes, took me by the hand, and led me silently behind a boarded-up kiosk on the platform.

"Don't say anything," Lyuba said.

She threw her arms around my shoulders and pressed her head against my chest as if looking for protection. I was silent. She held me tighter and tighter, and her head was trembling. Several minutes went by like this. The third warning sounded. Lyuba raised her head, quickly made the sign of the cross over me, turned away, and walked along the platform, holding the edge of her shawl to her face. I got back in the car. The train moved off.

THE RAW FEBRUARY

In Moscow I went straight from the station to the Union of Cities. The first man I saw there was Kedrin. We greeted each other happily and even embraced each other. It turned out that Kedrin had come from Minsk on some kind of mission.

I told him I wanted to return to the unit.

"That's a complicated problem," he answered. "We'll have to look into it."

He went off to look into it and did not come back for a long time. When he did, he told me confidentially that nothing could be worked out. The mood of the army was unreliable, the situation tense, and it would be better right then not to start any trouble at the front. This was the opinion of the leaders of the Union of Cities.

I was discouraged. Kedrin took off his glasses, wiped them, put them on again, and looked at me closely. Having finished with all this, he said:

"Don't be dejected. We'll find work to do. You don't write badly. Romanin showed me your sketch, 'The Blue Overcoats.' You have style."

He wrote me a letter of recommendation to a friend of his in the editorial office of one of the Moscow papers. I was greeted there by a bald man with the face of an old actor. He was writing in a dusty room at a table covered with galley proofs. In a soft armchair on the other side of the table sat a fat little man with shrewd, happy eyes and a gray Zaporozhe mustache, wearing a gray long-waisted coat and a lambskin hat. He looked very much like Taras Bulba.

The bald man read Kedrin's letter, said, "The man's himself again. Wait a minute," slipped the letter under a pile of proofs, and began to write again.

Taras Bulba pulled a silver box out of his pocket, winked at the bald man, tapped his finger on the table, and offered the box to me.

"Help yourself! This box was given to me personally by General Skobelyev after Plevna."

I thanked him and refused. Taras Bulba skillfully took a little snuff on his thumbnail, placed it in his nostril, and produced a deafening sneeze. There was a smell of dried cherries. The bald man did not pay the slightest attention to Taras Bulba.

Taras Bulba winked again, like a conspirator, at the bald man, picked up a horseshoe which was being used as a paperweight to hold the galleys on the table, and easily bent it into a straight bar of steel.

At this the bald man looked up.

"That's an old trick," he said. "You can't buy me that way. There's a war on. No more advances."

"You're keeping someone waiting." Taras Bulba pointed to me. "That's all I wanted to remind you of. Not another thing."

"Well, why not?" the bald man said lazily, and he glanced at me. "Let's try. Tell us what you want to do with yourself. By the way, I'm called Mikhail Alexandrovich. And he"—he pointed to Taras Bulba—"he's the king of Moscow reporters, poet, former boxer and actor, expert on Moscow slums, bosom friend of Chekhov and Kuprin, the famous Uncle Gilyai—Vladimir Alexandrovich Gilyarovsky."

I was overcome with embarrassment.

"Pay no attention to him, don't be scared!" Gilyarovsky reassured me, and he shook my hand so hard that my bones cracked.

He walked to the door. At the threshold he turned around, said, pointing at me, "I believe in him," and walked out, humming.

The bald man took me on the staff of the paper, congratulated me on this, and explained:

"These are critical times, fraught with uncertainty. It looks as if we're going to see a second Time of Troubles in Russia. On the surface, everything seems smooth enough, but inside everything's seething. The tighter the government screws down the top of the boiler, the bigger the explosion is going to be. We've got to watch this boiler. We've got to know what Moscow is talking about, and thinking about. What people say at the theater, and in their homes, at markets and in factories, in bathhouses and in trolley cars. What the workers are talking about, and cabdrivers and shoemakers and milkmen and actors and merchants, engineers, students, professors, soldiers, and writers. You go and take care of this. Just as a start. And then we'll see."

That very day I rented a little room on Granatny Lane, the same street on which I had been born twenty-three years before.

I had noticed that Russian people talk most freely on trains and in taverns. So I began with the suburban trains, full of noise and

cheap tobacco smoke. They never went farther than fifty versts
from Moscow. I would take a ticket to the last stop and travel there
and back. In a very short time I managed to get to most of the
little towns around Moscow. And I became convinced that the
capital city, Moscow, was surrounded by a moss-covered old Russia
that the oldest residents of the city had no conception of.

Fifty versts from Moscow the backwoods started—woods filled
with bandits, unusable roads, decayed old settlements, ancient
peeling churches, little horses with manure stuck to their skin,
drunken fights, cemeteries with overturned gravestones, sheep
living inside the peasants' huts, snotty children, straitlaced monasteries, God's fools clustered on church porches, markets filled with
rubbish and the squeal of pigs and obscene cursing, decay, poverty,
and thievery.

And through all this wilderness around Moscow, where the wind
whistled in the bare birch twigs, could be heard the repressed,
agonizing crying of women. They were crying for their soldiers—
mothers and wives, sisters and sweethearts. They were crying helplessly and hopelessly. It was as if no one expected any happiness
anywhere.

This land was growing cold, darkening the spruce palisades
with the crimson stripes of early winter sunsets, crackling with the
first granular ice, covering the fields with smoke from frozen villages. And Blok's words seemed prophetic:

> My Russia, my life, must we languish together?
> The Tsar, and Siberia, and Yermak, and prison . . .

I heard drunken and sober talk, bold and desperate talk, full of
humility and full of hatred, every kind of talk. In all the conversation there was only one common element: the hope for peace, the
hope that the soldiers would come back from the war and create
that better life without which there was nothing to do except to die
of hunger.

It was as if all the people's anger were concentrated there in
the west, with the army. The villages were waiting for it to flow
back from there, to wash their hateful life away, to clean up their
wretched existence, so that peasant and craftsman, factory worker
and artisan, might at last take power over the land.

Then life would start! Then hands would be reached out to
work, and such a clatter of saws and axes and hammers would rise
all over the land that you wouldn't be able to drown it out even if
you rang all the church bells in Russia.

Man is a strange creature. In all these places around Moscow I saw the poverty of Russia, but one thing produced in me a kind of repressed happiness—the people's habit of using speech which was amazing in its images and in its simplicity. It was the first time I had ever come so close to it. Turgenev's statement that such a language could have been given only to a great people sounded now like no exaggeration but like the simple truth.

It was different in Moscow. Some people argued fruitlessly while they sought a way out, others knew the way out and quietly prepared for it, while a third group—got rich. Businessmen appeared with a long reach and a clutch of iron. First place among them went to the Siberian industrialist Vtorov, a man like Lopakhin in Chekhov's *The Cherry Orchard.*

The shadow of Rasputin still stood over all this anxious life. Never before in Russian history had an illiterate old fox, a horse thief, and kulak arrived in Peterburg in a dirty third-class railroad car, looking for profits, and in a short time become almost the autocrat of the nation, the ruler of its destinies, the right hand of the Tsar and the possessor of a harem of court beauties. Imperial, wellborn, ministerial leaders bowed their haughty heads before him and waited, like cringing dogs, for him to throw them a bone from his table.

The country had never known such degradation and shame. Fateful times were upon us. Everyone, weary of the suspense, was waiting for the outcome.

And it started. It began with the killing of Rasputin. They threw his corpse under the ice in the Little Neva. Rasputin had been poisoned, shot, and strangled but according to the doctors his heart still beat for several minutes under the ice.

Everything in Moscow at that time was confused. Thousands of Uzbeks in green robes were marched through the streets under guard. A revolt had been put down in Central Asia and they were driving the Uzbeks to Murmansk to build a railroad in the Arctic north and to die. The first dry snowflakes fell on their black skullcaps embroidered with silver threads. This procession of the doomed went on for several days.

Moscow was flooded with refugees from Poland, the Baltic regions, and White Russia. Quick and sibilant accents could be heard more and more often mixed into the singing speech of Moscow. Old Jews who looked like rabbis walked up and down the streets with umbrellas to protect them from the sun. Symbolist poets who had completely lost all contact with reality sang about pale ghosts of passion and the fires of otherworldly lusts. They were not even noticed in the general turmoil of ideas and feelings.

In our editorial office life was never still for an hour, in the daytime or at night. All of us spent all our free time there. We argued, made a lot of noise, and waited for events.

Anxious rumors filtered through from Peterburg. Travelers reported threatening queues for bread, angry meetings in the streets and squares, strong feelings in the factories.

Shortly after Rasputin's murder, the bald man summoned me.

"Well," he said, "your sketches are wonderful. You've managed to catch something very . . . very much of the people. So I've had an idea. I want you to go to some godforsaken place in the provinces and write what Turgenev's Russia is thinking now."

I agreed. We began to speculate on where I should go, where I could find the most out-of-the-way district without going too far from Moscow. The well-known theater critic and Chekhov expert, the gentle Yuri Sobolyev, was taking part in the discussion. Everyone called him Yurochka, behind his back and to his face.

"Chekhov once wrote," Yurochka said, "that the incarnation of the Russian wilderness was for him the little town of Yefremov, in Tula province. It's somewhere near Yelets. By the way, it's also one of Turgenev's places. Yefremov is on the Krasivaya Mecha River. Remember 'Kassian from the Krasivaya Mecha'? That's where you ought to go."

I arrived in Yefremov at night. I sat in the cold station buffet until dawn. It was painted a dirty violet color. There was nothing at the buffet except cold tea. Kerosene lamps were smoking. A bearded station policeman walked by several times, looked sternly at me, and jingled his spurs.

As soon as it began to grow light I hired a cabdriver and drove to the only hotel in Yefremov. In the gray light of a winter morning the little town looked surprisingly small and shabby. A brick jail, a wine factory with a high, thin iron chimney, a scowling cathedral and little houses as alike as twins, all built of stone below and wood above, all these depressed your spirits in the light of the smothered street lamps which had not yet been put out. The only interesting buildings I saw were the rows of shops in the market. Something resembling columns and arches decorated them a little and spoke of the past.

Jackdaws were circling in the dank air. The streets had the sour smell of horse manure.

"Well, so that's the town!" I said to the cabdriver. "There's not much to look at."

"And why should you look at it?" he answered indifferently. "Nobody ever comes here to look at the town. It's not Moscow."

"Why do people come here?"

"For grain, or for apples. We used to have the richest grain-collecting station here. The merchants had a turnover of hundreds of thousands. And our apples, it's true, are excellent. Antonovka apples. If you're interested, go outside the town to the village of Bogovo. I can drive you there. Even in winter you can buy as many apples there as you want."

The hotel was dark and quiet. My room, although it had windows on the street, was also dark, but it was warm. A smell of sour cabbage soup and the steam from samovars floated up from the restaurant downstairs.

The bellboy, a freckled fellow with a mouth which seemed permanently opened in surprise, was reluctant to leave, and he stood and stared at me. He must have been wondering who I was, and what devil's business had brought me to Yefremov. I sent him packing. He was not offended, and when he walked out he said:

"Just think, we had a colonel in our hotel the other day. And right now we have a fortuneteller from Moscow. Madame Troma. She's as skinny as a cat. She smokes three packs of Ira cigarettes every day. And her fingers are all covered with rings. Nothing but diamonds. It's pretty gay here. This evening there will be dancing downstairs. Our boss organizes it all. For the money he makes from it. He's a hawk, all right."

The boy walked out. I hadn't slept all night long in the train and I undressed and went to bed with real enjoyment. For the first time in a long while I felt tired. It was cold, I had a chill, and I did not want to move or talk.

"That's all I need," I thought. "To get sick in this hole."

Thinking of sickness reminded me of what I always tried not to think about—my loneliness. Mama and Galya were far away, Romanin was at the front, Lelya was dead. There was absolutely no one who could have helped me in trouble or in sickness. Not a person! Hundreds of people had moved through my life for a short time, but no one had stayed in it. This was insulting, and unjust.

This was what I thought, trying to comfort myself. I fell asleep. I kept on having the same dream: a snowy plain with a paling of telegraph poles. I would wake a little, but as soon as I closed my eyes that unbroken snowy plain would appear again, with its telegraph poles leading no one knew where or why. I realized even in my sleep that they didn't lead anywhere; there was no town or village in front of me but only snow, and the boring, hard frost of winter.

I woke up at last with the feeling that someone was lightly shaking my bed. I opened my eyes, and I could hear the merry brassy sounds of a band. The glass was shaking in the windows. A Turkish drum was booming cheerfully and urgently. The dancing had started downstairs. I got dressed and went down. It was a good chance to look over the citizenry of Yefremov.

Streams of dampness were running down the walls of a low-ceilinged, half-dark room. The band was blowing away stormily. Girls with anxious faces were sitting on squeaky chairs and fanning themselves with their handkerchiefs.

A haggard-faced man in a worn evening coat was dancing in the middle of the empty floor. His gray hair bristled on his head which was as long as a melon. He was clearly drunk, but he was dancing skillfully and with some dash, doing tricky squatting steps, and crying out: "Ah, Nurka, don't you scold me; come instead, and you can hold me!"

Men were crowded in the doorways. There were almost no young ones, except for a few sickly fellows with long necks and watery eyes. These were obviously "white ticket men," excused from military service for physical reasons.

In a prominent place in the room, right next to a very thin woman whom I guessed to be the fortuneteller, I saw a snub-nosed man with a reddish spade beard, a wide-brimmed black hat, and long hair falling down on the collar of his checked raglan coat. He was slouched in his chair, with his legs crossed, and on his knees he was holding a cane with a silver head shaped like a naked naiad lying on the crest of a wave. He was playing with his cane and looking around the room through his small pince-nez, with a bored smile.

When he saw me he straightened up in his chair, stood up, and walked over to me, patronizingly brushing aside the man who was dancing.

"A thousand apologies!" he said, and he took off his hat with a theatrical gesture. "Judging by the entry in the hotel's registry, you are a literary man—a rare guest in these regions. So I, as your colleague of the pen, permit myself the liberty of introducing myself: Princess Greza."

I was struck dumb. The man with the hat was smiling cheerfully.

"You probably didn't expect to meet me in such a godforsaken place?" he asked. "Well, my old mother lives here, and I come down often from Moscow, seeking rest for both spirit and body."

"Princess Greza!" I had often seen the signature in cheap women's magazines in the section titled "Answers to Our Readers." "Princess Greza" answered their delicate and intimate questions with complete knowledge of what she was doing and in a highly perfumed and sentimental style. How to attract a blond man, what to do when your husband betrays you, what Platonic love is, and how to get rid of blackheads or morning sickness were typical questions.

"My real name," the man told me, "is Miguel Rachinsky. Allow me to introduce you to a guest of our town, the well-known fortune-teller, Madame Adelaide Tarasovna Troma."

He had led me up to the thin woman. She held out her bony hand flashing with paste diamonds, looked indifferently in my face, and said in a hoarse voice:

"Oh, what an extraordinarily lucky young man! Oh, a wonderful future is ahead of you. You were born under a good star."

She wanted to say something more but she began to cough chokingly, holding her black lace handkerchief pressed to her mouth. Her whole body shuddered with the coughing, and through her low-necked dress I could see her sharp collarbone and meager breasts dancing. Madame Troma could not stop coughing, and she got up and left the room.

Miguel Rachinsky invited me to the buffet to drink a bottle of wine with him. Over the bottle, he told me all the secrets of the town.

First of all he explained that the drunken man dancing in the ballroom was the local coffinmaker, a great artist of the dance. The owner of the hotel hired him as an entertainer to stimulate the other guests; otherwise the girls would sit there like stones all evening, waving their handkerchiefs and blushing, and the men would crowd together in the doorway and do nothing. Only a few would go to the buffet, where they would start heavy drinking that would last until morning.

According to Rachinsky, the town had no "intelligentsia of the spirit" except for himself, a young teacher of Russian literature named Osipenko, and a tax collector named Bunin who was the brother of the famous writer. But Bunin was an unsociable man interested only in the study of sorcerers, their plots, their slanders, and their exorcisms.

After making his acquaintance I saw Rachinsky every day and I became convinced that his principal misfortune was a pathological addiction to banality, boasting, and the cheap pose. He was, of course, an unintelligent, or rather, a naïve man, but his nature was kind and trusting. He was very sorry for the fortuneteller, who had been abandoned by her husband and who was sick with tuberculosis. The fortuneteller boarded with Rachinsky's mother, and he insisted that his mother cook separate fatty dishes for the fortune-teller because he had read somewhere that "a slight layer of fat" helps in cases of tuberculosis.

His banality was inexhaustible. Even in conversations about politics and the situation in Russia, Rachinsky loved to flash his dubious expressions. Speaking once about Rasputin, he said that this was "cynicism amounting to a state of grace." Bad poems and stupid aphorisms fell from him like hairs from a molting cat.

In his own home he was an attentive host. The more I observed him, the sorrier I became for this inadequate man.

Rachinsky invited me, too, to board at his mother's, and this was a real favor since the only restaurant in the town, at the hotel, was a stinking pothouse. I agreed, and I was surprised, the first time I went home with him, to find that his mother was a very pleasant and intelligent old lady, a former teacher. She treated her son, her Misha (at home the name Miguel was never used), as a clearly subnormal man, and his manner distressed her, but she was kind and compassionate toward him. It was the sympathetic tenderness of a mother to her black sheep son.

At Rachinsky's dinner table every day there gathered what he called his "fellow diners"—the fortuneteller, Osipenko, and I. The teacher turned out to be a very ardent man, sharp-witted and businesslike. He loved to argue, felt passionately about literature, and would never let Rachinsky get away with any of his "aesthetic tricks." When he had been shown up, Rachinsky would only smile embarrassedly and wipe his glasses. He never dared to argue with the teacher.

The fortuneteller wrapped herself up in her shawl and said nothing. She talked freely only with Rachinsky's mother, Varvara Petrovna, and this only when the men could not hear her. She was clearly ashamed of her occupation, and she often showed up with eyes red from crying. I learned only that she came from a Peterburg family and that the husband who had thrown her over was a lawyer. In her free time she worked in a military hospital where she helped the nurses. The hospital was located in the parochial school.

I decided to go out to the village of Bogovo to find out how the local peasants were living and what they were expecting. The village was on the bank of the Krasivaya Mecha River made famous by Turgenev. The river was covered with snow now, but black water roared down a millrace next to a mill. Melting icicles dripped into it with a loud, jangling noise. The first February thaw had come, with fog and the drip of thawing, a gusty wind, and the smell of smoke.

I met a curious man in Bogovo. At first, I thought of him only as a freak, and it was some days later before I realized the almost symbolic meaning of this encounter.

The peasants of Bogovo, just like those around Moscow, were waiting for only one thing—the end of the war. Nobody knew what would happen then. But all of them were convinced that the war would not just stop of its own accord, and that after it, at long last, justice would triumph.

"The chief thing is that there's no justice!" the village shoemaker, a hollow-chested little man, told me. "Travel all around Russia, ask all the inhabitants of all the towns, and you'll find that everyone has his own conception of justice. A local conception. And if you add all these local ideas of justice together, then you'll have a single, so to speak, all-Russian justice."

"Well, and what is your local justice here?" I asked.

"But there it is, right there, our justice!" the shoemaker answered, and he pointed to a hill above the river. There, in a rough apple orchard, I could see a half-destroyed manor house. It was not big, but it retained some features of that Empire style in country seats which flourished in Russia under Alexander I—a façade with peeling columns, narrow, high windows with a half-moon above each one, two small semicircular wings, and a broken iron grating of rare beauty.

"Explain to me," I asked, "just what that old house has to do with your local justice."

"Just walk up to that house, talk to its owner, and you'll understand. Draw your own conclusions as to who ought to own that house, and the orchard, and the land—there are five or six acres there—if you're going to talk about justice. The master's a queer one. The landowner Shuisky. An incredible scoundrel. He probably wouldn't let you in. You'd have to think up some excuse."

"What kind of an excuse?"

"Well, like wanting to rent a cottage from him for the summer. As if you'd come to talk with him about it."

I walked up to the house along a little path which could hardly be seen in the snow. The windows were all covered with rotting old boards. The front porch was piled deep with snow. I walked around the house and saw a narrow door covered with torn thick felt. I knocked loudly. Nobody answered. I listened. There was a silence like death about the house. "Well, I've tried," I thought. "Probably nobody's living here."

Then the door opened suddenly. A little old man was standing on the threshold in a black quilted dressing gown, ragged with wear, belted with an old towel. A little silk cap was on his head.

His face was covered with dirty bandages. Wisps of cotton, brown with iodine, stuck out from under the bandages.

The old man looked angrily at me through eyes as blue as a child's and he asked in a very high voice:

"What can I do for you, my dear sir?"

I answered as the shoemaker had instructed me.

"But you're not related to the Bunins?" the old man asked suspiciously.

"No, by no means!"

"Then come in."

He led me into what must have been the only living room in the house. It was filled with junk and trash. A little iron stove was glowing hot in the middle of the room. Every little gust of wind made smoke pour out of its cracks.

In a corner I saw a magnificent round stove made of glazed Dutch tiles. Almost half the tiles had been taken off, and the little niches which were left were filled with dusty bottles of medicine, yellowed paper bags, and dried-up, worm-eaten apples. Over the trestle bed, covered with a mangy sheepskin, there hung a gold-framed portrait of a woman in a blue gossamer dress, her powdered hair piled high on her head and her eyes as blue as those of the old man.

It seemed to me I had somehow fallen back into the beginning of the last century, into the world of Gogol's Plyushkin. I had never dreamed that such homes and such people still existed in Russia.

"Are you a member of the gentry?" the old man asked me.

It seemed the best thing to answer yes, that I was gentry.

"Then what you are doing now," the old man said, "does not interest me. Nowadays they've started such occupations that even a policeman can break his leg on them. Believe it or not, there's even something called an Assessor of Statutory Prices! Sheer rot! Those Romanovs' rot! I'll rent you a house for the summer, but on the one condition that you don't keep a goat. You know, three years ago Bunin lived here on my place. A very dubious gentleman! A real Judas! He brought goats with him and they liked it—they nibbled all the apples."

"The writer Bunin?" I asked.

"No. His brother, a tax collector. But the writer came, too. A little better than his brother, the official, but still, I must say, I don't understand what they have to pride themselves on! Small gentry, and nothing more!"

I decided to stand up for Bunin, adapting myself to the old man's sense of values.

"Well, what do you want?" I said. "Because the Bunins are from a very old and excellent family."

"Old?" the old man asked contemptuously. He looked at me as if I were a hopeless blockhead, and he shook his head. "Old? But mine is much older! I am registered in the velvet books of Russia's oldest aristocracy. If you have studied Russian history as you should have, you must know how old my family is."

I remembered only then that the shoemaker had told me the old man's name—Shuisky.* Was this man standing in front of me really the last scion of the family of Shuisky the Tsar? How incredible it was!

"I will charge you," the old man was saying, "fifty rubles for the summer. It's not a small sum, of course. But my expenses are not small. I divorced my wife last year. The old witch is living in Yefremov now, and I have to send her five rubles once in a while, and sometimes ten. It does no good. She just squanders the money on lovers. There isn't an aspen tree good enough to hang her on."

"How old is she?" I asked.

"She's passed her eightieth year, the good-for-nothing," Shuisky answered angrily. "But we will have to write a detailed agreement about your living on my place. Otherwise, it's out of the question."

I agreed to this. I felt as if a most extraordinary play was being acted in front of me.

Shuisky pulled a yellowed sheet of paper with a two-headed eagle embossed on it out of an old cardboard file, found a pen, sharpened it with a broken knife blade, and dipped it into a bottle of iodine.

"Fuii!" he said. "And why does this happen? Just because that old fool Vasilisa never leaves anything in its right place."

In later conversation it became clear that twice a week an old woman named Vasilisa, a former church servant, came out from Bogova to clean up somehow, to chop wood, and to cook *kasha* for the old man.

Shuisky finally found a little bottle of ink and started to write. At the same time he cursed out the new times.

"And nowadays people write and talk like Tartars. All around there's nothing but this Romanov rot. Assessors of Statutory Prices! They even say the little Nicholas allows a dissolute man to eat at the same table with him. Yet he considers himself the Tsar. A little boy he is, but not a Tsar!"

"Why do you put gauze around your face?" I asked him,

* Basil IV, who was a Shuisky, was one of the leading boyars of Muscovy during the reign of Boris Godunov, and became Tsar himself in 1606. He was deposed in 1610 and died two years later.

"I massage it with iodine, and then, naturally, I bandage it in gauze."

"Why?"

"It's for my nerves," Shuisky answered curtly. "Well, there it is. Read it through, and then sign it."

He handed me the paper, which was written in a precise, old-fashioned handwriting. Point by point, all the conditions of life in his broken-down house were listed. I remember especially one point:

"I, the aforementioned Paustovsky, undertake not to use the products of the fruit orchard in view of the fact that they have been sold as a standing crop to Gavrushka Sitnikov of Yefremov."

I signed this curious and completely unnecessary paper, and asked about a deposit. I realized that it would be stupid to pay any money for a house where I had no intention of living. But I had to play my role out to its end.

"What kind of a deposit!" Shuisky answered angrily. "If you are really a gentleman, how can you think of such things! When you come, we will settle up. I have the honor to salute you. I won't accompany you, I've caught a cold. Close the door tight."

I walked back to Yefremov on foot, and the farther I got away from Bogovo, the more fantastic this meeting seemed to me. In Yefremov Varvara Petrovna told me that the old man really was the last Prince Shuisky. It was true, he had had a son, but forty years ago Shuisky had sold him for forty thousand rubles to some childless Polish aristocrat. The latter had needed an heir, so that after his death his enormous properties—an entailed estate—would not be divided up among his relatives but would stay intact. Men skilled in problems of nobility found a little boy of good blood for the Polish count, who purchased him and made him his son.

It was a quiet snowy evening. Something was quietly buzzing in the hanging lamp. I had stayed after dinner at the Rachinsky's, and was reading Sergeyev-Tsensky's book, *The Sorrow of the Fields*.

Rachinsky was writing his advice to women at the dining room table. When he had written a few words, he would lean back in his chair, read them, and smirk—obviously everything he wrote pleased him enormously. Varvara Petrovna was knitting, and the fortuneteller, slumped in an armchair, was thinking about something, looking at her hands with their diamond rings folded on her knees.

Suddenly someone knocked loudly on the window. All of us started. From the knocking—quick and anxious—I realized something had happened.

Rachinsky went to open the door. Varvara Petrovna made the sign of the cross. Only the fortuneteller never budged.

Osipenko darted into the dining room, in his overcoat and hat, without even having taken off his galoshes.

"There's a revolution in Peterburg," he cried. "The government is overthrown." His voice gave out, he fell into a chair, and burst into tears.

For a moment there was complete silence. All that could be heard was the sound of Osipenko crying, gasping feverishly for breath, just like a little child.

My heart began to thump crazily. I gasped for breath, and I could feel tears rolling down my cheeks. Rachinsky grabbed Osipenko by the shoulders and shouted at him:

"When? How? Tell us."

"Look . . . Look . . ." Osipenko muttered, and he pulled a long, narrow telegraph form out of his pocket. "I've just come from the telegraph office. . . . Here it all is . . . all . . ."

I took the paper from him and started to read out loud the proclamation of the Provisional Government.

At last! My hands were shaking. Even though the whole country had been expecting the event for months, the blow was still too sudden.

Here in this sleepy, forgotten town, it was even more unexpected. Moscow papers arrived only on the third day after publication, and not many of them. Dogs barked in the evenings along the main street, and the night watchmen sounded their clappers as they made their rounds. It was as if nothing had changed since the sixteenth century in this little town, as if there were no railroad, no telegraph, no war, no Moscow, nothing happening anywhere.

And now—revolution! Thoughts crowded in disorder through my head, and only one thing was clear—something big had happened, something which nobody and nothing was powerful enough to stop. What had happened, on this seemingly ordinary day, was what people had been waiting for over more than a century.

"What's to be done?" Osipenko asked excitedly. "We must do something quickly."

Then Rachinsky said something for which all his sins could be forgiven:

"We've got to get this proclamation printed. And posted all over the town. And we must get in touch with Moscow. Come on!"

The three of us went out—Osipenko, Rachinsky, and I. Only Varvara Petrovna and the fortuneteller stayed at home. Varvara Petrovna was standing next to the icon in the corner, crossing herself often and quickly, and whispering: "Oh, God, at last! Oh, God,

at last!" The fortuneteller went on sitting motionless in her armchair.

A man was running toward us along the empty street. I noticed
in the faint light from the street lamps that he was hatless, wearing
only a blouse, and barefoot. He was holding a boot tree in his hand.
He rushed up to us.

"Dear friends!" he shouted, and he grabbed my arm. "Have you
heard? There's no more Tsar. Nothing's left but Russia."

He kissed us all and ran on farther, sobbing and mumbling
something.

"What's the matter with us?" Osipenko said. "We haven't even
congratulated each other." We stopped and embraced each other.

Rachinsky went to the telegraph office to check up on all mes-
sages coming in from Peterburg and Moscow, while Osipenko and
I went off to a little out-of-the-way printshop where posters and
official notices of the military authorities were usually printed.

It was closed. While we were trying to break the lock, a fussy
man with a key came along, opened the door, and lit some lights.
He turned out to be the only typesetter and printer in Yefremov.
What he was doing there at that moment, we did not ask.

"Stand next to the type fonts and start composing," I told him.
I began to dictate to him the text of the proclamation. He set the
type, interrupting his work only to wipe the tears from his eyes
with his sleeve.

Another piece of news was quickly brought to us—an order by
the Minister of Railroads of the Provisional Government, Nekrassov
—To all, to all, to all!—to hold the imperial train, wherever it
might be found.

History was moving across Russia like an avalanche.

I read the first reprint we made of the proclamation, and the
letters danced before my eyes. By now the printshop was full of
people who had found out somehow that a communication about
the uprising was being printed there. They took the proclamations
in their arms and ran out into the streets, nailing them on walls,
fences, and lampposts.

It was one o'clock in the night, a time when Yefremov was
usually fast asleep. Suddenly, at this odd hour, there sounded a
short, booming peal of the cathedral bell. Then another, and a third.
The pealing grew faster, its noise spread over the town, and soon
the bells of all the outlying churches started to ring.

Lights were lit in all the houses. The streets filled with people.
The doors of many homes stood open. Strangers, weeping openly,
embraced each other. The solemn, exultant whistling of locomotives
could be heard from the direction of the station. Somewhere far

down one street there began, first quietly, then steadily louder, singing of the "Marseillaise":

> *Ye tyrants quake, your day is over,*
> *Detested now by friend and foe!*

The singing brass sounds of a band joined the human voices in the chorus.

Osipenko wrote the first order of the Provisional Revolutionary Committee of Yefremov on a table smeared with printer's ink. No one had set up this committee. No one knew or could know who was on it, because it had no members. The order was improvised by Osipenko:

"Until the appointment by the government of liberated Russia of new authorities in the town of Yefremov, the Provisional Revolutionary Committee of Yefremov calls on all citizens to maintain calm, and it orders:

"The administration of the town shall be in the hands of the town council and its president, Citizen Kushelev.

"Citizen Kushelev is appointed Commissar of the government, to serve until further notice.

"The police are to surrender their arms at once to the town council.

"A people's militia will take charge of order in the streets.

"The work of all institutions and business is to go on.

"The garrison quartered in Yefremov [a reserve regiment] will swear allegiance to the new government as has been done by the garrisons of Petrograd, Moscow, and other cities of Russia."

Rachinsky showed up in the printshop at dawn, tired and pale but full of determination. A large red band was pinned to the sleeve of his overcoat. He walked in and threw down on the table, with a theatrical gesture, a policeman's cap, and his whip in its holster. It turned out that the railroad workers had disarmed the bearded station policeman and Rachinsky, who had been present, had brought his arms to the revolutionary committee as its first trophy.

Then a tall, white-haired man with a gentle, drawn face walked in: the new Commissar of the Provisional Government, Kushelev. He never even asked how he had been appointed to his high post. Another order was immediately issued, over his signature, congratulating the population of the town on the liberation of Russia from its ancient yoke. A meeting was called for one o'clock the next day of representatives of all groups in the town's population to consider urgent matters connected with recent events.

I have never in my life seen such happy tears as I saw that

night. Kushelev was crying while he signed the order. His daughter had come with him, a tall, shy girl with a short jacket worn over her dress. While her father signed the order, she stroked his white hair and told him, her voice trembling:

"You mustn't get so excited, Papa."

In his youth, Kushelev had spent ten years in exile in the north. He had been convicted of belonging to a revolutionary students' organization.

Noisy, muddleheaded, happy days had started. A people's assembly met around the clock in the hall of the town council. It was renamed the "Convention," in honor of the French Revolution. The Convention was smoky from the breathing of hundreds of people.

Red flags stood out straight in the February wind. The villages streamed into the town looking for news and directions. "The sooner we can get the land," the peasants said. Low, wide sledges were to be seen on all the streets around the council, and hay was scattered everywhere. They argued endlessly about land, about redemption prices, and about peace.

Older people stood at the crossings with red bands on their sleeves and revolvers on their belts—they were the people's militia.

Staggering news continued to arrive. Nicholas had renounced his throne at the station in Pskov. All passenger traffic in the country was stopped.

Priests held special services in the churches in honor of the new government. Almost all prisoners were released from the prisons. Work in schools stopped, and *gymnasium* students ran around the streets in ecstasy, carrying orders and directions from the Commissar.

On the fifth or sixth day, I met my shoemaker friend from Bogovo at the Convention. He told me that Shuisky had decided to leave for town as soon as he heard about the revolution. He put a ladder up against his Dutch-tiled stove and climbed up it to get a bag of gold coins from behind the top tile. He slipped and fell, and by evening he was dead. The shoemaker had come into town to give Shuisky's gold coins to the Commissar of the Provisional Government.

It was as if the town and the people had changed completely. Russia was talking. Magnificent orators showed up, from God knows where, in tongue-tied Yefremov. They were mostly workers from the railroad yards. Women burst out crying when they listened to them.

The dejected, frowning look which all the residents of Yefremov had had on their faces disappeared. Faces grew younger, there

were ideas and goodness in people's eyes. There were no more
vulgar Philistines, but only citizens, and this word carried responsibility.

As if by some great design, the days were sunny, with the
crystal-clear dripping of thaw, a warm wind, rustling flags, and
happy clouds floating over the town. You could feel the breath of
early spring all around you, in the heavy blue shadows, in the raw
nights filled with the noise of people.

I was dazed, intoxicated. I couldn't understand what would
happen next. I was eager to get back to Moscow, but no trains were
running.

"Wait," Osipenko told me, "this is only the prologue to great
events which are going to happen in Russia. This is why you must
try to keep your head cool and your heart warm. Save your
strength."

I left for Moscow on the first train with a pass signed by
Kushelev, Commissar of the Provisional Government. Nobody saw
me off. It was no time for that.

The train moved slowly. I did not asleep. I remembered my
life instead, month by month, trying to define the one purpose
which had moved me over the last few years. Try as I might, I could
not name it.

I knew only one thing firmly: that not once in these years had
I thought about prosperity or about organizing my life. I had been
possessed by one passion—writing. Now, on the train, I felt that
I could already express my understanding of what was beautiful
and just, my awareness of the world, and my feelings about
human happiness and human worth and freedom, and that I could
communicate all these to others, and that this must be the purpose
of my life which until then I had never understood.

What would happen now, I did not know. I knew only that I
would go on trying to be a writer with all the strength I had. I
would try to do it through serving my people, through love for the
fabulous Russian language and our amazing land. I would go on
working while my fingers could hold a pen and until my heart,
filled to its brim with this awareness of life, stopped beating.

At dawn on a misty March day I arrived at last in the happy,
excited, terrible city of Moscow.

At the beginning of this book, I wrote: "I knew that life would
bring me many fascinating things, meetings, loves and sadnesses,
joys and shocks, and that the greatest good luck of my youth was
in this preknowledge. Whether it would come true, the future would
show."

Now time had shown that the good luck had come true.

The Start of
An Extraordinary Era

The Whirlpool

IN A FEW MONTHS RUSSIA MANAGED TO UTTER EVERYTHING IT HAD been silent about for hundreds of years.

Day and night, across the whole country, a continuous, disorderly meeting went on from February until autumn in 1917.

Mobs of people shouted on city squares, around monuments, in railroad stations smelling of disinfectant, in factories, in villages, at markets, in every courtyard, on the stairway of every house that was inhabited. Oaths, challenges, accusations, oratorical fervor— all were drowned out by furious yells of "Down with him!" or by hoarse, excited cries of "Hurrah!" These yells sounded like cobblestones being thrown around at every street crossing.

This unending meeting was more inspired and more furious in Moscow than anywhere else.

A man would be dragged from Pushkin's monument by the belt of his overcoat. People would embrace each other, scratching their cheeks on unshaved bristles, you would shake someone's calloused hand, the crowd would knock off another man's hat. But then a moment later eager arms would lift the first man triumphantly back on the monument. Holding on to his trembling pince-nez, he would denounce someone else as the destroyer of Russian freedom. First here, then there, people would start clapping desperately; the noise of their hard palms beating together was like the sound of heavy hailstones falling on a paved road.

It was a cold spring in 1917, and the young grass along Moscow's boulevards was often covered by hailstones like frozen grain.

At meetings nobody ever asked for the platform. They took

it. Front-line soldiers were always listened to willingly, and so was a French officer who had got stuck in Russia, a member of the French Socialist party, later a Communist, named Jacques Sadoul. His blue greatcoat seemed always on the move between Moscow's two great meeting places—the monument to Pushkin and the monument to Skobelyev.

When a soldier called himself a front-line fighter, he was nearly always greeted by shouted questions from the crowd: "What front? Which division? Which regiment? Who was your regimental commander?" If the soldier, confused, could not manage to get out his answers, the crowd would yell: "He's a Moscow soldier. Down with him!" They would throw him off the platform, to be swallowed up in the crowd where he could sometimes be seen frowning, wiping his nose with the skirt of his overcoat, shaking his head with incomprehension.

It took a strong hand to hold that crowd, and to force it to listen. Once I saw a bearded soldier climb up to the pedestal of Pushkin's statue. The crowd started to yell: "Which division? Which regiment?" The soldier screwed his eyes up angrily.

"What are you yelling about?" he shouted. "If anyone looked carefully, he'd find the Kaiser's picture in the pocket of every third one of you. A good half of you are spies! That's a fact! Just what right do you have to shut a Russian soldier's mouth?"

This was a strong play. The crowd grew silent.

"Go off and feed the lice in the trenches," the soldier shouted, "and then you can ask me questions. Tsarist good-for-nothings! Swine! You've tied red bands around your arms, and you think we can't see through you? It isn't enough for you to sell us to the bourgeoisie like chickens, you want to pluck us, too, down to the last feather. Thanks to you, there's nothing but treachery and betrayal, at the front and in the rotten rear, too. Comrades, all of you who have been front-line soldiers! I appeal to you! I humbly beg you—cordon off all these citizens, search them, check their documents. If we find something on any of them, we can take care of him ourselves without waiting for any orders from the government commissar. Hurrah!"

The soldier took off his sheepskin hat and waved it over his head. A few people shouted "Hurrah!" but weakly, not in concert. Then a kind of ominous movement began in the crowd—soldiers, linking hands, were beginning to encircle it. I don't know how it would have ended if someone had not thought of telephoning to the Soviet of Deputies. They sent a truck filled with armed workers, and order was restored.

Meetings in various parts of Moscow gradually took on their own special character. At the Skobelyev monument the speakers were mostly representatives of the different parties, from the Cadets and the Popular Socialists to the Bolsheviks. The speeches were bitter here, but serious. Men were not supposed to prattle at the Skobelyev monument. When someone did, the crowd would yell at him cheerfully: "Go up to Taganskaya! To hell with you!"

On Taganskaya Square it was possible to talk about anything at all, about how Kerensky was really a converted Jew from Shpola, if you liked, or about how the monks in the Donskoy Monastery had been found to have a fortune in gold rubles hidden in the cores of pickled apples.

One day in the spring (May had started, but it seemed that no one had even noticed the ice breaking up in the Moscow River or the first flowering chokecherries) I was standing in the crowd at the Skobelyev monument. A fight was going on between Social Revolutionaries and Bolsheviks.

Suddenly Rachinsky appeared on the pedestal of the monument. I winced. I had not run into Rachinsky before in Moscow. He took off his wide-brimmed velvet hat, lifted his cane with its naked silver naiad high in the air, cried for silence, and then shouted:

"Black clouds are trying to blanket the radiant sun of our freedom! Permit me, a poor and modest poet, living in my attic, to raise my insignificant voice . . ."

"Take him to the dump!" someone in the crowd yelled in a clear, decisive, somewhat coarse voice.

"To Taganskaya!" the crowd yelled. "Hey there, whoever's closest, throw him off the monument."

"This is usurpation!" Rachinsky shouted in a desperate voice. "It's the voice of a mindless rabble!"

But they didn't let him speak. He raised his eyes dolefully to the heavens, waved his arms, and then jumped down from the pedestal, preserving his dignity, and disappeared back into the crowd.

Meetings around Pushkin's statue were varied in theme but speeches were kept on a high level. Students did most of the talking at the Pushkin monument.

I was working on a newspaper then and it was part of my job to attend these meetings. They registered the slightest changes in Moscow's mood. All of us reporters could pick up a lot of news at these meetings.

The paper on which I was working was curiously called *Register of the Borough of Moscow*. There was no longer any borough at that time, and there was no register. Maybe the paper took its name from the fact that its editorial office was in the former building of the town governor on Tverskoi Boulevard. It was a small paper, edited by a very free-and-easy, flippant poet and essayist called Don Aminado. No one knew his real name.

The paper published sensational dispatches from all over the country, a chronicle of Moscow life, and occasionally a few decrees issued by Dr. Kishkin, the Commissar of the Provisional Government. It never occurred to anyone to carry out these decrees, so Kishkin's position was purely decorative. He was a dryish man with a white beard and the eyes of someone who knew he was destined for sacrificial slaughter. He walked around in an elegant frock coat with a silk revers, and he always wore a red decoration in his buttonhole.

Every day the speeches at these meetings became more sharply defined, and soon it was possible to sort the slogans and the demands into two camps into which the whole country was already dividing: the camp of the Bolsheviks and the workers, and the camp of the Provisional Government, of the intelligentsia, of men who seemed to have the highest sort of principles but who turned out to be boneless, distraught people. Of course, this was not the whole intelligentsia, but it was an important part of it.

The state was falling to pieces like a handful of wet mud. The provinces and districts of Russia were no longer ruled by Petrograd, and no one knew what they lived on or what was seething inside them. The army at the front was melting fast.

Kerensky swept around the country, trying to paste the nation together with his ecstatic eloquence. For the power of an idea, for conviction, he was trying to substitute fancy phrases, an operatic pose, a grandiose but irrelevant gesture. He harangued thousands of soldiers at the front, in the trenches, without ever noticing how funny he was.

Once he ripped the epaulets off an elderly, sick soldier who had refused to go back to the trenches. He pointed to the east with the iron-hard manner of a Caesar, and told the soldier:

"Coward! Go on back to the rear! Not we but your own conscience will destroy you!"

He shouted this in a tragic voice, with tears in his eyes, and the soldiers turned away and swore.

I saw a good deal of this man with his puffy, lemon-colored face, his red eyelids, and his close-cropped, thinning, grayish hair. He walked at a fast pace, making his adjutants run behind him. Then he would turn around just as quickly, unexpectedly, frightening his companions. He held his injured arm in a black sling outside his rumpled field jacket, which lay in pleats on his stomach. Brown patent leather leggings glistened on his long thin legs.

He would throw short sentences at a crowd, in his baying, complaining voice, and then choke. He loved noisy words and believed in them. It seemed to him that they would resound like a tocsin across the desperate land and inspire people to sacrifices and achievements.

Having shouted his noisy words, Kerensky would fall back into an armchair, shuddering and in tears. His adjutants would give him a sedative. Like a nervous woman, he always smelled of spirits of valerian. This smell, suggesting the musty air of some closed, old-fashioned apartment, gave him away. At any rate, this is what I thought then. I was convinced that a smell of medicine and the high title of a people's tribune just could not go together. I quickly came to realize that Kerensky was simply a sick man with a large share of what one finds in many of Dostoievsky's characters—he was an actor who believed in his messianic mission and rushed headlong to disaster.

He was apparently sincere in his overwrought convictions, in his devotion to Russia, this hysterical man carried like a shaving on the crest of the first revolutionary wave. Russia has had its share of half-cracked God's fools ever since medieval times, and there was a good deal of this primitive kind of madness in Kerensky.

I had a chance to see almost all the leaders of the February Revolution. Even though I was confused by what was going on, I was struck by the ill-matched qualities they represented. There was nothing in common, for example, between Kerensky and his Foreign Minister, the historian Professor Miliukov. His gray-blue hair looked, somehow, ice-cold and sterile. And he himself was ice-cold and sterile, as was every careful, correct word he spoke. In those turbulent times, he seemed to be a refugee from some other, well-ordered, academic planet.

An enormous number of soapbox orators sprang up almost overnight. They grew like mushrooms. The most important thing for all of them was to outshout their opponents. Cheap demagoguery flourished in a well-manured soil. Shouters were even imported from abroad. One day the French Minister of War Supplies, Albert Thomas, arrived from Paris. He came to persuade "the magnificent Russian people" to remain loyal to their allies and not to get out of the war.

This short-legged, brown-bearded man in an elegant frock coat was a peerless master, in his speeches, of the shout and the expressive gesture. I heard him speak once from the balcony of what is now the Moscow Soviet (the building was then the headquarters of the Commissar of the Provisional Government).

Thomas spoke in French. There could not have been a dozen men who knew his language in the crowd that listened to him. It consisted chiefly of soldiers and residents of the suburbs of Moscow. But everything in his speech could be understood without words. Bobbing up and down on his bowed legs, Thomas showed us graphically what would happen to Russia, in his opinion, if it left the war. He twirled his mustaches like the Kaiser's, narrowed his eyes rapaciously, jumped up and down choking the throat of an imaginary Russia. He held it in a death grip, he started to hiss, he hurled it to the ground and began to stamp on it with his patent leather shoes. Through all this he kept shouting warlike noises and snarling like a frenzied tiger.

This terrifying dance of the Kaiser over the prostrate body of Russia lasted for several minutes. Fascinated by the circuslike spectacle, the crowd held its breath.

Then a hollow sort of roaring started in the crowd. Thomas wiped his flushed face with a scented handkerchief and put on his shining top hat, a little at an angle as he always wore it. He listened to the crowd and smiled. It seemed to him this roaring was approval. But the roaring got louder, and more and more threatening until, finally, you could make out separate phrases in it: "Shame!" "Clown!" "Down with him!" A sharp whistle could be heard. Someone took Thomas courteously by the elbow and led him off the balcony.

His place was taken by the Belgian socialist Vandervelde, a man with an incredibly pious face, tightly buttoned into a clergyman's coat. He started to speak very quietly, without any emphasis, chewing his words in his thin, dry lips. It looked as if he wanted to lull the crowd to sleep. It began to thin out quickly. Soon there was no one left except a small group of people who were obviously listening to Vandervelde only out of politeness.

Vandervelde said just what Thomas had said. He called humbly for loyalty to "the sacred war alliance." A column of workers was marching down the Tverskoi Boulevard. Red banners swam past Vandervelde, reading: "Peace to the peasants, war to the landowners!" "All power to the Soviets!" "Down with the war!" Vandervelde went on moving his lips for a few minutes, then he put away his notes and walked slowly away, leaning on a tightly rolled umbrella in a silk case.

The column of workers never even noticed him. They sang:

> *All that holds up thrones*
> *Is made by workers' hands.*
> *We'll make our own bullets,*
> *And fix the bayonets to our guns.*

Now, many years later, when you remember the first months of the Revolution, you begin to realize that those times were full of awareness of how unstable things were, and full of expectation of some inexorable change. The old system was destroyed. Almost no one thought, deep in his own heart, that this new February system was the completion of the Revolution. It was, of course, only a transitional step in the history of Russia.

It's possible that this was realized by those who were leading the country for a fleeting moment. It must have weakened their resistance to what was new, hostile to them, but inevitable, what was first expressed in the words Lenin spoke from the armored train in the Finland Station: "The dawn of an international socialist revolution has begun."

Everything which had been achieved so easily and so quickly since the February Revolution turned out to be only the first beginnings of the great change. This became clear to everybody later. But at that time one only sensed it. The times were too exciting; too many magical things were happening every day. There was neither enough emotional strength nor enough time to understand this great flight of history properly. The noises made by the collapse of the old regime were blurred in a confused rumbling.

The idyllic aspect of the first days of the Revolution was disappearing. Whole worlds were shaking and falling to the ground. Most of the intelligentsia lost its head, that great humanist Russian intelligentsia which had been the child of Pushkin and Herzen, of Tolstoy and Chekhov. It had known how to create high spiritual values, but with only a few exceptions it proved helpless at creating the organization of a state.

Russian culture had grown up chiefly in a struggle for freedom against autocracy. Thinking had been sharpened in this struggle, noble feelings and civil courage had been developed. Now the old system had crashed. The job was no longer to spread elementary ideas of what is "intelligent, good, and eternal" among the people, but to create new ways of life, quickly and with our own hands, boldly to govern a completely devastated, immense country.

The confused, almost unreal, condition of the country could not go on indefinitely. The very survival of the people demanded clarity of aims and precise application of effort. Men began to see that the establishment of justice and freedom was going to need hard physical work, and even some cruelty. They saw that these things were not born of themselves to the clash of cymbals and the delighted cries of the citizenry.

Such were the first lessons of the Revolution. Such was the first face-to-face confrontation by the Russian intelligentsia with its own ideals. It was a bitter drink, but no one could escape it. The strong in spirit drank it down, and stayed on the people's side; those who were weak either degenerated or perished.

So the nation moved into the threatening, drawn-out phase of creating a new kind of civic order. But, I repeat, all these ideas were not clearly understood then by everyone. They existed in embryo, more feelings than ideas. Most people swam with the current of events, trying only to survive, in order to see what turns the current would take and to what shore it would lead Russia in the end.

As for myself, I had greeted the February Revolution with the delight of a little boy, even though I was already twenty-five years old. I believed naïvely that this revolution would suddenly change people for the better and reconcile bitter enemies. It seemed to me that the incontrovertible gains of the Revolution had already made it easier for men to escape from the shadow of their past, from all that was mean and shabby, above all from the hunger to get rich, national enmities, and the oppression of one's fellow men.

I had always been convinced that the seeds of good were planted in every man and that all one had to do was to help them grow in the depths of his being. But I soon realized that these excellent convictions were based on smoke and shadow. Every day hurled hard evidence in my face that men did not change so easily, and that the revolution so far had eliminated neither hate nor mutual distrust.

I tried to drive this unhappy thought away, but it did not leave me and it poisoned my happiness. I was more and more often angry. I began to hate the smooth, liberal intelligentsia who were growing stupid so quickly because, in my opinion, of their ill will toward their own people. But this did not mean that I myself was prepared to accept the October Revolution completely. Much of it I took, but other parts I rejected, especially all that seemed to me neglectful of the culture of the past.

It was my idealist education which kept me from accepting the October Revolution in its entirety. This was why I lived through its first two or three years not as a participant, but as a deeply interested spectator.

It was only in 1920 that I realized that there was no way other than the one chosen by my people. Then at once my heart felt easier. A time for faith and for big hopes started. From that point on my life developed no longer accidentally but more thoughtfully, and more or less firmly along the path of service to the people in that province of life where I could use my strength most effectively —in literature. I still do not know which road is the better—the road from doubt to understanding, or the road which knows no doubt at all. In any case, a deep devotion to freedom, justice, and humanity, together with an honesty toward oneself, have always seemed to me the essential qualities of a man in our revolutionary times.

The cold spring of 1917 was followed by a sweltering summer. A hot wind blew piles of crumpled, torn newspapers along the streets. New papers appeared almost every day in Moscow with the most extraordinary ideas, including even theosophical and anarchist papers with the slogan: "Anarchy is the mother of order." These noisy, for the most part illiterate, sheets usually lived only for a day or two.

On the walls of buildings the wind ruffled dozens of posters. The air was filled with the kerosenelike smell of printer's ink, and the smell of rye bread. The army brought this second village smell with it. The city was filled with soldiers pouring back from the front in spite of Kerensky's strident orders.

Moscow was transformed into a turbulent military camp. The soldiers settled in around the railroad stations. The squares in front of them were wreathed in smoke like the ruins of a conquered city. This was the smoke not of gunpowder but of cheap tobacco. The breeze blew up little waterspouts of sunflower shells.

A red flag fastened to Skobelyev's militantly outstretched sword had faded from the sun a long time ago but it still snapped triumphantly in the wind. A shroud of dust hung over the city. Yellow street lamps burned day and night. People forgot to turn them off. To save electricity the government ordered all clocks turned ahead. The sun went down late in the evening.

The whole city was on its feet. Apartments were empty. People spoke at meetings for nights on end, loafed sleepily around the streets, then sat down and argued in public squares or on the sidewalks. Strangers thrown together at a meeting became either friends or enemies in a split second. Four months had gone by since the Revolution, but the excitement had not died down. Anxiety still filled people's hearts.

I decided to spend the autumn with my mother. I was exhausted by Moscow. I had not managed to read a thing in all this time except a lot of political pamphlets printed on newsprint, reflecting the bitter clash of political parties. I dreamed about the chance of reading Tolstoy's *War and Peace* again; even the thought of it was entrancing. It seemed to me then that this novel must have been written hundreds of years ago.

Mama was living with my sister Galya in Polessya, not far from the little town of Chernobuil, managing a small estate there, called Kopan, which belonged to my Aunt Vera in Kiev. Mama loved farm affairs. At one time she had dreamed of making me an agricultural expert.

I traveled through Kiev. Like Moscow, it was bubbling over with meetings. People yelled "Hurrah!" and "Down with him!" in Ukrainian instead of Russian, and they sang Shevchenko's "Zapovit" instead of the "Marseillaise."

I got to Chernobuil on a rusty little steamship, the *Volodya*, down the Dnieper and Pripyati Rivers. It was a hard-working little boat. Sometimes the captain—a white-haired Ukrainian with a red sash around his chest—would climb up on his bridge and, laughing, shout down to the engine room: "Come on, there, *Volodya*! Step on it! Try harder for the Revolution!"

And the *Volodya* would try harder. It would puff steam as hard as it could, churn the water with its paddles, and even pick up a little speed. But it never continued for long. Soon the paddles would be turning lazily again, the passengers would lie down to rest on the deck, the sweet smell of marsh flowers would float from the banks, and the noise of the grasshoppers would blur into a drowsy ringing.

I slept on the deck, too. Moscow seemed a bad dream I could hardly remember.

We had to go by horse and wagon forty versts beyond Chernobuil, through pine forests and quicksands. The horses plodded along, the wheels screeched, the old harness smelled of tar. The driver, who was a little fellow in a thin, brown peasant coat, kept asking me:

"I beg your pardon, but don't they really know up there in Moscow when the great permission will be given?"

"What permission?"

"For the peasants themselves to take the land. And to drive out all the big Pans and the little Pans with our spades, straight to the devil's mother. People say it's Kerensky who's blocking it. The devil with him, too!"

Kopan turned out to be a small country estate, or rather a

neglected farm. A large, ancient cottage stood in a clearing in the woods. Its thatched roof was rotting, the barns and sheds were tumbled down. There were no fences. The woods surrounded the cottage on all sides. The rustling of the pine trees, after the hurly-burly of Moscow, seemed majestic and relaxing.

Mama managed not to cry when she saw me. Only her lips trembled and her voice broke. She threw her arms around me, pressing her white head against my shoulder, and she stood there for a long time, motionless and quiet, swallowing her tears. She had never before embraced me this way, as if I were older, her defender, the only support left in her unhappy life.

Galya held on to my elbow, and tears dropped out from behind the bulging lenses of her glasses. She made no effort to wipe them away.

I comforted Mama clumsily. I had thought of her often, but it was only now that I realized that life had left her nothing except her bitter, deep-hidden love for two human beings—Galya and me. These were the last crumbs of love on which she was living. Thanks to them she was able to bear without a murmur her humiliation by her wealthy relatives, her heavy work, and this complete abandonment in these uninhabited woods.

When dusk came, Mama mentioned in a guilty voice that it had become quite impossible to get kerosene—there wasn't any even in Chernobuil—so she and Galya got through the evenings with pine splinters for light. I had never seen them used before. The clear, red light they gave delighted me.

Mama twisted the fringe of her shawl with her dry, earth-roughened fingers, and told me, hesitantly:

"How good it would be, Kostik, if you'd stay here with us for good. It's so dangerous now to go away. We could all manage together, somehow. On salt and potatoes, it's true, but we'd be all together. What do you think, Kostik?"

She didn't dare to look me in the face, and she sat there staring down at the ground.

I was quiet.

Mama began to fix a fresh splinter in its iron holder. Her hands were trembling.

"Galya and I have talked about it," she said, and she still did not turn toward me. "If you haven't yet given up your idea of becoming a writer, then it must be all the same where you work. And it's quiet here. Nobody would bother you."

I couldn't be silent any longer.

"I'll think about it," I answered.

Mama came up and stroked my hair.

"That's wonderful," she said, and she smiled sadly. "That's wonderful. You think about it, Kostik."

No matter how long you live in this world, you never stop being surprised at Russia. This surprise began in my childhood and has not stopped even now. There can be no country in the world more unexpected or more contradictory.

I became convinced of this again the day after my arrival at Kopan. I was telling Mama and Galya about revolutionary Moscow when I saw through the window a stooped-over, elderly monk in a dusty cassock and a peaked skullcap walk out of the woods on to the farm. He walked in, made the sign of the cross over the corner of the room where an icon should have been, bowed deeply to us, and asked Mama if she would trade some salt for some dried mushrooms. The monk might have walked out of a Russia which existed before Peter the Great.

Mama had salt. She poured out a quarter of a bag for the monk but she did not take the mushrooms—in these woods there was no way of using up one's own mushrooms. Mama poured him tea. He sat there at the table without taking off his cap and drank his tea while he sucked hard candy in his mouth, and tiny tears began to run down his cheeks, which were as yellow as the wax in churches. He wiped them away with the sleeve of his robe and said:

"May the Lord be thanked that I've had a chance to drink tea with sugar once more before I die. God must have had pity on me, and granted me this last indulgence."

Mama went into the next room to get something. I followed her, and asked her where the monk had come from. She told me that since very ancient times there had been a little monastery hidden deep in the woods some ten versts away on the bank of the Uzh River. Now, after the Revolution, all the monks who were at all physically capable had moved away, one by one, and there was no one left there except a few old, helpless men.

"You ought to go and see it," Mama advised me. "You should talk with them. It might be interesting for you."

A few days later I walked to the monastery. The woods were dark, filled with wind-fallen trees. Not in any clearing but right in the middle of the woods, I found a low stockade of darkened boards. I had seen such stockades in paintings by Roerich and Nesterov showing old monastic retreats.

I walked along the stockade until I found a gate. It was closed. I knocked for a long time before it was finally opened, by the same

monk who had come to get salt. I walked into a little courtyard
overgrown with grass, and saw a crooked little church made of pine
logs, and I dropped suddenly right out of my own century.

The chanting of elderly voices could be heard coming from the
church. A bell sounded occasionally in its belfry.

"We really don't know any longer," the monk told me, "whether
we should ring it or not. It's dangerous. It seems there is some
insult in it for those who are in power now. So we just ring it
gently. A crow sometimes sits on the bell and he doesn't even fly
away when we ring it so softly. Please come into the church."

We walked in. There were only three or four candles burning.
Some old men, in black monastic robes with white crosses and
skulls embroidered on them, never budged. Their narrow faces
glittered brown and gold in the darkness. There was the bitter
smell of roasted juniper berries—the monks were using them
instead of incense.

Somehow everything was churned up in my consciousness: the
ancient monastery, the dismal singsong, the rustling of the pine
trees outside the walls, the embroidered monastic robes, Moscow,
the cross on top of Lelya's grave, soldiers in the trenches, the
synagogue in Kobrin, the light of the signal buoy at Taganrog,
meetings, the Revolution, the "Marseillaise," Kerensky, "Peace to
the peasants, war to the landowners!" The fantastic course my life
had taken seemed like a crazy dream.

How could this be explained? How could I find any clarity in
this chaos? How could I find the truth without which nothing
honest and worth while could be accomplished? And how could I
explain to myself whatever it was that made me at one and the
same time a supporter of the Revolution, a believer in great progressive ideas, and a man who talked with Heine, as well as a con-
temporary of this ancient Russia singing here in the old monastery
in trembling voices about man's hope for the blessing of Heaven
"now and forever and for all eternity"?

After I walked out of the monastery it was a long time before
I could put my thoughts in any kind of order.

Since then, every time I went to the Uzh River to catch fish, I
went back to the monastery. The monks always gave me old honey
and cold water.

To get a newspaper, it was necessary to ride the lame old horse
all the way to Chernobuil. I did this once, and brought back to
Kopan news of the Kornilov revolt and that the Germans had taken
the offensive again and had captured Riga.

Mama would not let me go a second time. Some kind of bandits had appeared in the woods—some said they were escaped Austrian prisoners of war, some that they were convicts released from prison. No one had seen them, but everyone was frightened of them.

Time went on. People stopped talking about the bandits, and everything grew calm again. At last, late in the autumn, I went to Kiev and from there to Moscow. Mama made me promise to come back the next spring.

When I went away Polessya was covered by dry yellow leaves and soft mist. Several weeks later bandits descended on the monastery, rummaged through all the cells in search of silver, shot the monks, and set fire to the church. But the church proved to be made of petrified wood so that it did not burn but was only charred.

THE BLUE TORCHES

I took a room in Moscow in a two-storied house at the Nikitsky Gate. The house fronted on three streets: the Tverskoi Boulevard, Great Nikitskaya Street, and Leontyevsky Lane. Its fourth side was up against the fireproof wall of a six-story building.

Opposite it, at the end of Tverskoi Boulevard where the statue of Timirayazev now stands, was a long, uninteresting building in which there was a drugstore which kept its medical supplies in the basement. The window of my room looked out on this drugstore.

One autumn night, gray with frozen smoke, I woke up in my second-floor room with the strange feeling that someone had suddenly pumped all the air out of the room. The feeling made me deaf for several seconds. I jumped up. The floor was covered with broken glass from the window. The pieces glittered in the light of a high, misty moon which was dragging its way over sleeping Moscow.

A deep silence stood all around me.

Then there was a short explosion. A sharp howl rose to the level of the broken window and then rushed with a long rattling around the corner of the building into the Nikitsky Gate. I could hear children crying in my neighbor's apartment.

It was impossible to know in that first minute, of course, that a gun, set up near Pushkin's monument, was firing point-blank at the Nikitsky Gate. This became clear only later.

After a second shot, the silence rolled back again. The moon looked just as attentively out of its misty night sky at the broke.1 glass on the floor.

Several minutes later a machine gun at the Nikitsky Gate fired a long round.

This was how the October fighting started in Moscow. It was what was called then "the October Revolution." It lasted for several days.

Rifle fire answered the machine gun. A bullet smacked into the wall through a portrait of Chekhov. I found the portrait later under a pile of broken plaster. The bullet had hit Chekhov in the chest and gone right through his white piqué waistcoat.

The shooting crackled like dead branches breaking in the woods. Bullets clinked against the tin roof. My neighbor, an elderly architect, a widower, yelled to me to come into his back rooms. Their windows looked out on the courtyard.

Two little girls and an old nurse were sitting there on the floor. The old nurse had covered the girls with a warm shawl.

"It's safe here," my neighbor said. "The bullets won't come through the inside walls."

The older of the little girls asked from under the shawl:

"Papa, have the Germans attacked Moscow?"

"It's not the Germans."

"But then who's doing all the shooting?"

"Keep quiet!" the father yelled at her.

I went back to my own room and, hugging the wall, looked obliquely out of the window. The moon was now covered by black clouds. The outlines of unlighted buildings could hardly be seen in the darkness. The flashes of firing continued without a break, and the bullets all sang in different keys. One was a thin whistle, another a ripping sound, and still others made a strange screaming noise as if the bullets were turning somersaults in the air.

I looked for people but the flashes from the firing gave too little light. Judging by the firing, the Red Guards had advanced from Strastnoi Square as far as the middle of the boulevard where there stood the bizarre wooden pavilion of a summer restaurant. The

Junkers* were still in command of the square from their positions
at the Nikitsky Gate.

Suddenly a tall blue tongue of flame, swinging in the breeze,
leaped out with a quiet roar under the windows. It was like a torch.
In its pale light, at last, people could be seen running from tree
to tree in the middle of the boulevard. Soon a second blue torch
exploded on the opposite side. Bullets had broken the burners of
the gas-burning street lamps, and now the gas was ignited and
burning straight out of the pipes. Under this new flickering light,
the firing increased immediately.

I returned to my neighbor's.

"Well, how is it?" he asked.

"We must take the children out of here."

"But where?" he asked. "Tverskoi Boulevard is under fire."

"Onto Great Nikitskaya Street. Through the stores."

"No, the Red Guards are firing machine guns along that, and
at the Union cinema, where the Junkers' staff is located. They're
firing from Little Nikitskaya Street, across the boulevard."

"Then that leaves Leontyevsky Lane."

"Let's go and find out."

We climbed down the back stairs to the square courtyard. The
bullets sang a higher note here and sometimes you could hear a
cornice falling. At the back of the courtyard a few men were
standing around a little yardkeeper's lodge.

It turned out that the firing was even hotter on Leontyevsky
Lane than on Tverskoi Boulevard. The fourth side of the courtyard
was closed in by the fire wall of the next building. There was not a
single window in it.

The architect looked at the wall and swore.

"We're in a trap," he said. "Our building is surrounded on all
sides. There's no way to get out. We're really in no man's land."

It was already growing light. The people around the yardkeeper's hut turned out to be bakers from Bartels' bakery which
was in our building.

A bearded baker, white with flour, a Port Arthur veteran, proposed moving all the residents into the yardkeeper's lodge, the
safest place. There were very few residents, for the whole first floor
of the building was occupied by stores and warehouses.

This was the beginning of many days of sitting in that yardkeeper's lodge. One of the bakers, a young fellow, decided to join
the Red Guards. As soon as he jumped out of the gateway onto the

---

* Junkers in nineteenth-century Russia were army volunteers of low
rank but of noble birth; later the word was applied chiefly to cadets in
military schools.

pavement, he was cut down by machine-gun fire from the Nikitsky Gate.

Sitting there, we reviewed the last few days and were amazed at our own stupidity. The fighting had started without any of us expecting it. But we had known about the uprising in Petrograd, the storming of the Winter Palace, the firing by the *Aurora,* and we had known that Moscow had been placed under martial law, that well-armed Red Guards and soldiers had been assembling at Khodinka, and that the Alekseyev and Alexandrovsk military academies had been readied for immediate military action.

The Port Arthur baker took command of our building. Water was still flowing from the faucet in the yardkeeper's lodge, and the baker had us collect all the pails and basins from the apartments to make a reserve supply of water. At any moment it might stop running.

Then we collected all the bread and groceries we had. It turned out to be not a big supply.

We had no way of knowing what was going on around us, but we were convinced that fighting was general throughout Moscow. All we knew was that we found ourselves in a state of siege and were living in a fort surrounded by a ring of fire. The fort was not an impressive one. By the end of the first day bullets were beginning to come right into the courtyard.

We sat on the steps of the lodge throughout the first night, trying to guess who was winning by the intensity of the firing. Suddenly, in the middle of the night, the firing stopped. We all pricked up our ears. This quiet seemed more dangerous than the firing had been. But it didn't last long. Soon we could hear separate voices yelling in the pitch darkness: "Tell the commander! The Junkers are climbing up on the roofs!"

The cries became more hurried, more excited: "Tell the commander! The Junkers are climbing up on the roofs!" Suddenly the firing broke out again, and the hail of lead crackled against the waterpipes and street signs again.

By evening of the second day, the building on the corner of the boulevard, where the drugstore was, began to burn. It burned with flames of many colors, yellow, green, and blue, obviously because of the medical supplies. Hollow-sounding explosions could be heard in the basement, and these caused the building to cave in. The flames died down, but a thin, many-colored smoke hung over the ruins for several days.

The tin roof of our building started to warp, and the window frames turned black, but luckily the building itself did not catch fire. We panted, cried from the smoke in our eyes, and covered our faces with wet handkerchiefs, but this didn't help much.

On the third night the fighting died down again and we could hear someone yelling out on the boulevard in an uncertain, overstrained voice:

"Vikzhel [this was what people used to call the All-Russian Union of Railway Workers] urgently proposes that both sides stop firing and send out representatives. For negotiations about an armistice. Don't fire! The intermediary—representative of Vikzhel—will wait ten minutes. Don't fire!"

An unbelievable silence followed. It was so still that you could hear the street signs, riddled with bullets, swinging in the wind.

I looked at my watch in the dull glow left by the burned-out drugstore. All the others quietly looked at me. The second hand raced around the face of the watch faster than ever. Five minutes. Seven minutes. Would the Junkers really refuse the armistice? Ten minutes.

A single shot cracked out, then a second, and suddenly, like a tornado, the firing grew back to its former noise.

Then we heard several cannon firing somewhere in the direction of Arbat Square and something exploded dully in the building with the fire wall right next to us. A pillar of flame, twisting slowly, rose above its roof.

It turned out that the Junkers had set fire to the building with grenades to keep the Red Guards from storming it. This building, in military language, commanded the entire neighborhood. This second fire was much more dangerous to us than the burning of the drugstore had been. Pieces of red-hot tin roofing and charred timbers began to fall into our courtyard. We put them out with our meager reserves of water.

The old baker assured us that the danger would pass as soon as the top floor of the building had burned out. Unless, of course, the fire wall should be blown up. We agreed with him, although we all realized that our position was becoming truly desperate.

This same night, a man suddenly jumped through a broken first-floor window from Tverskoi Boulevard into our courtyard, which was lighted so brightly by the fire that you could see every crack in its stone paving. He was wearing a gray jacket with a soldier's belt, a Mauser at his side. He wore glasses and had a light brown beard. He looked like Dobroliubov.*

* N. A. Dobroliubov (1836–1861) was an important radical critic who has been claimed as a forerunner both by the *narodniks* and the Marxists; his name is highly honored in the Soviet Union.

"Quiet!" he shouted. "Residents—come over here. We've made a deal with the Junkers. We're all going to stop firing in a moment to let the women and children out of this building. Only women and children! They won't let men go out. Your position is pretty bad—the building will be on fire at any moment. So in my opinion, the men might as well take a chance, too. But, of course, only after the women and children have all got out. Go across Tverskoi Boulevard into Bronnaya Street. Go one by one. Line up at the gateway."

The man disappeared as quickly as he had come. We all assembled at the gateway. The firing died away, and the first to scuttle across the boulevard was the old nurse with the two little girls. The other women ran after them, one by one.

While the women were crossing the boulevard, the Red Guards began to shout at the Junkers.

"Ah, you snotty-nosed children!" the Red Guards yelled. "You've played the fool long enough. Drop your guns."

"We've taken our oath," the Junkers yelled back.

"To whom did you take it? To Kerensky? That son of a bitch has bolted to the Germans."

"Our oath is to Russia, not to Kerensky."

"But we are Russia!" the Red Guards shouted. "Use your heads."

As soon as the women had all gone, the old baker darted out of the gateway. I was supposed to run right after him. But the Junkers fired a machine gun straight at the corner of the gateway. The baker jumped back. The firing became general again, and pieces of broken bricks, window glass, and chips of wood began to fall on the pavement.

We went back to the yardkeeper's lodge.

The baker cursed, and said to me:

"Ah, if we'd only got through! You and I would have joined those Red Guards. If you'd been with me, they'd have taken you, too, even if you are a student. Look at it any way you like, there's just one Russia. Our Russia. We'll slap down all the others."

I remembered what the Red Guards had just shouted: "But we are Russia!" and suddenly I understood with extraordinary clarity and freshness what is meant by "the masses of the people." Yes, I belonged to "these masses of the people." I felt myself at home among these artisans, these peasants, these workers, these soldiers, one of this great people who have produced a Gleb Uspensky, and a Leskov, a Nikitin, a Gorky, and thousands of other talented men.

"Well, that's the way it is," I told the baker. "There's no life for me without the people. This much I know."

"That's right," the baker said, and he laughed. "Hang on tight to us, young fellow. Don't drag your heels."

Our food ran out on the fifth day. We stuck it out until the evening, swallowing our spit. Just beyond the wall of our lodge, the building next door had burned down.

There had been a small grocery store in our building. There was nothing left for us but to break into it. Its back door led into the courtyard. The baker broke its lock with an ax and we took turns at night in running into the store and taking as much sausage, canned goods, and cheese as we could carry.

Burned-out buildings still glowed at night, and we had to hide behind the counters so as not to be seen through the broken store window by one of the Junkers in the Union movie theater. Nobody knew what they might do. Everything went well the first night, but on the second night a Red Guard sharpshooter had been stationed on the roof of the corner building on Bronnaya Street. He could see our whole courtyard clearly in the light of the flames, and he sat there smoking and firing at anyone who went out in the courtyard.

It was my turn to go. I managed to get to the store all right— either the soldier failed to see me or he didn't manage to shoot in time.

I still remember that store. Smoked sausages, wrapped in silver paper, hung from a long wire. Round red cheeses on a shelf were covered with horseradish from cans which had been hit by bullets. There were pools of vinegar, mixed with cognac and liqueurs, on the floor. Firm, marinated white mushrooms, covered with a reddish film, were swimming in these pools. A big earthenware jar filled with the mushrooms had been smashed to smithereens.

I quickly collected some long sausages, piling them on my arm like sticks of wood. On top of them I put a heavy wheel of Swiss cheese and some canned goods. When I ran back across the courtyard something jingled under my arm, but I paid no attention to it.

I walked into the lodge, and the only woman left among us, the wife of the yardkeeper, a pale, sickly woman, started to scream. I dropped the food on the floor, and noticed that my hands were covered with blood. A minute later, everyone in the lodge was roaring with laughter, in circumstances that didn't make anything seem very funny. They were roaring with laughter while they scraped thick tomato paste off my arms. When I had been running back, the sharpshooter had fired at me, the bullet had hit a can in my arms, and I was covered with blood-red tomato sauce.

We did not have a crumb of bread. We ate the sharp cheese, the smoked sausages, and highly spiced canned goods without bread, and drank cold water from the tap. Then my neighbor remembered that he had left a bag of dried rusks in his kitchen. I volunteered to go and get them.

I climbed carefully up the back stairs, which were covered with broken brick fragments. Water was pouring out of a broken pipe in the kitchen, and the floor was a swamp of soaked plaster. I began to look through a cupboard for the bag of rusks. At just this moment I heard yells and heavy footsteps from the boulevard. I went into my own room in order to see what was happening. Red Guards were charging up the boulevard, with bayonets fixed to their rifles. The Junkers were falling back, without firing.

I had never seen fighting so close, right under the window of my room. I was fascinated by the men's faces, which were green, with sunken eyes. It seemed to me that these men saw nothing and understood nothing, deafened by their own yelling.

I turned away from the window when I heard hurried footsteps coming up the front stairway. The door opened with a crash and swung violently against the walls. Plaster fell from the ceiling. An excited voice yelled from the stair landing:

"Misha, bring your machine gun here!"

I turned around. An elderly man in a cap with earflaps and with a machine-gun strap over his shoulder was standing in the door. He held a rifle in his hands. For a second he stared carefully but fiercely at me, then he quickly lifted the rifle and shouted:

"Don't make a move. Raise your hands."

I raised my arms.

"What have you got there, Papa?" a young voice asked from the corridor.

"We've got one of them, anyway," the man with the earflaps answered. "He was shooting. Shooting at us out of the window, the snake. Shooting us in the back!"

It was only then that I realized I was dressed in a much-patched student's jacket, and I remembered the baker had told me that a group of students had been fighting at Nikitsky Gate on the side of the Provisional Government.

A young worker, with his cap pulled down over his ears, walked into the room. He waddled over to me, lazily took my right hand, and carefully examined its palm.

"It's clear he didn't shoot, Papa," he said cheerfully. "There's no spot from the bolt. His hand is clean."

"Shut your foolish mouth!" the man with earflaps shouted.

"What if he was shooting a pistol, and not a rifle? And then threw the pistol away? Take him out in the courtyard."

"Anything's possible," the young worker said, and he clapped me on the shoulder. "Well, forward march! And don't try anything foolish."

I had not said a word. Why—I don't know. Obviously all the circumstances were so hopelessly against me that it made no sense to try to explain. I had been found by a broken window in a room on the second floor in a building just captured by the Red Guards. I was wearing a student's jacket dusted thick with plaster and covered with suspicious brown spots. Whatever I had said, it would have made no difference, they would not have believed me. So I kept quiet, although I realized that my silence made one more serious count against me.

"He's a stubborn devil," the man in earflaps said. "You can see right away that he believes in what he's been doing."

They led me into the courtyard. The young Red Guard poked me in the back with the muzzle of his rifle.

The courtyard was full of Red Guards. They were pulling boxes out of a demolished warehouse and piling them on a barricade across Tverskoi Boulevard.

"What's this all about?" they shouted, and they crowded around me and my two captors. "Who is this?"

The man in earflaps said that I had been firing at their backs from the window.

"Let's exchange him," a young fellow with drunken eyes said in a happy voice. "Let's send him to join God's general staff."

"Send the commander here."

"The commander's not here."

"Where is he?"

"We had an order—not to harm any prisoners."

"That's all right for prisoners. But he was shooting us in the back."

"There's only one way to handle that—shoot him on the spot."

"We can't do that without the commander, comrades."

"What a lawyer we've found! Stand him up against the wall."

They pushed me over to the wall. The bareheaded wife of the yardkeeper ran out of the lodge. She threw herself on the Red Guards and began to grab frantically for their hands.

"My sons, comrades!" she yelled. "This is our boarder. He didn't shoot at you. My life's not worth anything, I'm a sick woman. It would be better to shoot me."

"Listen, mother," the man in earflaps said reasonably, "don't you

jump to conclusions either. We're not murderers. Go away. Don't
bother us."

I have never been able to understand—neither then, nor now—
why I felt absolutely nothing while I stood there against that wall,
hearing the gun bolts slapped back in those rifles. Whether it was
some sudden emotional stupidity, or an actual loss of consciousness, I do not know. I just stared carefully at the corner of the
gateway, which had been shattered by machine-gun fire, and
thought about nothing. But for some reason I remember the tiniest
details about that gate corner.

I remember seven dents made by bullets. On top they were
white (where there had been plaster), and below they were red
(where there had been brick). I remember the metal bracket,
painted white, of the yardkeeper's bell, now torn out, and a piece
of electric wire attached to the bell, and an ugly face drawn on the
corner of the wall with an enormous nose and hair standing out
like wires, with an inscription scrawled under it: "We've cheated
the fool all right."

It seemed to me that time itself had stopped, and I was weighed
down in a kind of complete dumbness. Actually it was only a few
seconds before I heard an unknown but somehow familiar voice
saying: "Who in hell are you shooting? Have you forgotten the
order? Put down your rifles."

With some difficulty I turned my eyes away from the gate
corner—my neck hurt terribly—and I saw the man with the
Mauser who had looked like Dobroliubov, the man who had come
to us in the night to get the women and children out. He was pale,
and he did not look at me.

"As you were!" he commanded sharply. "I know this man. He
was not a member of that students' group. The Junkers are still
attacking us, and you're fooling around with this kind of nonsense."

The man in earflaps took hold of my jacket, shook me hard, and
said spitefully:

"Well, you and your mother can still go to the devil! I came
close to having you on my own conscience, thanks to your stupid
noodle. What did you shut up for? And you're a student, too!"

But the young worker clapped me on the shoulder again, and
said cheerfully:

"Well, God be with you."

Out on the street the Junkers threw a hand grenade. The Red
Guards jumped over their barricade and began to run down the
boulevard. The building emptied. Machine guns barked again with
terrifying intensity.

So I never found out who was the young commandant with the Mauser who had saved the women and children in our building and then saved me. I never met him again. But I would recognize him among dozens or hundreds of people.

On the sixth night of our "Nikitsky siege" we were all sitting, unshaved and hoarse from the cold, on the steps of the yardkeeper's lodge and guessing when the long-drawn-out fighting would finally end. It seemed to be marking time. There was as yet none of the bitterness which came later, during the civil war. The Red Guards were fighting at random, sure of their victory, knowing that the Junkers' nerves would give out soon.

The new Soviet government had taken over power in Petrograd. The country was abandoning the Provisional Government, layer by layer. The Moscow Junkers, of course, knew this. Their game was already lost. The bullets which whistled around the buildings at the Nikitsky Gate were their last bullets.

We sat and talked about all this. The late night smelled of the smoke from burned-out buildings. The glow had died down. Only in the direction of the Kiev railroad station was the sky still filled with crimson smoke.

Then in the north, somewhere near Khodinka, we heard the noise of an artillery shell. It passed right over Moscow and we heard the sound of its explosion somewhere near the Kremlin. As if by command, all firing stopped at once. It was clear that both the Junkers and the Red Guards were waiting and listening for a second explosion, in order to find out where the artillery was in action.

At last it came, a second whistling noise. Again, the explosion sounded from the direction of the Kremlin.

"Are they really firing on the Kremlin?" the old baker asked quietly.

The architect jumped up. "I'll never believe it," he said. "It just can't be. Nobody would dare lift his hand against the Kremlin."

"You're right. Nobody would dare," the baker agreed in a low voice. "This must be just a warning. Wait. Let's listen."

We sat there, freezing. We were waiting for more artillery shots. An hour went by, without any. Two hours passed. Everything all around us was quiet.

A gray light began to spread from the east, the chilly light of early morning. It was unusually quiet for Moscow, so quiet that we could hear the noise made by the burning gas torches on the boulevards.

"It looks like the end," the old baker said. "We ought to go out and see."

We walked cautiously out on to Tverskoi Boulevard.

The linden trees with their shattered branches stood in the hoar-frost and the smoke. The torches of the broken street lamps blazed along the boulevard all the way to the Pushkin monument. The street was piled high with broken wires. They jingled complainingly as they swung against the pavement. A dead horse, showing its yellow teeth, lay across the trolley tracks.

Frozen blood lay in a ribbon on the stones around our gate. The buildings, riddled by machine-gun fire, were dropping sharp shards of glass out of their windows, and you could hear it breaking all around us.

Tired, quiet Red Guards were marching up the boulevard toward the Nikitsky Gate. Red bands were twisted tightly around their sleeves. Almost all of them were smoking, and the lights of their cigarettes, pricking the darkness, made it look like a soundless armed skirmish.

At the Union movie theater a white flag on a pole had been tied to a lamppost. The Junkers were standing in rows around the flag next to the wall of the building. Their caps were crumpled, and their coats were gray with plaster dust. Many of them were half asleep, leaning on their rifles.

An unarmed man in a short leather coat walked up to them. Several Red Guards were standing behind him. He raised his hand and said something quietly to the Junkers. A tall officer stepped out from their ranks. He took off his cap and his revolver, threw them at the feet of the man in the leather coat, saluted him, turned around and walked off slowly, weaving, toward Arbat Square.

All the Junkers in turn followed his example, piling up their rifles and cartridge belts in front of the man in the leather coat. Then they walked away, just as slow and tired as the officer, in the same direction. Some of them ripped off their epaulets as they walked.

The Red Guards watched the Junkers with quiet, dry, tense faces. There was not a single exclamation, not a single word.

It was all over. Through the cold dark there came from the Tverskoi the sounds of a band, and singing:

> *Nobody gives us our salvation*
> *Not God, the Tsar, nor anyone.*
> *We will win our liberation*
> *With a power all our own.*

THE JOURNALISTS' CAFÉ

The year 1918 began with short thaws, gray snow, and such a hazy sky that smoke from factory chimneys climbed up to the clouds, stopped, and spread out under them in heavy wreaths of black.

The Moscow streets still smelled of printer's ink. Gray scraps of paper and posters hung on the walls. Decrees of the new Soviet government were pasted on top of them. They were printed on crumbly gray paper.

Day by day, these sharp, ruthless decrees were cutting away whole layers of a way of life, throwing them away, and laying the basis for a new life. It was still hard to imagine what this new life might be. The change took place so unexpectedly that our very existence sometimes lost its reality and seemed as unstable as a mirage. A chill gripped one's heart. The weak in spirit reeled like drunkards.

My room at the Nikitsky Gate had been destroyed in the firing. I moved back to Granatny Lane, to a room in a brick building right next to the house where I had been born. I rented it from a gloomy widow who let out rooms only to students.

My neighbor, a freckled girl named Lipochka, daughter of a village teacher, was often visited by relatives and friends from her village near Ryazan. They brought with them the smell of frost, apples, and homespun coats. I asked them about the countryside. They sighed carefully, and told me in quiet voices that only God knew what was happening in the villages. It was as if a great flood had come, and no one knew what would come after it. Either it would cover the earth with a layer of good, new soil, or it would wash the seed right out of the ground. That's what it's like in the villages, friend, a mixture of terror and happiness. The big news was that the peasant had taken the land. Nobody could take it back from him now.

The smell of apples was strong, and the homespun clothes gave me a feeling of neatness and warmth, and for some reason this calmed my heart.

When I had come back from Kopan in September, I had gone
to work as a reporter on a newspaper called *The Power of the
People*. It was one of those short-lived papers of which a good many
were born in those days. Later on, they were all closed down
quickly.

It was published by the Popular Socialist party. Even some of
us who worked on the paper had little understanding of this party's
dim program. We knew only that the paper was run by quite intelligent people filled with liberal impulses which they were in no
position to carry out.

An imperious, good-looking, older woman named Yekaterina
Kuskova was the chief editor. She talked in a small, gypsy's voice,
smoked a great deal, and treated us reporters with disdain and
some dislike, especially after she found kidding poems about her
penciled on the door to her office. But the paper asked no political
angling from its reporters—this was supplied by those who wrote
the leading articles. I plunged desperately into the sleepless newspaper life of major and minor events, sensations, disputes, revolutionary meetings on the squares, demonstrations, and street
fighting.

The sharp air of revolutionary winter made one's head swim. A
misty romanticism filled our hearts. I could not resist it, nor did I
want to. Belief in universal happiness shone in us like the sun
rising over our disordered lives. It was sure to come. It seemed to
us, naïve as we were, that its guarantee was our desire to construct
it and to see it.

We were looking in poetry and in prose for something universal, international, all-inclusive. We tried to see the carry-over
from other epochs in many things around us. Stories of the French
Revolution, of the Decembrist uprising, of the Paris Commune,
and of the 1905 revolution colored what was happening around us
and made it all the more exciting.

Some old revolutionary spirit burned even in the contradictory
poetry of Verhaeren (I was still attracted to him at that time):

> *There where the guillotine's blade is sharp,*
> *Where the tocsin sounds along the street,*
> *Our dreams, in panic, stream.*

All the fever and the confusion of our ideas were justified then
by our youth and by our eagerness to see a new world established
as quickly as possible. My former judgments, born of my restless
youth and especially of the war, lost their luster. It was as if what
was happening had pushed me back ten years, to the time of my

unripe childhood convictions. I felt that I was growing stupid. The ground disappeared under my feet. My inability to work out any personal relationship to what was going on confused me, and sometimes made me angry.

For what was happening sometimes gladdened and excited me and sometimes seemed unreal, sometimes magnificent, and sometimes a vast unnecessary cruelty, sometimes radiant and sometimes dark and threatening, like the sky when it is covered with banks of crimson clouds.

Only one thing was clear—life was settling its accounts with the past and exploding into a new order. And this had to be free, of course, and just, it had to raise men to new heights and to let all their potentialities blossom. Revolution, in my opinion, had to recognize everything that can enrich the spirit of man. I saw its greatest meaning in the fact that it evoked all that is most valuable from the many aspects of our life and culture. People told me that this would be one of the results of revolution but that it was not its goal. I thought that a goal existed only in terms of results. This seemed to me an undeniable truth.

Mikhail Osorgin was the only Popular Socialist on the paper with whom we younger journalists made friends.* He had returned from abroad, he was confused, and he found it hard to cope with what was going on. You could see this confusion in his feverish and shining eyes.

He was indulgent and pleasant with everyone, and he trusted everyone and everything. There was a controlled grief in his manner, even in his tired voice. He was homesick for Italy where he had lived for many years. He lived in Russia like a man only half-awake.

Sometimes we urged him to go back to Italy, and we told him there was nothing for him to do here, while there he could at least go on writing his stories. Osorgin answered us guiltily:

"Don't forget that I'm a Russian, and that I love Russia so that my heart hurts with it. But I can't recognize it any more. Sometimes I think: stop now, is this really Russia? Even the tones of Russian speech have changed. Here I am pining for Italy, but there I would be desperately homesick for Russia. It's clear, there's no hope for me."

Osorgin was especially at a loss when the "king of the reporters," the ubiquitous old Gilyarovsky, burst into the office drown-

---

* Mikhail Osorgin, pen name of M. A. Ilyin (1879–1942), was a short-story writer and novelist; his *Moscow, a Quiet Street* was a Book-of-the Month Club choice in 1932.

ing out everything with his hoarse voice and his tobacco cough.

"You nursing babes!" he would shout at us younger reporters. "Popular Socialists! Moldering liberals! You don't know any more about the Russian people than that old fool Madame Kurdyukova: *Je ne vais pas, je ne sais pas, je ne mange que le repas.* A newspaper page ought to reek so loud that it's hard to hold it in your hands. There ought to be such writing in a paper that it makes the reader hold his breath. And what are you doing? You're all mumbling. You ought to be writing novels about anemic young ladies. I know the Russian people. And they'll show you yet where lobsters spend the winters!"

Osorgin smiled guiltily, and Kuskova slammed the door of her office in a temper. Gilyarovsky pointed at the door, and said in a clear whisper:

"Of course, it's possible to play politics even in a woman's office, on her little spider's legs. And to shed tears over your own articles about the Russian peasant. But one good peasant's word would give you all apoplexy. And the *narodniks*, too. Good-by. I'll drop in again sometime. Somehow I don't feel like talking with you now."

He walked out, but a tense silence gripped the office for a while —it was as if they were afraid the old man might come back.

All the young journalists loved Gilyarovsky for his noisy talent, his inexhaustible imagination, and his old man's despair. And he loved us in his own way, while he made fun of us. From *The Power of the People* he would go to some other editorial office near by. There, depending on circumstances, he would either organize another complete defeat of those who disagreed with him, or pick up some news, or just talk about his memories of Chekhov, Kuprin, Chaliapin, and General Skobolyev.

When he met me, he looked at me out of his round, angry eyes and said:

"It's high time, young man, to shift from little to medium-sized letters, and then to big ones. Little letters—they're for newspaper work; medium-sized are for poetry; while the really big letters are used for prose. Strap yourself down to your chair and work."

This gray-mustached old man in his Cossack hat personified the scope, wit, slyness, and goodheartedness of Russia. He was not only a journalist but also a poet, a prose writer, a connoisseur of painting, and a famous Muscovite. Tricks, games, and jokes flowed out of him. Without them he would probably have withered away.

In spite of his loudness he was really a child. He loved to send letters to nonexistent addresses in countries which fascinated him

—Australia or the Republic of Costa Rica. Since the letters could not be delivered, they would be sent back to Moscow bearing colored stamps and inscriptions in different languages. The old man would inspect them carefully, even sniffing them as if they had brought back with them the smell of tropical fruits. But the letters always smelled of sealing wax and leather.

Who knows, perhaps these letters were a sorry substitute for his dreams of traveling around the world—joking, and clapping on the shoulder the drivers of Paris fiacres and Negro chieftains on the shores of the Zambesi, and treating them all to a pinch of his snuff, and collecting such impressions as would make Moscow jaws hang open in amazement. Gilyarovsky saw the Revolution as a sensational news story and as another reflection of Russia's traditionally mutinous spirit. He looked for its roots in the peasant revolts led by Razin and Pugachev.

He knew the city's life thoroughly, especially those secret elements which tried to keep as far as possible from the Soviet authorities: the gypsies' home at Pokrovsky-Streshnev, the sectarian meetinghouse at Rogozhsky Gate, the gambling dens on Brestskaya Street, the howling group of aesthetes in Pertsov's house at the Cathedral of Christ the Savior. A certain lisping poet with a long child's forelock was in charge there. He wore a tuxedo and a monocle and was so frail that it was always dangerous to shake hands with him—it seemed as if his tender, transparent palm would stay in your hand.

The times were still unsettled. They threw together many quite different, curious people. These became more noticeable than they had been before. The Revolution flushed them out of their corners and stirred them up as when one shakes a can of stagnant water. Then sand, leaves, broken twigs, beetles, and grubs all appear suddenly from the bottom. And all of it turns and whirls in the moving water, bumping and colliding, until it settles again to the bottom.

In those young days of the Revolution, a lot of interesting people used to assemble in the journalists' café on Stoleshnikov Lane. By pooling their resources the journalists managed to lease an empty third-floor apartment, and a smoky, happy meeting went on there around its rickety tables for nights on end.

You could meet Andrei Byely* there, and the Mensheviks Martov, Brusov, and Balmont, the blind leader of Moscow's anarchists, Cherny, and the writer Shmelev, the actress Roksanova—the

---

* Andrei Byely, pen name of Boris Bugaev (1880–1934), was a Futurist poet and novelist who also experimented with Surrealist forms.

first of Chekhov's "sea gulls," Maximilian Voloshin, Potapenko, the poet Agnivtsev, and a great many journalists and writers of all ages, views, and characters.

The goodhearted Agnivtsev sang his simple songs. An enormous yellow necktie was wound around his long neck like a bandage, and his wide checked trousers were always full of cigarette burns. Coffee as bitter as quinine steamed in the little enamel cups. Even saccharine couldn't cut its bitterness. Frenzied arguments would break out at one table after another, and sometimes through the clamor you could hear the clear crack of someone being slapped in the face.

One handsome but malicious journalist with a dyed beard was on the receiving end of most of the slaps. He hissed like a snake, and he spread his poison over everyone without exception. The slaps he took represented a real fire risk, since he never removed the pipe from his mouth. Whenever someone struck him, the pipe would fly in the air, shooting sparks out like fireworks over the heads of the other patrons and pouring out shreds of burning tobacco. The smell of scorched cloth would promptly fill the room. Everybody would hurry to put out his burning coat or trousers or a tablecloth. The journalist with the dyed beard would coolly retrieve his pipe, fill it again, light it, and walk out with the comment to all who were listening that he would submit this scandalous incident at once to a comradely court.

"You can go to the devil!" the other patrons would yell after him. "Report it to a revolutionary court! Out of here! We're bored with you! You *provocateur!*"

One day the poet Maximilian Voloshin walked into the café, a heavily built, nearsighted man with a red beard. He invited all of us to his lecture on poetry at the Hermitage Theater. Only a few of us went. The others could not tear themselves away from the stormy political arguments at the shaky little tables.

I went. It was toward the end of March. It was dark and quiet in the park. Melting snow dropped from the trees. I caught the smell of rotten leaves, like the faint bouquet of wine, a smell of vegetable bitterness and the thawing of last year's flowers. It was as if it were percolating up through the damp earth, earth which had been uncared for, untended, unspaded for a long time.

A man forgot about nature in those days. Words thundered over the country, insistent summonses to struggle, impatient, exultant, accusing, threatening enemies. Millions clustered around these words as if they were magnetic poles. They were challenges to destroy and at the same time challenges to create. Those were days of sudden decisions and of constant agitation.

It was no time for nature. But the woods went on rustling just as vaguely, the ice on the rivers turned blue and watery. The same gloomy shaggy hoarfrost covered the linden trees on Moscow boulevards in the mornings. The sunsets died out humbly in the evenings and the stars shone timidly at night as if they understood that men—even astronomers and poets—had no time for them now.

Everyone was caught up and deafened by the storm raging in his own consciousness. A man did not even glance at nature. And if sometimes he did look, it was with unseeing eyes.

Other hopes and fears possessed people. Even love, as simple as air and as unconditional as sunshine, had to give way to the flood of events, and was regarded as a kind of sentimental sickness.

A sense of responsibility required avoidance of unnecessary and sometimes dangerous emotions. They were postponed to some distant future. Gigantic convulsions and reconstructions demanded all our energy. Not one gram could be wasted uselessly. Uselessly? The sacrifice of love could be, of course, excessive and truly heroic, especially if a man recognized what it was he was sacrificing.

Whatever my thoughts turned to in those days—love, poetry, thoughts of the past—I suffered from my unclear sense of values. I tried hard to find some clarity as quickly as I could. Without it, it would be hard for me—as for everyone—to go on living. But I soon realized that my time had clearly not yet come. Life was still too chaotic, and I would have to wait until, at long last, the features of a new world began to emerge from chaos.

Voloshin's lecture contributed even more to my confusion. The theater was almost empty. A few dusty electric lamps flickered under the ceiling. A brown mist filled the hall.

Voloshin seemed to be speaking for himself, having forgotten his audience. He talked about war, about the iron-hard times which had gripped the world, and in a hollow, tragic voice, staring at the back of the empty hall, he asked: "Well, what use are poets and artists in such tough times as these?"

In England they had hung the best of Irish poets. In France three hundred poets had been killed in the first days of the war. One French general, who was proud of his love for poetry and his knowledge of it, had said:

"Put these enthusiastic young men in the front ranks in the offensive. Let them stir up and lead the soldiers."

Verhaeren, in spite of the central ideas of his whole life, had been forced to hate. Jules Lemaître, appalled by the stupidity of war, had become ill and had forgotten how to read. He could no longer distinguish the meaning of symbols, and started to learn to read all over again, syllable by syllable.

The terrible list of the crimes of war against art went right on growing. Voloshin's voice grew hollower and hollower.

Well, then, this was how it was. What was the solution?

About this Voloshin had not a single word to say.

There were a good many amazing people among the regular patrons of the café. Each was all right in his own way, but taken together they made up a funny and ruthless band of newspapermen.

One young writer, a Bulgarian from Volsk named Alexander Yakovlev, held himself a little apart. He was a great expert on peasant life and he wrote wonderful stories about it. Everyone treated this modest, quiet man with real respect. It was called forth not only by his talent at writing first-class stories but also by his extraordinary ability, at that time of complete breakdown of the railroads, to make his way into the most out-of-the-way corners of Russia and come back unharmed. This required both fortitude and courage. He risked his life on almost every trip he made.

The army of demobilized soldiers had poured along the railroad tracks of Russia, recklessly destroying everything in its way. Everything in the trains themselves that could be taken or destroyed had been taken or destroyed. Sheets of metal were pried off the roofs of the cars. There was an active trade at the Sukharevsky market in washstands, mirrors, and pieces of red velvet ripped off the seats in trains.

A large number of bandits, dressed up as soldiers, incited the demobilized army to all kinds of outrages. They broke the windows in stations, tore down fences to fuel the engines, sometimes chopped up the houses of railroad workers. In trains that stopped near cemeteries the crosses stripped from graves were the first fuel fed to the engines. Twisted cemetery wreaths of lilies and roses, made of metal, were tied up with wire by the soldiers to decorate the cars. The wind made by the moving train whistled strangely through these roses.

Station officials would run away long before an echelon of demobilized soldiers pulled in with bandit yells, accordion music, and machine-gun fire. Any delay for the train resulted in cruel punishment for whoever was in charge of the station. Locomotive engineers turned pale when they heard a thousand voices shouting murder at them.

It was quite usual to throw off the moving train anyone who had managed to get on it in a civilian suit or an official's uniform. Yakovlev was thrown off three times, but he survived. The most amazing thing was that he came back from these brushes with death each time refreshed, excited, full of new things he had seen and heard, and convinced that no price was too high for a writer to pay for this kind of material.

Yakovlev managed to get to the most moss-covered little towns cut off from Moscow in the Russian wilderness, towns with names like Khvalinsk or Sarapul or Serdobsk, places which had become almost mythological. It was hard to believe even that they existed. For Russia was falling apart into separate little countries cut off from each other by the lack of roads, the destruction of the mails and the telegraph system, blown-up bridges, and the sudden elongation of all distance. Little homemade republics sprang up in these hidden corners of Russia, printing their own money on local printing presses or, most often of all, using postage stamps for money.

All this was mixed up with remnants of the past—balsam firs in the windows and the sound of church bells, prayer meetings and weddings accompanied by drunken salvos from sawed-off shotguns, plains filled thick with grain and yellow rapeseed, and talk about the end of the world when nothing would be left of Russia but "a black night with three columns of smoke." Yakovlev talked about all of this with great taste, unhurried, with the manner of a harness maker skillfully sewing a saddle girth with light, dry, waxended thread.

After that I ran into Yakovlev several times. He always impressed me with his unusual gentleness and his unconquerable love for the simple people of Russia. It was typical of him that when he died he asked to be buried not in Moscow but above the Volga in the town of Volsk where he was born.

A short, plain man in a hat with a drooping brim sometimes showed up at the café. It seemed he had been for a time a reporter either on a Tula paper or maybe one in Orlov. Prishvin had had an amusing experience with this man, one which Prishvin loved to tell about as something truly fantastic.

Prishvin had been traveling from Yelets to Moscow. At that time, all railroad junctions were under the control of antiprofiteer detachments made up of sailors from the Baltic Fleet. Prishvin had wrapped up all his things, his manuscripts and his books, in packages and taken them into the train with him. At some railroad junction near Oryol the sailors from an antiprofiteer brigade had taken the packages away from him, in spite of all his pleading and all his protests.

Prishvin dashed into the station to the head of the brigade. This turned out to be a sailor with high cheekbones, a Mauser on his belt, and a pewter earring in one ear. He was eating salt fish with a wooden spoon, like porridge, and he was not at all eager to talk with Prishvin.

"Of course, a member of the intelligentsia," he said. "And if you go on complaining, I'll arrest you for sabotage. It may not be quite clear under just which law the revolutionary tribunal will take you to its heart. But you, my friend, would do well to get out of here while you're still in one piece."

A short man in a hat with a drooping brim had followed Prishvin. He had stopped in the doorway, and now he said, quietly but distinctly:

"Give this citizen back his things at once."

"And just what kind of a joker is under that hat?" the sailor asked. "Who can you be, to order me around like that?"

"I'm Magalif," the plain little man said, just as quietly and distinctly, and he never took his piercing little eyes away from the sailor.

The sailor choked on his salted fish, and stood up.

"I beg your pardon," he said in an ingratiating voice. "My boys, it's clear, have made a mistake. They must have lost their heads. Lobov!" He was yelling like thunder. "Return his things to this citizen. The representative of Magalif has ordered it. Do you understand? Carry them all back into the train for him. And quickly, too."

On the platform Prishvin began to thank the plain little man, but in reply he got only the advice to write the word "folklore" clearly in indelible pencil on all his packages.

"Any Russian," the man told him, "treats what he doesn't understand with respect, especially if it's a foreign word. After this nobody will touch your things. I give you my word."

"Excuse my rudeness," Prishvin asked, "but what kind of a powerful institution is this Magalif which you represent? Why did just mentioning it produce such action from that antiprofiteer brigade?"

The frail little man smiled guiltily.

"It's no institution," he answered. "It's my name. Sometimes it helps."

Prishvin burst into laughter. He followed Magalif's advice and wrote the mysterious word "folklore" on all his packages. After that not a single antiprofiteering brigade ever dared to touch them.

This was when stupid contractions of words were first being used. In a few years their number would reach catastrophic size and threaten to transform the Russian language into something as tongue-tied as the international languages men have tried to invent.

Every evening the well-known journalist and bibliophile Shchelkunov walked into the café, rubbing the mist off his thick glasses and bumping blindly into the tables. He was always carrying heavy packages of dusty books tied together with pieces of telephone wire.

Shchelkunov would take off his old-fashioned coat with its shabby velvet collar and hang it carefully on a nail. The café would be filled immediately with the mewing of cats. Shchelkunov picked up abandoned kittens on the streets, put them in the pockets of his overcoat, and walked all over the city with them until late in the evening when he could turn the hungry animals over to his wife.

Shchelkunov was like a village doctor. His wet beard was always tousled and his jacket hung on him like a sack from the weight of the books and manuscripts in its pockets. There were no fountain pens in those days, and Shchelkunov carried around in his pocket a bottle of Vanka-Vstanka ink and several goose quills. He could never write with a pencil, and I was the only one who understood this and didn't laugh at him and his goose quills. Anything written with a pencil has always seemed to me careless and unfinished. I believed then that a clear idea required clear writing. Had it been possible, I myself would never have written except with India ink from China on very thick paper.

Shchelkunov would sit down at a table, carefully sharpen his goose quill with a razor blade, and begin to write his notes in the handwriting of a medieval scribe. He always wrote about rare books, the finding of famous pictures, exhibitions, bibliographical news, and all kinds of rarities.

He set out in the early morning on his search for rare books and news about them, and he could be found in the most unexpected places in Moscow. He had a notebook full of the addresses of religious elders, former bookstore buyers, bookbinders, receivers of stolen goods, and book hawkers. These were his suppliers. Most of them lived on the edges of the city, in Izmailov, or Cherkizov, or Kotlakh, beyond Presna. Shchelkunov made his rounds where he could by trolley, but most of the time he had to go on foot.

He had a kind of sixth sense where books were concerned. He would track down a rare book with the care and patience of a hunting dog following a bird. He was not the only bibliophile in Moscow. Knowing his skill in finding rarities, the other book lovers and bookstore owners would follow him stealthily and try to beat him to whatever he was looking for. So Shchelkunov was always trying to blur his tracks and to throw his rivals off the trail. This gave him many of the traits of a conspirator. Perhaps this was why he talked about everything in a smothered whisper, his narrow Tartar eyes shining suspiciously.

"It looks," he would say in a low voice across the table, forcing his companion to lean toward him, "as if any day now I'll find where Ivan the Terrible's library has been hidden. If only, please God, Lunacharsky doesn't find out about it. Keep it quiet!"

When someone brought Shchelkunov a rare book for appraisal, he would ruffle the pages, sniff at it a little, then smile broadly and say:

"A widely known edition. Can be bought any day for nothing in the stalls next to the Kitaigorod wall. You've simply been swindled. I'm sorry for you. But I guess I'd take it in exchange for a first edition of Chekhov's *Selected Tales*. Do you want to? What do you mean you don't want to? In a year's time you'll be sorry. Well, good! I'll give you an Italian edition of Marco Polo, instead. You'll get it tomorrow."

With this Shchelkunov, without waiting for any answer from the naïve owner, would hide the rare book in his bulging portfolio, lock it, and look for a chance to get up and go. I do not remember a single instance when the simpleton succeeded in getting back a book which had been locked up in Shchelkunov's portfolio.

It did no good to start a fight. At the first sign of a row, Shchelkunov would quietly put on his coat and walk out of the café, his head lowered like a bull's. There was no power that could stop him. He was stubborn in his silence, puffing heavily, and deaf to even the most terrible insults.

Shchelkunov proposed once that I go with him to a cheap lodging house near the Vindavsky station. A primitive poet from Tula who had gone to seed lived there. Shchelkunov hoped to swindle some rare books or manuscripts out of him.

We traveled to the Vindavsky station by trolley but we got out, cautiously, a stop before our destination. Some clue had made Shchelkunov suspect that his eternal enemies, the book dealers, were on the watch for him that day and would try to intercept the Tula poet. Suddenly Shchelkunov grabbed me by the arm and dragged me behind a billboard. While we hid there Shchelkunov, sighing, told me:

"I was right, there's a broker. Look, over there, on the pavement across from the lodging house. The old man in the torn straw hat, with the goat's beard. I brought you along to help me."

"How can I help?"

"I'll go into the drugstore. I can see the lodging house easily out of its window. And you get rid of him. I'll wait in the drugstore. If he notices me going into the lodging house, then I'm *kaput!* And I've been looking for this damned poet for two months."

"And just how am I to get rid of him?"

"Pretend you're a detective. That will scare him. His mug is in the police files. I myself have bought books from him which had been stolen from the Historical Museum."

Shchelkunov gave me no chance to collect my wits, but darted into the drugstore. There was nothing to do but to play out the role of detective he had assigned me. But how?

I pulled my cap down over my eyes, stuck my hands deep in my pockets, and walked up to the lodging house with a slouching gait. I stopped a few steps short of the old man, leaned against the fence, and began to examine the lodging house with great care—it was an old four-storied building with cracks in its wall from the roof to the cellar. On its door someone had posted a notice, written in alternate letters of red and blue: "Warning to all entering: please walk quietly on every floor."

The old man in the straw hat leaned toward me. I stood there with a face as indifferent and as insolent as I could muster, and then as if trying to hide it from the old man I began to look carefully at my own cupped hand, pretending that I held a photograph in it. The old man quickly turned around, stamped his foot, and began to walk off to the side. But at this moment he made a fatal mistake: he took out a cigarette case and lit a cigarette.

I walked behind him, watching his back. By some frightening tension in that spindly old back I knew that the old man was making a supreme effort to control himself and not to run. I caught up to him and politely accosted him:

"Excuse me, citizen, but may I have a light?"

And then something incredible happened, which frightened even me. The old man screamed, made an enormous jump to one side, and ran like a crab on his little bent legs, disappearing without a trace through the next gateway.

Shchelkunov rubbed his hands with satisfaction.

He succeeded in buying a letter of Leo Tolstoy's from the Tula poet, a victory over his professional rivals. I felt angry at him, as a result of this whole stupid incident, and I swore to have nothing more to do with Shchelkunov.

I thought that Shchelkunov, like most book collectors, never got around to reading, and that books interested him only as a collector, without regard to what was in them, but it turned out that this was wrong. Shchelkunov gave a lecture on the history of books in the journalists' café. His lecture might better have been called a poem about books, an enraptured eulogy in their honor.

The book, according to him, is the only repository of human thought, the vehicle for its transmission from generation to generation, from century to century. The book has carried thought throughout time in all its original purity and its fascinating subtlety, as fresh as when it first was written. The book, fashioned by man's hands, has become the same kind of eternal verity as space and time. A book is the only truly immortal thing ever made by mortal man. But in the hurly-burly of our lives we forget that we have done this.

We try to grasp the cadence of Homer's measured verses and a miracle takes place before us: his shepherd's crook, petrified for thousands of years, bursts into the flowers of living poetry.

Our first contact with an idea, handed down to us from time immemorial, is always fresh and young. We, people of the twentieth century, receive the idea with the same novelty and impact as our ancestors who first wrote it in a book.

The centuries have receded into an impenetrable fog. But human thought shines brightly through that fog like the blue star Vega, catching up within itself all the light of the universe. Not all the black coal sacks of the world can dim the light from that bright star. Nor can any convulsion of history or empty stretch of time destroy human thought, preserved as it is in hundreds and thousands and millions of books and manuscripts.

Shchelkunov was convinced that there are still manuscripts to be discovered in the world, especially in the ancient lands of the Bible. This will enrich humanity with unheard-of philosophical systems and pearls of poetry. An ancient city was recently discovered in the mountains of Sinai, built by the Ptolemies. It was buried in the hot canyons of a wilderness. Each building of that dead city is an architectural masterpiece. And if old cities can be found, then maybe we can find old scrolls and books, too.

After Shchelkunov's lecture and after I had first learned about unknown Arabian cities, I began to be attracted by the East. I set out to learn about Eastern poetry. Shchelkunov gladly loaned me books by Omar Khayyam, Saadi, and Hafiz.

It may seem strange that in a time of revolution, with the breaking up of all accustomed notions and habits, some people should have been attracted by the East, and poetry, and many other things. But there was really nothing strange about it. The inquisitiveness of the human spirit has proved to be greater than might have been expected.

The sense of something raw and fresh which was a feature of the first years of the Revolution was so strong and moving that it left its imprint on all we thought about. The idea that men of our time, children of the Revolution, must have not only the qualities which had once been reserved for a few outstanding people but also the spiritual riches of all preceding epochs and all countries seemed to me then an absolute truth. So I searched everywhere for this kind of personal enrichment, even in the poetry of the East.

The journalist Rozovsky encouraged me in this. He was an elderly, lazy man with a curly red beard. He went around all winter in a long bishop's coat reaching to his heels which had once been magnificent but was now shabby. In general, in spite of his Jewish origins, he looked not unlike an Orthodox priest. He spent all his free time in his room on a broken-down ottoman covered with a Turkish rug, reading books about the East.

He was something of an expert on Islam, especially on the different Mohammedan sects. He had singled out one Persian sect led by El-Baba, the so-called "Babists," which he considered truly revolutionary. He was convinced that this sect would destroy Islam and bring about a spiritual renaissance in the dormant countries of the Middle East.

Before the Revolution Rozovsky had traveled to Turkey and Persia to study the East at first hand. He was a free man, a bachelor, and it was easy for him to go. He had lived for almost a year in the old Turkish town of Bursa. He talked a lot about Turkey. He talked in his own way, not at all as one is supposed to talk.

He never started with the chief thing, but always with a part of it, sometimes a detail. But gradually these details would be linked together into a magnificent story. If it were written down, it could be published as it stood. But his incredible laziness kept Rozovsky from ever writing anything. As soon as he sat down at his table an almost fatal boredom would overcome him, and he would go off to his office or to a café to look for someone to talk with.

I remember Rozovsky's stories about the old wooden house in

which he lived in Bursa. He always began not with a description
of the house but with an elaborate description of the smell of
Turkish wooden houses. According to him, they smelled of the
warm dust of rotting wood, and of honey, especially on hot, still
days, when one couldn't lean on the railing of the terrace for fear
of burning the palms of the hands. In the smell of the rotting wood
there was also a slight fragrance of dried roses. And the houses
smelled of honey because so many bees lived in the gardens filled
with wild rose bushes. They built their hives in the garrets of the
houses, and this was why the houses were always full of the sweet
smell of honey and of roses.

Rozovsky noticed this first in Constantinople when he was being
shown the casket, strewn with roughly polished precious stones, in
which the green banner of the Prophet is kept. It was covered with
a disintegrating silk cloth, and powdered with rose petals.

Rozovsky cleared up for me the meaning of many of the dark
Eastern images in the poems of Bunin. Since that time Islam has
always seemed to me a religion of drowsiness, patience, and
indolence.

I said something once to Rozovsky about the passivity and
laziness of Islam. He called my idea sheer nonsense. On the contrary, he said, Islam was the most militant and fanatical of
religions. Once a holy war was declared, once the Prophet's green
banner had been raised, Islam might destroy the world, like a black
simoon blowing out of the desert. And I could picture that simoon
to myself, a low, whirling darkness out of which came the noise of
fighting horsemen, and the glitter of Mohammedan swords,
yataghans, held in the riders' hands like hundreds of little bolts of
lightning.

I cannot describe, of course, all the visitors to the journalists'
café. But I cannot leave out one fragment of old Moscow, the
president of the "Society of Lovers of Canary Singing," the reporter
Savelyev.

This always-chuckling old man was our chief source of political
gossip and legends. It didn't cost him anything, because he talked
through his nose in a kind of unintelligible patter. It required an
enormous effort even to guess what he was talking about.

The pockets of his slovenly jacket were always filled with sticky
sugar candies. He insisted on presenting them to anyone who
smoked. He simply forced them to suck these fruit drops coated
with dust from his dirty pockets. As soon as Savelyev showed up
in the office, everyone put out his cigarette quickly.

We called Savelyev "the undertaker" because his only job on the paper was to write obituary notices. They always began with the same words: either "Death has taken from our ranks . . ." or "Our community has suffered a heavy loss in . . ." These obituaries bored everyone so much that finally the editor in charge decided to liven up a routine notice, and at the same time play a joke on Savelyev, by writing in, just before the standard opening: "Death has taken from our ranks . . ." only two words—"at last."

The next day there was a noisy row in the office. The editor was fired. Everyone felt badly about it, even though the obituary had been about some unpopular and unpleasant professor. Savelyev sat all day long in the office frowning at his desk.

"I have ushered hundreds of people into the next world," he muttered, "but I have never once sinned against their memory. I'm not their judge. And about real rascals I have never written a single line."

In tears, Savelyev went to the chief editor and told him he could no longer work in an office where such dirty tricks were possible. No persuasion could change his mind. Savelyev left, and suddenly all the rest of us missed his patter, his chuckling, and even his fruit drops covered with dirt and lint.

Savelyev died soon after this. His obituary notice was no different from all the other banal, indifferent notices he had written: "Death has taken from our ranks a modest worker in the newspaper field . . ." And so on and so forth.

Savelyev had been a bachelor. He left nothing in his stuffy little room except an old parrot. It hung head downwards from a little stick, chuckled just like its master, and cried out in an angry voice: "Daddy, want a candy?" The janitor adopted the parrot, and Savelyev's accounts with life were finally balanced.

The last man to show up at the journalists' café every night was a polite but noisy man with merciless eyes—Oleg Leonidov, "the king of scoops." He came late on purpose, just at the time when the newspapers, with their ink still damp, were coming off the presses.

This was the time when Leonidov could safely tell the reporters from competing papers just what scoops he had developed during the day without fear that they would steal them for their own papers. His competitors turned white with envy but they were powerless to do anything about it.

Even trailing Leonidov led nowhere. He was unbeatable. Nobody knew how or when he wormed his way into the innermost offices of the new Soviet organizations and gently, with his indulgent smile, extracted from them their most astounding news items. It was foolish even to try to fool him. He was a past master himself at that kind of game. Only once, during the war, did a careless Kiev journalist try this, by passing on a false item to Leonidov. Leonidov was almost fired for it by his paper, but he took a revenge on the Kiev journalist which prevented anyone else from ever trying it again, or even joking with him.

Leonidov's revenge seemed simple enough. He sent the reporter in Kiev a telegram: "Kharkov Archangel Minsk give the turkey exclusively oat flour."

The war was going on. The telegram landed up in the military censor's office where it was seen to be in code. They arrested the journalist. It smelled of espionage.

I don't know how long the man would have had to sit in prison if it had not suddenly occurred to the prosecutor to read the first letters of all the words in the telegram. In Russian, they added up to an obscenity. The journalist was released, at no cost except his own fright, while Oleg Leonidov walked calmly around Moscow with the reputation of having taken a witty revenge.

The journalists' café was closed for lack of funds at the end of the summer in 1918. It was genuinely missed not only by the journalists of the most diverse papers but by writers and artists, too. It was missed by everyone for whom the apartment with its low ceilings and its tasteless pink wallpaper had become an inviting sort of club.

It had been especially pleasant in the café at twilight. Through the open windows, behind the fire tower and the pedestal on which Skobelyev's statue had once stood, the warm sunset glowed in gilded dust. The noise of the city, or rather the talk of the city (in those days there were very few automobiles and the trolleys went by only rarely), died down and from a great distance you could hear the winged words of some revolutionary song like the "Varshavyanka."

In these hours one's heart grew sick at the thought that there behind the Brest station, behind Khodinka, where the sun was slowly setting, the dew was already lying on the birch woods and the water was gurgling its way past the snags in the clear rivers outside of Moscow. The rivers smelled of cold, of slime, and of rotting piles. It was dark in the abandoned little country houses, and flowers planted long ago were blooming in solitude. The dew was dripping down onto the roofs of boarded-up porches, and except for the regular sound of these drops nothing was to be heard in the thickening dusk of the evening.

The parks and fields and woods, left for a while in peace, stood close to the anxious city of Moscow and listened through their sleep to its excited hum.

THE ROOM WITH THE FOUNTAIN

The government moved from Petrograd to Moscow.

Shortly after this the editors of *The Power of the People* sent me to the Lefortovsky barracks. Lenin was supposed to make a speech there to demobilized soldiers. It was a slushy evening. The enormous barracks hall was drowned in the smoke of cheap tobacco. Rain trickled down the dusty windows. There was a sour smell of wet overcoats and carbolic acid. Soldiers with rifles, dirty puttees, and worn-out boots were sitting on the wet floor.

The greater part of them were front-line soldiers who had come back to Moscow after the Brest-Litovsk peace. Nothing had gone right for them. They trusted nobody and nothing. Either they stormed and shouted for their immediate release to their homes, or they flatly refused to leave Moscow, crying out that they were being fooled and that they were being sent back to fight the Germans instead of being sent to their villages. Some traitors and deserters were inciting them. It is well known that a simple Russian soldier, when he is worried and confused, becomes angry and starts to revolt. In the end, those who suffer most from these revolts are always the army cooks and quartermasters. There was a persistent rumor in Moscow in those days that the soldiers at Lefortovsky were ready any day to mutiny.

I squeezed into the barracks hall with difficulty and stayed at the back. The soldiers looked sullenly and with contempt at my civilian clothes. I asked them to let me move closer to the flag-draped platform, but nobody budged to give me room. Here and there, a few soldiers slapped back the breech locks of their rifles, as if they were playing with them.

One of the soldiers yawned slowly.

"Ah! What a bore!" he said, and he scratched the back of his neck under his sheepskin hat. "They're going to mumble-bumble again. We're fed to the teeth with all this talking at us."

"Well, what do you want? There's tobacco, and they hand out some kind of food at least. That's enough!"

"Live in Moscow, take the girls out walking," a heavy-set, bearded soldier added, laughing. "There's enough to drink, and you'll have memories of the great city all your life. They're better than medals."

"What's holding them up?" somebody yelled behind us, and rifle butts began to be pounded on the floor. "Let's get started with the talking. If you're going to assemble us fellows from the front, don't keep us waiting."

"He's going to start talking right away."

"Who?"

"Lenin, I hear."

"Le-enin! That's a lie. He's never had to look at your ugly mug."

"He hasn't anyone to exchange a few words with except you, you regimental sewer."

"By God, he!"

"We already know what he'll say."

"They'll check all the night watches."

"We've had our stomachs full of slogans. Can them!"

"Listen, brothers, don't let anybody ship us back."

"Don't worry. We'll ship ourselves. Enough of that."

Suddenly the soldiers became noisy, and started to stand up. The *makhorka* smoke moved in great waves. I heard, long before I could see anything in the darkness and the layered smoke, a slightly burred, unusually quiet and high voice say:

"Let me through, comrades."

People in back began to press against those in front, in order to see better. They were met by bayonets. Swearing grew louder, threatening to turn into shooting.

"Comrades!" Lenin said.

The noise was cut, as by a knife. I could hear only the wheezing in the throats of people right around me.

Lenin began to speak. I could not hear well. I was squeezed tight in the crowd. Someone's rifle butt was pressing into my side. The soldier standing right behind me laid his heavy hand on my shoulder and squeezed it from time to time, convulsively tightening his fingers.

Cigarettes which were stuck to soldiers' lips burned themselves out. Their smoke rose in blue streams toward the ceiling. No one was inhaling; they all forgot about their cigarettes.

The rain was beating against the walls but I began to make out a few quiet, simple words through its noise. Lenin was not summoning anyone to anything. He was simply explaining to some angry but simplehearted men what they were grieving about and what they had already heard, perhaps, plenty of times. But they had not heard it in the words they needed.

He spoke slowly about the meaning of the Brest-Litovsk peace, about the treachery of the Left Social Revolutionaries, about the alliance of the workers with the peasants, and about bread, about how necessary it was to stop the endless meetings and noise in Moscow, waiting for no one knew what, and to start to work the land as quickly as possible and to trust the government and the party.

Only separate words came through. But I could guess what Lenin was talking about from the breathing of the crowd, from the way the sheepskin hats moved up and down on the backs of their necks, from the soldiers' half-open mouths, and from their curious sighs, not at all masculine but more like the drawn-out sighing of old women.

The heavy hand was now lying quietly on my shoulder, as if resting. I felt in its weight something like a friendly caress. This was the hand the soldier would use to stroke the shaved heads of his children when he got back to his village.

I wanted to look at the soldier. I glanced around. It turned out to be a tall civil guardsman with a blond unshaven face, very broad and very pale, without a single wrinkle in it. He smiled at me in embarrassment, and said:

"The President!"

"What president?" I asked, not understanding.

"The President of the People's Commissars, himself. He made promises about peace and the land. Did you hear him?"

"I heard."

"Now, that's something. My hands are itching for the land. And I've straggled clean away from my family."

"Quiet, you!" another soldier said to us, a frail little man in a cap.

"All right, I'll be quiet," the civil guardsman whispered and he started quickly to unbutton his faded shirt.

"Wait, wait, I want to show you something," he muttered as he fumbled inside his shirt until he pulled out, at last, a little linen

bag turned black with sweat, and slipped a much-creased photograph out of it. He blew on it, and handed it to me. A single electric
lamp was flickering high up under the ceiling. I couldn't see a thing.

Then he cupped his hands together, and lit a match. It burned
down to his fingers, but he did not blow it out. I looked at the
photograph simply in order not to offend the man. I was sure it
would be the usual peasant family photograph, such as I had often
seen next to the icon in peasant huts.

The mother always sat in front—a dry, wrinkled old woman
with knotty fingers. Whatever she was like in life—gentle and
uncomplaining or shrewish and foolish—the picture always showed
her with a face of stone and with tight-pressed lips. In the flash
of the camera's lens she always became the inexorable mother, the
embodiment of the stern necessity of carrying on the race. And
around her there always sat and stood her wooden children and
her bulging-eyed grandchildren.

You had to look at these pictures for a long time to see and
to recognize in their strained figures the people whom you knew
well—the old woman's consumptive, silent son-in-law—the village
shoemaker, his wife, a big-bosomed, shrewish woman in an embroidered blouse and with shoes with tops which flapped against
the bare calfs of her legs, a young fellow with a forelock and with
that strange emptiness in the eyes which you find in hooligans, and
another fellow, dark and laughing, in whom you eventually recognize the mechanic known throughout the whole region. And the
grandchildren—frightened kids with the eyes of little martyrs.
These were children who had never known a caress or an affectionate greeting. Or maybe the son-in-law who was the shoemaker
sometimes took pity on them quietly and gave them his old boot
lasts to play with.

The picture which the civil guardsman showed me was nothing
like these family horrors. It showed a carriage, pulled by a pair of
black trotters. My civil guardsman was sitting on the coach box,
dressed in a velvet sleeveless blouse. He was young and handsome
in the picture. He was holding the broad reins in his unnaturally
posed hands, and sideways in the carriage sat a young peasant
woman of extraordinary beauty.

"Light another match," I said to the civil guardsman.

He quickly lit a second match, and I noticed that he was looking
at the picture just as I was, carefully and even with amazement.

The young woman in the carriage was wearing a long satin
dress with flounces, and a white kerchief tied low over her eyebrows as nuns wear them. She was smiling, barely opening her

mouth. There was such tenderness in her smile that my heart winced. Her eyes were big, obviously, and gray, and languishing.

"I worked for two years as coachman for the landowner Velyaminov," the soldier whispered to me hurriedly. "They took my picture on the quiet, in the master's carriage. With my bride. Before our wedding."

He was silent for a moment.

"Well, can't you say anything?" he suddenly asked me in a rough, challenging voice. "As if you'd seen thousands of girls as pretty as that?"

"No," I answered. "I've never seen anyone like her. Never."

"Ryabinka was her name," the soldier said, reassured. "She died just before the war. In childbirth. So I have a daughter, she's just like her mother. You come and see me, my dear comrade, in Orlov province . . ."

The crowd suddenly surged forward and separated us. Caps and hats were flying in the air. A fierce "Hurrah!" exploded from near the platform, bounced back and forth across the hall and out into the street. I watched Lenin walking quickly out, surrounded by soldiers. He held one hand against his ear, so as not to be deafened by the shouting, he was laughing, and he said something to the frail little soldier in the cap who had stood beside us.

I searched through the crowd for my civil guardsman, failed to find him, and walked out onto the street. The cheers were coming now from around the corner. Clearly, they were shouting after Lenin as he drove away.

I walked back to the city along a dark street. It had stopped raining. A rain-soaked moon appeared among the clouds.

I thought about Lenin and about the enormous movement which that amazingly simple man was leading, the man who had just walked through that cheering, excited crowd of soldiers. I thought about my civil guardsman, and about his young peasant wife, with whom I was already in love, across a distance of many years, just as I was in love with Russia, and this three-way meeting held something indefinably important for me which filled my spirit with light and with emotion. I couldn't explain the reason for this emotion. Maybe it was just a consciousness of the unprecedented times, and a presentiment of a good future—I don't know. Again I had the happy thought, as I had already had it many times before, that Russia is an extraordinary land resembling nothing else in this world.

On the façade of the Hotel Metropole, just under the roof, Vrubel's picture "Princess Greza" had been reproduced in colored tiles. The tiles had been heavily broken and chipped by bullets.

The Central Executive Committee of the Soviet Union—known as TSIK, which was the parliament of those times—used to hold its sessions in the Metropole. It met in what had once been the restaurant, which had a concrete fountain in its middle. To the left of the fountain and in the center (if you were looking from the tribune) the Bolsheviks and Left Social Revolutionaries sat, while on the right sat the less numerous but noisy Mensheviks, Social Revolutionaries, and Internationalists.

I was present at many sessions of TSIK. I liked to go long before they opened, sit in a niche not far from the tribune, and read. I liked the dark room, its resonant emptiness, the two or three lamps in crystal lampshades burning in different corners of the room, even the hotel smell of dusty rugs which never disappeared from the Metropole. But most of all I liked to wait for the moment when the empty room would become the scene of bitter wordy fights and brilliant speeches, the arena of stormy historical events.

Rozovsky and Shchelkunov also reported the TSIK sessions. Rozovsky could predict with great accuracy the verbal heat to be expected from any session. "Hang around today," he would warn me. "There's going to be an explosion." Or he would say, in a bored manner: "There's tea at the buffet. Let's go and have some. They're about to have a feast of legal vermicelli."

For some reason Shchelkunov was frightened of Sverdlov, the president of TSIK, especially of his attentive, imperturbable gaze. Whenever Sverdlov accidentally glanced at the reporters, Shchelkunov would either look away quickly or hide behind his neighbor.

An iron will could be felt in every word and gesture of Sverdlov, a short, pale man who wore a shabby short leather coat, and especially in his powerful bass voice which had no relation to his sickly appearance. Even his most ruthless and savage opponents, like the Mensheviks Martov and Dan, acknowledged the authority in Sverdlov's voice.

Martov sat closest to the reporters and we had a chance to study him carefully. Tall, emaciated, and fierce, with a sinewy neck wrapped in a torn scarf, he jumped up often, interrupted the speaker, and shouted his impatient words in a hoarse, broken voice. He was the instigator of most of the fights, and could be calmed down only by denial of the right to speak or expulsion from the hall for several sessions.

But occasionally he was in a good mood. Then he would walk over to us, pick up a book from someone, and settle down to read it avidly, as if forgetting time and place and the events still going on in the room with the fountain. Once he borrowed a *History of Islam* from Rozovsky and immersed himself in it. While he was reading, Martov would slouch far down in his chair, sticking his thin legs out far in front of him.

Discussion was going on of a decree sending food industry workers out to the villages. A fight was expected. But neither Martov nor Dan had pulled any surprises, and things were growing calmer. Newspapers rustled, and pencils scratched. Sverdlov took his hand away from his bell and smiled while he listened to the man next to him. This calmed the deputies more than anything else, because Sverdlov smiled rarely.

The list of speakers was drawing to its end. Then Martov stood up and asked for the floor in a sluggish voice. The room started to sit up. A premonitory rumbling ran along the rows.

Stooping over and rocking on his heels, Martov slowly drew himself up to the tribune, moved his empty eyes across the room, and started to speak, slowly, as if unwillingly. He said the decree needed, if you please, more exact juridical and stylistic editing. Such and such a point, for example, could be expressed more simply, eliminating some unnecessary words, and in another place they might eliminate the repetition of what had already been stated earlier.

Martov fumbled for a long time in his notes, failed to find what he was looking for, and shrugged his shoulders sadly. The room was now convinced there would be no explosion. Newspapers started to rustle again. Rozovsky, who had predicted a fight, began to wonder. "He's simply evaporated, like spirits of ammonia," he whispered to me. "Let's go out to the buffet."

Suddenly a shudder ran through the room. I did not realize right away what had happened. Martov's voice was thundering from the tribune, shaking the very walls. Bitterness gurgled in it. The scrappy pages of his notes were sailing in the air like snow and settling on the front rows of chairs.

Martov was shaking his two fists in front of him and shouting, breathlessly:

"It's treachery! You've dreamed up this decree just to clean all the discontented workers, the finest flower of the proletariat, out of Moscow and Petrograd. And to stifle the healthy protest of the working class!"

After a moment's silence, everyone jumped up from his place. A storm of shouts echoed through the room. Separate cries cut through it: "Down with the tribune!" "Traitor!" "Bravo, Martov!" "How does he dare!" "The truth will open their eyes!"

Sverdlov rang his bell furiously, calling Martov to order. But Martov went right on shouting, more bitterly than ever.

Finally Sverdlov denied Martov the floor, but the latter went right on talking. Sverdlov then formally expelled him for three sessions, but Martov just waved his arms and went on making accusations each of which was more sinister than the one before it. Sverdlov summoned the guard. Then, finally, Martov left the tribune and walked out of the room with deliberate slowness in a storm of whistling, foot stamping and applause.

The walls of the Metropole shook with these wordy battles at almost every session of TSIK. The Mensheviks and Social Revolutionaries often organized these fights on purpose, on such useless pretexts as an orator's use of a wrong word or his manner of talking. Sometimes instead of wild shouting they organized sardonic laughter, or at a speaker's first words, as if by command, they would all stand up and walk out of the room, talking with each other as noisily as they could. There were both helplessness and little boys' bravado in this kind of behavior. Protest became a fight.

The whole life of the country had been shaken down to its thousand-year-old roots, the times were threatening and filled with dark predictions, expectations, cruel passions, and contradictions. This made it still harder to understand this kind of combat, this fruitless and noisy nonsense.

Obviously, their party dogmas were more important to these people than the fate of the nation, the happiness of ordinary people. There was something dead and mechanical in these dogmas, which had been worked out in smoke-filled rooms far from Russia, far from the people's life. Some wanted to confine the new life within the framework of these schemes worked out by *émigrés* outside of Russia. This desire showed both contempt for the human spirit and a very bad knowledge of the country.

One day, a session of TSIK was held in deep silence. It was the day of the murder of the German Ambassador, Count Mirbach. The German government had presented an ultimatum demanding the admission of German military units to Moscow, ostensibly for the protection of the German Embassy, and German military control over the entire region around Denezhny Lane where the embassy was located. There had probably never been a more brazen or cynical ultimatum in history.

Immediately after its delivery, a special session of TSIK was called. I remember well that stifling summer day, drawing toward evening. The whole city was white with the reflection of the sun from windowpanes, and yellow with the dusk of evening. I walked into the room with the fountain, and I was struck by the silence, even though the room was crowded. There was not even that faint rustling which comes from the whispering of many people.

The pendulum of a clock on the wall was marking off the passing time by its regular beat. But it was clear that everyone felt, as I did, that time had stopped and that the sound of the pendulum was nothing but the faint noise of its dying.

Sverdlov walked in, rang for order, and announced in a hollow voice that he was giving the floor at this special session to the President of the Council of People's Commissars, Vladimir Ilyich Lenin.

The room shuddered. Everyone knew that Lenin was ill and that he was not supposed to speak.

Lenin walked quickly up to the tribune. He looked pale and thin. A gauze bandage was wrapped around his throat. His hands gripped the edges of the tribune while he looked slowly around the room. We could hear his broken breathing.

Quietly and slowly, raising a hand occasionally to his bandaged throat, Lenin said that the Council of People's Commissars had categorically rejected the brazen German ultimatum and had decided to mobilize immediately all the armed strength of the Russian Federation.

Arms were raised and lowered in dead silence as approval of what the government had done was voted.

We walked out on to Theater Square stunned by what we had heard. Twilight had already started, and a Red Army detachment, its bristling bayonets moving up and down in regular rhythm, was marching past the Metropole.

THE ZONE OF SILENCE

Now and then I had a free day. I would leave the house early in the morning and walk through the whole city to the Noyevsky Park or I would loaf around the outskirts, most often of all beyond Presna and in the fields around Devichi.

These were hungry times. The ration was a quarter pound of black bread a day. I would take this, two or three apples (which my neighbor Lipochka supplied me with), and a book, and go out for the whole day until it was dark.

The outskirts of Moscow then were just like the so-called "demoted" Russian towns which had lost their provincial status. A circle of godforsaken little places surrounded the big, anxious capital. The noise of Moscow did not reach as far as this circle. Once in a while a puff of wind would bring, along with its dry swirls of dust, some distant sounds of the "Internationale" or of rifle fire. There were short bursts of shooting fairly often in the city then, but they aroused little interest. They started suddenly and stopped suddenly, too.

The outskirts of the city were thinly populated then. Maybe this was what most attracted me. Was it a desire for a short rest from the excitement of those days, or was it perhaps a search for silence, when a man could breathe deeply, look around him, and examine what was happening a little from one side, so as to cope with it better?

I always had one other feeling as soon as I arrived in the outskirts—a certainty that the most varied kind of life, perhaps too varied and too interesting, was lying in wait for me. I still do not understand just why this feeling was always so strong for me in the outskirts of Moscow. But I often found myself speculating, while I looked at some back road grown up to stunted grass, with laundry drying on a clothesline, that in a few years I must come back to this dusty corner just to measure how much I had changed in the interval, while it stayed just as neglected as it had always been.

The cupolas of the peeling churches would look just as dull and muddy, and the laundry would still be flapping in the wind, while I would have long travels behind me, perhaps, and my own books written, and even, best of all, some extraordinary girl in love with me. It was as if I were taking that back street as a witness to my life. I wanted to use this ordinary corner of the city as a measure of the change I expected in myself.

But I turned out to be wrong, of course. When I returned to Moscow, five years later, to one of these dusty back streets in the outskirts, I found a new white building, girdled by young linden trees, with a sign saying: "District Music School."

The outskirts had their own charm—in their crooked wooden houses propped up by dark boards, in the overgrown little workshops with rusty boilers lying among the weeds, and in the lumber sheds smelling of birchbark. The charm was in the benches, shiny with time, at the gates, where the earth had been pounded into a kind of asphalt made with sunflower seeds. The charm was in the roads, soft with goose grass, and in the long-disused barriers at railroad crossings. Black locomotives, now cold forever, which dated probably from Stephenson's time, stood there. Swallows had built their nests in the cabins of those engines.

The charm was also in the dark elm trees, so frail with age that by the end of summer they could hardly cover half their branches with leaves, and in the piles of slag covered with dandelions, in the birdhouses, and the fences made of broken steel beds and church gratings. They were covered with morning-glories. Geraniums flamed in the windows in old tin cans, like fireflowers by the sea.

In one courtyard I saw a strange sight—a doghouse and in it a crimson cockerel with a black tail, tied to a chain by its foot (in place of the missing dog) obviously to correct its impudent, pugnacious habits.

There was a kind of charm in the down from poplar leaves rolling along the streets in silver-gray coils, in the mewing, shabby cats playing in the backyards, in the old women who looked as if they had been carved out of brown, wrinkled wood, in the nasturtiums flaunting their round, juicy leaves and the red hoods of their flowers, even in the sparrows drinking water out of puddles around the water hydrants, in a fly-specked oleograph, "The Kissing Ceremony," seen through the open window of a dark room, in a cage of canaries cheeping out of boredom, in the potted fig trees, in a broken and crudely glued-together porcelain dog, in a stuffed oriole nibbled by moles, and finally, in smoke from a samovar streaming straight up out of a courtyard into the white sky, even though the samovar was crooked. As is well known, when a samovar acts like this, it forecasts terribly hot weather.

Some child's hand had written, with a piece of coal, the words "Paradise," "Hell," "Treasure Island," and "Winter Palace" on enormous cement pipes lying about in the wilderness. "Winter Palace" was covered with fresh red scars from little pieces of brick; it had obviously been recently fired at.

Sometimes the breeze would fill the street with the smell of stagnant water and of tomato plants. Gardens waved behind many of the houses. Children's windmills, made of many-colored glazed paper, whirled on little sticks set among the garden beds, acting as scarecrows.

Far over the dust, over the grayish haze, there shone the dark gold cupolas of Moscow and the dome of the Cathedral of Christ the Savior. Clouds stood over the churches like beaten egg whites just barely reddened by the sun. Seen from here, Moscow was part of Asia, a heathen temple of Orthodox saints sculptured out of brown clay or cast in iron, with its heavy crosses held up by chains, and the round towers of the Kremlin wreathed by unending flights of pigeons.

The ponds covered with silt were especially wonderful in the outskirts. Discarded tin cans glittered through the olive-oil-green water. Rotting piles stuck out of the ponds, with slime dangling from them in long threads. They smelled like a drugstore. Willow trees, their crowns burned out by lightning, stood on the banks leaning over the water.

I would read in their shade, sitting on the warm ground and watching bubbles of swamp gas stream up from the bottom, never overtaking each other. Beetles would race across the water on their long legs; little boys in the district called them "water racers." If you threw a match into the water, the water racers would dart up to it from all directions, assembling in a little knot, and then when they were convinced it was only an inedible match, they would dart away again. Ponds like this always had a rusty pipe pouring in foaming water. Where the water poured into the pond, gulls would be standing in clusters.

Small boys launched flat little boards as steamships. Older girls, rinsing clothes, would slap and pound the laundry and shriek whenever some unseen water creature squirmed over their feet. The girls were always sure that these were leeches.

At one of these ponds I often met a gardener who wore torn, loose overalls. He used to fish there, using five or six lines fastened to the shore. Once in a while he would catch little carp, no bigger than a five-kopeck piece. The old man could sit there for hours, chewing black bread like myself.

I used to talk with him, and he showed me his kitchen garden. It seemed to me more beautiful than any rose garden I had ever seen. Its damp greenness was full of the fresh smell of mint and dill.

"Just see, my dear comrade," the gardener told me, "it's quite possible to live like this. Everyone could live, and fight for freedom, and perhaps make people better, and grow tomatoes, too. Every man has his own honor, his own price, and his own glory."

"What does that prove?" I asked him.

"The need for patience and understanding. It's in these, I'm convinced, that true freedom lies. Every man should turn his hand willingly to whatever occupation he loves. And nobody should bother him. Then nothing will frighten us, and no enemy will ever hurt us."

Sometimes I walked through the little garden and the fields where the sun, reflected from broken glass, made your eyes blink, to the sloping bank of the Moscow River. Waving hills of green ran down from Noyevsky Park right to the water. Thin films of oil floated on the water in rainbow patterns like those in a gypsy's shawl.

A little boy would row me across to the other bank, to the Noyevsky Park. It was magnificent there under the tall linden trees and their green shadows. The lindens were in blossom. Their strong fragrance seemed to have been brought here from some distant southern springtime. I loved to imagine that spring. It strengthened my love for the world. I could not share these dreams, except on paper. I wrote a little, but usually I lost what I wrote and did not regret it. I was ashamed of this writing. It had no link with the stern times we were living through.

Noyevsky Park had been famous for its flowers for a long time. Gradually it had grown poorer, run wild, and at the beginning of the Revolution there was nothing left in the park except one small greenhouse. But some elderly women and the old gardener were still working in it. They soon grew used to me and even started to talk to me about their affairs.

The gardener complained that flowers were needed now only for funerals and memorial meetings. Every time he talked about this, one of the women—thin, with pale, light eyes—seemed to grow embarrassed for him and told me that very soon they would probably be growing flowers for the city squares and for sale to all citizens.

"No matter what you say," the woman assured me, although I

had not contradicted her, "men just can't get along without flowers. For example, there have been, are, and always will be lovers. And what's a better way to show your love than with flowers? Our profession will never die out."

Sometimes the gardener would pick some stock or a few double carnations for me. I was ashamed to carry them through the hungry, anxious city; I always wrapped them so carefully in paper that no one could guess I had flowers in the package.

Once the package came undone in the trolley. I did not notice it until an elderly woman in a white kerchief asked me:

"And where did you get such beauty nowadays?"

"Hold them more carefully," the woman conductor of the trolley warned me. "Or else someone will shove you, and the flowers will all die. You know how people are."

"Who's that shoving?" a sailor wearing a cartridge belt asked challengingly, and then he bristled up against a knife grinder who was pushing his way through the crowd of passengers with his machine. "Where do you think you're going? Look—flowers. You dunderhead!"

"Just look, how sensitive you are!" the knife grinder said, sarcastically. "And from the navy, too."

"You leave the navy out of this. Or you'll be wiping your own eyes soon enough."

"My God, they're barking at each other, and about flowers," a young woman with a baby said, sighing. "You know, my husband, he's a very serious man, a solid man, but he brought me cherry blossoms to the hospital when I had this baby, my first one."

Someone was breathing feverishly down my back and I heard a whispering so low that at first I couldn't even make out where it came from. I looked around. A pale girl about ten years old was standing behind me in a homemade pink dress and looking at me imploringly out of gray eyes that were like pewter saucers.

"Little uncle," she said huskily and mysteriously, "give me a flower. Please, please, give me one."

I gave her a carnation. The girl made for the back platform of the trolley at once, through the resentful and jealous comments of the other passengers, jumped off while it was moving, and disappeared.

"She's out of her mind," the woman conductor said. "A crazy fool. Everybody would ask for a flower if his conscience let him."

I took a second carnation out of the bouquet and gave it to the conductor. She blushed almost to the point of tears, staring at the flower with shining eyes.

At once several hands were quietly held out to me. I divided up the whole bouquet, and suddenly saw in the trolley around me more shining eyes, more friendly smiles, more excitement than I had ever seen before, it seemed to me, in all my life. It was as if a blinding sun had risen in that dirty trolley car and brought youth to all those exhausted, anxious people. They wished me happiness, good health, the most beautiful bride in all the world, and all the brides I wanted.

An elderly, bony man in a worn black jacket bent his shaved head, opened his canvas briefcase, carefully placed the flower in it, and I thought I could see a tear fall into it before he closed it.

I could not control myself, and I jumped off the trolley. I walked and I thought, how many bitter or happy memories had that flower brought back to the old man, and how long had he hidden in his spirit the pain of his old age and of his young heart, if he had not been able to keep from crying in public?

Everyone treasures in his soul, like the thin fragrance of the linden trees in Noyevsky Park, the memory of some happiness buried by the litter of daily life.

During my wanderings around the outskirts of Moscow and in Noyevsky Park I moved into the zone of silence which surrounded the city, so incredibly close to it. These escapes from the tumult of life were understandable. For great events could no longer even follow each other in order, but were piling up every day in greater and greater confusion.

Yet ordinary life was still going on only a few steps away from these great historic happenings. There was in this too, probably, a kind of sense.

REVOLT

The big deserted stage of the Bolshoi Theater was filled with the sets for the Granovitaya Palata scene from *Boris Godunov*.

A woman in a black dress ran up to the footlights, her high heels clicking against the floor. A scarlet carnation was pinned to her corsage.

From a distance the woman looked young, but in the glare of the footlights it was clear that her yellow face was furrowed with little wrinkles and her eyes shone with a tearful, unhealthy glitter.

The woman was clutching a small steel Browning in her hand. She raised it high above her head, her heels clicked again, and she cried out in a shrill voice:

"Long live the revolt!"

The audience answered her with the same cry:

"Long live the revolt!"

The woman was the well-known Social Revolutionary, Marusya Spiridonovna. This was how we newspapermen learned about the begining of the revolt of the Left Social Revolutionaries in Moscow. Many events had led up to it.

The Council of Soviets was meeting. The best places had been given to the newspapermen who were in the orchestra pit. From there we could see and hear everything perfectly.

The only one of the orators whom I remember well was Lenin. And I don't remember what he said as clearly as his gestures and his way of talking.

Lenin sat at the very end of a long table, leaning way over and writing quickly; it looked as if he were paying no attention to the other orators. You could see only his beetled forehead, and sometimes a laughing look in his eyes as he glanced up at someone speaking. Sometimes he raised his head from his writing and made a cheerful or a caustic comment on some point in a speech. The audience would burst into laughter or applause. Lenin would lean back in his chair and laugh infectiously with all the others.

He did not make a speech, but simply talked, very lightly, as if he were carrying on conversation not in an enormous auditorium but with some of his friends. He talked without any pathos and without pressure, using ordinary intonation and slightly rolling his r's, which gave his voice a feeling of sincerity. But sometimes he would stop for a moment, and then throw out a sentence in a metallic voice which did not know any doubt.

He walked along the footlights while he spoke, sometimes pushing his hands deep in his trouser pockets, sometimes holding with both hands, and without embarrassment, the armholes of his black waistcoat. There was nothing monumental about him, no awareness of his own importance and no pomposity, no desire to utter sacred truths.

He was simple and natural in his voice and in his movements. It was clear from his eyes that he was prepared at any moment to talk not only about affairs of state but about any interesting human subject—perhaps about gathering mushrooms, or about fishing, or about our need for scientific weather forecasting.

Lenin spoke at this session about the country's need for peace and a breathing space, about food supplies, and about the harvest. The word "bread," which sounded in other speeches like something abstract, a purely economic and statistical concept, became for him, thanks to his graphic way of pronouncing the word, that same black rye bread for which the whole country was hungry.

The German Ambassador, Count Mirbach, was sitting in a side box at this Council of Soviets. He was a tall, balding, haughty man, who wore a monocle. At this time the Germans occupied the Ukraine, and peasant uprisings were breaking out under them, flaring up and dying down in region after region.

The Left Social Revolutionary Kamkov spoke on the first day of this session. He shouted out an angry speech against the Germans. He demanded a break with the Germans, immediate war, and support for the peasant uprisings. A threatening roar swept over the crowd. Kamkov walked almost directly up to the box where Mirbach was sitting, and shouted in his face:

"Long live the rebellion in the Ukraine! Down with the German occupation! Down with Mirbach!"

All the Left Social Revolutionaries jumped up from their places. They yelled and shook their fists. Kamkov shook his fists, too. Under his jacket, as he raised his arms, you could see the revolver hanging on his belt.

Mirbach sat there motionless, never taking the monocle out of his eye, reading a newspaper.

The yelling, whistling, and stamping reached a climax. It seemed as if the enormous chandelier would shatter, and the stucco moldings around the walls of the theater crumble. Even Sverdlov's powerful voice could not control the hall. He kept on ringing for order, but his bell could be heard only by the newspapermen in the orchestra pit. It could not penetrate through the wave of shouts coming from the theater itself.

Then Sverdlov closed the session. Mirbach stood up and walked slowly out of his box, leaving his newspaper on the railing.

It was impossible to force your way through the corridors of the theater. Security officers opened all the doors wide but the theater emptied very slowly. The excitement reached such fever pitch that an explosion of violence might have been expected at any moment. But the rest of the day went by in Moscow with unexpected calm.

On the next day, July 6, I got to the Bolshoi Theater very early, but I found all the other newspapermen already in their places. Everyone had come early in the expectation of excitement. Everyone was waiting for a government announcement about yesterday's demonstration by the Left Social Revolutionaries.

The theater was crowded. The session had been announced for two o'clock. But by that time nobody had appeared at the table of the praesidium. A half hour went by. The session did not start. Puzzled talk ran through the theater.

Then Smidovich, the Secretary of the Council of People's Commissars, walked out on the stage and announced that the session would be delayed a little, and he asked the Bolsheviks to go out to a party meeting in one of the buildings next to the theater. The Bolsheviks walked out. The theater emptied. No one remained except the Left Social Revolutionaries.

Everyone realized that only the most unusual circumstances could have postponed the opening of the session. The newspapermen dashed for the telephones to call their offices and find out what had taken place. But an armed solider was standing next to every telephone. No one was allowed to make a call. All exits from the theater were closed. Armed guards were standing at them, too. They had orders to let nobody leave.

A little later, from some unknown source, the rumor began to spread through the theater that three hours earlier Mirbach had been killed in his embassy.

Confusion swept through the newspapermen. The Left Social Revolutionaries stood up and gathered around all the exits. Strange noises began to be heard from outside the theater—a deafening crash and then heavy, dull blows, as if someone were driving wooden piles into the ground around the theater with a heavy hammer.

A gray-haired usher beckoned to me with his finger, and said: "If you want to know what's going on in the city, climb up this iron staircase to the roof. Up there on the left side you'll find a little window. Only don't let anyone notice you. Look out that window. God save us all!"

I climbed up an iron staircase without any railing to a dusty little window, or rather a deep hole left in the wall of the theater. I could see through it the edge of Theater Square and the side wall of the Metropole Hotel.

Red Army soldiers were running toward the Metropole from the direction of the Municipal Duma, leaping up and then lying flat, almost falling down on the pavement, firing short bursts from their rifles. Then from somewhere to the left, toward Lubyanskaya Square, a machine gun began to clatter. It was clear that while we had been sitting in the theater, locked in with the Left Social Revolutionaries, a revolt had broken out in Moscow.

I returned quietly to my place. This was the moment when Spiridonovna ran out to the footlights, as I described at the beginning of this chapter. Now it was all clear—it was the Left Social Revolutionaries who had started the revolt.

In answer to Spiridonovna's cry, all the Left Social Revolutionaries took revolvers out from under their coats and from their pockets. But at the same moment the quiet, hard voice of the commandant of the Kremlin was heard speaking from the gallery:

"Gentlemen, Left Social Revolutionaries! At the first attempt to leave the theater or to use your weapons, we will open fire from the upper galleries. I advise you to sit down quietly and wait for a decision on your fate."

None of us newspapermen was eager to be killed through the negligence of the security forces, which had obviously forgotten to let us get out in time. So we sent a deputation, headed by Oleg Leonidov, to the commandant. He answered politely but firmly that he regretted having received no instructions about newspapermen. But he gave in finally to our persuasion, and instructed us to assemble quietly in the vestibule of the theater, where the guards, quickly opening the door, let us out into Theater Square.

After the half-darkened theater, I was blinded at first by the bright sunshine. A second later, a bullet struck one of the columns of the theater, hissed, and then seemed to bounce back in the direction it had come from. Then, as if by command, bullets started to crackle all along the wall, fortunately above our heads.

"To Kopyevsky Lane!" Oleg Leonidov shouted, and he ran, crouching as low as he could, around the corner of the theater. All the rest of us ran after him.

Around the corner, everything was quiet. Bullets were still flying close to us, but to one side. We knew about them only from their light whistling noise, the breaking of windows in buildings across from the theater, and the little white fountains of plaster spurting out of the walls.

A tattered old book had slipped out of Shchelkunov's portfolio while he was running. He tried several times to dart around the corner and recover it, but we held him by the arms and wouldn't let him go. In the end he broke away from us, crawled out to the book, and came back red and dusty but happy.

"You're a dangerous maniac with your books," Oleg Leonidov yelled at him. "You're out of your mind!"

"What do you mean?" Shchelkunov retorted. "That was a first edition of Jean Jacques Rousseau's *Confessions*. It's you who are crazy, not I."

The firing shifted quickly up beyond Lubyanskaya Square. The Left Social Revolutionaries were retreating.

Back at the office I learned that Count Mirbach had indeed been killed that morning by the Left Social Revolutionary Blumkin. This had been the signal for the revolt. The rebels had managed to seize the Pokrovsky barracks and the telegraph office on Myasnitskaya Street, and had advanced almost as far as Lubyanskaya Square. The Left Social Revolutionaries who had been locked in the theater were arrested shortly after our escape.

By evening, the rebels had been driven out of the city. They retreated to the Kazan railroad freight station and to the Ryazansky highway, where they broke up and scattered.

The revolt ended as suddenly as it had started.

NOTES FOR
A HISTORY OF MOSCOW PRIVATE HOUSES

The history of houses is sometimes more interesting than that of human beings. Houses live longer than people, watching generation after generation come and go. Except for a few regional historians, nobody bothers to study the history of an old house. And it is the fashion to treat regional historians condescendingly, like harmless eccentrics. But it is they who are collecting, grain by grain, our history and our traditions, and who are are fostering a love of our country.

I am convinced that if one could assemble the history of a house in all its detail, follow the lives of all who lived in it, learn their characters, describe the events which took place inside the house, one would have a social novel more meaningful, perhaps, than any Balzac ever wrote.

Besides, the story of every house is bound up with the existence of a lot of things which have also lived for a long time, been moved across great distances, and seen a thing or two. But it is unfortunately impossible to write the history of things. Things do not talk, and people are forgetful, not curious, and inclined to treat things— their true assistants in life—with an insulting carelessness.

For things are made by our own hands, just as the big-nosed Buratino was carved out of a dry log by the old carpenter Carlo. Buratino came to life, and so much happened to him then that it required the intervention of magic and of fairies. If things could come to life, what a wonderful muddle they would introduce among us, and how much richer history would be! For they would have a lot to tell.

No one can tell now exactly how many private houses there were in Moscow at the time of the October Revolution. People say there were as many as two hundred. They were mainly the homes of merchants. There were very few left belonging to the gentry— most of those had been burned in 1812.

Most of the merchants' homes were taken over after October by the anarchists. They lived freely and happily with all the elegant antique furniture, the chandeliers, the thick rugs, and there were many cases in which they treated them after their own fashion. Portraits served as targets for revolver practice. Expensive rugs were used, like tarpaulins, to cover boxes of cartridges piled up in the courtyards. Window openings were barricaded, for protection, with piles of rare and valuable books. Ballrooms with patterned parquet floors were used as dormitories. The houses were lived in, together with the anarchists, by all sorts of dubious characters.

Moscow was full of rumors about the loose life of these anarchists in the private homes they had taken over. Prim old ladies whispered to each other about scandalous orgies. But they were really not orgies, but ordinary drinking bouts with bad vodka instead of champagne, to wash down hard Caspian salt fish instead of caviar. They were assemblies of riffraff, unstrung adolescents and starry-eyed girls, nests of delinquents in the heart of Moscow.

The anarchists even had their own theater. It was called "Izid." Its posters announced that it was a theater of mysticism, eroticism, and anarchy of the spirit, and that its goal was "the idea raised to the level of fanaticism." What kind of an idea this was, the posters did not state. Every time I saw one of those posters, I thought that the theater could not possibly have been started without Rachinsky.

I stayed often at the office until late at night, and sometimes until morning, writing my first novel. I slept on an old couch with broken springs. Sometimes in the middle of the night a spring would break with an evil twang and stab me in the side.

I preferred to write in the office rather than in my own sleepy, musty room where water was always dripping in the bathroom and my landlady shuffled along in her bedroom slippers outside my door. The light in my room worried her, and she would get up several times a night to check the electricity meter.

At the office I usurped Kuskova's spacious, carpeted room and her writing table. Sometimes I would fall asleep at the table, and wake up again after ten or fifteen minutes, refreshed and full of energy. The editorial cat slept on the table next to me. Sometimes he would open his eyes and look at me good-naturedly, as if to say: "You working? Well, go on and work. I'll go on dreaming for a little while."

But one night the cat's ears stood up at an angle. He looked at me with eyes as green as gooseberries and mewed hoarsely. I listened. Distant firing could be heard in the sleeping city, and it was approaching the office. From its persistence it was clear that

this was no accidental street shooting. At that moment the telephone rang. The head of our Moscow desk was calling.

"They've started disarming the anarchists," he told me. "They're
taking the private houses by assault. It's good that you're in the
office. I'm coming down right away, but meanwhile go on out, my
boy, to Morozov's house on Vozdvizhenka and see what's going on
there. But be careful."

I walked out on the street. It was dark, deserted. Wild firing
could be heard from the direction of the Malaya Dmitrovka, where
the anarchists were established in the former Merchants' Club and
had even set up two field guns at the gate.

I went through some small lanes to the Vozdvizhenka and
Morozov's house. All Muscovites know that fantastic building, like
a castle, with seashells fastened to its gray walls. Until very recently the old millionairess, Morozova, had lived there.

But that night the building was dark and sinister. I walked up
the granite steps to the heavy door, like the bronze door of a
medieval cathedral, and listened. Not a sound came from inside.
I decided that the anarchists had left, but I knocked cautiously.

The door opened suddenly and easily. Someone grabbed me by
the arm, pulled me in, and the door swung shut. I found myself in
complete darkness. Some people were holding me tightly by the
arms.

"What's the matter?" I asked carelessly. The question itself
seemed to me stupid. There was nothing the matter except utter
nonsense. And I could guess that this nonsense might end with
great unpleasantness for me.

"He's clearly been sent here," a young woman's voice said right
next to me. "We must report it to Comrade Ognyev."

"Listen," I answered, determined to laugh the matter off, "the
times of the Count of Monte Cristo have gone by. Light a light, and
I'll explain everything to you. And, if you please, let me get out
again."

"Well, just listen to him," the same woman's voice said. "All he
wants is that we should let him go. Listen, you rat, you're a Bolshevik scout, we know you, and you'll be staying here. I promise
you, not a hair will fall from your head unless you start to flutter
and make trouble."

I became angry.

"Princess of anarchism," I said to the woman I couldn't see,
"stop playing the fool. You've just been reading too many bad
novels. At your innocent age that can be dangerous."

"Search him, and then lock him up in the left-hand drawing

room," the woman said in an icy voice, as if she had not heard me, "and I'll report it to Comrade Ognyev."

"Please do," I said. "Report it to your Ognyev, and to anyone else you like. I spit on them all."

"My, aren't you ashamed of your insolence, you rat?" the woman said in a singsong voice.

Two men pushed me down a corridor in the dark. One of them was wearing a cold leather jacket. Without a word, they shoved me up a short stairs, then down one, and into a room which they locked from the outside, telling me that if I tried to pound on the door they would simply shoot me through the panel, and then they went away, one of them saying to me as they left, in a pleasant enough tone:

"So this is how your scouts work, you Bolshevik swine. If you were working for us, I'd teach you a thing or two."

I had matches with me, but I didn't dare to light one, to look around me. There was no telling what those anarchists might think. They could take the light of a match to be a signal and then, for all I knew, they really might begin to shoot through the panel of the door.

I felt the panel. It was covered with fancy fretwork. Then I began to feel the wall and I hurt myself—I tore a fingernail on a silken hanging. In the end I bumped into a soft armchair with elbow rests and I sat down in it and began to wait.

For a while this incident amused me. It was clear the anarchists took me for a scout sent by the Bolsheviks. This was stupid on their part, but I couldn't do anything about it. And what kind of a girl was this? Her voice had seemed familiar to me. I began to search my memory and I recalled an anarchist with a voice like hers who had made a speech once at a meeting near the monument to Gogol. She had had long black bangs, her eyes had shone hungrily like those of a drug addict, and she was wearing enormous turquoise earrings. She had not been allowed to finish. Then she had taken out a cigarette, lit it, and walked away through the crowd, swinging her hips and smiling scornfully. Yes, of course, she was the one.

I was not unhappy to be sitting there in the comfortable chair, waiting for what would happen next. I was sure they would let me go, as soon as I showed them my credentials from *The Power of the People.*

More than an hour went by. Rifle firing could be heard from far away. I heard one hollow rolling explosion. I wanted desperately to smoke. In the end I couldn't resist, took out a cigarette, squatted on my heels behind the back of the chair, and lit a match. It flared up like a torch and for a second lit the whole room. I could see the flame reflected in the mirrors and in crystal vases. I lit my cigarette quickly and put out the match, only then guessing why it had burned so brightly—it was a defective match with a double phosphorous head.

Then something else quite unexpected happened—rifle fire suddenly began from the street at the windows of the house. The air was full of plaster dust. I stayed on the floor. The firing became heavier. I guessed then that the light of my match had served as a kind of signal to the Red Army soldiers who had quietly surrounded the building.

Most of the firing was aimed at the room where I was sitting on the floor. Bullets hit the chandelier. I could hear its crystals tinkling as they fell to the floor.

I had unknowingly played exactly the role of scout which the anarchists had falsely accused me of. I realized that my position was no longer an attractive one. If the anarchists had noticed that match, they would soon come back to the room and shoot me.

But apparently the anarchists had never seen the light of the match, for they were not interested in me. They were returning the fire. I could hear something heavy being dragged down the corridor, probably a machine gun. Someone, swearing jerkily, gave the command: "Four men up to the second floor! Don't let them in the windows!"

Something exploded with a crash. Then a lot of people ran past my room noisily, the familiar woman's voice yelled out: "This way, comrades! Through the hole in the wall!" and then after a little confusion, everything grew quiet again. Only once in a while, as if checking to see if anyone were still besieged in the house, the Red Army soldiers would fire at the windows.

Then there was complete silence. The anarchists, obviously, had fled.

But this silence did not last long. I heard heavy steps again, a kind of clanking, voices shouting: "Search the whole house! Give us some light! Light!" "Look what a soft life they had here, the dirty pigs!" "Watch your step, or they'll throw a grenade out of the corner."

The heavy steps stopped outside my door. Someone pushed heavily against the knob, but the door did not give.

"They locked it, the snakes," a hoarse voice said wonderingly.

The door began to yield. I kept silent. What could I do? I couldn't begin a long and confused explanation through the locked door of how the anarchists had captured me and locked me in. No one would have believed me.

"Open up, you shaggy devil!" Several voices were yelling through the door. Then someone shot into the lock, and the door began to give. It was being battered with rifle butts.

"They built this door to last," the same hoarse voice said cheerfully.

Half the door flew open and an electric lamp was flashed into my face.

"There's one of them here," a young Red Guard said happily, and he aimed his rifle at me. "Well, come on, stand up, anarchist. Off to headquarters with you! You've had your fun, and this is the end!"

I went willingly back to staff headquarters. The staff was housed in a little building on Povarskaya Street. An extraordinarily thin man in a battle jacket was sitting there at a table. He had a sharp, light-colored beard, and laughing eyes.

He looked at me quietly, and suddenly smiled. I smiled back at him.

"Well, tell your story," the thin man said, and he lit his pipe. "But keep it short. We have no time to waste on you."

I told everything honestly, and I showed my documents. The thin man glanced at them quickly.

"We ought to lock you up for a week or two for excessive curiosity. But unfortunately, there's no law that permits that. On your way! If you want my advice—to hell with your paper *The Power of the People.* What's it to you? What's the matter with you, aren't you content with the Soviet setup?"

I replied that on the contrary all my hopes for the happiness of the Russian people were based on this setup.

"Well, then," the thin man answered, frowning from the smoke of his pipe, "we'll try our hardest, of course, to justify your confidence, young man. I assure you, it's most flattering to us. Most flattering. And now—get the hell out of here!"

I went out on the street. Somewhere firing was still going on. I felt my face red with shame. The thin man had been laughing at me. But deep in my heart I knew he had been right, and, no matter how many sharp and clever answers I thought up afterwards, they did not meet his scornful words.

By midday the anarchists had been driven out of all the private houses they had occupied. Some of them fled from Moscow, some of them scattered through the city and gave up their military nonsense.

The residents of the city, who had slept through this event, looked with astonishment the next day at the bullet-riddled houses, at the yardkeepers sweeping the broken glass into piles, and at the gap made by the only artillery shot of the engagement, in the wall of the Merchants' Club on Malaya Dmitrovka.

In those days events took place so suddenly that it was even possible to sleep through them.

SOME EXPLANATIONS

In the middle of the summer of 1918 they closed *The Power of the People*, as well as all the other papers which called themselves independent.

Soon after this I received a letter from my sister Galya, from Kopan. A conductor from Bryansk brought the letter to my house when I was not at home. He left no trace by which I could find him. The letter was smeared with grease and had been folded many times. It had taken a month to reach Moscow from Kopan.

Galya wrote me:

"You promised Mama to come in the spring but you are not here yet and we have despaired of seeing you. Mama has suddenly grown very old and you would not recognize her. She is silent for whole days, and at night when she thinks I am asleep she cries so loud that even I can hear it. And I, Kostik, have become almost completely deaf in this last year.

"Can't you really give her this last happiness? We talk only about you and we don't know what has happened to you, or if you are well. It is terrible for us to think that any day something might happen to you. There is a great deal in your life, but there is nothing except you for Mama. You must understand this, Kostik.

"Yesterday morning Mama said that if you don't get here by the middle of August, we will start out on foot for Moscow. Mama is sure that we can somehow make it. We'll leave everything here—

what good is it to us?—and go with just our knapsacks. We have very little money, but Mama says that there are good people in the world and so she isn't afraid of anything. We'll have to start while it's still warm, and winter is still far away. And maybe someplace we'll be able to get on a train, although they say here that the trains are not running.

"Kostik, darling, answer this somehow, let us know how you are and whether we should wait for you here. We sit here all alone in the woods, as if we were in a den, and we don't understand how it is that we haven't been killed yet."

This letter cut into my heart like a razor. I had to go. But how? How was I to get to the Ukraine?

At that time, the Ukraine, the Don basin, and the Crimea were held by the German army. Kiev was held by a hetman who had been invented by the Germans—Pavel Skoropadsky, a long-legged, polished, stupid officer. Ukrainian newspapers credited him with a dislike for low-cut women's dresses, but no other personal qualities of any kind were ever attributed to Skoropadsky. Even the Germans laughed rudely at this fake hetman.

To get permission from the Commissariat of Internal Affairs to leave Soviet Russia meant to waste not less than a month. July was ending, and I figured that I could not expect such permission before the end of August. But I knew Mama, and I knew that in the middle of August, risking her own and Galya's life, she would set out on foot for Moscow. So I could not lose a single day. I had to leave at once.

It seemed that in order to enter the Ukraine I would need also a permit from the Ukrainian consul. I went to his office. It was located in the courtyard of a big building on Tverskaya Street. A faded yellow and blue flag hung from a staff fixed to the railing of a balcony. Laundry was drying on the balcony, and the consul's child was sleeping in a carriage. An old nurse was sitting next to it, rocking the baby carriage with her foot, and singing sleepily.

It proved to be impossible even to get inside the door of the consulate. Hundreds of people were sitting and lying on the dusty ground, waiting their turn. Some of them had been waiting more than a month, listening to the old nurse's song, completely in the dark about what was happening to their applications. So I would have to go without the permit.

I learned that some Leningrad newspapermen, from some of the cheap, so-called boulevard papers, were going to the Ukraine. Their documents were all in order. Someone introduced me to them. Somewhat reluctantly, it is true, they agreed to take me with them and to help me on the frontier, but as their leader—a yellowish man with gray spats and gold pince-nez—told me, "only within the bounds of reason." He did not explain what were the bounds of reason. I knew very well myself that if I had trouble, none of them would stand up to help me.

Their departure was set for three days later. During these three days nothing happened except that I heard that Romanin had arrived in Moscow. I went immediately to Yakimanka, to the house where he lived, but a shrewish old woman there would not even let me in the vestibule and said that Romanin only slept there two or three nights a month. I left a letter for him, went away, and lost my last trace of him forever. And again I felt the old familiar pain from losing, one after the other without exception, all the people whom I had learned to love.

A long file of people still moved past me, but not one of them stayed with me even for a few years. People appeared for a moment and then moved on, and I knew I was unlikely ever to see them again. Obviously to console myself, I remembered Lermontov's words about "the fever of the spirit, squandered in the desert."

Before I left I made the round of all my favorite places in Moscow. I looked at the Kremlin from the Noyevsky Park. A thunderstorm was moving quickly over it. The cupolas of the churches shone with a dark flame, the wind that comes before a storm was stiffening the red flags, and a yellow ball of cloud was lighted up by flashes of lightning. Suddenly, scudding away from the crowded city, the thunder roared out over my head. The cloudburst roared down onto the trees.

I took refuge in an empty hothouse. A single vase of flowering pelargonium, covered with sickly red spots, stood on the shelf. I touched the flower, which had been forgotten or left there on purpose. It was stretching with all its leaves and petals toward the air and the streams of rain which were falling down outside. I put the flower under the rain. It trembled under the heavy rain drops. It seemed to take on new life while I was watching it.

This flower symbolized my love for Russia. The memory of it is fused with my last days in Moscow. I went away in great uncertainty, not suspecting, of course, that it would be five years before I would return and that a life was waiting for me which was so like something made up by a fiction writer that I am a little afraid to tell about it.

In these chapters I have written only about what I myself saw and heard. For this reason, many well-known events of these years are missing from my story. But I am writing only my own testament, and I have neither the intention nor the ability to give any broad picture in this book of the early period of the Revolution.

I began to write this story about my life a long time ago. I am very old, and yet I have brought the story only up to times when I was still a young man. I do not know if I will manage to finish it. If I could wipe ten years out of my life, I would have time to write a second tale perhaps more interesting than this one—a second book about my life. But not about my life as it actually was lived, but about life as it should have been and might have been if its arrangement had been left only to me, and had not depended on a lot of external and partly hostile forces.

That would be a story about what did not really happen, about all the things that conquered my consciousness and my heart, about a life which held within itself all the colors, all the light and all the feeling of the world. I can see many chapters of that book as clearly as if I had lived them several times.

THE HEATED BOXCAR

I have had a passion for railroads ever since I was a child, perhaps because my father worked for them. It showed itself, of course, in ways peculiar to little boys. When our family would spend a summer somewhere near a railroad, I would spend hours at the nearest station, meeting every train together with the station official in his red cap.

Everything connected with railroads has had the poetry of travel for me ever since then, even the smell of coal smoke from a locomotive. I would watch the green, oily locomotive with sheer delight as it slowed its shining driving rods to stop next to the water tower, puffing out into the sky a whistling stream of steam as if it were panting after an exhausting race. I would imagine to myself how that engine had thrust its steel chest into the wind, the night and the thick woods, through the shining wilderness of the earth, and I would hear the sound of its whistle carried far from the railroad, maybe to some forester's lodge. And there might be a little boy there, like myself, imagining how the shining express train was flying across the country through the night, and perhaps a fox, lifting its paw, watching it from a distance and giving a little yelp of grief it could not understand. Or, perhaps, of admiration.

When a passenger train had left, a sleepy quiet would reign over the station. A hot railroad boredom settled down. Warm water dropped from the green tub on the platform. Hens wandered impudently across the rails. The nicotiana in the little station garden held their flowers closed for evening. The rails shone blindingly, polished by hundreds of steel wheels. A little chestnut horse, harnessed to a wagon, would be tethered to the back of a freight car standing on a siding. It would be asleep, but it would twitch the skin on its back from time to time, trying to shake off the flies.

Then from a distance one would hear a loud, quavering whistle. This would mean a freight train, going through without stopping. Beyond the station a stretch of the line bent in a great arc into a pine forest. The train would always burst out of the woods unexpectedly, twisting and leaning on the curve.

It seemed to me then that I had never seen a more beautiful sight. Mountains of thick steam flew up from the engine. The locomotive roared for a long time, frighteningly. The train would rush through the station and sweep past like an attack of dizziness, with a steel clanging, the fast clatter of its wheels, and wild clouds of dust. It seemed as if with just a little more speed it would rise right into the air and carry away with it all the people at the station, like dry leaves. And first of all, of course, the official in his red cap.

The freight cars swept by quickly. They dazzled my eyes, but I managed somehow to read the white letters on their sides showing the railroads they belonged to: RO (Riga-Orlov), MKV (Moscow-Kiev-Voronezh), SPBW (St. Petersburg-Warsaw), RU (Ryazan-Uralsk), PRIV (Privislinshy), MVR (Moscow-Vindavo-Ryabinsk), SV (Sizrano-Vyazemsky), MKS (Moscow-Kharkov-Sevastopol), and dozens of others. Sometimes I found railroads I did not know, like USS or PRIM, and I found out from my father that USS was the Ussuri Railroad in the Far East, and PRIM the Primorsky Railroad, a little line running from Peterburg to Oranienbaum and going up to the shore of the Gulf of Finland.

What can I say? I envied these inanimate freight cars just because they themselves did not know where they were being sent, perhaps to Vladivostok and from there to Viatka, from Viatka to

Grodno, from Grodno to Feodosia, from Feodosia to the station at
Navlya, in the very heart of the wide-sounding Bryansk forests.
Had it been possible, I would have sat in a corner of any one of
those freight cars and traveled with it. What wonderful days I
would have spent on the sidings where freight trains would stand
for hours at a time! I would have wallowed in the warm grass next
to the embankments, I would have drunk tea with the conductors,
I would have bought strawberries from long-legged peasant girls,
and swum in the little rivers where yellow water lilies were in cool
full blossom. And then, on the way again, I would have sat in the
open door of the freight car swinging my legs, the wind warmed
all day by the earth would have blown in my face, the long hurrying shadows of the cars have fallen across the fields, and the sun
have dropped like a golden shield into the dark distance of the Russian plains, leaving its wine-gold traces on the burned-out sky.

I remembered this little boy's passion for freight cars when I
hunted through the sidings of the Kiev station for the Riga-Orlov
railroad heated boxcar number 717,802. I found my companions already in it, the journalists from Petrograd. They had
fixed themselves up in comfort, were drinking tea on a turned-over
box, and telling each other delicately bawdy stories. They paid no
attention to me, barely returned my greeting, and tried in every
way to show that they had no desire to know me. Why, then, had
they agreed to take me with them?

I lost myself in wondering about this. Could it have been only
to save themselves in any trouble with the authorities? Their documents were all in order, but anything could still happen. Suppose
the authorities should suddenly start to make trouble for them? In
that case a man like myself, with permission neither to leave
Russia nor to enter the Ukraine, would be simply a windfall for
them. I would give them a chance to protect themselves, to prove
their devotion to the Soviet authorities and to say: "Look, comrades, you're making trouble for us, honest Soviet citizens, while
in the same boxcar there's a very dubious character without
any documents at all. It's our obligation to report him to you. You'd
better check him carefully."

I dismissed these thoughts from my mind. I was ashamed of
them. Five years before I would never have thought such evil of
strangers. But I could not define my suspicion of these free and
easy journalists. A short little man with round, oily eyes was the
one I disliked most of all. His name was Andrei Borelli, but this
was only a pen name, of course, for the stunning reports he was
going to write. Among themselves the journalists called him Dodya.

He was always pulling up his short khaki trousers, and laughing, spraying out saliva as he laughed. His face was covered with gray, spongy skin like rubber. He never stopped making puns and wisecracks, and he talked about everything with a kind of sick irony. Even the chief of this corrupt little gang—the jaundiced man in gray spats—sometimes could not control himself, and he would say, frowning:

"You're a genius at fornication with words, Dodya. Stop playing the clown. You bore me."

Without thinking, Dodya would answer him with a sarcastic pun. The jaundiced man would threaten to throw him out of the boxcar, and for a little while Dodya would remain silent.

The first night passed calmly. The train hardly moved. I did not talk with my companions and tried to think up some pretext for moving into another car. But this was impossible. There were armed soldiers and sailors all through the train, and some of the cars were filled with cavalry horses.

The next day I noticed a strange circumstance. There was a blue teapot tied to Dodya's suitcase, its enamel badly dented and chipped. It seemed to me curious that my companions used a big tin mug to get hot water for tea at the stations where we stopped. They never used the teapot, although the mug was not big enough for all of them.

The mystery was cleared up on our second day. The train, stopping often, was hesitantly pulling in to the station at Bryansk. A Red Army soldier from the next car looked in our door.

"Brothers," he said, "imagine what bad luck we've had. We've lost our teapot along the way. Our government-issued teapot. It's enough to make you cry. You wouldn't have an extra teapot?"

"No," Dodya answered sharply. "We're drinking out of a mug ourselves."

"But you've got an enamel teapot tied on there," the Red Army soldier said coolly. "Lend it to us for a day. We'll return it safely."

"That teapot can't be used," the man in spats said, his pince-nez flashing angrily.

The soldier took offense.

"What do you mean, it can't be used?" he asked. "Is it made of gold, or what?"

"It leaks, understand? It leaks. It's good for nothing. All full of holes."

The Red Army soldier laughed in a knowing way.

"Queer!" he said, his voice cool again. "I wonder why you want to carry such old junk around with you. As if you were poor people.

But you're not poor, that's clear. You drink your tea with real sugar, not with saccharine. Excuse me for having bothered you."

The soldier went away. My companions looked at each other, and one of them said to Dodya in a whistling kind of whisper:

"You idiot! Your teapot stuck out like a sore thumb."

They talked in low voices for quite a while, and then they put another package on top of the suitcase with the teapot, and put an overcoat on top of that.

"In which car?" a disgruntled voice suddenly asked outside. "In this one?"

"Exactly, Comrade Commissar. The Riga-Orlov car."

Dodya leaned quickly over to the teapot, grabbed it, put it on his knees, and with an effort which turned his face red and made tears come to his eyes, broke off the spout and put it in his pocket.

An elderly, disgruntled commissar climbed, groaning, into the car. Behind him came the Red Army soldier we had seen before.

"What's all this about a teapot here?" the commissar asked. "Where is it? Show it to me."

Dodya pulled the mutilated article out from under the package.

"Look, it's lost its spout," the Red Army soldier said, and he whistled. "It was here a few minutes ago, but now it's flown away like a bird."

The commissar looked at the teapot, thought for a while, and then told the soldier:

"Well, run along, and bring back two men from the guard."

He turned to the journalists.

"Your documents."

They produced their documents eagerly, but their hands were trembling. The commissar waited patiently. He looked at them slowly, and then stuffed them in the pocket of his coat.

"Our documents are completely in order, Comrade Commissar," the man in spats said. "Why are you taking them away from us?"

"I can see that they're in order," the commissar answered, and he turned expectantly toward me.

"Look, Comrade Commissar," the man in spats blurted out hurriedly. "Here's what's really wrong. This citizen just showed up in our car. He got on in Moscow, even though we protested. As far as we know, he has no permit to leave Moscow, and no permission to cross the frontier. You ought to check him first of all. As loyal Soviet citizens, we were going to report him to you. But we hadn't got around to it yet."

"And just how do you know, you loyal Soviet citizens," the commissar asked, "that he has no permit and no exit visa? Do you know him?"

"No, we don't know him at all."

"To slander a man, you need to know him," the commissar said, like a teacher. "And we know a lot of types with diamonds in the spouts of teapots; we pick up a half dozen every week. Imagination is needed for business like that. Imagination!"

The commissar drummed his fingers against the teapot.

"Well, citizens, if you please. Let's talk things over. Meanwhile we'll leave your things here. Sidorov, Ershikov"—he turned to two soldiers standing next to the car—"bring them to my office. And leave this one"—he pointed to me—"here for a while. And be careful they don't drop anything out of their pockets on the way. Understand?"

"We understand," the Red Army men said cheerfully. "We've done this before, Comrade Commissar."

They led the journalists away. The commissar followed them. I was left alone in the boxcar. Soon the soldiers returned and quietly took away the journalists' baggage.

I waited. An hour went by. A sleepy, barefoot man with a lot of tousled hair and a wispy beard, naked to the waist, climbed out of a boxcar reserved for political propaganda work. He took out a sheet of plywood, some brushes and some cans of paint, leaned the plywood against the car, spat on his hands, and with a few strokes drew a fat man in a top hat. From the fat man's stomach, ripped open by a bayonet, money was pouring out. Then the artist scratched his ear for a moment, and wrote sideways on the board:

> The bourgeois belly, full of gold,
> Never expected a stroke so bold.

The sailors in the other boxcars roared with laughter. The hairy man paid them no attention, sat down on the step of the car, and lit a fat *makhorka* cigarette.

Then the Red Army soldier came back to take me to the commissar. This was the end. I picked up my bag and we walked away.

The commissar was housed in a boxcar on a siding overgrown with dandelions. A shining machine gun stood in the door. He was sitting, smoking, at a table made of rough boards. He looked at me thoughtfully, for a long time.

"Unbosom yourself," he said finally. "Where are you going, and what for? And, by the way, show me your documents."

I realized that I had to come clean. I told the commissar about my efforts to get a permit.

"And as far as documents are concerned, my most important one is this letter," I said, and I put my sister Galya's letter down on the table in front of him. "I have no others."

The commissar frowned, and began to read the letter slowly. He looked up at me several times while he was reading it. Then he folded the letter, put it back in its envelop, and handed it to me.

"It's an authentic document," he said. "Do you have any identification?"

I handed him my identification card.

"Sit down," he said, as he picked up an official form and began to write something very carefully, glancing occasionally at my identification card.

"There!" he said, at last, and he handed me the form. "There's your permission to leave."

"Thank you," I said in confusion, and my voice broke. The commissar stood up and clapped me on the shoulder.

"Well, well," he said, embarrassed. "It does no good to get emotional about it. Give my compliments to your mother. Tell her they come from Commissar Anokhin, Pavel Zakharovich. An amazing old woman she must be. Just think what she was planning—to go all the way to Moscow on foot."

He held out his hand. I shook it firmly, unable to say a thing. He straightened the belt which held his revolver, and commented:

"We'll have to shoot that little fellow with the diamonds in his teapot. We've let the others go. I've given orders to transfer you to another car. You shouldn't be traveling with them. Well, have a good trip. And don't forget to give my compliments to your mother."

I walked out in a daze. I held back my tears only by a great effort. The soldier who was leading me back to another car noticed this.

"For a commissar like him," he said, "it would be worth dying twice. He's a worker from the Obukhovsky factory, a Petrograd man. You remember his name—Anokhin, Pavel Zakharovich. You might meet up with him again somewhere."

They put me in a car where there were only two other men—an elderly singer and a skinny, talkative fellow named Vadik, an incoherent, sympathetic, responsive boy. They were both traveling from Petrograd, the singer to see his only daughter who was working as a doctor in Vinnitsa, and Vadik to his mother in Odessa. Vadik had gone from Odessa to Petrograd to visit his grandfather in his winter vacation in 1917 and had got stuck there for a year and a half. Everything that had happened seemed extremely interesting to him.

We traveled quietly to the frontier, which was at that time at the station Zernovo. The train stopped for the night at a little station on the edge of a forest. The Bryansk forests stretched southward from there, and I found myself in the wonderful region where I had been so often when I was a child.

I couldn't sleep. The singer and I got out of the boxcar and walked along a country road. It wound along the edge of the woods and into the fields which were dark with night. The grain rustled, and summer lightning played low over it. We sat down on an old fallen elm tree beside the road. Single, weathered elm trees in the middle of meadows and fields always remind me somehow of strong old men in caftans with their white beards blowing in the wind.

The singer said, out of the silence:

"Everyone believes in Russia in his own way. Everyone has his own evidence for that belief."

"And what's your evidence?"

"I'm a singer. So it's clear what kind of evidence mine is." He was quiet for a little, and then he sang, sorrowfully and slowly, a verse by Lermontov:

> *I walk out on the road alone,*
> *The stony path shines through the fog . . .*
> *The night is quiet, the wilderness worships God,*
> *And the stars talk to each other.*

The wind was running over the grain, which moved with a kind of whispering rustle. The heat lightning increased, and a half-awake thunderstorm began to rumble. We walked back to the little station. In the darkness I picked a handful of grass, and only in the morning noticed that it was sweet clover, the shyest and most beautiful flower of the Russian land.

THE NEUTRAL ZONE

The train pulled into Zernovo in the morning. The border control went through the cars, checking all permits to leave the country. Our car was detached from the train, with several others, and an old yard engine pulled us to the frontier, to the so-called neutral zone. The doors of all the boxcars had been closed and Red Army men with rifles stood beside them.

The train stopped at last. We all got out. The cars were standing in a dry field next to a track watchman's cabin. The wind was driving dust across the field. Some peasant carts were tied up to the buffer on the tracks. Their drivers—old men with whips— yelled out: "Who's going to the other side, to the Ukraine? Come along."

"Is it far?" I asked an old man with a sparse beard.

"What do you mean—far? A couple of miles, and you'll see the Germans. Let's go!"

We loaded our things in his cart, and walked along beside it. The other carts followed along behind us. In the rear I saw my companions from the Riga-Orlov heated boxcar. They were walking behind a wagon and talking about something excitedly and happily. Dodya was not with them. The man in gray spats looked like a crazy man here on the road where the wind was whirling up little columns of dust and the underbrush was rustling its leaves in the ravines we passed.

When we had gone almost a mile, the man in spats stopped, turned back to the north, facing Russia, shook his fist, and swore coarsely. The driver looked at him frightened, and shook his head with sorrow.

I think I have already written that my mother believed in the law of retribution. Any kind of mean, inhuman, perfidious act, she used to say, was sure to be punished. Sooner or later, retribution was certain. I used to laugh at Mama's superstitions, but this was a day when I too almost came to believe in the law of retribution.

We were descending into a hollow overgrown with brush. Our

driver started to get nervous, and kept clucking to his horse. We crossed the bottom of the hollow and began to ascend the slope on the other side. At that moment a man in a tall sheepskin hat and dusty violet riding breeches walked out of the brush. He held a Mauser in his hand. He wore two canvas bands filled with cartridges across his chest. Some young fellows followed him out of the bushes, dressed in overcoats, pea jackets, and embroidered Ukrainian shirts. They were all carrying sawed-off shotguns and swords, and some of them had grenades hanging on their belts.

The man with the violet riding breeches raised his Mauser and fired into the air. All the carts stopped immediately.

"Who let you through?" he yelled in a whining voice.

"The border detachment," the journalist in the gray spats answered, in confusion. The man in the riding breeches had walked onto the road right next to the cart carrying the journalists' baggage.

"They must have been looking in their own pockets!" he shouted. "Did they inspect your things?"

"They inspected them."

"They inspected their own pockets! Did they check your documents?"

"They checked them."

"They must have checked their own pockets! Well, come on, fellows, take what you like. All at once!"

The young fellows began to throw the baggage off the cart. The journalist in spats started to scream. The man in the violet riding breeches hit him in the mouth with the handle of his Mauser, and said:

"Is that what you wanted? Shut up, you bourgeois spawn, before I put a bullet in your boiler."

The man in spats, holding a bloody handkerchief to his mouth, was fumbling in the dust on the road, looking for his pince-nez.

The fellows began to slit the leather bags with their swords. They sliced them cleverly, with one slash in each direction. Obviously there wasn't time to open the bags, or even to break their locks. The boys were obviously hurrying, and they kept looking in the direction of the Soviet frontier.

Our driver quietly moved his horse forward a few paces, and then stopped. The fellows were pulling things out of the bags, examining shirts and linen in the light and trampling what they didn't want in the dust.

"They're busy," our driver told us quietly. "Walk on ahead, but just as quietly as you can, as far as that bush there. There's a turn right beyond it, and then we won't be seen. And I'll come on little by little, maybe they won't notice us."

We walked up beyond the bush, and our driver, urging his horse on and then stopping him, quickly caught up to us, and then he began to whip his horse. We got over a little hillock and the horse broke into a full gallop. We ran after the cart for ten minutes. Then the driver stopped.

We lit cigarettes, while the driver told us that a gang led by the *ataman* Kozyuba was wandering around the neutral zone and robbing everyone passing through it. They were looking chiefly for precious stones and money. They always had to hurry, because the Soviet frontier guards, although they were not supposed to go into the neutral zone, sometimes swooped down on the bandits and shot them mercilessly.

We were despondent and silent. For some reason none of us felt happy over our narrow escape from the bandits.

The road wound along a wide clearing through a lot of stumps. The sun was setting. Its reddish light fell on the tops of a few undamaged pine trees. I walked along, thoughtfully. Suddenly I started and raised my eyes when I heard a sharp metallic command:

"Halt!"

Two German soldiers in dark overcoats and steel helmets were standing in the middle of the road. One of them was holding our driver's thin, sickly horse by the bridle. The Germans demanded an entry permit. I had none.

One stocky German apparently guessed this from my face. He walked up to me, pointed in the direction of Russia, and barked out: *"Zurück!"*

"Give him five rubles in Tsarist money," the driver told me, "and we'll drive on to Mikhailovsky's farm. Don't let the son of a bitch bamboozle us."

I held out a ten-ruble note to the German. "No, no!" he shouted in irritation, and he shook his head.

"What are you giving him ten for?" the driver asked me angrily. "I told you: give him five. They don't take anything else. That's because the Tsarist five-ruble notes are printed by them in Germany."

I gave the German a five-ruble note. He lifted one finger to his helmet and then waved his hand:

"Fa-hr!"

We drove on. I looked around. The Germans were standing in the middle of the sandy road, stretching their legs in their heavy

boots, laughing and lighting cigarettes. The sun was reflected on
their helmets.

There was a bitter lump in my throat. It seemed to me that
there was no longer any Russia and would never be one, that all
was lost, and that there was nothing more to live for. It was as if
the singer guessed my thoughts, for he said:

"Most gracious God, what has happened to Russia? It's some
kind of bad dream."

Vadik stopped, too, and looked at the Germans. The corners of
his lips drooped and trembled, and he started to cry, loudly, like a
child.

"Never mind, lad," the driver muttered. "Maybe it won't happen
quickly, but we'll pay them back for our tears."

He slapped his reins, and the cart squeaked on through the deep
red sand imprinted with the marks of German horseshoes.

In the north, where Russia remained, a pink evening haze was
thick over the clearing. Little islands of purple clover were in
blossom on the side of the road. For some reason, this made my
heart feel lighter. "We'll see," I thought. "We'll see."

"OUR VAGABOND HETMAN"

I stayed in Kopan until late in the autumn, and then I went to Kiev
to get settled there so I could bring Mama and my sister to the city.

It was not easy to get established. In the end I took a job as
proofreader on the only fairly decent newspaper, *The Thought of
Kiev.* This was a paper which had seen better days. Korolenko,*
Lunacharsky, and other important people had worked on it. The
paper tried to be independent even under the Germans and the
hetman, but it was not always successful. It was constantly being
fined, and several times threatened with suspension.

* Vladimir Korolenko (1853–1921) was a *narodnik* writer of Ukrainian-
Polish origin; he also edited a monthly, *The Wealth of Russia.*

I rented two small rooms near the Cathedral of St. Vladimir from an extraordinarily sentimental German spinster named Amalie Knoster. But I couldn't bring Mama and Galya to Kiev—the city was suddenly surrounded by Petliura's troops. They started a real siege.

The windows of my room looked out toward the Botanical Gardens. I was wakened every morning by the cannon fire which went on steadily in a circle around Kiev. I would get up, fix the stove, look at the Botanical Gardens where the hoarfrost was being shaken from the twigs by the artillery fire, and then I would go back to bed, to read or think. The shaggy winter morning, the crackle of the wood in the stove, and the noise of the shooting on the edges of the city—all these gave me an unusual and precarious but real feeling of peace and quiet. My head felt light and fresh after I had washed in the icy water at the sink. The smell of coffee from the landlady's room somehow reminded me of Christmas Eve.

I began to write a great deal. Strange as it may seem, the siege helped. The city was caught in a ring, and so were my thoughts. The knowledge that Kiev was cut off from the world, that there was no way of getting out of it, that the siege would clearly go on for a long while, that there was nothing to do now but wait, this knowledge made life seem simple and carefree.

Even Amalie Knoster grew used to the cannon fire as a normal part of daily life. When it died down occasionally, she grew nervous. The quiet threatened something unexpected, and this was dangerous. But as soon as the roar started to sweep through the city again, everyone relaxed. You could read again, or work, or think, in the regular cycle of every day: waking up, work, hunger (or, rather, half-hunger), and then blissful sleep.

I was Amalie's only boarder. She rented out rooms only to single men, but there was no cunning purpose in this. She simply could not stand women. She fell in love quietly with every one of her boarders, but never showed it except in little services and in a sudden, heavy blushing. This would cover her long yellow face at any word which could be construed as even an indirect reference to the dangerous worlds of love or marriage. She spoke of all her previous boarders with enthusiasm and was deeply disappointed that all of them, as if in a conspiracy, had finally married evil, greedy women and moved away from her apartment.

Amalie had worked in the past as a governess in wealthy Kiev homes, and she had saved up a little money and rented the apartment. She lived on the rent paid by her boarders, and on her sewing. But in spite of her earlier profession, there was nothing stiff or prim about Amalie. She was just a goodhearted, dull, lonely woman.

I was surprised to find that Amalie, although she herself was German, felt hostile to the Germans who were occupying the city, and thought them churlish boors. She treated me with a somewhat shy respect, obviously because I read and wrote at night. She considered me a writer, and sometimes she even worked up the courage to talk to me about literature, and about her favorite writer, Shpielhagen. She cleaned my room herself, and sometimes I would find in my books either a pressed flower, or a fresh dahlia. She was never intrusive in her little attentions, and nothing ever jarred our friendship.

Her friends came to visit her only on holidays. They were all aged German or Swiss governesses in old-fashioned capes with satin ribbons, and with reticules and gaiters. Amalie would take out her piles of little napkins embroidered with cats, pug dogs, pansies, and forget-me-nots, spread them around the table, and serve her famous Basel coffee. The old nurses ate and drank with great delicacy and carried on a conversation consisting exclusively of exclamations of surprise and terror.

Only one man was admitted to this select society, the superintendent of the building who was an accountant on the Southern-Western Railroad, a man with an elegant name—Pan Sebastian Kturenda-Tsikavsky. He was a cocky little man with close-cropped hair, the dyed mustaches of a pimp, and insolent little button eyes. He wore a blue jacket with tobacco-colored stripes, too short and too tight for him, and it had a piece of lilac-covered cloth sewed over its breast pocket to look as if it held a dandy's handkerchief. Besides this, he affected pink celluloid collars and butterfly neckties. These collars, which were always dirty, used to be called "bachelors' friends." Instead of washing them, you were supposed to rub the dirt off them with an ordinary eraser.

Pan Kturenda gave off a complicated smell of mustache dye, tobacco ashes, and home-brewed vodka. He made the vodka himself out of millet in his darkened room. He was a bachelor and he lived with his mother—a timid old lady. She was frightened by her son, and especially by his learning. Pan Kturenda loved to impress the residents of our building with this learning, and he expressed it in florid sentences.

"I have the honor to inform you," he would say, "that Weininger's book *Sex and Character* is the formulation of the sexual problem in its best aspect."

Pan Kturenda did not not expound the sexual problem in his

conversations at Amalie's but he used to make the old governesses quiver with his accounts of the origins of "the most noble Pan and Hetman Skoropadsky."

I have seen many fools in my life, but I never met a more thickheaded idiot than Pan Kturenda.

In those days life in Kiev was like a banquet in the middle of a plague. A lot of coffee houses and restaurants were opened. In its external appearance, the city made an impression of shabby wealth. Refugees from Moscow and Petrograd had doubled the size of the city. Artzibashev's *Jealousy** and Viennese operettas were playing in the theaters. Patrols of German Uhlans marched through the streets with lances and black-red flags.

Papers printed little about what was going on in Soviet Russia. This was an embarrassing subject. People preferred not to talk about it. Everyone tried to pretend that life was cloudless and serene.

The oxeyed beauties of Kiev roller-skated on the city's rinks with the hetman's officers. Gambling dens and houses of assignation sprang up overnight. Cocaine was sold openly on the Bessarabka, where ten-year-old prostitutes offered themselves to passers-by.

What was going on in the factories and in the workers' districts, nobody knew. But the Germans felt unsure of themselves, especially after the murder of General Eichhorn.† Kiev itself seemed to be hoping to go on living carefree through the blockade. It was as if the Ukraine had ceased to exist—it lay outside the ring of Petliura's troops.

Sometimes in the evenings I went to a literary-artistic society on Nikolayevskaya Street. Poets, singers, and dancers who had fled from the north appeared in a restaurant there. Drunken shouts interrupted the poetry readings. It was always stifling in the restaurant, so the windows were sometimes opened, although it was winter. Then snow would blow through them into the lighted room, together with the frosty air, and melt on the floor. The nighttime bombardment could be clearly heard.

Vertinsky sang there once. I had never heard him on a stage before. I remembered him when he had been a *gymnasist*, a young poet already writing delicate verses.

A lot of snow blew through the windows that evening, circling

* Michael Artzibashev (1878–1927) was a novelist and playwright whose contempt for any code of morality gave him a considerable popularity in the years before 1917; he emigrated in 1923.

† Field Marshal Hermann von Eichhorn (1848–1918) was commander-in-chief of all German troops on the eastern front; he was assassinated at Kiev on July 30, 1918.

through the air as far as the piano on the stage. The cannon fire
had come appreciably closer. It made the bottles on the tables
jingle. This noise of glass was like a danger warning to the people,
but they went right on smoking, arguing, drinking toasts, and
laughing. A young woman in evening dress, with narrow, Egyptian
eyes, was laughing hardest of all. The snow was melting on her bare
back, and she kept on shuddering and looking around as if she
wanted to watch it melt.

Vertinsky came out on the stage in a black dress coat. He was a
tall, lean man, incredibly pale. Everything grew quiet. The waiters
stopped carrying around their trays of coffee, wine, and cakes, and
lined up in ranks at the back of the room.

Vertinsky twisted his long fingers together, held them out in
front of him with an air of long suffering, and began to sing. He
sang about the Junkers who had been killed not long before in the
village of Borshchakovka near Kiev, about the youth sent to certain
death in fighting against bandits.

> *Who needed this and why?*
> *What ruthless hand sent them to their death?*

The song was about the funeral of the Junkers. Vertinsky finished it with the words:

> *The watchers huddled in their coats.*
> *A woman with a frenzied face*
> *Kissed one of the dead on his blue lips*
> *And tossed to the priest her engagement ring.*

He was singing about a real incident which had taken place at the
Junkers' funeral.

There was a storm of applause. Vertinsky bowed. A drunken
officer, sitting in the back of the room yelled out stupidly:

"Sing 'God, Save the Tsar!' "

The noise grew. A thin old man with a pointed, quivering beard,
pince-nez, and a jacket shiny with age, rushed over to the officer.
The old man looked like a teacher. He began to pound on the officer's marble table with his thin fists, and to shout out, foaming at
the mouth:

"Riffraff! Scum! How do you dare insult the people of free
Russia? You belong at the front fighting Bolsheviks and not here!
You café idler!"

Everyone jumped up. The old man tried to fight the officer but
people grabbed his arms and dragged him away. The officer's face
turned red, he stood up slowly, pushed his chair away with his

foot, and grabbed a bottle by the neck. The waiters swarmed over
him. The woman in the evening dress screamed and covered her
face with her hands.

Vertinsky struck the piano keys loudly, and held up his hand.
Everything grew quiet suddenly.

"Gentlemen!" Vertinsky said distinctly and arrogantly. "This
is very boring."

He turned around and walked slowly off the stage. People were
pouring water on the man in the pince-nez. The officer sat down
again at his table, as if nothing had happened, and declared into
empty space:

"I've thrashed Jews and I'll go right on thrashing Jews until I
die. I'll show you what riffraff is, Mr. Movshenson from Gomel-
Gomel."

The row broke out again. A patrol of the hetman's guards, with
yellow-blue bands around their sleeves, marched into the restaurant.

I walked out onto the street. I walked, and I swore at myself
in dull anger. How much riffraff there was in guardsman's uniforms, in pink celluloid collars, and in heavy German helmets, all
across my country! My own excuse seemed to me inadequate—I
was writing a great deal, and thus living a double life. The world I
was imagining had overwhelmed me, and I could not resist it.

What I was writing then was a sort of useless pictorial experi-
mentation. There was no integrity in it, but a good deal of lightness,
and of disorderly imagination. I could write for hours, for example,
just describing different lusters, wherever I found them—in a piece
of a broken bottle, in the brass railing of a ship's ladder, in window
glass, in a tumbler on the table, in dew, in the mother-of-pearl in a
seashell, or in human eyes. These all blurred together for me in a
surprising way. Honest imagination required sharpness and defini-
tion, but I achieved these only rarely. Most of the pictures in my
mind were diffused and dim. I did not drive myself then to give
them the clearness of reality, and I forgot about real life.

In the end I worked out an indisputable catalog of these kinds of
light and shining. But I soon discovered that they made a boring,
sugary list. I grew confused. The strength and severity which are
essential to good prose were transformed into a kind of sherbet,
a Turkish Delight, a collection of dainties. These lists of words
were all too sweet. It was hard to wash them off.

I sometimes managed to clean off this cloudy, florid quality of
my style by hard work, but not always successfully. This was a
stage that passed quickly, to my good fortune, and I destroyed

almost everything I wrote at that time. But even now I sometimes catch myself with a predilection for words that are too fancy, too dressed-up.

Both my writing and my self-doubting were soon interrupted in an unexpected way. Petliura kept tightening his noose around Kiev. Then the hetman Skoropadsky decreed the mobilization of all men between eighteen and thirty-five. The superintendent of every building in the city was held personally responsible for every man in his house who did not appear. The decree said simply that in every case of the "nonappearance" of a man in this age group, the superintendent of his building would be shot.

The decree was posted up throughout the city. I read it casually. I considered myself a citizen of Soviet Russia and therefore not subject to any of the hetman's decrees.

Late one winter evening I was returning home from the newspaper plant. A cold wind was blowing. The poplars along Bibikovsky Boulevard were sighing mournfully. A woman wrapped up in a shawl was standing in the garden next to my building. She ran up to me and seized my hand. I drew back.

"Quiet!" the woman said, and I recognized Amalie's voice, shaking with emotion. "Let's get away from here."

We walked to the Cathedral of St. Vladimir. Awkward buttresses arched up against its heavy walls. We stopped behind one of them, where there was no wind, and Amalie told me in a quick whisper, although there was nobody near us:

"Thanks be to God you've been away all day. He's been sitting in the vestibule since ten o'clock this morning. And he doesn't budge. It's terrible."

"Who?"

"Pan Kturenda. He's lying in wait for you."

"But why?"

"Ah, my God!" Amalie exclaimed, and she held her hands in their little muff imploringly up to her breast. "Run away! I implore you. Don't come back home. I'll give you the address of my friend— she's a very good old woman, there aren't any more like her in this world. I've written a note to her. Go to her. It's pretty far, out in Glubochitsa, but it will be better there. She lives all alone in a little house. She'll hide you. And I'll bring you something to eat every day, until the danger's over."

"What's happened?" I said. "I don't understand a thing."

"Haven't you read the hetman's decree?"

"I read it."

"Kturenda has come for you. To turn you in to the army."

Finally I understood it all, for the first time.

"He's weeping," Amalie said in a cold voice. "He's all wet with tears, and he keeps saying that if you've run away they'll shoot him like a bandit at nine o'clock tomorrow morning."

She took a letter out of her muff and stuffed it into the pocket of my overcoat.

"Go now. Hurry."

"Thank you, Amalie Garlovna. Nothing is threatening me. I'm a citizen of the Russian Federated Republic. I can spit on all the hetman's decrees."

"Oh God, how wonderful!" Amalie said, either not noticing or forgiving my rough language. She pressed the muff to her bosom and laughed. "I didn't know about that. That means, they won't touch him, either."

"Nothing will happen. Tomorrow I'll go along with Kturenda to the recruiting station, and they'll release me right away."

"Well, that's fine," Amalie agreed, reassured. "Let's go back home. I'll go first, and you follow in two or three minutes, so he won't suspect anything. Ah, how tired I am!"

When I took her arm, to help her, I could feel her trembling all over. I waited for a few minutes on the stairs, and then went into the apartment. Pan Kturenda was sitting on a chair in the vestibule. He hurled himself on me, grabbed my arm with his chicken's claws, and muttered in a quivering voice:

"In the name of Jesus Christ, don't kill me. I've been waiting for you all day. Have pity, if not on me, then at least on my old mother."

I told him I would go with him the next morning to the recruiting station and they would let me go, of course, as a Russian citizen. Pan Kturenda sobbed, bent down, and started to kiss my hand. I drew my hand away. Amalie was standing in the doorway, watching Pan Kturenda with screwed-up eyes. I had never seen her look like that before. And I suddenly understood that if I had run away, as Amalie advised me to, they really would have shot this shabby little man. I thought about this, and marveled at the quiet hardness of that extraordinarily sentimental woman.

Pan Kturenda went away, calling down blessings on my head. He added the most lively agreement that they would let me go, of course, because "the Pan Hetman" would have no desire to have people from Red Moscow in his army.

When I had washed at the sink in the kitchen and was going to my room, Amalie stopped me in the corridor.

"Not a word!" she said mysteriously, taking me by the hand and leading me on tiptoe through the tiny drawing room into the vestibule. She pointed to the door and pushed my shoulder to show that she wanted me to look through the keyhole.

I looked. Pan Kturenda was sitting on an egg crate on the stair landing, yawning and covering his mouth with his hand. Of course, he had not trusted me and he had decided to guard me until morning.

"The beast!" Amalie said quietly when he had gone back into the drawing room. "And to think that I invited him into my home! I hate him so much I have a headache. I've left you some breakfast in the kitchen cabinet."

Precisely at eight o'clock the next morning, Kturenda rang the doorbell. I opened the door. His red eyes were full of tears. His butterfly tie was drooping its crumpled ends, giving him a most woebegone appearance.

We walked to the mobilization headquarters at the Galitsky Bazaar. Pan Kturenda, pleading dizziness, held tightly to my arm. He was clearly scared that I might dash away from him at any moment. We had to stand in line. Building superintendents, with their thick registers, were fussing around the men being mobilized. They all looked guilty and fawning at the same time. They kept giving cigarettes to their wards, yessing them constantly, but they never left them for a moment.

An officer of the hetman's, with yellow-blue epaulets, was sitting at a table in the back of the room. His foot kept tapping the floor under the table.

A skinny, unshaved boy with glasses stood in front of me. He waited quietly, downcast. When his turn came, he answered the officer's question about his profession:

"I'm an accountant."

"A count?" the officer interrupted, leaning back in his chair and examining the lad with undisguised pleasure. "That's a rare bird. I've had the gentry here, and even some barons, but you're the first count."

"I'm not a count, but an accountant."

"Shut up!" the officer said calmly. "We're all counts. We know all about your counts and your accountants. For any more stupid talk I'll put you in kitchen police."

The young fellow simply shrugged his shoulders.

"Next!"

I was the next. I showed my documents to the officer and told him firmly that as a citizen of the Russian Soviet Federation I was not subject to mobilization in the hetman's army.

"What a surprise!" the officer said, and he lifted his eyebrows and made a face. "I am simply shattered by what you say. If I had known you were going to be good enough even to appear, I would have had a military orchestra for you."

"Your jokes have nothing to do with this business."

"What does, then?" the officer asked angrily, and he stood up. "Maybe this?"

He made a fist and held it up to my face.

"Fiddlesticks!" he said. 'Fiddlesticks with poppyseed is all your Soviet-Jewish citizenship is worth. I spit on it from a high tree."

"Don't you dare talk like that," I said, trying to remain calm.

"Everyone tells me right to my face what I don't dare to do," the officer said sadly, and he sat down. "Enough! Out of respect for your sham citizenship I'm putting you in the Cossack infantry regiment. In the Pan Hetman's personal guard. You can thank God. I'll keep your documents. Next!"

During this conversation with the officer, Pan Kturenda had disappeared. All of us who had been mobilized were led off, under guard, to barracks on the Demievka.

This whole comedy, played with bayonets, had been so crude and incredible that I felt its real bitterness for the first time only in the cold barracks. I sat down on a dusty window sill, lit a cigarette, and thought things over. I was quite ready to run any risks or to do any job, but not to play this farce with the hetman's army. I decided to look around, and to run away as quickly as I could.

But the farce turned out to be a bloody one. That night two young fellows were shot and killed by the guards just because they walked out through the gates and did not stop at once when challenged.

The sound of the cannon firing was growing louder. This reassured those of us who had not lost our ability to worry. It was an augury of some change, what kind of change we did not know but probably a quick one.

Most of us who had been mobilized were what were then called "motor boys"—the gangsters and petty thieves from the desperate outskirts of Kiev—Solomenka and Shulyavka. They were arrant, shameless fellows. They entered the hetman's army willingly. It was clear that it was nearing its last days, and the "motor boys" knew better than anyone else how easy it would be in the inevitable confusion to keep their weapons, loot whatever they liked, and raise hell. So the "motor boys" tried for a while to disarm suspicion by acting as much like serious hetman's soldiers as they could.

The regiment was called "the Cossack infantry regiment of His Radiant and Noble Pan Hetman Pavel Skoropadsky." I was put in a company commanded by a former Russian pilot, whom we called "Pan Horse's Tail." He did not know a word of Ukrainian except for a few commands, and these he gave hesitantly. When he wanted to say "left" or "right" he had to think for a moment, afraid that he might make a mistake and confuse everyone. He was openly contemptuous of the hetman's army. Sometimes he would look at us, shake his head, and say:

"Well, you're an army for some shah! Convicts, tramps, and scoundrels, every one of you!"

For several days he gave us some casual lessons in marching, handling our rifles, and throwing hand grenades. Then they dressed us in tobacco-green overcoats and caps with the Ukrainian coat-of-arms, in old boots and puttees, and paraded us down the Kreshcha-tik, promising to send us to the Petliura front the next day. With a few other regiments we marched down the Kreshchatik, past the building of the Municipal Duma where I had been under fire when I was still a little boy. The golden archangel Michael was still balancing on one leg on his pedestal over the round building of the *Duma*.

The hetman himself was waiting there on an English horse. He was wearing a white sheepskin coat and a soft little hat. He held a riding crop in his hand. Behind him, like monuments on black iron horses, were the mounted German generals, wearing helmets with gilded spikes. Nearly all of them wore monocles. Shifting crowds of curious Kiev citizens were gathered on the pavements.

The regiments marched by and shouted "Hurrah!" to the hetman. In reply he would raise his riding crop to the edge of his hat and spur his horse a little.

Our regiment had decided to startle the hetman. When we came up to him, the whole regiment began to sing:

> *Our vagabond Hetman is a tramp,*
> *Our Pavel Skoropadsky.*
> *Our vagabond Hetman is a tramp.*
> *Pavel Skoropadsky.*

The "motor boys" sang with a special dash, with a whistle before each couplet and a great swing to the song. They were all angry because we were being sent to the front so soon, and were feeling mutinous.

Skoropadsky never even quivered. He went right on lifting his riding crop to his hat, smiling as if he had just heard a pleasant joke, and looking at the German generals. Their monocles sparkled a little, the only sign that perhaps they had understood some of the words of the song. And the crowds of Kiev citizens on the sidewalks gave a muffled roar of sheer delight.

They woke us up in the dark. The dawn we didn't want to see was just beginning to light up the east. In the kerosene fumes of the barracks that morning, with the smell of stale tea and salt herring, the quiet despair in the faded eyes of Pan Horse's Tail, in the cold wet boots which we couldn't pull on, there was such unutterable grief, such an enormous, exhausting pain, that I decided to desert that very day, without fail, from the Cossack infantry regiment of His Radiant and Noble Pan Hetman Pavel Skoropadsky.

At the roll call it turned out that we were already short twelve men. The pilot hopelessly shrugged his shoulders and said:

"Well, you can all go to the devil's mother. Attention!"

We formed ranks somehow.

"Squads right!" the pilot commanded and we marched out of the raw and dubious warmth of the barracks into the biting air of an early winter morning.

"And just where is this alleged front?" a sleepy voice asked from the rear. "Are we really going to have to walk to it on foot?"

"Haven't you heard of Madame Tsimkovich's whore house? At Priorka? That's where the front is. The whole staff of the commander-in-chief is always there."

"Why don't you all shut up?" Pan Horse's Tail asked pleadingly. "By God, it's disgusting to listen to you. Besides, you're not supposed to talk while you're marching."

"We know all right what we're supposed to do."

Pan Horse's Tail just sighed and walked a little farther away from us. It was clear that he was a little frightened of the "motor boys."

"You've sold the Ukraine for a bottle of champagne," an angry deep voice said. "And now you're dirtying all this clean snow with horse droppings. It's scandalous."

"We ought to send them all to the devil's grandmother, and be rid of them!"

"Who do you mean—all of them?"

"Just that—all of them. And Petliura, too, and this Hetman son of a bitch, and the whole pack. And give people a chance to breathe easy again."

"Pan Horse's Tail, why are you so quiet? Just where is the front?"

"Beyond Priorka," the flier said, reluctantly. "Near Pushcha-Voditsa."

"We-e-ll! God knows that's not good news. That means a hike of at least ten versts."

"Don't worry," the flier said. "They'll carry us there."

A laugh ran along the ranks.

"They're going to take us in the Tsar's carriage. We're unselfish heroes, so it couldn't be any other way."

I still don't understand what stupid inertia kept us walking and walking while each one of us, including Pan Horse's Tail, knew perfectly well that there was no sense in going to the front and that any one of us could have walked away to his home at any moment without any trouble at all. But we did go on walking, down to Podol and on to Kontraktovaya Square. There the life of a peaceful ordinary morning was stirring—little boys were going to the *gymnasium* in their gray overcoats, the Bratsky Monastery was ringing its bells for a service, old women in boots were driving fat cows through the street, a barber shop was opening, and janitors were sweeping the melting snow off the sidewalks.

Two ancient open trolley cars were standing on the square.

"Into the trolleys!" the flier shouted, suddenly coming to life. The company stopped, blank with astonishment.

"You heard me. Into the trolleys!" the flier repeated angrily. "I told you they'd transport us. These are military trolley cars."

The soldiers all began to talk noisily and happily.

"Well, it's a cultured war, after all!"

"It's one of Father Gervasiya's miracles! Going to the front in a trolley car!"

"Climb in, fellows, Don't hold us up."

We filled the trolley cars quickly and they moved off, rattling and clanking, along the cobblestoned Podol and through drab Priorka toward Pushcha-Voditsa. Just beyond Priorka the cars stopped. We got out and followed the pilot along a little bystreet lined with crooked hovels and across a snow-covered field on which piles of manure were steaming in the cold air. In front of us was the huge and ancient park, "Good-by to Care," which I had known so well in my childhood.

On a snow-covered slope at the edge of the park foxholes had been dug with passages between them and with dugouts. The trenches pleased the "motor boys"; their protection seemed to promise some hope. The pilot settled in a dugout, while the "motor boys" picked out foxholes where in a few minutes they had established a kind of fort behind some trestle tables made of old boards.

I stood at an observation post. The pine forest of Pushcha-Voditsa looked green, and dry from the warm wind, beyond a broad field in front of us. The Petliura troops were firing at us lazily from the woods. The bullets flew quietly and safely over our heads, only rarely thudding into our breastworks.

The pilot ordered us not to show ourselves above the breast-works, and not to return the fire. A leaden sky hung over the Dneiper to our right. A dirt road, brown with manure, wandered off into the woods. To our left, from the direction of Svyatoshina, we could hear heavy artillery fire. No matter how hard I stared into the woods, trying to glimpse a Petliura soldier, I could see nothing. I thought once I could see a bush moving, but I was wrong.

Standing there was boring. I lit a cigarette. I had recently acquired three packages of Odessa cigarettes, of which I was very proud. They were thick, strong, and aromatic. So I smoked, and thought about my life over the last few years. It made a very mixed picture.

It seemed to me that it was high time to bring some kind of order into my life and to subordinate even my desire to be a writer to some plan. I was twenty-six years old and I had not yet written anything of any value—nothing more than a few sketches, fragments, and exercises. I needed to achieve some clarity of purpose, and to make some choices.

Then I thought I saw something vague, hardly noticeable, moving to my right, along the little dirt road. There was an old cemetery there. A leaning cross was standing on one of the graves. And suddenly the sullen day, the cross, the thawing air around me, and the gulls screaming behind me in the dark park, and the little road covered with manure and rotting straw, all seemed old and familiar. The feeling made me groan out loud. It had been on just such a day and on just such a little hill outside a village that Lelya had been buried three years before. Three years as long, it seemed to me, as three decades. There were still the same damned Germans, the same slush. Maybe the last traces of her grave had disappeared. I could never imagine for a moment that her bones were lying there under the earth. I never believed this. It always seemed to me that she would stay forever as we had seen her in her wooden coffin—pale and incredibly beautiful, quiet and young, with the sad shadow of her eyelashes falling on her cheeks.

I had never been able to tell anyone about this, even Mama. I was condemned to carry this burning pain inside my heart. There had not been a day when I had not felt it, not a single day, even if I have not referred to it in the preceding pages of this book.

Nor was there any point, I guess, in referring to it. Can any writer be sure that a critic's cold hands or the peevish glance of a reader will not handle rudely and laughingly what is trembling in the writer's heart, like a single tear on the point of falling to the ground? Can any writer know that nobody will shake off that tear, as he passes by, and leave a bleeding scar on his spirit?

I thought about Lelya, lit another cigarette, and then squeezed the trigger of my rifle just to break the terror which was gripping me. It was lying in a groove on top of the breastworks. The shot made a loud noise. Then a wild firing came back at us from the cemetery. It was clear the Petliura troops had gathered there, and my shot had scared them.

The pilot leaped out of his dugout, and we all started to fire into the cemetery. We could see little chips fly off the crosses, then some people jumped up from the ground and started to run back into the woods. The "motor boys" fired wildly at them, whistled with two fingers in their mouths, and swore by everybody's mother. The Petliura attack had been beaten off.

I was relieved in the observation post by a shaggy student with thick glasses, probably the son of a priest. I went back into the foxhole. A little kerosene lamp was burning there. I got some bread and some stale smoked sausage from my knapsack, and started to eat. The soldier on duty came up to me. He was a man with very bright eyes, an enormous number of white scars on his face, and tattooing on his palm. A pair of woman's lips, shaped in a bow, had been tattooed there. When he opened his hand, the lips opened, as if for a kiss, and when he closed it again, the lips closed tight. This had already won him enormous prestige in the eyes of the "motor boys."

The bright-eyed man poured me a mug of hot tea, handed me three pieces of sugar, slapped me on the shoulder, and said:

"The tea belongs to the Tsar, the sugar to Brodsky, and Russia to Trotsky. Isn't that so?"

Without waiting for an answer, he walked back to the table and some foul-mouthed, clowning soldiers who were playing cards. The artillery fire from Svyatoshina sounded louder and louder. After every explosion, the kerosene lamp would smoke more heavily. I gradually grew warmer and fell asleep, leaning against the wall of the foxhole.

A confused racket, with a lot of swearing, woke me in the middle of the night. The card players were fighting. They had pinned the bright-eyed man with his back against the table and were beating him mercilessly. He was not fighting back and not saying a word—it was clear they had good reason to beat him.

An order came from the trench outside for three men. The "motor boys" released the bright-eyed man, and he, I, and a tall man in a cavalry overcoat went out into the trench. I was assigned a place there right next to the bright-eyed man.

It grew warmer in the middle of the night. The snow started to rustle, and it sounded as if mice were all around us.

The bright-eyed man swore for a long time, fiercely, until the man in the cavalry overcoat told him, in an angry, hoarse voice:

"Shut up, you bastard, or I'll carve you up. Like a dog."

The bright-eyed man spat, walked over to me, squatted on his heels, and, after a little silence, said:

"Nobody's going to carve me up, brother. I carved myself up once, like a picture. My snout's all in scars already. Have you noticed it?"

"I saw it," I answered. I had no desire to talk with this trivial man.

"But, you know, they're not really scars at all," the bright-eyed man said, with a sudden sadness in his voice. "They're a great love story, written on my ugly skull. That's what they are."

He laughed in a curious way. It sounded as if he were choking.

"I worked once on a Volga River steamship which belonged to the Caucasus and Mercury Company. I was a waiter in the restaurant. And once, when we were in Kostroma, a *gymnasium* student in her last year came aboard. She was going to Simbirsk. In those days I'd had a lot of women, shipboard friends, you know. I always had an easy time with them. There are some men who cry or beat their heads against the wall when a woman stops loving them. But it never made me suffer. I just took what was coming to me. Then, if she fell out of love, well, that was the end of it. Clear off the table! I always had good luck with the greedy ones, and every woman is greedy either for money or for love. They'll take waiters or dishwashers then, whichever are younger. . . . Yes. . . . Well, this student got on the boat and came into the restaurant for supper. All alone. She was pale, and beautiful, and you could see all this was new to her, she was embarrassed. Her hair was gold colored, and heavy, and it lay in a coil on the back of her neck. When I was serving her, I touched her hair with my hand. And I shivered all over, it was so cold and—somehow—sort of elastic. I begged her pardon, of course, but she just frowned, looked at me, said, 'It's nothing,' and quietly straightened her hair. You could see she was a proud one.

"Well, I thought, you've fallen! The big thing that knocked me over was something pure about her—apple trees blossom like that, all a mass of fragrance. And right away, it made me sad. I started

to groan because of her. No matter how you beat your head against
the wall and fight the idea that she's going to leave at Simbirsk,
you'll still be left alone on the ship with your ugly broken heart. But
while I suffered, I counted the hours—there were still two full days
to Simbirsk. I served her with the best of everything. I even promised to pay the cook myself to garnish her dishes specially. But she,
of course, without any experience, never noticed it. She was a very
young woman, really nothing but a girl. I tried to start a conversation with her, even though this was strictly forbidden for us waiters.
The rule was: serve the food quietly and quickly, and never try to
start a conversation with the ladies and gentlemen, remember
you're just a mug, never dare even to think about it. You're a servant, so you'd better act like one. Just 'Yes, Sir,' or 'Right away,'
or 'May I serve you now?' or, when they gave you a tip, 'My most
humble thanks.'

"I couldn't manage to find time to talk with her—the other
waiter, Nikodim, was always hanging around. Then finally I had
a break: Nikodim went out to the kitchen. So I asked her right
away: 'Where are you going?' She looked at me out of her dark
gray eyes, with eyelashes like a velvet night, and she answered: 'To
Simbirsk. But why?' It was that 'But why?' which really finished
me. 'Well, no reason,' I told her. 'Only I wanted to warn you that,
after all, you're traveling alone, and there are all kinds of people on
a ship. Sometimes they're bad people, one might say, without any
conscience, especially in respect to defenseless young women.' She
looked at me, said, 'I know,' and smiled. And that was when I knew
that for every smile she gave me I was ready to give my blood, drop
by drop, and nobody would even hear me cry.

"I had no more chances to talk with her. Of course, I managed
to put all the flowers from three or four tables on hers. Although
it wasn't much, I thought, it would show her how much dearer she
was to me than everything else in the world. But again it was as if
she didn't notice it.

"Just before we got to Simbirsk, Nikodim raised a row. Right in
front of her, too. 'What are you trying to do?' he told me, 'taking
away my flowers? What kind of a fool do you take me for?' She
guessed what it was all about, of course, and she blushed, but she
never looked up.

"You've got to believe this. What I'm telling you I'm telling for
the first time in my life. You don't tell things like this to just anybody. They make it dirty just by listening to it. And there was never
anything better than this in all my life, I swear it by my old mother.
And no matter how crooked I may be, or even, one might say, how

honest a thief I am, I'll never stoop so low as to talk about this to ordinary rabble. Do you believe me?"

"I believe you," I answered. "Tell me how it ended."

"It had no end yet," the bright-eyed man went on, and he repeated it with something ominous in his voice. "There was no end to it. But I kept thinking that there would be. And you don't have the right to make me doubt it now. Don't interrupt me. Yes. . . . The next morning our ship was supposed to tie up at Simbirsk, and you'd never believe what went through my head. I only knew one thing—I wasn't going to be separated from her now. Even at a distance, even very quietly, I was going to stay with her until my lousy death. I didn't ask for much, just to breathe the same air as she was breathing. Can you even understand that? You've read all the books about love—it must be written down there. By morning I had a plan all worked out in my head, just what I had to do. While it was still dark, I took all the cash from the restaurant, and as soon as we got to Simbirsk I ran ashore, dressed just as I was in my waiter's uniform, as if I wanted to go to the market and buy some radishes. But I stayed on shore.

"I had enough money for a while, but my clothes, of course, were suspicious. So I bought a jacket. And I followed her, of course. And my good luck was that diagonally across from the house where she lived with her grandmother—an old house with a garden and gooseberries—right across from it there was a tavern. A poor sort of tavern, small, and without even canaries singing. So I sat myself down in that tavern. I made up a story that I'd agreed to buy a goose from a comrade in Simbirsk, and the comrade must have been delayed, he hadn't shown up. So I was sitting there, bored with myself, and waiting for him. I didn't even remember that you buy geese in the autumn, not in the summer."

"Well, what happened? Did you see her?" I asked.

"I saw her. Twice. She walked right through my soul and took everything clean away with her. I couldn't make any plans then. All I knew was that I was happy. She didn't suspect anything, of course, and she'd probably forgotten all about me—I'm not a good man to look at, anyway, I know it myself, with teeth like a polecat, and a mouse's eyes. And my eyes keep wandering, damn them! To hell with them! You can't buy good looks and you can't steal them, either, no matter how you try."

A Petliura machine gun fired a short burst from the woods and then was silent.

"That's all nonsense," the bright-eyed man said. "Both the hetman and Petliura, too. And all this mess, this fluttering around with war. I don't understand who the devil makes anything out of it. I don't even want to understand."

He was silent for a little.

"Well, what's the matter with you?" I said. "You started to tell a story, and then quit."

"No, I haven't quit. I lived there in Simbirsk for ten days in all, and then the tavern owner—he was a sick man, and a good one—came up to me and whispered: 'Detectives have been here today, asking about you. Watch out, fellow, or they'll pick you up. Are you a thief?' No, I told him, I'm not a thief and never was one, except for love of a woman. 'The court won't take love for a woman into account,' he told me. 'It's not a juridical concept. You'd better not come back here. Be careful.' And I decided that no, I'd not go to jail. I needed all the freedom I could get right then, so as not to lose that woman. I had to turn around a little and mix up my traces.

"So I moved on that same day to Sizran, to sit it out for a while, but two days later they picked me up there like a snotty lost child. They sent me to Samara for trial. There were two guards taking me. We got as far as Simbirsk on a ship. I looked out of the little window, and from the river I could see the house where she lived, and the garden. I asked the guards: 'Take me up to the third-class buffet. I haven't eaten for two days.' Well, they took pity on me, of course, and they took me up. I asked the woman at the buffet quietly for a glass of vodka. She poured it for me. I drank it down in one gulp, and then I broke the glass in this hand, and I rubbed it all around my face. It was like washing my face with bloody chunks of glass. Out of unbearable grief. The whole counter was covered with blood. The scars have been all over my muzzle ever since then, adding to my good looks."

"Well, and afterwards?" I asked.

The bright-eyed man looked at me, spat, and answered:

"As if you didn't know. Afterwards—*borshch* with shit in it. Give me a pack of those Odessa cigarettes or I'll grab you by the neck—I've got a real grip—and you'll never break away. I've been lying to you, Friar. And I've made you run at the nose, by God."

I gave him a package of cigarettes.

"Well, that's all," he said, and he stood up and walked slowly along the trench. "And if you talk about it to this riffraff, either now or thirty years from now, I'll kill you with my bare hands. Make up some poetry instead: 'Ah, love, that entrancing dream.' "

I couldn't understand the evil which had suddenly swept through him, and I watched his back.

The whistle of a shell, from the direction of Kiev, came out of the early morning mist. It seemed to me to be coming straight at us. I was not mistaken. It hit the breastworks and exploded with a noise as if all the air around us had exploded like an empty iron ball. Shell fragments flew around us. The bright-eyed man turned around in surprise, leaned his face against the wall of the trench, spat out his last mother-oath with a mouthful of blood, and slipped down into the mud and snow on the bottom of the trench. A crimson spot began to grow in the snow.

Then a second shell hit right next to the foxhole. Pan Horse's Tail jumped out of his dugout. A third shell hit the breastworks.

"It's our own!" Pan Horse's Tail yelled out in a desperate voice, and he shook his fist in the direction of Kiev. "Our own guns are firing on us. Idiots! Scoundrels! Who are you shooting at? You're shooting at your own men, you sons of bitches!"

Pan Horse's Tail turned to us:

"Get out of here, back to Priorka. Quickly! No panic! Your hetman can go to the devil's mother."

Bending over, and falling down every time we heard the whistle of a shell, we ran back to Priorka. First of all, of course, ran the "motor boys."

It turned out that the hetman's artillery had decided our positions must have been taken by Petliura's men, and had concentrated their fire on them.

As he left the trench Pan Horse's Tail stepped across the body of the bright-eyed man and said to me, without turning around:

"Take his documents, just in case. Maybe you can find his relatives. He was a man, after all, not just a dog."

The bright-eyed man was lying face down, and I turned him on his side. His body was still warm and, in spite of his thinness, quite heavy. A shell fragment had gone right through his neck. The woman's lips tattooed on the palm of his hand were smeared with blood. I unbuttoned his blue Austrian overcoat and took out of the pocket of his shirt a creased and obviously forged identification card and an empty envelope with an address written on it: "Elizaveta Tenishevaya, Sadovaya Street 13. Simbirsk."

The shabby, dwindling troops of the hetman were lining up across the straw-covered square in the middle of Priorka. Civilians were pouring into the streets and watching our departure with unconcealed relish. But in spite of everything, the streets were still being patrolled by German cavalry calmly sitting on their well-fed horses. Hetman or Petliura, it was all the same to the Germans, but order had to be preserved first of all.

We threw all our rifles and grenades into a big pile on the

square, on the order of Pan Horse's Tail. The Germans rode up to the pile at once, and coolly set up a guard around it. They did not even look at us.

"And now—everybody go home!" Pan Horse's Tail said. He took off his own yellow-blue epaulets and threw them on the pavement. "Any way you like. You're on your own. The city's in a mess. Petliura's troops hold some streets, while the hetman's are retreating from others. So when you come to a corner, look first to the left and then to the right. I wish you all good health."

He gave a forced smile at his own unsuccessful joke, waved his hand to us like a civilian, and walked away without looking back.

Some of the soldiers sold their overcoats right on the square for a few kopecks or gave them away free, walking away in their shirts or blouses. I felt cold, so I kept my overcoat and only ripped the buttons off. Cotton came out of the holes where the buttons had been, and it was easy to guess who I was by a single glance at me.

I walked as far as the Kirillovsky Church where I had once been a long time ago with my father and Vrubel. At that time all the area around the church had been cut by deep ravines overgrown with hawthorn, and the knotty elm trees had seemed mysterious to me, and frightening. This time, I walked slowly up the steep, dusty road to Lukyanovka, and I had no feeling of the strangeness of the place or of the time. Probably because I was tired.

I know now, of course, that the times were unusual, almost fantastic, not unlike delirium, but I didn't see this then. A dark sky hung over the side streets and hovels of the region just as it had thirty years before. Gray thoughts ran through my head and I thought dimly: "When will there be an end to this third-rate comedy with hetmans, *atamans*, Petliuras, all this yelling of slogans and pompous ideas, this complete muddle of evil, all of it much worse than it needs to be? When will the curtain come down on this improvised stage where unfortunately it's not cranberry extract but real human blood which flows along the floor?"

At crossings inside the city I looked neither to the left nor to the right. I felt, to hell with all this political and military nonsense, and anger took any sense of danger away from me. I walked right through a column of Petliura's soldiers with my overcoat clearly showing that I had ripped the buttons off, and only twice was I hit hard in the back by rifle butts.

Crowds of fat Ukrainians standing in little rows along the streets were yelling "Hurrah!" at Petliura's troops, and they all looked at me with fanatical hatred.

But still I managed to get home. I rang the bell, and I heard Amalie's happy shout. I held on to the side of the door, let myself down into a chair in the vestibule, and light, happy thoughts went whirling through my head although my overcoat was pressing hard against my chest, harder and harder every minute as if it were a living creature and trying to strangle me. Then I realized that it was not my overcoat, but the long, knotty fingers of the bright-eyed man reaching for my throat because of the package of Odessa cigarettes. And a pair of blue woman's lips, bow-shaped, tattooed on the palm of his hand, were also choking me. I groaned, and forgot everything.

Such short fainting fits used to happen to me fairly often in my youth. They came from being tired.

THE VIOLET RAY

When from my room I heard shouting in the streets next morning, I could guess that Pan Petliura, the "*ataman* of Ukrainian troops and *gaidamak* cavalry forces"* was riding into Kiev on his white horse. Posters had been pasted up around the city the night before. With a fatuous self-confidence and a complete lack of any sense of humor, they had announced that Petliura would enter the city at the head of his government—the Directory—riding a white horse given to him by the railroad workers of Shmerinsky.

No one could understand just why they had given him a horse, instead of a handcar or perhaps a shunting engine. But Petliura did not disappoint the maidservants, the merchants, the governesses, and the retired generals of the city: he actually did ride into the conquered city on a big, rather indolent, white horse.

The horse was wearing a blue saddlecloth with an embroidered

---

* *Gaidamaks* were Ukrainian peasants who revolted in the eighteenth century against their Polish overlords; the name was later taken by Petliura's troops in their fighting against the Red Army.

yellow border. Petliura himself wore a khaki padded coat. His only adornment—a curved Zaporozhe saber obviously taken from a museum—bounced against his thighs. The fat Ukrainians along the streets looked with awe at this Cossack weapon, at the white-faced, bloated Petliura himself, and at the *gaidamak* cavalrymen prancing behind him on their shaggy horses.

These *gaidamaks*, with their long blue-black forelocks swinging down from the sheepskin hats they wore on their shaved heads, reminded me of my childhood and of Saksagansky's Ukrainian theater. Nearly every play produced there included some of these *gaidamaks*, their eyes made up with blue paint, swinging into the old Ukrainian folk-dance, the *gopak*.

Every people has its own character, its own distinguishing traits. But those whose mouths drool with tender emotions for their people and who have lost all sense of measure always push these special characteristics to a ridiculous extreme, to pathos, and to something close to disgusting. No people has more dreadful enemies than its own chauvinists.

When I was a boy in Kiev, we lived once next door to the well-known "artist of the Ukraine," the painter Pimonenko.* This elderly man worked alone in his studio and exclusively from memory. With incredible speed and carelessness, he painted all kinds of pretty-pretty cottages, vineyards, hollyhocks, sunflowers, and girls bedecked with ribbons from head to toe. Then he painted the same things in the reverse order—first the girls, then the sunflowers, the hollyhocks, the vineyards, and the cottages. And so on with no end to it. He poured out his energy in the creation of a post-card Ukraine, as sweet as honey. Even as children we found that Pimonenko's landscapes set our teeth on edge.

Petliura was trying to revive this kind of sugar-and-honey Ukraine. But, of course, nothing came of it.

Behind Petliura, on his horse, came the Directory, the loose, slack, neurasthenic writer Vinnichenko,† and then some moss-covered and utterly unknown ministers. This was the beginning in Kiev of the short, lightminded rule of Petliura.

The people of Kiev, who are as given to irony as all southern peoples, made the new government a target for a fantastic number of jokes. They were especially delighted by the activity of some

* N. K. Pimonenko (1862–1912) was a painter who specialized in Ukrainian peasant scenes; his pictures are in the Tretyakovsky Gallery in Moscow and the Historical Museum in Kiev.

† Vladimir Vinnichenko (1880–1951) was a writer of the Decadent school; he was influenced, like Artzibashev, by Nietzschean ideas and a strong interest in eroticism.

gaidamaks, in the first few days of Petliura, who walked along the Kreshchatik with stepladders and replaced all the Russian signs with Ukrainian ones.

Petliura brought with him a so-called Galician language—a heavy speech filled with words borrowed from neighboring languages. And the sharp, singing common speech of the Ukraine, full of pearls as shining as the teeth of healthy boys and girls, retreated before the new language into the ancient Shevchenko huts and quiet country fields. It lived there quietly through all the hard years, retaining its poetry and its integrity.

Everything under Petliura seemed invented—the *gaidamaks* and the language and all his policies, and the gray-bearded chauvinists who emerged in enormous numbers from their dusty holes, and the money, everything including the Directory's reports to the people. But more about this later. When you encountered the *gaidamaks*, you went nearly crazy asking yourself if they were real or actors. The squeezed-out sounds of the new language evoked the same question—was this Ukrainian or something invented? And when you were given change in a store, you looked distrustfully at the gray pieces of paper with their dull little spots of yellow and blue color, and asked yourself: is this real money or counterfeit? They were the kind of tired pieces of paper children like to play with, pretending they are money.

There was a great deal of counterfeit money, and so little real money that the population quietly agreed to recognize no difference between them. Counterfeit money passed quite freely at the same value as real money. There was not a printshop in Kiev where the typesetters and lithographers were not cheerfully producing Petliura money from *karbovantsi* (worth about a ruble) down to *shagi* (the smallest unit, worth a half a kopeck). Many enterprising citizens made money at home with brushes and cheap water colors. They did not even bother to hide their tools when strangers walked into the room.

Pan Kturenda's room was now given over entirely to the production of counterfeit money and his vodka made out of millet. After this pompous little man had shoehorned me into the hetman's army, he developed feelings toward me like those a hangman has for his victim. He went out of his way to be nice to me, and was always inviting me to visit him. I was interested in this last survivor of the small Polish gentry who had somehow managed to last into our—as Pan Kturenda himself called them—"upsetting times."

One day I walked into his stifling room which was filled with bottles of his muddy vodka. It had the sour smell of paint and of the special drug—I forget its name—which was used in those days to cure gonorrhea. I found Pan Kturenda busy making Petliura hundred-ruble notes. These pictured two sultry-eyed girls in embroidered blouses, with thick bare legs. For some reason, they stood in graceful ballet poses on some intricate scallops and curls which Pan Kturenda was at that moment drawing with a paint brush. His mother—a thin old woman with a trembling face—was sitting behind a screen, reading a Polish prayer book in a low voice.

"The scallop is the alpha and the omega of all Petliura's money," Pan Kturenda told me in a professorial tone. "Instead of these Ukrainian girls, you could paint the bodies of two fat women without any risk at all. They are completely unimportant. What matters is that the scallops should look like the government bills. If they are, nobody will miss those pretty girls for a minute, and they'll take the hundred-ruble note with pleasure."

"How many of them do you make?"

"I can paint up to three in a day," Pan Kturenda said, and he proudly stuck out his lip with its little mustache. "Sometimes I can do five. It depends on my mood."

"Basya!" the old woman said from behind the screen. "My son. I am afraid."

"Nothing is going to happen, Mama. Nobody would dare to take any liberties with a person like Pan Kturenda."

"I'm not afraid of prison," the old woman answered suddenly and unexpectedly. "I'm afraid of you, Basya."

"Softening of the brain," Pan Kturenda told me, and he motioned toward the old woman. "Excuse me, Mama, but can't you please keep quiet?"

"No," the old lady said. "No, I can't. God will punish me if I don't tell everyone I can"—the old woman was crying—"that my son, like Judas Iscariot . . ."

"Quiet!" Pan Kturenda shouted angrily. He jumped up from his chair, grabbed the screen behind which the old woman was sitting, and shook it violently. The screen danced up and down on its little legs and yellow dust came up from the floor.

"Quiet, you crazy old fool, or I'll tie up your mouth with a rag soaked in kerosene."

The old lady wept, and blew her nose.

"What does that mean?" I asked Pan Kturenda.

"It is my personal business," he answered defiantly. His twisted face was covered with red veins and it looked as if blood would pour out of them at any moment. "I advise you not to stick your nose into my affairs unless you want to end up in a common grave with the Bolsheviks."

"You scoundrel," I said quietly. "You're such a petty scoundrel that you're not even worth a forged hundred-ruble bill."

"Under the ice!" Pan Kturenda shouted hysterically, and he stamped his foot. "Pan Kturenda disposes of people like you in the Dnieper, under the ice!"

I told Amalie about this. She told me it was her guess that Pan Kturenda was working as an informer for everybody, for the old Rada, which had been the legislative body in the Ukraine until the revolution, for the Germans, for the hetman, and for Petliura. Amalie was convinced that Pan Kturenda would carry out his threat and would denounce me. So, as a careful and practical woman, she set up her own watch on Pan Kturenda. But all her plans to render him harmless were made unnecessary by that very evening. Pan Kturenda died while we were watching, and his death was as stupid as his nasty life had been.

We heard some pistol shots on the street in the early evening. I went out on the balcony, as I always did on such occasions, to see what was going on. I saw two men in civilian clothes running across the dusty square in front of the Cathedral of St. Vladimir toward our house, with some Petliura soldiers and officers chasing them but clearly not eager to catch up to them. The officers were firing as they ran, and furiously yelling "Stop!"

Then I noticed Pan Kturenda. He darted out of his room in the wing of the building, ran up to the heavy gate leading out to the street, and took out of its keyhole the heavy key, which looked like the ancient key to some medieval town. Holding the key in his hands, he hid behind the gate. When the two men ran by, he opened the gate, stuck out his arm with the key (he was holding it like a pistol, and from a distance it really looked as if he had one in his hand), and shouted in a piercing voice:

"Stop! You Bolshevik filth! Or I'll kill you!"

Pan Kturenda wanted to help the Petliura soldiers by holding up the fugitives, if even for only a moment. A few seconds, of course, would have settled their fate. From the balcony I could see clearly everything that happened. The second of the two men raised his pistol while he ran and fired to the side, without even looking at Pan Kturenda. The latter, screaming and spitting blood, danced back into the cobblestoned courtyard, stumbled, and fell and died, the key still in his hand. Blood was flowing over his pink celluloid collar, and there was a look of terror and of evil in his open eyes.

It was an hour before a shabby ambulance arrived and took Pan Kturenda away to the morgue. His old mother had slept through her son's death and learned about it only that night. A few days later she was sent off to the old Sulimovsky almshouse. I used to see its inmates fairly often when I took a walk. They always went in pairs, like students in a school procession, in identical dark cotton dresses. When they walked, they made me think of a solemn parade of large ground beetles.

I have described the meaningless end of Pan Kturenda simply because it was so typical of what was going on in Kiev under the Directory. Everything was petty and mean, like some bad and disorderly, but occasionally tragic, vaudeville.

One day all of Kiev was plastered with enormous posters telling the population that the Directory would give an accounting to the people in the Ars motion picture theater. The whole city tried to be present at this accounting, anticipating something unexpected. And they got it.

The long, narrow theater was plunged in a mysterious darkness. No lights were lit. The crowd rustled cheerfully in the dark. Then someone struck a resounding gong on the stage, the footlights were turned on, and in front of a backdrop which illustrated in garish colors "the wonderful Dnieper in good weather" there stood an elderly but well-built man in a black suit and with an elegant beard—the Prime Minister Vinnichenko.

He delivered a short, dull speech about the international position of the Ukraine, speaking unhappily and clearly embarrassed, continually straightening his necktie. Everyone applauded him.

Then an incredibly thin and heavily powdered woman in a black dress walked out on the stage. She extended her arms in obvious despair and began to recite verses by the poetess Galinaya to the accompaniment of heavy chords struck on a piano. She was applauded, too.

All the speeches by ministers were sandwiched in between acts like this. After the Minister of Roads had spoken, some boys and girls danced the *gopak*.

The audience was really having a good time, but it was discreetly quiet when the Minister of Finance walked out on the stage. He had a disheveled, quarrelsome look; he was clearly angry and he was puffing hard. His close-cropped round head was shining with sweat.

Blue-gray Zaporozhe mustaches hung down to his collar. He was
dressed in very large gray-striped trousers, an equally large jacket
made of silk, and an embroidered shirt tied at the throat with a
braid dangling large red pompons.

He had no intention of making a speech. He walked up to the
footlights and began to listen to the crowd in the theater. The
Minister even cupped his hand around his hairy ear to hear better.
There was a good deal of laughter. The Minister laughed, too, as if
he were satisfied, nodded at some thought going through his head,
and then asked:

"Are you all from Moscow?"

Actually, the theater was filled mainly with Russians. Un-
suspectingly, they answered calmly that, yes, many of them came
from Moscow.

"So-o-o!" the Minister said angrily, and he blew his nose into a
large checked handkerchief. "It's all very clear. But not at all
pleasant."

The theater grew quiet; something extraordinary seemed sure
to follow.

"To hell with all of you!" the Minister shouted out suddenly in
Ukrainian, and he turned beet-red. "So you've all sneaked here out
of your rotten Moscow. Like flies to honey. Why didn't you stay
there? God should wipe you all out with one thunderclap. Back
there in Moscow things have got so bad that there's nothing to buy,
and nothing to buy it with."

The audience began to hoot. You could hear whistles. Some
little man jumped up on the stage, took the Minister of Finance
by the elbow, and tried to lead him away. But the old man was
incensed, and he pushed the little man away so that he almost fell.
The Minister was by now under full steam, and he could not stop.
He denounced us and cursed us in a Ukrainian full of peasant
profanity.

By now two men were discreetly pulling at the tail of the
Minister's silk jacket, but he turned on them angrily and yelled:

"Beggars! Parasites! Crawl back to your Moscow! There you can
suffer under your Yiddish government! Crawl off!"

Vinnichenko appeared in the wing of the stage. He shook his
fist angrily, and the old man finally, red with indignation, was led
off the stage. Then, to ease the situation, a chorus of young fellows
came out on the stage with tambourines and began to sing and
dance.

This ended the accounting of the Directory to the people of Kiev.
Happily shouting "Crawl back to Moscow!" and "There you can

suffer under your Yiddish government," the audience filed out of the theater on to the street.

The regime of Petliura and the Directory gave the city a very provincial look. The once glittering Kiev was transformed into a slightly bigger Shpola or Mirgorod. Everything was reconstructed to look like an old-fashioned Ukraine, including a cake store named for Taras Bulba. The long-mustached Taras who ran it was so impressive and his embroidered Ukrainian shirt was so shiningly white that many people hesitated to buy cakes and honey from such an operatic personage. It was hard to know if something serious were happening to the city, or if the city were simply acting out a play with characters dressed up like *gaidamaks*.

It was impossible in general to know what was going on. These were feverish, violent times, and upset followed upset in the government. In the very first days after each new government took office there were clear and threatening signs of its early and ignominious defeat. Every regime hurried to issue a maximum number of declarations and decrees, hoping that a few of them might trickle down into real life and leave a trace.

Petliura's government, like that of the hetman, gave an impression of total lack of confidence in its own future, and of complete confusion of ideas. Petliura's chief hope was in the French, who were then occupying Odessa. Soviet forces were threatening him from the north. So the Petliura agents spread rumors that the French were going to take over Kiev, that they were already in Vinnitsa, in Fastova, and that by tomorrow the brave French Zouaves in their red trousers and their handsome fezzes might well show up at Boyarsk right next to Kiev itself. Petliura's bosom friend, the French consul, had promised him that this would happen. Newspapers, confused by the contradictory rumors, gladly printed all this nonsense even though everyone knew that the French were sitting quietly in Odessa in the French zone of occupation, and that the zones of influence in that city (French, Greek, and Ukrainian) were divided from each other by nothing but rows of dilapidated old chairs.

Rumors became almost an elemental force under Petliura, a kind of cosmic development like a plague of madness. It was an epidemic of hypnosis. Rumors entirely lost their primary purpose— to communicate invented facts. They acquired a new character, becoming a sort of self-reassurance, a powerful narcotic drug. People could hold on to hope for the future only by means of rumors.

Some of them were transient, some lasted for a long while. Most of them held people in a kind of trance for two or three days. Even the most cynical skeptics believed all sorts of stories, such as that the Ukraine would be made a department of France and that President Poincaré himself was coming to Kiev for the triumphal announcement, or that the actress Vera Kholodnaya had recruited an army which she led, like Joan of Arc, on a white horse, and that she was basing her gallant troops on the town of Priluka where she had declared herself Empress of the Ukraine.

I started once to keep a record of these rumors but then I gave it up. It was enough to give you a bad headache, or to drive you into a kind of quiet insanity. Then you wanted just to liquidate them all, from President Poincaré and President Wilson to Makhno and the famous *ataman* Zelony who kept his headquarters in the village of Tripolye near Kiev. I regret now that I destroyed my list of rumors. It was a magnificent collection of lies, and of the irrepressible fantasies of helplessly disorganized people.

To keep my own sanity, I went back to rereading some of my favorite books: Turgenev's *Torrents of Spring*, Boris Zaitsev's *The Blue Star, Tristan and Isolde, Manon Lescaut*. These books really shone like imperishable stars in the dim twilight of those Kiev evenings.

I was living alone. Mama and my sister were still completely cut off from Kiev. I heard nothing from them. So I decided to go on foot to Kopan in the spring, even though I was warned that the wild "Dimersky" Republic lay across my road and that I had no chance of getting through it alive. But then new events took place, and there was no point in even thinking about walking to Kopan.

I was alone with my books. I tried to write a little, but everything came out shapeless and sounded like ravings. My solitude was punctuated only by the nights when quiet would possess our building and the whole neighborhood, and everything slept except the street patrols, the clouds, and the stars. The footsteps of the patrols carried a long way in the night. I used to turn out the lamp each time I heard them, so as not to attract their attention to our building. Sometimes at night I could hear Amalie crying, and I thought how much harder her loneliness was than mine.

Each time after she had cried at night, she would speak to me haughtily for a few days and even with hostility, but then suddenly she would smile shyly and guiltily and start again to fuss over me just as she fussed over all her boarders.

The revolution began in Germany. The German regiments stationed in Kiev duly and accurately elected their Soviet of Soldiers' Deputies, and began to get ready to return to their fatherland. Petliura decided to take advantage of their weakness and to disarm them. But the Germans learned about his plan.

On the morning of the day appointed for the disarming of the Germans, I woke up with the feeling that the walls of our building were shaking in rhythm. Drums were being beaten. I walked out on the balcony. Amalie was already there. The German troops were marching heavily down Fundukleyevskaya Street. Their hobnailed boots jingled the glass in the windows. The drums sounded warningly. The cavalry followed the infantry, just as gloomily, their hoofbeats just as regular, and still farther behind, clattering along the paved street, came dozens of cannon.

Without a single word, with no noise but the drums, the Germans circled through the city and returned to their barracks. Petliura immediately canceled his secret order to disarm the Germans.

Soon after this quiet German demonstration, distant artillery fire began to be heard from the left bank of the Dnieper. The Germans evacuated Kiev in a hurry. The shooting grew louder, and the city learned that Soviet regiments from Nezhin were rapidly moving into battle. When fighting broke out right next to Kiev, in Brovorov and Darnitsa, and it became clear to everyone that Petliura had played out his hand and lost, his commandant of the city issued a special order. It stated that on the following night Petliura's army was going to employ a deadly violet ray against the Bolsheviks. It was a weapon which had been loaned to Petliura by French military forces, thanks to that "friend of a free Ukraine," the French consul. The population of the city was warned to take refuge in the cellars during the night, not going out until morning, in order to avoid unnecessary casualties.

The citizens of Kiev were used to sleeping in their cellars where they took refuge whenever there was a change of government. The next safest place, besides the cellar, and in its way a citadel of tea drinking and endless conversation, was the kitchen. Most of Kiev's kitchens were located near the backs of the buildings, where bullets seldom penetrated. There was something comforting in the smells of food which clung to the kitchens, and sometimes a little water would trickle out of a faucet. In an hour, you might collect a whole teapotful and brew yourself some strong tea out of dried bilberry leaves.

Anyone who ever drank that tea will agree that it was our only strong support in those times, a kind of elixir of life and a panacea against all grief and misfortune.

It seemed to me then that the country was drifting into an

impenetrable fog. It was impossible to believe that any kind of dawn could follow those deep nights, compounded of soot and despair, under the wind whistling through the bullet-riddled roofs. Any dawn that might come would show us the same empty streets, the same people turning green with cold and hunger running through them in their frozen puttees, with their rifles of all makes and calibers.

It was murderously still on the night of the violet ray. Even the artillery fire died down and the only thing to be heard was a distant rumbling of wagon wheels. This sound told experienced citizens that army supplies were being transported in a hurry out of the city in some unknown direction.

This was just what happened. In the morning the city was free of all Petliura's men, clean of them all. The rumors about the violet ray had been started solely to allow them to clear out in the night without hindrance.

As had happened often enough before, Kiev was left without anyone in power. But the local *atamans* and the neighboring bandits failed to take it over this time. By midday, across the Tsepny Bridge, with steam from horses' flanks, the clatter of wheels, shouting, singing, and the cheerful sound of accordions, the Bogunsky and Tarashchansky Regiments of the Red Army were entering the city, and once more the entire life of Kiev was changed right down to its foundations.

As theater people say, it was "a complete change of scene." But no one could guess what it promised to the starving people. Only time could show this.

A BOLSHEVIK WEDDING

Sodden posters appeared on the walls of Kiev announcing the grim new decrees of the Military Revolutionary Committee. They were all short and momentous. Mercilessly and without any reservations, they divided the population of the city into worthwhile people and human rubbish.

The rubbish began to be cleaned out, but there was not much of it as things worked out. Most of it scurried away into inaccessible places where it settled down to wait for better days. What had already happened in Moscow began all over again here, but there was something new about it. There was an added sense of freedom and of recklessness.

The Bogunsky Regiment (named in honor of its desperately courageous colonel, Bogun) was quartered in private houses. Four of them moved into our apartment. They brought with them a bomb, put it down carefully in the vestibule next to the curved hat-stand, and told Amalie:

"Just walk around it on tiptoe, and don't bump into it carelessly. Or else it will go off with such a bang that your house and all your furniture will be just a dream. Understand?"

"I understand," Amalie answered, tightening her lips, and she immediately opened the door to the long-disused backstairs. From then on, no one walked through the vestibule.

It was hard to understand how the Bogunsky soldiers could move around at all with the weapons they carried. They had everything: machine guns, rifles, grenades, sawed-off guns, bayonets, revolvers, Finnish daggers, swords, knives, and in addition, to remind them sentimentally of peaceful times, they carried red and purple gramophone horns.

As soon as they occupied a town, the melodies of long-forgotten love songs began to pour out of all the windows. The gloomy baritone complained again that he had nowhere to go and no one to love, the lisping tenor lamented that it was not for him that spring was coming, not for him the beech trees bursting into bloom, no, not for him, not for him.

Everything was all mixed up—sopranos and hand grenades, the smell of chloroform and Ukrainian songs, red ribbons on the sheepskin hats and symphony concerts, the soldiers' dreams about quiet lakes surrounded by peaceful meadows and the hysterical screaming of illegal traders being rounded up in the market places.

A gentle, decrepit old engineer named Belelubsky lived directly beneath us in an apartment filled with pug dogs. In his day he had been famous throughout the world for having built the Sizran Bridge across the Volga. But fame vanishes like smoke, and by now Belelubsky had nothing to do except in the mornings when he walked his repulsive, snorting dogs with their round, insolent little eyes which looked just like Bismarck's.

The Belelubskys had a red-cheeked, cheerful servant girl named Motrya. The sergeant living in our apartment fell in love with her. Motrya hesitated. She had some old-fashioned notions about marriage. She was afraid that the sergeant, who was a happy-go-lucky fellow and an arrogant one, would live with her for a few days and then throw her over.

One day Motrya came to me and told me, with the frankness of a country girl, that she had all but given the sergeant up but that she had now reconsidered and decided to accept him on condition that he should marry her "by the rules" and agree to love her forever. She dictated a letter to him. It consisted of only three words: "Agreed, if forever." I wrote them in big, block letters.

In about an hour, after he had received the letter, the sergeant started to storm through the apartment, swearing a blue streak, waving a gun, stamping his boots, demanding the regimental seal.

"Where in hell have you hidden it, you bandits?" he yelled at all the soldiers. "I'll shoot you all. I want that seal, and right away!"

The whole building shook. The sergeant was ransacking his soldiers' knapsacks. Finally, the seal was found. The sergeant wrote on a piece of paper, "I swear to you, it's forever," stamped it with the regimental seal, to make assurance doubly sure, and sent it to Motrya. And Motrya surrendered.

A wild wedding took place the next day. Some gun carriers drove up to the house. The horses had red ribbons plaited into their manes. Although it was only two hundred meters to the Cathedral of St. Vladimir, where the ceremony was to take place, the procession drove off in high style and circled the cathedral several times with the sound of bells, whooping, whistles, and singing. At every chorus of the regimental song the horses stopped and danced and pranced, shaking their bells, in perfect time to the song. This was a truly virtuoso performance, and an enormous crowd of curious onlookers cheered in admiration.

On the third day after the wedding (for some reason, everything unpleasant always happens on the third day) the soldiers
were summoned suddenly in the middle of the night. They assembled morosely, saying little, and they answered all our questions
curtly:

"We're being sent to Zhitomir. Pacification work. A lot of priests
are raising hell there."

Motrya was sobbing. Her worst fears were coming true. The
sergeant, of course, would throw her over and never come back
again.

Then the sergeant flew into a rage.

"Drive everyone in the building into the courtyard," he shouted
at his soldiers, and to underline the order he fired from the
staircase into the ceiling. "Get them all out here, the parasites!
To hell with them!"

The frightened residents all assembled in the courtyard. It
was a late winter night. Biting frost was seeping down from a
muddy sky. Women were crying, holding their shivering, sleepy
children close to them.

"Don't worry," the soldiers said. "Nothing is going to happen to
you. It's just our sergeant and his godforsaken Motrya."

The sergeant made his entry across from the crowd of frightened
civilians and marched forward. He was holding the wailing Motrya
by the hand. In the middle of the ice-covered courtyard he stopped,
drew his Hussar's sword out from its scabbard, cut a big cross with
its blade in the ice, and shouted out:

"Soldiers and free citizens of a free Russia! Be witnesses that
I swear on this cross on my native soil in front of you that I will
not desert my wife, and that I will certainly come back to her. And
we will live together in my house in the village of Moshna near the
town of Kaneva, to which I sign my name and I take an oath."

He embraced the weeping Motrya, then he gently pushed her
away and shouted:

"Into your wagons! Forward march!"

The soldiers jumped into their wagons. They drove off whistling
and singing and we could hear the clatter of their wheels down
Bibikovsky Boulevard to the highway to Zhitomir.

It was all over. Motrya dried her tears and said: "Well, he said
it, the damned Mohammedan!" and then went back to the
Belelubsky apartment where the pug dogs were barking frantically.
Life went on in its accustomed way.

Everything suddenly lost some of its luster. And after a little
while the people of Kiev began to recall the Bogunsky Regiment

with real regret. They had been simple and happy but desperately brave fellows. They carried with them the smell of gunpowder, and red flags with bullet holes in them, bold songs, and an unswerving devotion to the Revolution. They had come and then disappeared, but a little breeze of revolutionary spirit rustled over the city for a long time, without blowing itself out, and made the citizens of Kiev, who were used to everything, smile happily.

Shchors was in command of the Bogunsky Regiment then. His name was soon to become a legendary one. I heard about him for the first time from those soldiers. I heard enthusiastic tales about an unbending, courageous, and talented commander.

I remember being most impressed by the soldiers' almost child-like love for Shchors. In their eyes he had all the best qualities of an officer: firmness, resourcefulness, a sense of justice, love for the common man, and a sober kind of romanticism which never seemed false.

The Bogunsky soldiers were a young crowd. Shchors, too, was young. Their youth and their belief in the victory of the Revolution transformed a military regiment into a kind of fraternity, held together by a common impulse and by the blood they had spilled together.

There are no external forces which can slow up the movement of sap in trees. So spring came in its good time, the Dnieper overflowed its banks, weeds in the fields grew higher than a man's head, and the battle-scarred chestnut trees were covered with succulent leaves and then with blossoms of a special elegance.

Sometimes it seemed as if the only thing left unchanged in the world was the foliage of the chestnut trees. It murmured over the pavements just as before, throwing its heavy shadows. And the straight candles of its spotted pink and yellow flowers began to rise just as delicately and gradually as before. But you no longer saw the tender-eyed schoolgirls walking in the shade of the chestnut trees. Instead, the fallen dry chestnut blossoms were swept along the sidewalks with greenish cartridge shells and scraps of hardened, dirty bandages.

The spring flamed up over Kiev, covering the city with a cloud of blue until the lindens blossomed in the parks. Their fragrance filtered into rooms which had been battened tight through the winter, forcing the townsfolk to throw open their windows and their balconies. Then summer stole into the rooms with all its little breezes and its warmth. And in this summer serenity all terrors and all misfortunes disappeared.

It's true, there was no bread and we ate old frozen potatoes instead.

I got myself a job in a strange organization. It was almost impossible to pronounce the shortened name coined from its initials; it went something like "Obgubsnabchuprod . . ." and what followed these syllables was so complicated that even the director, a fat Armenian with a black beard and a Mauser hung around his neck the way cameras are often carried, snorted and grew embarrassed every time he had to sign a paper.

It would also be hard to say just what this organization did. It had something to do with calico cloth. All the rooms and corridors in its offices were filled with bales of cloth. It was never given out to anyone, under any circumstances, but it was always being brought in or shipped back to warehouses and then brought back to the office and piled up again in the corridors. This incomprehensible movement back and forth of the same bales of calico cloth drove most of the workers in the office into a stupor.

I had a lot of free time. I tried to find some of my friends with whom I had studied in the *gymnasium,* but almost none of them were left in the city except for Shmukler. And I saw him rarely. He had become very quiet and sad, perhaps because he had had to abandon the painting he loved to take care of his family. His father had died, and the whole support of his family fell on him. He had to protect them from hunger, from requisitions of their property, from being squeezed into a smaller apartment, from being dispossessed entirely, from billeting officers, and from Petliura's pogroms.

I went sometimes in the evenings to concerts in the garden of the former Merchants' Club, as I had done while I was in the *gymnasium.* There were no longer any roses or canna lilies in the garden. They had been replaced by peppermint and wormwood. Unscored noises—distant explosions or rifle fire—were woven often enough into the music at these concerts, but no one paid any attention to them.

It was during these days in Kiev that I first became engrossed in the books of the great French writer and literary hoaxer, Stendhal. But his plagiarisms and his mystifications never bothered me. I considered them quite legitimate, as I still do. They are legitimate because they reveal such a wealth of different ideas and images that it would have been unthinkable to publish them over one name. Nobody would have believed that any single man could have dug so deep into so many areas of human life—into painting, the terms of trade in the steel business, French provincial life, the confusion of the Battle of Waterloo, the science of seducing women, the corruption of his bourgeois century, how to run a commissariat, the music of Cimarosa and Haydn.

When I learned that Stendhal's extensive diaries, filled with exciting events and ideas, were in large part fictitious, but so artfully invented that even the best scholars on Stendhal's times can not fault them, I felt an instinctive admiration for the genius and the literary courage of this puzzling, lonely man. Ever since then he has been my secret friend. It would be hard to say how many walks I've taken through Rome or the Vatican with this clumsy friend or how many trips through the ancient towns of France, how many plays I've seen at La Scala Theater with him, how many of his conversations with the wisest men of the nineteenth century I have overheard.

I soon had a piece of luck. The writers Mikhail Koltsov and Efim Zozulya came to Kiev from Moscow. They began to issue an art magazine, and I took over the job of literary secretary. There was very little work. The magazine always came out as thin as a school notebook with half its pages torn out.

I showed Zozulya the beginning of my first and still unfinished story, "The Romantics." He praised it sincerely, although he pointed out that I was extraordinarily prone to self-analysis and that, besides, I wrote at too great length. Zozulya was then writing a cycle of stories with only five or six lines in each. He said himself that they were "shorter than a sparrow's nose." They were much like little fables. Each contained an unmistakable moral.

Zozulya believed that literature was a kind of teaching, or instruction. I thought it deserved something much higher than this utilitarian description, so we were always quarreling. I was convinced then that real literature was the purest possible expression of a free human mind, that only through literature could a man open up all the richness and the complexity of his spirit and his internal strength, and thus make up for what is commonplace in all of us. I saw literature as a present given to us from a distant and priceless future. Generation after generation pour into literature their dreams of the perfection of the world, its harmony, and the immortality of love, in spite of the fact that every day the world is born again and dies. In the same way the quiet hum of a seashell creates a desire to see the endless blue and quiet waters in the haze of dawn, and creates a yearning for the silver clouds flying across the sky, for the oceans of air rising from damp woods and refreshing our eyes, for eternal summer, for a child's voice, for the deep, peaceful quiet which is the true companion of reflection.

Literature does these same things. By a kind of underwater vibration, far away and yet very close to us, it brings us closer to the golden age of all our thoughts, our acts, and our feelings.

While Zozulya and I were arguing about literature, the insolent *atamans* Zelony and Struk were galloping around Kiev and making raids here and there on the outskirts of the city. Once Struk even seized all of Podol, and he was not driven out except with difficulty.

Denikin's forces were moving up from the south. In the steppes around Kremenchug, Nestor Makhno was committing his outrages. People talked little about them in the city, as if they didn't think these events had great significance. There were so many false rumors in the air that no one any longer believed in actual facts.

THE CRIMSON RIDING BREECHES

My good-humored arguments with Zozulya about art were unexpectedly interrupted by my conscription into the army. Because of my extreme shortsightedness I had always been exempted from military service. I was what was then called "a white-ticket man." But now the army suddenly conscripted everyone who had been exempt before.

I was quickly examined, along with some sick young fellows, and we were all enrolled in a guard regiment. It turned out to be, beyond any doubt, the most fantastic regiment that has ever existed anywhere in the world.

In one of the skirmishes with Makhno's forces, his adjutant had been captured, a man named something like Antoshchenko or Antonyuk. I have forgotten his name. I will call him Antoshchenko. This man deserved shooting for the crimes he had already committed. But while he was sitting in Lyukanovka Prison, awaiting execution, he took it into his crazy head to try to save himself.

Antoshchenko summoned the prosecutor and dictated to him a letter addressed to the president of the CHEKA (the Extraordinary

Commission dealing with political crimes). He wrote that the Soviet powers clearly did not know what to do with captured bandits. There were too many of them. You couldn't shoot them all, but to keep these parasites in prison, especially in those hungry times, was foolish. This was why bandits, after they had been disarmed, were so often released to go where they wanted to. The majority of them went right back to their *atamans* to start their bloody looting and chasing around the Ukraine all over again.

Antoshchenko suggested a solution: to release him from prison, instead of shooting him, in gratitude for which he would undertake to organize a completely disciplined regiment of bandits of all kinds. He mentioned his own authority among the bandits, and added that this task would be beyond the powers of anyone else.

The government accepted the risk and freed Antoshchenko. In a short time he did organize a regiment, in which the captured bandits were enrolled in companies: Makhno's men, Strukov's men, Zelony's men, the Black Angels, the Red Coats, and one more company made up of members of smaller and less well-known gangs of bandits. It was in this regiment that we, the former "white-ticket men," were enrolled.

It all started when a convoy picked us up at the mobilization station and took us to regimental staff headquarters on Pechersk. The convoying soldiers would not answer any of our questions on the road, but from time to time they would mutter angry and profane phrases which clearly referred to our new commander, Antoshchenko.

We soon found out for ourselves. They lined us up across from a little house with lilacs in its garden growing up to the roof. There was no overt sign of disaster awaiting us, except that the tense, white faces of the soldiers convoying us seemed to promise nothing very good.

A little man with black sidewhiskers walked out of the house on curved crab's legs. He was wearing a red woolen shirt, and crimson riding breeches with silver stripes down their sides. Enormous spurs dragged behind his red leather boots. Red leather gloves were wrinkled over his fat fingers. A round fur hat with a scarlet leather top was on his head. This was a caricature of a "Red Commander" as one of Makhno's shameless followers would have imagined him.

Not one of the conscripted men even smiled. On the contrary, many shuddered when they saw the man's eyes, which were light in color, almost white with evil. We guessed that this was Antoshchenko.

A Mauser with a big wooden butt hung at his belt, and at his side was a curved sword in a scabbard decorated with silver. He pulled a snow-white handkerchief out of the pocket of his riding breeches, opened it delicately in the air, and wiped his lips. Then he asked in a husky voice:

"Who are these men you've brought me, lads? The dregs of the dregs?"

The convoying soldiers were silent.

Antoshchenko walked slowly along our ranks, looking each man over from head to foot. Two tall officers followed him. We guessed that they must be his battalion commanders. Suddenly Antoshchenko pulled out his curved sword, and cried out in a high whining voice:

"I'll teach you how to serve the Revolution, and I'll do this and that to your mothers! Rascals! Do you know who I am? I'm the man who carved up General Kaledin with this sword, so do you think I'm going to handle you with kid gloves? I haven't seen the day when I didn't cough up a dozen glasses of blood. I've been all shot up for my fatherland, and that's why Moscow sends me thirty thousand gold rubles every month for pocket expenses. Did you know about that? But maybe you do know that when I have to talk with scoundrels like you, it's very short—a bullet in the back of your neck and into the ditch with you!"

His voice had risen to a screech. Little bubbles of spit collected at the corners of his mouth. It was clear that the man in front of us was either insane or an epileptic.

He walked straight up to a tall fellow in glasses, who must have been a student, and hit him in the chin with the hilt of his sword.

"Who are you?" he asked, looking drunkenly up at the tall fellow. "So you've put on glasses? Look, with these hands I killed my own wife for betraying me." He spread his hands wide and showed us his short, stubby fingers in the wrinkled red gloves which were clearly much too big for him. "So you think that I'll just look at you because you're wearing glasses? Listen, I'll strip the skin off you, and nobody will say a word to me about it."

We were all silent, defeated, not understanding what was going on or even where we were. The soldiers who had brought us watched Antoshchenko with a kind of tense anger. Only the battalion commanders stood there in complete indifference, watching us with bored eyes. Obviously, they were used to spectacles like this.

Antoshchenko jumped back and cried out in an affectedly cheerful tone:

"Well, which of you knows how to read and write? Be so obliging as to march three steps forward!"

And he made a gesture of invitation with his naked sword.

I wanted to step forward, but one of the soldiers who had brought us there, standing right next to me, said in a whisper I could hardly hear:

"Stand still! Don't move forward!"

I stood still. We were all literate, of course, but a good many suspected something in Antoshchenko's voice, so only ten or fifteen men stepped forward. This did not surprise Antoshchenko in the slightest.

"Are any of you musicians?" he asked again in his cheerful voice, and again the soldier whispered to me:

"Don't move forward!"

Then Antoshchenko sorted out, joking and laughing, all the shoemakers, the singers, and the tailors. People felt more calm, and a good many stepped forward each time. The rest of us, illiterate and uncultured, numbered not more than a dozen men—obviously those whom the convoying soldiers had managed to warn.

Antoshchenko turned to one of the officers behind him and said in a tired voice:

"Battalion commander! Do you see these windbags who want to be clerks at headquarters or to mend the soldiers' pants instead of risking a heroic death for a peaceful peasantry? Do you see these intelligent snakes who want to fix themselves up with nice jobs, without having any right to them?"

"I see them, Comrade Commander," the officer answered in a dejected voice.

"Send them into action today, against Zelony near Tripolye. And if a single one of them comes back to the regiment alive, you'll answer for it with your head. I swear it by my mother!"

"Yes, Comrade Commander," the officer said in the same doleful voice.

Antoshchenko glanced at the rest of us, the illiterates, slipped his sword skillfully back into its scabbard, and said:

"And I don't want even to look at this rubbish. Put them in the kitchen police! To the devil's mother, forward march!"

They separated us from the others and led us to the Nikolsky Fort where the guard regiment was quartered.

This semicircular building, surrounded by slopes overgrown with elder, stood on a cliff above the Dnieper near Marinsky Park. I had spent a lot of time, when I was a boy, especially in the spring, in that shaded, empty park. That was where I met my first sailor and felt for the first time a deep yearning for distant voyages. Under the sound of bees buzzing in the jasmine bushes I had read poetry there endlessly, almost to the point of stupor, memorizing the lines which delighted me. So Nikolsky Fort, constructed of gray brick and covered with embrasures and arches, with its decrepit drawbridge hanging on rusty chains, with bronze lion heads on its iron gates, had always seemed to me one of the most romantic places in the world.

It had stood empty and neglected. The grass grew high on the parade ground intended for practice and inspection. Swallows had nested under the roof of the fort. A sluggish smell of warm summer leaves drifted in through the broken windows. This was a fort that had never been besieged. For many years it had been an abandoned ruin.

This impression of Nikolsky Fort had sunk so deep into my consciousness that I felt glad now that I was going to serve inside its walls. But this was a naïve impression which disappeared like dust after the first minute of my service. The fort was dirty and gloomy inside. The walls were scrawled over with obscenities, and they shook in the waves of stamping, shouts, yells, cursing, and singing which rolled through the building. The inside of the fort had such a corrosive barracks smell that clothing became saturated with it in a minute and held the smell forever.

We were lined up again in a dusty corridor with a floor of unplaned boards. The pale, effeminate commander of kitchen police, obviously a former officer, came up to us. He looked at us sympathetically, tapped his riding crop against his boot, and said:

"Well, what's the matter? You've seen the mad dog? Killing would be too good for a commander like him."

He was either talking with great sincerity or trapping us, and this we understood clearly. So none of us said a word.

"Ah, what can I expect?" the company commander said. "You're all right out of the mire. March down to the cellar and start peeling potatoes."

We peeled rotten, wet potatoes until evening in a cold underground basement. Dampness was running off the walls. Rats scurried around in the dark corners. Light barely came through a narrow slit in the wall. Our fingers grew numb from the cold and the slippery potatoes.

We talked with each other in low voices. I learned that my neighbor—a meek little man in glasses with sad, reddened eyes— was called Iosif Morgenstern and that before the war he had been a worker in a razor factory in Lodz. We went back to our barracks in the evening. I lay down on the bare boards, and fell asleep at once.

In the middle of the night the hollow sound of horse's hoofs woke me up. I opened my eyes. One electric lamp was hanging from the ceiling on a long cord. Snoring in different keys was to be heard all around me. The clock on the wall showed that it was three o'clock.

In the yellow light I could see Antoshchenko. He was riding a plump horse down the arched corridor and the stones rang under his horse's hoofs. The wire of a field telephone had been stretched across the corridor, and it kept Antoshchenko from riding on. He stopped, pulled out his sword, and cut the wire. Then he rode out of the corridor into the barracks where we were, stopped his horse, and shouted:

"Kitchen police! Form ranks!"

Frightened, sleepy men jumped up from their cots and lined up in a hurry. Almost none of us had our shoes on, and we stood there barefoot on the stone floor, shivering and half awake.

"Right now," Antoshchenko said quietly, "I'm going to have a machine gun brought in here to shoot you all, like quail. Do you think I don't know that you're planning to murder your commander, and that you've called him a mad dog?"

A note of hysteria was quivering in his voice.

"Send the machine gunner here!" he shouted, turning around, and then we noticed for the first time that two of his orderlies were standing behind Antoshchenko, in the door to the barracks. "Where's he disappeared to, the son of a bitch?"

"Comrade Commander," one of the orderlies said carefully, "let's go home now, by God."

"I'll kill you," Antoshchenko yelled wildly, and he turned around in his saddle. "I'll cut you into strips, you bespectacled Jews. I'll cut you up with a buzz saw like mutton."

Antoshchenko's voice broke. Foam began to pour out of his mouth, and he started to slip slowly out of his saddle. We stood there without moving. We learned later that each of us had had the same idea at that moment—if Antoshchenko had brought in his machine gunner, we would have broken ranks, rushed to the corner where our rifles were piled up, grabbed them, and opened fire.

The orderlies picked up Antoshchenko, led him out into the corridor and from there into the open air. His plump horse walked along behind like a piece of clockwork.

Not one of us soldiers, who had landed up in this regiment by accident, could understand how it was possible that in Kiev, right next to the Kreshchatik, right next to theaters and the university, libraries and symphony concerts, right next to ordinary good people of all sorts, there could exist this sinister gang of bandits led by a half-crazy, sick commander. The very existence of this regiment was a disaster. At any moment Antoshchenko might shoot any one of us. Our lives depended on his whims.

We expected some kind of humiliating trick from him every day, and he never disappointed us. We were penned up in Nikolsky Fort with no way of getting out. There were no passes given into the city. But even if we had been allowed to go into Kiev, there would have been nobody there to tell what was going on in the regiment. And it would have done no good anyway—nobody would have believed us.

We decided to write about Antoshchenko to the government and to the Commissar of Military Affairs, Podvoisky, but events moved faster than we did.

Several days went by in relative quiet. Part of the regiment had been sent to Tripolye against Zelony, and the rest of us were carrying out guard duties in Kiev, protecting warehouses and freight stations and taking part in raids on the speculators along the Bessarabka and around the notorious Semadeni Café on the Kreshchatik.

But late one night the regiment was summoned by an alarm signal and lined up in a large square on the parade ground in front of the fort. Nobody knew what was going on. Some said that a new gang of bandits was threatening Kiev from the direction of Svyatoshin and that we were supposed to drive it away from the city. The excitement infected even us in the kitchen police who were equipped with Japanese rifles without a single cartridge.

We stood on the parade ground and waited. A rainy dawn began to show over the Dnieper. The chestnut trees drooped down their leaves like wide green fingers. There was a smell of dusty grass, and we could hear the bell in the Pechersk Monastery strike four o'clock.

"Regiment, attention!" the officers barked out in different voices. The soldiers drew themselves up and stood stock-still. A black lacquered landau drove into the middle of the square. Two Orlov trotters, dapple-grays, stopped and began to paw the ground. Antoshchenko was standing in the landau, and two girls in broad-brimmed hats were sitting in it. The girls were elbowing each other, squealing with delight and giggling.

"Regiment, listen to me!" Antoshchenko said in a drunken voice and he waved his sword over his head. "By platoons, around my carriage, singing my song, march! March! March!"

He lowered his sword. The regiment stood without moving. Then the first company of Makhno's men began to move around the carriage hesitantly, out of step. The singers among them started to sing, "Don't cry, Marusya, you will be mine," but stopped suddenly, and the company stood there in confusion.

"March!" Antoshchenko yelled in a wild voice. The whole regiment stood just as motionless and quiet as before. The girls stopped giggling. The silence was so heavy that we could hear Antoshchenko's broken, angry breathing.

"Ah, you sons of bitches!" Antoshchenko said hoarsely, and he yanked his Mauser out of its holster. At that moment someone yelled from a back row:

"A hell of a way to please your girls, you skunk! Kill him, fellows, let's get him!"

Rifles started to fire. Antoshchenko's driver turned the landau around sharply—the trotters were prancing in the air—and the carriage clattered off the parade ground on to the street along the slope of Marinsky Park.

A few shots were fired after him. Then the ranks broke, and a desperate yelling and swearing started among us. The company of Makhno's men were pushed back against the wall, and they started to fight back with their rifle butts. The piercing two-fingered whistle of the bandits rose over the parade ground and the fort and—it seemed—all of Kiev.

The Makhno men were being beaten, clearly, because they had been Antoshchenko's favorites. They retreated into the first floor of the fort and began to fire back. It was hard to see what was going on. A crazy kind of fighting was swirling all across the parade ground, up the staircases and in the casemates. Fortunately no one paid any attention to us in the kitchen police, and we managed to get back to our barracks, without any casualties, and barricade ourselves.

The mutiny lasted for two hours before the fort was surrounded by an international regiment made up of former Hungarian and Austrian prisoners of war. Surprising as it might seem, nobody had been killed. There were a few wounded.

At eleven o'clock the next morning the regiment was lined up again on the parade ground. The men were still swearing at each other, and they formed ranks sullenly and angrily. It was announced that members of the government were coming to talk with the soldiers and to find out what had happened. A sigh of relief ran along the ranks.

A tribune made of rough planks was set up in the center of the square. Some members of the government, headed by Rakovsky, drove up in automobiles. The regiment presented arms. A band played the "Internationale." Looking at the motionless rows of soldiers, no one could have believed that a mutiny had taken place in this regiment a few hours before. Only a few heads were freshly bandaged after the wounds and contusions of the night before.

Antoshchenko slipped up onto the platform. He did not greet the regiment. He stood there trying to talk to the members of the government, but nobody would answer him.

Rakovsky spoke first. He talked softly and gently, calmed the soldiers down, and told them that a special commission would spend three days hearing all complaints against the commander of the regiment and that, if they were justified, the strongest measures would be taken.

Antoshchenko was standing behind Rakovsky. His face was flushed and a red scar on his cheek began to twitch nervously. He kept clenching and unclenching his hand on the hilt of his sword. In the end he could not control himself, he pushed Rakovsky aside, and shouted:

"How is it possible, Comrade Rakovsky, to talk so delicately with this cattle! The government can be lenient, but I don't have to be. Why should I have to put up with every kind of shit? I'll talk to them in my own way. First of all, what do you sons of bitches mean by complaining about your father-commander to our great and respected government? Who put this idea into your thick heads? You should not complain, you should kiss my hand. Which one of you, with your bandit snouts, has made this regiment? I, Antoshchenko! Who's given you boots, and uniforms? Again, it's I, Antoshchenko! Who feeds you with eggs in your porridge, and fresh butter, and full tobacco rations? Your commander, Comrade Antoshchenko. Without me, you'd have all been shot, I swear it by my dear father, the shoemaker in Khristinovka. But you complain! And you mutiny! Scoundrels! You, there, with the red face—three steps forward! No, not you, but the one in the Austrian coat. Who gave you that overcoat, a friend? Answer me!"

A soldier in an Austrian greatcoat moved three steps forward out of the ranks, stood at attention, but remained silent.

"I gave you everything. I, you snub-nosed fool! And who gave you those blue woolen puttees, made of pure English cloth? You don't know, you keep your eyes closed. I gave them to you illegally,

I, your commander Antoshchenko, because they're officer's puttees. I was sorry for you vermin. Why do you keep your eyes and your trap shut, like a dead man? Now, in the second place. You're all so brave in complaining about your commander, but you yourselves sell your bread rations to the monks in the Lavra. And you think I don't know about it. And who's trading in army overcoats on the Zhitny market? And who undressed those girls on Vladimir Hill and sent them back stark naked? I know it all. I've got you all right here"—Antoshchenko clenched and unclenched his red fist—"I can have every one of you shot right now!"

An adjutant tried to stop Antoshchenko, but the latter did not even look at him.

"You're making home-brew vodka in all your barracks, and you're using gas masks for the coils. You waste cartridges for fun and for making trouble when there aren't enough at the front for the struggle against the Ukrainian *atamans!* Well, that's enough. Good. I forgive you, in front of the government. To hell with you, there's no hate for you in my heart. Now, regiment, listen to me!"

Antoshchenko drew his curved sword. Its sharp blade glistened in the raw morning air.

"With a song, in front of the tribune of the government, from the right flank, by platoons, march!"

The band began to play, and the regiment moved awkwardly into a march in front of the tribune. The front ranks sang. The members of the government, without waiting for the march to end, jumped quickly down from the tribune, and went away.

The whole regiment wondered how it would all end. We were convinced that Antoshchenko would be removed from his command and disgraced. But the days went by, and nothing changed. Obviously, the government was not up to handling Antoshchenko. Denikin took Odessa. The situation was alarming.

Antoshchenko continued to strut around the fort, and he handled the regiment worse than before the mutiny.

The stormy, unhappy existence of the whole regiment came to an end at last, thanks to a soldier in our company, the same short, quiet-spoken Iosif Morgenstern whom I mentioned at the beginning of this chapter. This mild little man hated Antoshchenko fiercely, with a cold passion, especially after Antoshchenko threatened to "carve up" all the Jews in the regiment and clean it of its "Jerusalem gentry."

One day our company had been sent to mount a guard around some warehouses at the Baikovi Cemetery. We were even issued two cartridges each. It was a warm night. There was a smell of flowers in blossom. In the middle of the night the sickle of a dying moon rose over Kiev and swam through a soundless Ukrainian night.

To keep myself awake I was singing songs to myself. Suddenly I heard a horse running. Someone was riding up to the warehouse, dismounting, swearing heavily. I recognized Antoshchenko's voice. Sometimes he used to check the guards at night.

Antoshchenko walked up to the warehouse. Morgenstern was standing on sentinel duty at its door.

"Who goes there?" he cried out in his thin little voice.

"What's wrong with you, you pig?" Antoshchenko answered him. "Can't you see who it is?"

Then Morgenstern, who had of course immediately recognized the commander, yelled out three times, very quickly and without any pause but scrupulously following the rules: "Who goes there? Who goes there? Who goes there?" and then without waiting for any answer from Antoshchenko, he fired point-blank at him between the eyes.

They had to arrest Morgenstern but they let him go after one day's detention, and the whole regiment was quickly reorganized. Those of us who had been assigned to kitchen police were sent back to our homes.

I walked home in late twilight along Institutskaya Street, past the building of the Government Bank which had been designed, by the caprice of its architect, to look like the Palace of the Doges in Venice. The night was close, a storm was threatening, and little flashes of summer lightning were reflected against the polished columns of the bank. A light breeze murmured among the chestnut trees, and then grew still.

Someone was playing a piano behind an open window and he sang in a baritone voice: "He's far away, he doesn't know, he doesn't care about your grief." The gardens were filled with the smell of grass.

And I suddenly remembered the night after our final *gymnasium* ball when I had taken Olya Bogushevich home along Institutskaya Street under these same chestnut trees. Her dress had seemed to me too beautiful even for that beautiful night, and she herself had been all joy and loveliness.

I remembered that night, the girl's fingers cold with emotion when we said good night at her house, and her incredibly shining eyes in the light of the street lamp. And everything that had happened then seemed to me now an incredible dream of hundreds of years ago.

I couldn't believe that right next to this world of summer lightning and chestnut trees, fresh grass and quiet human voices, the tender trembling of a young girl, and books, and poetry, and secret hopes, right next to this clear and simple world there could exist a wild fanatic with stark madness in his eyes, the blood-hardened Antoshchenko, the man whom Morgenstern called "the fiend from hell." I couldn't help thinking how thin the film of civilization still is over our lives, and what depths of dark madness surge beneath it. But the light of the human mind can illuminate those depths to their very bottom. This was the great challenge of our future, of our work, of our still unconstructed life.

Twenty-odd years later I had to deliver a lecture in the municipal library in the city of Alma-Ata.

It was late in the autumn and the hard, dry poplar leaves were rustling. Irrigation ditches ran with ice-cold mountain water, which smelled like the sea. A thick sky hung over the Ala-Tau mountain tops, and behind those mountain tops lay India.

After my lecture, a short white-haired man with sad eyes came up to me.

"Don't you recognize me?" he asked.

"No. I don't remember your face."

"I'm Morgenstern. We served together in that guard regiment in Kiev."

"What are you doing now?" I asked him.

"It makes no difference," he answered, and he laughed. "But I'm glad for you. You have got to speak, in what you write, for all the people you've met and known in your life. Including your fellow soldier Morgenstern."

PUFF PASTRY

It was a summer morning with a gusty wind. The chestnut trees were making their untidy noise outside the windows, and cannon were barking far away in the direction of Fastov. Fighting was going on there against the Denikin forces advancing from the south.

Amalie's warm apartment smelled of fresh-ground coffee. She ground the last bean and the little coffee mill squeaked as if the coffee bean knew it was nearing the end of its existence.

As always, the smell of the coffee made the apartment seem cozier, even though the "present from the sea"—a broken thermometer decorated with seashells which hung on the wall—read the same in summer as in winter—always three degrees below zero. Those unchanging three degrees of frost sometimes made the apartment seem cooler than it was.

Someone knocked at the kitchen door. I heard Amalie opening it. After a short silence, she suddenly screamed:

"Yes! He's here! Right here! Of course!"

Amalie's voice broke. I ran into the kitchen. Two dust-covered beggars were standing there. Their heads were so wrapped around in old shawls that their eyes could not be seen.

A woman exclaimed, "Kostik!" in a lower voice and then sank down on a bench and dropped her head onto the kitchen table. A homemade cane fell out of her hand and clattered on the floor.

I recognized Mama's voice, knelt down beside her, and tried to see her face. Without looking at me she pressed my cheeks in her dry, cold hands and cried, almost without tears. Only her convulsive breathing betrayed that she was crying.

Galya just stood there, afraid to move; she probably could not see a thing. I noticed that her feet were wrapped in rags torn from a piqué bedspread, tied with string. I can still remember the green pattern of that old cloth. She had no glasses. She peered intently, stretching out her neck, into the corner of the kitchen where a sideboard stood, and asked Mama: "Well, what about it? Is he here, Kostik? Why don't you answer me? Where is he?"

Mama and Galya had come on foot from Kopan to Kiev. There had been no sense in staying any longer in Kopan. Little gangs of bandits had been descending on the farm nearly every day, but they seldom touched Mama or Galya, obviously because they had nothing which could have been looted. Other bandits even pitied Mama and, when they left, gave her a handful of dried rusks or some vegetable oil, and one bandit gave her a beautiful Spanish shawl which was full of holes. His story was that he had picked it up in the theater in Zhitomirsk.

Mama was all but finished by the last bandit, a man with the nickname "Angel of Vengeance." Having already seen dozens of *atamans,* she was amazed to find this "Angel of Vengeance" a bearded philosopher, wearing glasses. He had run a drugstore in Radomisl in the past, and considered himself an ideological anarchist. He called Mama "Madame" and took everything she had, down to her last needle, but he left her a detailed list of all the things he had taken, acknowledging her right to reclaim payment by means of this list "as soon as anarchism has embraced the whole world."

It took Mama and Galya two weeks to walk to Kiev. They deliberately dressed to look like beggars; in actual fact, this is what they were. Galya went without glasses, and walked holding on to Mama's shoulder, like a blind woman. No one would have believed them to be poor if Galya had worn her glasses. Everyone treated people in glasses suspiciously in those violent times. They thought them cunning enemies, and hated them bitterly. It is amazing that this distrust of people wearing glasses has persisted up to the present time.

Mama and Galya just rested for several days, making up for lost sleep, and a look of calm and happiness never left their faces. Then Mama decided to act, as she always did, and she began to help with Amalie's sewing. They had become friends at once, and two sewing machines were soon humming away in the apartment, while Galya settled down to making artificial flowers.

She made them slowly and carefully, out of different-colored pieces of cloth. I was amazed to see her set of metal tools and punches. She would stamp out rose petals, daisy blossoms, and different kinds of leaves from starched calico. Stamens and buds required a great deal of work. The flowers were fine, but they smelled of paint and glue and they became dusty very quickly.

I was sure in my heart that Galya was doing something quite useless, especially in times of revolution, hunger, and civil war. Who would ever buy flowers like these, when people had to risk fatal, skull-breaking expeditions to get a pound of barley flour or a glass full of sunflower oil? But it turned out that I was wrong.

Cloth flowers sold very well in little shops near the Baikovi Cemetery which specialized in cheap wreaths, gratings for tombs (these were made chiefly out of old bedsprings), sugary marble monuments, and florid steel crucifixes. Once a week an old woman who was a secondhand dealer would come to Galya, pick out her flowers, and advise Galya not to sweat too hard over them—they would sell anyway, because there weren't any others to be had. This advice always troubled Galya, and she would proceed to spend an entire day working on just one tea rose. She was conscientious to the point of self-torture.

The old secondhand dealer, who had a philosophic temperament, held fairly gloomy views on the human condition. She loved to expound them in her monotonous voice.

"When times are like ours," she said, "you can earn a living only with things that have always been, that are, and that will be on the earth, in spite of all our wars and revolutions. First of all, a man's hair never stops growing as long as the earth turns on its axis. And the earth turns, mind you, both day and night. So you can draw the conclusion, I think, that the best trade of all is the barber's. And then, second, men never stop dying. No matter what party is in power, dead people have to be buried. A dead man cannot dig his own grave, place a wreath on it, or write on it: 'Sleep well, dear husband Yasha,' or, 'You died fighting magnificently against the enemy.' This means that some kopecks can always be earned in this way, too. This is the way it all works out. What's one man's grief means bread for me. What's tears for somebody means a jug of milk for me."

Everyone in our house was frightened of this evil-mouthed old graveyard woman except Galya. She alone had the courage to engage her in long, useless arguments.

The cannon fire in the south grew louder. Soviet troops were fighting those of Denikin at the approaches to the city.

The calico cloth organization where I had returned to work after my time in the army began to evacuate the city. They took the bales of cloth to the railroad station and sent them to the north.

I arrived at the office one morning to find a notice pinned on the door. It had been printed on a typewriter I knew, which had no letter "r": "Oganization evacuated Addess all queies by telephone." I climbed the dark staircase, covered with scraps of matting, hoping to find some of my colleagues. Not one showed up.

I went back to the street, confused, and saw about twenty wounded Red Army soldiers. Dusty and exhausted, they were limping heavily along the pavement. Some had fresh white bandages around their arms, some around their heads.

I followed them. It was clear that these men had just come out of heavy fighting and had got to the city on foot. They went along Vassilkovskaya Street, then along the Kreshchatik, and started to go down to the Dnieper at Podol. As they walked along, the noisy trading streets grew quieter and quieter. Passers-by stopped and watched them for a long time. Terror started to follow the wounded men down the Kreshchatik, and quickly spread into all the neighboring streets.

I caught up with one of the Red Army men and asked him where the fighting was taking place.

"Near Krasny Kabachok," he answered without looking at me. "It's hot there right now, comrade."

The Denikin troops were coming up from the south, and Krasny Kabachok lay to the west of Kiev.

"Has Denikin already surrounded the city? Are there many of his troops?" someone asked from the crowd.

"What kind of Denikin troops?" the Red Army soldier answered sadly. "I never saw a single one there."

"With whom were you fighting, then?"

"Against the enemy, of course," the soldier said, and he laughed and went on with his comrades.

It was all impossible to understand. When shells began, an hour later, to scream over the city with the sound we all recognized, exploding on Podol and on the river docks, complete confusion seized the city. A move to the cellars started all over again. Again we set up duty watches in the courtyards, got out oil lamps which flickered with each explosion, filled receptacles with water, listened to rumors, and sat up through sleepless nights.

It may well be that night watch was the calmest occupation a man could have in those violent times. I came to love my assignment in our little courtyard next to the rusty iron window in the equally rusty old gate. For some reason, in that crowded little courtyard, with its single spreading chestnut tree, I felt as safe as if I were in an impregnable fortress. Civilians assigned to such watches had no weapons, and could have none. Men were shot out of hand for possession even of a child's Monte Cristo air rifle. The only thing one had to do on watch was to waken all the residents of the building at the slightest alarm, so that danger might not hit them unawares. A copper pan and a hammer hanging in the courtyard served to do this.

It must be that I loved these nights because of their strange, completely false feeling of safety right next to great danger. The danger was always hiding right there, on the other side of the quarter-inch sheet metal covering the window. You had only to open the little door and walk across its threshold to come face to face with the unknown and terrible things which possessed the dead streets of Kiev on a dark night, to hear something stealing along the little garden, and to feel with all your nerve ends the lead bullet which was whistling through the air, coming straight for you.

This terror disappeared inside the courtyard. You had only to sit very still and listen hard and not give yourself away by any move. Instinct tells wild animals that their only safety is in complete silence and total dark, which will prevent them from being noticed.

An elderly history teacher at the former Levandovsky girls' *gymnasium* named Avel Isidorovich Stankover sometimes sat out the night watch with me. In spite of the fact that he taught in a girls' school, he hated women bitterly. A short man, with a long disheveled beard and red cheeks, slovenly and always angry, he never tired of calling down curses, like the prophet Jeremiah, on all women without exceptions.

He could talk calmly only about the Middle Ages. He held that they had been the finest time in human history. He had his own reasons for this belief, excluding of course the medieval worship of beautiful damsels and of Madonnas. All the rest suited Stankover perfectly.

He used to number the attractions of the Middle Ages on his fingers. First, the world was more spacious. Second, the woods and the rivers ran right up to the thresholds of men's dwellings. A man could breathe the life-giving air of the forests and eat the simple fruits of the earth, and not have to live on kerosene fumes and canned goods. Third, magnificent poetry flourished in those times, and human thinking was no less brilliant than today. Fourth, man himself was simpler, clearer, and more attractive than he became after the blossoming of modern civilization.

Stankover never missed a chance to show me the beauty of the Middle Ages. He talked as if he could have moved me bodily back to those distant times, and as if I could freely choose the epoch in which I lived. He spoke like a recruiting agent, like an inspired adherent to a cause, like the official representative of the Middle Ages, and he talked about them as if he himself had just returned from there.

Stankover used even the civil war in the Ukraine and our night watches to celebrate the Middle Ages. On the night when the Red forces evacuated Kiev and no one knew whose artillery was throwing an arc of fire over the city, Stankover told me:

"I don't know how you feel, my young friend, but I'd like to live in a medieval castle. That was the only place, in those dangerous times, where a man could experience blessed peace and safety. He could walk out of the woods, where he ran a risk at every step of being hung on the first oak bough, into the eternal sanctuary of its crenellated walls. The drawbridge would be raised after him against the closed castle gates, and a man could enjoy not only the happiness of being safe, but all the fullness of life. The sunny quiet of enormous courts shone with life, the air was full of it, it sounded in the song of the horns summoning the people in the castle to their meals. It was bound into the illuminated manuscripts in the library where the breeze rustled the heavy pages. A man was relaxed about his life, and only in that condition, my young friend, can a man create things of immortal value."

In the daytime, Stankover showed me plans and drawings of old castles, with their great towers, their dungeons, their loopholes, their corridors, their labyrinths of darkened rooms, their two-meter-thick walls, their inside gardens, and their wells. All castles used to stand on the tops of hills, protected by unclimbable cliffs. And from all directions blew the winds of Normandy and the Ile de France, of Lotharingia and Savoy, Bohemia and the Apennines. From the lofty sun, like a great crown, light fell on the towers, the waving standards, and the tiles covered with moss.

Mama liked especially to listen to Stankover. When I was on duty, she would get up in the night, put on a warm dress and come out to the courtyard. We would sit behind a jut in the building and talk in whispers, stopping often to listen to some mysterious sound.

Mama, who like all mothers still thought of Galya and me as quite small children, urged me simpleheartedly to talk with Stankover as often as possible.

"He's like a deep well of every kind of wisdom," Mama said. "A walking university. It would be very useful to you to meet him more often, Kostik. Don't underestimate such people."

No, I have never neglected such people. On the contrary, I could listen to them for hours. I have always been grateful to them for their wide understanding and for the generosity with which they shared it with me.

It has always surprised me that they, in their turn, were grateful to me for listening to them. It was clear that they were not spoiled by attention, and I could explain this only by the fact that, in Pushkin's precise phrase, we Russians are "lazy and uncurious." Neither the *gymnasium* nor the university taught me as much of what is deeply and absorbingly interesting as have books and meetings with people. And I, an extraordinarily shy man, have always envied others who can meet the people around them easily and start lively conversations with them quickly. It has always taken me a lot of time to do this.

Shells whistled over the city all through the night. They exploded on Podol with a noise as if someone were beating the ground with sheaves of iron rods.

At dawn the Soviet forces moved out of the city and up the Dnieper, and it grew quiet.

Early in the morning Mama, who had an unusual curiosity and a complete disregard of danger, went out in the city, as she said, to reconnoiter. She came back quickly and announced that the city was empty, that Denikin's troops had not yet entered it, but that in places some foresighted citizens were already hanging out their red, white, and blue Tsarist flags.

While we were drinking carrot tea in the kitchen, we could hear shouting outside on Fundukleyevskaya Street. We went out on the balcony. Not Denikin's troops but Petliura's were marching down the street with their yellow and blue flags. They were marching calmly and confidently, showing off their Austrian uniforms. And all the fat Ukrainians who had disappeared a short time ago were out in their embroidered shirts, shouting greetings to the troops and throwing their moth-eaten astrakhan hats into the air.

The city was puzzled. Instead of Denikin, Petliura had marched in. His troops marched up to the Kreshchatik, occupied it, set up a bivouac, and hung their flag from the Municipal Duma. Any flag on this building was a kind of declaration. Every new occupying power hung one there as a sign that it would not be driven out without a struggle.

Rumors immediately began to fly that Denikin was giving Kiev to Petliura and that the White forces, bypassing the city from the south, were moving in the direction of Orlov. Dazed by all the unexpected changes and overturns of government, the population no longer cared much who held the city if only the newcomers would not shoot many people, or loot, or throw them out of their homes. So the arrival of the Petliura troops was greeted with complete indifference.

But at one o'clock the first cavalry detachments of General

Denikin, followed by a regiment of Don Cossacks, moved into the city across Pechersk, from the direction of the Lavra. They advanced as far as the Kreshchatik, were enormously surprised to find Petliura's men already there—as surprised as the citizenry—and began to try to find out just what had happened.

It turned out that an entire division of Petliura's had been hiding in the villages west of the city for a long time, waiting for its chance. No one knew about them. Taking advantage of the Soviet withdrawal, this division had decided to get ahead of Denikin, advanced on the city, and occupied it after two days of fighting.

This, of course, did not please the Denikin soldiers. Some secret and complicated negotiations began between them and Petliura's men. Then a red, white, and blue flag was broken out on the balcony of the Municipal Duma, right next to the Petliura flag, showing that there was now a dual rule over the city.

This completely confounded the citizens of Kiev. It was impossible to know who really held power in the city. But all doubts were ended by evening when Denikin's men brought up reinforcements. Two of his Cossack regiments suddenly poured down like lava from the Pechersk hills on the unsuspecting Petliura forces.

The Cossacks were carrying their booty on their lances, whooping, firing into the air, and waving their drawn swords. No nerves were strong enough to stand up against this kind of sudden attack. The Petliura men ran away without firing a shot, throwing their guns away as they ran. And the same fat old Ukrainians who had greeted them that morning stood now on their balconies and on the pavements, shaking their fists in rage and shouting "Shame!" at them. But Petliura's soldiers paid no attention and went right on running, looking back and stuffing things in their pockets as they ran.

They recovered themselves only outside the city, when they had run as far as Svyatoshin. They stopped there to catch their breath. And the only battery they had left fired a dozen shells blindly back at the city. There were no casualties, if you don't count a shattered ice-cream stand on Vladimir Hill and an ear knocked off by a shell from the plaster monument to one of the great enlighteners of Russia—perhaps it was Kyril, perhaps Mefodi.

By morning a proclamation signed by General Bredov, one of Denikin's officers, was pasted up all over the city announcing that, from that day on and forever, Kiev had become again a part of the one and indivisible Russia.

THE CRY IN THE NIGHT

It must have been that late hour of the night when everything slowly dies a little in a swamp of darkness and of silence. Even the water dried up in its rusty pipes in the middle of the night and stopped dripping, drop by drop, out of the faucet into the iron kitchen sink.

It is in this numbness of the night that the most tangled dreams occur. These are the dreams that make your heart ache afterwards.

Someone was trying to rouse me for a long time, but I could not wake up. Or rather, I did not want to wake up, and I groped agonizingly in a dim blurring of consciousness for some strip of light which eluded me.

Suddenly a sobbing broke through this tangled struggle with sleep. I opened my eyes, sat up quickly on my bed, and saw Mama. She was sitting at my feet. Her hair fell in gray braids across her face. She was holding on to the bed and crying, dully, feverishly.

"What's the matter?" I asked in a whisper. "What's happened?"

"Quiet," Mama said, swallowing her tears. "You'll wake Galya."

"But what's wrong? Tell me."

"I don't know," Mama answered, in confusion, and her head was trembling. It seemed to me that Mama was losing her mind. "I don't know what's happened, but it must be something terrible. Get up and listen. Go out on the balcony."

I groped my way to the balcony. Its door was half open. I walked out, listened, and suddenly froze—from far away in the direction of Vassilkovskaya Street, pouring over the whole city closer and closer to our building, came a many-voiced scream of terror, the death cry of a large number of people. You could not hear a single separate voice.

"What is it?" I asked in the darkness.

"It's a pogrom," Amalie answered unexpectedly behind my back. Her teeth were chattering. She could no longer stand it, obviously, and was on the edge of hysteria.

I listened again. Only the scream could be heard, and there were no other signs of a pogrom—no shots, no sound of breaking glass, no sign of fire over the buildings, none of the things which go with a pogrom.

It had been quiet for a little while after the terrible *gaidamak* pogroms. And it stayed quiet for a while after Denikin took over. For the present they were not touching the Jews. Occasionally, but only at some distance from the more populated streets, a few Junkers with drug-crazed eyes, prancing on their horses, would sing their favorite song:

> *Black Hussars!*
> *Save our Russia, beat the Jews.*
> *For they are the commissars!*

But after the Soviet forces had thrown Denikin's out of Oryol and begun to drive southwards, the mood of the Whites changed. Pogroms started in the little towns and villages of the Ukraine.

The ring of these pogroms had been tightening around Kiev and finally, on the night I am describing, the first night pogrom began on Vassilkovskaya Street. The thugs surrounded one of the big buildings but did not succeed in breaking into it. In the dark, quiet building, shattering the evil silence of the night, a woman screamed, piercingly, in terror and despair. She had no other way to defend her children—nothing but this unbroken, unwavering shriek of fear and helplessness.

Suddenly the woman's single scream was answered by an exactly similar cry from the whole building, all the way from the ground floor to the roof. The thugs could not stand it, and started to run. But there was no place for them to hide; outstripping them, all the buildings along Vassilkovskaya Street were now screaming, and along all the little lanes which led away from it.

The cry grew like the wind, covering block after block. The most frightening thing about it was that it was coming from dark buildings, which seemed uninhabited, and that the streets were all deserted and dead with nothing but an occasional dull street lamp seeming to light the way for the quivering, wailing scream.

I learned about this later. At the moment, without knowing what was going on, I started to get dressed in a hurry, to go out where this heartrending cry was coming from. Mama also started to get dressed. She was determined to go with me.

I had no clear idea of why I was going. I couldn't stay at home. I knew I would not feel quiet until I had learned the reason for that cry. Not knowing was the most evil thing of all for anyone near those accursed city streets that night.

We never had to go out. While we were dressing, Fundukleyev-skaya Street right next to us and a three-story building next door to us began to scream. Not a single light was burning in the windows. I went out on the balcony again, and I saw some men dash out of the screaming buildings and race down the street. They must have been the thugs who were starting the pogrom.

I had a real attack of nerves. Amalie was sitting on the floor, rocking back and forth, her face in her hands, groaning. Mama was giving her spirits of valerian. I kept on listening. By now Podol was screaming, and Bessarabka, and the whole enormous city. The cry must have been heard far beyond the city limits. It beat up against the low dark sky and bounced back again, a cry for mercy and compassion.

The pogrom did not take place. The Denikin commanders, who had not expected this turn of affairs, grew confused. Armed detachments were sent into all sections of the city. All the street lamps were lighted. By morning a reassuring order by the commander-in-chief of the Denikin forces had been pasted up on the walls. And the next day the well-known conservative Shulgin published an article in the *Kievlyanin* titled "Torture by Fear," which sharply criticized the Denikin command for its toleration of pogroms.

I had heard individuals cry in fear, and even crowds of people, but never before had I heard an entire city cry. It was unbearably frightening, because it drove out of one's consciousness all notion —naïve as it may be—of the basic humanity required of everyone. These people had been crying to the very last remnants of man's conscience.

During those days in Kiev these last remnants of conscience went to work, and there was no pogrom. But this was sheer accident. It could have happened—indiscriminate killings of innocent people are not rare in history. Man's progress toward justice, freedom, and happiness has been truly frightening at times. And only a deep faith in the victory of light and intelligence over black stupidity has kept despair from full possession of our minds.

The strength of the human conscience is indeed so immense that one should never completely lose faith in it. Not long ago, a writer told me an amazing story about this.

This writer had grown up in Latvia, and he spoke Latvian perfectly. Soon after the war, he was traveling from Riga to Vzmorye by electric train. An old, quiet, gloomy Latvian was sitting across from him. I don't know how the conversation started which gave the old man his chance to tell this story.

"Listen to this," the old man had said. "I live on the outskirts of Riga. A man moved in, sometime before the war, into the house next to mine. He was not much of a man. I would even have said that he was a dishonorable and evil man. He was a speculator. You know yourself that people like that have neither heart nor conscience. I know, some people say that speculation is just a way of getting rich. But on what? On human grief, on the tears of children, and mostly on our greed. This man was engaged in all kinds of speculation, with his wife. Yes . . .

"Well, the Germans captured Riga and drove all the Jews into a ghetto, so that they could kill part of them and leave the rest to starve to death. The whole ghetto was ringed off, and a cat couldn't have got out of it. Anyone who walked up to within fifty paces of the guards was shot on the spot. The Jews, and especially the children, were dying by the hundreds every day, and this was when my neighbor had a bright idea—to load his cart with potatoes, bribe the guards to let him drive into the ghetto, and trade the potatoes for gold and precious stones. And people used to say that the Jews still had a lot of these, even in the ghetto.

"So that is what he did. I ran into him in the street just before he went, and just listen to what he told me. 'I'll offer the potatoes,' he said, 'only to women with children.'

" 'Why?' I asked.

" 'Because they'll be ready to give anything to save their children and so I'll make a lot more.'

"I kept silent, but it wasn't easy. Can you see this?"

The Latvian took his pipe out of his mouth and showed his teeth. Several of them were missing.

"I didn't say a word, but I bit my pipe so hard that I broke it and two of my teeth. People say that blood rushes to the head. I don't know. With me, blood rushes not to my head, but to my hands and my fists. They felt as heavy as if they had been poured out of steel. And if he hadn't walked away, I might have killed him, right there on the street. He must have guessed it, because he sort of darted away from me and scurried off like a polecat. . . . But that's by the way. That night he loaded up his cart with sacks of potatoes and drove into the Riga ghetto. The German guard stopped him but, you know, wicked people can make a deal just by looking at each other. He gave the guard a bribe, and the guard told him: 'You're a fool. Go on in, but they haven't got anything left except their empty stomachs. You'll find out. You'll be driving back with all your rotten potatoes. I'll bet you on it.'

"Once in the ghetto, he drove into a large courtyard. Women

and children were swarming around his cart with the potatoes. They just watched quietly while he untied the first sack. One woman was standing there with a little boy's dead body in her arms, and holding out a broken gold watch in the palm of her hand. 'You're crazy!' this man shouted suddenly. 'What do you want potatoes for when he's already dead? Get away from here!' He told me himself later that he didn't understand what happened to him then. He clenched his teeth, started to rip open the tops of the potato sacks and to spill the potatoes on the ground.

" 'Quick!' he told the women. 'Give me your children. I'll take them out. But be sure they shut up, and don't move around. Hurry!' The mothers, hurrying, began to hide their frightened children in the sacks, and he tied up the tops again. Do you realize, those women didn't even have time to kiss their children? And they knew perfectly well they'd never see them again. He piled his cart full with these sacks of children, and he just left a few sacks of potatoes around the edges, and then he drove out. The women were kissing the muddy cart wheels, and he drove on without looking around. He shouted at his horses with all the voice he had, because he was afraid one of the children might start to cry, and give them all away. But the children kept quiet.

"Well, the guard he knew spotted him from quite a distance and shouted at him: 'What did I tell you? I knew you were a fool. Get the hell away from here now, with your stinking potatoes, before the lieutenant shows up.'

"So he drove by the guards, swearing as loud as he could against those damned Jews and their children. He did not go home, but along a deserted little country road to a place in the woods near Tukumso where there were some of our guerillas, and he gave the children to them, and they hid them in a safe place. He told his wife that the Germans had confiscated all his potatoes and held him under arrest for two days. When the war was over, he got a divorce and left Riga."

The old man was silent for a while.

"Now I think," and for the first time he smiled, "that it would have been a mistake if I had let myself go and hit him with my fist."

THE WEDDING PRESENT

The train took eighteen days to go from Kiev to Odessa. I have never counted up how many hours this was, but I know that every hour of that exhausting trip seemed twice as long as normal to us who were passengers on it. The reason must have been that every hour hid within itself the threat of death.

It's true that only three men were killed and a few more wounded by stray bullets in our heated boxcars, but all of us, and especially the young priests—students at the Zhitomir Catholic Seminary—considered these low casualties a miracle. The priests were trying to get through to Poland by an incredible route, through Constantinople, Salonika, Belgrade, and Budapest. None of us, of course, really believed that a single one of them would ever get to Poland alive.

In the autumn, while the Whites were still holding a line between Oryol and Kursk and felt themselves in no danger, Kiev was suddenly startled on a warm early morning by the noise of heavy machine-gun firing. As was always the case, nothing could be learned except by reconnaissance, and Mama undertook to find out. While all the rest of us were dressing in a hurry, she went out in the streets and quickly came back, cheerful and excited.

I was always amazed at Mama's bravery. The explanation was that she was a convinced fatalist and really believed that every life was controlled by an immutable fate. You can never escape your destiny. What was written down at your birth—this will happen to you.

Mama brought back amazing news. Soviet forces were attacking Kiev from the west and had already captured part of the city as far as the Galitsky market. But it was a long way from Kiev to the nearest Soviet territory. It was impossible to believe that any Soviet troops had been able to cover that distance unnoticed by the Whites. So their very appearance seemed something of a miracle. But it was a tangible one, and the proof of it was the bullets which were biting into the brick walls of our long-suffering building.

It turned out that some Soviet regiments, retreating from the south at the very start of the Denikin offensive, had moved into the vast, almost impassable Irpensky swamps near Kiev, and had settled down there for the whole summer. Not only the Denikin command but even the citizens of Kiev had not suspected their presence. Peasants in the villages around the swamps had never breathed a word about the existence of these Soviet regiments.

Now they had suddenly erupted on Kiev, seized half the city, captured a good deal of provisions and weapons, and prepared to fight their way northward to join up with their own forces. The fighting was severe. It flared up in savage battles, first in one section of the city, then in another, and died down only in the evening.

The next day it became known that General Bredov, who was in command of the Denikin forces, had decided to demand the mobilization of all men up to the age of forty. So I decided to run away from this mobilization, to Odessa.

Mama was already much calmer. She had a room in Kiev, and I left her almost all my money. By this time Galya had started to earn quite a lot from her artificial flowers. Besides, Mama and Galya had both become Amalie's friends, and I knew that she would not desert them.

We agreed that I would come back to Kiev as soon as everything had settled down. So I went off to Odessa with an easy heart.

The first night passed quietly enough, although some fires danced in the wind on the horizon. The train crept stealthily along, without any lights. It stopped often and stood for long times, as if listening to the muddled noises of the night, unable to make up its mind to go on. Sometimes it even reversed and went backwards a little, and seemed to be hiding in the shadows from some fire that was too bright. And every time it seemed to me that black horsemen, who had not seen us, were riding along the railroad embankment far in front of us.

Five priests were traveling in our car, a journalist from *The Russian Word* named Nazarov, and a thin, fidgety Odessan with the ribbon of the Legion of Honor in his buttonhole. His name was Victor Khvat. He had served with the French Army and had even taken part in the famous Battle of the Marne. Khvat spent most of the time making jokes, chiefly about his Jewish origin. He joked, probably, to hide his fright. We all realized that if we ran into any bandits—and they were then swarming all over the Ukraine—Khvat would be the first of us to be shot.

There were many expressions current in those days for being shot: "being put against the wall," "being exchanged," "being liquidated," "transferred to Dukhonin's staff," "written off to expenses." Every region of the country had its own favorite phrase for it. Khvat's wit was a real asset. A successful wisecrack might mean the difference between life and death.

Nazarov had his assets, too, which had saved him several times from disaster—a simple heart and very bad eyes. His simple heart made even the most indomitable bandits like him, and his near-sightedness was considered by them to be a sure sign of complete helplessness and harmlessness.

The priests were all pale, quiet, and excessively polite young men. In moments of danger, they made the sign of the cross and watched the rest of us with frightened eyes. But by the end of the third day, they had lost their clean-shaven, elegant appearance. We all had to go for days without a chance to wash. Their robes were torn while they were loading wood for fuel—the priests were the most zealous choppers of wood for the engine and they became specialists at breaking up the fences around stations and the signalmen's cottages along the track. Victor Khvat was in charge of this work.

A plump, cheerful woman climbed into our car at Fastova. She had young, furious eyes. Her name was Lusena. Before she climbed in, she threw in through the door a dusty package sewed up in an old torn gypsy's shawl. The priests were sitting on rough planks next to the door, chewing some bone-hard cookies made of rye flour.

"Ah, you louts!" Lusena called to the priests. "Give a woman a hand. You can see for yourselves that I can't climb in."

The priests jumped up, embarrassed at not having noticed her, and with their combined efforts they managed to pull Lusena into the car.

"Foo-oo," she sighed, and she looked around the boxcar, "you don't seem to have a very stylish setup here."

The priests said nothing, still embarrassed.

"All right, you abbots!" Lusena said when she had finished her inspection and pulled up a much-darned silk stocking. "I'll take that dark corner over there. Just so you won't think I have any designs on your virginity. Which you need, by the way, about as much as a dead man needs a poultice."

One of the priests started to giggle, but Victor Khvat said in an easy, familiar way:

"I'm convinced, my dear, that we'll be done for now, with your assistance. But at least we'll die happily, and with some flourish."

"Shut up, pipsqueak!" Lusena answered him in an affected

bass voice. "Or don't you know that I come from Odessa and that
I've seen a lot of friars cleaner than you are? I don't dance the
cancan, even though I used to work as a singer at the Tivoli Café
in Kharkov. I can sing you songs, my boy, that will make your thin
blood boil. And anyway it wouldn't hurt you to treat a young lady
to one of those cookies, especially when she hasn't tasted a thing
for two whole days. No joking!"

We gave her some cookies, and at that moment what Khvat
called "a new and happy life" began in our boxcar. There were
no limits to Lusena's temperament nor to her appetite for life.
Lusena transformed everything, even the constant threat of shooting and capture by bandits, into an excuse for laughter, and for
making fun of the priests who were driven to their wit's end by
her presence. She competed with Khvat in making jokes, she sang
music-hall songs, she treated the priests to her most seductive
anecdotes. The priests just sighed, but we could see more and more
often in their eyes a spark of real admiration for this woman they
called "the great adulteress Panna Lusena." They clearly liked her
very much. In the end they were looking for justifications for her
in all the dogmas of the Catholic Church, in both the Old and New
Testaments, and in the Papal encyclicals.

Finally they called her the Mary Magdalene of our times. They
explained to all of us that that beautiful red-haired prostitute, who
had sinned day and night for years, had been added to the list of
saints for her honorable love for Christ when she had thrown herself on the crucifix on Golgotha, covered his wounded feet with the
thick coils of her splendid hair, and soothed the pain from his
wounds.

How many women have followed that same path of sin and then
become saints! The proof of their salvation is in the little golden
halos painted over their heads by all the great masters of the
Renaissance. It is also in the white lilies brushed by the hem of
their skirts, sweetening the air with the fragrance of chastity.

The priests talked about all this in low voices. I understood
Polish and while I listened to them I began to suspect that
Catholicism, with its cult of the Madonna, is another manifestation
of man's delicate, clear, and eternal sensuality. I became completely
convinced of this much later when, in the many-colored half-light
of the cathedrals of Rome and Naples, I saw the pale Madonnas
with their long eyelashes and the mysterious Gioconda smiles on
their little, red, quivering lips.

Now, many years later, these conversations and these ideas
seem to me unlikely ever to have happened at all in that half-

demolished boxcar where the autumn wind whistled through
the bullet holes and utterly different people lived a friendly, happy
life together—the impoverished prostitute Lusena, a chevalier
of the legion of Honor, the weaksighted philosopher Nazarov,
clutching his little volume of Heine, the priests, and I—at that time
a man without any profession, much addicted to flights of imagination.

The train stopped often, and the engine would start to emit
imploring little whistles. This meant that there was no more fuel
and that the passengers, if they wanted to proceed farther and not
wait for bandits to descend upon them, would have to jump out of
the cars and chop up the nearest fences or the storehouses which
lined the station markets. Then Khvat would open the heavy door
with a laugh and shout to the priests:
"Hey, Your Reverences! To your axes!"
We had a crowbar and two axes in our car. The priests would
grab them and jump out, holding up their robes and revealing heavy
soldiers' boots and puttees under them. The rest of us would jump
out, too, and run up to the nearest fence. These raids were not
always successful. Sometimes the owners of the fences would open
fire on us with sawed-off shotguns. Then the engineer would start
his engine without blowing the whistle, Khvat would yell: "Christ-
loving legion! To horse!" and we would all have to jump aboard
while the train was moving.
Beyond Belaya Tserkov the train was shot up frequently. The
firing usually came from woods and thickets next to the right of
way, and we could not see who was firing at us. We would lie flat
on the floor or, as Khvat put it, "try to reduce the size of the target."
Khvat asserted that a man lying down was sixteen times less
visible than a man standing up.
This didn't reassure us much, especially after a stray bullet
came through the wall right next to Lusena's head and knocked a
tall Spanish comb out of her luxuriant hair. The comb had been
an inheritance from her grandmother, who had sold little ring-
shaped rolls in the town of Ribnitsa on the Dniester River. Glancing
off the comb, the bullet ricocheted around the car and seemed, for
a few seconds, to have gone crazy looking for a way out. But the
bullet hit the wall again and fell next to one of the priests. He
picked it up, put it away in his little bag, and swore that he would
hang it on a silver chain on the Chenstokhov icon of the Mother
of God in gratitude for our escape from death.
Lusena straightened her hair, sat on a plank, and sang a shrill

rollicking song which delighted all the priests. Then she thought
for a minute and said:

"If I get killed, be sure to bury me in my gypsy shawl. And I
haven't any doubt you priests will sing me out of this world in
first-class style."

A strange kind of stirring could be seen among the priests, who
were lying face downwards on the floor; there were fewer bullets
now, but the firing continued. It looked as if they were all trying
hard not to burst out laughing.

"And they'll let me into Heaven," Lusena went on. "They'll
even be very glad to. Because I'll sing Peter such a fine little song
that he'll double over with laughter and he'll blow his nose, and
then he'll say: 'Mademoiselle Lusena, I am terribly sorry to have
met you in this tedious heaven and not on the sinful earth. You
and I could have lived together so wonderfully that people would
have shaken their heads in wonder and delight.' "

Then one of the priests said:

"That's blasphemy, Panna Lusena. But the Blessed Virgin will
forgive you for it. As we forgave you a long time ago."

"Thanks for that," Lusena answered, and then she added in a
very low voice, "You fellows are all dear to me. If you only knew
how good I feel! Nobody badgers me, nobody says anything mean to
me, nobody treats me like a tart. And none of you even knows that
I've been shot already, in the breast. I shot myself in Lugansk.
That's a damned bad town. That's where my little son died. My
little boy . . ."

She lay face down on the floor and grew still. We were all silent.

"And why in the devil am I going to Odessa? Just what in hell
do I need there?" Lusena suddenly said, without raising her head.

I stood up and opened the door carefully. A blue little river
was looping through the dry steppes. A white autumn sun shone
in the sky. Its tender warmth slanted down against my face. And
to the south, toward the distant sea, where our grunting, jerking
train was taking us, a flock of cranes flew by in the mist high above
us.

A pockmarked, red-haired old woman got on our train at Korsyn.
She was going to Znamenka to celebrate the marriage of her
daughter and she was taking along a heavy chest filled with the
dowry. She was a loud, frantic old woman. Dirty yellow lace hung
down below her skirt and brushed against her blackened, hobnailed
boots.

She ordered the hungry railroadmen around like an *ataman*.
She shouted at them, demanding that her chest be put in the

heated boxcar. But we wouldn't let her and her chest in the car.
The whole train by now was infuriated at her and her chest and her
flushed face and her shrill voice.

This was the first time, I think, that I ever saw a real and
typical kulak, or rich peasant living on the labor of others—
greedy, wicked, brazen in her knowledge of her own worth and
her own wealth in the midst of general ruin and poverty. The
Ukraine was full of cruel, arrogant kulaks in those days. One of
these women would strangle her own father for the profit that
might be in it, and their "little sons" flocked in bands to the
atamans, to Makhno and Zelony, where they cold-bloodedly buried
people alive in the ground, split open children's heads with their
gun butts, and cut strips of leather from the backs of Jews and
Red Army men.

This old lady fussed around her chest, first untying and then
tying up again the warm shawl around her neck, and she cried out
in a strained voice:

"You've filled the train full of hungry tramps, so there's no
place for us, the masters. They've got nothing but a hole in their
pants, all these city characters with their girls. They ought to be
stamped on, like worms, not go gallivanting between Kiev and
Odessa."

A stoop-shouldered station official was standing next to the
mutinous old lady, humble and silent.

"And what are you standing there for like an old goat? Why
do you think I gave you bread and lard? Just so every no-good
tramp here could laugh at me? You promised to get me a seat—
well, get me a seat. Or I'll take the bread and the lard back from
you."

The official shrugged his shoulders and walked along the train.
He looked in the doors and asked the passengers, in a low voice
so the old woman could not hear him:

"Let her in, the old bitch, do it for me as a favor. Her husband
is the village elder here, a bandit. He'll beat me to death. There's
not a crumb of bread anywhere around here, and she gave me a
loaf."

But the people in the cars were unyielding. Then the official
made a deal with the engineer, and the latter agreed, for a promise
of bread and lard, to put the chest between the lamps on the very
front of the locomotive. They dragged it up there, with difficulty,
and tied it with a heavy rope. The old woman sat on it like a brood
hen, covering it with her dirty skirt, tightened the warm shawl
around her neck, and the train moved off.

So we traveled, with the chest on the front of the engine, the old woman white with rage sitting on it, and all the little boys along the track whistling and hooting at her. She untied her bag at every stop and ate, greedily and enormously. Maybe she didn't want to eat each time, but she was doing it on purpose, with evil in her heart, to have her revenge on the hungry passengers and to gloat over them. She carved enormous pieces of tender pink suet, tore a roast chicken apart with her greasy fingers, and stuffed her mouth with soft white bread. Her cheeks were drenched with sweat. After eating, she would belch loudly, and then pant. She almost never got off the chest and even her most personal needs never led her more than two or three paces from the engine. This showed not only a lack of modesty but a massive contempt for everyone and everything. The engineer grunted and turned away, but he said nothing. He had not yet received a crumb of bread or a smidgeon of lard. They had been promised him only at Znamenka when he delivered the old woman and her daughter's dowry.

The entire train bitterly hated her and her chest. In some, this hatred overcame even the fear of death. They were waiting impatiently for the first "good gang of bandits" to shoot up our train efficiently. We were all sure the old woman would be the first to be killed—with her chest she made a perfect target.

Somewhere beyond Bobrinsk our dreams of revenge came true, but only in part. Just before evening a Makhno gang shot up the train. Several bullets hit the chest. The old woman remained whole, but the bullets damaged some of the dowry and left holes in it. From that point on she sat as if made of stone, pressing her blue lips tight together, and there was so much black hatred in her eyes that during our stops the passengers chose not to walk past the locomotive without some special reason.

We were still waiting for revenge. I remembered Mama's favorite law of retribution. When the priests heard about it, they brightened up and cheerfully affirmed that such a law really does exist and had not lost its power even in days of civil war, but Lusena said that there was no such law, but only little men who couldn't make up their minds to drop the old woman and her chest over the first bridge we came to.

But finally retribution came. As might have been expected, the sky was filled with torn black clouds. They were scudding over the hungry fields with incredible speed. Sheets of rain were beating like hail against the decrepit walls of the station at Znamenka. It seemed the gods of retribution must have unleashed those black clouds, that rain, and the wet, cutting wind across the earth.

It all started when the old woman gave the engineer only one loaf of bread and a pound of lard instead of the two loaves and five pounds he had been promised. The engineer did not say a word. He even thanked her and, with the fireman's help, began to unload the chest from the front of the engine. It must have weighed at least fifteen *poods* [540 pounds]. They finally managed to get it off the engine and put it down on the track.

"Two perfectly healthy bums," the old woman said, "and you haven't got the strength to wrestle with one chest. Move it further over here."

"Just try to move it yourself, by God!" the engineer said. "It won't work without a crowbar. I'll get one right away."

He climbed back up in his cab for the crowbar. But instead of getting it, he released two streams of hot whistling steam from both sides of the engine. The old woman screamed and jumped away. Then the engineer started the locomotive and ploughed straight into the chest, which broke to pieces with a great crash. All the dowry—quilted bedclothes, shirts, dresses, towels, German silver knives, spoons, pieces of material, and even a big nickel-plated samovar—erupted into the air.

With a triumphant whistle, belching out steam, the locomotive moved over the dowry up to the water tower, crushing the samovar into a pancake. But this wasn't all. The engineer then put the train in reverse, backed right on top of what had been the dowry, and suddenly poured out a boiler full of hot water mixed with engine grease.

The old woman ripped off her shawl and started to tear her hair. She fell down on the ground and screamed in a heart-rending voice. Her arms were stretched out, holding a few hairs she had torn from her own head, over the puddle between the rails, just as if she were getting ready to swim across the puddle.

Then she jumped up and threw herself on the engineer.

"I'll claw your eyes out," she cried, and she began to roll up her sleeves. People held her back.

A little man pushed his way through the crowd. He consisted of an enormous checked hat, a pair of new galoshes, and a sharp nose sticking out from under the cap. This was the old woman's son-in-law. He had been coming to meet her, and he was late.

The son-in-law looked at the piles of ruined dowry, picked up the flattened samovar, dropped it at the old woman's feet, and then told her in a squeaky high-pitched voice: "Thank you, Mama darling, thank you very much indeed for delivering the last of our property so efficiently."

The old woman turned to her son-in-law, grabbed him by the

lapels, and spat straight into his face. The crowd roared with laughter.

We stayed for several days at the station at Bobrinsk. In front of us a section of the line had been destroyed by Makhno's men. And to the south were the black Ukrainian freebooters, storming, whooping, rumbling along on their gun carts, firing as they went, whistling, looting, raping women, and vanishing at the sight of any determined opposition.

These *ataman* fanatics came out of their holes in little villages, pink with tall hollyhocks, which were truly medieval. These were bloody times, with swords whistling through the air to cut with equal ease the heads of thistles or of men. Black flags with the skull and bones on them fluttered in the wind which blew across the steppes around Kherson and Nikolayevsk. And the Middle Ages seemed dim and pale compared to the cruelty, the violence, and the ignorance of the twentieth century.

Where had all this been hiding, ripening, gathering strength, and waiting for its hour to strike? Nobody could answer this question. History was moving swiftly backwards. Everything was all mixed up, and for the first time after many years of quiet, men felt their own helplessness before the evil of other men.

Nazarov talked about this most of all. The priests kept mum, Lusena slept for days on end, and Khvat disliked this topic—it gave few openings for his bantering wit.

Four kilometers from Bobrinsk was the town of Smela, the little town where I had gone as a child with my Aunt Nadya and had met the bearded young artist who was in love with her. On the second day of our wait I walked there. To visit places where one has been before is for the most part a sad business. Its sadness is compounded by the discovery of forgotten things—an old curved porch, a poplar tree, or the rusted mailbox into which I had once dropped a letter with my first declaration of love to a blue-eyed girl in the *gymnasium* in Kiev.

Everything was quiet and empty in Smela. The townsfolk never went outside their houses unless they had to, to avoid running into drunken Denikin soldiers. The Tyasmin River was covered with a thick carpet of bright green duckweed, just as it had been when I was a child, making it look like a bright spring meadow. You could smell the marigolds along the fences.

All these places—Smela and the next little town of Cherkasy —were linked with memories of my family. I walked through Smela's quiet streets, and my life, which before then had seemed short to me, suddenly stretched out in my mind's eye as a long series of years filled with big events and little happenings.

Most people like to remember the past, apparently, because what really happened in years gone by becomes clearer at a distance in time. My own passion for remembering developed much too early, when I was still a child, and became a kind of game. I remembered not the consecutive progress of my life, but categories within it. I could recall all the hotels I had stayed at, and all the rivers I had seen in my life, all the ships I had sailed on, or all the girls with whom, I thought, I might have fallen in love.

My addiction to this kind of remembering turned out to be less stupid than it seemed while I was indulging in it. When I would recall hotels, for example, I would remember every detail connected with them—the color of the carpet in the halls, the design of the wallpaper, the smells, the pictures, the faces of the maids and their way of talking, the furniture, everything down to the inkwells made of Ural stone which looked like wet sugar, in which there had never been ink but only the dried bodies of a few dead flies.

While I recalled these things, I tried to see them fresh. Only later, when I began to write, did I realize that this was helping me a great deal in my work. This kind of remembering trained me in concreteness, in visual memory, and piled up a great store of details. I could then choose from it what I needed.

I walked back to Bobrinsk in the twilight. I walked along the railroad embankment. The moon was already hanging high in the sky. I could hear rifle fire from the direction of Bobrinsk. Suddenly my heart beat faster with the thought that I had managed to live in a most interesting time, full of contradictions and events, full of great hopes. "You've been really lucky," I told myself. "You were born under a lucky star."

Our train pulled in to the station at Pomoshna early in the morning. It was shunted at once onto a siding where dry goosefoot plants were turning black where they grew on piles of old slag.

Later in the morning we jumped out of our car and were surprised to find that our engine had been uncoupled from the train and had disappeared. There was not a single person to be seen anywhere along the tracks, at any of the switches, or on the station platform. It was as if the station had died.

I went out to investigate. There was a kind of gray air inside the cold station. All the doors were open but there were no passengers in the waiting room, or in the buffet. The station was abandoned.

I wandered around its hollow-sounding stone floors, walked out into the square behind the station, and found a half-open door. I pushed it open. A man in a red cap, obviously the station official on duty, was sitting hunched over a table in a high, narrow room. He was sitting there morose, his hands in the frayed sleeves of his overcoat, motionless. But he did turn his little inflamed eyes at me. A lock of greasy hair was sticking out under his red official's cap.

"What's happened?" I asked him. "Why isn't there anybody around the station?"

He took his hands out of his sleeves and mysteriously beckoned me up to the table. I went. He took my hand in his cold, damp fingers and whispered to me:

"Everyone's gone out on the steppe. I'm the only one that stayed. It's not my turn to be on duty, mind you, it's Bondarchuk's. But he's got a wife, and children. And I'm a bachelor. So that's how it worked out. He didn't ask me, mind you, but I offered to take his turn."

He kept squeezing my hand harder and harder. I began to be frightened. "He's crazy," I thought, and I pulled my hand away. He looked at me in surprise, and then broke out laughing.

"You scared?" he asked. "I'm scared myself."

"What are you scared of?"

"Bullets," he answered. He stood up and began to straighten his overcoat. "Who can know where the bullet is now that's going to smash my skull in? So I just sit, and wait."

He looked at his watch. "There's a half an hour to go."

"Until what?"

"Makhno's coming," the official said suddenly in a loud, clear voice. "Can you imagine it? He'll be here in half an hour."

"Where did you hear this?"

"Right here." He pointed to the telegraph key on the table. "From Edison. Before that man Edison, people lived quiet lives, they didn't know a thing. Now we know everything in advance, and as a result there's nothing but trouble. Makhno took a beating near Golta. He's pulling back to his base at Alexandriya. He sent a telegram—he's going to come through with three echelons of his fellows, right through Pomoshna without stopping. He's going to Zlatopol. His order—leave all the switches set for a clear run, open the signals, and wait. In case of disobedience, everyone to be shot, right on the spot. Here, read it, that's what it says: 'universal execution.'"

The official pointed to a snarled telegraph ribbon lying on the table, and he sighed.

"It's our bad luck that brings him through here, the son of a bitch. Are you from the passenger train?"

I answered that I was, and I smiled—what kind of a passenger train was that row of dirty, broken boxcars?

"Well then, go back to it and tell them they should lock themselves in the cars and not stick even their noses out. If Makhno's boys see them, they'll push them all into a ditch and machine-gun them."

I went back to the train with this shattering piece of news. The doors were all closed at once, and all the iron stoves extinguished, so as not to betray the train by their smoke. We were all glad to notice that there was a long train of empty freight cars standing beween us and the track along which the military trains would pass.

But this did not suit Khvat and me. We wanted to see Makhno's forces. Ducking behind cars and switch boxes, we went back to the station. The official was glad to see us—anyone feels better with others around.

"Go into the buffet; you can see everything from the window there," he told us.

"How about you?"

"I'm going out on the platform to pass the train through the station. With the green flag."

Khvat looked at him wonderingly.

"But maybe it would be better not to go out?"

"What do you mean? Not go out? But I'm the official in charge here. If I weren't out there, the engineer might stop the train, and then—good-by to my sweetheart, she'd have to write me in Heaven."

Khvat and I walked into the buffet. There was a bulletin board there with a prehistoric train schedule. We moved it over to the window so we could look out from behind it, without being noticed. In case of danger inside the buffet, we could slip back into the kitchen where there was a stairway down into a dark cellar.

A gray cat with red spots came up out of the cellar. He glanced at us, walked by all the tables and the empty counter, jumped up on the window sill where he sat with his back to us, and looked out at the tracks. It was clear that he didn't like the confusion in the station: the end of his tail was twitching with irritation.

He bothered us, but we decided not to drive him away. He was, after all, a railroad cat, he had a right to sit there, while we, passengers without any rights, ought to know our place better. From time to time the cat looked at us in exasperation.

Then his ears went up sharply, and we heard the warning whistle of a train approaching the station. Through the window I could see the official walk hurriedly out on the platform, straightening his overcoat, and holding a rolled-up little green flag.

Blowing puffs of steam into the sky, the locomotive roared up to us, pulling heated boxcars and open flatcars. What went by us on the open flatcars seemed to me pure delirium.

I could see the laughing faces of young fellows loaded down with weapons—curved swords, naval broadswords, daggers with silver handles, revolvers, rifles, and oilskin cartridge cases. Enormous black and red ribbons flew from every kind of hat, cap, bowler hat, sheepskin hat. The biggest ribbon I saw was tied around a dented top hat. Its owner, in a cut-off Siberian fur coat, was firing into the air—obviously he was saluting the fear-paralyzed station of Pomoshna.

One of the Makhno men lost his straw hat in the wind. It soared in slow circles over the platform and finally landed almost at the feet of the station official. It had a kind of slap-happy look, in spite of its ominous black ribbon. This was the kind of hat that provincial Don Juans dream about; it must have covered the head of some small-town barber not long ago. Maybe its owner had paid with his life for his dandy's taste.

Then I noticed a thin, hook-nosed sailor with a long neck like a giraffe's, in a flesh-colored shirt torn open to the navel. It had clearly been ripped on purpose, to show the magnificent and terrifying tattooing on his chest. I did not manage to see it all. I remember only a tangle of women's legs, hearts, daggers, and snakes. The blue outline of the tattooed design had been covered with some pink paint, the color of strawberry juice. If there are styles in tattooing, this one was clearly a rococo piece of work.

Then I saw a fat Georgian in green velvet trousers with a woman's fur piece around his neck. He was standing on a machine-gun carrier and we could see two gun muzzles, right next to him, which were pointed straight at us. The cat kept staring at this fantastic procession going by us, quivering with excitement and moving his claws in and out.

Following a drunken man who held a roast goose in his hands came a white-haired old man wearing a student's cap with a broken visor. He was holding a Cossack lance with a black petticoat tied to it. A rising sun was painted in white on the petticoat. Each of the flatcars poured sound against the platform as it passed—

snatches of accordion music, earsplitting whistles, the broken words of songs.

The first train went by and the second followed close after it. A whole forest of shafts of machine-gun carts pointed upwards, jouncing and bouncing with the movement of the trains. Shaggy little horses stood sideways in the freight cars, shaking their heads. Instead of blankets, the horses were covered with Jewish prayer shawls. The soldiers sat on the sides of the cars, swinging their legs. We could see the shine of yellow boots, felt boots, shoes laced up to the knees, silver spurs, Hussars' boots with officers' cockades on the sides, orange slippers, red and roughened bare feet, puttees cut out of red plush and out of the green felt covering of billiard tables.

Suddenly the train slowed down. The official looked around helplessly, then suddenly stood stock-still. We drew away from the window, and got ready to run. But the train did not stop. It kept on moving slowly and steadily through the station and we saw another flat car. There was nothing on it except a luxuriously lacquered carriage with a prince's golden coat of arms on its doors. One of its shafts stuck straight up in the air, with a black flag tied to it announcing: "Anarchism—Mother of Law and Order." Bandits in brown English overcoats sat at all four corners of the flatcar with machine guns next to them.

On the red Morocco leather of the back seat in the carriage a little man with a green, sallow face, wearing a black hat, was lying. His legs were stretched over the coach box and his whole pose was one of lazy, sleepy, well-fed calm. He was holding a Mauser in his outstretched hand, balancing it and playing with it.

When I saw this man's face a hard lump of disgust formed in my throat. A damp lock of hair fell over his narrow frowning forehead. His eyes were both evil and empty-looking, the eyes of a paranoiac and a skunk. Some kind of madness, it was clear, possessed this man, even now in spite of his relaxed and easy pose.

This was Nestor Makhno.

The station official straightened up, thrust his right hand with the green flag out in front of him, and saluted Makhno with his left hand. At the same time his lips formed a little smile. It would be hard to imagine anything more frightening than that smile. It wasn't really a smile, but a humble prayer for mercy; it was straight terror for his insignificant life, and a hopeless attempt to evoke some human pity.

Makhno raised his revolver lazily and, without even looking at the official or aiming, fired. Why? No one could know. No one could even guess what went on inside the head of a fanatic like him.

The official spread his hands out awkwardly, spun around, fell on his side, and began to twist there on the platform, holding his throat with both hands and vomiting blood. Makhno waved a hand. A burst of machine-gun fire rattled on the asphalt of the platform all around the official. He twitched a couple of times, and then lay still.

We ran out on to the platform. The last boxcar was going by us. A girl with curly hair and a snub nose, dressed in an astrakhan jacket and riding breeches, smiled at us happily and took aim at us with the Mauser in her hand. But a swarthy Makhno man in a French steel helmet pushed her arm. The bullet buried itself in the wall behind us.

We ran up to the official. He was dead. The same humiliated little smile was on his face. We picked him up, trying not to slip in the puddle of blood, carried him into the buffet and put him down on a long table with a dying palm tree in a green tub at its end. The earth in the green tub was covered with the yellow stubs of old burned-out cigarettes.

It was not until the next morning that they sent our train on farther, to the station at Golta. The priests were very quiet, reading their prayers all day in whispers. Lusena lay on her planks without talking, staring at the watery sky outside the door. Khvat was frowning sadly to himself, and only Nazarov tried to talk, but no one answered him and he too grew quiet.

We arrived in Golta a few hours after a pogrom against the Jews. People told us there were still a great many dead lying in the streets. We never found out who had organized the pogrom. No one could make up his mind to venture into the town.

Lusena began to cry in the middle of the night, at first very quietly and then more loudly. Then the crying turned into feverish sobbing and a real paroxysm. By dawn the attack was finished, and in the morning, when we pulled in to some way station, there was no Lusena in the boxcar. Nobody had seen her leave. She had just disappeared, leaving behind the package wrapped in her gypsy shawl—obviously she did not need it any longer.

THE SILVERSIDES,
THE WATER PIPE, AND SMALL DANGERS

Silversides are a small Black Sea fish, about the size of a safety pin. They were popular in the markets because there were no other fish and all Odessa seemed to be living on this insignificant little fish. Sometimes even the silversides ran out. We ate them either raw and slightly salted, or chopped up and fried in cutlets. You could manage to get those cutlets down only as a last, desperate resort or, as people in Odessa used to say, "garnished with tears."

Both Nazarov and I had run almost completely out of money. So we ate nothing but silversides and soggy bread made out of corn-meal. This looked like a kind of granular plum cake, but it tasted like little drops of anise. After eating it, you had to rinse your mouth out to get rid of its overpowering taste.

Sometimes I bought roasted chestnuts. They were sold by old women, wrapped in heavy, fringed shawls, who sat on little stools on the pavement and roasted the chestnuts in braziers. When the chestnuts split open, they gave off a smell of slightly burned bark, but sweeter and more fragrant.

There was little light in Odessa then. The street lamps were lighted late or not at all, and sometimes the pavements would be lighted on a quiet autumn evening only by the reddish glow of these braziers. This light, rising almost from the ground, gave the streets a look of fairyland. The old women were wrapped in their shawls and the city was wrapped in its thick fog which lasted all through the autumn. I must confess that I have liked foggy days ever since then, especially in the autumn when they take on the limp, lemon-yellow color of fallen leaves.

It was very hard to find a place to live in Odessa, but we were lucky. Dr. Landesman's private sanatorium for patients with nervous diseases stood on a hill overlooking the sea in Lanzheron, on quiet, empty Black Sea Street. The troubled life of those years saw a sharp rise in nervous diseases, but nobody had the money to pay for treatment, especially in such an expensive sanatorium as Landesman's. So it had been closed.

Nazarov ran into a woman he knew in Odessa, a Moscow nerve specialist, and she arranged things for us in this empty sanatorium. Landesman, a very majestic, courteous character, let us have two small white cubicles on condition that we guard the sanatorium. We had to make sure that the little garden around the building was not cut down for firewood, and that the house itself was not taken to pieces for the same purpose.

The central heating was not working. My room had a very high ceiling and a wide window, and the little iron stove could never get it warm, no matter how I tried. There was almost no fuel. Sometimes I could buy acacia wood, which was sold by the pound. I could never buy more than three or four pounds—all I could afford. And it was terribly cold, especially when the wind blew from the north. The whiteness of the glazed tile walls made it seem even colder.

I was working again as proofreader on a newspaper. I've forgotten its name. It was published by Ovsyaniko-Kulikovsky, a member of the Academy.* I worked only one day in three and was paid very little in "bells"—this is what we used to call the Denikin money with its picture of the Tsar-bell in the Kremlin.

I was delighted with life in this deserted private building overlooking the sea. I loved the solitude. I even liked the cold air inside its walls, a cold that felt like rough sand and smelled like ocean salt. I read a great deal, wrote a little, and for want of anything better to do took up the study of mists and fog.

In the mornings I would walk out through the little garden to the bluff overlooking the sea. The fog horn would be blowing dolefully on Vorontsovsky lighthouse, through the regular ringing of its bell. Little gray drops would be glittering on the dried grass and on the twigs of the acacia. Through the fog the rumble of unseen breakers came up from the pebbled beach below.

Fog has been linked for me ever since then with solitude, quiet, and concentration. It shut out the world, and enclosed only a small circle one could really see. This circle included a few things worth really careful observation—a few trees, some yellow-flowered shrubs like broom, a column built of rough stones, an iron wicket gate, and an anchor chain which had been left in this garden for reasons I couldn't guess.

Fog made one look at these things more carefully and much

* Dmitri N. Ovsyaniko-Kulikovsky (1853–1920) was a critic and journalist who contributed occasionally before 1917 to Marxist journals.

longer than we usually do, revealing many things about them that one never noticed before. You could see, for example, an enormous number of little seashells embedded in the porous yellow stone, and a few little blossoms sitting on the stiff branches of the broom bushes, like soaked and wrinkled golden butterflies waiting patiently for the sun. But the sun managed very seldom to shine even a dull whiteness through the fog, and this made neither warmth nor shadows. Under a single old plane tree with yellow splotches on its trunk, leaves were scattered like pieces cut out of dull green velvet cloth. Files of ants moved across the iron gate, carrying their last winter supplies to their underground anthills, and there was a small, shy toad living under the anchor chain.

The fog had its own noises. Some of them would begin just before the fog started to thin out, when you could hear a confused little rustling. This was the moisture collected from the sea spray into drops on the black branches of the trees and starting to fall to the ground with thousands of dull, tiny splashes. Then you could sometimes hear a clear, ringing little sound in this soft murmur, which meant that the first drop of water precipitated from the fog had fallen from the roof on to an empty tin can lying upside down next to the house.

I loved the smell of fog—a faint smell of coal smoke and steam. It's the smell of railroad stations, of docks, of the decks of ships, of everything connected with great distances, with islands far in the sea where the breeze blows a faint fragrance from the lemon trees, with the raw winds and the flashing beacon lights of northern channels, with the steady roaring of a railroad train through our drowsy Russian forests, with what holds the human heart in captivity for life.

In those days in Odessa I dreamed of spending my whole life traveling, so that I might live whatever years were granted me in constant contact with new things and new places, writing books about them with all the skill I had, and giving those books—giving the whole, wide world with all the enchantment it holds—to some woman I had not yet met whose very presence would transform my days and my years into an unbroken flow of happiness and sorrow, of sheer delight at the beauty of the world as it always ought to be, but seldom really is.

In those days I was quite certain that this was just how my life would work itself out.

Everything a writer gives to his beloved, he gives to all humanity. I was convinced of this vague law of generosity, and of the need to give oneself fully. To give, expecting nothing in return and asking nothing, nothing greater than a grain of sand from the warm hand of someone loved and cherished, this was all that mattered.

Literary theoreticians would call everything I have just written a sort of lyrical deviationism; they advise a writer not to lose control over himself, and not to confuse the natural order of things. But it still seems to me that it would be possible to write a whole book in this way, freely and without any strain, paying attention to nothing but the headlong rush of imagination and of ideas. Maybe only in this way is it possible to achieve truly full expression.

But I must come back to the silversides and the cornmeal bread and those autumn days in Odessa.

The skimpy diet did not bother me in the slightest, especially after I managed to acquire two cans of concentrated Holland coffee from the cook on the *Dumont-Durville,* a French ship anchored in the harbor. I traded him a box of Stamboli tobacco for the coffee. The box had been left by my father and given me by Mama who had managed to preserve it somehow for many years.

The *Dumont-Durville* was anchored off the breakwater in the Quarantine Harbor, next to an English destroyer. The sailors from the destroyer played football all day long on the breakwater. The black and yellow steamships of the Lloyd Triestino Line came regularly to Odessa from Trieste and Venice. Greek sailors patroled the streets of the city. Their blue uniforms, and their white gaiters with little round buttons, and their broad cutlasses made them look old-fashioned and theatrical.

Odessa was filled with an amazing mixture of people that year. Small local gamblers and speculators could not meet the competition of the cruel and brazen types who were pouring into the city from the Soviet-controlled part of the country. The little businessmen could only sigh bitterly—this was the end of an old way of life in which a single crumpled waybill for a single carload of lemon extract in Archangel could pass from hand to hand in Fankone's café for an entire month, rising or falling in price from day to day and giving everyone a chance to turn a profit. Archangel was now as far away as Mars, and lemon extract had become something out of mythology. This in itself never bothered the little speculators. Their business was like the noisy games of men in a lunatic asylum. They traded until they were hoarse, they pounded with their fists, they insulted each other, and sometimes a carload of lemon extract or an equally mythological consignment of sponges (f. o. b. at Patras in Greece) would lead to long-drawn-out and screaming riots.

Sometimes these small gamblers did a little real business, for a package of saccharine, or a gross of old suspenders, or a dubious box of ammonium chloride in powder. Ammonia was terribly expensive, and was traded literally in drops.

The speculators pouring into the city from the north overwhelmed their local counterparts with bold and ruthless trading. They flashed diamonds, which always came from the Tsar's crown, of course, they handled brand new pound sterling and franc notes, and the rarest furs from the shoulders of famous Petrograd beauties passed into the hands of Greek traders in the city. There was an extensive trading of famous landed properties in all the provinces of "long-suffering Russia."

Any evening along Deribasovskaya Street you could see a great many famous people around the flower stalls. Most of them, it is true, were out at the elbows, and in a violent temper over the crazy rumors which spread like fever. Odessa easily outstripped all the cities of the south in rumors. Some of them were not only crazy, but also ominous. They literally blew into the city on the gusty north wind from the Kherson steppes. Soviet troops were driving southwards, hacking Denikin's rear guards to pieces, tightening their semicircle around the White armies, cutting the roads of their escape. The thin chain of the White front was breaking like rotten thread in place after place.

Deserters flooded into Odessa after each new break in the front. The taverns were noisy into early morning. Women screamed, there was the crash of broken dishes, shots could be heard as the fugitives settled accounts among themselves in their effort to discover who had betrayed them and sold out Russia. The white death's-heads on the sleeves of officers of the so-called "battalions of death" turned yellow with dirt and grease and lost their power to frighten anyone.

The city was living on a hopeless gamble. Supplies of food and fuel should have given out long ago, but by some miracle a trickle continued to flow. There was electricity only in the center of the city, and even there it burned only dully and hesitantly. Nobody paid any attention to the White officials, even the Whites themselves.

Three thousand bandits from Moldavanka, led by Misha Yaponchik, looted lazily, clumsily, halfheartedly. All the bandits were sated with the fabulous loot they had already acquired. They wanted nothing more than a rest from all the bother of pillaging. They cracked jokes now more than they robbed, they packed the restaurants, singing, in tears, a heart-rending song about the death of Vera Kholodnaya:

Poor Runich is weeping bitter tears,
For Vera's in her grave.

Runich had been Vera Kholodnaya's leading man. According to the song, Vera lay down herself in her grave, and asked Runich:

Cover my breasts
With blue cornflowers
And wet them
With your bitter tears.

One day I went home from the printing shop with Yakob Lifshitz, a Petrograd journalist. He had no place to live, so he became the third boarder in Dr. Landesman's sanatorium. He was a short, untidy man who was nicknamed "Yasha on Wheels." He had an unusual way of walking, putting down his foot at each step with a kind of rolling motion like a curved blotter drying the ink on a piece of paper. This made Lifshitz look as if he were not walking but rolling. And his shoes always looked like curved blotters, or like pieces of a wheel, with their soles bent into convex arcs.

We walked out to Black Sea Street along quiet side streets, in order to meet as few patrols as possible. Two young men in identical jockey's caps stepped out of a gate in front of us. They stood there, smoking. We were walking toward them, but they did not move. It looked as if they were waiting for us.

"Bandits," I said quietly to Yasha, but he only snorted in disbelief, and muttered:

"What stupidity! Bandits wouldn't be working a deserted little street like this. Let me show you."

"How?"

"Walk right up and talk to them. Everything will be all right."

Yasha had a theory about life—one should never hesitate but walk right up to any danger. He was convinced that this theory had saved him in many serious situations.

"But what will we talk to them about?" I asked, distrustfully.

"That makes no difference. Anything will do."

Yasha walked briskly up to them and suddenly asked:

"Tell me, please, how do we get from here to Black Sea Street?"

The young men began to explain to Yasha very politely how to get there. It was a complicated route, and they took a long time explaining, especially since Yasha kept interrupting them on details. Then he thanked them, and we went on.

"There you see," Yasha said triumphantly. "My system works perfectly."

I was ready to agree, but at that moment the young men called to us. We stopped. They came up, and one of them said:

"You know, of course, that on the way to Black Sea Street, outside Alexandrovsky Park, they take the overcoats away from anyone walking by?"

"Well, probably not from everyone," Yasha answered cheerfully.

"Almost everyone," the young man corrected himself, and he smiled. "But they're sure to take yours. Beyond any doubt. So it's much better for you to lose it here. It's all the same to you, after all, where you lose it, outside the park or right here on this street. Don't you agree?"

"Well, maybe you're right . . ." Yasha started to answer in a flustered voice.

"So, if you will be so good . . ."

The young man took a dagger out of his pocket. I had never seen such a long, beautiful, or razor-sharp dagger. The blade seemed to be floating in the air at just about the level of Yasha's stomach.

"I hate to bother you," the young man went on, "but take out of the pockets everything you need except for money. That's the way. Thank you very much. And good night to you. No, no, don't worry," he turned to me. "One overcoat is enough for us. Greed is the mother of all the other vices. Go on your way in peace, but don't look around. You'll never achieve anything serious in life, you know, by looking backwards."

We went on. We were not even very much depressed by the incident. Yasha kept hoping that I would lose my coat, too, along the way, but I didn't. And then Yasha suddenly became very surly and pouted at me, as if I could have known they would take only his coat or as if I had been in cahoots with the bandits.

Yasha always had bad luck. Nazarov was sure he belonged to a special type of people who attract bad luck. He used to cite two instances to prove this, and I could hardly argue because they both took place before my eyes. One had to do with a large glass carboy for holding water, and the other with a thermometer.

The water supply was very bad in Odessa in those days. It was pumped from the Dniester, some sixty kilometers away, and the pumps were barely working. Bandits kept shooting them up, and the city came very close to losing its water supply completely.

There was a little in the pipes, not always and only in the lowest-lying sections of the city. These lucky districts were jammed from morning to night with lines of people from all over Odessa carrying pails, jugs, and tea kettles. Only a few lucky ones—the owners of carts—could carry their water in large quantities. These few were envied and hated at the same time, in spite of the fact that they often made a sorry sight when they were driving their carts up or down a steep hill and splashing out half their water.

We used to take turns walking about two kilometers to Uspenskaya Street. I knew every cellar on this street which had a faucet and I could have found them with my eyes closed. When we stood in line, we exchanged all the latest news and rumors, and we came to know the others in the line as good and old friends.

The poetess Vera Imber* lived not far from us, on Observatory Lane. She used to get her water in a large flower vase made of frosted glass of many colors with purple irises on its sides. One day Imber, who was tiny and frail, slipped and broke her vase. The next day she showed up with one just like it. Out of simple compassion I carried it home for her full of water. She was so afraid that I might slip and break her last vase that her worrying exhausted me and my legs began to shake.

When I carried water I used to watch the ground carefully, of course, and I came to know intimately all the pavements and streets from Uspenskaya Street to where we lived. I learned that watching the ground can be an entrancing and sometimes rewarding occupation. One could see all kinds of little things which were worth thinking about, some of them pleasant, some neutral, and some unpleasant.

The most unpleasant of them all were drops, and sometimes little pools, of blood, and only slightly less unpleasant were the empty cartridge shells. These still had the sour smell of gunpowder. I also included empty purses and torn-up papers among the unpleasant things. But one did not see these often.

The pleasant small objects were fewer, but they were of many different kinds. Usually they would be something quite unexpected —dried flowers from a bouquet, or pieces of crystal, the dried-out claws of a crab, the wrappers of Egyptian cigarettes, ribbons lost by little girls, rusted fishhooks. All of these things suggested a world at peace. Grass, of course, growing in places between the stones of the pavement, belonged among the pleasant things. And little flowers, dead before they had blossomed, and smooth, round, rainwashed stones in the cemented gutters.

---

* Vera Imber, who was born in 1892, was one of the Constructivist poets in 1924; she has become well known in the Soviet Union for her poems on World War II themes.

Most of the things were neither pleasant nor unpleasant—buttons, copper coins, pins, cigarette butts. No one paid them any attention.

When we had carried our water home, we poured it into a big glass carboy in the hall. One day Yasha Lifshitz went out into the hall and started to shout. I jumped out of my room, and saw something quite inexplicable. While Yasha and I watched it, the big glass container started to lean over, looking for a moment like the leaning tower of Pisa, and then suddenly collapsed on the floor and shattered into thousands of splinters. The precious water ran gurgling down the stairs. We could have picked up the carboy when it started to lean over, but we had both stood there watching it as if bewitched.

The incident with the thermometer was even more startling. I was sick with influenza. Thermometers were as hard to get then in Odessa as pineapples; there were only a few of them in the city. People treasured a thermometer as shipwrecked sailors guard their last match.

Nazarov asked to borrow one for a couple of days from the editor of the paper, the respectable, venerable, illustrious Ovsyaniko-Kulikovsky. This academician was well-known as a humanist and a defender of the traditions of liberal Russian society, so he could hardly refuse Nazarov's request. He chewed his lips and grumbled, showing his extreme reluctance, but he gave him the thermometer with strict orders to wrap it up in cotton and to guard it like the pupil of his eye.

Nazarov turned it over to me but he forgot the editor's strict orders. He put it on the table, and walked out. I fell asleep. Yasha woke me up. He had opened the door carefully, but it squeaked a little and I opened my eyes. I looked at the table and I could feel the hair rising on my head—the thermometer had suddenly started to roll toward the edge of the table.

I wanted to yell, but I had no breath for it. I saw Yasha's terror-stricken eyes. He, too, was watching the thermometer, and making no move. It rolled slowly to the edge of the table, fell off on to the floor, and broke to pieces. My temperature immediately fell, obviously from sheer fright. I got well again almost at once.

For a long time we broke our heads over the problem of replacing the thermometer. For two days Nazarov pleaded illness so he could stay away from the office and avoid the editor. In the end we were driven to crime. We contrived a key to Dr. Landesman's office and found a thermometer in a drawer of his desk. In the evasive language of thieves, who do not like the word "steal," we "took" it and turned it over to Ovsyaniko-Kulikovsky.

After these two incidents Nazarov tried to convince me that Yasha was a dangerous man and urged me not to go out on the street with him. I just laughed at this, but not for long. In order to explain what happened next, I must say a few words about Sturdzovsky Lane, a little street which could not be avoided on our way home each night to the sanatorium.

This lane, named for the Jesuit Sturdzo, who was famous in Pushkin's time, always gave us a feeling of some hidden danger. Perhaps this was because it ran next to the stone walls of big gardens which stretched down to the sea. These walls offered no cover, no hiding place. In those days, everyone had developed the habit, when walking through the streets, of picking in advance the nearest hiding place in case of shooting in the street or an encounter with a drunken patrol.

There was not a single such place on this street except for a two-storied house with a narrow, dark gateway. No one lived there, and weeds were growing out of its broken window frames. Not having taken Nazarov's warning, I found myself walking along this street with Yasha late one autumn night on my way home from work.

One could walk through the streets at night then only by strictly obeying a series of unwritten laws. It was impossible to smoke, to carry on conversation, to cough, or to let your heels make a noise on the sidewalk. You had to walk, or rather pick your way, close to the walls or in the shadow of trees. Every forty or fifty steps you had to stop, listen, and stare into the darkness. At crossings it was obligatory to examine all four corners carefully, and then dart across with great speed.

We had got as far as Sturdzovsky Lane successfully, stopping often, looking around corners, listening and peering into the pitch darkness. The darkness favored us in one sense: it hid us. But in another sense it was dangerous, for it might lead us into an ambush. Everything was quiet, so quiet that we could hear the faint roaring of the breakers on the beach.

We moved stealthily along the lane. I had told Yasha that we ought to walk along the side with the house and the narrow gateway on it, stopping to listen carefully and then dashing quickly and silently past the gateway. This plan had a mathematical exactitude about it which pleased me. If there were people in the gateway, they might not notice us. But if we were on the other side of the lane, they would see us from farther away. I figured that in the second case we would be in the danger zone, visible to anyone standing in the gateway, five times longer than in the first case.

And therefore there would be five times as much chance that we would be noticed.

But Yasha had started to whisper his old theory that one must always walk straight into the jaws of danger. I had not really argued it with him, in order not to make any extra noise, and we walked along the side of the street opposite the deserted house and its gateway.

Yasha was counting the seconds to himself. We knew that there were seven minutes of walking between this lane and the sanatorium. There, behind its high fence and its iron gates, we always felt completely safe, especially if we did not light the lamps.

When we had got up to the gateway, Yasha stumbled. He claimed later, when we talked about it, that whenever you try to do something as carefully as you possibly can, it is always some tiny little accident which brings failure. I thought to myself that the blame belonged rather to Yasha's impossible way of walking, but I didn't tell him so.

Anyway, when he stumbled, instead of cursing to himself, he suddenly said, in a very audible voice:

"Excuse me, please."

"Halt!" a husky voice called from the gateway, and the sharp beam of an electric flashlight fell on us. "Hands out of your pockets! Quick, now, you sons of bitches!"

Several armed men came up to us. It was a Cossack patrol.

"Your documents!" the same husky voice said.

I held out my identification card. The Cossack shone his flashlight on it, then on me.

"You Greek," he declared. "Mackerel with a little lemon. Take your papers back."

He handed my card back to me and then examined Yasha.

"You don't have to show your papers," he said. "I can see you're a Jerusalem general. Well, all right. Go along."

We took several steps.

"Halt!" the same Cossack shouted. "Don't move a step!"

We stood still.

"What are you standing there for? Didn't I tell you—go along!"

We started off again, but very slowly, so as not to show our confusion. My nerves were so tense that behind my back I could feel with all my body the Cossacks opening the bolts of their guns. I never heard them. I realized that this was a cat and mouse game, that they were going to kill us anyway, and that any movement by us might be our last.

"Halt!" the Cossack commanded, and he added an obscenity about our mothers. The rest of the armed men were laughing.

We stopped again, right next to the wall. I could not see it in the darkness, but I knew that it was made of rough stone and that there were projections and dents in it.

"Climb over the wall," I whispered to Yasha. "In one scramble. Otherwise it's all over with us!"

I was thin. It was easy for me to scramble up the wall. But Yasha, with his round shoes, almost fell. I grabbed him by the arm and yanked. We swung our legs over the top and jumped. Behind us we heard some shots, and pieces of broken stone fell from the top of the wall.

We tore off through a dark garden. The trunks of the trees, painted with lime, shone in the darkness, and this helped us. The Cossacks climbed the wall right after us. Bullets were whistling all around us. We ran up to the garden's other wall, and there was a big breach in it. The Cossacks were already running through the garden, but their rifles slowed them up, and we scrambled through the breach in the wall. Three steps beyond it, the ground fell sharply down to the sea. We slithered down and ran off along the beach. The Cossacks went on firing from on top but they had already lost us in the darkness and their shots went wild.

For a long time we climbed along the shore, past ravines and caves. The surf was beating along the shore line just as regularly and as sleepily as ever. It was hard to believe that a man could thoughtlessly kill another man just like himself on such a warm autumn night, smelling of wild savory, right next to those gently murmuring waves. In my innocence then I thought that evil always retreated before beauty, that it would be impossible to kill a man in front of the Sistine Madonna or on the Acropolis.

I wanted desperately to smoke. The shooting had died down. We climbed into the next cave, and lit cigarettes. I doubt if a cigarette has ever tasted so good to me. We sat there for three hours, then climbed out and made our way stealthily along the shore to Landesman's sanatorium. Hanging on to bushes and stones, we climbed up the cliff to the high fortresslike wall on top. A round opening had been made in the base of the wall for the pipes carrying rain water. We climbed through this hole, then filled it with stones, although this wasn't really necessary, and went into the house.

Nazarov was not sleeping. He was astounded by our tale. We lit a lamp in the bathroom, where there was no window, and saw ourselves for the first time. Our clothing was in rags, and our hands were caked with blood. But we had escaped death cheaply.

We gulped down hot tea, and got drunk on it. It was not from the tea, of course, but from the amazing feeling of being safe, a feeling not to be compared with any other. If there is such a thing as complete happiness, we felt it that night.

I wanted to prolong the feeling as long as I could. I got dressed, took a blanket, and went out on the loggia, a deep bay on the second floor with an overhanging balcony. It was dark there. Even the wind did not blow into it, and no one could see me from the street. I sat on a chaise longue, wrapped myself in the blanket, and listened to the sounds of the night.

The limitless roaring of the sea never stopped for a minute. It came up in long waves, rising, then falling away again. And the wind would start a whisper in the bare branches of the trees, and then grow silent, just like myself listening to the flowing of the night. But it never went away completely. I could tell this by the smell of the wet pebbled shore, and by the barely audible quivering of a single leaf left on the plane tree. I had already noticed that stubborn gray-blue leaf in the daytime but now, at night, it seemed like a small living being, my one friend keeping vigil with me.

Sometimes out of the dark, out of the city, came the sounds of rifle firing. Dogs would bark for a long time after each shot. Then a dull light flared up far out at sea, and went out again.

Everything around me was asleep. I dozed off myself for a few minutes, but it was troubled sleep. It was that half sleep in which you can see great white flowers floating on the night sea as clearly as when one is wide awake, and hear a violinist playing notes as light as the palm of a child's hand.

In that half sleep I was aware of a world quite different from the one I knew—a quiet, trusting, welcoming world. And I heard poetry coming from the darkness of the sea, like a woman's whisper.

THE LAST SHRAPNEL

Life in Odessa grew more alarming every day. Fighting was already going on against Soviet troops around Voznesensk.

Ships loaded with fugitives were leaving for Constantinople. Almost all of these grimy boats, the black paint peeling off their sides, pulled out of the port with a heavy list, loaded down beyond their water line, smoking so heavily that the smoke lay heavy over all of Lanzheron and our Black Sea Street.

But the newspapers still came out. The White command knew that the end was approaching, literally hour by hour, but it concealed this fact as completely as it could from the population, and especially from the fugitives from the north. The papers published telegraphic reports that each Bolshevik attack had been repulsed, and that strong French forces, equipped with artillery and with poison gas, were on their way to Odessa from Salonika.

These rumors were spread to keep the fugitives from the north from streaming still farther south in panic, toward Constantinople, and from thus hampering the flight of the White army itself. There were not many ships in the port, and Denikin's men were saving them for themselves.

The papers continued to appear, and officers in the Yellow Canary Café still insisted loudly that all was not lost. The papers tried to reassure the people by repeating the hackneyed truth that "when Moscow was burned, Russia did not fall." The paper where I was employed as a proofreader was also working hard along the same lines in its articles, its stories, and its poems, even though its founder, the academician Ovsyaniko-Kulikovsky, had already fled to Turkey on a shabby little Greek freighter, the *Venera*.

One day Ivan Bunin walked into the office. He was worried, and he wanted to know what was happening at the front. He stood in the door and tugged for a long time at the glove on his right hand. A cold rain was falling, and his glove had become wet and stuck to his hand.

Finally he pulled it off. His quiet, gray eyes wandered around the smoke-filled room where we were sitting, and he said:

"Well, you haven't much of a place here."

We were all embarrassed, but Nazarov answered him:

"What kind of a place could we have, Ivan Alexeyevich? We all have one foot in the grave these days."

Bunin took a chair and sat down next to Nazarov's desk.

"By the way," he said, "do you know where that expression comes from—to have one foot in the grave?"

"No, I don't know."

"In general, it's the end of everything," Bunin said, and he was silent for a while. "Rain, cold, dark, and peace in the soul. Or rather, emptiness. A little like death."

"You've grown sad, Ivan Alexeyevich," Nazarov said cautiously.

"Not really," Bunin answered him. "It's just that everything has turned unpleasant in this world. Even the sea smells of rusty iron now."

He got up and walked into the editor's office.

From my earliest years I have loved Bunin for the merciless precision of his writing and for his sadness, for his love of Russia and his amazing knowledge of its people, for his delight in the world and all its varied beauties, for his vigilance, and for his clear awareness that happiness can be found everywhere and not only by the knowing ones. Bunin was already a classic in my eyes. I knew many of his poems by heart, and even some passages of prose. Greatest of all in its bitterness, its suffering, and its faultless language was a little story he wrote—not more than two or three pages long—called "Ilya the Prophet."

This was why I was afraid to say a word in his presence. I was frightened. I hung my head, listening to his hollow voice, and only glanced at him a few times, afraid to look into his eyes.

It was many years later that I read his *Life of Arseniev*. Some chapters of this book have seemed to me on a higher level than almost any poetry and prose I know. I feel this way especially about the passages in which Bunin wrote about his mother's bones, buried in the cold clay, about the unavoidable loss of loved ones, and about despair in love. He knew the simple words which wring our hearts.

Bunin soon left the office. I could not work any longer, correcting the fabricated, illiterate stories of Odessa reporters, and I went home by myself to Black Sea Street.

A black wind was blowing off the lead-colored sea. Sullen curtains of rain were hanging down through it. Acacia leaves no longer floated on the puddles. They had long since drowned in them and were lying under the water in yellow, rotting layers on the pavement. Only the wet ivy shining against the walls of kitchen gardens spoke of life.

I walked down to the sea, to Arkadia. Wastes of water swirled evenly and quietly across the packed sand. All the sullenness and hostility of the sea in autumn flowed into a feeling of complicated, cold unhappiness. I did not fight against it.

Again, as so many times before, I thought about my life. I took it to pieces year by year, and I suddenly realized that nothing could give any sense, any meaning, or any justification to all the contradictions of my past except the future. Perhaps the future might sort out of my life and out of all I had lived through whatever had been illuminated and warmed by honest humanity and by poetry, whatever would make me able to tie the broken links of my life into a whole story. Who could know? Perhaps this story might be needed by other people, and not just by myself, and it might help them to struggle through stormy times to a far-off, blinding strip of clear sky.

Who could know? It might be to that strip of sky which was just then spreading over the sea to the southward, promising release from the clouds to the autumn sun.

During the night that strip of clear sky widened, and in the morning I saw an incredibly blue sea out of the window of my room.

A weak but steady northeast wind was blowing. As always, it brought cold with it, and a clean sky, and clear air. The dry grass was sheathed in frost, and it swung, tinkling and shining, in the wind. The surf pounded heavily and lazily against the bluffs along the shore, leaving a white bark of ice on them. The wind whipped thick salt foam off the waves, like beaten egg whites. Ragged scraps of it quivered along the shore, and it was easy to credit the ancient Greeks who believed that the fabulously beautiful goddess Aphrodite had been born of such foam.

The heavy roar of cannon interrupted these thoughts. It seemed to slap down on the city like a great steel paw. The whole sanatorium rattled like an old cupboard with glass doors. Tiles fell off the roof and broke noisily on the ground.

There was another roar, a third, a fourth . . .

The French cruiser was firing, standing in the roadstead. It was firing into the steppe north of the city. The shells screamed over the city and fell so far away that the noise of their explosion could not be heard in Odessa.

From my window I could see "Yasha on Wheels" racing through

the courtyard. He opened the door to the stairway and shouted up, filling the empty sanatorium with his voice:

"The Bolsheviks have appeared at Tiligulsky Lagoon! They're advancing on Kuyalnik! It's the end!"

Kuyalnik was only a few kilometers east of Odessa.

Yasha dashed into my room. Nazarov followed him. Yasha told us that the Whites were running away without firing a shot, that there was panic in the port, that the French cruiser was firing at random into the steppe, and that we must quickly collect whatever we needed most, pack it into a small bag, and run to the port. Loading of the last ships there had already started.

"Well, what of it?" I told him. "Go along. It's a matter of your own conscience. But I know that I can't quit my country like that, ever, under any circumstances. Or my people."

"Yes," Nazarov added. "Life outside of Russia makes no sense and wouldn't be worth living. And if your life, Yasha, is so damned valuable—I don't know to whom—why, just run along. To hell with you!"

"What stupidity!" Yasha muttered, and he blushed until tears came into his eyes. "Everybody's running away. It must have infected me. Why, of course, I'm not going anywhere."

Decisions in those days had to be quick ones. One moment of indecision could ruin a life, or save it.

Yasha stayed. He was rapturously happy that he no longer had to worry about anything, and that there was no reason to hesitate. He even made us tea, which we drank in a hurry, and then we all went down to Alexandrovsky Park.

An ancient pavilion stood on a cliff in that park, and from it we could see the whole port and everything that was going on. For a long time afterwards I could not get rid of a feeling that I had seen that Homeric flight in the picture of some cruel painter. There were mouths twisted in cries for help, eyes popping out of their sockets, faces green with terror, the deep wrinkles of imminent death, the blindness of fear when people can see only one thing—the rickety gangway of a ship with its steps broken under the weight of human bodies, soldiers' rifle butts over people's heads, children held up in their mothers' arms over the mad stampede of hurrying men, their desperate crying, a woman trampled underfoot and still wriggling, screaming, on the pavement . . .

People literally destroyed each other, not letting even those save themselves who could manage to crawl up the gangways and grab a railing of a ship. Several arms would reach out at once to clutch the lucky man, and to hang on to him. He would inch forward, along the gangway, dragging the other fugitives behind him, until the gangway itself collapsed and dropped him into the sea to drown, unable to free himself from his living, terrifying burden.

All the roads leading down to the port were jammed with people. It looked as if the fences and the houses were bending under their pressure and would soon collapse. This would have happened, except that buildings made of rough stone do not collapse. Only the unbroken sound of breaking glass and splitting wood showed how people were being pressed against doors and windows.

Bulging suitcases, packages, and baskets slithered along under the legs of the people like some horrible living creatures. Their contents poured out of them, getting tangled in people's legs, and men dragged along with them women's chemises, lace, children's garments, and long ribbons. These peaceful-looking objects made still more tragic the total picture of this frenzied flight.

A frozen dust was hanging in the air over all the streets leading down to the port.

The crowd of officers and soldiers would freeze solid, and then break apart, and only the felt boots of the Caucasians stood in the jam of people like black bells, keeping their owners from running. Some men discarded them, and the boots, like black goats, seemed to be moving by themselves, crowding toward the port.

The ships slowly listed far over under the weight of people scrambling aboard them. Sailors and soldiers were trying to thin out the crowd, but they were thrown down and crushed.

The crowd of people grew minute by minute. You could no longer hear the roaring of the surf, crashing against the breakwater. Then we heard shots fired around the gangways. They were fired in an effort to stop the crowds, but they only increased their fury.

And in the city itself, behind the maddened crowd, everything was quiet and deserted. It was clear that the Soviet troops had not yet entered Odessa. If they had come in, if just one horseman had shown up in the rear of that crowd or announced his presence by a single shot, the panic would have passed all bounds.

We learned the next day that Soviet scouts had entered the city but, staggered by the sight of this mad flight, had stopped at the edges of the port district and had not opened fire.

We could see men on the ships chopping through the mooring lines, and the ships pulled away from the docks without even raising their gangplanks. These broke away under the strain and slipped down into the sea with the people who were on them. It was impossible to hear the cries, the oaths, and the weeping of those who were left behind, separated and abandoned.

The ships slowly stood out toward the roadstead, smoking

heavily and furiously racing their propellers. Suddenly the port emptied. People hurled themselves back into its little alleys and into all the holes and chinks of a great harbor.

A mounted detachment of Soviet cavalry slowly rode down one of the streets leading to the port, filled with broken suitcases and trunks, and lined with the bodies of people who had been crushed to death.

The soldiers were riding with their heads lowered, as if they were thinking, and they stopped next to the bodies, leaning over from their saddles. They were apparently looking for those who might still be alive. There were none.

The detachment rode out to the end of the breakwater and stopped there and the soldiers looked at the ships for a long time.

The ships were steaming out to the roadstead past the ancient Vorontsovsky lighthouse, which had seen many sights in its time. Everything was quiet. From the city one could hear, faintly, the singing of a stanza of the "Internationale."

One of the ships puffed out a ball of steam into the gray sky and blew out a shuddering whistle. All the other ships followed it with whistles in all keys and all degrees of loudness. These were the parting salutes of the dying. They sounded like the dying salutes of men who were quitting their fatherland, abandoning their own people, the Russian fields and forests, springtimes and winters, their sufferings and their joys, breaking away from the past and from the present, from the radiant genius of Pushkin and Tolstoy, from the great filial love for every blade of grass, for every drop of water from a well somewhere in our simple and beautiful land.

The cavalrymen stayed motionless on the end of the breakwater.

A mine layer, convoying the ships, fired two shots. Two useless shells filled with shrapnel exploded over the city with a thin, whining noise. These were the fugitives' last gifts to the country where they had been born.

The Soviet artillery did not fire back. People stood on the breakwaters, on the boulevards, on the bluffs hanging over the sea, and watched the heavy hulks of the ships turn dark in the smoke and the twilight. There was something heavy and reproachful in this silence of the conquerors.

The ships disappeared in the mist. It was as if the winter wind out of the northeast had blown open a clean, new page. There was still to be written on it a new and heroic story of Russia—the long-suffering and extraordinary land which we love until our dying breath.

PANTHEON MODERN CLASSICS

MEMED, MY HAWK
by Yashar Kemal

The most important novel to come out of modern Turkey, this vital and exciting story of a latter-day Robin Hood is set against the beauty and brutality of Turkish peasant life. "Exciting, rushing, lyrical, a complete and subtle emotional experience."—*Chicago Sun-Times*

0-394-71016-9 $6.95

THE LEOPARD
by Giuseppe di Lampedusa

This powerful novel of a Sicilian prince perched on the brink of great historic change is widely acknowledged as a masterpiece of European literature. "The finest historical novel I have read in years."—*Saturday Review*

0-394-74949-9 $5.95

YOUNG TÖRLESS
by Robert Musil

Taut, compelling, pitiless first novel by the author of *The Man Without Qualities*. A meticulous account, set in an Austrian military academy, of the discovery and abuse of power—physical, emotional, and sexual. "An illumination of the dark places of the heart everywhere."—*Washington Post*

0-394-71015-0 $5.95

THE STORY OF A LIFE
by Konstantin Paustovsky

Universally acclaimed memoir of Russian boyhood coming of age amidst war and revolution. A startlingly vivid, deeply personal yet panoramic view of Russia during the tumultuous first two decades of the twentieth century. "A work of astonishing beauty . . . a masterpiece."—Isaac Bashevis Singer

0-394-71014-2 $8.95